Java™: A Framework for Programming and Problem Solving

Second Edition

Kenneth A. Lambert

Washington and Lee University

Martin Osborne

Western Washington University

BROOKS/COLE

THOMSON LEARNING

Australia ▪ Canada ▪ Mexico ▪ Singapore ▪ Spain ▪ United Kingdom ▪ United States

BROOKS/COLE

™

THOMSON LEARNING

Sponsoring Editor: *Kallie Swanson*
Marketing Team: *Christopher Kelly,*
  Samantha Cabaluna
Editorial Assistant: *Carla Vera*
Production Editor: *Kelsey McGee*
Production Service: *Forbes Mill Press*
Manuscript Editor: *Frank Hubert*
Permissions Editor: *Sue Ewing*

Media Editor: *Burke Taft*
Interior Design: *Robin Gold*
Cover Design: *Laurie Albrecht*
Cover Photo: *Photodisc*
Print Buyer: *Vena M. Dyer*
Typesetting: *Wolf Creek Press/Linda Weidemann*
Cover Printing, Printing and Binding:
  R. R. Donnelley and Sons Co./Crawfordsville

For more information about this or any other Brooks/Cole product, contact:
BROOKS/COLE
511 Forest Lodge Road
Pacific Grove, CA 93950 USA
www.brookscole.com
1-800-423-0563 (Thomson Learning Academic Resource Center)

10   9   8   7   6   5   4   3   2   1

Library of Congress Cataloging-in-Publication Data

Lambert, Kenneth Alfred, [   ]
   Java a framework for programming and problem solving / Kenneth Lambert, Martin Osborne.--2nd ed.
     p. cm.
   Includes index.
   ISBN 0-534-38277-0
   1. Java (Computer program language) I. Osborne, Martin, [   ] II. Title.
QA76.73.J38 L354 2002
005.2'762--dc21   2001035180

Contents

Preface

This text is intended for a first course (CS1) in programming and problem solving. It focuses on traditional introductory computer science concepts, but in the modern context of object-oriented programming (OOP), Java™, and graphical user interfaces (GUIs). The book presents seven major aspects of computing, some in stand-alone chapters and others spread across several chapters:

1. **Programming Basics.** This deals with the basic ideas of problem solving with computers, including primitive data types, control structures, methods, and algorithm analysis.

2. **Object-Oriented Programming.** OOP is today's dominant programming paradigm. All the essentials of this subject are covered.

3. **Data and Information Processing.** Fundamental data structures are discussed. These include strings, arrays, files, lists, and maps. The general concept of abstract data type is introduced, and the difference between abstraction and implementation is illustrated.

4. **Software Development Life Cycle.** Rather than isolate software development techniques in one or two chapters, the book deals with them throughout in the context of numerous Case Studies.

5. **Graphical User Interfaces and Event-Driven Programming.** Many books at this level restrict themselves to character-based terminal I/O. The reason is simple: Graphical user interfaces and event-driven programming are usually considered too complex for beginning students. In this book, we circumvent the complexity barrier and show how to develop programs with graphical user interfaces with the same ease as their terminal-based counterparts.

6. **Graphics.** Problem solving with simple graphics is explored. This includes drawing basic geometric shapes, representing data graphically, and implementing a rudimentary sketching program.

7. **Web Basics.** The programming of Web pages with HTML and applets is introduced.

Focus on Fundamental Computer Science Topics

There seem to be two types of introductory Java textbooks. The first emphasizes basic problem solving and programming techniques, and the second emphasizes language features. This book takes the former approach and introduces Java features only as needed to support programming concepts. In this way, most of Java's core syntax is covered without succumbing to the temptation of discussing Java's many powerful and popular advanced features, such as threads and beans. Anyone who intends to program extensively in Java will need to master the language's advanced features eventually; however, CS1 is not the best place for this endeavor.

Methods and Objects, Early or Late?

Occasionally, people argue about whether methods and objects should be introduced early or late in CS1 courses. In Java, even the simplest program involves both, so the problem really becomes one of how to introduce these concepts in a clear and meaningful manner from the outset. Starting with the first program, we show how to instantiate and send messages to objects. The book's early chapters (2 through 4) focus on the use of objects, arithmetic expressions, control constructs, and algorithms in the context of short, simple programs. As programs become more complex, it becomes advantageous to decompose them into cooperating components. With this end in mind, Chapter 6 shows how to develop systems of cooperating methods, and Chapter 9 does the same for classes. Thus, we take a pragmatic rather than an ideological approach to the question of when to introduce methods and objects with complete confidence that students will master both by the end of the course.

Case Studies, the Software Life Cycle, and Comments

The book contains numerous Case Studies. These are complete Java programs ranging from the simple to the substantial. To emphasize the importance and usefulness of the software development life cycle, Case Studies are presented in the framework of a user request followed by analysis, design, and implementation, with well-defined tasks performed at each stage. Some Case Studies are carried through several chapters or extended in end-of-chapter programming projects.

Programming consists of more than just writing code, so we encourage students to submit an analysis and design as part of major programming assignments. We also believe that code should be properly commented, and for purposes of illustration, we include comments in most of the listings in the book. Many of these comments take the form of pre- and postconditions.

Early, Easy GUIs with BreezySwing

There is some debate concerning the role of user interface design in CS1. While interfaces are obviously necessary, they typically are not a primary focus. Consequently, in most CS1 courses, programming assignments usually involve straightforward terminal-based interfaces that can be implemented with a modest effort, and when GUI interfaces are desired, professors often feel compelled to provide them. However, there is an alternative. This book uses a freely available software package called BreezySwing that allows students to develop GUIs with the same ease as terminal-based interfaces. BreezySwing extends Java's Abstract Windowing Toolkit (AWT) and Swing in a manner that hides most of the underlying complexities from the beginning programmer. Using BreezySwing, students write event-driven programs with realistic graphical interfaces, but without becoming entangled in numerous and difficult details.

People sometimes argue that students need to know how to develop GUIs the real way—that is, using AWT and Swing—and of course they are correct; however, CS1 is probably not the right place to master this material. In the meantime, BreezySwing provides a useful introduction to GUI-based programming. It is easy to learn and use, and it provides a bridge to AWT and Swing. For those who are interested and highly motivated, Chapter 18 explains the details of AWT and Swing. After mastering Chapter 18, students are ready to abandon BreezySwing and undertake full-fledged Java GUI development with all its power and complexity.

BreezySwing is available on the CD accompanying this book and from the Web site cs.wwu.edu/BreezySwing/. The Web site is the preferred source because it contains the latest release of BreezySwing together with online documentation and other related materials. BreezySwing is a free educational product, and everyone is invited to use it either with or without this textbook.

Terminal I/O Not Forgotten

In this book's first edition, there were very few and only very simple examples of programs that used terminal I/O. Some instructors found our nearly exclusive emphasis on GUI-based programming one-sided, so in this edition, we provide a more balanced approach. Chapters 2 through 4 use only terminal I/O and demonstrate standard terminal-based interface techniques such as how to write menu driven programs. Chapter 5 presents BreezySwing, and after that, instructors have the choice of asking students to write terminal-based or GUI-based programs. The book makes a smooth transition from terminal I/O to GUIs by presenting both in the context of very similar frameworks.

In Chapters 2 through 4, we do terminal I/O using our own TerminalIO package. We hope that instructors will appreciate the simplicity and pedagogical advantages of statements such as

```
hourlyRate = keyboard.readDouble();
```

and

```
screen.println ("Your gross pay is " + grossPay);
```

versus the complexity of doing the same things with Java's standard stream classes; however, later in the book, we show how to use the standard stream classes.

Exercises

The book contains two different types of exercise. First, most sections end with self-test questions that reinforce the reading by asking basic questions about the material in the section. All these questions are answered at the end of the chapter. Second, each chapter includes programming projects of varying degrees of difficulty.

CS Capsules

Scattered throughout the book are short essays called CS Capsules. These present historical and social aspects of computing. Special attention is paid to issues in computer ethics and security.

Alternative Paths Through the Book

The standard path through the book is to cover the first ten chapters and then select material from the remaining chapters according to interests and time constraints. However, it is possible to cover some chapters early.

1. Those who want to do applets early can insert Chapter 17 between Chapters 5 and 6.
2. Those who want to do graphics early can jump ahead to Chapter 13 after finishing Chapter 6.
3. Files (Chapter 14) can be presented after Chapter 7.

Those who do not have time to cover advanced CS1 topics (recursion, complexity analysis, and linked lists) can omit Chapters 12, 15, and 16, while those who would rather postpone inheritance until CS2 can skip Chapter 11. In a typical 15-week semester, it should be possible to cover all chapters, while in a 10-week quarter, Chapters 1 through 10 can be covered followed by two or three of the remaining chapters.

We have tried to produce a high quality text, but should you encounter any errors, please report them to klambert@wlu.edu. A listing of errata, should they exist, and other information about the book will be posted on the Web site www.wlu.edu/~lambertk/java/.

Acknowledgments

We would like to thank the following reviewers for their time and efforts: Stephen Fyfe, Central College; Adrian German, Indiana University–Bloomington; John Hansen, Iowa Central Community College; David Housman, Goshen College; John Hynd, Queensland University of Technology; Joe Lynn Look, Valencia Community College; Richard Mallory, University of Texas at Austin; Benjamin B. Nystuen, University of Colorado at Colorado Springs; Andrew Rock, Griffith University; and Emily Wenk, Gettysburg College.

We would also like to thank several other people whose work made this book possible: Robin Gold, production service; Frank Hubert, copy editor; Christopher Kelly, marketing manager; Samantha Cabaluna, marketing; Kelsey McGee, project editor; Kallie Swanson, editor; and Carla Vera, editorial assistant.

Kenneth A. Lambert
Martin Osborne

1 Background

This is the only chapter in the book that is not about the details of writing Java™ programs. Here we say something about computing in general, about hardware and software, about the representation of information in binary (i.e., as 0s and 1s), and about general concepts of object-oriented programming. All this material will give you a broad understanding of computing and a foundation for your study of programming.

1.1 History of Computers

ENIAC, built in the late 1940s, was one of the world's first computers. It was a large stand-alone machine that filled a room and used more electricity than all the houses on an average city block. ENIAC contained hundreds of miles of wire and thousands of heat-producing vacuum tubes. The mean time between failures was less than an hour, yet because of its fantastic speed when compared to hand-operated electromechanical calculators, it was immensely useful.

In the early 1950s, IBM sold its first business computer. At the time, it was estimated that the world would never need more than ten such machines, yet its awesome computational power was a mere 1/800 of the typical 800-megahertz Pentium personal computer purchased for about $1000 in 2000. Today, there are hundreds of millions of computers in the world, most of which are PCs. There are also billions of computers embedded in such everyday products as hand-held calculators, cars, refrigerators, and soon even clothing.

The first computers could perform only a single task at a time, and input and output were handled by such primitive means as punch cards and paper tape.

Figure 1.1 An interconnected world of computers

In the 1960s, time-sharing computers, costing hundreds of thousands and even millions of dollars, became popular at organizations large enough to afford them. These computers were sufficiently powerful that 30 people could work on them simultaneously, and each felt as if he or she were the sole user. Each person sat at a teletype connected by wire to the computer. By making a connection through the telephone system, teletypes could even be placed at a great distance from the computer. The teletype was a primitive device by today's standards. It looked like an electric typewriter with a large roll of paper attached. Keystrokes entered at the keyboard were transmitted to the computer, which then echoed them back on the roll of paper. In addition, output from the computer's programs was printed on this roll.

In the 1970s, people began to see the advantage of connecting computers in networks, and the wonders of e-mail and file transfers were born.

In the 1980s, PCs appeared in great numbers, and soon thereafter, local area networks of interconnected PCs became popular. These networks allowed a local group of PCs to communicate and share such resources as disk drives and printers with each other and with large centralized multiuser computers.

The 1990s saw an explosion in computer use, and the hundreds of millions of computers now appearing on many desktops and many homes are connected through the Internet (Figure 1.1).

And the common language of all these computers is fast becoming Java.

1.2 Computer Hardware and Software

Computers can be viewed as machines that process information. They consist of two primary components: hardware and software. *Hardware* consists of the physical devices that you see on your desktop, and *software* consists of the programs that give the hardware useful functionality. The main business of this book, which is programming, concerns software, but before diving into programming, let us take a moment to consider some of the major hardware and software components of a typical PC.

Bits and Bytes

It is difficult to discuss computers without referring to bits and bytes. A *bit,* or *binary digit,* is the smallest unit of information processed by a computer and consists of a single 0 or 1. A *byte* consists of eight adjacent bits. The capacity of computer memory and storage devices is usually expressed in bytes.

Computer Hardware

As illustrated in Figure 1.2, a PC consists of six major subsystems. Listed in order from outside and most visible to inside and most hidden, these are:

1. the *user interface,* which supports moment-to-moment communication between a user and the computer
2. *auxiliary I/O devices* such as printers and scanners
3. *auxiliary storage devices* for long-term storage of data and programs
4. a *modem* for connecting to the Internet and thus the rest of the world
5. *internal memory,* or *RAM,* for momentary storage of data and programs
6. the all important *CPU,* or *central processing unit*

Now we explore each of these subsystems in greater detail.

User Interface

The user interface consists of several devices familiar to everyone who has used a PC. In this book, we assume that our readers have already acquired basic computer literacy and have performed such common tasks as using a word processor or surfing the Internet. The *keyboard* and *mouse* are a computer's most frequently used input devices and the *monitor* or *screen* is the principal output device. Also useful, but less common, are a *microphone* for input and *speakers* for output.

Auxiliary I/O Devices

Computers have not yet produced a paper-free world, so we frequently rely on the output from *printers. Scanners* are most commonly used to enter images, but in

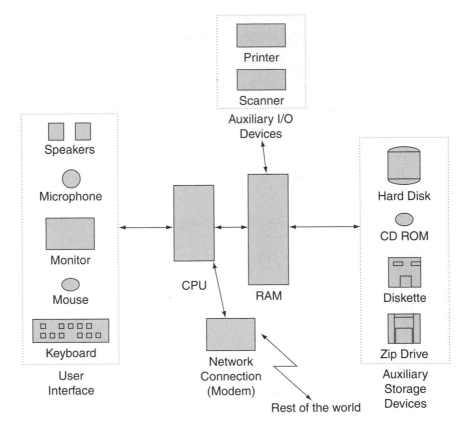

Figure 1.2 A PC's six major subsystems

conjunction with appropriate software, they can also be used to enter text. In case you have not already guessed, I/O stands for input/output. Numerous other I/O devices are available for special application, such as joysticks for games.

Auxiliary Storage Devices

The computer's operating system, the applications we buy, and the documents we write are all stored on devices collectively referred to as auxiliary storage or *secondary memory.* The current capacity of these devices is incredibly large and continues to increase rapidly. In 2000, as these words are being written, *hard disks* typically store tens of billions of bytes of information, or gigabytes (Gbytes) as they are commonly called. In addition to hard disks, which are permanently encased within computers, there are several *portable storage media.* Most computer software is now purchased on *CD ROM*s. CD stands for compact disk and ROM for read only memory. The term *ROM* is becoming somewhat misleading in this context as PCs are increasingly being equipped with CD devices that can read and write. Most CDs have a capacity of about 600 million bytes (megabytes or Mbytes), enough for an hour of music or a typical PC software package. Currently, CDs are being supplanted by *DVD*s, which have about ten times a CD's capacity. *Zip drives* with a capacity of 100–200 Mbytes are the most convenient portable storage device, but *diskettes* with a capacity of a mere 1 Mbyte are still widely used. Both support input and output and are used primarily for transporting data between computers that are not interconnected and for making backup copies of crucial computer files.

Network Connection

A network connection is now an essential part of every PC, connecting it to all the resources of the Internet. For home computer users, a modem has long been the most widely used connection device. Modem stands for modulator–demodulator and refers to the fact that the device converts the digital information (0s and 1s) of the computer to an analog form suitable for transmission on phone lines, and vice versa. Of course, as phone technology becomes increasingly digital, modem is fast becoming a misnomer. Other devices for connecting to the Internet include cable modems, which use TV cable rather than a phone connection, and Ethernet cards, which attach directly to local area networks and from there to the Internet.

Internal Memory

Although auxiliary storage devices have great capacity, access to their information is relatively slow in comparison to the speed of a computer's central processing unit. For this reason, computers include high-speed internal memory, also called *random access memory* (RAM) or *primary memory.* The contents of RAM are lost every time the computer is turned off, but when the computer is running, RAM is loaded from auxiliary storage with needed programs and data. Because a byte of RAM costs about 100 times as much as a byte of hard disk storage, PCs usually contain only about 32–128 Mbytes of RAM. Consequently, RAM is often unable to hold simultaneously all the programs and data a person might be using during a computer session. To deal with this situation, the computer swaps programs and data backward and forward between RAM and the hard disk as necessary. Swapping takes time and slows down the apparent speed of the computer from the user's perspective, so often the cheapest way to improve a computer's performance is to install more RAM.

Central Processing Unit

The central processing unit (CPU) does the work of the computer. Given the amazing range of complex tasks performed by computers, one might imagine that the CPU is intrinsically very complex, but such is not the case. In fact, the basic functions performed by the CPU consist of the everyday arithmetic operations of addition, subtraction, multiplication, and division together with some comparison and I/O operations. The complexity lies in the programs that direct the CPU's operations rather than in the CPU itself, and it is the programmer's job to determine how to translate a complex task into an enormous series of simple operations, which the computer then executes at blinding speed. Martin Osborne's current computer operates at 800 million cycles per second (800 MHz), and during each cycle, the CPU executes all or part of a basic operation.

Perhaps we have gone too far in downplaying the complexity of the CPU. To be fair, it too is highly complex, not in terms of the basic operations it performs, but rather in terms of how it achieves its incredible speed. This speed is achieved by packing several million transistors onto a silicon chip roughly the size of a postage stamp. Since 1955, when transistors were first used in computers, hardware engineers have been doubling the speed of computers about every 18 months, principally by increasing the number of transistors on computer chips. However, basic laws of physics guarantee that the process of miniaturization that allows ever greater numbers of transistors to be backed onto a single chip will soon end. How soon this will be no one knows.

The *transistor,* the basic building block of the CPU and RAM, is a simple device that can be in one of two states—ON, conducting electricity, or OFF, not conducting electricity. All the information in a computer—programs and data—is expressed in terms of these ONs and OFFs, or 1s and 0s as they are more conveniently called. From this perspective, RAM is merely a large array of 1s and 0s, and the CPU is merely a device for transforming patterns of 1s and 0s into other patterns of 1s and 0s.

To complete our discussion of the CPU, we describe a typical sequence of events that occurs when a program is executed, or run:

1. The program and data are loaded from disk into separate regions of RAM.

2. The CPU copies the program's first instruction from RAM into a decoding unit.

3. The CPU decodes and executes the instruction; for instance, add a number at one location in RAM to one at another location and store the result at a third location.

4. The CPU determines the location of the next instruction and repeats the process of copy, decode, and execute until the end of the program is reached.

5. After the program has finished executing, the data portion of RAM contains the results of the computation performed by the program.

Needless to say, this description has been greatly simplified. We have, for instance, completely ignored all issues related to input and output; however, the description provides a view of the computational process that will help you understand what follows.

Computer Software

Computer hardware processes complex patterns of electronic states or 0s and 1s. Computer software transforms these patterns, allowing them to be viewed as text, images, and so forth. Software is generally divided into two broad categories: system software and application software.

System Software

System software supports the basic operations of a computer and allows human users to transfer information to and from the computer. This software includes:

- the operating system, especially the file system for transferring information to and from disk and schedulers for running multiple programs concurrently
- communications software for connecting to other computers and the Internet
- compilers for translating user programs into executable form
- the user interface subsystem, which manages the look and feel of the computer, including the operation of the keyboard, the mouse, and a screen full of overlapping windows

Application Software

Application software allows human users to accomplish specialized tasks. Examples include:

- word processors
- spreadsheets
- database systems
- other programs we write

Self-Test Questions

1. What is the difference between a bit and a byte?
2. Name two input devices and two output devices.
3. What is the purpose of auxiliary storage devices?
4. What is RAM and how is it used?
5. Discuss the differences between hardware and software.

1.3 Binary Representation of Information and Computer Memory

As we saw in the previous section, computer memory stores patterns of electronic signals, which the CPU manipulates and transforms into other patterns. These patterns in turn can be viewed as strings of binary digits, or bits. Programs and data are both stored in memory, and there is no discernible difference between program instructions and data; they are both just sequences of 0s and 1s. To determine what a sequence of bits represents, we must know the context. We now examine how different types of information are represented in binary notation.

Integers

We normally represent numbers in decimal (base 10) notation, whereas the computer uses binary (base 2) notation. Our addiction to base 10 is a physiological accident

(10 fingers rather than 8, 12, or some other number). The computer's dependence on base 2 is due to the on/off nature of electric current.

To understand base 2, we begin by taking a closer look at the more familiar base 10. What do we really mean when we write a number such as 5403? We are saying that the number consists of 5 thousands, 4 hundreds, 0 tens, and 3, or expressed differently:

$$5 * 10^3 + 4 * 10^2 + 0 * 10^1 + 3 * 10^0$$

In this expression, each term consists of a power of 10 times a coefficient between 0 and 9. In a similar manner we can write expressions involving powers of 2 and coefficients between 0 and 1. For instance, let us analyze the meaning of 10011_2, where the subscript 2 indicates that we are using a base of 2:

$$10011_2 = 1 * 2^4 + 0 * 2^3 + 0 * 2^2 + 1 * 2^1 + 1 * 2^0$$
$$= 16 + 0 + 0 + 2 + 1$$
$$= 1 * 10^1 + 9 * 10^0$$
$$= 19_{10}$$

The inclusion of the base as a subscript at the end of a number helps us avoid possible confusion. Here are four numbers that contain the same digits but have different bases and thus different values:

1101101_{16}

1101101_{10}

1101101_8

1101101_2

Computer scientists use bases 2 (**binary**), 8 (**octal**), and 16 (**hexadecimal**) extensively. Base 16 presents the dilemma of how to represent digits beyond 9. The accepted convention is to use the letters A through F, corresponding to 10 through 15. For example:

$$3BC4_{16} = 3 * 16^3 + 11 * 16^2 + 12 * 16^1 + 4 * 16^0$$
$$= 3 * 4096 + 11 * 256 + 12 * 16 + 4$$
$$= 15300_{10}$$

As you can see from these examples, the next time you are negotiating your salary with an employer, you might allow the employer to choose the digits as long as she allows you to pick the base. In closing, Table 1.1 shows some base 10 numbers and their equivalents in base 2.

Floating-Point Numbers

Numbers with a fractional part, such as 354.98, are called *floating-point numbers.* They are a bit trickier to represent in binary than integers. One way is to use the *mantissa/exponent notation* in which the number is rewritten as a value between 0 and 1 ($0 \leq x < 1$) times a power of 10. For example,

$$354.98_{10} = 0.35498_{10} * 10^3$$

Table 1.1

Some Base 10 Numbers and Their Base 2 Equivalents	
Base 10	**Base 2**
0	0
1	1
2	10
3	11
4	100
5	101
6	110
7	111
43	101011

where the mantissa is 35498, and the exponent is 3. Similarly, in base 2,

$$10001.001_2 = 0.10001001_2 * 2^5$$

with a mantissa of 10001001 and exponent of $5_{10} = 101_2$. In this way, we can represent any floating-point number by two separate sequences of bits, with one sequence for the mantissa and the other for the exponent.[1]

Characters and Strings

To process text, computers must represent ***characters*** such as letters, digits, and other symbols on a keyboard. There are many encoding schemes for characters. One popular scheme is called ***ASCII*** (American Standard for Information Interchange). In this scheme, each character is represented as a pattern of 8 bits or 1 byte.[2] In binary notation, byte values can range from 0000 0000 to 1111 1111, allowing for 256 possibilities. These are more than enough for the characters

- A . . . Z
- a . . . b
- 0 . . . 9
- +, −, *, /, etc.
- and various unprintable characters such as carriage return, line feed, bell, and command characters

---

[1] Many computers follow the slightly different IEEE standard in which the mantissa contains one digit before the decimal or binary point. In binary, the mantissa's leading 1 is then suppressed.

[2] Originally, this was a 7-bit code, but it has been extended in various ways to 8 bits.

Table 1.2 shows some characters and their corresponding ASCII bit patterns. Java, however, uses a scheme called *Unicode* rather than ASCII. In this scheme, each character is represented by a pattern of 16 bits, ranging from 0000 0000 0000 0000 to 1111 1111 1111 1111. Unicode allows for 65,536 possibilities and can represent many alphabets simultaneously. Within Unicode, the patterns 0000 0000 0000 0000 to 0000 0000 1111 1111 duplicate the ASCII encoding scheme.

Table 1.2

Some Characters and Their Corresponding ASCII Bit Patterns					
Character	**Bit Pattern**	**Character**	**Bit Pattern**	**Character**	**Bit Pattern**
A	0100 0001	a	0110 0001	0	0011 0000
B	0100 0010	b	0110 0010	1	0011 0001
. . .	. . .	. . .	. . .	. . .	. . .
Z	0101 1010	z	0111 1010	9	0011 1001

Strings are another type of data used in text processing. Strings are sequences of characters, such as "The cat sat on the mat." The computer encodes each character in ASCII or Unicode and strings them together.

Images

Representing *images* in a computer is straightforward. For example, consider a black-and-white picture. To represent this image, we superimpose a fine grid on the image or, for better resolution, an even finer grid. If a grid cell, or *pixel,* contains black, we encode it as 0; otherwise, we encode it as 1. Color images are encoded in a similar manner but use several bits to represent the color value of each pixel. This is done in terms of the color's composition as a mixture of varying intensities of red, green, and blue. Typically, 8 bits are used to represent each intensity for a total of 24 bits or 16,777,126 color values per pixel.

Sound

We can digitize sound as follows:

- For each stereo channel, every 1/44,000 of a second measure the amplitude of the sound on a scale of 0 to 65,535.
- Convert this number to binary using 16 bits.

Thus, 1 hour of stereo music requires

$$2 \text{ channels} * \frac{1 \text{ hour}}{\text{channel}} * \frac{60 \text{ minutes}}{\text{hour}} * \frac{60 \text{ seconds}}{\text{minute}} * \frac{44,000 \text{ samples}}{\text{second}} * \frac{16 \text{ bits}}{\text{sample}}$$

$= 5,068,800,000$ bits

$= 633,600,000$ bytes

which is the capacity of a standard CD. By the way, the sampling rate of 44,000 times a second is not arbitrary, but corresponds to the number of samples required to reproduce accurately sounds with a frequency of up to 20,000 cycles per second. Sounds above that frequency are of more interest to dogs, bats, and dolphins than people.

Program Instructions

Program instructions are represented as a sequence of bits in RAM. For instance, on some hypothetical computer, the instruction to add two numbers already located in RAM and store their sum at some third location in RAM might be represented as follows:

```
0000 1001 / 0100 0000 / 0100 0010 / 0100 0100
```

where

- the first group of 8 bits represents the ADD command and is called the *operation code,* or *opcode* for short
- the second group of 8 bits represents the location (64_{10}) in memory of the first operand
- the third group of 8 bits represents the location (66_{10}) in memory of the second operand
- the fourth group of 8 bits represents the location (68_{10}) at which to store the sum

In other words, add the number at location 64 to the number at location 66 and store the sum at location 68.

Computer Memory

We can envision a computer's memory as a gigantic sequence of bytes. A byte's location in memory is called its *address.* Addresses are numbered from 0 to 1 less than the number of bytes of memory installed on that computer, say, 32M−1, where M stands for *megabyte*; that is, $2^{20} = 1,048,576$, or approximately 1 million bytes.

A group of contiguous bytes can represent a number, a string, a picture, a chunk of sound, a program instruction, or whatever, as determined by context. For example, let us consider the meaning of the two bytes starting at location 3 in Figure 1.3. The several possible meanings include these:

1. If it is an ASCII encoded string, then the meaning is "Hi".
2. If it is a binary encoded integer, then the meaning is 18537_{10} .
3. If it is a program instruction, then it might mean ADD, depending on the type of computer.

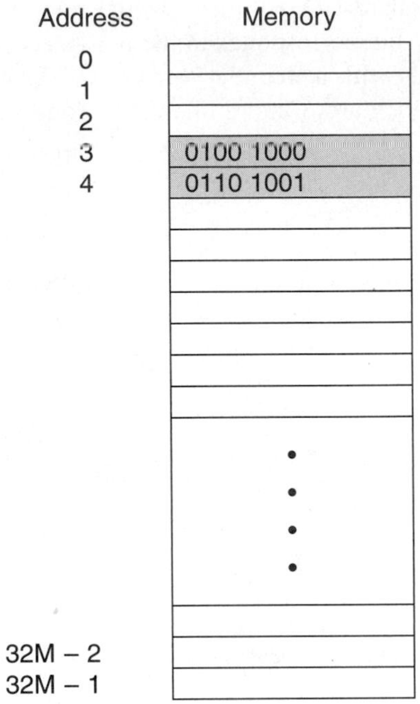

Address   Memory

0	
1	
2	
3	0100 1000
4	0110 1001

·
·
·
·

32M − 2

32M − 1

Figure 1.3 A 32 Mbyte RAM

Self-Test Questions

6. Translate 11100011_2 to a base 10 number.

7. Translate $45B_{16}$ to a base 10 number.

8. What is the difference between Unicode and ASCII?

9. Assume that 4 bits are used to represent the intensities of red, green, and blue. How many total colors are possible in this scheme?

10. An old-fashioned computer has just 16 bits available to represent an address of a memory cell. How many total memory cells can be addressed in this machine?

CS Capsule: The ACM Code of Ethics

The Association for Computing Machinery (ACM) is the flagship organization for computing professionals. The ACM supports publications of research results and new trends in computer science, sponsors conferences and professional meetings, and provides standards for computer scientists as professionals. The standards concerning the conduct and professional responsibility of computer scientists have been published in the ACM Code of Ethics. The code is intended as a basis for ethical decision making and for judging the merits of complaints about violations of professional ethical standards.

The code lists several general moral imperatives for computer professionals:

- Contribute to society and human well-being.
- Avoid harm to others.
- Be honest and trustworthy.
- Be fair and take action not to discriminate.
- Honor property rights, including copyrights and patents.
- Give proper credit for intellectual property.
- Respect the privacy of others.
- Honor confidentiality.

The code also lists several more specific professional responsibilities:

- Strive to achieve the highest quality, effectiveness, and dignity in both the process and products of professional work.
- Acquire and maintain professional competence.
- Know and respect existing laws pertaining to professional work.
- Accept and provide appropriate professional review.
- Give comprehensive and thorough evaluations of computer systems and their impacts, including analysis of possible risks.
- Honor contracts, agreements, and assigned responsibilities.
- Improve public understanding of computing and its consequences.
- Access computing and communication resources only when authorized to do so.

In addition to these principles, the code offers a set of guidelines to provide professionals with explanations of various issues contained in the principles. The complete text of the ACM Code of Ethics is available at the ACM's World Wide Web site, www.acm.org.

1.4 Programming Languages

Question: "If a program is just some very long pattern of electronic states in a computer's memory, then what is the best way to write a program?" The history of computing provides several answers to this question in the form of generations of programming languages.

Generation 1 (Late 1940s to Early 1950s)—Machine Languages

Early on, when computers were new on this earth, they were very expensive, and programs were very short. Programmers toggled switches on the front of the computer to enter programs and data directly into RAM in the form of 0s and 1s. Later, devices were developed to read the 0s and 1s into memory from punched cards and paper tape. There were several problems with this *machine language* coding technique:

1. Coding was error prone (entering just a single 0 or 1 incorrectly was enough to make a program run improperly or not at all),
2. Coding was tedious and slow.
3. It was extremely difficult to modify programs.
4. It was nearly impossible for one person to decipher another's program.
5. A program was not portable to a different type of computer because each type had its own unique machine language.

Needless to say, this technique is no longer used!

Generation 2 (Early 1950s to the Present)—Assembly Languages

Instead of the binary notation of machine language, *assembly language* uses mnemonic symbols to represent instructions and data. For instance, here is a machine language instruction followed by its assembly language equivalent

```
0011 1001 / 1111 0110 / 1111 1000 / 1111 1010
ADD       A,          B,           C
```

meaning

1. add the number at memory location 246, which we refer to as A
2. to the number at memory location 248, which we refer to as B
3. and store the result at memory location 250, which we refer to as C

Each assembly language instruction corresponds to exactly one machine language instruction. The standard procedure for using assembly language consists of several steps:

1. Write the program in assembly language.
2. Translate the program into a machine language program—this is done by a computer program called an *assembler.*
3. Load and run the machine language program—this is done by another program called a *loader.*

When compared to machine language, assembly language is

- more programmer friendly
- still unacceptably tedious to use, difficult to modify, and so forth
- no more portable because each type of computer still has its own unique assembly language

Assembly language is used as little as possible, although sometimes it is used when memory or processing speed are at a premium. Thus, every computer science major probably learns at least one assembly language.

Generation 3 (Middle 1950s to the Present)—High-Level Languages

Early examples of **high-level languages** are FORTRAN and COBOL, which are still in widespread use. Later examples are BASIC, C, and Pascal. Recent examples include Smalltalk, C++, and Java. All these languages are designed to be human friendly—easy to write, easy to read, and easy to understand—at least when compared to assembly language. For example, all high-level languages support the use of algebraic notation, such as the expression $x + y * z$.

Each instruction in a high-level language corresponds to many instructions in machine language. Translation to machine language is done by a program called a **compiler.** Generally, a program written in a high-level language is portable, but must be recompiled for each different type of computer on which it is going to run. Java is a notable exception because it is a high-level language that does not need to be recompiled for each type of computer, but more about this in Chapter 2. The vast majority of software is written in high-level languages

Self-Test Questions

11. State two of the difficulties of programming with machine language.
12. State two features of assembly language.
13. What is a loader and what is it used for?
14. State a difference between a high-level language and assembly language.

1.5 Software Development Process

High-level programming languages help programmers write high-quality software in much the same sense as good tools help carpenters build high-quality houses, but there is much more to programming than writing lines of code, just as there is more to building houses than pounding nails. The more consists of organization and planning and various diagrammatic conventions for expressing those plans. To this end, computer scientists have developed a view of the software development process, known as the **software development life cycle.** We now present a particular version of this life cycle, called the **waterfall model.**

The waterfall model consists of several phases:

1. **Customer request**—In this phase, the programmers receive a broad statement of a problem that is potentially amenable to a computerized solution. This step is also called the **user requirements** phase.
2. **Analysis**—The programmers determine what the program will do. This is sometimes viewed as a process of clarifying the specifications for the problem.
3. **Design**—The programmers determine how the program will do its task.
4. **Implementation**—The programmers write the program. This step is also called the **coding** phase.

5. **Integration**—Large programs have many parts. In the integration phase, these parts are brought together into a smoothly functioning whole, usually not an easy task.

6. **Maintenance**—Programs usually have a long life; 5–15 years are common. During this time, requirements change and minor or major modifications must be made.

The interaction between the phases is shown in Figure 1.4. Note that the figure resembles a waterfall, in which the results of each phase flow down to the next. A mistake detected in one phase often requires the developer to back up and redo some of the work in the previous phase. Modifications made during maintenance also require backing up to earlier phases.

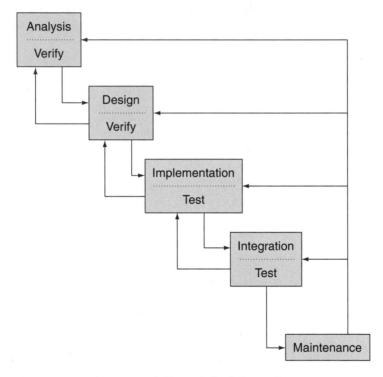

Figure 1.4 The waterfall model of the software development life cycle

Programs rarely work as hoped the first time they are run; hence, they should be subjected to extensive and careful testing. Many people think that testing is an activity that applies to only the implementation and integration phases; however, the outputs of each phase should be scrutinized carefully. In fact, mistakes found early are much less expensive to correct than those found late. Figure 1.5 illustrates some relative costs of repairing mistakes when found in different phases.

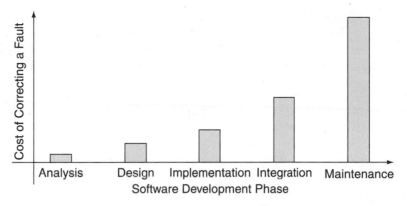

Figure 1.5 Relative costs of repairing mistakes when found in different phases

Finally, the cost of developing software is not spread equally over the phases. The percentages shown in Figure 1.6 are typical.

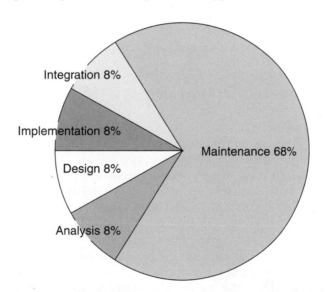

Figure 1.6 Percentage of total cost incurred in each phase of the development process

Most people probably think that implementation takes the most time and therefore costs the most. However, maintenance is, in fact, the most expensive aspect of software development.

As you read this book and begin to sharpen your programming skills, you should remember two points:

1. There is more to software development than hacking out code.

2. If you want to reduce the overall cost of software development, write programs that are easy to maintain. This requires thorough analysis, careful design, and good coding style. We will have more to say about coding style throughout the book.

For a thorough discussion of the software development process and software engineering in general, see Stephen R. Schach, *Software Engineering with Java* (Chicago: Irwin, 1997).

Self-Test Questions

15. What happens during the analysis and design phases of the software development process?

16. Which phase of the software development process incurs the highest cost to developers?

17. How does the waterfall model of software development work?

18. In which phase of the software development process is the detection and correction of errors the least expensive?

1.6 Basic Concepts of Object-Oriented Programming

The high-level programming languages mentioned earlier fall into two major groups, and these two groups utilize two different approaches to programming. The first group, consisting of the older languages (COBOL, FORTRAN, BASIC, C, and Pascal), uses what is called a ***procedural approach.*** Inadequacies in the procedural approach led to the development of the ***object-oriented approach*** and to several newer languages (Smalltalk, C++, and Java). There is little point in trying to explain the differences between these approaches in an introductory programming text, but suffice it to say that everyone considers the object-oriented approach to be the superior of the two. There are also several other approaches to programming, but that too is a topic for a more advanced text.

Most programs in the real world contain hundreds of thousands of lines of code. Writing such programs is a highly complex task that can only be accomplished by breaking the code into communicating components. This is an application of the well-known principle of divide and conquer that has been applied successfully to many human endeavors. There are various strategies for subdividing a program, and these depend on the type of programming language used. We now give an overview of the process in the context of ***object-oriented programming*** (OOP)—that is, programming with objects. Along the way, we introduce fundamental OOP concepts, such as class, inheritance, and polymorphism. Each of these concepts is also discussed in greater detail later in the book. For best results, reread this section as you encounter each concept for a second time.

We proceed by way of an extended analogy in an attempt to associate something already familiar with something new. Like all analogies, this one is imperfect but ideally useful. Imagine that it is your task to plan an expedition in search of the lost treasure of Balbor. How familiar can this be, you ask? Well, that depends on your taste in books, movies, and video games. Your overall approach might consist of the following steps.

Planning. You determine the different types of team members needed: leaders, pathfinders, porters, trail engineers. You then define the responsibilities of each type in terms of

- a list of the resources used—these include the materials and knowledge needed by the type
- the rules of behavior followed—these define how the type behaves and responds in various situations

Finally, you decide how many of each type will be needed.

Execution. You recruit the team members and assemble them at the starting point, send the team on its way, and sit back and wait for the outcome. There is no sense in endangering your own life too.

Outcome. If the planning was done well, you will be rich; otherwise, prepare for disappointment.

How does this analogy relate to OOP? We give the answer in two columns. On the left we describe various aspects of the expedition and on the right corresponding aspects of object-oriented programming.

The World of the Expedition	The World of OOP
The trip must be planned.	Computer software is created in a process called ***programming.***
The team is composed of different types of team members, and each type is characterized by its list of resources and rules of behavior.	A program is comprised of different types of software components called ***classes.*** A class defines or describes a list of data resources called ***instance variables*** and rules of behavior called ***methods.*** Combining the description of resources and behavior into a single software entity is called ***encapsulation.***
First the trip must be planned. Then it must be set in motion.	First a program must be written. Then it must be ***run,*** or ***executed.***
When the expedition is in progress, the team is composed of individual members and not types. Each member is, of course, an instance of a particular type.	An executing program is composed of interacting ***objects,*** and each object's resources (instance variables) and rules of behavior (methods) are described in a particular class. An object is said to be an ***instance*** of the class that describes its resources and behavior.

At the beginning of the expedition, team members must be recruited.

Team members working together accomplish the mission of the expedition. They do this by asking each other for services.

When a team member receives a request for service, she follows the instructions in a corresponding rule of behavior.

If someone who is not a pathfinder wants to know where north is, she does not need to know anything about compasses. She merely asks one of the pathfinders, who are well-known providers of this service. Even if she did ask a pathfinder for his compass, he would refuse. Thus, team members tell others about the services they provide but never anything about the resources they use to provide these services.

The expedition includes general-purpose trail engineers plus two specialized subtypes. All trail engineers share common skills, but some specialize in bridge building and others in clearing landslides. Thus, there is a hierarchy of engineers.

While a program is executing, it creates, or *instantiates,* objects as needed.

Objects working together accomplish the mission of the program. They do this by asking each other for services or, in the language of OOP, by sending *messages* to each other.

When an object receives a message, it refers to its class to find a corresponding rule or method to execute.

If an object A needs a service that it cannot provide for itself, then A requests the service from some well-known provider B. However, A knows nothing of B's data resources and never asks for access to them. This principle of providing access to services but not to data resources is called *information hiding.*

Classes are organized into a hierarchy also. The class at the *root,* or base, of the hierarchy defines methods and instance variables that are shared by its *subclasses,* those below it in the hierarchy. Each subclass then defines additional methods and instance variables. This process of sharing is called *inheritance.*

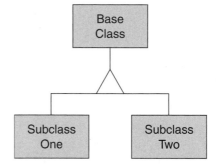

At the end of the day, the leader tells each member to set up camp. All members understand this request, but their responses depend on their types. Each type responds in a manner consistent with its specific responsibilities.

During the trip, everyone is careful not to ask an individual to do something for which he is not trained—that is, for which he does not have a rule of behavior.

One can rely on team members to improvise and resolve ambiguities and contradictions in rules.

Different types of objects can understand the same message. This is referred to as *polymorphism.* However, an object's response depends on the class to which it belongs.

When writing a program, we never send a message to an object unless its class has a corresponding method.

In contrast, a computer does exactly what the program specifies—neither more nor less. Thus, programming errors and oversights, no matter how small, are usually disastrous. Therefore, programmers need to be excruciatingly thorough and exact when writing programs.

Self-Test Questions

19. In what way is programming like planning?
20. An object-oriented program is a set of objects that interact by sending messages to each other. Explain.
21. What is a class and how does it relate to objects in an object-oriented program?
22. Explain the concept of inheritance with an example.
23. Explain the concept of information hiding with an example.

CS Capsule: Copyright, Intellectual Property, and Digital Information

For hundreds of years, copyright law has existed to regulate the use of intellectual property. At stake are the rights of authors and publishers to a return on their investment in works of the intellect, which include printed matter (books, articles, etc.), recorded music, film, and video. More recently, copyright law has been extended to include software and other forms of digital information. For example, copyright law protects the software on the disk included with this book. This prohibits the purchaser from reproducing the software for sale or free distribution to others. If the software is stolen or "pirated" in this way, the perpetrator can be prosecuted and punished by law. However, copyright law also allows for "fair use"—the purchaser may make backup copies of the software for personal use. When the purchaser sells the software to another user, the seller thereby relinquishes the right to use it, and the new purchaser acquires this right.

When governments design copyright legislation, they try to balance the rights of authors and publishers to a return on their work against the rights of the public to fair use. In the case of printed matter and other works that have a physical embodiment, the meaning of fair use is usually clear. Without fair use, borrowing a book from a library or playing a CD at a high school dance would be unlawful.

With the rapid rise of digital information and its easy transmission on networks, different interest groups—authors, publishers, users, and computer professionals— are beginning to question the traditional balance of ownership rights and fair use. For example, is browsing a copyrighted manuscript on a network service an instance of fair use? Or does it involve a reproduction of the manuscript that violates the rights of the author or publisher? Is the manuscript a physical piece of intellectual property when browsed or just a temporary pattern of bits in a computer's memory? Users and technical experts tend to favor free access to any information placed on a network. Publishers and, to a lesser extent, authors tend to worry that their work, when placed on a network, will be resold for profit.

Legislators struggling with the adjustment of copyright law to a digital environment face many of these questions and concerns. Providers and users of digital information should also be aware of the issues. For a detailed discussion, see Pamela Samuelson, "Regulation of Technologies to Protect Copyrighted Works," *Communications of the ACM,* Vol. 39, No. 7 (July 1996), 17–22.

1.7 Summary

This chapter has provided an overview of computing that is relevant to programming. We have traced a simple history of computing and sketched an outline of the basic ideas of computer hardware, software, programming languages, and the binary representation of information. A brief outline of the software development process and the fundamental concepts of object-oriented programming has set the stage for a more detailed discussion of these topics in later chapters.

1.8 Key Terms

If you have difficulty finding the definitions of any key terms in the body of this chapter, turn to the Glossary at the end of the book.

application software	high-level language	output device
assembler	information hiding	polymorphism
assembly language	inheritance	program
bit	input device	root
byte	instance variable	secondary storage device
central processing unit (CPU)	instantiation	software
class	loader	software life cycle
coding	machine language	subclass
compiler	message	system software
data	method	user requirements
encapsulation	object	waterfall model
hardware	object-oriented programming	

1.9 Answers to Self-Test Questions

1. A bit can be either 1 or 0 and is the smallest unit of information in computer memory. A byte is a unit of storage that consists of 8 bits.

2. Two input devices are a mouse and a keyboard. Two output devices are a monitor screen and a printer.

3. An auxiliary storage device serves as permanent storage medium for information. Because it is less expensive than primary storage, auxiliary storage can also accommodate large quantities of information.

4. RAM stands for random access memory. Also known as primary memory, RAM holds all the information, both program instructions and data, in cells that are very quickly accessible.

5. Hardware consists of the physical components of a computer. Software consists of the program instructions and data representations that give hardware its functionality.

6. $11100011_2 =$

$$1 * 2^7 + 1 * 2^6 + 1 * 2^5 + 0 * 2^4 + 0 * 2^3 + 0 * 2^2 + 1 * 2^1 + 1 * 2^0 =$$

$$128 + 64 + 32 + 0 + 0 + 0 + 2 + 1 = 227$$

7. $45B_{16} =$

$$4 * 16^2 + 5 * 16^1 + 11 * 16^0 =$$

$$1024 + 80 + 11 = 1115$$

8. ASCII is a coding scheme that uses 7 bits to represent 128 different character values, which include the English alphabet, punctuation marks, and some control codes. Unicode, which contains ASCII as a subset, uses 16 bits to represent 65,536 characters, including many alphabets.

9. Using 4 bits for each primary color, we get $2^4 * 2^4 * 2^4$ or 4096 possible colors.

10. 16 bits can address 65,536 different memory cells.

11. One difficulty in programming with machine language is that the programmer must translate all operation codes and addresses by hand to binary form. Another difficulty is that each type of computer has its own machine language, so a program must be rewritten to run on each type of machine.

12. One feature of assembly language is the use of mnemonic labels to name operations and symbolic labels to name data addresses. Another feature is automatic translation to machine language.

13. A loader is a software tool that automatically places program instructions and data in machine cells before a program is run.

14. One difference between a high-level language and an assembly language is the use of algebraic expressions in the high-level language.

15. During the analysis phase of software development, the programmer states what the system will do. During the design phase, the programmer states how the system will do what it does.

16. The maintenance phase of software development incurs the highest cost.

17. The result or output of each phase in the waterfall model trickles down to the next phase and becomes its input. When an error is detected in a given phase, the developers can back up to a previous phase to fix the error. This process resembles swimming upstream.

18. The least expensive phase in which to detect and correct an error is the first one, the analysis phase.

19. Programming is like planning in the sense that a plan or a program is a document drawn up to guide a process before that process begins to execute.

20. Computer software systems can be built from reusable components called objects. An object contains data and manipulates these data in response to messages. At program startup, objects are created and a message is sent to one of them. This object responds by sending messages to other objects. The resulting behavior constitutes the behavior of the software system.

21. A class is a template that describes the data and the behavior of a set of objects. An object is created by instantiating its class. When a message is sent to an object, the object looks in its class for the behavior to execute in response to the message.

22. Clerk, driver, machine worker, and manager are all subclasses of the class employee. Each employee has a name, social security number, and address. The subclasses inherit these attributes from the employee class. By default, an employee's salary is computed and paid on a weekly basis. However, managers receive a monthly salary.

23. A bank account object hides the balance from users of accounts, unless they enter a password and select the appropriate message to send to the account. Messages can be withdraw, deposit, or get the balance.

2 First Java

Programs are written in programming languages, and the language used in this book is Java. This chapter gets you up and running with a couple of simple Java programs. We show how to write these first programs, compile them, and run them. In the process, you will become acquainted with a Java programming environment, the structure of a simple Java program, and the basic ideas of variables, input and output statements, and sending messages to objects.

2.1 Why Java?

Java is the fastest growing programming language in the world. Companies such as IBM and Sun have adopted Java as their major application development language. There are several reasons for this.

First, Java is a modern object-oriented programming language. The designers of Java spent much time studying the features of classical object-oriented languages such as Smalltalk and C++ and made a successful effort to incorporate the good features of these languages and omit the less desirable ones.

Second, Java is secure, robust, and portable. That is, the Java language

- enables the construction of virus-free, tamper-free systems (secure)
- supports the development of programs that do not overwrite memory (robust)
- yields programs that can be run on different types of computers without change (portable)

These features make Java ideally suited to develop distributed, network-based applications, which is an area of ever increasing importance.

Third, Java supports the use of advanced programming concepts such as threads. A *thread* is a process that can run concurrently with other processes. For example, a single Java application might consist of two threads. One thread transfers an image from one machine to another across a network, while the other thread simultaneously interacts with the user.

Fourth and finally, Java bears a superficial resemblance to C++, which is currently the world's most popular industrial strength programming language. Thus, it is easy for a C++ programmer to learn Java and for a Java programmer to learn C++. However, compared to C++, Java is easier to use and learn, less error prone, more portable, and better suited to the Internet.

On the negative side, Java runs more slowly than most modern programming languages because it is interpreted. To understand this last point we must now turn our attention to the Java virtual machine and byte code.

Self-Test Questions

1. What is a portable program?
2. Describe two features of Java that make it a better language than C++.
3. What is a thread? Describe how threads might be used in a program.

2.2 The Java Virtual Machine and Byte Code

Compilers usually translate a higher-level language into the machine language of a particular type of computer. However, the Java compiler translates Java not into machine language, but into a pseudomachine language called Java *byte code.* Byte code is the machine language for an imaginary Java computer. To run Java byte code on a particular computer, you must install a *Java virtual machine (JVM)* on that computer.

A JVM is a program that behaves like a computer. Such a program is called an interpreter. An interpreter has several advantages and disadvantages. The main disadvantage of an interpreter is that a program pretending to be a computer runs programs more slowly than an actual computer. However, Java virtual machines are getting faster every day. For instance, some JVMs translate byte code instructions into machine language when they are first encountered—called *just-in-time compilation (JIT)*—so that the next time the instruction is encountered it is executed as fast machine code rather than being interpreted as slow byte code. Also, new computer chips are being developed that implement a JVM directly in hardware, thus avoiding the performance penalty.

The main advantage of an interpreter is that any computer can run it. Thus, Java byte code is highly portable. For instance, many of the pages you download on the Web contain small Java programs already translated into byte code. These are called *applets,* and they are run in a JVM that is incorporated into your Web browser. These applets range from the decorative (displaying a comical animated character on the Web page) to the practical (displaying a continuous stream of stock market quotes).

Because Java programs run inside a virtual machine, it is possible to limit their capabilities. Thus, ideally, you never have to worry about a Java applet infecting your computer with a virus, erasing the files on your hard drive, or stealing sensitive information and sending it across the Internet to a competitor. In practice, however, computer hackers have successfully penetrated Java's security mechanisms in the past and may succeed again in the future. But all things considered, Java applets really are very secure, and security weaknesses are repaired as soon as they become known.

For a discussion of the current impact of Java, see "The Java Factor," *Communications of the ACM,* Vol. 41, No. 6 (June 1998), 34–76.

Self-Test Questions

4. What does JVM stand for?

5. What is byte code? Describe how the JVM uses byte code.

6. What is an applet? Describe how applets are used.

2.3 Choosing an Interface Style

Before writing our first program, we must make a difficult decision. What type of user interface do we want to use? There are two choices: the *graphical user interface (GUI)* familiar to all PC users and the less common *terminal I/O interface.* Figure 2.1 illustrates both in the context of a program that converts degrees Fahrenheit to degrees Celsius. The graphical interface on the left is familiar and comfortable. The user enters a number in the first box, clicks the Command button, and the program displays the answer in the second box. The terminal based interface on the right begins by displaying the prompt "Enter degrees Fahrenheit:". The user then enters a number and presses the Enter key. The program responds by displaying the answer.

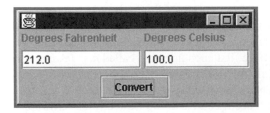 

Figure 2.1 Two interfaces for a temperature conversion program

We begin with terminal I/O and in Chapter 5 make a swift and easy transition to GUIs. Thereafter, you can choose the style you consider most suitable to the problem at hand. In the long run, you will discover that this book's core material is independent of interface issues. There are three reasons for beginning with terminal I/O. First, in Java and many other languages, a terminal interface is easier to implement than a GUI, although in other languages, such as Visual BASIC, the opposite is true. Second, there are programming situations that require terminal I/O rather than a GUI, so familiarity with the techniques of terminal-oriented programming is important. Third, terminal-oriented programs are similar in structure to programs that process files of sequentially organized data, and what we learn here will be transferable to that setting.

2.4 Hello World

In conformance with a long and honorable tradition dating back to the early days of the language C, a textbook's first program often does nothing more than display the words "Hello World" in a terminal window. Actually, as you can see in Figure 2.2, we could not resist adding few embellishments. In case you have not guessed, "Hello World" is the steam wafting upward from a cup of hot Java.

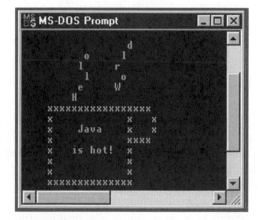

Figure 2.2 Hello World

The Source Code

Just as a recipe is a sequence of instructions for a chef, a program is a sequence of instructions for a computer. And just as a recipe does nothing until executed by a chef, so a program does nothing until executed by a computer. With that in mind, here is the bulk of the instructions, or *source code,* in our hello world program:

```
writer.println("                    d              ");
writer.println("            o      l              ");
writer.println("          l      r              ");
writer.println("          l          o          ");
writer.println("        e      W              ");
writer.println("      H                        ");
writer.println("    xxxxxxxxxxxxxxxxx          ");
writer.println("    x                x    x    ");
writer.println("    x    Java      x    x    ");
writer.println("    x              xxxx      ");
writer.println("    x    is hot!  x          ");
writer.println("    x              x          ");
writer.println("    x              x          ");
writer.println("    xxxxxxxxxxxxxx            ");
```

The Explanation

In this code:

- writer[1] is the name of an object that knows how to display or print characters in a terminal window
- println is the name of the message being sent to the writer object
- the strings enclosed in quotation marks contain the characters to be printed
- semicolons (;) mark the end of each *statement* or sentence in the program

As mentioned at the end of Chapter 1, an object-oriented program accomplishes its task by sending messages to objects. In this program, a writer object responds to a println message by printing a string of characters in the terminal window. The string of characters that appears between the parentheses following the message is called a *parameter.* Some messages require several parameters, separated from each other by commas, while other messages have no parameters. The "ln" in the message println stands for "line" and indicates that the writer object should advance to the beginning of the next line after printing a string.

The ScreenWriter Class

As mentioned in Chapter 1, an object is always an instance of a class and must be created or instantiated before being used. In general, instantiation is done like this:

```
SomeClass someObject = new SomeClass();
```

---

[1] We could have used System.out.println here, but to achieve symmetry with our approach to input, we have developed and use a ScreenWriter class. To learn more about System.out in the broader context of streams, readers, and writers, see Chapter 14.

The statement looks a little strange, but it will make more sense as we proceed. We must add similar code to the beginning of our hello world program:

```
ScreenWriter writer = new ScreenWriter();
```

In this line, we are free to choose any name we wish for the object, but the class's name has already been fixed by its authors.

The Larger Framework

The program as presented so far is not complete. It must be embedded in a larger framework defined by several additional lines of code.[2] No attempt will be made to explain this code until Chapter 3, but fortunately, it can be reused with little change from one program to the next. Here then is the complete program with the new lines shown in blue:

```
import TerminalIO.*;

public class HelloWorld {

    ScreenWriter writer = new ScreenWriter();

    public void run() {
        writer.println("                    d        ");
        writer.println("             o     l        ");
        writer.println("           l     r          ");
        writer.println("           l       o        ");
        writer.println("           e     W          ");
        writer.println("         H                  ");
        writer.println("       xxxxxxxxxxxxxxxx      ");
        writer.println("       x             x   x  ");
        writer.println("       x    Java     x   x  ");
        writer.println("       x            xxxx    ");
        writer.println("       x   is hot!  x        ");
        writer.println("       x             x      ");
        writer.println("       x             x      ");
        writer.println("       xxxxxxxxxxxxx         ");
    }

    public static void main (String [] args) {
        HelloWorld tpo = new HelloWorld();
        tpo.run();
    }
}
```

---

[2] There are several different ways to do this, and we have chosen an approach that makes the transition to GUIs as smooth as possible. In Chapter 9, we consider one of the alternatives.

To reuse the framework, replace `HelloWorld` with the name of another program:

```
import TerminalIO.*;
public class <name of program>  {

   . . .

  public void run() {
     . . .
  }

  public static void main (String [] args) {
     <name of program> tpo = new <name of program>();
     tpo.run();
  }
}
```

Self-Test Questions

7. Give a short definition of "program."
8. What is the effect of the message `println`?
9. Describe how to create and use a `ScreenWriter` object.

2.5 Edit, Compile, and Execute

In the preceding section, we presented the source code for our first program. Now we discuss how to enter it into a computer and run it. There are three steps.

1. **Edit.** In the first step, the programmer uses a word processor or editor to enter the source code into the computer and save it in a text file. The name of the text file must match the name of the program with the extension `.java` added, as in `HelloWorld.java`.

2. **Compile.** In the second step, the programmer invokes the Java language compiler to translate the source code into Java byte code. In this example, the compiler translates source code in the file `HelloWorld.java` to byte code in the file `HelloWorld.class`. The extension for a byte code file is always `.class`.

3. **Execute.** In the third step, the programmer instructs the JVM to load the byte code into memory and execute it. At this point, the user and the program can interact, with the user entering data and the program displaying instructions and results.

Figure 2.3 illustrates the steps. The ovals represent the processes edit, compile, and execute. The names of the files `HelloWorld.java` and `HelloWorld.class` are shown between parallel lines.

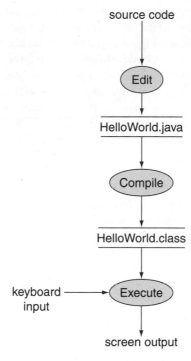

Figure 2.3 Editing, compiling, and running a program

Development Environments

The details involved in editing, compiling, and running a program vary with the development environment being used. Some common development environments available to Java programmers include:

1. UNIX using a standard text editor with command line activation of the compiler and the JVM.

2. Windows 9x using Notepad for the editor with command line activation of the compiler and the JVM from inside a command or DOS window. We call this the ***DOS development environment.***[3]

3. Windows 9x or MacOS using an ***integrated development environment (IDE)*** such as Symantec's Visual Café, Microsoft's Visual J++, or Borland's JBuilder.

The first two options are free and merely require you to download and install the Java software development kit (JDK) as described in Appendix A. The third option, an integrated development environment, costs money, but it has the advantage of combining an editor, a Java compiler, a debugger, and a JVM in a manner

---

[3] DOS was Microsoft's original PC operating system and had a terminal-based interface.

intended to increase programmer productivity. However, IDEs take time to master and can obscure fundamental details of the edit, compile, run sequence.[4]

As we cannot possibly discuss all of these environments simultaneously, we will give our instructions in terms of the DOS development environment; however, the installation and use of the major alternatives are presented in our supplemental materials on the book's Web site (the URL is in Appendix A). This supplemental material is broken down into chapters that parallel those in this book, thus making it easy for you to find the instructions that match your development environment. Please feel free to print the Web site material so that you can always have it close at hand.

Step-by-Step Instructions

We are now ready to present step-by-step instructions for editing, compiling, and running the Hello World program. After reading what follows, read the supplemental material for an explanation that matches the development environment on your computer.

Step 1. Use Windows Explorer to create the directory in which you intend to work (for instance, C:\A\JavaCollege\Ch2). Open a terminal window by selecting **MS-DOS Prompt** (or something similar) from the **Start/Programs** menu. In the terminal window, use the **cd** command to move to the working directory as illustrated in Figure 2.4.

Figure 2.4 Using the cd command to move to the working directory

Step 2. Open the Notepad editor on the file HelloWorld.java (Figure 2.5). Once Notepad opens, type in the program. Select menu option **File/Save** and save the file using the name HelloWorld.java. You can now close Notepad or leave it open. Figure 2.6 shows a snapshot of the Notepad window after the program has been entered.

Step 3. Now that the program has been saved, switch back to the terminal window and compile the program by typing javac HelloWorld.java.

Step 4. Run the program by typing java HelloWorld. Figure 2.7 shows a snapshot of this and the previous step.

---

[4] Needless to say, people argue heatedly about whether or not IDEs should be used in introductory programming classes.

MS-DOS Prompt
C:\A\JavaCollege\Ch2>notepad HelloWorld.java
C:\A\JavaCollege\Ch2>_

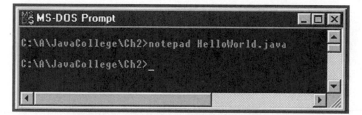

Figure 2.5 Activating Notepad to edit the program

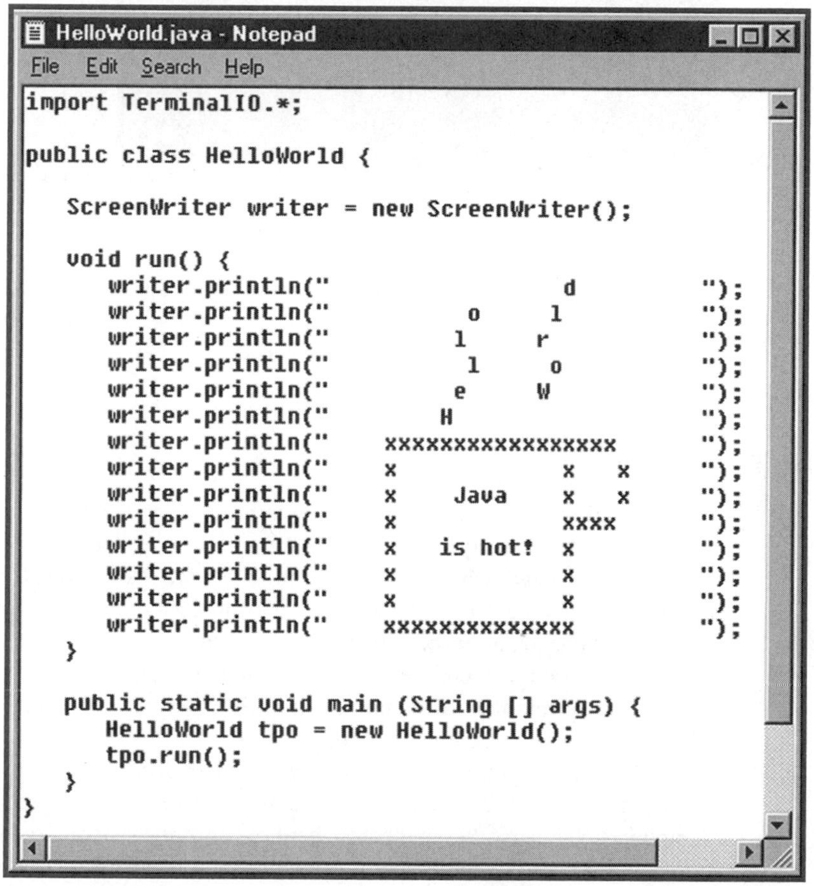

HelloWorld.java - Notepad
File Edit Search Help
import TerminalIO.*;
public class HelloWorld {
ScreenWriter writer = new ScreenWriter();
void run() {
writer.println("   d   ");
writer.println("   o   l   ");
writer.println("   l   r   ");
writer.println("   l   o   ");
writer.println("   e   W   ");
writer.println("   H   ");
writer.println("   xxxxxxxxxxxxxxxxx   ");
writer.println("   x   x   x   ");
writer.println("   x   Java   x   x   ");
writer.println("   x   xxxx   ");
writer.println("   x   is hot! x   ");
writer.println("   x   x   ");
writer.println("   x   x   ");
writer.println("   xxxxxxxxxxxxxx   ");
}
public static void main (String [] args) {
HelloWorld tpo = new HelloWorld();
tpo.run();
}
}

Figure 2.6 The program as typed into Notepad

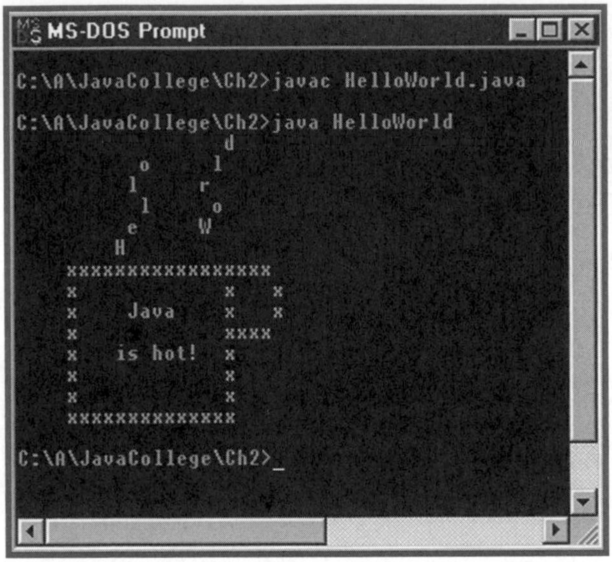

Figure 2.7 Compiling and running the program

WARNING: In some development environments, the terminal window disappears immediately after the JVM executes the program's last instruction. We will show you how to overcome this problem later in the chapter when we present a temperature conversion program.

Compile-Time Errors

It is inevitable that we will make typographical errors when we edit programs, and the compiler will nearly always detect them. Mistakes detected by the compiler are called *compile-time errors.* To illustrate these, we modify the program so that it includes two such errors. After reading this subsection, read the supplemental material that matches your development environment.

For the first error, on line 8, we misspell `println` as `pritnln`. For the second, we omit the semicolon at the end of line 12. Figure 2.8 contains a snapshot of the program as it now appears in Notepad.

When the program is compiled, the compiler prints a list of errors in the terminal window (Figure 2.9). Unfortunately, some of the error messages are difficult to decipher, but at least they indicate where the compiler encountered text it could not translate into byte code. The first error message is easy to understand. It says that `pritnln` is not a method in the `ScreenWriter` class. Notice that the second error generates two error messages, neither of which makes any sense at this point.

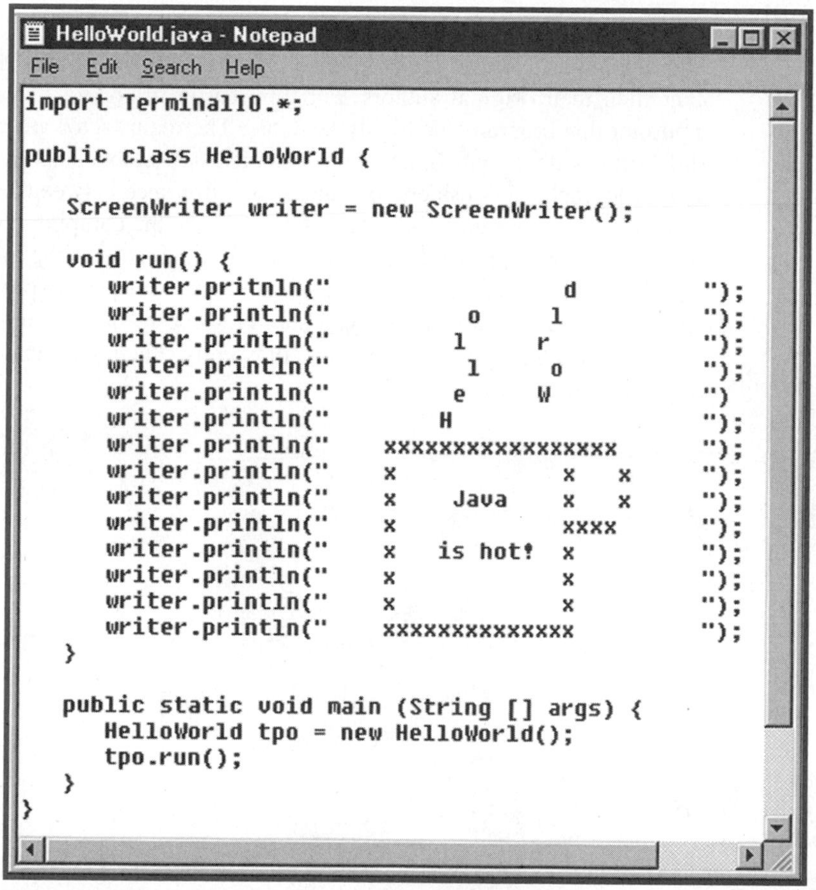

```
HelloWorld.java - Notepad
File  Edit  Search  Help
import TerminalIO.*;

public class HelloWorld {

    ScreenWriter writer = new ScreenWriter();

    void run() {
        writer.pritnln("                    d        ");
        writer.println("              o      l        ");
        writer.println("            l        r        ");
        writer.println("             l       o        ");
        writer.println("            e      W        ")
        writer.println("           H                 ");
        writer.println("      xxxxxxxxxxxxxxx        ");
        writer.println("      x              x   x   ");
        writer.println("      x     Java     x   x   ");
        writer.println("      x              xxxx    ");
        writer.println("      x   is hot!  x         ");
        writer.println("      x              x       ");
        writer.println("      x              x       ");
        writer.println("      xxxxxxxxxxxxx          ");
    }

    public static void main (String [] args) {
        HelloWorld tpo = new HelloWorld();
        tpo.run();
    }
}
```

Figure 2.8 The program with compile-time errors on lines 8 and 12

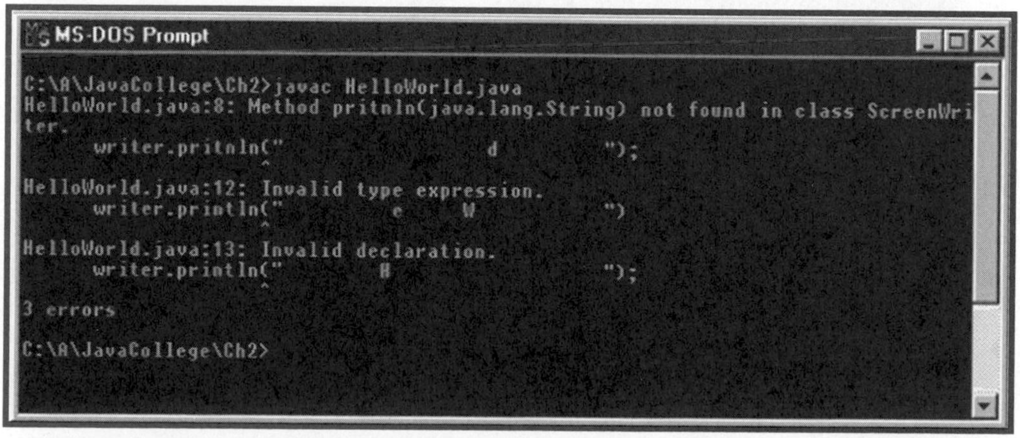

```
MS-DOS Prompt
C:\A\JavaCollege\Ch2>javac HelloWorld.java
HelloWorld.java:8: Method pritnln(java.lang.String) not found in class ScreenWri
ter.
        writer.pritnln("            d        ");
               ^
HelloWorld.java:12: Invalid type expression.
        writer.println("        e    W      ")
               ^
HelloWorld.java:13: Invalid declaration.
        writer.println("      H              ");
               ^
3 errors

C:\A\JavaCollege\Ch2>
```

Figure 2.9 The compiler's error messages

Readability

Programs typically have a long life and must be read and modified by many people other than their original authors. For this reason, if for no other, it is extremely important that programs be highly readable. The main factor affecting a program's readability is its layout. Indentation, the inclusion of blank lines and spaces, and other typographical considerations make the difference between an intelligible program and an incomprehensible mess. Interestingly, the compiler completely ignores a program's format, provided that there are no line breaks in the middle of words or quoted strings. Throughout the book, we attempt to format our programs in a pleasing and consistent manner, and you should strive to do the same. Here for your enjoyment is a highly unreadable, but completely functional, rendering of the hello world program:

```
import TerminalIO.*; public class HelloWorld
     {
ScreenWriter writer = new ScreenWriter(); public void run
(){writer.println("                d           ")
;writer.println("         o    l            ");writer.println
("      l    r          ");writer.println(
     "        l    o          ");
writer.println("         e    W            ");
     writer.println("         H              ");
        writer.println("    xxxxxxxxxxxxxxxxx       ");
  writer.println("    x          x   x     ");
writer.println("    x    Java    x   x     ");
     writer.println("    x            xxxx      ");
        writer.println("    x   is hot!  x          ");
   writer.println("    x            x        ");writer
.
println("    x            x        ");
     writer.println("    xxxxxxxxxxxxx          ");
}public static void main (String [] args){HelloWorld
tpo = new HelloWorld();tpo.run();}}
```

Self-Test Questions

10. Name the three steps in writing and running a program.

11. What are compile-time errors? Give an example.

12. Why is readability a desirable characteristic of a program?

CS Capsule: Intrusive Hacking

Hacking is a term whose use goes back to the early days of computing. In its original sense, a "hack" is a program that exhibits rare problem-solving ability and commands the respect of other programmers. The culture of hackers began in the late 1950s at the MIT computer science labs. These programmers, many of them students and later professionals and teachers in the field, regarded hacking as an accomplishment along the lines of Olympic gymnastics. These programmers even advocated a "hacker ethic," which stated, among other things, that hackers should respect the privacy of others and distribute their software for free. For a narrative of the early tradition of hacking, see Steven Levy, *Hackers: Heroes of the Computer Revolution* (Garden City, NY: Anchor Press/Doubleday, 1984).

Unfortunately, the practice of hacking has changed over the years, and the term has acquired darker connotations. Programmers who break into computer systems in an unauthorized way are called hackers, whether their intent is just to impress their peers or to cause actual harm. Students and professionals who lack a disciplined approach to programming are also called hackers. An excellent account of the most famous case of intrusive hacking can be found in Clifford Stoll, *The Cuckoo's Egg: Tracking Through the Maze of Computer Espionage* (New York: Doubleday, 1989).

2.6 Temperature Conversion

We now present code for the temperature conversion program illustrated earlier in the chapter. To refresh your memory, we show the interface again in Figure 2.10. This program is fundamentally more interesting than the hello world program because it reads user inputs and performs computations. Despite being short and simple, the program demonstrates several important concepts.

Figure 2.10 Interface for the temperature conversion program

The Source Code

Here is the program's source code:

```
import TerminalIO.*;

public class Convert {

    KeyboardReader reader = new KeyboardReader();
    ScreenWriter writer = new ScreenWriter();

    double fahrenheit;
    double celsius;

    public void run() {
        writer.print ("Enter degrees Fahrenheit: ");
        fahrenheit = reader.readDouble();
        celsius = (fahrenheit - 32.0) * 5.0 / 9.0;
        writer.print ("The equivalent in Celsius is ");
        writer.println (celsius);
        reader.pause();
    }

    public static void main (String [] args) {
        Convert tpo = new Convert();
        tpo.run();
    }
}
```

The Explanation

Here is a line-by-line explanation of the portions of the program shown in black. The blue lines will be explained in Chapter 3.

```
KeyboardReader reader = new KeyboardReader();
ScreenWriter writer = new ScreenWriter();
```

In these statements, we instantiate `KeyboardReader` and `ScreenWriter` objects. A `KeyboardReader` object can read inputs entered at the keyboard.

```
double fahrenheit;
double celsius;
```

In these statements, we declare that the program will use two numeric variables called `fahrenheit` and `celsius`. A numeric variable names a location in RAM in which a number can be stored. The number is usually referred to as the *variable's value.* During the course of a program, a variable's value can change, but its name remains constant. The variables in this program are of type `double`, which means they will contain only floating-point numbers. It is customary, though not required, to begin variable names with a lowercase letter, thus "fahrenheit" rather than "Fahrenheit." We are allowed to declare as many variables as we wish in a program, and we can name them pretty much as we please. Restrictions are explained in Chapter 3.

```
writer.print ("Enter degrees Fahrenheit: ");
```

This statement is similar to those we saw in the hello world program, but there is a minor difference. The message here is `print` rather than `println`. A `print` message positions the cursor immediately after the last character printed rather than moving it to the beginning of the next line.

```
fahrenheit = reader.readDouble();
```

In this statement, the `reader` object responds to the message `readDouble` by waiting for the user to type a number and then press the Enter key, at which point the `reader` object returns this number to the program. This number is then assigned to the variable `fahrenheit` by means of the *assignment operator* (=), or in other words, the number entered by the user becomes the variable's value. Note that although the `readDouble` message has no parameters, the parentheses are still required. As the user types at the keyboard, the characters are automatically echoed in the terminal window, and not until the user presses the Enter key does this input become available to the program.

```
celsius = (fahrenheit - 32.0) * 5.0 / 9.0;
```

In this statement, the expression to the right of the assignment operator (=) is evaluated, and then the resulting value is stored in memory at location `celsius`. The variable `fahrenheit` in the expression indicates that the variable's value is to be used. Notice that all the numbers (32.0, 5.0, and 9.0) contain a decimal point. In Java, some unexpected rules govern what happens when integers and floating-point values are mixed in an expression. Until we learn those rules (Chapter 3), we will not mix. In the expression:

- * indicates the *multiplication operator*
- / indicates the *division operator*
- - indicates the *subtraction operator*

```
writer.print ("The equivalent in Celsius is ");
```

Here the `writer` object prints the string "The equivalent in Celsius is ". The cursor is positioned after the last character in preparation for the next line of code.

```
writer.println (celsius);
```

Here the `writer` object prints the value of the variable `celsius`. The parameter for a `print` or `println` message can be a string in quotes, a variable, or even an expression. When a variable is used, the variable's value is printed, not its name. When an expression is used, the expression is evaluated before its value is printed.

```
reader.pause();
```

This statement is optional and is needed only in some development environments. The statement's purpose is to prevent the terminal window from disappearing immediately after the JVM executes the program's last statement. We discussed this problem when presenting the hello world program. Sending the `pause` message to the `reader` object displays the string "Press Enter to continue . . ." in the terminal window, after which the program pauses until the user presses the Enter key.

Variables and Objects

Figure 2.11 depicts the variables and objects used in the program. All of these exist in the computer's memory while the program is running. The variables `fahrenheit` and `celsius` each hold a single floating-point number. At any given instant, the value stored in a variable depends on the effect of the preceding lines of code. The variables `reader` and `writer` are very different than the variables `fahrenheit` and `celsius`. Instead of holding numbers, they hold references to objects. The arrows in the figure are intended to suggest this fact. During the course of the program, we think of these variables as being the names of the objects. As the figure indicates, we know nothing about what lies inside the objects (information hiding), but we do know that a `KeyboardReader` object responds to the message `readDouble`, and a `ScreenWriter` object responds to the messages `print` and `println`. One of the really significant facts about object-oriented programming is that we can use objects without having the least idea of their internal workings. Likewise, we can design objects for others to use without telling them anything about the implementation details.

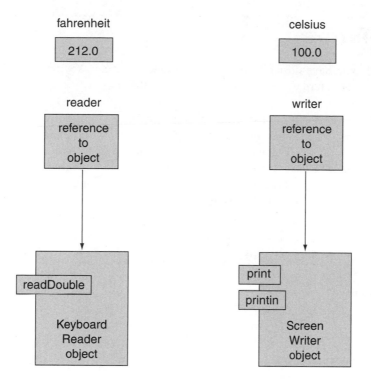

Figure 2.11 Variables and objects used in the program

Self-Test Questions

13. What is a variable in a program and how is it used?
14. Describe the role of the assignment (=) operator in a program.
15. What is a `KeyboardReader` object?
16. Explain the difference between a variable of type `double` and a variable of type `ScreenWriter`.

2.7 Summary

In this chapter, we have shown how to get started with some short Java programs. These programs perform simple input and output using a keyboard and terminal screen. An overview of the edit, compile, execute cycle was given, and the fundamental concepts of variables, input and output statements, and assignment statements were introduced. A brief discussion of compile-time errors and sending messages to objects has set the stage for a more detailed treatment in later chapters.

2.8 Key Terms

If you have difficulty finding the definitions of any key terms in the body of this chapter, turn to the Glossary at the end of the book.

applet	integrated development	statement
assignment operator	environment (IDE)	terminal I/O interface
byte code	Java virtual machine (JVM)	thread
graphical user interface (GUI)	just-in-time compilation (JIT)	variable
hacking	parameter	virus
	source code	

2.9 Answers to Self-Test Questions

1. A portable program can be written once and recompiled to run on any machine.

2. Java has standard features for writing programs with graphical user interfaces. Java also has standard features for writing network-based applications.

3. A thread is a process that can run concurrently with other processes. One program can consist of several threads. In a given program, one thread might be loading an image while another thread takes input from the user.

4. JVM stands for Java virtual machine.

5. Byte code is the code to which a Java source program translates during compilation. The JVM executes the byte code by interpreting its instructions.

6. An applet is a Java program that runs in a Web browser. The user launches an applet by selecting a hot spot in a Web page. The hot spot asks the Web page's server to transmit the applet's byte code to the client's Web browser. The byte code is checked for security, and then the Web browser's JVM executes the code.

7. A program is a sequence of instructions and data that solves a problem or accomplishes a task.

8. The message `println` causes the object to which it is sent to run the corresponding method. This method displays the message's parameter, a string or a number, on the terminal screen.

9. A `ScreenWriter` object is instantiated by executing the expression `new ScreenWriter()`. This object can then be sent the messages `print` or `println`.

10. Three steps in writing and running a program are editing, compilation, and execution.

11. Compile-time errors occur while a program is being compiled. An example is the failure to include a semicolon where it is expected.

12. A readable program is more easily understood and modified by others and even by its original author.

13. A variable is a name of a storage location in computer memory. Programs can store values, such as numbers or reference to objects, in variables and use these values whenever they are needed. In general, a variable provides a convenient way of remembering a value that might be modified during the course of a program.

14. The assignment operator causes a value to be stored in a variable.

15. A `KeyboardReader` object receives messages to input data from a human user. For example, when sent the message `readDouble`, a `KeyboardReader` object causes a program to wait for a user to enter the digits of a number. When the user presses the Enter key, the object returns the corresponding floating-point number.

16. A variable of type `double` names a storage location for a floating-point number. A variable of type `ScreenWriter` names a storage location for a reference to a `ScreenWriter` object.

2.10 Programming Problems and Activities

Beginning with this chapter, we conclude each chapter with a set of programming problems and activities. We wish to emphasize that programming is not just coding. Thus, a complete solution to each exercise in this section would include not just a set of `.java` and `.class` files for the program but also a report that covers the analysis, design, and results of testing the program. Ideally, you would do analysis and design before coding, and perhaps turn in this work for review before coding proceeds. How this is done depends on the size of the class and the time available to the instructor. In any case, when you see the words "write a program that . . . ," you should at least pause to reflect on the nature of the problem before coding the solution. For example, your analysis might consist of a description of how the program would be used. Your design might consist of a pseudocode algorithm that describes how the results are computed in the program.

1. Write a program that displays your name, address, and telephone number.

2. A yield sign encloses the word YIELD within a triangle. Write a program that displays a yield sign (use stars to represent the sides of the triangle).

3. Write a program that takes as input a number of kilometers and prints the corresponding number of nautical miles. You may rely on the following items of information:
   - A kilometer represents 1/10,000 of the distance between the North Pole and the equator.
   - There are 90 degrees, containing 60 minutes of arc each, between the North Pole and the equator.
   - A nautical mile is 1 minute of arc.

4. Write a program that calculates and prints the number of minutes in a year.

5. An object's momentum is its mass multiplied by its velocity. Write a program that expects an object's mass (in kilograms) and velocity (in meters per second) as inputs and prints its momentum.

3 Syntax, Errors, and Debugging

To use a programming language, one must become familiar with its vocabulary and the rules for forming grammatically correct sentences. One must also know how to construct meaningful sentences and sentences that express the programmer's intent. Errors of form, meaning, and intent are possible, so one must finally know how to detect these and correct them. This chapter discusses the basic elements of the Java language in detail and explores how to find and correct errors in programs.

3.1 Language Elements

Before writing code in any programming language, we need to be aware of some basic language elements. Every natural language, such as English, Japanese, and German, has its own vocabulary, syntax, and semantics. Programming languages also have these three elements.

Vocabulary

The vocabulary is the set of all of the words in the language. Here are examples taken from Java:

arithmetic operators	`+    −    *    /`
assignment operator	`=`
numeric literals	`5.73    9`
programmer-defined variable names	`fahrenheit celsius`

Syntax

Syntax consists of the rules for combining words into sentences, or **statements** as they are more usually called in programming languages. Here are two typical syntax rules in Java:

1. In an expression, the arithmetic operators for multiply and divide must not be adjacent. Thus,

   ```
   (f - 32) * / 9
   ```

   is invalid.

2. In an expression, left and right parentheses must occur in matching pairs. Thus,

   ```
   )f - 32( * 5 / 9
   ```

   and

   ```
   f -32) * 5 / 9
   ```

   are both invalid.

Semantics

Semantics define the rules for interpreting the meaning of sentences. For example, the expression

```
(f - 32.0) * 5.0 / 9.0
```

means "subtract 32.0 from the variable quantity indicated by f, multiply the result by 5.0, and finally divide the whole thing by 9.0."

Programming and Natural Languages

Despite their similarities, programming languages and natural languages have important differences. First, programming languages have small vocabularies and a simple syntax and semantics when compared to natural languages. Thus, their basic elements are not hard to learn. Second, in a programming language, one must get the syntax absolutely correct, whereas an ungrammatical English sentence is usually comprehensible. This strict requirement of correctness often makes writing programs difficult for beginners, though no more difficult than writing grammatically correct sentences in English. Third, when we give a friend instructions in English, we can be a little vague, relying on the friend to fill in the details. In a programming language, we must be exhaustively thorough. Computers do exactly what they are told, neither more nor less. When people blame problems on computer errors, they should more accurately blame sloppy programming. This last difference is the one that makes programming difficult even for experienced programmers.

Although programming languages are simpler than human languages, the task of writing programs is challenging. It is difficult to express complex ideas using the limited syntax and semantics of a programming language.

Self-Test Questions

1. What is the vocabulary of a language? Give an example of an item in the vocabulary of Java.

2. Give an example of a syntax rule in Java.

3. What does the expression `(x + y) * z` mean?

4. Describe two differences between programming languages and natural languages.

3.2 Basic Java Syntax and Semantics

Having seen two examples of Java programs in Chapter 2, we are ready for a more formal presentation of the basic elements of the Java language. Some points have already been touched on in Chapter 2, but most are new.

Literals

Literals are items in a program whose values do not change. Examples from the conversion program in Chapter 2 include the numbers 5.0 and 9.0 and the string "Enter degrees Fahrenheit:". Here are other examples of numeric literals (note that numeric literals never contain commas):

51	an integer
–31444843	a negative integer
3.14	a floating-point number
5.301E5	a floating-point number equivalent to $5.301 * 10^5$, or 530,100
5.301E-5	a floating-point number equivalent to $5.301 * 10^{-5}$, or 0.00005301

Numeric Data Types

Java programs can manipulate several different types of numeric data, but in this and the next few chapters, we will restrict ourselves to `int` (for integer) and `double` (for floating-point numbers). The range of values available with these two data types is as follows:

Type	Storage Requirements	Range
`int`	4 bytes	–2,147,483,648 to 2,147,483,647
`double`	8 bytes	–1.79769313486231570E+308 to 1.79769313486231570E+308

Variables

A *variable* is an item whose value can change during the execution of a program. A variable can be thought of as a named location or cell in the computer's memory.

Changing the value of a variable is equivalent to replacing the number that was in the cell with another number (Figure 3.1). For instance, at one point in a program, we might set the value of the variable `fahrenheit` to 78.5. Later in the program, we could set the variable to another value such as –23.7. When we do this, the new value replaces the old one.

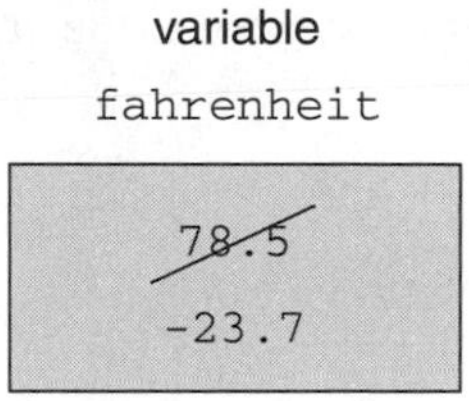

variable

`fahrenheit`

```
  78.5
 -23.7
```

Figure 3.1 Changing the value of a variable

Variable Declarations and Object Instantiation

During the course of a program, a specific variable can hold only one *type* of data. Some common types include integer, floating point, character, string, and reference to an object. Before using a variable for the first time, the programmer must declare its type. This is done in a *variable declaration statement.* For instance, a program might contain the statements:

```
int age;
double celsius;
KeyboardReader reader;
ScreenWriter writer;
```

From this point forward in the program, `age` can hold only integers, `celsius` only floating-point numbers, `reader` only references to `KeyboardReader` objects, and `writer` only references to `ScreenWriter` objects. It is also possible to declare several variables in single declarations and to simultaneously assign them initial values. For instance:

```
int x, y, z = 7;
double p, q = 1.41, pi = 3.14, t;
KeyboardReader reader = new KeyboardReader();
```

The last statement declares the object variable `reader`, instantiates or creates a `KeyboardReader` object, and finally assigns the object to the variable. Instantiation takes the form:

```
new <name of class>()1;
```

---

[1] The format is slightly more general than shown here, as will be explained in Chapter 5.

Assignment Statements

An assignment statement has the following form:

```
<variable> = <expression>;
```

where the value of the expression on the right is assigned to the variable on the left. For instance:

```
fahrenheit = reader.readDouble();
celsius = (fahrenheit  - 32.0) * 5.0 / 9.0;
```

Arithmetic Expressions

An *arithmetic expression* consists of operands and binary operators combined in a manner familiar from algebra. The usual rules apply:

- multiplication and division are evaluated before addition and subtraction
- operations of equal precedence are evaluated from left to right
- parentheses can be used to change the order of evaluation

Unlike in algebra, multiplication must be indicated explicitly: thus, a * b cannot be written as ab. Table 3.1 shows several operands from the conversion program, and Table 3.2 shows some common operators.

Table 3.1

Examples of Operands	
Type	**Example**
literals	32.0 5.0 9.0
variables	fahrenheit celsius
parenthesized expressions	(fahrenheit - 32.0)

Several points concerning operators need explanation. First, the semantics of division are different for integer and floating-point operands. Thus,

5.0 / 2.0 yields 2.5

5 / 2   yields 2   (the fractional portion of the answer is simply dropped)

The operator % yields the remainder obtained when one number is divided by another. Thus,

9 % 5   yields 4

9.3 % 5.1 yields 4.2

Table 3.2

Common Operators and Their Precedence

Operator	Symbol	Precedence (from highest to lowest)	Association
Grouping	( )	1	Not applicable
Method selector	.	2	Left to right
Unary plus	+	3	Not applicable
Unary minus	–	3	Not applicable
Multiplication	*	4	Left to right
Division	/	4	Left to right
Remainder or modulus	%	4	Left to right
Addition	+	5	Left to right
Subtraction	–	5	Left to right
Assignment	=	6	Right to left

When evaluating an expression, Java applies operators of higher *precedence* before those of lower precedence unless overridden by parentheses. The highest precedence is 1.

```
3 + 5 * 3    yields 18
-3 + 5 * 3   yields 12
+3 + 5 * 3   yields 18  (use of unary + is uncommon)
3 + 5 * -3   yields -12
3 + 5 * +3   yields 18  (use of unary + is uncommon)
(3 + 5) * 3  yields 24
3 + 5 % 3    yields 5
(3 + 5) % 3  yields 2
```

The column labeled **Association** in Table 3.2 indicates the order in which to perform operations of equal precedence. Thus,

```
18 - 3 - 4 yields 11
18 / 3 * 4 yields 24
18 % 3 * 4 yields 0
```

Some more examples of expressions and their values are shown in Table 3.3. In this table, we see the application of two fairly obvious rules governing the use of parentheses:

1. Parentheses must occur in matching pairs.

2. Parenthetical expressions may be nested but must not overlap.

Table 3.3

Examples of Expressions and Their Values		
Expression	**Same As**	**Value**
3 + 4 − 5	7 − 5	2
3 + (4 − 5)	3 + (−1)	2
3 + 4 * 5	3 + 20	23
(3 + 4) * 5	7 * 5	35
8 / 2 + 6	4 + 6	10
8 / (2 + 6)	8 / 8	1
10 − 3 − 4 − 1	7 − 4 − 1	2
10 − (3 − 4 − 1)	10 − (−2)	12
(15 + 9) / (3 + 1)	24 / 4	6
15 + 9 / 3 + 1	15 + 3 + 1	19
(15 + 9) / ((3 + 1) * 2)	24 / (4 * 2)	3
	24 / 8	
(15 + 9) / (3 + 1) * 2	24 / 4 * 2	12
	6 * 2	

Mixed-Mode Arithmetic

When working with a hand-held calculator, we do not give much thought to the fact that we intermix integers and floating-point numbers. This is called *mixed-mode arithmetic*. For instance, if a circle has radius 3, we compute the area as follows:

```
3.14 * 3 * 3
```

In Java, when there is a binary operation on operands of different numeric types, the less inclusive type (int) is temporarily and automatically converted to the more inclusive type (double) before the operation is performed. Thus, in

```
double d;
d = 5.0 / 2;
```

the value of d is computed as 5.0/2.0 yielding 2.5. However, problems can arise when using mixed-mode arithmetic. For instance,

```
3 / 2 * 5.0   yields   1 * 5.0   yields   5.0
```

whereas

```
3 / 2.0 * 5   yields   1.5 * 5   yields   7.5
```

Mixed-mode assignments are also allowed, provided the variable on the left is of a more inclusive type than the expression on the right.[2] Otherwise, a syntax error occurs, as shown in the following code segment:

```
double d;
int i;

i = 45;           ← OK, because we assign an int to an int.
d = i;            ← OK, because left is more inclusive than right. 45.0 is stored in d.
i = d;            ← Syntax error because left is less inclusive than right.
```

User-Defined Symbols

Variable and program names are examples of user-defined symbols. We will see other examples later in the book. In this section, we explain the rules for forming and naming user-defined symbols. These names must consist of a letter followed by a sequence of letters and/or digits. Letters are defined to be

- A ... Z
- a ... z
- _ and $
- symbols that denote letters in several languages other than English

Digits are the characters 0 . . . 9. Names are case sensitive; thus, celsius and Celsius are different names.

Some words cannot be employed as user-defined symbols. These words are called *keywords* or *reserved words* because they have special meaning in Java. Table 3.4 shows a list of Java's reserved words. You will encounter most of them by the end of the book.

---

[2] In Chapter 8, we show how to overcome this restriction on assignment statements.

Table 3.4

Java's Reserved Words			
abstract	double	int	static
boolean	else	interface	super
break	extends	long	switch
byte	final	native	synchronized
case	finally	new	this
catch	float	null	throw
char	for	package	throws
class	goto	private	transient
const	if	protected	try
continue	implements	public	void
default	import	return	volatile
do	instanceof	short	while

Here are examples of valid and invalid names:

Valid Names	surfaceArea3	_$_$$$	
Invalid Names	3rdPayment	pay.rate	abstract

Well-chosen variable names greatly increase a program's readability and maintainability; consequently, it is considered good programming practice to use meaningful names such as

radius	rather than	r
taxableIncome	rather than	ti

When forming a compound variable name, programmers usually capitalize the first letter of each word except the first. For instance:

taxableIncome	rather than	taxableincome
	or	TAXABLEINCOME
	or	TaxableIncome

On the other hand, all the words in a program's name typically begin with a capital letter; for instance, ComputeEmployeePayroll. The goal of these rules and of all stylistic conventions is to produce programs that are easier to understand and maintain.

Self-Test Questions

5. State whether each of the following are valid or invalid user-defined symbols in Java:

   a. `pricePerSquareInch`

   b. `student2`

   c. `2GuysFromLexington`

   d. `PI`

   e. `allDone?`

6. What is the difference between a variable and a literal?

7. Assume that the integer variable x is 5 and the integer variable y is 10. Give the values of the following expressions:

   a. `x + y * 2`

   b. `x - y + 2`

   c. `(x + y) * 2`

8. How does mixed-mode arithmetic work?

3.3 Case Study: Income Tax Calculator

It is now time to write a program that illustrates some of the concepts we have been presenting. We do this in the context of a case study that adheres to the software development life cycle discussed in Chapter 1. This life cycle approach may seem overly elaborate for small programs, but it scales up well when programs become larger. Each year nearly everyone with an income faces the unpleasant task of computing his or her income tax return. If only it could be done as easily as suggested in this case study.

Request. Write a program that computes a person's income tax.

Analysis. Here is the relevant tax law (mythical in nature):

- There is a flat tax rate of 20%.
- There is a $10,000 standard deduction.
- There is a $2000 additional deduction for each dependent.
- Gross income must be entered to the nearest penny.
- The income tax is expressed as a decimal number.

The user inputs are the gross income and number of dependents. The program calculates the income tax based on the inputs and the tax law and then displays the income tax. Figure 3.2 shows the proposed terminal interface. Characters in bold italics indicate user inputs. The word **Enter** indicates that the user must press the Enter key. The program prints the rest. The inclusion of an interface at this point is a good idea because it allows the customer and the programmer to discuss the intended program's behavior in a context understandable to both.

```
Enter the gross income: 50000.50 Enter
Enter the number of dependents. 4 Enter
The income tax is $6400.1
```

Figure 3.2 Interface for the income tax calculator

Design. During analysis, we specify what a program is going to do, and during design, we describe how it is going to do it. This involves writing the algorithm used by the program. *Webster's New Collegiate Dictionary* defines an ***algorithm*** as "a step-by-step procedure for solving a problem or accomplishing some end." A recipe in a cookbook is a good example. Program algorithms are often written in a somewhat stylized version of English called ***pseudocode.*** Here is the pseudocode for our program.

```
read grossIncome
read numDependents
compute taxableIncome = grossIncome - 10000 - 2000 * numDependents
compute incomeTax = taxableIncome * 0.20
print incomeTax
```

Although there are no precise rules governing the syntax of pseudocode, you should strive to describe the essential elements of the program in a clear and concise manner. Over time, you will develop a style that suits you.

Implementation. Given the preceding pseudocode, an experienced programmer would now find it easy to write the needed Java program. For a beginner, on the other hand, writing the code is the most difficult part of the process. Here then is the program:

```
import TerminalIO.*;

public class IncomeTaxCalculator {

    KeyboardReader reader = new KeyboardReader();
    ScreenWriter writer = new ScreenWriter();

    double grossIncome;
    int     numDependents;
    double taxableIncome;
    double incomeTax;
```

```
public void run() {
   writer.print ("Enter the gross income: ");
   grossIncome = reader.readDouble();
   writer.print ("Enter the number of dependents: ");
   numDependents = reader.readInt();

   taxableIncome = grossIncome - 10000 - 2000 * numDependents;
   incomeTax = taxableIncome * 0.20;

   writer.print ("The income tax is $");
   writer.println (incomeTax);
}

public static void main (String [] args) {
   IncomeTaxCalculator tpo = new IncomeTaxCalculator();
   tpo.run();
}
}
```

In this program, notice that:

- We have used mixed-mode arithmetic, but in a manner that is not going to produce any undesired effects.

- To read integer data from the keyboard, we send the message `readInt` to the `reader` object.

CS Capsule: Computer Viruses

A *virus* is a computer program that can replicate itself and move from computer to computer. Some programmers of viruses intend no harm; they just want to demonstrate their prowess by creating viruses that go undetected. Other programmers of viruses intend harm by causing system crashes, corruption of data, or hardware failures.

Viruses migrate by attaching themselves to normal programs and then become active again when these programs are launched. Early viruses were easily detected if one had detection software. This software examined portions of each program on the suspect computer and could repair infected programs.

However, viruses and virus detectors have coevolved through the years, and both kinds of software have become very sophisticated. Viruses now hide themselves better than they used to; virus detectors can no longer just examine pieces of data stored in memory to reveal the presence or absence of a virus. Researchers have recently developed a method of running a program that might contain a virus to see whether or not the virus becomes active. The suspect program runs in a "safe" environment that protects the computer from any potential harm. As you can imagine, this process takes time and costs money. For an overview of the history of viruses and the new detection technology, see Carey Nactenberg, "Computer Virus-Antivirus Coevolution," *Communications of the ACM*, Vol. 40, No. 1 (Jan. 1997), 46–51.

3.4 Programming Errors

According to an old saying, we learn from our mistakes, which is fortunate because most people find it almost impossible to write even simple programs without making numerous mistakes. These mistakes, or errors, are of three types: syntax errors, run-time errors, and logic errors.

The Three Types of Errors

Syntax errors, as we learned in Chapter 2, occur when we violate a syntax rule, no matter how minor. These errors are detected at compile time. For instance, if a semicolon is missing at the end of a statement or if a variable is used before it is declared, the compiler will be unable to translate the program into byte code. The good news is that when the Java compiler finds a syntax error, it prints an error message, and we can make the needed correction. The bad news, as we saw previously, is that the error messages are often quite cryptic. However, knowing that there is a syntax error at a particular point in a program is usually enough of a clue to find the error.

Run-time errors occur when we ask the computer to do something that it considers illegal, such as dividing by 0. For example, suppose that the symbols x and y are variables. Then the expression x/y is syntactically correct, so the compiler does not complain. However, when the expression is evaluated during execution of the program, the meaning of the expression depends on the values contained in the variables. If the variable y has the value 0, then the expression cannot be evaluated. The good news is that the Java run-time environment will print a message telling us the nature of the error and where it was encountered. Once again, the bad news is that the error message might be hard to understand.

Logic errors (also called *design errors* or *bugs*) occur when we fail to express ourselves accurately. For instance, in every day life, we might give someone the instruction to turn left when what we really meant to say is turn right. In this example:

- the instruction is phrased properly, and thus the syntax is correct
- the instruction is meaningful, and thus the semantics are valid
- but the instruction does not do what we intended and thus is logically incorrect.

The bad news is that programming environments do not detect logic errors automatically. However, we offer many useful tips on how to prevent logic errors and how to detect them when they occur.

Next we show examples of each of these types of errors.

Illustration of Syntax Errors

We have already seen examples of syntax errors in Chapter 2; however, seeing a few more will be helpful. Here is a listing of the income tax calculator program with the addition of two syntax errors. See if you can spot them. The line numbers are not part of the program but are intended to facilitate the discussion that follows the listing.

```
1    import TerminalIO.*;
2
3    public class IncomeTaxCalculator {
4
5       KeyboardReader reader = new KeyboardReader();
6       ScreenWriter writer = new ScreenWriter();
7
8       double grossIncome;
9       int    numDependents;
10      double taxableIncome;
11      double incomeTax;
12
13      public void run() {
14         writer.print ("Enter the gross income: ");
15         grossIncome = reader.readDouble();
16         writer.print ("Enter the number of dependents: ");
17         numDependents = reader.readInt();
18
19         taxableIncome = grossincome - 10000 - 2000 * numDependents;
20         incomeTax = taxableIncome * 0.20
21
22         writer.print ("The income tax is $");
23         writer.println (incomeTax);
24      }
25
26      public static void main (String [] args) {
27         IncomeTaxCalculator tpo = new IncomeTaxCalculator();
28         tpo.run();
29      }
30   }
```

Just in case you could not spot them, the errors in the code are:

- in line 19, where `grossIncome` has been misspelled as `grossincome` (remember Java is case sensitive)
- in line 20, where the semicolon is missing at the end of the line

When the program is compiled, the terminal window contains the following error messages. We could show a snapshot of the window, but we think the following plain text is more readable:

```
C:\A\JavaCollege\Ch3\IncomeTaxCalculator.java:19: Undefined variable: grossincome
    taxableIncome = grossincome - 10000 - 2000 * numDependents;
                    ^
C:\A\JavaCollege\Ch3\IncomeTaxCalculator.java:20: Invalid type expression.
    incomeTax = taxableIncome * 0.20
              ^
C:\A\JavaCollege\Ch3\IncomeTaxCalculator.java:22: Invalid declaration.
    writer.print ("The income tax is $");
                 ^
3 errors
```

Error 1: The compiler says that line 19 contains an undefined variable called `grossincome`. This is just what we expected. As you can see, a copy of line 19 is printed for our further edification with a carat mark (^) immediately under the word that contains the error.

Error 2: The compiler says that line 20 contains an invalid type expression. This message makes no sense, and the carat mark is under an equal sign. However, when we look at the line, we notice that a semicolon is missing from the end. At least the compiler realizes something is wrong with this line.

Error 3: The compiler says that line 22 contains an invalid declaration. Sorry, but this is not so. This line is fine. However, when the compiler is thrown off balance by a syntax error, it often spits out misleading error messages for several lines thereafter.

The corrective action is to go back into the editor, fix all the errors that make sense, save the file, and compile again. We must repeat this process until the compiler stops finding syntax errors. (Now you can turn to the supplemental materials and read any additional instructions that apply to your development environment.)

Illustration of Run-Time Errors

To illustrate run-time errors we write a small program that attempts to perform division by 0. As is well known, division by 0 is not a well-defined operation and should be avoided. Nonetheless, we must ask what happens if we accidentally write a program that does it. Here then is a trivial program that illustrates the situation:

```java
import TerminalIO.*;

public class DivideByIntegerZero {

    ScreenWriter writer = new ScreenWriter();
    int i, j = 0;
```

```
    public void run() {
       i = 3 / j;
       writer.print ("The value of i is  ");
       writer.println (i);
    }

    public static void main (String [] args) {
       DivideByIntegerZero tpo = new DivideByIntegerZero();
       tpo.run();
    }
}
```

Figure 3.3 shows what happens when we attempt to run this program. The JVM *throws an exception,* which is another way of saying that the program stops executing and a message is printed in the terminal window. The message indicates the nature of the problem, "/ by zero," and its location in line 9 of method run, which was called from line 16 in method main.[3]

Figure 3.3 Run-time error when dividing by integer 0

Interestingly, the JVM responds rather differently when the division involves a floating-point rather than an integer 0. Consider the following nearly identical program:

```
import TerminalIO.*;

public class DivideByFloatingPointZero {

   ScreenWriter writer = new ScreenWriter();
   double i, j = 0.0;

   public void run() {
      i = 3.0 / j;
```

Continues

---

[3] We discuss Java exceptions in greater detail in Chapter 14 and Appendix F.

Continued

```
      writer.print ("The value of i is  ");
      writer.println (i);
   }

   public static void main (String [] args) {
      DivideByFloatingPointZero tpo = new DivideByFloatingPointZero();
      tpo.run();
   }
}
```

The result obtained when running this program is shown in Figure 3.4. As you can see, the program completes execution without error; however, the value of the variable i is considered to be `Infinity`, which is to say it falls outside the range of a `double`. If we now extend the program to divide some number by i, say 3, we will obtain 0. Try it and see.

Figure 3.4 Result obtained when dividing by a floating-point zero

Here is a final and puzzling example of a run-time error. You might not notice it, even after you examine the error message in Figure 3.5. Look again at the code. The word `main` has been misspelled as `Main`. Remember that Java is case sensitive, and computers are exasperatingly literal-minded. They never try to guess what you meant to say, so every mistake, no matter how small, is significant.

```
import TerminalIO.*;

public class PuzzlingRuntimeError {

   ScreenWriter writer = new ScreenWriter();

   public void run() {
      writer.println ("Hello World!");
   }

   public static void Main (String [] args) {
      PuzzlingRuntimeError tpo = new PuzzlingRuntimeError();
      tpo.run();
   }
}
```

Figure 3.5 A puzzling run-time error

Illustration of Logic Errors

Incorrect output is the most obvious indication that there is a logic error in a program. For instance, suppose our temperature conversion program converts 212.0 degrees Fahrenheit to 100.06 instead of 100.0 degrees Celsius. The error is small, but we notice it. And if we do not, our customers, for whom we have written the program, surely will. We caused the problem by incorrectly using 31.9 instead of 32 in the following statement:

```
celsius = (fahrenheit  - 31.9) * 5.0 / 9.0;
```

Errors of this sort are usually found by running a program with test data for which we already know the correct output. We then compare the program's output with the expected results. If there is a difference, we reexamine the program's logic to determine why the program is not behaving as expected.

But how many tests must we perform on a program before we can feel confident that it contains no more logic errors? Sometimes the fundamental nature of a program provides an answer. Perhaps your mathematical skills are sufficiently fresh to recognize that the statement

```
celsius = (fahrenheit  - 32.0) * 5.0 / 9.0;
```

is actually the equation of a line. Because two points determine a line, if the program works correctly for two temperatures, it should work correctly for all. In general, however, it is difficult to determine how many tests are enough. We can often break the data down into categories and test one number in each, the assumption being that if the program works correctly for one number in a category, it will work correctly for all the other numbers in the same category. Careful choice of categories then becomes crucial.

We can also reduce the number of logic errors in a program by rereading the code carefully after we have written it. This is best done when the mind is fresh. It is even possible to use mathematical techniques to prove that a program or segment of a program is free of logic errors.[4] Because programming requires exhausting and excruciating attention to detail, avoid programming for long stretches of time or when tired, a rule you will break frequently unless you manage your time well.

---

[4] We will return to this topic in a somewhat informal manner in Chapter 8 when we discuss loop invariants.

Usually, we can never be certain that a program is error free, and after making a reasonable but large number of tests, we launch the program on the world and wait for some complaints. If we launch too soon, the number of errors will be so high that we will look ridiculous, and we will lose customers, but if we wait too long, the competition will beat us to the market.

Self-Test Questions

9. At what point in the program development process are syntax errors, run-time errors, and logic errors detected?

10. Give an example of a run-time error and explain why it cannot be caught earlier in the program development process.

3.5 Debugging

After we have established that a program contains a logic error, or bug as it is more fondly called, we still have the problem of finding it. Sometimes the nature of a bug suggests its general location in the program. We can then reread this section of the program carefully with the hope of spotting the error. Unfortunately, the bug often is not located where we expect to find it, and even if it is, we will probably miss it. After all, we thought we were writing the program correctly in the first place, so when we reread it, we tend to see what we were trying to say rather than what we actually said.[5]

Thus, programmers are frequently forced to resort to a rather tedious, but powerful, technique for finding bugs. We add to the program extra lines of code that print the values of variables in the terminal window. Of course, we add these lines where we anticipate they will do the most good—that is, preceding and perhaps following the places in the program where we think the bug is mostly likely located. We then run the program again, and from the extra output, we can determine if any of the variables deviate from their expected values. If one of them does, then we know the bug is close by, but if none do, we must try again at a different point in the program. A variable's value is printed in the terminal window as follows:

```
writer.print ("<some message>");
writer.println (<variable name>);
```

Now let us try to find a bug that has been secretly introduced into the temperature conversion program. Suppose the program behaves as shown in Figure 3.6. Something is seriously wrong. The program claims that 212 degrees Fahrenheit converts to 41.1 degrees Celsius instead of the expected 100.

---

[5] That's the advantage of having two authors. One can insert the errors and the other can find them.

Figure 3.6 Incorrect output from the conversion program

Perhaps we can find the problem by checking the value of `fahrenheit` just before `celsius` is calculated. The needed code looks like this:

```
writer.print ("fahrenheit = ");          ← This is debugging code
writer.println (fahrenheit);             ← This is debugging code
celsius = (fahrenheit  - 32.0) * 5.0 / 9.0;
```

When we run the program again with the debugging code included, we get the output shown in Figure 3.7. We entered 212, but for some reason, the program says the value of `fahrenheit` is 106.

Figure 3.7 Running the program after adding extra lines of debugging output

Perhaps we should look at the surrounding code and see if we can spot the error. Here is the relevant code:

```
. . .
writer.print ("Enter degrees Fahrenheit: ");
fahrenheit = reader.readDouble() / 2.0;
writer.print ("fahrenheit = ");
writer.println (fahrenheit);
celsius = (fahrenheit - 32.0) * 5.0 / 9.0;
. . .
```

Ah, there is the error. It looks as if the value entered by the user is divided by 2 just before being assigned to the variable `fahrenheit`. Devious, but we cannot be fooled for long.

Now you can turn to the supplemental material and read additional information related to debugging in your development environment.

Self-Test Question

11. Describe how one can modify code so that the cause of a logic error can be discovered.

3.6 Comments

When we first write a program, we are completely familiar with all its nuances; however, 6 months later, when we or someone else has to modify it, the code that was once so clear now seems confusing and mysterious. There is, however, a technique for dealing with this situation. The remedy is to include comments in the code. *Comments* are explanatory English sentences inserted in a program in such a manner that the compiler ignores them. There are two styles for indicating comments:

> *End of line comments*: These include all of the text following a double slash (//) on any given line.

> *Multiline comments*: These include all of the text between an opening /* and a closing */.

The following code segment illustrates the use of both kinds of comments:

```
/* This code segment illustrates the
use of assignment statements and comments */

a = 3;        // assign 3 to variable a
b = 4;        // assign 4 to variable b
c = a + b;    // add the number in variable a
              //    to the number in variable b
              //    and assign the result, 7, to variable c
c = c * 3;    // multiply the number in variable c by 3
              //    and assign the result, 21, to variable c
```

While this code segment illustrates the mechanics of how to include comments in a program, it gives a misleading idea of when to use them. The main purpose of comments is to make a program more readable and thus easier to maintain. With this end in mind, we usually:

- begin a program with a statement of its purpose and other information that would help orient a programmer called on to modify the program at some future date
- accompany a variable declaration with a comment that explains the variable's purpose

- precede major segments of code with brief comments that explain their purpose
- include comments to explain the workings of complex or tricky sections of code

The case study in the next section follows these guidelines and illustrates a reasonable and helpful level of comments. Too many comments are as harmful as too few, because over time, the burden of maintaining the comments will become excessive. No matter how many comments are included in a program, future programmers must still read and understand the region of code they intended to modify. Common sense usually leads to a reasonable balance. We will always avoid comments that do nothing more than restate the obvious. For instance, the next comment is completely pointless:

```
a = 3;      // assign 3 to variable a. Duh!
```

The best-written programs are self-documenting, that is, the reader can understand the code from the words used and from structure of the sentences and paragraphs or larger units of organization.

Self-Test Questions

12. Describe the difference between an end-of-line comment and a multiline comment.
13. State two rules of thumb for writing appropriate comments in a program.

3.7 Case Study: Count the Angels

Computers have been applied to many complex problems, from predicting the weather, to controlling nuclear power plants, to playing the best chess in the world. Now we extend computing into the realm of metaphysics.

Request. Write a program that determines how many angels can dance on the head of a pin.

Analysis. To solve this problem, we first consulted several prominent theologians. From them we learned that the pertinent factors are the size of the pinhead, the space occupied by a single angel, and the overlap between adjacent angels. Although angels are incorporeal beings, there are limits to the amount of overlap they can tolerate. Also, no region of space is ever occupied by three angels simultaneously. Based on this perhaps imperfect understanding of the problem, we proceed as follows, and herein lies a significant difficulty. The people who write programs usually are not the people who know the most about the problems. Consequently, many programs fail to solve problems correctly either because they completely ignore important factors or because they treat factors inaccurately. To emphasize our point, we are purposely going to introduce two significant errors into our analysis, and we invite you to discover them.[6] These errors are somewhat subtle, so do not feel bad if you cannot spot them. At the end of the chapter, we will suggest what they are. The fact that the eventual program will run perfectly and with blinding speed simply means that it produces an incorrect answer more quickly than would be humanly possible.

The inputs are fairly obvious: the radius of the pinhead, the space occupied by an angel, and the overlap factor. Based on these inputs, we will calculate:

- area of pinhead = πr^2
- nonoverlapping space required by an angel = space occupied by an angel * (1 – overlap factor)
- number of angels on pinhead = area of pinhead / nonoverlapping space required by an angel

The proposed interface is shown in Figure 3.8.

```
Enter the radius in millimeters: 10 Enter
Enter the space occupied by an angel in square micrometers: 0.0001 Enter
Enter the overlap factor: 0.75 Enter
The number of angels = 1.256E7
```

Figure 3.8 Proposed interface for the count angels program

Design. Our rather crude estimate for π is 3.14. Obviously, more accurate estimates yield more accurate calculations of the area. Later we will see how Java itself can provide an excellent estimate. Here is the pseudocode:

```
read radius
read angelSpace
read overlapFactor
area = 3.14 * radius * radius
nonOverlapSpace = angelSpace * (1.0 - overlapFactor)
numberAngels = area / nonOverlapSpace
print numberAngels
```

We have introduced another error in the pseudocode. Can you find it? Again the error is somewhat subtle, and again we will suggest what it is at the end of the chapter. We are not going to make a practice of making analysis and design errors, and we are doing so just this once to make an important point: Analysis and design are significant and worthy of careful thought. After you know what the errors are, you will see that they have nothing to do with programming per se, and they could occur even if we were solving the problem with paper and pencil. Before writing a program to solve a problem, we definitely need to know how to do it correctly by hand.

---

[6] There might be more, but there are at least two. Well, that should cover any mistakes we might be making.

Implementation. The code is a straightforward translation of the pseudocode into Java. Comments are included. Although the code is written correctly, it incorporates the errors made during analysis and design.

```
/*CountAngels.java
Count the number of angels that can dance on the head of a pin.
1) The user inputs are:
        The radius of the pinhead
        The space occupied by an angel
        The allowed overlap between angels subject to the restriction
        that no space can simultaneously be occupied by more than two
2) The program computes:
        The area of the pinhead based on its radius
        The amount of nonoverlapping space required by an angel
        The number of angels based on the preceding two values
3) The program ends by printing the number of angels.
*/

import TerminalIO.*;

public class CountAngels {

   KeyboardReader reader = new KeyboardReader();
   ScreenWriter writer = new ScreenWriter();

   double radius;           //Radius of the pinhead in millimeters
   double angelSpace;       //Space occupied by an angel in square micrometers
   double overlapFactor;    //Allowed overlap between angels from 0 to 1
   double area;             //Area of the pinhead in square millimeters
   double nonOverlapSpace;  //Nonoverlapping space required by an angel
   double numberAngels;     //Number of angels that can dance on the pinhead

   public void run() {

      //Get user inputs
      writer.print ("Enter the radius in millimeters: ");
      radius = reader.readDouble();
      writer.print
        ("Enter the space occupied by an angel in square micrometers: ");
      angelSpace = reader.readDouble();
      writer.print ("Enter the overlap factor: ");
      overlapFactor = reader.readDouble();

      //Perform calculations
      area = 3.14 * radius * radius;
```

Continued

```
      nonOverlapSpace = angelSpace * (1.0 - overlapFactor);
      numberAngels = area / nonOverlapSpace;

      //Print results
      writer.print ("The number of angels = ");
      writer.println (numberAngels);
   }

   public static void main (String [] args) {
      CountAngels tpo = new CountAngels();
      tpo.run();
   }
}
```

3.8 The Lines in Blue

The time has come to remove some of the mystery surrounding the lines of code originally shown in blue. Here they are again.

```
import TerminalIO.*;

public class <name of program> {

   . . .

   public void run() {
      . . .
   }

   public static void main (String [] args) {
      <name of program> tpo = new <name of program>();
      tpo.run();
   }
}
```

In what follows, we make no attempt to explain the meaning of the words public, static, and void or the phrase "String [] args". All this is postponed until Chapters 6 and 9. However, the rest can be understood now.

The import Statement

All our programs have utilized KeyboardReader and ScreenWriter objects, which raises two questions. How does the compiler know what messages can legally be sent to these objects? And during execution, where does the code for the corresponding methods come from? The answer to both of these questions is the same. The information is contained in a package called `TerminalIO`. A ***package*** is a byte code file that defines a collection of related classes. Most packages are added automatically to the development environment when Java is first installed on a computer, and others are added later as needed. We wrote the `TerminalIO` package because the classes `KeyboardReader` and `ScreenWriter` are easier to use than their counterparts in the standard Java packages. The standard classes are presented in Chapter 14. `import` statements are the mechanism for telling the compiler and the JVM the names of any packages needed by a program. The `.*` indicates that all classes in the package are available.

The Program Class and Program Object

In addition to using objects, our programs are objects themselves at the time they are run in the JVM, and thus, they must be defined in a class and instantiated. We illustrate the following discussion by referring to the convert program. The program or class definition is contained within the following lines of code:

```
public class Convert {
    . . .
}
```

The word `class` indicates that we are defining a class.

Instantiating and Running the Program Object

The code that instantiates the program object is contained in the line:

```
Convert tpo = new Convert();
```

This line has the same form as the lines in which we instantiate reader and writer objects. The name `tpo` is of course completely arbitrary and was chosen because it is an acronym for "the program object." Figure 3.9 provides a conceptual view of the `tpo` object. Notice that the object responds to one message, which we have arbitrarily but suggestively called `run`. Also, the object contains four variables, which in accordance to the terminology introduced at the end of Chapter 1 are called instance variables.[7]

Objects do nothing until they are sent a message. The next line of code sends the `run` message to the `tpo` object:

```
        tpo.run();
```

---

[7] There are two other types of variables. In Chapter 6, we present local variables and, in Chapter 9, static variables.

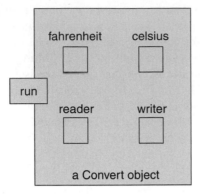

Figure 3.9 A `Convert` object with its four instance variables

The object responds by executing the code in the `run` method as defined in the lines:

```
public void run() {
       . . .
   }
```

The Method `main`

The lines that instantiate and run the program object must be located somewhere, and the developers of Java have decreed that this be in a method called `main`:

```
public static void main (String [] args) {
     Convert tpo = new Convert();
     tpo.run();
   }
```

The method `main` itself must also be located somewhere, and we have chosen what amounts to the simplest option. You will understand more about this after reading Chapters 6 and 9. Whenever we attempt to run a program, the JVM begins by looking for a `public static` method `main`. If exactly one is found, execution begins with the method's first statement. If there is no `public static main` method or more than one, the JVM quits.

Self-Test Questions

14. Describe the purpose of a Java package and give an example of one.
15. In what sense are programs objects?
16. What role does the method `main` play in a Java program?
17. Suppose a programmer forgets to include the method `main` in a program. What happens when the program compiles and runs?

3.9 Summary

This chapter has covered some basic elements of the Java language, such as its vocabulary and the syntax and semantics of variables, arithmetic expressions, and assignment statements. In addition, we have distinguished syntax errors, run-time errors, and logic errors and shown how to detect and correct them.

3.10 Key Terms

If you have difficulty finding the definitions of any key terms in the body of this chapter, turn to the Glossary at the end of the book.

arithmetic expression	logic error	syntax
assignment statement	package	syntax error
comments	pseudocode	type
debugging	reserved words	variable declaration
exception	run-time error	statement
import statement	semantics	virus
literal	statement	

3.11 Answers to Self-Test Questions

1. The vocabulary of a language is the set of words used in forming its sentences. Examples in Java are `class`, `main`, and `{`.

2. A java syntax rule for assignment statement is `<variable> = <expression> ;`.

3. The expression `(x + y) * z` means add the values of x and y and multiply the result by the value of z.

4. One difference between a programming language and a natural language is that people often can understand the meaning of a grammatically incorrect expression in a natural language, whereas a computer must always execute grammatically correct expressions in a programming language. Another difference is that a sentence in a natural language often can have more than one meaning, whereas a sentence in a programming language must have exactly one meaning.

5. a. Valid.

   b. Valid.

   c. Invalid. A user-defined symbol must begin with a letter.

   d. Valid.

   e. Invalid. A user-defined symbol cannot contain a question mark.

6. A variable is a user-defined symbol that names a storage location whose contents or value can change. A literal is a value that cannot change.

7. a. 25

    b. −3

    c. 30

8. When the operands are of different types, the operand of the less inclusive type is automatically converted to a value of the more inclusive type before the operation is performed. The result of the operation is of the more inclusive type.

9. Syntax errors are detected at compile time. Run-time and logic errors are detected at run time.

10. The attempt to divide by 0 is a run-time error. This error cannot be caught before run time, if the divisor operand is a variable, because a variable cannot receive a value until run time.

11. To track down the cause of a logic error, one can examine the values that variables have at a spot close to the suspected source of the error. One does this by inserting output statements with these variables before and after the suspected code. Of course, one needs an idea about which piece of code is under suspicion before inserting these output statements.

12. An end-of-line comment is prefixed with the // symbol. This kind of comment can go anywhere on a line and extends from the // symbol to the end of the current line. A multiline comment begins with the symbol /* and ends with the symbol */. This kind of comment can extend for several lines.

13. Do not undercomment. At least provide comments that name the author, describe the purpose of the program, and explain any complex code that might be unclear to a reader. Do not overcomment. Most of the time, code should be self-documenting; that is, it should be written in a way that the reader understands the meaning just from the words used.

14. The purpose of a Java package is to provide a group of classes for use in a program. An example is the package `TerminalIO`, which provides the classes `ScreenWriter` and `KeyboardReader` for terminal I/O programs.

15. Programs are objects insofar as they are instances of classes.

16. A Java application is a class that contains a `main` method. When an application is run, the `main` method executes, creates an instance of the program class, and sends this object the `run` message.

17. The program compiles successfully and begins execution but terminates instantly because no `main` method is available.

3.12 Programming Problems and Activities

1. Describe the two errors in analysis and the one error in design in the angels case study. (*Hints*: The user can enter any number for the overlap factor, and the spaces occupied by angels are little squares.)

2. The surface area of a cube can be known if we know the length of an edge. Write a program that takes the length of an edge as input and prints the cube's surface area as output. (*Remember*: ADIT—analyze, design, implement, test.)

3. The kinetic energy of a moving object is given by the formula $KE = (1 / 2)mv^2$, where m is the object's mass and v is its velocity. Modify the program of Chapter 2, Problem 5 so that it prints the object's kinetic energy as well as its momentum.

4. An employee's total weekly pay equals the hourly wage multiplied by the total number of regular hours plus any overtime pay. Overtime pay equals the total overtime hours multiplied by 1.5 times the hourly wage. Write a program that takes as inputs the hourly wage, total regular hours, and total overtime hours and displays an employee's total weekly pay.

5. Modify the program of Problem 4 so that it prompts the user for the regular and overtime hours of each of five working days.

4. Control Statements

All the programs to this point have consisted of short sequences of instructions that were executed one after the other. Such a scheme, even if we allowed the sequence of instructions to become extremely long, would not be very useful. In computer programs as in real life, instructions must express repetition and selection. Expressing these notions in Java is the major topic of this chapter, and we start with a very down to earth example.

4.1 A Visit to the Farm

Once upon a time in a faraway land, Jack visited his cousin Jill in the country and offered to milk the cow. Jill gave him a list of instructions:

```
fetch the cow from the field;
tie her in the stall;
milk her into the bucket;
pour the milk into the bottles;
drive her back into the field;
clean the bucket;
```

Although Jack was a little taken aback by Jill's liberal use of semicolons, he had no trouble following the instructions. A year later, Jack visited again. In the meantime, Jill had acquired a herd of cows, some red and some black. This time, when Jack offered to help, Jill gave him a more complex list of instructions:

```
herd the cows from the field into the west paddock;
while (there are any cows left in the west paddock){
    fetch a cow from the west paddock;
    tie her in the stall;
    if (she is red){
       milk her into the red bucket;
       pour the milk into red bottles;
    }else{
       milk her into the black bucket;
       put the milk into black bottles;
    }
    put her into the east paddock;
}
herd the cows from the east paddock back into the field;
clean the buckets;
```

These instructions threw Jack for a loop (pun intended) until Jill explained

```
while (some condition){
    do stuff;
}
```

means do the stuff repeatedly as long as the condition holds true, and

```
if (some condition){
    do stuff 1;
}else{
    do stuff 2;
}
```

means if some condition is true, do stuff 1, and if it is false, do stuff 2.

"And what about all the semicolons and braces?" asked Jack.

"Those," said Jill, "are just a habit I picked up from programming in Java, where `while` and `if-else` are called ***control statements***."

Self-Test Questions

1. Why does Jill use a `while` statement in her instructions to Jack?
2. Why does Jill use an `if-else` statement in her instructions to Jack?

4.2 The `if` and `if-else` Statements

We now explore the `if-else` statement and the slightly simpler but related `if` statement in greater detail. The meanings of `if` and `else` in Java sensibly adhere to our everyday usage of these words. Java and other high-level programming languages achieve their programmer friendly qualities by combining bits and pieces of English phrasing with some of the notational conventions of elementary algebra.

To repeat, in Java, the `if` and `if-else` statements allow for the conditional execution of statements. For instance:

```
if (condition){
   statement;             //Execute these statements if the
   statement;             //condition is true.
}
```

```
if (condition){
   statement;             //Execute these statements if the
   statement;             //condition is true.
}else{
   statement;             //Execute these statements if the
   statement;             //condition is false.
}
```

The indicated semicolons and braces are required; however, the exact format of the text depends on the aesthetic sensibilities of the programmer, who should be guided by a desire to make the program as readable as possible. Notice that braces always occur in pairs and that there is no semicolon immediately following a closing brace.

The braces can be dropped if only a single statement follows the word `if` or `else`; for instance:

```
if (condition)
   statement;
```

```
if (condition)
   statement;
else
   statement;
```

```
if (condition){
   statement;
      ...
   statement;
}else
   statement;
```

```
if (condition)
    statement;
else{
    statement;
       ...
    statement;
}
```

In general, it is better to overuse braces than to underuse them. Likewise, in expressions, it is better to overuse parentheses. The extra braces or parentheses can never do any harm, and their presence helps to eliminate logic errors.

The condition of an if statement must be a ***Boolean expression.*** This type of expression returns the value true or false.

Figure 4.1 shows a diagram, called a ***flowchart,*** that illustrates the behavior of if and if-else statements. When the statements are executed, either the left or the right branch is executed depending on whether the condition is true or false.

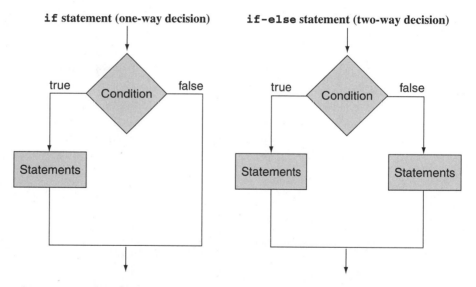

Figure 4.1 Flowcharts for the if and if-else statements

Examples

Here are some examples of if statements:

```
//Increase a salesman's commission by 10% if his sales are over $5000
if (sales > 5000)
    commission = commission * 1.1;
```

```
//Pay a worker $14.5 per hour plus time and a half for overtime
pay = hoursWorked * 14.5;
if (hoursWorked > 40){
    overtime = hoursWorked - 40;
    pay = pay + overtime * 7.25;
}
```

```
//Let c equal the larger of a and b
if (a > b)
    c = a;
else
    c = b;
```

Self-Test Questions

3. What type of expression must the condition of an `if` statement contain?
4. Describe the role of the curly braces (`{}`) in an `if` statement.
5. What is the difference between an `if` statement and an `if-else` statement?

4.3 Relational and Logical Operators

We introduced a new symbol in the preceding examples, at least new from your perspective as beginning Java programmers. It is the greater than symbol (>). In Java, it is one of six *relational operators,* and its meaning conforms to that already established in elementary algebra. Here is a list of Java's relational operators:

<	less than
>	greater than
<=	less than or equal to
>=	greater than or equal to
==	equal to
!=	not equal to

The notation for the last two relational operators is rather peculiar, but there it is. The double equal signs (==) distinguish *equal to* from *assignment* (=). In the *not equal* to operator, the exclamation mark (!) is read as *not*. When these expressions are evaluated, their values will be either true or false depending on the values of the variables involved. For example, suppose

```
a = 3        c = 10
b = 7        d = -20
```

then

a < b	is true	
a <= b	is true	
a == b	is false	
a != b	is true	
a - b > c + d	is true	(the precedence of > is lower than + and -)
a < b < c	is invalid	
a == b == c	is invalid	

In addition to the six relational operators, Java also provides three *logical operators* equivalent in meaning to the English words AND, OR, and NOT. The symbols for these operators are &&, ||, and !, respectively. The operands of logical operators must be Boolean expressions. The behavior of the logical operators can be completely specified in a *truth table.* A truth table lists all of the possible values of the operand expressions and the resulting values of the operations on these expressions. Tables 4.1(a) and 4.1(b) are truth tables for &&, ||, and !. The symbols A and B in the two tables stand for any Boolean expressions.

Table 4.1(a)

The Truth Table for || and &&			
A	B	A || B	A && B
true	true	true	true
true	false	true	false
false	true	true	false
false	false	false	false

Table 4.1(b)

The Truth Table for !	
A	! A
true	false
false	true

To help you understand the meaning of the logical operators, we will write some code in a mixture of Java and English, which we call *Javish.*

AND. First we illustrate the && operator:

```
if (the sun shines && it is 8 AM)      // AND
    let's go for a walk;               // Both conditions are true
else
    let's stay home;                   // One or both conditions are false
```

In conformance with the usual meaning of the word AND, we will go for a walk if both conditions are true; otherwise, we will stay at home.

OR. Rewriting the example using the | | operator yields:

```
if (the sun shines || it is 8 PM)    // OR
   let's go for a walk;              // One or both conditions are true
else
   let's stay home;                 // Both conditions are false
```

Again applying standard English usage, we will go for a walk if either or both conditions are true; otherwise, we will stay home.

NOT. Here is an illustration of the ! operator:

```
if (! the sun shines)            // NOT
   let's go for a walk;          // The sun is not shining
else
   let's stay home;             // The sun is shining
```

Some people obviously prefer to walk in the rain.

Mixture. Even a condition involving all three operators simultaneously is fairly easy to understand:

```
if ((the sun shines && it is 8 AM) || your brother visits))
   let's go for a walk;
else
   let's stay home;
```

So now when do we go for a walk? The answer is at 8 A.M. on sunny days or when your brother visits.

Pure Java. Finally, here is an example in pure Java. Suppose

$$a = 3 \qquad c = 10$$
$$b = 7 \qquad d = -20$$

Then let us determine what sage advice is offered by the next segment of code:

```
if (a > b || c > d)
   writer.println("Lottery tickets are a waste of money");
else
   writer.println("Someone always wins so buy today");
```

Well, a > b is false and c > d is true. The operator is OR. The conclusion is, "Lottery tickets are a waste of money." But perhaps you would rather make up your own mind on a matter of such great financial importance.

Precedence Rules. We close the section by presenting Table 4.2, which shows how the relational and logical operators fit into the operator precedence scheme.

Table 4.2

Positions of the Logical and Relational Operators in the Precedence Scheme

Operation	Symbol	Precedence (from highest to lowest)	Association
Grouping	( )	1	Not applicable
Method selector	.	2	Left to right
Unary plus	+	3	Not applicable
Unary minus	–	3	Not applicable
Not	!	3	Not applicable
Multiplication	*	4	Left to right
Division	/	4	Left to right
Remainder or modulus	%	4	Left to right
Addition	+	5	Left to right
Subtraction	–	5	Left to right
Less than	<	6	Not applicable
Less than or equal to	<=	6	Not applicable
Greater than	>	6	Not applicable
Greater than or equal to	>=	6	Not applicable
Equal to	==	7	Not applicable
Not equal to	!=	7	Not applicable
And	&&	8	Left to right
Or	||	9	Left to right
Assignment	=	10	Right to left

Self-Test Questions

6. What is a truth table?

7. Assume that X is 3 and Y is 2. Write the values of the following expressions:

   a. X <= Y

   b. X > Y

   c. X != Y

   d. X == Y

8. Assume that A is true and B is false. Write the values of the following expressions:

   a. A || B

   b. A && B

   c. A && ! B

   d. ! (A || B)

9. List the logical operators in the order in which each one would be evaluated at run time.

10. Construct a Boolean expression that tests whether the value of variable x is within the range specified by the variables min (the smallest) and max (the largest).

4.4 Case Study: Compute Weekly Pay

We illustrate the use of if statements and relational operators by writing a program to compute weekly pay.

Request. Write a program to compute the weekly pay of hourly employees.

Analysis. Employees are paid at a base rate for the first 40 hours they work each week. Hours over 40 are paid at an overtime rate equal to twice the base rate. An exception is made for part-time employees, who are always paid at the regular rate no matter how many hours they work. Figure 4.2 shows the user interface.

```
Enter type of employee (1 full-time, 2 part-time): 1 Enter
Enter the hourly rate (double): 10.50 Enter
Enter the hours worked (int)   : 50 Enter
The weekly pay is $630
```

Figure 4.2 Interface for the compute weekly pay program

Design. Here is pseudocode for the program:

```
read employeeType
read hourlyRate
read hoursWorked
if (hoursWorked <= 40 || employeeType == 2)
   weeklyPay = hourlyRate * hoursWorked
else
   weeklyPay = hourlyRate * 40 + hourlyRate * 2 * (hoursWorked - 40);
print weeklyPay
```

Implementation. The implementation is now straightforward:

```
/* ComputeWeeklyPay.java
Compute an employee's weekly pay. Employees are paid at a base
rate for the first 40 hours they work each week. Hours over 40
are paid at an overtime rate equal to twice the base rate, except for
part-time employees who are never paid overtime.
1) The user enters the employee type, hourly rate, and the number of
   hours worked.
2) The program computes and displays the employee's pay.
*/

import TerminalIO.*;

public class ComputeWeeklyPay {

   KeyboardReader reader = new KeyboardReader();
   ScreenWriter   writer = new ScreenWriter();

   int    employeeType;   //Type of employee
                          //1 full-time, 2 part-time
   double hourlyRate;     //An employee's hourly rate
   int    hoursWorked;    //The hours worked in one week
   double weeklyPay;      //The employee's pay for the week

   public void run() {

      //Read the employee type, hourly rate, and hours worked
      employeeType = reader.readInt
         ("Enter type of employee (1 full-time, 2 part-time): ");
      hourlyRate  = reader.readDouble("Enter the hourly rate (double): ");
      hoursWorked = reader.readInt   ("Enter the hours worked (int)  : ");
```

Continues

Continued

```
    //Calculate the weekly pay
    if (hoursWorked <= 40 || employeeType == 2)
       weeklyPay = hourlyRate * hoursWorked;
    else
       weeklyPay = hourlyRate * 40
                 + hourlyRate * 2 * (hoursWorked - 40);

    //Print the weekly pay
    writer.print ("The weekly pay is $");
    writer.println (weeklyPay);
 }

 public static void main (String [] args) {
    ComputeWeeklyPay tpo = new ComputeWeeklyPay();
    tpo.run();
 }
}
```

In this listing, we have introduced new versions of the `readDouble` and `readInt` messages that accept a string as a parameter. The `reader` object prints the string in the terminal window and then waits for the user's input. For a complete list of `KeyboardReader` and `ScreenWriter` methods, see Appendix H.

4.5 Testing

Quality assurance is the ongoing process of making sure that a software product is being developed to the highest standards possible subject to the ever-present constraints of time and money. As we learned in Chapter 1, faults are fixed most inexpensively early in the development life cycle; however, no matter how much care is taken at every stage during a product's development, at the end the product must be run against well-designed test data. Such data should exercise a program as thoroughly as possible. In particular, the test data should try to achieve *complete code coverage,* which means that every line of a program is executed at least once. This standard is easily applied to the payroll program by testing with an hourly rate of $10 and the hours worked equal to 30 and 50 hours. Because we must compare the program's output with the expected results, we have chosen numbers for which it is easy to perform the calculations by hand. Having tested the program for 30 hours, we feel no need to test it for 29 or 31 hours because we realized that exactly the same code is executed in all three cases. Likewise, we do not feel compelled to test the program for 49 and 51 hours. All the sets of test data that exercise a program in the same manner are said to belong to the same *equivalence class,* which is to say they are equivalent from the perspective of testing the same paths through the program. Test data for the payroll program falls into just two equivalence classes: hours between 0 and 40 and hours greater than 40.

The test data should also include cases that explore a program's behavior under *boundary conditions*—that is, on or near the boundaries between equivalence classes. It is common for programs to fail at these points. For the payroll program, this requirement means testing with hours equal to 39, 40, and 41. Finally, we should test under *extreme conditions*—that is, with data at the limits of validity. For this, we choose hours worked equal to 0 and 168 hours. We will encounter other types of tests later in the chapter, but for now, we have enough. Table 4.3 summarizes our planned tests. Notice the last row, which contains an additional test needed to make sure that the OR operator is having the planned effect.

Table 4.3

Test Data for the Payroll Program	
Type of Test	**Data Used**
Code coverage	employee type: 1
	hourly rate: 10
	hours worked: 30 and 50
Boundary conditions	employee type: 1
	hourly rate: 10
	hours worked: 39, 40, and 41
Extreme conditions	employee type: 1
	hourly rate: 10
	hours worked: 0 and 168
Further tests of `if` condition	employee type: 2
	hourly rate: 10
	hours worked: 30 and 50

Self-Test Questions

11. What happens when we provide complete code coverage of a program?
12. What is an equivalence class? Give an example.
13. What are boundary conditions? Give an example.
14. What are extreme conditions? Give an example.
15. Suppose a teacher uses grades from 0 to 100 and wants to discount all grades below 60 in her records. Discuss the equivalence classes, boundary conditions, and extreme conditions used to test a program that processes this information.

4.6 The `while` Statement

The `while` statement implements a *loop*. It allows the statement or group of statements inside the loop to execute repeatedly while a condition remains true. Here is the `while` statement's format:

```
while (condition)          // loop test
    statement;                 // inside the loop
```

```
while (condition){         // loop test
    statement;                 // inside
    statement;                 // the
    ...                        // loop
}
```

If the condition is false from the outset, the statement or statements inside the loop never execute. Figure 4.3 uses a flowchart to illustrate the behavior of a `while` statement.

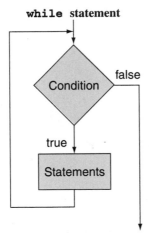

Figure 4.3 Flowchart for a `while` statement

Three Short Examples

To help you become familiar with `while` statements, we now present three short examples. Here is the first one:

```
//Print the sum of the integers from 1 to 100
sum = 0;
i = 1;
while (i <= 100){
```

```
    sum = sum + i;      // point p (we will refer to this later)
    i = i + 1;
}
writer.println (sum);
```

The behavior of the snippet is clear. The variable sum starts at 0 and i starts at 1. The code inside the loop executes 100 times, and each time through the loop, sum is incremented by increasing values of i.

To understand a loop fully, we should think about the way in which the variables change on each pass or *iteration* through the loop. Table 4.4 helps in this endeavor. On the 100th iteration, i is increased to 101, so there is never a 101st iteration, and we are confident that the sum is computed correctly.

Table 4.4

Trace of How Variables Change on Each Iteration Through a Loop

Iteration Number	Value of i at point p	Value of sum at point p
1	1	1
2	2	$1 + 2$
. . .	. . .	. . .
100	100	$1 + 2 + \cdots + 100$

Here are two more examples in the same vein:

```
//Print the product of the even integers from 2 to 100
product = 1;
i = 2;
while (i <= 100){
    product = product * i;
    i = i + 2;
}
writer.println (product);
```

```
//Print the first value n for which 1 + 2 + . . . + n
//is greater than a million
sum = 0;
n = 0;
while (sum <= 1000000){
    n = n + 1;
    sum = sum + n;
}
writer.println (n);
```

To verify that these examples work as intended, we could construct tables similar to Table 4.4.

A Common Loop Structure

The loops in the first two examples share a structure that is both common and useful. You will find that many of your `while` statements will fit this pattern:

```
initialize an accumulator;
initialize a counter;
while (some condition is true about the counter){
   make a calculation;
   store the result in the accumulator;
   increment the counter;
}
```

Logic Errors in Loops, Including Infinite Loops

It is easy to make logic errors when coding loops, but we can avoid many of these errors if we have a proper understanding of a loop's typical structure. A loop usually has four component parts:

1. **Initializing statements.** These statements initialize variables used within the loop.
2. **Terminating condition.** This condition is tested before each pass through the loop to determine if another iteration is needed.
3. **Body statements.** These statements execute on each iteration and implement the calculation in question.
4. **Update statements.** These statements, which usually occur at the bottom of the loop, change the values of the variables tested in the terminating condition.

A careless programmer can introduce logic errors into any one of these parts. To demonstrate, we first present a simple but correct `while` loop and then show several revised versions, each with a different logic error. All the loops can be tested in a program with the following structure:

```
import TerminalIO.*;

public class QuickTest {

   ScreenWriter writer = new ScreenWriter();

   int i, product;

   public void run() {
      . . .
```

```
      while (. . .){
         . . .
      }
      writer.println (product);
   }

   public static void main (String [] args) {
      QuickTest tpo = new QuickTest();
      tpo.run();
   }
}
```

The correct version is:

```
//Compute the product of the odd integers from 1 to 100
//Outcome - product will equal 3*5*...*99
product = 1;
i = 3;
while (i <= 100){
   product = product * i;
   i = i + 2;
}
writer.println (product);
```

First Error. We first introduce an error into the initializing statements. Because we forget to initialize the variable product, it retains its default value of zero.

```
//Error - failure to initialize the variable product
//Outcome - zero is printed
i = 3;
while (i <= 100){
   product = product * i;
   i = i + 2;
}
writer.println (product);
```

Second Error. This error involves the terminating condition:

```
//Error - use of "< 99" rather than "<= 100" in the
//        terminating condition
//Outcome - product will equal 3*5...*97
product = 1;
i = 3;
```

Continues

Continued

```
while (i < 99){
   product = product * i;
   i = i + 2;
}
writer.println (product);
```

This is called an *off-by-one error,* and it occurs whenever a loop goes around one too many or one too few times. This is one of the most common types of looping errors and is often difficult to detect. Do not be fooled by the fact that in this example the error is glaringly obvious.

Third Error. Here is another error in the terminating condition:

```
//Error - use of "!= 100" rather than "<= 100" in the terminating condition
//Outcome - the program will never stop
product = 1;
i = 3;
while (i != 100){
   product = product * i;
   i = i + 2;
}
writer.println (product);
```

The variable i takes on the values 3, 5, . . . , 99, 101, . . . and never equals 100. This is called an *infinite loop.* Anytime a program responds more slowly than expected, it is reasonable to assume that it is stuck in an infinite loop. Do not pull the plug. Instead, on a PC, select the terminal window and type Ctrl-c; that is, hold down the Control key and c simultaneously. This will stop the program. (Turn to the supplemental materials for special instructions relating to your development environment.)

Fourth Error. Here is an error in the body of the loop:

```
//Error - use of + rather than * when computing product
//Outcome - product will equal 3+5+...+99
product = 1;
i = 3;
while (i <= 100){
   product = product + i;
   i = i + 2;
}
writer.println (product);
```

Fifth Error. We conclude with an error in the update statements:

```
//Error - placement of the update statement in the wrong place
//Outcome - product will equal 5*7*...*99*101
product = 1;
i = 3;
while (i <= 100){
    i = i + 2;
    product = product * i;
}
writer.println (product);
```

Debugging Loops

If you suspect that you have written a loop that contains a logic error, inspect the code and make sure the following are true:

- Variables are initialized correctly before entering the loop.
- The terminating condition stops the iterations when the test variables have reached the intended limit.
- The statements in the body are correct.
- The update statements are positioned correctly and modify the test variables in such a manner that they eventually pass the limits tested in the terminating condition.

In addition, when writing terminating conditions, it is usually safer to use one of the operators

```
<    <=    >    >=
```

than either of the operators

```
==    !=
```

as was demonstrated earlier.

Also, if you cannot find an error by inspection, then use `writer.println` statements to dump key variables to the terminal window. Good places for these statements are

- immediately after the initialization statements
- inside the loop, at the top
- inside the loop, at the bottom

You will then discover that some of the variables have values different than expected, and this will provide clues that reveal the exact nature and location of the logic error.

Self-Test Questions

16. When does a `while` loop terminate execution?

17. List the four components of a `while` loop.

18. List two possible causes of infinite loops.

19. Why is it usually a bad idea to terminate loops with conditions that use `==` or `!=`?

20. Suppose Jack wants to write code to input a number until it falls within a given range, specified by the variables `min` and `max`. Jill shows him the following loop, which contains a logic error. Find and correct the error.

```
int number = reader.readInt("Enter a number: ");
while (number >= min && number <= max)
    number = reader.readInt("Enter a number again: ");
```

4.7 Case Study: Count the Divisors

This case study illustrates the use of `while` statements. It is fairly straightforward, and we combine analysis, design, and implementation into a single step.

Request. Write a program that computes the number of proper divisors of an integer.

Analysis, Design, and Implementation. The program considers only positive numbers and positive divisors. We do not include 1 or the number itself when counting the proper divisors. If the user enters a negative number, the program computes the answer for the corresponding positive number.

The proposed interface is shown in Figure 4.4. A number A is a divisor of a number B if the remainder produced by dividing B by A is equal to 0. Thus, the test for this condition in Java is `B % A == 0`. Here is code for the core of the program (the missing lines are left as an exercise):

```
int number;          //The number entered by the user
int count;           //A count of the divisors
int trialDivisor;    //A trial divisor
int limit;           //The limit for the while loop

. . .
if (number < 0)
    number = -number;
count = 0;
trialDivisor = 2;
limit = number / 2 + 1;
while (trialDivisor < limit){
```

```
    if (number % trialDivisor == 0)
      count = count + 1;
    trialDivisor = trialDivisor + 1;
}
. . .
```

```
Enter a positive integer: 24 Enter
The number 24 has 6 proper divisors.
```

Figure 4.4 Interface for the divisors program

Note that in the code, if `trialDivisor` is greater than or equal to `limit`, then it is too large to be a divisor of `number` and the loop terminates. For example:

If number **is:**	**Then** limit **is:**
100	51
101	51

Obviously, 51 is too large to be a divisor of 100 or 101.

4.8 More Testing

The presence of looping statements in a program increases the challenge of designing good test data. Frequently, loops do not iterate some fixed number of times, but instead iterate zero, one, or more times depending on a program's inputs. In these situations, we strive to develop test data that cover all three possibilities.[1] With this requirement in mind, Table 4.5 provides test data for the count divisors program. Note that a single test can sometimes serve several different purposes. When looking at the table, we cannot help being surprised by how many tests are required, but at the same time, we are left wondering if perhaps there should be more.[2] Note the extreme conditions test. How long does it take on your computer? In general, should we assume that just because a program works well for small numbers, it will work equally well for large numbers? Chapter 12 has some answers to the latter question.

---

[1] For greater insight into why these three possibilities are the most significant, see the discussion of loop invariants and mathematical induction in Chapter 8.

[2] We postpone until Chapter 8 how the test data should be modified in response to changes in the program, the difference between white box and black box testing, and regression testing.

Table 4.5

Test Data for the Count Divisors Program	
Type of Test	**Data Used**
Code coverage	number: −10 and 10 (first `if` statement)
	number: 10 and 11 (second `if` statement)
Boundary conditions	number: −10, 0, and 10 (first `if` statement)
Loop limits	number: 0, 1, 2, or 3 (no iterations)
	number: 4 or 5 (one iteration)
	number: 10 (more than one iteration)
Extreme conditions	number: 2000000000

Consider the following question: Suppose a program is composed of three parts and that it takes five tests to verify each part independently. Then how many tests does it take to verify the program as a whole? In the unlikely event that the three parts are independent of each other and in addition can utilize the same five sets of test data, then five tests suffice. However, it is far more likely that the behavior of each part affects the other two and also that the parts have differing test requirements. The total number of tests could then be at least 125 (5 * 5 * 5). We call this multiplicative growth in test cases a *combinatorial explosion,* and it pretty well guarantees the impossibility of exhaustively testing large complex programs; however, it does not diminish our responsibility to test our programs intelligently and well. Fortunately, although combinatorial explosion is our nemesis when testing, equivalence classes are our allies.

So far, we have focused on developing test data that confirm a program produces correct results when provided with valid inputs, but surprisingly, this is not good enough. We should also determine how a program behaves when confronted with invalid data. After all, users frequently make mistakes or do not fully understand a program's data entry requirements. A program that tolerates errors in user inputs and recovers gracefully is said to be *robust.*

The best and easiest way to write robust programs is to check user inputs immediately on entry and reject invalid data. We illustrate this technique in the next case study. At this stage, there are limits to how thorough we can be when checking inputs, and in the next case study, we will merely make sure that inputs are positive when it is reasonable to expect them to be so.

Self-Test Questions

21. What would be reasonable test data for a loop that does not execute a fixed number of times?

22. What is a robust program? Give an example.

CS Capsule: Artificial Intelligence, Robots, and Softbots

You have seen in this chapter that a computer not only calculates results but also responds to conditions in its environment and takes the appropriate actions. This additional capability forms the basis of a branch of computer science known as *artificial intelligence,* or AI. AI programmers attempt to construct computational models of intelligent human behavior. These tasks involve, among many others, interacting in English or other natural languages, recognizing objects in the environment, reasoning, creating and carrying out plans of action, and pruning irrelevant information from a sea of detail.

There are many ways to construct AI models. One way is to view intelligent behavior as patterns of *production rules.* Each rule contains a set of conditions and a set of actions. In this model, an intelligent agent, either a computer or a human being, compares conditions in its environment to the conditions of all of its rules. Those rules with matching conditions are scheduled to fire—meaning that their actions are triggered—according to a higher-level scheme of rules. The set of rules is either hand-coded by the AI programmer or "learned" by using a special program known as a *neural net.*

AI systems have been used to control *robots.* While not quite up to the performance of Data in the TV series *Star Trek: The Next Generation,* these robots perform mundane tasks such as assembling cars.

AI systems are also embedded in software agents known as *softbots.* For example, softbots exist to filter information from electronic mail systems, to schedule appointments, and to search the World Wide Web for information.

For a detailed discussion of robots and softbots, see Rodney Brooks, "Intelligence Without Representation," in *Mind Design II*, ed. John Haugeland (Cambridge, MA: MIT Press, 1997), and Patti Maes, "Agents That Reduce Work and Information Overload," *Communications of the ACM,* Vol. 37, No. 7 (July 1994): 30–40.

4.9 Case Study: Fibonacci Numbers

There is a famous sequence of numbers that occurs frequently in nature. In 1202, the Italian mathematician Leonardo Fibonacci presented the following problem concerning the breeding of rabbits. Assume somewhat unrealistically that:

1. Each pair of rabbits in a population produces a new pair of rabbits each month.
2. Rabbits become fertile 1 month after birth.
3. Rabbits do not die.

Then if a single pair of newborn rabbits is introduced into an environment, how rapidly does the rabbit population increase on a monthly basis?

To answer the question, we proceed 1 month at a time:

- At the beginning of month 1, there is one pair of rabbits. (total = 1 pair)
- At the beginning of month 2, our initial pair of rabbits, A, will have just reached sexual maturity, so there will be no offspring. (total = 1 pair)
- At the beginning of month 3, pair A will have given birth to pair B. (total = 2 pair)
- At the beginning of month 4, pair A will have given birth to pair C and pair B will be sexually mature. (total = 3 pair)
- At the beginning of month 5, pairs A and B will have given birth to pairs D and E, while pair C will have reached sexual maturity. (total = 5 pair)
- And so on.

If we continue in this way, we obtain the following sequence of numbers

$$1 \quad 1 \quad 2 \quad 3 \quad 5 \quad 8 \quad 13 \quad 21 \quad 34 \quad 55 \quad 89 \quad 144 \quad 233 \quad \ldots$$

called the **_Fibonacci numbers_**. Notice that each number, after the first two, is the sum of its two predecessors. Referring back to the rabbits, see if you can demonstrate why this should be the case. Although the sequence of numbers is easy to construct, there is no known formula for calculating the nth Fibonacci number, which gives rise to the following program request.

Request. Write a program that can compute the nth Fibonacci number on demand, where n is a positive integer.

Analysis, Design, and Implementation. The user input should be a positive integer, and other inputs will be rejected. The proposed interface is shown in Figure 4.5. Here is the code:

```
/*Fibonacci.java
Calculate the nth Fibonacci number.
1) The user should enter a positive integer n. Other inputs are
   rejected.
2) The program computes and displays the nth Fibonacci number.
*/

import TerminalIO.*;

public class Fibonacci {

   KeyboardReader reader = new KeyboardReader();
   ScreenWriter   writer = new ScreenWriter();

   int n;          //The number entered by the user
   int fib;        //The nth Fibonacci number
   int a,b,count;  //Variables that facilitate the computation
```

```
public void run() {

    //Keep asking the user for inputs until a positive integer is entered
    n = reader.readInt("Enter a positive integer: ");
    while (n <= 0)
       n = reader.readInt("Please, you must enter a positive integer: ");

    //Calculate the nth Fibonacci number
    fib = 1;                    //Takes care of case n = 1 or 2
    a = 1;
    b = 1;
    count = 3;
    while (count <= n){   //Takes care of case n >= 3
       fib = a + b;       //Point p. Referred to later.
       a = b;
       b = fib;
       count = count + 1;
    }

    //Print the nth Fibonacci number
    writer.print ("Fibonacci of ");
    writer.print (n);
    writer.print (" is ");
    writer.println (fib);
}

public static void main (String [] args) {
    Fibonacci tpo = new Fibonacci();
    tpo.run();
}
}
```

```
Enter a positive integer: 8 Enter
Fibonacci of 8 is 21
```

Figure 4.5 Interface for the Fibonacci program

Loop Analysis

The workings of the loop in the Fibonacci program are not obvious at first glance, so to clarify what is happening, we construct Table 4.6, which traces the changes to key variables on each pass through the loop.

Table 4.6

count at point p	a at point p	b at point p	fib at point p
3	1	1	2
4	1	2	3
5	2	3	5
6	3	5	8
. . .	. . .	. . .	. . .
n	$(n-2)$th Fibonacci number	$(n-1)$th Fibonacci number	nth Fibonacci number

Changes to Key Variables on Each Pass Through the Loop

Test Data

What we have learned so far about designing test data suggests the tests shown in Table 4.7. You are probably surprised that 80 represents a test of extreme conditions; however, the program returns the value 285,007,387 when n equals 80. The problem is due to *arithmetic overflow.* In Java and most programming languages, integers have a limited range (see Chapter 3), and exceeding that range leads to strange results. Adding 1 to the most positive integer yields the most negative integer, and likewise, subtracting 1 from the most negative integer yields the most positive integer. Welcome to the strange world of computer arithmetic, where bizarre events are always waiting to trip the unwary. See if you can find the largest number for which the Fibonacci program works correctly. To avoid our problem, we could include extra lines of code that test for an unexpected switch to negative values. A somewhat similar problem cost the French space program half a billion dollars and a great deal of embarrassment when a computer guided rocket and its payload exploded shortly after takeoff.

Table 4.7

Test Data for the Fibonacci Program

Type of Test	Data Used
Robustness and limits on first loop	*n:* 1 (no iterations)
	n: 0 followed by 1 (one iteration)
	n: −1 followed by 0 followed by 1 (one iteration)
Limits on second loop	*n:* 1 or 2 (no iterations)
	n: 3 (one iteration)
	n: 8 (more than one iteration)
Extreme conditions	*n:* 80

4.10 Nested `if` Statements

The complexities of programming sometimes require `if` and `if-else` statements to be nested in various combinations. Here is an everyday example written in Javish:

```
if (the time is after 7 PM){
   if (you have a book)
      read the book;
   else
      watch TV;
}else
   go for a walk;
```

Although this code is not complicated, it is a little difficult to determine exactly what it means. A truth table can help a great deal. Table 4.8 provides an example. The first two columns of this table show the conditions being tested. Each condition can be true or false, giving rise to four combinations of true and false and thus to four rows in the table. The last column shows the outcome for each combination.

Table 4.8

Truth Table for Reading a Book, Watching TV, or Going for a Walk		
After 7 P.M.	**Have a book**	**Outcome**
true	true	read book
true	false	watch TV
false	true	walk
false	false	walk

Having made the table, we can be certain that we understand exactly what the code does. Of course, it would probably be better to make the table first and then write the code to match. As an alternative to a truth table, we can draw a flowchart as shown in Figure 4.6. Again it would be better to draw the flowchart before writing the code. Truth tables and flowcharts can also represent more complex situations involving any number of conditions. The prudent programmer uses them frequently.

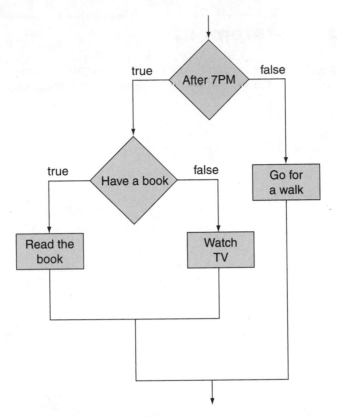

Figure 4.6 Flowchart for reading a book, watching TV, or going for a walk

Here is a second example of nested `if` statements written in Javish. The code determines a student's grade based on test average:

```
if (average >= 90)
   grade is A;
else{
   if (average >= 80)
      grade is B;
   else{
      if (average >= 70)
         grade is C;
      else{
         if (average >= 60)
            grade is D;
         else{
            grade is F;
```

```
            }
        }
      }
}
```

By remembering that, in the absence of braces, an else is associated with the preceding if, we can rewrite the code as follows:

```
if (average >= 90)
   grade is A;
else
   if (average >= 80)
      grade is B;
   else
      if (average >= 70)
         grade is C;
      else
         if (average >= 60)
            grade is D;
         else
            grade is F;
```

or after some reformatting as

```
if (average >= 90)
   grade is A;
else if (average >= 80)
   grade is B;
else if (average >= 70)
   grade is C;
else if (average >= 60)
   grade is D;
else
   grade is F;
```

This last format is very common and is used whenever a variable must be compared to a sequence of threshold values. This form of the if statement is sometimes called an *extended if statement* or a *multiway if statement,* as compared to the two-way and one-way if statements we have seen earlier.

Self-Test Questions

23. Construct a truth table that shows all the possible paths through the following nested if statement:

```
If (the time is before noon)
    If (the day is Monday)
        Take the computer science quiz
    Else
        Go to gym class
Else
    Throw a Frisbee in the quad
```

24. What is the difference between a nested `if` statement and a multiway `if` statement?

4.11 Design, Testing, and Debugging Hints

- Most errors involving selection statements and loops are not syntax errors caught at compile time. Thus, you will detect these errors only after running the program, and perhaps then only with extensive testing.

- The presence or absence of the `{ }` symbols can seriously affect the logic of a selection statement or loop. For example, the following selection statements have a similar look but a very different logic:

```
if (x > 0){
    y = x;
    z = 1 / x;
}

if (x > 0)
    y = x;
    z = 1 / x;
```

The first selection statement guards against division by 0; the second statement only guards against assigning x to y. The next pair of code segments shows a similar problem with a loop:

```
while (x > 0){
    y = x;
    x = x - 1;
}

while (x > 0)
    y = x;
    x = x - 1;
```

The first loop terminates because the value of x decreases within the body of the loop; the second loop is infinite because the value of x decreases below the body of the loop.

- When testing programs that use `if` or `if-else` statements, be sure to use test data that force the program to exercise all of the logical branches.

- When testing a program that uses `if` statements, it helps to formulate equivalence classes, boundary conditions, and extreme conditions.

- Use an `if . . . else` statement rather than two `if` statements when the alternative courses of action are mutually exclusive.

- When testing a loop, be sure to use limit values as well as typical values. For example, if a loop should terminate when the control variable equals 0, run it with the values 0, –1, and 1.

- Be sure to check entry conditions and exit conditions for each loop.

- For a loop with errors, use debugging output statements to verify the values of the control variable on each pass through the loop. Check this value before the loop is initially entered, after each update, and after the loop is exited.

4.12 Summary

This chapter has introduced you to the basic control structures of selection and iteration. Selection allows a computer to choose among alternative courses of action as the result of evaluating one or more conditions. Iteration allows a computer to perform repetitive tasks. You also learned how to compose appropriate conditions using the comparison and logical operators. The use of control structures adds a layer of complexity to program testing. We examined the use of equivalence classes, boundary conditions, and extreme conditions as means of implementing appropriate tests of control structures.

4.13 Key Terms

If you have difficulty finding the definitions of any key terms in the body of this chapter, turn to the Glossary at the end of the book.

arithmetic overflow	flowchart	production rules
artificial intelligence	infinite loop	quality assurance
boundary condition	Javish	relational operator
combinatorial explosion	justification	robust
complete code testing	logical operator	selection statement
equivalence class	loop	softbot
extended `if` statement	nested `if` statement	text area
extreme condition	neural net	truth table
Fibonacci numbers	off-by-one error	

4.14 Answers to Self-Test Questions

1. Jill uses a `while` statement in her instructions because there might be more than one cow to milk.

2. Jill uses an `if-else` statement in her instructions because there are two different types of cows, leading to two different cases (colors of buckets) for depositing the milk.

3. The condition of an `if` statement must contain a Boolean expression.

4. The curly braces enclose a sequence of statements that are treated as a logical unit.

5. An `if` statement provides a one-way decision. A single action is executed if the condition is true; otherwise, control proceeds to the next statement after the `if` statement. An `if-else` statement provides a two-way decision. The action following the condition is executed if the condition is true; otherwise, the action after the `else` is executed.

6. A truth table completely specifies the values of a Boolean expression for all possible values of its operands. The top row contains the operand symbols and the Boolean expression. The remaining rows contain the values true and false.

7. a. false

   b. true

   c. true

   d. false

8. a. true

   b. false

   c. true

   d. false

9. `!, &&, ||`

10. Two possible answers: `min < x && max > x, x >= min && x <= max`

11. Complete code coverage of a program guarantees that each of the program's instructions has been executed at least once.

12. Equivalence classes are sets of test data that execute a program's instructions in the same manner. For example, the datum 30 belongs to the equivalence class of a program that computes a weekly pay based on 40 or fewer hours per week.

13. Boundary conditions are test data that are at or near the limits of a program's valid data. For example, the data 0, 1, 39, and 40 are the boundary conditions of a program that computes a weekly pay based on 40 or fewer hours per week.

14. Extreme conditions are test data that are invalid and might cause strange behavior if not detected and handled properly. For example, the data –1 and 41 are among the extreme conditions of a program that computes a weekly pay based on 40 or fewer hours per week.

15. The program has two equivalence classes consisting of data ranging from 0 to 59 and from 60 to 100. The boundary conditions are 0, 1, 58, 59, 60, 61, 99, and 100. Extreme conditions are –1 and 101.

16. A `while` loop terminates its execution when its condition becomes false.

17. The four components of a `while` loop are initializing statements, termination condition, loop body statements, and update statements.

18. Two possible causes of infinite loops are an incorrectly formed termination condition and an incorrect or missing update statement.

19. It is usually a bad idea to terminate a loop with ! = or == because these conditions are more likely to remain true than <, >, <=, and >=.

20. The condition in the loop returns true when the number is valid. This will cause the loop to continue when the user enters valid data and to stop when the user enters invalid data. Here is a correct version of the condition:

```
min > number || max < number
```

21. Reasonable test data for a loop that does not execute a fixed number of times would be a datum that causes the loop not to execute at all, a datum that cause one pass through the loop, and a datum that causes ten passes through the loop.

22. A robust program is one that responds gracefully to invalid data. An example is a program that prints an error message when a negative number is entered for the number of hours worked.

23.

Before Noon	It's Monday	Outcome
true	true	Take quiz
true	false	Go to gym class
false	true	Throw Frisbee
false	false	Throw Frisbee

24. A nested if statement contains an if statement in the action that follows the condition. A multiway if statement contains an if statement in the action that follows the else.

4.15 Programming Problems and Activities

In keeping with the spirit of this chapter, each program should be robust and validate the input data. You should try also to formulate the appropriate equivalence classes, boundary conditions, and extreme conditions and use them in testing the programs.

1. When you first learned to divide, you expressed answers using a quotient and a remainder rather than a fraction or decimal quotient. For example, if you divided 9 by 2, you gave the answer as 4 r. 1. Write a program that takes two integers as inputs and displays their quotient and remainder as outputs. Do not assume that the integers are entered in any order, but be sure to divide the larger integer by the smaller integer.

2. Write a program that takes the lengths of three sides of a triangle as inputs. The program should display, in a text area, whether or not the triangle is a right triangle. You should assume that the side with the rightmost, lowest field is the longest one.

3. A 2-minute telephone call to Lexington, Virginia, costs $1.15. Each additional minute costs $0.50. Write a program that takes the total length of a call in minutes as input and calculates and displays the cost.

4. The German mathematician Leibniz developed the following method to approximate the value of π:

$$\pi/4 = 1 - 1/3 + 1/5 - 1/7 + \ldots$$

Write a program that allows the user to specify the number of iterations used in this approximation and displays the resulting value.

5. A local biologist needs a program to predict population growth. The inputs would be the initial number of organisms, the growth rate (a real number greater than 0), the number of hours it takes to achieve this rate, and a number of hours during which the population grows. For example, one might start with a population of 500 organisms, a growth rate of 2, and a growth period to achieve this rate of 6 hours. Assuming that none of the organisms die, this would imply that this population would double in size every 6 hours. Thus, after allowing 6 hours for growth, we would have 1000 organisms, and after 12 hours, we would have 2000 organisms. Write a program that takes these inputs and displays a prediction of the total population.

6. Computers use the binary system, which is based on powers of 2. Write a program that displays the first ten powers of 2, beginning with 2^0. The output should be in headed columns.

7. Modify the program of Problem 6 so that the user can specify the number of powers of 2 to be displayed.

8. Modify the program of Problem 7 so that the user can specify the base (2 or higher) as well. The header of the output should display which base was entered.

9. Teachers in most school districts are paid on a schedule that provides a salary based on their number of years of teaching experience. For example, a beginning teacher in the Lexington School District might be paid $20,000 the first year. For each year of experience after this up to 10 years, a 2% increase over the preceding value is received. Write a program that displays a salary schedule for teachers in any district. The inputs are the starting salary, the percentage increase, and the number of years in the schedule.

10. John has $500 to invest. Sue knows of a mutual fund plan that pays 10% interest, compounded quarterly (that is, every 3 months, the principal is multiplied by the 2.5% and the result is added to the principal). Write a program that will tell John how much money will be in the fund after 20 years. Make the program general: That is, it should take as inputs the interest rate, the initial principal, and the number of years to stay in the fund. The output should be a table whose columns are the year number, the principal at the beginning of the year, the interest earned, and the principal at the end of the year.

11. The TidBit Computer Store has a credit plan for computer purchases. There is a 10% down payment and an annual interest rate of 12%. Monthly payments are 5% of the listed purchase price minus the down payment. Write a program that takes

the purchase price as input. The program should display a table, with appropriate headers, of a payment schedule for the lifetime of the loan. Each row of the table should contain the following items:

- the month number (beginning with 1)
- the current total balance owed
- the interest owed for that month
- the amount of principal owed for that month
- the payment for that month
- the balance remaining after payment

The amount of interest for a month is equal to balance * rate / 12. The amount of principal for a month is equal to the monthly payment minus the interest owed.

12. Modify the program of Problem 11 so that it displays the total interest paid and the total of the monthly payments at the end of the loan.

13. Modify the program of Problem 12 so that it allows the user to specify the interest rate and the percentage of the purchase price representing the monthly payment amount.

5 Improving the User Interface

You do not judge a book by its cover because you are interested in its contents, not its appearance. However, you do judge a software product by its interface because you have no other way to access the product's functionality. In this chapter, we explore two ways to improve program interfaces. First, we present some standard techniques for enhancing terminal-based interfaces, and then we show how to develop programs with graphical user interfaces (GUIs). Making the transition to GUIs will be easy because in this book terminal-based and graphical-based programs have a similar structure and both rely on objects to perform I/O operations. Along the way, we will introduce character and string-based variables.

5.1 Repeating Sets of Inputs

Accepting repeated sets of inputs is the most obvious improvement we can make to a terminal-based interface. To avoid the distraction of defining and explaining a new problem, we now illustrate the technique in the context of the familiar temperature conversion program. Consider the modified interface shown in Figure 5.1. The interface allows the user to enter repeated temperatures without having to start and stop the program between conversions.

```
Enter degrees Fahrenheit: 212 Enter
The equivalent in Celsius is 100

Do it again (y/n)? y Enter
Enter degrees Fahrenheit: 32 Enter
The equivalent in Celsius is 0

Do it again (y/n)? n Enter
```

Figure 5.1 Interface for a temperature conversion program that processes multiple sets of inputs

Here is pseudocode for the program:

```
doItAgain = 'y'
while (doItAgain == 'y'){
    read fahrenheit
    calculate and display celsius
    read doItAgain                    //The user should respond with 'y' or 'n'
}
```

The key to this pseudocode is the character variable doItAgain. This variable controls how many times the loop repeats. Initially, the variable equals 'y'. As soon as the user enters a character other than 'y', the program terminates. Here is a partial listing of the Java code. We challenge you to fill in the missing pieces and run the program.

```
    . . .
    char doItAgain = 'y';
    while (doItAgain == 'y'){
        . . . code to read, convert, and print goes here . . .
        writer.print ("Do it again (y/n)? ");
        doItAgain = reader.readChar();
    }
    . . .
```

In this code, note that a character literal is enclosed within apostrophes. A character variable can hold a single character and is declared using the keyword char. The readChar method reads the first character entered on a line. Finally, 'Y' and 'y' are not the same character.

Self-Test Questions

1. Describe the structure of a loop that processes repeated sets of inputs.
2. What is a character literal?

5.2 Strings

We have included string literals in all the programs we have written so far, but this has given us only a very limited notion of what can be done with strings. We now explore some elementary features of string variables and string expressions. In Chapter 7, we will explore more advanced aspects of the topic.

Strings are objects in exactly the same sense that keyboard readers and screen writers are objects. This is in contrast to integers, floating-point numbers, and characters, which are examples of ***primitive data types.*** The distinction is important when we talk about variables. A variable that represents a primitive data type contains a number or character, whereas a variable that represents an object contains a reference to that object (see Figure 2.10).

String Literals

So far, we have only used string literals in the context of `print` and `println` messages:

```
writer.print ("Enter the gross income: ");
```

The characters in a string literal are always enclosed in double quotes. Thus, `453` is a number of type `int`, whereas `"453"` is a string. Occasionally, a programmer wants to use a string literal that contains no characters, called an ***empty string.*** This is represented as a pair of double quotes with nothing in between (`""`) and must not be confused with a string containing a single space character (`" "`). Also, we must not confuse a character literal (such as `'A'`) with a string literal consisting of one character (such as `"A"`).

String Variables and String Concatenation

String variables are declared and initialized in much the same way as variables of other types. The following code declares four strings and initializes them in various ways:

```
String firstName;
String middleInitial;
String lastName = "Smith";
String fullName;

firstName = "Bill";
middleInitial = "J";
fullName = firstName + "  " + middleInitial + ". " + lastName;
```

The last line of code uses the ***concatenation operator*** (+) to create a new string consisting of the three names plus a period. The concatenation operator has exactly the same precedence as the numeric addition operator, and the only thing that distinguishes the two is the context in which they are used. Notice that to insert spaces between the various parts of the name, we concatenate a string containing a single space. The variable `fullName` now refers to the string `"Bill J. Smith"`.

Strings can also be concatenated with other data types. When this happens, the other data types are first automatically converted to their string representations. For instance:

```
int number = 2;
String message1, message2;

message1 = "I would like " + number + " fried eggs please.";

        //Yields "I would like 2 fried eggs please."

message2 = "5 times 6 is " + 5 * 6;

        //Yields "5 times 6 is 30"
```

In the second assignment statement, the expression 5 * 6 is evaluated *before* the concatenation takes place; however, this is only because the * operator has higher precedence than the + operator and not because arithmetic operations take precedence over string operations. The next example illustrates this point:

```
String message1, message2;

message1 = "5 plus 6 is " + 5 + 6;      // Yields "5 plus 6 is 56"
message2 = "5 plus 6 is " + (5 + 6);    // Yields "5 plus 6 is 11"
```

In the first assignment statement, `"5 plus 6 is "` is concatenated to 5 and then to 6 with automatic conversion of 5 and 6 to strings. In the second expression, 5 and 6 are first added, yielding 11, before being concatenated to the rest of the string. Here is a final example:

```
String message;

message = 15 + " divided by " + 6 " is " + 15 / 6;

        //Yields "15 divided by 6 is 2"
```

Adding Newline Characters to Strings

Occasionally, we want a single string to contain multiple lines of text. We embed *newline characters* in a string to accomplish this. In Java, the newline character is represented as `'\n'`. For example, the following code segment constructs and prints a multiline message:

```
String nameAndAddress = "Mary Roe\nLexington, Virginia\n"
int age = 19;
String message = nameAndAddress + "Age " + age + "\n";
writer.print (message);
```

The output from this code is

```
Mary Roe
Lexington, Virginia
Age 19
_
```

where the "_" on the last line indicates the final position of the cursor. Notice that the cursor is on a new line even though we used the print message rather than the println message.

Reading Strings

The KeyboardReader class includes the method readLine that can be used to read strings. For instance:

```
String name;

writer.print ("Enter your name: ");
name = reader.readLine();
```

The readLine method reads everything that the user enters up to but not including the terminating Enter key. This includes space characters.

Self-Test Questions

3. When used with strings, what does the + operator mean?
4. What is the difference between a string and a character?
5. Write the values returned by the following expressions:
    a. "Hi " + "there! "
    b. "6 + 3 is " + 6 + 3
    c. "6 * 3 is " + 6 * 3
6. How does one include a newline character in a string?

5.3 A Menu-Driven Conversion Program

Menu-driven programs begin by displaying a list of options from which the user selects one. The program then prompts for additional inputs related to that option and performs the needed computations, after which it displays the menu again. Figure 5.2 shows how this idea can be used to extend the temperature conversion program.

```
1) Convert from Fahrenheit to Celsius
2) Convert from Celsius to Fahrenheit
3) Quit
Enter your option: 1 Enter

Enter degrees Fahrenheit: 212 Enter
The equivalent in Celsius is 100

1) Convert from Fahrenheit to Celsius
2) Convert from Celsius to Fahrenheit
3) Quit
Enter your option: 2 Enter

Enter degrees Celsius: 0 Enter
The equivalent in Fahrenheit is 32

1) Convert from Fahrenheit to Celsius
2) Convert from Celsius to Fahrenheit
3) Quit
Enter your option: 3 Enter
```

Figure 5.2 Interface for a menu-driven version of the temperature conversion program

Here is the corresponding pseudocode followed by a listing of the program.

```
menuOption = 4
while (menuOption != 3){
   print menu
   read menuOption
   if (menuOption == 1){
      read fahrenheit
      convert to celsius and print
   }else if (menuOption == 2){
      read celsius
      convert to fahrenheit and print
   }else if (menuOption != 3)
      print "Invalid option"
}
```

```java
/* TempConversion.java
This menu-driven temperature conversion program can convert from
Fahrenheit to Celsius and vice versa.
*/

import TerminalIO.*;

public class ConvertWithMenu {

    KeyboardReader reader = new KeyboardReader();
    ScreenWriter   writer = new ScreenWriter();

    String menu;            //The multiline menu
    int menuOption;         //The user's menu selection
    double fahrenheit;      //Degrees Fahrenheit
    double celsius;         //Degrees Celsius

    public void run() {

        //Build the menu string
        menu = "\n1) Convert from Fahrenheit to Celsius"
            + "\n2) Convert from Celsius to Fahrenheit"
            + "\n3) Quit"
            + "\nEnter your option: ";

        //Set up the menu loop
        menuOption = 4;
        while (menuOption != 3){

            //Display the menu and get the user's option
            menuOption = reader.readInt(menu);
            writer.println ("");

            //Determine which menu option has been selected

            if (menuOption == 1){

                //Convert from Fahrenheit to Celsius
                fahrenheit = reader.readDouble("Enter degrees Fahrenheit: ");
                celsius = (fahrenheit - 32.0) * 5.0 / 9.0;
                writer.println ("The equivalent in Celsius is " + celsius);

            }else if (menuOption == 2){

                //Convert from Celsius to Fahrenheit
                celsius = reader.readDouble("Enter degrees Celsius: ");
```

```
            fahrenheit = celsius * 9.0 / 5.0 + 32.0;
            writer.println
               ("The equivalent in Fahrenheit is " + fahrenheit);

        }else if (menuOption != 3){

            //Invalid option
            writer.println ("Invalid option");

        }
      }
   }

   public static void main (String [] args) {
      ConvertWithMenu tpo = new ConvertWithMenu();
      tpo.run();
   }
}
```

Self-Test Questions

7. What role does a menu play in a program?

8. Describe the structure of a menu-driven command loop.

9. Write the code for a menu that gives the user options to add a student, remove a student, and display all students in a database of students.

5.4 A GUI-Based Conversion Program

Because developing GUIs in Java is usually quite complicated, many introductory textbooks either restrict themselves to terminal-based I/O or present a rather limited and distorted version of GUIs. This book avoids both of these unappealing alternatives by using a package called BreezySwing®. This package extends Java's built-in facilities for creating GUIs in a manner that is powerful yet easy to use. Having mastered the basics of GUI-based programming with BreezySwing, you will be in an excellent position to make the transition to Java's standard GUI building facilities, the Abstract Windowing Toolkit (AWT), and the Swing Toolkit. Chapter 18 covers the details, and if you are eager to master the toolkits as soon as possible, you can jump ahead to Chapter 18 immediately after finishing this one.

Figure 5.3 shows the interface for a GUI-based temperature conversion program. To use the program, one enters a temperature in one of the fields and clicks the button below it. The converted temperature is then displayed in the other field.

One repeats the processes as many times as desired and clicks the close icon when finished (top right corner).

Figure 5.3 Interface for the GUI-based temperature conversion program

Here is a listing of the program. Code that is common to all GUI programs is shown in blue. This code defines a structure that is very similar to the structure of our terminal-based programs:

```
/* ConvertWithGUI.java
This GUI-based temperature conversion program can convert from
Fahrenheit to Celsius and vice versa.
*/

import javax.swing.*;
import BreezySwing.*;

public class ConvertWithGUI extends GBFrame{


   //Declare and instantiate the window objects
   JLabel        fahrenheitLabel  = addLabel        ("Fahrenheit" ,1,1,1,1);
   JLabel        celsiusLabel     = addLabel        ("Celsius"    ,1,2,1,1);
   DoubleField   fahrenheitField  = addDoubleField (32.0          ,2,1,1,1);
   DoubleField   celsiusField     = addDoubleField (0.0           ,2,2,1,1);
   JButton       fahrenheitButton = addButton        (">>>>>>"    ,3,1,1,1);
   JButton       celsiusButton    = addButton        ("<<<<<<"    ,3,2,1,1);

   //Declare other instance variables
   double fahrenheit;          //Number of degrees Fahrenheit
   double celsius;             //Number of degrees Celsius

   //This method responds to button clicks.
   public void buttonClicked (JButton buttonObj){

      //When more than one button, determine which one was clicked.
      if (buttonObj == fahrenheitButton){
```

```
        //Convert from Fahrenheit to Celsius
        fahrenheit = fahrenheitField.getNumber();
        celsius = (fahrenheit  - 32.0) * 5.0 / 9.0;
        celsiusField.setNumber (celsius);

    }else{

        //Convert Celsius to Fahrenheit
        celsius = celsiusField.getNumber();
        fahrenheit = celsius * 9.0 / 5.0 + 32.0;
        fahrenheitField.setNumber (fahrenheit);
    }
}

public static void main (String[] args){
    ConvertWithGUI tpo = new ConvertWithGUI();
    tpo.setSize (250, 100);    //Set the window's size in pixels
    tpo.setVisible (true);     //Make the window visible
}
}
```

Wow! This fabulous GUI program is actually shorter than its terminal-based counterpart, and once you become familiar with its conventions, you will probably agree that it is easier to write. There are several points to explain in this code, and we deal with them in the sections that follow.

5.5 The GUI Program Explained

Despite the similarity in general structure between terminal-based and GUI-based programs, there are some fundamental but subtle differences. In a terminal-based program, execution proceeds as follows:

1. The *program begins* its execution in method main. The tpo object is instantiated and sent the run message.

2. Execution transfers to the tpo object's run method and proceeds through the method until the last line has been executed, at which point execution returns to method main.

3. Execution recommences in main, where there are no more statements to execute, so execution in main terminates, and the *program ends*.

In a GUI-based program, on the other hand, execution proceeds like this:

1. The *program begins* with execution in method main. The tpo object is instantiated and sent the setSize and setVisible messages. At this point, the GUI is visible, there are no more statements to execute in main, and execution in main terminates; however, the *program does not end,* but instead becomes inactive until the user clicks a command button or the GUI's close icon.

2. Every time the user clicks a command button, the JVM sends the `buttonClicked` message to the `tpo` object. Execution then begins anew in the `tpo` object's `buttonClicked` method, proceeds through the method until the last line has been executed, and terminates. The program then becomes inactive again.

3. When the user clicks the GUI's close icon, the *program ends.*

We now begin a line-by-line explanation of the code.

```
import javax.swing.*;
import BreezySwing.*;
```

GUI programs must import the two packages `javax.swing` and `BreezySwing`. These packages contain classes that support the overall behavior of a GUI-based program and the window objects.

```
public class ConvertWithGUI extends GBFrame{
```

A GUI program must be a subclass of `GBFrame`, which unfortunately is a statement that will not make any sense until you read Chapter 11.

```
//Declare and instantiate the window objects
JLabel        fahrenheitLabel  = addLabel        ("Fahrenheit" ,1,1,1,1);
JLabel        celsiusLabel     = addLabel        ("Celsius"    ,1,2,1,1);
DoubleField   fahrenheitField  = addDoubleField (32.0          ,2,1,1,1);
DoubleField   celsiusField     = addDoubleField (0.0           ,2,2,1,1);
JButton       fahrenheitButton = addButton       (">>>>>>"     ,3,1,1,1);
JButton       celsiusButton    = addButton       ("<<<<<<"     ,3,2,1,1);
```

GUI-based programs must declare and instantiate objects that correspond to the labels, fields, and buttons in the user interface. We call these *window objects.* The `add` methods instantiate, initialize, and position the window objects. Each type of window object has a different purpose:

- A *label object* displays text in the window. This text is normally used to label some other window object, such as a data entry or data display.

- A *double field object* can accept user input and/or display program output.

- A *button object* activates the `buttonClicked` method when clicked by the user.

Window objects are positioned in an imaginary grid (see Figure 5.4), and the grid automatically adjusts itself to the needed number of rows and columns. The syntax for defining a window object indicates its position and size in this grid:

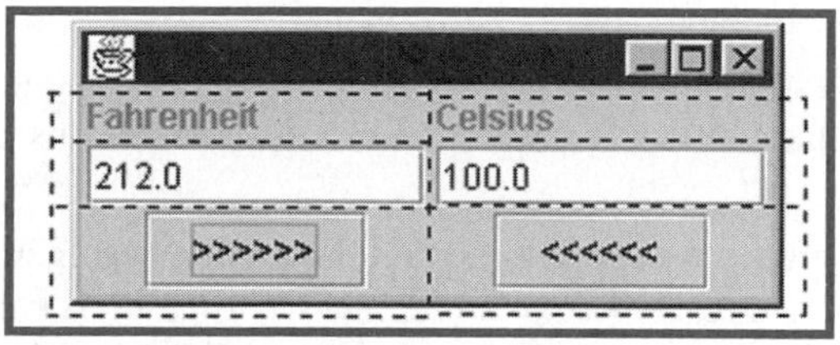

Figure 5.4 An imaginary grid superimposed on the program's interface

```
<type of object> <name of object> = <add type>
   (<initial value>,    //The object's initial value, varies depending on type.
   <row #>,             //Row position in grid. Our example has 3 rows.
   <column #>,          //Column position in grid. Our example has 2 columns.
   <width>,             //Width of object, usually 1 grid cell.
   <height>);           //Height of object, usually 1 grid cell.
```

```
//Declare other instance variables
double fahrenheit;          //Number of degrees Fahrenheit
double celsius;             //Number of degrees Celsius
```

These lines are exactly the same in the terminal-based version of the program.

```
//This method responds to button clicks
public void buttonClicked (JButton buttonObj){
```

When the user clicks a command button, the JVM sends the `buttonClicked` message to the `tpo` object. These lines begin the method's definition. Notice that the method has one parameter, a button object. When the method is called, this parameter corresponds to the button clicked by the user.

```
if (buttonObj == fahrenheitButton){
```

Here we determine if the button clicked by the user equals the `fahrenheitButton`.

```
//Convert from Fahrenheit to Celsius
fahrenheit = fahrenheitField.getNumber();
celsius = (fahrenheit - 32.0) * 5.0 / 9.0;
celsiusField.setNumber (celsius);
```

The `getNumber` and `setNumber` methods read and write numbers from and to the numeric fields. To make sure this is clear, let us quickly review messages, methods, and parameters. Sending an object a message, as we already know, activates in the object a method that accomplishes the desired task. In addition:

- The message and the method have the same name.

- In response to a message, an object may or may not return a value. For instance, the `getNumber` method returns a value, and `setNumber` returns nothing (also called `void`).

- When an object is sent a message, additional information is sometimes required as part of the message, and each piece of additional information is called a parameter. If a method expects parameters, the message must include them in the designated order. Thus, the variable `celsius` is a parameter in the following message:

```
celsiusField.setNumber (celsius);
```

In general, several parameters may be included or passed at once. For instance:

```
someObject.someMethod (parm1, parm2, . . ., parmn);
```

Sometimes no parameters are needed. For instance:

```
fahrenheit = fahrenheitField.getNumber();
```

The rest of the program should now be fairly self-explanatory.

Self-Test Questions

10. Explain how a GUI program runs in contrast to a terminal I/O program.

11. What is `BreezySwing`?

12. What is the role of the method `buttonClicked`?

13. Explain how a window object is positioned in a window with `BreezySwing`.

14. Describe the behavior of a double field.

15. Why does a GUI program require no menu-driven command loop to process a sequence of commands?

5.6 Other Window Objects and Methods

In our sample program, we encountered three types of window objects and several of the messages that they recognize. We now build on that foundation and introduce some additional window objects with their methods. For a complete list, see Appendix H. When presenting methods, we usually use the format:

```
<return type> <method name> (<parameter list>)
```

as in

```
void setNumber(aDouble).
```

Before looking at the details, however, it is helpful to make a distinction between those classes and methods that are part of the standard Java Swing and those that are unique to BreezySwing. All the methods for adding window objects to the user interface and for responding to user events are part of BreezySwing. The window objects themselves are either part of Swing or are derived from objects in Swing. For instance, labels and command buttons are part of Swing, while double fields are derived from Swing's standard text fields. Appendix H makes the distinctions clear. Programs that use Swing must import javax.swing.* and those that use BreezySwing must also import BreezySwing.*.

Integer Field Objects

An object of class IntegerField is called an ***integer field object,*** and as the name suggests, it can be used to enter or display an integer value. An integer field should always be initialized to an integer and never to a floating-point value. The principal methods for manipulating integer fields are:

int getNumber()   which reads an integer from an input field

void setNumber(anInteger)   which prints a number in an output field

These are, of course, the same as the method names used for manipulating a double field. As we learned in Chapter 1, using the same method name with different classes is called polymorphism.

Text Field Objects

An object of class JTextField is called a ***text field object*** and can hold one line of string data. A text field is useful for entering or displaying such things as a person's name and must be initialized to a string. The principal methods for manipulating text fields are:

String getText()   which reads a string from an input field

void setText(aString)   which prints a one-line string in an output field

Text Area Objects

An object of class JTextArea is called a ***text area object*** and is similar to a text field object except that it can handle several lines of text at a time. A text area can be used for entering or displaying a person's address or any other multiline descriptive information. Whereas a text field typically has a width and height of one, a text area is usually several cells wide and high. The principal methods for manipulating a text area are:

String getText()   which reads a multiline string from an input field

void setText(aString)   which prints a multiline string in an output field

void append(aString)   which appends a multiline string to the end of
                              the text already present in the output field

Declaring Window Objects

Here is a list that shows how to declare and instantiate the window objects discussed so far:

```
JLabel          <name> = addLabel          ("..."     ,r,c,w,h);
IntegerField    <name> = addIntegerField (<integer>,r,c,w,h);
DoubleField     <name> = addDoubleField  (<double> ,r,c,w,h);
JTextField      <name> = addTextField     ("..."     ,r,c,w,h);
JTextArea       <name> = addTextArea      ("..."     ,r,c,w,h);
JButton         <name> = addButton        ("..."     ,r,c,w,h);
```

The `messageBox` Method

We close the section by presenting message boxes. A ***message box*** is a convenient device for popping up messages outside an application's main window. For instance, we might want to tell the user of our temperature conversion program that he must not enter a temperature greater than 10,000 (Figure 5.5).

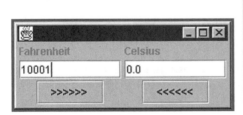

(a) Main window

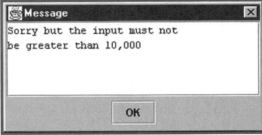

(b) Message box

Figure 5.5 A pop-up message box for the temperature conversion program

The code for activating a message box always appears inside a GUI class, which in our example is the `ConvertWithGUI` class. The key piece of code consists of sending the message `messageBox` to the object `this`:

```
this.messageBox ("Sorry but the input must not \nbe greater than 10,000");
```

In the line of code, the word `this` refers to the tpo object itself. For the convenience of programmers, Java allows the word `this` to be omitted, so the code can be written as:

```
messageBox ("Sorry but the input must not \nbe greater than 10,000");
```

Setting the Look and Feel

Each GUI-based operating system, such as Windows, MacOS, and Motif (for UNIX), has its own look and feel. Java's Swing toolkit provides a default look and feel called **Metal** that is system-independent and is used in most GUIs in this book. However, Swing allows the programmer to set the look and feel of a window and all of its subcomponents. To accomplish this with `BreezySwing`, one simply calls the method `setLookAndFeel` with the `String` parameter "METAL", "MOTIF", or "OTHER". On a Windows system, "OTHER" would change the look and feel to Windows. An appropriate place to call this method is in the method `main`. The following code segment shows how to do this in the converter program, and Figure 5.6 compares the Metal look and the Motif look.

```java
public static void main (String[] args){
   ConvertWithGUI tpo = new ConvertWithGUI();
   tpo.setLookAndFeel("MOTIF");
   tpo.setSize (250, 100);     //Set the window's size in pixels
   tpo.setVisible (true);      //Make the window visible
}
```

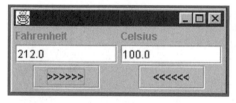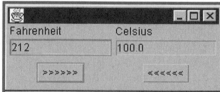

Figure 5.6 The Metal and the Motif looks and feels

Self-Test Questions

16. What is the difference between a text field and a text area?

17. Write a code segment that displays an exit message in a message box.

18. Why are there integer fields in addition to double fields?

19. Visit the `BreezySwing` Web site at `http://turing.cs.wwu.edu/martin/BreezySwing/`. Review the documentation on integer and double fields and describe the role of the method `isValid()` for these fields.

20. What is the effect of the `doubleField` method `setPrecision(anInteger)`?

5.7 Summary

In this chapter, you learned how to extend the terminal I/O interface to handle repeated sets of inputs. In the process, we introduced the use of character data and variables, string variables, and string concatenation. We then showed that programs with graphical user interfaces provide a simpler, more natural way to handle repeated sets of inputs. Along the way, you learned how to use BreezySwing to lay out window objects in a GUI, how to do input and output with data fields, and how to implement a method to take action when a button is clicked. For complete documentation on BreezySwing, including a tutorial and downloadable source code and byte code, consult the BreezySwing Web site at http://turing.cs.wwu.edu/martin/BreezySwing/.

5.8 Key Terms

If you have difficulty finding the definitions of any key terms in the body of this chapter, turn to the Glossary at the end of the book.

button	empty string	text area
close box	integer field	text field
concatenation	message box	window object
double field	newline character	

5.9 Answers to Self-Test Questions

1. A loop that processes repeated sets of inputs takes the inputs from the user, processes them, and asks the user for a confirmation to continue, until the user says, in some specified way, "No."

2. A character literal is one of the letters, digits, or punctuation marks on the keyboard enclosed in single quotes.

3. The + operator means concatenation when used with strings. This operation returns a new string consisting of the left operand string followed by the right operand string.

4. A string is a sequence of zero or more characters, whereas a character is a single letter, digit, or punctuation mark.

5. a. "Hi there!"

   b. "6 + 3 is 63"

   c. "6 * 3 is 18"

6. One includes a newline character in a string by including the sequence \n wherever needed; for example, "\nHello there!\n" begins and ends with newline characters.

7. A menu displays a set of options, such as commands, from which a user can select, in much the same way as a diner would order a meal from a restaurant's menu.

8. A menu-driven command loop displays a menu, receives a command from the user, and executes that command, repeating this process until the user selects a command to exit.

9.
```
writer.println("1    Add a student");
writer.println("2    Remove a student");
writer.println("3    Display all students");
writer.println("4    Exit");
```

10. A GUI program instantiates the window class, sets its size, shows the window, and waits for user actions such as button clicks. When a button is clicked, a method handles this event by extracting inputs from data fields, processing the data, and inserting the results into data fields. This process of waiting for and responding to user events is repeated until the user clicks the close box. A terminal I/O program instantiates a keyboard reader and a screen writer and then enters a menu-driven command loop as described in Exercise 8. No mouse input is used in this type of program.

11. `BreezySwing` is a package of Java code that extends Java's GUI classes with a framework for construction GUI programs quickly and easily.

12. The method `buttonClicked` is activated by the JVM when the user selects a button in a GUI. The programmer can place any appropriate code in this method, including code that determines which button has been clicked (the parameter of the method) and takes the appropriate action.

13. The programmer specifies the row and column position of the window object as well as the width in columns and the height in rows of the window object's extent.

14. A double field allows the user to enter numbers with a decimal point or just whole numbers. A program can extract these data by sending the `getNumber()` message to a double field. A program can also insert an integer or a double value into a double field by sending the `setNumber(aNumber)` message to a double field. In that case, the number is always displayed with a decimal point.

15. The user waits and acts in a command loop with a GUI program, but that loop is written in the JVM instead of the Java program.

16. A text field can input or display a single line of text as a string. A text area can input or display a piece of text consisting of several lines.

17. `messageBox("That's all for now; have a nice day!");`

18. An integer field restricts input and output to whole numbers.

19. The method `isValid()` returns `true` if the user has entered a well-formed number into a numeric field or `false` otherwise. This method allows a program to check for invalid input data.

20. The method `setPrecision(anInteger)` allows a program to specify the number of digits to the right of a decimal point for the display of a number in a double field.

5.10 Programming Problems and Activities

When developing a program that uses a GUI, much of the analysis phase is occupied with sketching layouts of the user interface. These drawings help the programmer to determine which window objects are needed and to determine their arrangement, position, and extent in the window. Moreover, the design of the computation can be postponed until the user interface part is coded and tested. When the look of the interface matches the sketches resulting from analysis, the remaining parts of the program, which handle button clicks and so forth, can be designed, coded, and tested. We recommend that you follow this incremental development strategy in the problems and activities that follow. Because most solutions recast ones already done in Chapter 4, you can borrow code from the previous versions.

1. Redo Programming Problem 4, Chapter 4 (computing the value of π) with a GUI.

2. Redo Programming Problem 5, Chapter 4 (predicting population growth) with a GUI.

3. Redo Programming Problem 8, Chapter 4 (displaying n powers of a given base) with a GUI. (*Hint*: Use a text area for the output.)

4. Redo Programming Problem 10, Chapter 4 (return on investment) with a GUI.

5. Newton's method for computing the square root of a number consists of approximating the actual square root by means of a set of transformations. Each transformation starts with a guess at the square root. A better approximation is then (guess + number / guess) / 2. This result becomes the guess for the next approximation. The initial guess is 1. Write a GUI program that allows the user to view successive approximations of the square root of a given input number by clicking a button.

6. Modify the program of Problem 5 so that the user can enter more than one input number. When the user selects the **Reset** button, the input field and the output field are reset to 0.

6 Cooperating Methods

The programs we have written so far have been short and simple, but soon we will tackle problems of greater complexity. To manage the complexity, we apply a strategy that has proven successful in many areas of human endeavor—divide and conquer. Thus, when confronted by the task of writing a long and difficult method, we divide or decompose it into a number of shorter methods that cooperate to achieve the same result. We will call these *cooperating methods,* and we explore how to write them in this chapter. Although all the examples in the chapter involve GUI-based programs, the ideas discussed apply equally to terminal-based programs.

6.1 First Look at Cooperating Methods

As a first example of cooperating methods, we write a simple program that computes either a circle's area from its radius, or vice versa (Figure 6.1). For this program, we present two versions of the `buttonClicked` method, one without and one with cooperating methods. Normally, we would not bother to decompose such a simple method; however, it is best to begin with a straightforward example.

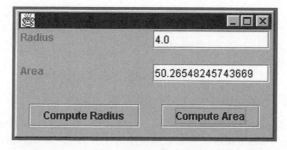

Figure 6.1 Interface for a circle area/radius program

The Complete Program Without Decomposition

The program has the standard structure for GUI programs described in Chapter 5. Here is the listing. For the sake of brevity we omit comments:

```
import javax.swing.*;
import BreezySwing.*;

public class CircleAreaAndRadius extends GBFrame{

    JLabel radiusLabel       = addLabel       ("Radius"          ,1,1,1,1);
    DoubleField radiusField  = addDoubleField (0                 ,1,2,1,1);
    JLabel areaLabel         = addLabel       ("Area"            ,2,1,1,1);
    DoubleField areaField    = addDoubleField (0                 ,2,2,1,1);
    JButton radiusButton     = addButton      ("Compute Radius",3,1,1,1);
    JButton areaButton       = addButton      ("Compute Area"  ,3,2,1,1);

    double radius, area;

    public void buttonClicked (JButton buttonObj){
        if (buttonObj == areaButton){
            radius = radiusField.getNumber();
            area = Math.PI * radius * radius;
            areaField.setNumber (area);
        }else{
            area = areaField.getNumber();
            radius = Math.sqrt (area / Math.PI);
            radiusField.setNumber (radius);
        }
    }

    public static void main (String[] args){
        CircleAreaAndRadius tpo = new CircleAreaAndRadius();
        tpo.setSize (200, 150);
        tpo.setVisible (true);
    }
}
```

Although the code is easy to understand, it does contain two new features: `Math.PI` and `Math.sqrt`. We discuss the `Math` class in Chapter 7, but for now suffice it to say that `Math.sqrt` is a method that returns the square root of a number, and `Math.PI` is a high-precision estimate of π.

Decomposed Version of the `buttonClicked` Method

Here is a decomposed version of the `buttonClicked` method. Notice as you read the code that we have tried to choose descriptive names for the methods. Doing so makes the code much easier to understand. There are now three methods:

```
public void buttonClicked(Button buttonObj){
   if (buttonObj == areaButton)
      this.computeArea();          //Here the tpo object sends a
                                   //message to itself

   else
      this.computeRadius();        //Here the tpo object sends another
                                   //message to itself

}


private void computeArea(){
   radius = radiusField.getNumber();
   area = Math.PI * radius * radius;
   areaField.setNumber (area);
}


private void computeRadius(){
   area = areaField.getNumber();
   radius = Math.sqrt (area / Math.PI);
   radiusField.setNumber (radius);
}
```

Analysis of the Running Program

To understand the code, we analyze what happens when the program is running and the user clicks one of the command buttons:

1. The JVM sends the `buttonClicked` message to the `tpo` object.

2. The `tpo` object executes the `buttonClicked` method and in the process determines which button was clicked and sends a message to itself, as indicated in the lines

   ```
   this.computeArea();
   ```

   and

   ```
   this.computeRadius();
   ```

3. The `tpo` object then executes the indicated method, which reads the user input, does the needed calculation, prints the result, and returns to the `buttonClicked` method.

4. There is nothing left to do in the `buttonClicked` method, so the `tpo` object is now finished and execution terminates until the user clicks another command button.

In other words, as the computer runs a program, it executes only one instruction at a time, and the point of execution shifts from object to object and within an object from method to method. Figure 6.2 illustrates how this point of execution (also called the *flow of control*) shifts when the **Compute Area** button is clicked. Execution starts in the `buttonClicked` method and remains there until the `computeArea` method is called. Then, when the `computeArea` method completes its task, execution returns to the `buttonClicked` method immediately following the point of departure.

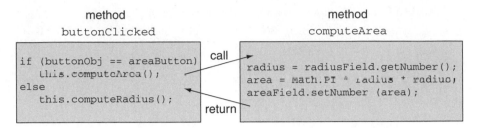

Figure 6.2 Flow of control when the **Compute Area** button is clicked

Basic Terminology

We will call a method's first line its ***header*** and the rest its ***body.*** By looking at the header, we can determine how to call a method and whether or not it returns a value. The body describes the processing performed by a method.

When talking about the program, we normally say that the buttonClicked method ***calls*** one of the other methods rather than saying the tpo object sends a message to itself. Also, we usually drop the optional phrase "this." when an object sends a message to itself.

The relationship between methods that call each other is traditionally represented in a diagram called a ***structure chart,*** as illustrated in Figure 6.3. The downward pointing arrows stand for **calls.**

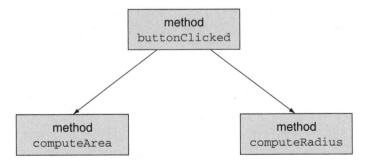

Figure 6.3 A structure chart showing the decomposition of the buttonClicked method

Referring back to the listing, notice that the buttonClicked method is public, while the other two are private. ***Private methods*** are accessible only when an object sends messages to itself—in other words, only from inside an object. ***Public methods,*** on the other hand, are accessible from inside and outside an object. Thus, the JVM can send a buttonClicked message but not a computeArea message to the tpo object. The tpo object, on the other hand, can send either message to itself if it needs to do so.

By the way, the order of the methods defined in a program is merely a matter of the programmer's personal taste. However, from the perspective of someone reading the program, it is probably better to list calling methods before those they call. By reading the calling method first, the reader gets an overview of the task at hand and can find the details in the called methods. This top-down order also corresponds to the order in which programmers tend to develop the methods, an approach called *top-down design.*

Self-Test Questions

1. What is divide and conquer? How is it exemplified in cooperating methods?
2. Describe how the flow of control works when one method calls another method.
3. What is the difference between a method header and a method body?
4. Describe the difference between public methods and private methods.
5. What is the role of the keyword `this`?

6.2 How Methods Share Information

Methods that work together usually need to share information. There are generally two ways they can do so. They can either access a common pool of variables, or they can communicate via parameters and return values. Sometimes a mixed approach is used.

Accessing a Common Pool of Variables

The first approach is illustrated in the area/radius program presented earlier. As shown in Figure 6.4, the `buttonClicked` method and the two computational methods all have equal access to the instance variables (consisting of the window objects, `radius`, and `area`). The next line of code, taken from the program, accesses two of these shared variables:

```
radius = radiusField.getNumber();
```

Parameters and Return Values

We illustrate the use of parameters and return values in the context of a GUI-based program for counting divisors. We encountered a terminal-based version of this program in Chapter 4, and we now convert it to suit our present purposes. Figure 6.5 shows the interface. We first present the code and follow that with a detailed explanation of how it works. As you read the code, pay close attention to the comments.

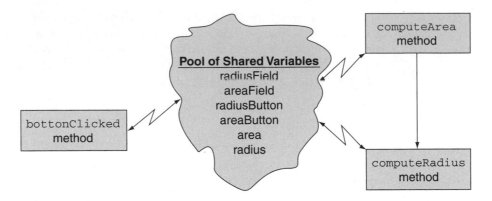

Figure 6.4 Methods with equal access to a pool of shared variables

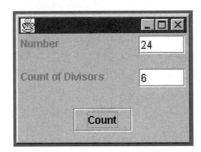

Figure 6.5 Interface for the GUI-based count divisors program

```
import javax.swing.*;
import BreezySwing.*;

public class CountDivisors extends GBFrame{

    JLabel numberLabel        = addLabel ("Number"              ,1,1,1,1);
    JLabel countLabel         = addLabel ("Count of Divisors",2,1,1,1);
    IntegerField numberField  = addIntegerField (0             ,1,2,1,1);
    IntegerField countField   = addIntegerField (0             ,2,2,1,1);
    JButton countButton       = addButton ("Count"             ,3,1,2,1);

    public void buttonClicked (JButton buttonObj){
        int number;                      //Local variable
        int count;                       //Local variable

        number = numberField.getNumber();
        if (number < 0)
            number = -number;
        count = computeCount (number);   //Call method computeCount using
                                         //the parameter 'number' and assign
                                         //the returned value to 'count'
```

```
        countField.setNumber (count);
}


private int computeCount (int nmbr){ //One parameter called 'nmbr'
    int cnt;                           //Local variable
    int trialDivisor;                  //Local variable
    int limit;                         //Local variable

    cnt = 0;
    trialDivisor = 2;
    limit = nmbr / 2 + 1;
    while (trialDivisor < limit){
        if (nmbr % trialDivisor == 0)
            cnt = cnt + 1;
        trialDivisor = trialDivisor + 1;
    }

    return cnt;                        //Return the value of 'cnt'
}

public static void main (String[] args){
    CountDivisors tpo = new CountDivisors();
    tpo.setSize (200, 150);
    tpo.setVisible (true);
}
}
```

First, notice that several variables are declared at the beginning of the `buttonClicked` and `computeCount` methods. These are said to be *local variables* because they are visible strictly within the body of the method that declares them and exist only while the method is executing. The difference between the local variables and the shared variables is a consequence of where they are declared. Local variables are declared within a method, while shared variables are declared outside all the methods and exist for the lifetime of the object. We will say more about this in Section 6.3.

In the foregoing code, the line

```
private int computeCount (int nmbr){
```

indicates that the `computeCount` method returns an integer value and expects an integer parameter, which here is called `nmbr`. In the line

```
return cnt;
```

the method returns an integer value to the calling method. There can be more than one `return` statement in a method; however, the first one executed ends the method.

Now consider the `buttonClicked` method. The line

```
count = computeCount (number);
```

activates the `computeCount` method, passing it the value of the variable `number`. When `computeCount` has completed its calculations and returns, the `buttonClicked` method assigns the returned integer value to the variable `count`.

Formal and Actual Parameters

We now introduce some more terminology, which is used in Figure 6.6. Parameters listed in a method's definition are called *formal parameters.* Values passed to a method are called *arguments* or *actual parameters.* In our example, `number` is an actual parameter, and `nmbr` is a formal parameter. When a method is called, the values of the actual parameters are automatically transferred to the corresponding formal parameters immediately before the method is activated. Thus, the value of `number` is transferred to `nmbr` immediately before `computeCount` is activated. It is important to understand that the variables `number` and `nmbr` are otherwise completely independent of each other. For instance, changing the value of `nmbr` has no effect on the value of `number`.

```
public void buttonClicked (JButton buttonObj){
     int number;                                          Local variables
     int count;
     number = numberField.getNumber();                    Actual parameter
     if (number < 0)
        number = -number;
     count = computeCount(number);
     countField.setNumber(count);                         Returned value
  }                                                        assigned to count

                                                           Return type
  private int computeCount(int nmbr){
     int cnt;                                              Formal parameter
     int trialDivisor;
     int limit;                                            Local variables
     cnt = 0;
     trialDivisor = 2;
     limit = nmbr / 2 + 1;
     while (trialDivisor < limit){
        if (nmbr % trialDivisor == 0)
           cnt = cnt + 1;
        trialDivisor = trialDivisor + 1;
     }
     return cnt;                                           Value returned
  }
```

Figure 6.6 The `buttonClicked` and `computeCount` methods with explanatory tags

Diagramming the Relationship Between the Methods

We can better understand the relationship between the `buttonClicked` and `computeCount` methods by means of the diagrams in Figure 6.7. Part (a) gives an overview of the communications between the two methods. The `buttonClicked` method passes the actual parameter `number` to the `computeCount` method and gets back a value that is assigned to the variable `count`. Part (b) goes into greater detail and shows the correspondence between variables in the two methods. Note that although the variable `number` and the parameter `nmbr` have the same value, they refer to different areas of storage.

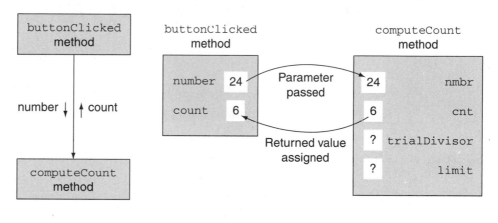

(a) Overview   (b) Correspondence between the methods

Figure 6.7 Communications between the methods

Multiple Parameters

Sometimes a method has many parameters, as shown in Figure 6.8. Notice in this figure that the number, type, and order of the actual parameters must match exactly the number, type, and order of the formal parameters. Also notice that the actual parameters can be variables, literals, or expressions.

Four Possibilities

A method does not have to use a return type and parameters simultaneously. Four possibilities are allowed:

1. `void` return type and no parameters
2. `void` return type and some parameters
3. a return type and no parameters
4. a return type and some parameters

The preceding examples have illustrated only the first and last of these possibilities.

```
public class ParameterDemo extends GBFrame{
    ...
    public void buttonClicked (Button buttonObj){
        double x;
        int i;
        ...
        x = myMethod (i*3, 2.4, i);
        ...
    }

    private double myMethod (int parm1, double parm2, int parm3){
        ...
        return aDouble;
    }
    ...
}
```

Figure 6.8 Calling a method that has many parameters

Sharing Variables versus Passing Parameters

As shown in the previous examples, methods can communicate by sharing a common pool of variables or by the more explicit means of parameters and return values. Years of software development experience have convinced computer scientists that the second approach is better even though it seems to require more programming effort. There are three reasons to prefer the use of parameters:

1. Suppose that several methods share a pool of variables and that one method misuses a variable. Then other methods can be affected, and the resulting error can be difficult to find. For example, if method m1 mistakenly sets the variable x to 0 and if method m2 uses x as a divisor, then when the program is run, the computer will signal an error in m2, even though the source of the error is in m1.

2. It is easier to understand methods and the relationships between them when communications are explicitly defined in terms of parameters and return values.

3. Methods that access a pool of shared variables can be used only in their original context, whereas methods that are passed parameters can be reused in many different situations. Reuse of code boosts productivity, so programmers try to create software components (in this case, methods) that are as reusable as possible.

Self-Test Questions

6. How do cooperating methods access a common pool of variables?

7. What is the difference between a formal parameter and an actual parameter?

8. How are data transmitted by means of parameters from a caller to a method?

9. Write method headers for methods that perform the following tasks (use parameters and return values):

   a. Return the square root of a given number.

b. Return the result of raising a number to a given power.

c. Determine whether a given number is a prime number.

d. Determine whether a given number is between two numbers (inclusive between).

10. What is a local variable?

11. State two reasons it is often better for methods to transmit information by means of parameters and return values than by means of a common pool of variables.

6.3 Scope and Lifetime of Variables

As we have seen repeatedly, a class definition consists of two parts: a list of instance variables and a list of methods. For example, in the class CountDivisors, the instance variables are the window objects, and the methods are buttonClicked and computeCount. When an object is instantiated, it receives its own complete copy of the instance variables, and when it is sent a message, it activates the corresponding method in its class. Thus, it is the role of objects to contain data and to respond to messages, and it is the role of classes to provide a template for creating objects and to store the code for methods. When a method is executing, it does so on behalf of a particular object, and the method has complete access to the object's instance variables. From the perspective of the methods, the instance variables form a common pool of variables accessible to all the class's methods. For this reason, we sometimes refer to them as *global variables*, in contrast to the variables defined within a method, which we have already called local variables.

Scope of Variables

The *scope* of a variable is that region of the program within which it can validly appear in lines of code. We now know that the scope of a local variable is restricted to the body of the method that declares it, while the scope of a global or instance variable is all the methods in the defining class. Fortunately, the compiler flags as an error any attempt to use variables outside of their scope. Here is an example that illustrates the difference between local and global scope:

```
public class ScopeDemo extends GBFrame{

    int iAmGlobal;

    public void buttonClicked (Button buttonObj){

        int iAmLocal;
        ...
    }
```

Continues

Continued

```
    private int helperMethod (int parm1, int parm2){

       int iAmLocalToo;
       ...
    }
    ...
}
```

The following table shows where each of the variables and parameters can be used (i.e., its scope):

Variable	helperMethod	buttonClicked
iAmGlobal	Yes	Yes
buttonObj	No	Yes
iAmLocal	No	Yes
parm1 and parm2	Yes	No
iAmLocalToo	Yes	No

Notice that formal parameters are also local in scope.

Lifetime of Variables

The *lifetime* of a variable is the period during which it can be used. Local variables exist during a single execution of a method. Each time a method is called, it gets a fresh set of local variables, and once the method stops executing, the local variables are no longer accessible. Instance variables, on the other hand, last for the lifetime of an object. When an object is instantiated, it gets a complete set of fresh instance variables. These variables are available every time a message is sent to the object, and they in some sense serve as the object's memory. When the object stops existing, the instance variables disappear too.

Duplicating Variable Names

Because the scope of a local variable is restricted to a single method, the same variable name can be used within several different methods without causing a conflict. In the computeCount method, we could have named the variables as follows, which duplicates names in the buttonClicked method:

```
private int computeCount (int number){
   int count;
   int trialDivisor;
```

```
    int limit;
    ...
    return count;
}
```

Whether or not we use the same variable name in several different methods is merely a matter of taste. When the programmer reuses the same local variable name in different methods, the name refers to a different area of storage in each method. In the next example, the name iAmLocal is used in two methods in this way:

```
public class ScopeDemo extends GBFrame{

    int iAmGlobal;

    public void buttonClicked (Button buttonObj){

        int iAmLocal;
        ...
    }

    private int userMethod (int parm1, int parm2){

        int iAmLocal;
        ...
    }
    ...
}
```

The names of a local variable and a global variable can also be the same, as shown in the next code segment:

```
public class ScopeDemo extends GBFrame{

    int iAmAVariable;

    public void buttonClicked (Button buttonObj){

        int iAmAVariable;
        ...
        iAmAVariable = 3;            //Refers to the local variable
        this.iAmAVariable = 4;       //Refers to the global variable
        ...
    }

    ...
}
```

In this example, the local variable `iAmAVariable` is said to *shadow* the global variable with the same name. When the variable name is used in the method, it refers to the local variable, and the global variable can be referenced only by prefixing "`this.`" to the name. Shadowing is considered a dangerous programming practice because it greatly increases the likelihood of making a coding error.

Self-Test Questions

12. Define the concept of the scope of a variable.

13. What are the lifetimes of an instance variable, a local variable, and a parameter?

14. What is shadowing? Give an example and describe the bad things that shadowing might cause to happen in a program.

6.4 Preconditions and Postconditions

It is often difficult to tell whether or not cooperating methods are working together correctly, but the task is simplified by specifying what each method is supposed to do in terms of *preconditions* and *postconditions.*

We can think of preconditions and postconditions as the subject of a conversation between the user and implementer of a method. Here is the general form of the conversation:

Implementer: "Here are the things that you must guarantee to be true before my method is invoked. They are its preconditions."

User: "Fine. And what do you guarantee will be the case if I do that?"

Implementer: "Here are the things that I guarantee to be true when my method finishes execution. They are its postconditions."

A method's preconditions describe what should be true before it is called, and its postconditions describe what will be true after it has finished executing. The preconditions describe the expected values of parameters and instance variables that the method is about to use. Postconditions describe the return value and any changes made to instance variables. Of course, if the caller does not meet the preconditions, then the method probably will not meet the postconditions.

Preconditions and postconditions are conveniently written as comments placed directly below a method's header:

```
private int computeCount (int number){
//Count the divisors of a given number
//   Preconditions  -- number is an integer >= 0.
//   Postconditions -- return the number of divisors.

   int count = 0;
   int trialDivisor = 2;
```

```
    int limit = number / 2 + 1;
    while (trialDivisor < limit){
        if (number % trialDivisor == 0)
            count = count + 1;
        trialDivisor = trialDivisor + 1;
    return count;
    }
}
```

Writing preconditions and postconditions for every method can be tedious, but it is generally worth the effort, especially in complex situations.

Self-Test Questions

15. Why is it important to write preconditions and postconditions for a method?

16. Write preconditions and postconditions for the method that raises a number to a given power in Self-Test Question 9.

6.5 Overloaded Methods

Two methods in a class can have the same name, provided the number and types of their parameters are not both identical. Whether or not the methods have the same return type is immaterial. Such methods are said to be *overloaded.* Here is an example:

```
private int doIt (int parm1, double parm2){
    ...
}

private int doIt (int parm1, int parm2){
    ...
}
```

The headers of these two methods differ only in the second parameter's type.

6.6 Cohesion and Coupling

Whenever we break a task down into cooperating methods, we create what in everyday parlance is called a division of labor. However, all divisions of labor are not equally effective. Imagine you are in charge of organizing a large party with the help of some friends. You could make a list of all the individual tasks involved and assign them at random to your friends. But random assignments are not a good idea because each friend's tasks would be unrelated, making life chaotic for you and your friends. It would make more sense to give each friend a single clearly defined responsibility, which in turn would encompass a set of related tasks. The party would then come off smoothly and easily.

The same principle applies to programming. When a method has a single clearly defined responsibility, we say that it has **high cohesion,** but if it implements unrelated or loosely related tasks, it has **low cohesion. Cohesion** is thus a measure of a method's unity of purpose. In writing programs, we strive for methods whose cohesion is as high as possible. In this chapter, the computeCount method has high cohesion. It has a single clearly defined purpose: to count the number of divisors. The computeArea method, despite being shorter, has lower cohesion. Rather than doing a single task, it performs three related ones: gets data from the screen, performs a computation, and displays the result.

Coupling is another characteristic to consider when decomposing methods. It is a measure of how tightly methods are bound together. **Low coupling** is desirable, while **high coupling** should be avoided. Methods are bound together by the information they share. Less is better. Again think about the party. If the overall task is decomposed sensibly, the instructions given to each helper will be short and simple (low coupling) rather than long and complex (high coupling). In this chapter, the coupling between the buttonClicked method and the computeCount method is low. They communicate by means of a single parameter and a return value. In the circle area/radius program, coupling at first glance seems nonexistent. The three methods (buttonClicked, computeArea, and computeRadius) work together without the need for parameters or return values; however, a closer look reveals that they share access to a common pool of instance variables. This is not bad in itself, but it must be considered when evaluating the degree of coupling between the methods.

For now, do not be overly concerned about cohesion and coupling, but nonetheless, keep them in mind.

CS Capsule: Function-Oriented Programming

In 1977, John Backus, the inventor of the programming language FORTRAN, was given the ACM Turing Award for his contributions to computer science at the annual meeting of the Association for Computing Machinery. Each recipient of this annual award presents a lecture. Backus discussed a new discipline in his talk called *function-oriented programming.* This style of programming was developed to address concerns about the reliability and maintainability of large software systems. One of the principal causes of errors in large programs is the presence of side effects and unintentional modifications of variables. These modifications can occur anywhere in a program with assignment statements whose targets are global variables. Backus proposed that function-oriented programming could eliminate side effects by eliminating the assignment statement and keeping global variables to a minimum. Function-oriented programs consist of sets of function declarations and *function applications.* A function application simply evaluates the parameters to a function, applies the function to these values, and returns a result to the caller. No assignment statements to global variables are allowed within a function. No side effects occur.

The philosophy of function-oriented programming has motivated the design of function-oriented languages. These languages do not allow the programmer to perform assignments to global variables within functions. The closest thing in Java to a function is a method. However, Java methods allow this kind of side effect. In fact, as we will see when we introduce cooperating classes in Chapter 9, many important Java methods exist just for the purpose of modifying global variables within objects. However, by exercising some discipline, Java programmers can still emulate a function-oriented style to guard against unwanted side effects in their programs.

6.7 Case Study: Tally Grades

Successful completion of large complex programs requires the use of good design and implementation strategies. We now present these in the context of a case study.

Request. Write a program that allows a teacher to tally the grades on a test.

Analysis. The input consists of student scores on a test. The program calculates the number of As, Bs, and so on, and a running average, and it displays the tallies and the running average. We provide a facility to reset the program so that more than one set of scores can be entered.

The program should be robust, meaning that it responds sensibly when invalid scores are entered. As we know from Chapter 4, robust should not be confused with correct. A program is *correct* if it produces correct output when presented with correct inputs. A score is considered invalid if it is:

- outside the range 0 to 100 (for instance, –6 and 105)
- nonnumeric (for instance, "cat")
- numeric but not an integer (for instance, 3.14).

A message box should be used to display an appropriate error message in response to invalid inputs.

The proposed interface is in Figure 6.9. The user must click the **Tally Score** button after entering each score, at which point one of the tallies is incremented and the running average is updated. Clicking the **Reset** button reinitializes the program, resetting the variables in preparation for another batch of scores. After either button is clicked, the program moves the cursor back to the score field and selects the text already there. This makes the program easier to use.

Design. Let us begin by determining the variables needed by this program:

- The variables for window objects consist of all the usual suspects and can be chosen during implementation.

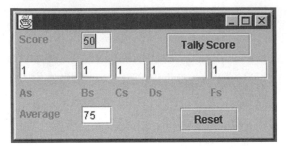

Figure 6.9 Interface for the tally grades program

- The variables to tally the number of As, Bs, and so on are

  `tallyA, tallyB, tallyC, tallyD, tallyF`
- The variables needed to compute the average are

  `numberOfTests`, the number of test scores entered so far

  `totalOfTests`, the total of the test scores entered so far

  `average`, the average of the test scores entered so far

In developing the pseudocode, we take a top-down approach and decompose the `buttonClicked` method into a hierarchy of cooperating methods. Starting at the top of this hierarchy, we write the `buttonClicked` method in terms of its immediate subordinate methods, and these in their turn we write in terms of their subordinates. We continue in this manner until we reach the bottom level, at which point we write methods that are not decomposed any further. Typically with this approach, the methods toward the top of the hierarchy coordinate the activity of their subordinates, while methods toward the bottom take care of the nitty-gritty details, rather like the situation in many human organizations. Unfortunately, there is no formula that you can learn for doing this activity; but fortunately, with exposure to examples and practice, you will get the hang of it. We use a structure chart to describe our overall strategy for decomposing the `buttonClicked` method (Figure 6.10).

Here is the pseudocode with calls to subordinate methods shown in *italics*:

```
buttonClicked(){
   if (reset button clicked)
     resetGlobalVariables()
   else
     processScore()
   set the focus to the input field for the score
}

resetGlobalVariables(){
   set the tallies to zero (tallyA, etc.)
   set the totals to zero (numberOfTests, etc.)
   set the average to zero
```

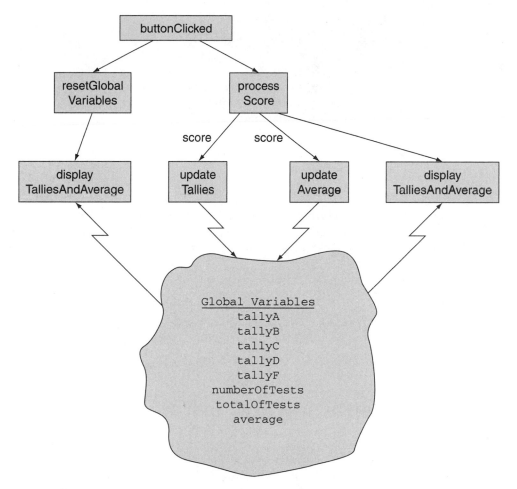

Figure 6.10 Decomposition of the `buttonClicked` method in the tally program

```
   display zero in the score field
   displayTalliesAndAverage()
}

displayTalliesAndAverage(){
   display the tallies and the average on the screen
}

processScore(){
   if (score entered by user is invalid)
      display an error message;
   else{
```

Continues

Continued

```
      get the score from the screen
      if (score is out of the range 0 to 100)
         display an error message
      else{
        updateTallies (score)
        updateAverage (score)
        displayTalliesAndAverage()
      }
    }
}

updateTallies (int score){
   update one of the tallies based on the value of score
}

updateAverage (int score){
   update the totals based on the score
   compute the average
}
```

6.8 Implementation and Testing Strategies

At this point, we could write the complete code for the program; however, it makes more sense to implement and test a program of this size incrementally. In this manner, we test the validity of our program step-by-step. At each small step, it is easy to find and remove any errors we may have made and then to proceed from a firm basis to the next step. In contrast, if we go for broke and implement the whole program at one shot, we may never unravel the errors.

In this section, we illustrate how this can be done using several different incremental approaches. People sometimes argue quite heatedly about which of these approaches is the best; however, in doing so, they obscure the main point, namely, that the benefit comes just from being incremental.

Top-Down Implementation and Testing Strategy

We begin with a *top-down implementation* strategy that mirrors the process utilized during design. In the first step, we implement the interface and the `buttonClicked` method fully; however, the methods called by `buttonClicked` will contain only enough code to indicate that they are called appropriately. Such simplified methods are called *stubs*. After making the usual number of programming errors and testing thoroughly, we arrive at the following code:

```java
import javax.swing.*;
import BreezySwing.*;

public class TallyGrades extends GBFrame{

   //Window objects
   JLabel scoreLabel   = addLabel ("Score"  ,1,1,1,1);
   JLabel AsLabel      = addLabel ("As"      ,3,1,1,1);
   JLabel BsLabel      = addLabel ("Bs"      ,3,2,1,1);
   JLabel CsLabel      = addLabel ("Cs"      ,3,3,1,1);
   JLabel DsLabel      = addLabel ("Ds"      ,3,4,1,1);
   JLabel FsLabel      = addLabel ("Fs"      ,3,5,1,1);
   JLabel averageLabel = addLabel ("Average",4,1,1,1);

   IntegerField scoreField   = addIntegerField (0,1,2,1,1);
   IntegerField AsField      = addIntegerField (0,2,1,1,1);
   IntegerField BsField      = addIntegerField (0,2,2,1,1);
   IntegerField CsField      = addIntegerField (0,2,3,1,1);
   IntegerField DsField      = addIntegerField (0,2,4,1,1);
   IntegerField FsField      = addIntegerField (0,2,5,1,1);
   IntegerField averageField = addIntegerField (0,4,2,1,1);

   JButton tallyScoreButton = addButton ("Tally Score",1,4,2,1);
   JButton resetButton      = addButton ("Reset"      ,4,4,2,1);

   public void buttonClicked (JButton buttonObj){
      if (buttonObj == resetButton){
         scoreField.setNumber (0);
         resetGlobalVariables();
      }else
         processScore();
      scoreField.requestFocus();
      scoreField.selectAll();
   }

   private void resetGlobalVariables(){
      messageBox ("I am resetGlobalVariables");
   }

   private void processScore(){
      messageBox ("I am processScore");
   }

   public static void main (String[] args){
      TallyGrades tpo = new TallyGrades();
```

Continues

Continued

```
      tpo.setSize (300, 150);
      tpo.setVisible (true);
   }
}
```

In the second step, we introduce the global variables, expand down one level in the structure chart, and test the logic for detecting invalid user input. We are introducing sufficient complexity in this step to make our job challenging without making it overly difficult:

```
. . . same as previous version

//Window objects
. . . same as previous version

//Other global variables
int tallyA = 0;
int tallyB = 0;
int tallyC = 0;
int tallyD = 0;
int tallyF = 0;
int numberOfTests = 0;
int totalOfTests = 0;
int average;

public void buttonClicked (JButton buttonObj){
   if (buttonObj == resetButton)
      resetGlobalVariables();
   else
      processScore();
   scoreField.requestFocus();       //See Appendix H
   scoreField.selectAll();          //See Appendix H
}

private void resetGlobalVariables(){
   //on next step reset variables here
   scoreField.setNumber (0);
   displayTalliesAndAverage();
}

private void processScore(){
   int score;
   if (!scoreField.isValid()){
      messageBox ("SORRY: The score must be an integer.");
```

```
        }else{
            score = scoreField.getNumber();
            if (score < 0)
                messageBox
                ("SORRY: Test scores must be between 0 and 100, inclusive.");
            else if (score > 100)
                messageBox
                ("SORRY: Test scores must be between 0 and 100, inclusive.");
            else{
                updateTallies (score);
                updateAverage (score);
                displayTalliesAndAverage();
            }
        }
    }

private void updateTallies(int score){
    messageBox ("I am updateTallies");
}

private void updateAverage(int score){
    messageBox ("I am updateAverage");
}

private void displayTalliesAndAverage(){
    messageBox ("I am displayTalliesAndAverage");
}

. . . same as previous version
```

In the third and final step, we complete the program and the testing. Here we include comments. Notice the use of pre- and post-conditions. It requires a lot of work to write all these comments, and it is very tempting simply to leave them out. After all, at this point, we know how the program works and hardly need comments to remind us; however, as said before, programs in the real world typically have a long life, and the comments will be immensely useful to whoever has the job of doing maintenance on the program 6 months from now:

```
/* TallyGrades.java
Accept test scores and display a running tally of the number
of A's, B's,  etc., and the average.
1) Reject scores which are not numeric, not integer, or not
   between 0 and 100.
2) Allow user to reset all counter and the average back to zero.
```

Continues

Continued

```
*/

import javax.swing.*;
import BreezySwing.*;

public class TallyGrades extends GBFrame{

   //Window objects
   JLabel scoreLabel   = addLabel ("Score"  ,1,1,1,1);
   JLabel AsLabel      = addLabel ("As"      ,3,1,1,1);
   JLabel BsLabel      = addLabel ("Bs"      ,3,2,1,1);
   JLabel CsLabel      = addLabel ("Cs"      ,3,3,1,1);
   JLabel DsLabel      = addLabel ("Ds"      ,3,4,1,1);
   JLabel FsLabel      = addLabel ("Fs"      ,3,5,1,1);
   JLabel averageLabel = addLabel ("Average",4,1,1,1);

   IntegerField scoreField   = addIntegerField (0,1,2,1,1);
   IntegerField AsField      = addIntegerField (0,2,1,1,1);
   IntegerField BsField      = addIntegerField (0,2,2,1,1);
   IntegerField CsField      = addIntegerField (0,2,3,1,1);
   IntegerField DsField      = addIntegerField (0,2,4,1,1);
   IntegerField FsField      = addIntegerField (0,2,5,1,1);
   IntegerField averageField = addIntegerField (0,4,2,1,1);

   JButton tallyScoreButton = addButton ("Tally Score",1,4,2,1);
   JButton resetButton      = addButton ("Reset"      ,4,4,2,1);

   //Other instance variables
   int tallyA = 0;
   int tallyB = 0;
   int tallyC = 0;
   int tallyD = 0;
   int tallyF = 0;
   int numberOfTests = 0;
   int totalOfTests = 0;
   int average;

   public void buttonClicked (JButton buttonObj){
   //Respond to button clicks
   //   resetButton      -- see method resetGlobalVariables for details
   //   tallyScoreButton -- see method processScore for details
   //      Postconditions -- additional: focus has been set to the scoreField
   //                     -- additional: content of scoreField has been
   //                        selected
      if (buttonObj == resetButton){
```

```
        scoreField.setNumber (0);
        resetGlobalVariables();
    }else
        processScore();
    scoreField.requestFocus();        //See Appendix H
    scoreField.selectAll();           //See Appendix H
}

private void resetGlobalVariables(){
//Reset the instance variables to zero
//  Preconditions  -- none
//  Postconditions -- all instance variables reset to zero
    tallyA = 0;
    tallyB = 0;
    tallyC = 0;
    tallyD = 0;
    tallyF = 0;
    numberOfTests = 0;
    totalOfTests = 0;
    average = 0;
    displayTalliesAndAverage();
}

private void processScore(){
//Read score entered by user and add it to various tallies, etc.
//Reject invalid inputs
//Nonnumeric data are filtered out automatically by the scoreField object
//  Preconditions  -- next number has been entered in scoreField
//  Postconditions -- the score has been added to totalOfTests
//                 -- numberOfTests has been incremented by 1
//                 -- the appropriate tally has been incremented by 1
//                 -- the average has been adjusted
    int score;
    if (!scoreField.isValid()){
        messageBox ("SORRY: The score must be an integer.");
    }else{
        score = scoreField.getNumber();
        if (score < 0)
            messageBox
            ("SORRY: Test scores must be between 0 and 100, inclusive.");
        else if (score > 100)
            messageBox
            ("SORRY: Test scores must be between 0 and 100, inclusive.");
        else{
            updateTallies (score);
```

Continues

Continued

```
        updateAverage (score);
        displayTalliesAndAverage();
      }
    }
  }

  private void updateTallies (int score){
  //Update the appropriate tally
  //  Preconditions  -- none
  //  Postconditions -- the appropriate tally has been incremented by 1
    if       (score >= 90) tallyA = tallyA + 1;
    else if (score >= 80) tallyB = tallyB + 1;
    else if (score >= 70) tallyC = tallyC + 1;
    else if (score >= 60) tallyD = tallyD + 1;
    else                  tallyF = tallyF + 1;
  }

  private void updateAverage (int score){
  //Update the average
  //  Preconditions  -- none
  //  Postconditions -- totalOfTests incremented by score
  //                 -- numberOfTests incremented by 1
  //                 -- average updated
    totalOfTests = totalOfTests + score;
    numberOfTests = numberOfTests + 1;
    average = totalOfTests / numberOfTests;
  }

  private void displayTalliesAndAverage(){
  //Display tallies and average
  //  Preconditions  -- none
  //  Postconditions -- tallies and average displayed in window
    AsField.setNumber (tallyA);
    BsField.setNumber (tallyB);
    CsField.setNumber (tallyC);
    DsField.setNumber (tallyD);
    FsField.setNumber (tallyF);
    averageField.setNumber (average);
  }

  public static void main (String[] args){
    TallyGrades tpo = new TallyGrades();
    tpo.setSize (300, 150);
    tpo.setVisible (true);
  }
}
```

Finding the Location of Run-Time Errors

We now digress somewhat to demonstrate how to find the location of run-time errors. In Chapter 3, we explored the consequences of division by zero. If a program attempts to divide by integer zero, the Java interpreter generates or throws an arithmetic exception. When this happens, the Java interpreter writes messages in the command prompt window that direct the programmer's attention to the erroneous line of code. Now we see what these messages look like when the error is several levels deep within a stack of user-defined methods. Suppose we introduce a divide-by-zero error into the `updateAverage` method. Figure 6.11 shows a snapshot of the error messages that are generated when the user now clicks the **Tally Score** button. Here is the modified code:

```java
private void updateAverage (int score){
//Update the average
//   Preconditions  -- none
//   Postconditions -- totalOfTests incremented by score
//                  -- numberOfTests incremented by 1
//                  -- average updated
   totalOfTests = totalOfTests + score;
//   numberOfTests = numberOfTests + 1;      <<< numberOfTests stuck at 0
   average = totalOfTests / numberOfTests;  // Divide by zero here
}
```

We have commented out the line that increments the `numberOfTests` with the consequence that the next line will involve division by zero.

Figure 6.11 The call stack that results when we divide by zero

The error messages in Figure 6.11 show which methods were being called by which other methods at the time the error occurred. This is known as a ***call stack.*** The last method called is listed first. Thus, the error messages say that division by zero occurred in method `updateAverage` (line 122), which at the time was being called by method `processScore` (line 97), which at the time was being called by method `buttonClicked` (line 55). Below this point, the listed methods belong to parts of `BreezySwing` or the Java virtual machine and are beyond the scope of this book. Here are the contents of lines 122, 97, and 55:

```
line 122 in updateAverage: average = totalOfTests / numberOfTests;
line 97  in processScore  : updateAverage (score);
line 55  in buttonClicked: processScore();
```

Expanding Capabilities Implementation and Testing Strategy (Optional)

We now demonstrate another incremental approach that we call the **expanding capabilities** strategy. At the first step, we develop and test a program that fully implements some aspect of the problem. At the second step, we add additional capabilities and so on until the program fully satisfies the requirements as specified during analysis. When taking this approach, we must avoid painting ourselves into a corner. In other words, at each step we want a program that expands naturally in the direction of the final solution. The best way to ensure this is to complete the analysis and design before starting the implementation. Let us begin the process.

In the first step, the program has a simplified interface and does not check the validity of the user's input. The program computes the tallies but not the average. Figure 6.12 shows a snapshot of the interface. Here is a listing of the code:

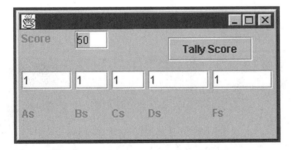

Figure 6.12 First step in the expanding capabilities approach

```
. . .

public class TallyGrades extends GBFrame{

    //Window objects
    JLabel scoreLabel   = addLabel ("Score"  ,1,1,1,1);
    JLabel AsLabel      = addLabel ("A's"     ,3,1,1,1);
    JLabel BsLabel      = addLabel ("B's"     ,3,2,1,1);
    JLabel CsLabel      = addLabel ("C's"     ,3,3,1,1);
    JLabel DsLabel      = addLabel ("D's"     ,3,4,1,1);
    JLabel FsLabel      = addLabel ("F's"     ,3,5,1,1);
```

```
IntegerField scoreField   = addIntegerField (0,1,2,1,1);
IntegerField AsField      = addIntegerField (0,2,1,1,1);
IntegerField BsField      = addIntegerField (0,2,2,1,1);
IntegerField CsField      = addIntegerField (0,2,3,1,1);
IntegerField DsField      = addIntegerField (0,2,4,1,1);
IntegerField FsField      = addIntegerField (0,2,5,1,1);

JButton tallyScoreButton = addButton ("Tally Score",1,4,2,1);

//Other instance variables
int tallyA = 0;
int tallyB = 0;
int tallyC = 0;
int tallyD = 0;
int tallyF = 0;

public void buttonClicked (JButton buttonObj){
   processScore();
   scoreField.requestFocus();
   scoreField.selectAll();
}

private void processScore(){
   int score;
   score = scoreField.getNumber();
   updateTallies (score);
   displayTallies();
}

private void updateTallies (int score){
   if      (score >= 90) tallyA = tallyA + 1;
   else if (score >= 80) tallyB = tallyB + 1;
   else if (score >= 70) tallyC = tallyC + 1;
   else if (score >= 60) tallyD = tallyD + 1;
   else                  tallyF = tallyF + 1;
}

private void displayTallies(){
   AsField.setNumber (tallyA);
   BsField.setNumber (tallyB);
   CsField.setNumber (tallyC);
   DsField.setNumber (tallyD);
   FsField.setNumber (tallyF);
}

 . . .
}
```

In the second step, we add code to process the average. In the third and final step, we add code to validate user inputs and to implement the **Reset** button. We omit the details.

Bottom-Up Implementation and Testing Strategy (Optional)

Another strategy worth mentioning is called ***bottom-up implementation.*** In this approach, we first implement the methods at the bottom of the structure chart. To test these, we must of course create a context in which they can be run. This context often includes simplified versions of the calling methods, known as ***drivers.*** After the methods at the bottom of the hierarchy are thoroughly tested and known to work correctly, we then move up a level and so on until we reach the top.

Now we illustrate the first step in this process (Figure 6.13). For this particular problem, it seems appropriate to include the complete user interface, but the only methods developed completely are `updateTallies`, `updateAverage`, and `displayTalliesAndAverage`.

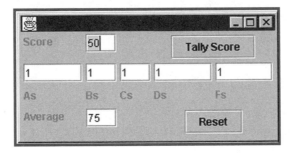

Figure 6.13 Interface for the bottom-up approach

```
.  .  .

public class TallyGrades extends GBFrame{

    //Window objects
    JLabel scoreLabel    = addLabel ("Score"  ,1,1,1,1);
    JLabel AsLabel       = addLabel ("As"     ,3,1,1,1);
    JLabel BsLabel       = addLabel ("Bs"     ,3,2,1,1);
    JLabel CsLabel       = addLabel ("Cs"     ,3,3,1,1);
    JLabel DsLabel       = addLabel ("Ds"     ,3,4,1,1);
    JLabel FsLabel       = addLabel ("Fs"     ,3,5,1,1);
    JLabel averageLabel  = addLabel ("Average",4,1,1,1);

    IntegerField scoreField   = addIntegerField (0,1,2,1,1);
    IntegerField AsField      = addIntegerField (0,2,1,1,1);
    IntegerField BsField      = addIntegerField (0,2,2,1,1);
    IntegerField CsField      = addIntegerField (0,2,3,1,1);
    IntegerField DsField      = addIntegerField (0,2,4,1,1);
```

```
IntegerField FsField      = addIntegerField (0,2,5,1,1);
IntegerField averageField = addIntegerField (0,4,2,1,1);

JButton tallyScoreButton = addButton ("Tally Score",1,4,2,1);
JButton resetButton      = addButton ("Reset"     ,4,4,2,1);

//Other global variables
int tallyA = 0;
int tallyB = 0;
int tallyC = 0;
int tallyD = 0;
int tallyF = 0;
int numberOfTests = 0;
int totalOfTests = 0;
int average;

// Dummy driver to call bottom-level methods
public void buttonClicked (JButton buttonObj){
    tallyA = 1;
    tallyB = 1;
    tallyC = 1;
    tallyD = 1;
    tallyF = 0;
    numberOfTests = 4;
    totalOfTests = 90 + 80 + 70 + 60;
    updateTallies (50);
    updateAverage (50);
    displayTalliesAndAverage();
}

private void updateTallies (int score){
    if      (score >= 90) tallyA = tallyA + 1;
    else if (score >= 80) tallyB = tallyB + 1;
    else if (score >= 70) tallyC = tallyC + 1;
    else if (score >= 60) tallyD = tallyD + 1;
    else                  tallyF = tallyF + 1;
}

private void updateAverage(int score){
    totalOfTests = totalOfTests + score;
    numberOfTests = numberOfTests + 1;
    average = totalOfTests / numberOfTests;
}

private void displayTalliesAndAverage(){
    AsField.setNumber (tallyA);
```

Continues

Continued

```
    BsField.setNumber (tallyB);
    CsField.setNumber (tallyC);
    DsField.setNumber (tallyD);
    FsField.setNumber (tallyF);
    averageField.setNumber (average);
  }
}
```

Mixed Implementation and Testing Strategy (Optional)

There is no rule that says one must follow any of the suggested strategies exactly. Each has its strengths and weaknesses, so programmers often choose a mixed approach. They implement and test methods at the top of the structure chart in a top-down fashion and those at the bottom in a bottom-up fashion. As already discussed, methods at the top of the structure usually contain the logic that orchestrates the cooperation between methods. This logic is best tested in a top-down fashion. Methods at the bottom of the structure usually do the nitty-gritty work of the application. The easiest way to subject these methods to the varying conditions in which they have to operate is bottom-up.

Because of the extra work required to write the stubs needed for the top-down approach and drivers for the bottom-up approach, you will probably find yourself using the expanding capabilities strategy most frequently. In any event, some form of an incremental approach is highly recommended. Nothing more surely spells doom and hours of frustration than trying to debug a large, completely untested program.

Self-Test Questions

17. What is top-down testing?

18. What is bottom-up testing?

6.9 Summary

In this chapter, we showed how complex tasks can be decomposed into a set of cooperating methods. A method allows a task to be named and filed away for later use. It consists of a header, which includes its name, return type, and parameter list, and a body, which includes the code for accomplishing its task. Methods can communicate with each other by sharing a common pool of variables, also called global variables. They can also receive information by means of parameters and return information to callers by means of return values. Methods that use the latter form of communication can be used in different situations without changes to their code. Methods can also contain locally declared variables. All three kinds of variables—global variables, local variables, and parameters—have a scope and a lifetime that is suited to their particular roles in a program. The different strategies for testing programs with cooperating methods include top-down testing and bottom-up testing.

6.10 Design, Testing, and Debugging Hints

- Be sure that a method is cohesive; that is, it should perform a single, well-defined task.
- Begin the definition of a method as a stub. When tested, a stub allows you to verify that the method receives and transmits data properly. Then fill in the code for manipulating these data and retest.
- As a rule of thumb, use global variables (declared within a class) only to share data among methods or for storing data that should survive a method call. If the data should not be shared, use local variables (declared within a method).
- Resist the temptation to use a global variable for the work of several methods when each method could declare its own local variable for that purpose.
- Use a parameter when the data transmitted to a method might be sent from more than one variable in a program. For example, `Math.sqrt(data)` can return the square root of many different data variables.
- Write preconditions and postconditions for each method you define. This information will help you during testing and debugging, and it will help your readers during program maintenance.
- To debug a method, perform the following steps:
  1. Examine the preconditions and postconditions by placing output statements with the appropriate variables before and after the calls of the method. If a precondition is not satisfied, fix it and retest.
  2. Place output statements with the appropriate variables at the beginning and at the end of the method body. Observe the outputs, and move the statements toward the middle of the method, until you discover the source of the error.
  3. If a method invokes another user-defined method, repeat steps 1 and 2 for this method.

6.11 Key Terms

If you have difficulty finding the definitions of any key terms in the body of this chapter, turn to the Glossary at the end of the book.

activate	function-oriented	postcondition
actual parameter	programming	precondition
body	global variable	return type
bottom-up implementation	header	scope
call stack	high cohesion	shadow
cohesion	instance variable	structure chart
driver	lifetime	stub
flow of control	local variable	top-down design
formal parameter	low cohesion	top-down implementation
function applications	overloaded method	

6.12 Answers to Self-Test Questions

1. Divide and conquer is a strategy that decomposes a complex task into smaller, simpler subtasks to solve a problem. A large, complex program can be decomposed into smaller, simpler methods that cooperate to solve a problem.

2. When a method is called, control is transferred from the caller to the method's first statement. The method's statements are executed until the end of the method's body is reached or a return statement is executed. Control then returns to the caller's next statement.

3. A method header contains the method's name, return type, and parameter list. A method body contains statements and locally declared variables.

4. A public method is visible within a class and to all clients of a class. A private method is visible only within a class.

5. The keyword `this`, when used within a method, refers to the object that has received the message which activated the method.

6. A common pool of variables for cooperating methods is typically a set of instance variables within the methods' class. The methods can access and modify these variable directly or by prefixing them with the keyword `this`.

7. A formal parameter is a parameter's name as it appears in a method header and in its body. An actual parameter is an expression that is passed to a method when the method is called.

8. The expressions which are the actual parameters are first evaluated. These values are then assigned to temporary storage locations, which are referenced by the corresponding formal parameters of the method.

9. a. `double squareRoot(double n)`
   b. `int raise(int base, int exponent)`
   c. `boolean isPrime(int n)`
   d. `boolean isBetween(int min, int n, int max)`

10. A local variable is a variable that is declared within the body of a method.

11. One reason that it is often better to transmit information by means of parameters and return values is that the user of such a method knows exactly which data are being accessed and modified by the method, whereas a method that accesses a common pool of variables does so only in its body, which may be hidden from the user. Another reason is that such a method can be used with different variables in different contexts, whereas access to a common pool is restricted to one context, that common pool.

12. The scope of a variable is that region of the program within which it can validly appear in lines of code.

13. The lifetime of an instance variable is the lifetime of the object that owns it. The lifetime of a local variable is the activation of the method in which it is declared. The lifetime of a parameter is also the activation of the method in which it is declared.

14. Shadowing occurs when a local variable or parameter and a global variable have the same name. Shadowing can cause incorrect behavior if the programmer thinks that a variable reference in a method is to a common pool of variables, whereas it really is to a local variable or a parameter, which likely has a different value.

15. Preconditions give users and implementers of a method a rule about what must be true for a method to execute correctly. Postconditions state what must be true after the correct execution of a method. Both kinds of conditions spell out the assumptions we make about methods and consequences that ensue from running them.

16. `int raise(int base, int exponent)`
    ```
    // Preconditions: base and exponent are greater than or equal to 0
    // Postcondition: returns the result of raising base to the given exponent
    ```

17. Top-down testing follows the path of top-down design, which starts with the implementation of a main method that calls other methods to accomplish its subtasks. Top-down testing uses stubs, or methods that have not been completed, to allow the programmer to examine how several methods cooperate.

18. Bottom-up testing starts with short, complete methods and uses drivers, or methods whose sole purpose is to test how the completed methods run independently of all other methods.

6.13 Programming Problems and Activities

Structure your solutions to the following problems in terms of Java methods. Use preconditions and postconditions to specify what each method does. When relevant, test your methods in the context of a short terminal I/O program before integrating them into GUI applications.

1. Modify the program of Problem 1, Chapter 4 so that the program displays an error message (in a message box) when the user enters a zero as one of the inputs.

2. Write a program that takes as inputs the lengths of three sides of a triangle and displays in a message box whether the triangle is scalene, isosceles, or equilateral.

3. The tax rate for a mythical state is based on the following table:

Income	Tax Rate
$0–5,000	0%
$5,001–10,000	5%
$10,00 –20,000	10.5%
$20,001–30,000	15%
Over $30,000	25.5%

Note that this is a graduated tax rate. For example, the tax on each dollar over $5,000 up to $10,000 is 5%, whereas the tax on each dollar after that, up to $20,000, is 10.5% and so on. Write a program that, when given a person's income as input, displays the tax owed rounded to the nearest dollar.

4. An object floats in water if its density (mass/volume) is less than 1 g/cm³. It sinks if its density is 1 or more. Write a program that takes the mass (in grams) and volume (in cubic centimeters) of an object as inputs and displays whether it will sink or float.

5. A quadratic equation has the form

$$ax^2 + bx + c = 0$$

where $a \neq 0$. Solutions to this equation are given by

$$x = \frac{-b \pm \sqrt{b^2 - 4ac}}{2a}$$

where the quantity $(b^2 - 4ac)$ is referred to as the *discriminant* of the equation. Write a program that takes three integer inputs as the respective coefficients (*a, b,* and *c*), computes the discriminant, and displays the real number solutions. Use the following rules:

   a. discriminant $= 0 \rightarrow$ single root

   b. discriminant $< 0 \rightarrow$ no real number solution

   c. discriminant $> 0 \rightarrow$ two distinct real solutions

   You should define a method, `discriminant`, that takes *a, b,* and *c* as parameters and returns the discriminant.

6. Write a program that takes as input a positive integer *N* and displays as output the Fibonacci numbers from 1 to *N*. You should define a method that computes the Fibonacci number for any value of *N* that is greater than zero.

7. A perfect number is a positive integer such that the sum of the divisors equals the number. Thus, $28 = 1 + 2 + 4 + 7 + 14$ is a perfect number. If the sum of the divisors is less than the number, it is deficient. If the sum exceeds the number, it is abundant. Write a program that takes a positive integer as input and displays a message box that indicates whether the number entered is perfect, deficient, or abundant. Your program should define the following two methods:

```
boolean isDivisor (int number, int divisor)
```

```
int divisorSum (int number)
```

The method `isDivisor` returns `true` if the `divisor` parameter is a divisor of the `number` parameter and `false` otherwise. The `divisorSum` method uses `isDivisor` to accumulate and return the sum of the divisors of the `number` parameter. Be sure to design and test the program incrementally; that is, verify that `isDivisor` works correctly before using it in `divisorSum`.

8. The least common multiple (LCM) of two positive integers *X* and *Y* is the positive integer *Z*, such that *Z* is the smallest multiple of both *X* and *Y*. For example, the LCM of 8 and 12 is 24. Write a program that takes two positive integers as inputs and displays as output the LCM of the two integers.

7 More Data Types, Operators, and Control Statements

I t is rather amazing how many data types, operators, and control statements there are in a typical programming language. So as not to overwhelm you with unnecessary details, we presented only the most essential of these in the first six chapters. We now discuss a few more of the most popular ones.

7.1 Data Types

Until this point in the text, we have limited our use of primitive data types to `char`, `int`, and `double`; however, Java supports several others. In this section, we introduce the primitive types `boolean`, `byte`, `short`, `long`, and `float`. We also say more about type `char`.

Booleans

The values `true` and `false` are called **Booleans** in honor of George Boole, a 19th-century British mathematician and one of the originators of mathematical logic. In Java, a `boolean` variable is one that can assume only two values: `true` and `false`. For instance, here is a simple, but ridiculous, example:

```
boolean b1, b2;
int i = 3, j = 4, k = 5;

b1 = i < j;       // The result of this comparison is either true or false
                  // and can be assigned to the Boolean variable b1
```

Continues

Continued

```
b2 = j < k;

if (b1 && b2)
   writer.println ("i is less than j and j is less than k");
else
   writer.println ("i, j, and k are not in order");
```

Not all examples need to be so silly. A `boolean` variable is useful when determining if a number is prime:

```
int number, divisor;
boolean isPrime;

number = ...;      // Assume number >= 3
isPrime = true;    // This means we start with the assumption that the
                   // number is prime
divisor = 2;
while (divisor < number && isPrime){
   if (number % divisor == 0)
      isPrime = false;          // We now know the number is not prime.
   divisor = divisor + 1;
}
if (isPrime)
   writer.println ("The number is prime");
else
   writer.println ("The number is NOT prime");
```

Characters

In Chapter 5, we saw a very limited use of character variables; however, programs frequently need to manipulate characters in other settings. Word processors are an obvious example. Let us quickly review what we know about characters from Section 1.3. When we think of characters, the letters of the alphabet immediately spring to mind. To these we must add the ten digits needed to represent numbers and various punctuation marks. Not so obvious are the nonprintable characters needed to represent carriage returns, linefeeds, tabs, backspaces, command key sequences, and other items more familiar to computer users than to the general public. The total number of all these special characters is not large, so the entire set of characters is easily represented by a 7-bit code that provides 128 possibilities. Of course, there needs to be agreement among computer users concerning which code, or pattern of 0s and 1s, represents which character. Until recently, the most widely used coding scheme in the English-speaking world was the ASCII standard. The addition of 1 bit allows for an extended ASCII character set of 256 codes. The need to represent more of the world's alphabets led to the adoption of the 16-bit Unicode scheme that is used in Java and which provides 65,536 patterns. For the sake of convenience, the first 256 Unicode characters match the extended ASCII character set. A table listing the basic ASCII character set can be found in Appendix D.

Here is a snippet of code in which we declare some character variables and assign them values using character literals:

```
char c1, c2, c3, c4;
c1 = 'a';
c2 = 'b';
c3 = ' ';
c4 = '8';
c5 = ';';
```

For the purposes of this book, we have little need to know which ASCII values represent which characters; however, it is important to remember that the letters a to z are represented by consecutive integer values (that is, when viewed as binary numbers), as are the letters A to Z and the digits 0 to 9. Therefore, it is not surprising that arithmetic operations can be performed on characters:

```
char chr;
chr = 'a';                 // chr equals 'a'
chr += 2;                  // and now 'c'
chr++;                     // and finally 'd'

chr = chr + ('A' - 'a');   // convert from lower- to uppercase by adding the
                           // difference between an upper- and lowercase letter
writer.println(chr);       // 'D' displayed
```

However, not all arithmetic operations on characters make sense. Adding a large number, say, 1000, to 'a' yields a Unicode value that does not correspond to a familiar character and, if displayed on a computer set up for an English alphabet, yields '?'. Similarly, multiplying 'a' by 6 would not make much sense either.

Because int is more inclusive than char, character values can be assigned to integer variables, but going in the other direction yields a compile-time error:

```
char chr;
int i;

chr = 'A';
i = chr;
writer.println(chr);       // 'A' displayed
writer.println(i);         // 65  displayed
chr = i + 1;               // Syntax error: cannot assign int to char.
```

Character variables and character literals can be compared to each other. For instance, to see if a character variable contains a lowercase letter, we write code like this:

```
char chr;
chr = ...;
if ('a' <= chr && chr <= 'z')
   writer.println("lowercase");
else
   writer.println("not lowercase");
```

A simpler alternative is to use one of the static[1] methods in the Character class. For example, the following code segment uses the Character methods isUpperCase, isLowerCase, and isDigit to determine if a character variable represents a lowercase letter, an uppercase letter, or a digit:

```
char chr;
chr = ...;
if (Character.isLowerCase(chr))
   writer.println("lowercase");
else if (Character.isUpperCase(chr))
   writer.println("uppercase");
else if (Character.isDigit(chr, 10))
   writer.println("digit");
else
   writer.println("unknown");
```

For a complete list of the Character class's methods, go to Sun's official Java Web site and consult the extensive documentation (see Appendix A for guidance).

Representing nonprintable characters as literals presents a dilemma. After all, if they are not printable, how are we supposed to type them between apostrophes? Java solves the problem by encoding them as a combination of a backslash followed by a designated letter as in:

```
chr = '\b';    // backspace
chr = '\t';    // tab
chr = '\n';    // linefeed
chr = '\r';    // carriage return
```

A related problem is how to represent as literals characters which are printable but which have special significance—for instance, the double quote, apostrophe, and backslash. Java again uses a combination of characters beginning with a backslash as in:

```
chr = '\"';    // double quote
chr = '\'';    // apostrophe
chr = '\\';    // backslash
```

---

[1] We discuss static variables and methods in Chapter 9. For now, the examples that follow will provide adequate guidance to correct usage.

Finally, it is always possible to use a Unicode value to designate a character literal. Unicode values are in the form **\uxxxx**, where **x = 0 . . 9** or **A . . F**:

```
chr = '\u0043';
writer.println(chr);  // 'C' displayed
```

This example uses hexadecimal numbers. See Section 1.3 and Appendix E for more details.

Other Numeric Data Types

In addition to int and double, Java supports several other numeric types. A complete list is in Table 7.1. When memory is at a premium, the types short and float are used instead of the types int and double, respectively. We will continue to use int and double for numbers in this text.

Table 7.1

Numeric Data Types

Type	Storage Requirements	Range
byte	1 byte	−128 to 127
short	2 bytes	−32,768 to 32,767
int	4 bytes	−2,147,483,648 to 2,147,483,647
long	8 bytes	−9,223,372,036,854,775,808L to 9,223,372,036,854,775,807L
float	4 bytes	−3.40282347E+38F to 3.40282347E+38F
double	8 bytes	−1.79769313486231570E+308 to 1.79769313486231570E+308

Self-Test Questions

1. List two uses of Boolean variables.
2. How many character values are in the ASCII set, the extended ASCII set, and the Unicode set, respectively?
3. What happens when we assign a character value to an integer variable?
4. When would one use the types long, short, and float?
5. Look up the definitions of the methods digit and forDigit in Sun's Java documentation (in the Character class in the package java.lang). What do these methods do?

7.2 Symbolic Constants and the `Final` Qualifier

We already know that we can declare and initialize a variable in a single step. If in addition we precede the declaration with the qualifier `final`, then no further changes can be made to the variable during the course of the program, and any attempt to change it is flagged as a compile-time error. Here is an example:

```
final double SALES_TAX_RATE = 0.08;
```

Such variables are sometimes called *symbolic constants,* and it is customary to use underscores and capitalize all the letters in their names.

Symbolic constants are useful because they make programs easier to read and maintain. Consider, for example, a program that computes a customer's bill in a state that has a sales tax rate of 8%. Then, when computing an invoice's total, we could write

```
invoiceTotal = subtotal * 1.08;
```

or

```
invoiceTotal = subtotal * (1.0 + SALES_TAX_RATE);
```

Even though the second alternative is a little longer than the first, its meaning is stated more explicitly, and thus, it is easier to understand. Now imagine what happens if the sales tax rate changes to 9%. If we have used a symbolic constant, then it is very clear where we need to modify the program. If not, we must search the program for all instances of 1.08 and replace them by 1.09. But wait! Perhaps 1.08 is also used in our program in a context other than the sales tax rate, and perhaps there are other places in the program where we use the rate in the form 0.08 rather than 1.08. In a large program containing lots of constants, the maintenance implications are significant.

Self-Test Questions

6. Define symbolic constants for the following values:

   a. the newline character

   b. the number of hours in a standard workweek (40)

   c. the minimum wage ($8.50)

7. List the names of the symbolic constants that represent the largest and smallest integers in Java (you can find these in the documentation for the `Integer` class).

7.3 The Cast Operator and Mixed-Mode Arithmetic

Now that we have so many different data types, we are going to encounter situations in which we desire to mix them in arithmetic expressions and assignment statements, a situation called *mixed-mode arithmetic*. When using mixed-mode arithmetic, we must remember that some types are considered more inclusive than others. The numeric types from least to most inclusive are:

```
byte   short   int   long   float   double
```

We have already dealt with mixed-mode arithmetic on a minor scale in Section 3.2, where we saw that we can always assign a less inclusive type to a more inclusive one, but not conversely. However, we can overcome this restriction by using the cast operator. The *cast operator* converts a more inclusive type to a less inclusive one. The form of the operator is:

```
(<less inclusive type name>) <more inclusive value>
```

For instance, here is a sequence of assignment statements in which we begin with a double, cast to an int, and finally cast to a char:

```
double d;
int i;
char c;

d = 65.57;
i = (int) d;          // i contains 65, due to truncation.
c = (char) i;         // c contains 'A'.
writer.println(c);    // Displays 'A'.
```

As we notice in this example, the cast operation can destroy information. In general, the fractional part of a double or float is thrown away when cast to byte, short, int, or long. In addition, if the number being cast is outside the range of the target type, unexpected values can result. Thus,

```
(int)8.88e+009   becomes   290065408
```

The cast operator can also be used within expressions. Normally, when an operator involves mixed data types, the less inclusive type is automatically converted to the more inclusive before the operation is performed. For instance:

```
2 / 1.5              becomes      2.0 / 1.5
2 + 1.5              becomes      2.0 + 1.5
aByte  / aLong       becomes      aLong   / aLong
aFloat - anInt       becomes      aFloat  - aFloat
aFloat % aDouble     becomes      aDouble % aDouble
```

We could present other examples in a similar vein. Sometimes, though, we want to override this automatic conversion and, for instance, to treat

```
aFloat / anInt     as     anInt / anInt
```

This can be achieved by using the cast operation again, as illustrated next:

```
(int)aFloat * anInt            becomes    anInt  * anInt
aByte        / (byte)aLong     becomes    aByte  / aByte
aFloat       + (float)aDouble  becomes    aFloat + aFloat
```

In these expressions, the unary cast operator has higher precedence than the binary arithmetic operators (see Table 7.2 for details).

Self-Test Questions

8. State the purpose and a common use of the cast operator.

9. Give two examples of the manner in which information can be lost by using a cast operator.

10. Assume that the `double` variable `d` has the value 6.55 and the `int` variable `i` has the value 2. Write the value of the target variable after each of the following assignment statements:

   a. `d = i;`

   b. `d = i * d;`

   c. `i = (int)d;`

   d. `d = (int)d * i;`

   e. `d = (int)(d * i);`

7.4 Arithmetic and Assignment Operators

There really is no need for additional arithmetic and assignment operators in Java; however, using those that follow can save a few keystrokes in a typical program. Whether or not such a minor convenience is worth making the language larger and more complex is debatable; however, once such features are included, we must learn them if we are to read each others' programs.

Increment and Decrement Operators

One of the most common programming tasks is incrementing or decrementing a numeric variable by 1. This task is easily accomplished through the use of an assignment statement:

```
x = x + 1;
```

However, in imitation of C++, on which it is modeled, Java provides two more operators that make the task even easier. These are ++ (increment) and -- (decrement), as illustrated next:

```
x++;      // Increment x by 1.       Called postfix increment.
++x;      // Also increment x by 1.  Called prefix increment.
x--;      // Decrement x by 1.       Called postfix decrement.
--x;      // Also decrement x by 1.  Called prefix decrement.
```

The difference between the postfix and prefix versions of these operators is illustrated in the next snippet of code:

```
double x = 3.1, y = 3.1, z;
z = 2 * x++;  // z equals 6.2 because x is incremented after it is used.
z = 2 * ++y;  // z equals 8.2 because y is incremented before it is used.
```

Caution is advised when using these operators because it is easy to interchange the postfix and prefix versions accidentally. In this text, we use only the postfix versions and then only in stand-alone statements, such as

```
x++;
```

Increment and decrement operators are used frequently in the context of `for` statements.

Extended Assignment Operators

Again in imitation of C++, Java provides operators that combine the assignment operator (=) with various binary operators (+, -, *, /, %) to yield +=, -=, *=, /=, and %=. For instance, the following are equivalent:

```
sum = sum + i;
sum += i;

product = product * i;
product *= i;
```

We can, at the risk of some confusion, place several assignment operators in the same statement, called a *cascaded assignment statement*:

```
int a = 1, b = 2;
a += b += 3;        // This is evaluated from right to left so that
                    // first 5 is assigned to b and then
                    // 6 is assigned to a
```

Generally, we avoid writing such tricky code because it is hard to understand and maintain. Considering the overwhelming cost of maintenance, doing anything to make reading code more difficult is strongly discouraged.

Table 7.2 shows how the new operators fit into Java's overall precedence scheme.

Table 7.2

The Extended Operator Precedence Scheme

Operation	Symbol	Precedence (from highest to lowest)	Association
Grouping	( )	1	Not applicable
Method selector	.	2	Left to right
Unary plus	+	3	Not applicable
Unary minus	−	3	Not applicable
Not	!	3	Not applicable
Cast	(<type>)	3	Not applicable
Increment	++	3	Not applicable
Decrement	−−	3	Not applicable
Multiplication	*	4	Left to right
Division	/	4	Left to right
Remainder or modulus	%	4	Left to right
Addition	+	5	Left to right
Subtraction	−	5	Left to right
Less than	<	6	Not applicable
Less than or equal to	<=	6	Not applicable
Greater than	>	6	Not applicable

Table 7.2 *(continued)*

Operation	Symbol	Precedence (from highest to lowest)	Association
Greater than or equal to	>=	6	Not applicable
Equal to	==	7	Not applicable
Not equal to	! =	7	Not applicable
And	&&	8	Left to right
Or	||	9	Left to right
Assignment operators	= += -= *= /= %=	10	Right to left

Self-Test Questions

11. Convert each of the following assignment statements to a simpler form using an extended assignment operator, increment operator, or decrement operator:

    a. `x = x + 2;`

    b. `x = x % 3;`

    c. `x = x + 1;`

    d. `x = x - 1;`

12. Assume that the variables `x` and `y` have been declared to be of type `double`. Show how both variables can be set to the value 10.08 using a cascaded assignment statement.

7.5 The Math Class

While we are on the topic of arithmetic operators, we make a small digression to introduce Java's Math class. Many computations involve the use of standard mathematical constants such as π and standard mathematical functions such as sine, cosine, square root, and logarithm. For programmer convenience, these and other constants and functions have been implemented in the Math class as static variables and methods. Here are several snippets of code that illustrate their use.

```
radius = Math.sqrt (area / Math.PI);
```

Given the area of a circle, we compute its radius by using `Math.PI` for a highly accurate approximation of π and `Math.sqrt` to obtain the square root.

```
radians = Math.PI * angle / 180.0;
length = height / Math.tan (radians);
```

Given a person's height, we compute the length of her shadow when the sun is at a known angle above the horizon by using the tangent function `tan`.

```
amount = 100 * Math.pow (1.05, 8);
```

How much is $100 compounded annually for 8 years at 5% interest? This can be answered by computing $100 * 1.05^8$ with the aid of the power function `pow`.

```
int a = 7, b = 19;
number = (int)(a + Math.random() * (b - a + 1));
```

Here we generate a random integer between `a` and `b` inclusive. First, the method `Math.random()` returns a floating-point number that is greater than or equal to 0 and less than 1.0. Next, this random number is scaled and translated to the interval [a, b]. Finally, the `(int)` cast operator converts the result from a `double` to an `int`.

Table 7.3 summarizes several of the most frequently used methods and constants in the `Math` class. For a complete list of the `Math` class's methods, consult Java's Internet accessible documentation (see Appendix A for instructions).

Table 7.3

Frequently Used Methods and Constants in the `Math` Class	
Constant / Method	**Explanation**
double abs(double) float abs(float) int abs(int) long abs(long)	Returns the absolute value of a number.
double exp(double)	Returns e raised to the power of a `double` value, where e = 2.718 . . .
double log(double)	Returns the natural logarithm (base e) of a `double` value.
double max(double, double) float max(float, float) int max(int, int) long max(long, long)	Returns the greater of two values.
double min(double, double) etc.	Returns the smaller of two values.
double pow(double, double)	Returns a value of the first parameter raised to the power of the second parameter.

Table 7.3 *(continued)*

Constant / Method	Explanation
double random()	Returns a random number greater than or equal to 0.0 and less than 1.0.
long round(double)	Returns the nearest `long` integer to the parameter. *Warning*: Be sure to cast this to an `int` if your intent is to round to an `int`.
double sin(double)	Returns the trigonometric sine of an angle expressed in radians.
double cos(double)	Ditto for cos and tan.
double tan(double)	
double sqrt(double)	Returns the square root of a `double` value.
double E	The `double` value that is closer than any other to e, the base of the natural logarithms.
double PI	The `double` value that is closer than any other to π, the ratio of the circumference of a circle to its diameter.

Self-Test Questions

13. What is the `Math` class?

14. Assume that the `double` variable d has been given a value. Write the expressions that perform the following tasks:

    a. truncate d to an `int`

    b. round d to an `int`

    c. compute the square root of d

    d. raise d to the fourth power

15. Look in Sun's documentation for the definitions of the `Math` class methods `floor` and `ceil`. Write an expression using one of these methods that rounds the `double` variable d to the nearest `int`.

16. What does the `Math` method `random` return?

7.6 Two Sample Programs

We now present two short programs that illustrate some of the ideas presented in the preceding sections.

Using the Cast Operator and Symbolic Constants

Our first program converts from meters to yards, feet, and inches. This is an excellent opportunity to use symbolic constants and the `round` method. The interface is shown in Figure 7.1. We present most of the code and leave the rest as an exercise. In the code, we take advantage of the fact that integer division discards the fractional portion of the result. By the way, `Math.round` returns a `long`, which must be cast to an `int` before being assigned to the integer variable `inchesLeft`.

```
final double CENTIMETERS_PER_INCH = 2.540005;
final int    INCHES_PER_YARD = 36;
final int    INCHES_PER_FOOT = 12;

double meters;
int    inchesLeft, feet, yards;

public void buttonClicked (JButton buttonObj){
   meters = metersField.getNumber();

   inchesLeft = (int)(Math.round(meters * 100 / CENTIMETERS_PER_INCH));

   yards = inchesLeft / INCHES_PER_YARD;
   inchesLeft = inchesLeft % INCHES_PER_YARD;    //0 <= inchesLeft <= 35

   feet = inchesLeft / INCHES_PER_FOOT;
   inchesLeft = inchesLeft % INCHES_PER_FOOT;    //0 <= inchesLeft <= 11

   yardsField.setNumber (yards);
   feetField.setNumber (feet);
   inchesField.setNumber (inchesLeft);
}
```

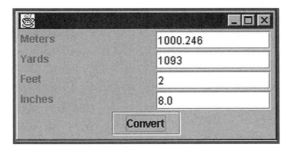

Figure 7.1 Interface for a metric conversion program

Using the `random` Method

The `random` method is frequently used in computer simulations. By way of illustration, we use it to simulate rolls of a pair of dice. Figure 7.2 shows our program's interface. Every time the **Roll** button is clicked, two random numbers between 1 and 6 are generated and displayed. Just to give the user some confidence that the dice are unbiased, the running average of each die is also displayed. The program has the typical structure, so again we present only some of the code and leave the rest as an exercise. Notice the use of the `cast` operator.

```
int numberOfRolls = 0;
int dice1, dice2;
```

```
double dice1Total = 0;
double dice2Total = 0;

public void buttonClicked (Button buttonObj){
   numberOfRolls = numberOfRolls + 1;
   dice1 = (int)(1 + Math.random() * (6 - 1 + 1));
   dice2 = (int)(1 + Math.random() * (6 - 1 + 1));
   dice1Total = dice1Total + dice1;
   dice2Total = dice2Total + dice2;

   dice1Field.setNumber (dice1);
   dice2Field.setNumber (dice2);
   average1Field.setNumber (dice1Total / numberOfRolls);
   average2Field.setNumber (dice2Total / numberOfRolls);
   rollsField.setNumber (numberOfRolls);
}
```

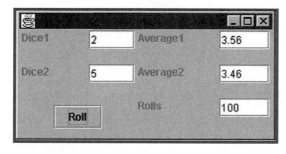

Figure 7.2 Interface for the dice program

7.7 Control Statements

At this point, we have developed considerable facility in working with if and while statements. Although these two control statements are adequate for all of our programming needs, there are many situations in which the following additional control statements are convenient and useful.

do-while Statement

The do-while statement is a slight variant of the while statement. Its syntax is:

```
do {block of statements} while (some condition);
```

Figure 7.3 illustrates the behavior of this looping construct. The block of statements is executed before the condition is tested, in contrast to the `while` statement, which tests the condition before entering the loop. Consequently, the `do-while` statement always executes the block of statements at least once. The next example shows a `do-while` loop that sums the numbers between 1 and 10:

```
int counter = 1;
int sum = 0;
do{
    sum = sum + counter;
    counter++;
}while (counter <= 10);
```

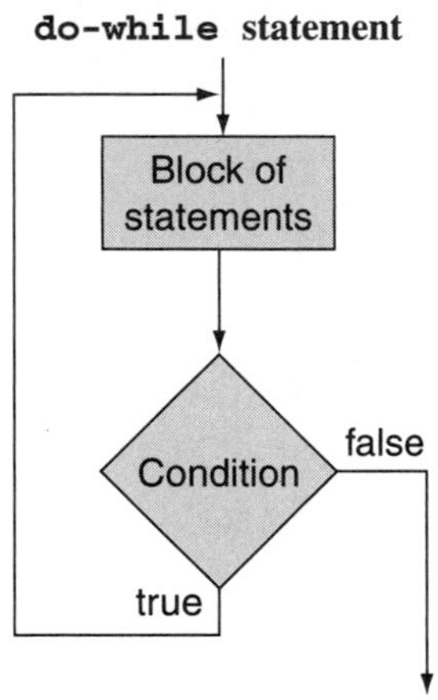

do-while statement

Figure 7.3 The `do-while` statement

`for` Statement

The `for` statement provides yet another looping construct. The syntax of the statement is:

```
for (statement1; condition; statement2)
    statement;
```

or

```
for (statement1; condition; statement2) {
    statement;
    . . .
    statement;
}
```

In this code,

- `statement1` does initialization needed before entering the loop for the first time
- `condition` is the test that is executed at the beginning of each iteration
- `statement2` does what is needed to prepare for the next iteration around the loop

This is most clearly demonstrated by rewriting the `for` loop using an equivalent `while` loop:

```
statement1;                 // Initialize
while (condition){          // Test
   block of statements;
   statement2;              // Prepare for next iteration
}
```

Here is a `for` loop that adds the numbers between 1 and 100:

```
sum = 0;
for (i = 1; i <= 100; i++)
   sum += i;
```

And here is another that does the same thing counting backward from 100 to 1:

```
sum = 0;
for (i = 100; i >= 1; i--)
   sum += i;
```

Some care must be taken when writing `for` loops. A loop that adds the numbers 1.00, 1.01, 1.02 . . . , 1.99 might be written as follows:

```
double sum, x;
sum = 0.0;
for (x = 1.0; x != 2.0; x += 0.01)
   sum += x;
```

Because of the limited precision of floating-point numbers, there is no guarantee that x will equal 2 exactly, with the consequence that the loop could be infinite. A minor modification corrects the problem:

```
double sum, x;
sum = 0.0;
for (x = 1; x < 2; x += 0.01)      // < instead of !=
   sum += x;
```

`switch` **Statement**

The `switch` statement behaves very much like an extended `if` statement, and although it is not as general as an extended `if` statement, it is considerably less cumbersome to use. Here is the syntax:

```
switch (expression){
   case literal 1:
      group of statements;
      break;
   case literal 2:
      group of statements;
      break;
   ...
   case literal n:
      group of statements;
      break;
   default:                    // This part
      group of statements;     // is
      break;                   // optional.
}
```

The `switch` statement begins by comparing the expression to the literals. If there is a matching literal, the corresponding group of statements is executed; otherwise, the statements following the keyword `default` are executed (if this optional group is present). If the keyword `break` is missing, execution continues into the next group. The expression must yield a value of type `byte`, `long`, `int`, or `char`, and the literals must be of the same type as the expression. Figure 7.4 illustrates the logic of the `switch` statement. Here is an example:

```
lotteryNumber = <generate a random number between 1 and 100>

switch (lotteryNumber){
   case 100:
      writer.println("Congratulations, you have won first prize");
      break;
   case 99:
      writer.println("Congratulations, you have won second prize");
      break;
   case 98:
      writer.println("Congratulations, you have won third prize");
      break;
   default:
      writer.println("Sorry, you didn't win a prize");
      break;
}
```

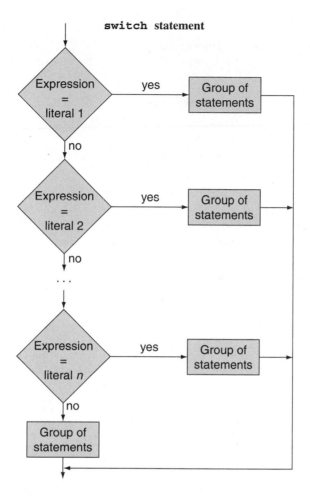

switch statement

Figure 7.4 The switch statement

break Statement

Sometimes we want to break out of a loop prematurely. The break statement provides a simple mechanism for doing so. It works equally well with for, while, and do-while loops. For instance, here we rewrite the code for determining if a number is prime using a combination of a break and for statement:

```
int number, isPrime, divisor;

number = ...;    // Assume number >= 3
isPrime = 1;     // This means we start with the assumption that the
                 // number is prime

for (divisor = 2; divisor < number; divisor++){
   if (number % divisor == 0){
```

Continues

Continued

```
     isPrime = 0;      // We have now discovered that the number is not
     break;            // prime, so we break out of the loop prematurely.
   }
}
if (isPrime == 1)
   writer.println("The number is prime");
else
   writer.println("The number is NOT prime");
```

The `break` statement in the form just presented breaks out of the immediately enclosing loop. The `labeled break`, on the other hand, can be used to break out of nested loops. A label is a user-defined symbol, and it is placed immediately before the loop from which we want to break. For instance:

```
thisIsALabelWithAStrangeName:
while (...){
   ...
   for (...){
      ...
      if (...) break thisIsALabelWithAStrangeName;
      ...
   }
   ...
}
```

`continue` Statement

The `continue` statement is similar to the `break` statement and is used in exactly the same manner; however, its effect is less drastic. When encountered, the `continue` statement causes the next iteration of the loop to start immediately, with the consequence that the statements following `continue` are completely skipped on the current iteration.

Self-Test Questions

17. Translate the following `while` loop into an equivalent `for` loop:

```
int i = 1;
int sum = 0;
int max = keyboardReader.readInt("Enter a number: ");
while (i <= max){
   sum = sum + i;
   i++;
}
```

18. Can the `while` loop in Question 17 be translated into an equivalent `do-while` loop? If not, why not?

19. Describe the situation in which a `do-while` loop is the appropriate choice of a loop.

20. Translate the following extended `if` statement into an equivalent `switch` statement:

```
char grade = keyboardReader.readChar("Enter a grade[a, b, or c]: ");
String message = "";
if (grade == 'a')
   message = "Excellent";
else if (grade == 'b')
   message = "Very good";
else if (grade == 'c')
   message = "Average";
else
   message = "Unacceptable";
```

21. When is the use of a `break` statement called for?

7.8 Strings Revisited

`String` Methods

To do more with strings than we have seen so far, we must send them messages. Class `String` includes methods for examining individual characters in a string, comparing the lexicographical order of two strings, searching for characters or substrings, extracting substrings, and creating a copy in which all characters are translated to uppercase or lowercase.

Many of the `String` methods refer to specific locations within a string, and locations are numbered starting with 0. For instance, in the three-character string `"abc"` the character `'a'` is considered to be at location 0 and not, as we might reasonably expect, at location 1. The characters `'b'` and `'c'` are at locations 1 and 2, respectively. This rather strange way of counting is a symptom of Java's historic ties to C++, and thus to C, and finally to assembly language, where counting from 0 is generally more convenient than counting from 1.

Table 7.4 provides a list of frequently used `String` methods. For more complete information, access the online documentation (see Appendix A).

Conversion Between Strings and Primitive Data Types

We have seen that Java automatically converts primitive data types to their string representation prior to concatenation. It is also possible to do these conversions outside

Table 7.4

Frequently Used `String` Methods	
Method	**Description**
`charAt (anIndex)` returns `char`	Ex: `chr = myStr.charAt(4);` Returns the character at the position `anIndex`. Remember that the first character is at position 0. An exception is thrown (i.e., an error is generated) if `anIndex` is out of range (i.e., does not indicate a valid position within `myStr`).
`compareTo (aString)` returns `int`	Ex: `i = myStr.compareTo("abc");` Compares two strings lexicographically. Returns 0 if `myStr` equals `aString`; a value less than 0 if `myStr` string is lexicographically less than `aString`; and a value greater than 0 if `myStr` string is lexicographically greater than `aString`.
`equals (aString)` returns `boolean`	Ex: `bool = myStr.equals("abc");` Returns `true` if `myStr` equals `aString`; else returns `false`. Because of implementation peculiarities in Java, **never test for equality like this**: `myStr == aString`

`equalsIgnoreCase`
   `(aString)`
   returns `boolean`
	Similar to `equals` but ignores case during the comparison.

`indexOf (aCharacter)` returns `int`	Ex: `i = myStr.indexOf('z')` Returns the index within `myStr` of the first occurrence of `aCharacter` or –1 if `aCharacter` is absent.

`indexOf (aCharacter,`
   `beginIndex)`
   returns `int`
	Ex: `i = myStr.indexOf('z', 6);`
	Similar to the preceding method except the search starts at position `beginIndex` rather than at the beginning of `myStr`. An exception is thrown (i.e., an error is generated) if `beginIndex` is out of range (i.e., does not indicate a valid position within `myStr`).

`indexOf (aSubstring)` returns `int`	Ex: `i = myStr.indexOf("abc")` Returns the index within `myStr` of the first occurrence of `aSubstring` or –1 if `aSubstring` is absent.

`indexOf (aSubstring,`
   `beginIndex)`
   returns `int`
	Ex: `i = indexOf("abc", 6)`
	Similar to the preceding method except the search starts at position `beginIndex` rather than at the beginning of `myStr`. An exception is thrown (i.e., an error is generated) if `beginIndex` is out of range (i.e., does not indicate a valid position within `myStr`).

`length()` returns `int`	Ex: `i = myStr.length();` Returns the length of `myStr`.

`replace (oldChar,`
   `newChar)`
   returns `String`
	Ex: `str = myStr.replace('z', 'Z');`
	Returns a new string resulting from replacing all occurrences of `oldChar` in `myStr` with `newChar`. **`myStr` is not changed.**

Table 7.4 *(continued)*

Method	Description
substring (beginIndex) returns String	Ex: str = myStr.substring(6); Returns a new string that is a substring of myStr. The substring begins at location beginIndex and extends to the end of myStr. An exception is thrown (i.e., an error is generated) if beginIndex is out of range (i.e., does not indicate a valid position within myStr).

substring (beginIndex,
       endIndex)
   returns String
	Ex: str = myStr.substring(4, 8);
	Similar to the preceding method except the substring extends to location endIndex-1 rather than to the end of myStr.

toLowerCase () returns String	Ex: str = myStr.toLowerCase(); str is the same as myStr except that all letters have been converted to lowercase. **myStr is not changed.**
toUpperCase () returns String	Ex: str = myStr.toUpperCase(); str is the same as myStr except that all letters have been converted to uppercase. **myStr is not changed.**
trim () returns String	Ex: str = myStr.trim(); str is the same as myStr except that leading and trailing spaces, if any, are absent. **myStr is not changed.**

the context of concatenation. Here are some representative examples in which the String class method valueOf is used to perform the conversions:

```
String s1 = String.valueOf (true);   // Boolean to string
String s2 = String.valueOf ('A');    // Character to string
String s3 = String.valueOf (3);      // Integer to string
String s4 = String.valueOf (3.14);   // Double to string
```

Conversion in the other direction is also supported, but it is more awkward. Here are some examples:

```
byte   b = Byte.valueOf ("12").byteValue();          // String to byte
double d = Double.valueOf ("3.14e4").doubleValue();  // String to double
float  f = Float.valueOf ("3.14e4").floatValue();    // String to float
int    i = Integer.valueOf ("12").intValue();        // String to int
long   l = Long.valueOf ("12").longValue();          // String to long
short  s = Short.valueOf ("12").shortValue();        // String to short
```

Short Examples of String Manipulations

We now present several short examples of string manipulations:

```
// Count the number of uppercase letters in a string

String str;
int count, i;
char chr;

str = " + A x ...G;H";
count  = 0;
for (i = 0; i < str.length(); i++){
   chr = str.charAt(i);
   if (Character.isUpperCase(chr)) count++;
}
writer.println ("str contains " + count + " uppercase letters.");
```

```
// Create a string that consists of all the digits
// in another string.

String digitStr, mainStr;
int i;
char chr;

mainStr = "a12bc3d";
digitStr = "";                         // An empty string

for (i = 0; i < mainStr.length(); i++){
   chr = mainStr.charAt(i);
   if (Character.isDigit (chr))
      digitStr += chr;
}
writer.println (digitStr);
```

```
// Extract the substring starting with the first '*' and
// ending with the second '*'

String str, substr;
int first, second;

str = "ab*cdef*xyz*";
first = str.indexOf ('*');
if (first == -1)
   writer.println ("not present");
else{
   second = str.indexOf ('*', first+1);
   if (second == -1)
      writer.println ("not present");
```

```
    else{
        substr = str.substring (first, second+1);
        writer.println (substr);
    }
}
```

```
// Determine the lexicographical order of two strings

String str1 = "Charles", str2 = "Chuck";
int outcome;

outcome = str1.compareTo (str2);

if (outcome == 0)
    writer.println ("str1 equals str2");
else if (outcome < 0)
    writer.println ("str1 comes before str2");
else
    writer.println ("str1 comes after str2");
```

Self-Test Questions

22. Assume that a string `str` has been assigned a value. Write expressions to perform the following tasks:

    a. Find the position of the letter `'a'` in the string.

    b. Find the position of the string `"the"` in the string.

    c. Determine if the string is the same as the string `"quit"`.

23. How does one use the method `compareTo` to compare two strings?

24. Write a code segment that counts the number of instances of a character in a string. You can assume that the variables `str` and `ch` refer to the string and the character, respectively.

25. Describe how to convert values of primitive types to the corresponding string values.

26. Describe how to convert the strings that represent primitive values to values of the corresponding primitive types.

7.9 Case Study: Palindromes

We now present a case study that involves some basic string manipulations.

Request. Write a program that determines whether or not an input string is a palindrome.

Analysis. A palindrome is a string that reads the same forward and backward. We accept an input string from a text field. We ignore the case of the letters in the string. All characters, including internal spaces, are examined; however, leading and trailing spaces are ignored. We display "Yes, you entered a palindrome" or "No, you did not enter a palindrome" in a message box. Figure 7.5 shows the proposed interface.

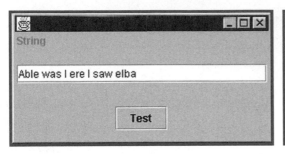
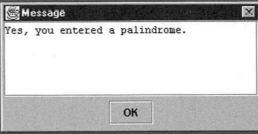

Figure 7.5 Interface for the palindrome program

Design. Here is pseudocode for the buttonClicked method:

```
buttonClicked (aButton){
    get aString from the text field
    if isPalindrome (aString)
        output yes
    else
        output no
}
```

The buttonClicked method calls the palindrome method:

```
boolean palindrome (aString){
    convert the string to uppercase and trim off leading and trailing spaces
    forward = first position in string
    backward = last position in string
    while forward < backward{
        if string.charAt (forward) != string.charAt (backward)
            return false
        forward++
        backward--
    }
    return true
}
```

In this method, the loop drives the two position indicators forward and backward from opposite ends of the string toward the middle. If unequal characters are encountered at these opposing positions, then the string is not a palindrome; otherwise, it is.

Implementation

```
/* Palindrome.java
Determine if a string is a palindrome.
```

```
1) The user enters a string and clicks the Test button.
2) The program examines the string and pops up its answer in a message box.
*/
import javax.swing.*;
import BreezySwing.*;

public class Palindrome extends GBFrame{

   JLabel stringLabel     = addLabel     ("String",1,1,2,1);
   JTextField stringField = addTextField (""      ,2,1,2,1);
   JButton testButton     = addButton    ("Test" ,3,1,2,1);

   public void buttonClicked(JButton buttonObj){
   // Read the string, call palindrome, and display the response
   //    Preconditions  -- none
   //    Postconditions -- the response is displayed

      String aString = stringField.getText();
      if (isPalindrome (aString))
         messageBox("Yes, you entered a palindrome.");
      else
         messageBox("No, you did not enter a palindrome.");
   }

   private boolean isPalindrome (String s){
   // Determine if a string is a palindrome. Omit leading and trailing spaces.
   //    Preconditions  -- s is a string
   //    Postconditions -- return true if a palindrome else false

      int forward, backward;

      s = s.toUpperCase().trim();     // Convert to uppercase and trim spaces.

      for (forward = 0, backward = s.length() - 1; // Initialize
           forward < backward;                     // Test
           forward++, backward--){                 // Prepare next iteration

         if (s.charAt (forward) != s.charAt (backward))
            return false;
      }
      return true;
   }

   public static void main (String[] args){
      Palindrome tpo = new Palindrome();
      tpo.setSize (300, 150);
      tpo.setVisible (true);
   }
}
```

There are three points to note in the foregoing code. First, the string is converted and trimmed in a single statement. This is possible because the `toUpperCase` method returns a string, which is then immediately sent the `trim` message. Second, although we used a `while` loop in the pseudocode, here we use a `for` loop. Third, the `for` statement illustrates a new feature, namely, a series of comma-separated statements can be used in the "initialize" and "prepare next iteration" sections.

CS Capsule: Data Encryption

Data encryption involves the translation of data into a code that cannot be read by unauthorized users. *Cryptography* is the formal study of methods of data encryption, and *cryptanalysis* is the branch of cryptography that deals with "breaking" codes. The practice of data encryption is hundreds of years old, and its use with computers is almost as old as the computer itself. One of the first uses of a computer was to break German codes during World War II, and Alan Turing, one of the first computer scientists, was a leading engineer in this project.

Though the algorithms for encryption and decryption have become very sophisticated, the processes are straightforward. The inputs to an encryption algorithm are a code (a string of bits) and the source data; the output is the encrypted data. Decryption reverses this process.

Needless to say, the primary use of data encryption during the Cold War (from 1946 to 1992) was military, and the United States government closely regulated any new data encryption algorithms. With the advent of networks and their use for commerce, electronic mail, and so forth, the use of data encryption has spread, mainly to protect the privacy, security, and reliability of these transactions. For an overview of the technology and policy issues concerning data encryption, see the entire issue of *Communications of the ACM,* Vol. 35, No. 7 (July 1992).

7.10 Design, Testing, and Debugging Hints

- A `for` loop's logic is similar to that of a `while` loop and should be designed and tested accordingly.
- Remember to include a `break` statement for each case of a `switch` statement and a `default` statement where relevant.
- The individual characters in a string are located at positions 0 through the length of the string minus 1. An attempt to access a character at a position outside this range will result in a run-time error.

7.11 Summary

In this chapter, we added a few operators, such as increment, decrement, and extended assignment, and control statements, such as `do-while` loops, `for` loops, and `switch` statements to our arsenal of Java tools. We also surveyed the primitive data types for Booleans, characters, and numbers, showed how to convert them to each other with the cast and assignment operators, and showed how to name them as symbolic constants. We introduced several useful methods in the `Math` class and the `Character` class for manipulating numbers and characters. Finally, we examined some methods in the `String` class that are handy for processing strings.

7.12 Key Terms

If you have difficulty finding the definitions of any key terms in the body of this chapter, turn to the Glossary at the end of the book.

cascaded assignment statement	cryptanalysis	decrement
	cryptography	increment
cast operator	data encryption	symbolic constant

7.13 Answers to Self-Test Questions

1. A Boolean variable can be used to control an exit condition of a loop. Such a variable, say, done, is initialized to false before the loop starts, and set to true when the loop should terminate. The loop condition then says `while (! done)`. Another use of a Boolean variable is to simplify a complex expression. For example, one can assign the result of a comparison to a Boolean variable and then use the variable in an expression with a logical operator.

2. There are 128 values in the ASCII set, 256 values in the extended ASCII set, and 65,536 values in the Unicode set.

3. When a character value is assigned to an integer variable, the character's Unicode value is used.

4. One would use the types `short` and `float` when memory is at a premium and the numbers used are not very large. One would use the type `long` when the integer is larger than the maximum allowed by type `int`.

5. The method `digit` expects a digit (a character) and a base (an integer) as parameters and returns the integer represented by that digit in that base. The method `forDigit` expects a number (an integer) and a base (an integer) and returns the digit representing that number in that base.

6. a. `final char NEWLINE = '\n';`

   b. `final int WEEKLY_HOURS = 40;`

   c. `final double MINIMUM_WAGE = 8.50;`

7. `Integer.MAX_VALUE` and `Integer.MIN_VALUE`.

8. A cast operator is used to convert a value of one type to a value of another less inclusive type. For example, one must use a cast operator before assigning a value of a more inclusive type to a variable of a less inclusive type.

9. When one casts a `double` to an `int`, the fractional part of the `double` is dropped. When one casts a `long` to an `int` and the `long` exceeds the range allowed by `int`, only the data in the least significant 32 bits are retained.

10. a. 2.0

    b. 13.1

    c. 6

    d. 12.0

    e. 13.0

11. a. `x += 2;`

    b. `x %= 3;`

    c. `x++;`

    d. `x--;`

12. `x = y = 10.08;`

13. The `Math` class includes several commonly used methods for manipulating numbers, such as functions for computing square roots and trigonometry.

14. a. `(int)d`

    b. `(int)Math.round(d)`

    c. `Math.sqrt(d)`

    d. `Math.pow(d, 4)`

15. `(int)Math.floor(d + 0.5)`

16. `Math.random` returns a random number greater than or equal to 0 and less than 1.

17.
```
int i;
int sum = 0;
int max = keyboardReader.readInt("Enter a number: ");
for (i = 1; i <= max; i++){
    sum = sum + i;
    i++;
}
```

18. No, one cannot in general translate a `while` loop to a `do-while` loop because the body of a `do-while` loop must execute at least once, whereas the body of a `while` loop might not execute at all.

19. A `do-while` loop is appropriate when the body of the loop must execute at least once.

20.
```
char grade = keyboardReader.readChar("Enter a grade[a, b, or c]: ");
String message = "";
switch (grade){
    case 'a':
        message = "Excellent";
        break;
    case 'b':
        message = " Very good ";
```

```
          break;
      case 'c':
          message = " Average ";
          break;
      default:
          message = " Unacceptable ";
  }
```

21. A break statement is needed in a switch statement to separate the cases. A break statement is also handy in a search loop to quit when an item is found.

22. a. str.indexOf('a')

    b. str.indexOf("the")

    c. str.equals("quit")

23. The method compareTo uses the form string1.compareTo(string2) and returns an integer. If the integer equals 0, the strings are equal. If the integer is greater than 0, string1 occurs after string2. If the integer is less than 0, string1 occurs before string2.

24.
```
int count = 0;
for (int i = 0; i < str.length(); i++)
    if (ch == str.charAt(i))
        count++
```

25. To convert a primitive value to its string representation, use the concatenation operator with "" as the first operand and the primitive as the second operand, or use the method String.valueOf(aPrimitive).

26. To convert a string to the primitive value it represents, use a method in the primitive's corresponding class. For example, to convert a value of type double to a string, use the method Double.valueOf(aDouble).

7.14 Programming Problems and Activities

1. A number is prime if it has no divisors (other than 1) that are less than or equal to its square root. The number 1 is not prime. Design and implement a method, isPrime, that returns true if its parameter is a prime number and false otherwise. You should use the isDivisor method developed in Problem 7, Chapter 6, in the implementation of isPrime. Then use these methods in a program that takes as input a number *N* and displays as output a list of the first *N* prime numbers.

2. Write a terminal I/O program that displays the characters that have the ASCII values 0 through 127.

3. A number guessing game begins with one player saying, "I'm thinking of a number between *x* and *y*," where *x* is the smaller number and *y* is the larger number. The other player responds with a guess. The first player then replies, "it's larger" or "it's smaller" or "you've got it!" This process goes on until the second player guesses the number. Write a program that plays this game. At startup, the program should use two randomly generated integers. When the user correctly guesses the number, the program should display a count of the number of guesses. You should

use Java's `Math.random()` method to generate your random numbers. `Math.random()` returns a `double` that is less than 1 and greater than or equal to 0. Thus, to generate a random integer between 1 and an upper bound, you can use the expression `(int) (1 + Math.random() * upperBound)`.

4. In the game of PNZ, one player thinks of a number consisting of three unique digits. The other player repeatedly guesses the number and receives the following evaluation of the guess from the opponent:

   - PPP means that each digit is in the correct position—the player has guessed the number.

   - Each P means that a digit is in the correct position, without saying which position that is.

   - Each N means that a digit occurs in the number, but it's not in the correct position.

   - A single Z means no digits are in the number.

   Assuming that the number is 123, here are some sample guesses and evaluations:

Guess	Evaluation
134	PN
213	PNN
143	PP
300	N
555	Z
123	PPP

   So as not to provide too many clues, the evaluator always displays the Ps before the Ns in the output.

   Write a program that plays this game with the user. The interface should have three window objects: a text field for entering a three-digit string, a button to register the guess, and a text area to display the results. The results should be displayed in a format similar to the one just shown. Your program should have the following methods:

   - `char randomDigit()` returns a randomly generated digit between 0 and 9.

   - `String randomString()` returns the string representation of a number that has three unique, randomly generated digits.

   - `String evaluateGuess(String target, String guess)` takes the target string and the guess string as parameters and applies the rules of PNZ to generate and return a result string.

   - `void displayResults(String guess, String result)` takes the guess string and the result string as parameters and updates the text area by adding a new line to its text.

   At program startup, the computer generates the target string by running `randomString`. When the **Guess** button is clicked, the program responds by evaluating the guess and displaying the results. The program should handle invalid guesses (strings not having three unique digits) by displaying the error in a message box.

8 In Greater Depth

I n this chapter, we examine more closely several topics introduced in earlier chapters. None of the material is essential to understand the rest of the book; however, for those with the time and interest, reading the chapter will be rewarding. First, because computers represent numbers with only limited precision, programs can easily generate erroneous results that in certain circumstances lead to financial loss and danger to human life. To avoid these problems, we must have a deeper understanding of the peculiarities of computer arithmetic. Second, as `if` statements are sometimes rather complex, we need the tools to understand their meaning and techniques to rewrite them in simpler forms. Third, to gain assurance that our looping statements are really behaving as intended, we should learn how to use loop invariants. Finally, we close the chapter by examining some additional aspects of strings and showing how to format tables of output in readable columns.

8.1 Peculiarities of Computer Arithmetic

We have already seen that truncation in integer division can lead to unexpected results:

```
5 / 2 + 1.0        yields 3.0
5 / 3 * 3          yields 3
5 * 3 / 3          yields 5
```

These problems are easily avoided by using floating-point numbers:

```
5 / 2.0 + 1        yields  3.5
5.0 / 3.0 * 3.0    yields  5.0
5.0 * 3.0 / 3.0    yields  5.0
```

However, there are worse situations to consider. Computers represent numbers with a fixed and limited precision. For instance, type `int` is limited to values between plus and minus 2 billion, which leads to results such as the following:

```
int b;
b = 1000000 * 1000000;
writer.println (b);              // yields -727379968


b = 2000000000 + 1000000000;
writer.println (b);              // yields -1294967296
```

The problem, which is referred to as *arithmetic overflow,* is the same in both examples: The results of the operations lie outside the allowed range of type `int`. Just because the computer performs an operation does not mean the result is meaningful. Arithmetic overflow is a potential problem whenever we work with integer types (`byte`, `short`, `int`, `long`), and you probably remember that we encountered it when we wrote a program to calculate Fibonacci numbers.

Floating-point types (`float`, `double`) have a large range but limited precision with consequences such as this:

```
float c;
int i;

c = 1.0E8F + 5.0F;
writer.println (b);    //Yields 100,000,008 but 10,000,000,005 is
                       //expected. The problem is due to the limited
                       //precision of floating-point arithmetic.

c = 1.0E8F;
for (i = 1; i <= 1000000; i++)
   c = c + 1.0F;
writer.println (b);    //However, this yields 100,000,000 because
                       //by itself each 1 is too small to have an effect.
```

The suffix `F` appended to the numeric literals indicates that they are to be treated as type `float` rather than type `double`. Type `double` has greater precision but is subject to similar problems. Sometimes a number that can be expressed precisely as a floating-point number in base 10 does not have a precise representation as a floating-point number in base 2 with results such as the following:

```
int count = 0;
double x;
for (x = 0.0; x != 1.0; x = x + 0.1)
```

```
   count++;
writer.println (count);   //Statement never executed because of infinite loop
```

The logic is impeccable, but the results are disastrous because x is never exactly equal to 1.0 even though it comes extremely close (the error is beyond the 15th decimal place). To avoid the preceding problem, we should rewrite the code as follows:

```
int count = 0;
double x;
for (x = 0.0; x <= 1.0001; x = x + 0.1)
   count++;
writer.println (count);   //11 is printed
```

It is easy to imagine how problems like those just illustrated and minor variants could lead to very nasty errors in computer programs. Next time your life is in the hands of a computer—as it is when you fly in an airplane, get a dental x-ray, or drive a recent model car—ask yourself if the programmer was guarding against the treacherous proclivities of computer arithmetic. On second thought, perhaps you will sleep better if you just try to forget this paragraph.

Even when precision is not an issue, we can experience annoying difficulties when working with floating-point values. Usually, Java uses double rather than float to represent floating-point literals, which can lead to unexpected compile-time errors as illustrated next:

```
float x = 1.0;         //Invalid because 1.0 is assumed to be double
float y = 1.0F;        //OK because the 'F' indicates a float literal
float z = (float)1.0;  //OK because we cast

double c = 1.0;        //OK

float d;
d = 3.0 * x;           //Invalid because 3.0 is assumed to be double
                       //and thus the product is double.
d = 3.0F * x;          //OK because the 'F' indicates a float literal
d = (float)3.0 * x;    //OK
d = (float)(3.0 * x);  //OK
```

Advice: To avoid these annoying errors, declare variables to be double rather than float.

Self-Test Questions

1. What is arithmetic overflow?

2. What does the JVM do when it detects arithmetic overflow?

3. Describe an error that can result from the imprecision of floating-point numbers and explain why the error occurs.

8.2 Nested `if` Statements Revisited

It is easy to write nested `if` statements, but it is sometimes difficult to understand their implications. Here are two examples that illustrate how small changes in the positioning of braces can dramatically change the meaning of nested `if` statements.

```
// Version 1
if (the weather is wet){
   if (you have an umbrella)
      walk;
   else
      run;
}

// Version 2
if (the weather is wet){
   if (you have an umbrella)
      walk;
}else
   run;
```

To demonstrate the differences between the two, we construct a truth table:

The Weather Is Wet	You Have an Umbrella	1st Example's Outcome	2nd Example's Outcome
true	true	walk	walk
true	false	run	
false	true		run
false	false		run

The truth table shows exactly how different the two versions are. This example raises an interesting question. What happens if the braces are removed? In such situations, Java pairs the `else` with the closest preceding `if`. Thus,

```
if (the weather is wet)
   if (you have an umbrella)
      walk;
   else
      run;
```

Remember that indentation is just a stylistic convention intended to improve the readability of code. It means nothing to the computer. Consequently, reformatting the preceding code as follows does not change its meaning but will almost certainly mislead the unwary programmer.

```
if (the weather is wet)
   if (you have an umbrella)
      walk;
else
   run;
```

Now let us consider one final variation:

```
if (the weather is wet)
   if (you have an umbrella)
      open umbrella;
      walk;
   else
      run;
```

Whoops, this contains a syntax error. Can you spot it? The second if is followed by more than one statement, so braces are required:

```
if (the weather is wet)
   if (you have an umbrella){
      open umbrella;
      walk;
   }else
      run;
```

Remembering that it is better to overuse than to underuse braces, we should perhaps write:

```
if (the weather is wet){
   if (you have an umbrella){
      open umbrella;
      walk;
   }else{
      run;
   }
}
```

Logical Errors: Calculating a Salesperson's Commission

Nesting must be done with care if the desired effect is to be achieved and logical errors are to be avoided. As an example, consider increasing a salesperson's commission as follows:

- 10% if sales are greater than or equal to $5,000
- 20% if sales are greater than or equal to $10,000

Here is a first attempt at writing the code:

```
if (sales >= 5000)
   commission = commission * 1.1;        // line a
else{
   if (sales >= 10000)
      commission = commission * 1.2;     // line b
}
```

Let us see if the code works correctly. We do so by checking the three principal regions: sales less than $5,000, sales between $5,000 and $10,000, and sales greater than $10,000. We also check the boundary conditions: sales equal to $5,000 and $10,000.

Value of Sales	Lines Executed	Validity
1,000	neither line a nor line b	correct
5,000	line a	correct
7,000	line a	correct
10,000	line a	incorrect
12,000	line a	incorrect

Maybe it would have worked better without nesting:

```
if (sales >= 5000)
   commission = commission * 1.1;        // line a
if (sales >= 10000)
   commission = commission * 1.2;        // line b
```

Value of Sales	Lines Executed	Validity
1,000	neither line a nor line b	correct
5,000	line a	correct
7,000	line a	correct
10,000	line a and line b	incorrect
12,000	line a and line b	incorrect

We try once more, this time with greater success:

```
if (sales >= 10000)
   commission = commission * 1.2;        // line b
else{
   if (sales >= 5000)
      commission = commission * 1.1;     // line a
}
```

Value of Sales	Lines Executed	Validity
1,000	neither line a nor line b	correct
5,000	line a	correct
7,000	line a	correct
10,000	line b	correct
12,000	line b	correct

Rewriting Nested if Statements

Nested `if` statements are convenient but sometimes confusing. It is always possible to rewrite them as a sequence of independent `if` statements. Here is a demonstration involving the calculation of sales commissions:

```
if (5000 <= sales && sales < 10000)
    commission = commission * 1.1;
if (10000 <= sales)
    commission = commission * 1.2;
```

And here is another involving the calculation of student grades (the original nested version is in Chapter 4):

```
if (90 <= average                ) grade is A;
if (80 <= average && average < 90) grade is B;
if (70 <= average && average < 80) grade is C;
if (60 <= average && average < 70) grade is D;
if (                average < 60) grade is F;
```

The first question people usually ask when confronted with these alternatives is which is faster, by which they mean which will execute more rapidly. In nearly all situations, the difference in speed is insignificant and irrelevant, so a much better question is: Which is easier to write and maintain correctly?

Rewriting Complex Conditions

Even when they are not nested, `if` statements can be complex. Consider:

```
if (the sun shines && (you have the time || it is Sunday))
    let's go for a walk;
else
    let's stay home;
```

This statement can be replaced by a number of simpler ones, and there is a purely mechanical, if somewhat verbose, technique for doing so. Create a truth table for the complex `if` statement and then implement each line of the truth table by a separate `if` statement involving only `&&` (AND) and `!` (NOT). Applying the technique here yields:

```
if ( the sun shines &&  you have time &&  it is Sunday) walk;
if ( the sun shines &&  you have time && !it is Sunday) walk;
if ( the sun shines && !you have time &&  it is Sunday) walk;
if ( the sun shines && !you have time && !it is Sunday) stay home;
if (!the sun shines &&  you have time &&  it is Sunday) stay home;
if (!the sun shines &&  you have time && !it is Sunday) stay home;
if (!the sun shines && !you have time &&  it is Sunday) stay home;
if (!the sun shines && !you have time && !it is Sunday) stay home;
```

In this particular example, the verbosity can be reduced without reintroducing complexity by noticing that the first two `if` statements are equivalent to

```
if ( the sun shines &&  you have time) walk;
```

and the last four `if` statements are equivalent to

```
if (!the sun shines) stay home;
```

Putting this together yields:

```
if ( the sun shines &&  you have time) walk;
if ( the sun shines && !you have time &&  it is Sunday) walk;
if (!the sun shines) stay home;
```

Of course, it is also possible to go in the other direction; that is, combine several `if` statements into a single more complex one, but remember that no matter how we choose to represent complex alternatives, truth tables are an essential tool for verifying the accuracy of the result. We should use them whenever we have the slightest doubt about the meaning of the `if` statements we write.

Self-Test Questions

4. Find the error in the following code segment and write a correct version.
   ```
   if (income >= 5000)
      rate = 0.10;
   else if (income >= 10000)
      rate = 0.20;
   else
      rate = 0.00;
   ```

5. Construct a truth table for the correct version of code in Question 4.

8.3 Loop Invariants

The examples of loops thus far in this text have been so simple that it was fairly obvious that they were coded correctly; however, many programs include complex loops whose correctness cannot be determined at a glance. With that in mind, we need to learn how to demonstrate that a loop is correct. Let us reconsider the code for computing the sum $1 + 2 + 3 + \ldots + 100$. We choose this simple example so that we can focus on the demonstration's structure rather than on its contents. We will then apply this same structure to several more difficult examples. We strongly recommend that you apply the techniques you learn here whenever you are uncertain of a loop's behavior.

Here is the loop:

```
//Compute the sum of the integers from 1 to 100
sum = 0;
i = 1;
while (i <= 100){
    sum = sum + i;      // point p (we will refer to this later)
    i = i + 1;
}
```

Table 8.1

Trace of Variables While Computing a Sum		
All Possible Iterations	**Value of i at Point p**	**Value of sum at Point p**
1	1	1
2	2	$1 + 2$
3	3	$1 + 2 + 3$
. . .	. . .	. . .
k	k	$1 + 2 + 3 + \ldots + k$
. . .	. . .	. . .
100	100	$1 + 2 + 3 + \ldots + k + \ldots + 100$

Table 8.1 traces how the variables change during each iteration of the loop. In other words,

1. initially sum equals 0 and i equals 1
2. because $1 <= 100$, the loop is entered for a first time
3. at point p, on the kth iteration through the loop, sum = 1 + 2 + . . . + k

4. this is true the first time through the loop, when $k = 1$

5. this is true on each subsequent pass through the loop

6. after the 100th iteration

   a. i equals `101`

   b. the condition i `<= 100` becomes false

   c. the looping stops

   d. and sum ends up being equal to `1 + 2 + 3 + . . . + 100`

7. therefore, it is fair to say that the code does exactly what was intended

The statement "at point p, on the kth iteration through the loop, sum = `1 + 2 + . . . + k`" is called *a **loop invariant.***

Programmers do not usually do all this work every time they write a loop, but if they want to verify a loop's correctness, they must complete these steps:

1. Show that the loop is entered for a first time if appropriate.

2. Identify a relevant loop invariant.

3. Verify that the invariant is true the first time the loop is executed.

4. Verify that the invariant remains true on each subsequent pass through the loop.

5. Verify that the looping stops after the correct number of iterations.

This approach incorporates an informal use of the principle of ***mathematical induction.*** We now show three more examples of the use of loop invariants.

Computing the gcd of Two Numbers

Consider the problem of computing the greatest common divisor (gcd) of two positive integers a and b. The problem is solved by making the following observations:

```
if a = b then gcd (a,b) = a and/or b
if a < b then gcd (a,b) = gcd (a,b-a)
if a > b then gcd (a,b) = gcd (a-b, b)
```

To illustrate, suppose a is 15 and b is 24. Then

```
gcd (15,24) = gcd (15,9)
            = gcd (6,9)
            = gcd (6,3)
            = gcd (3,3)
            = 3
```

Here is a `while` loop that automates the computation:

```
//Compute the gcd of two positive integers
a = 15;
```

```
b = 24;
while (a != b){
    if (a > b)
        a = a - b;
    else
        b = b - a;
    // point p
}
gcd = a;
```

Table 8.2

Trace of Variables While Computing the gcd

All Possible Iterations	Value of **a** at Point *p*	Value of **b** at Point *p*
1	15	9
2	6	9
3	6	3
4	3	3

A trace of the loop helps to verify its correctness (see Table 8.2). In other words,

1. If a is not equal to b, then the loop is entered for a first time. Otherwise, there is no need to enter the loop at all.

2. At point *p*, on the *k*th iteration through the loop, the gcd of a and b is unchanged because of the way in which a and b are reduced.

3. This is true the first time through the loop, when $k = 1$.

4. This is true on each subsequent pass through the loop.

5. The looping stops because on each pass through the loop the difference between a and b is reduced by at least 1.

6. After the last iteration,

   a. a equals b

   b. so the gcd equals a

7. Therefore, it is fair to say that the code does exactly what was intended.

Balzano Bisection

If the graph of some function *f(x)* is known to cross the *x*-axis once between two numbers *a* and *b*, the crossing point can be estimated with fairly good accuracy using a method called Balzano bisection. The method works as follows (Figure 8.1):

1. Let $m = (a + b) / 2$.

2. If $f(m)$ and $f(a)$ are on the same side of the x-axis, then let $a = m$; else let $b = m$.

3. If a and b are now very close together, then $(a + b) / 2$ is an adequate approximation of the crossing point; else return to step 1.

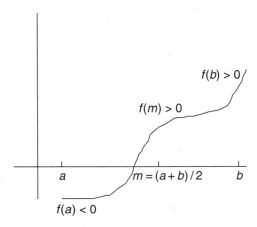

Figure 8.1 Balzano bisection

To illustrate the use of this algorithm, suppose that we want to approximate the cube root of 107, a number that lies somewhere between 0 and 107. This is equivalent to finding where in the interval (0,107) the function $f(x) = x^3 - 107$ crosses the x axis. Here is some code that performs the needed calculations:

```
a = 0;
b = 107;
while (b - a > 1e-10){
    m = (a + b) / 2;
    fAta = a * a * a - 107;
    fAtm = m * m * m - 107;
    if (fAta * fAtm > 0)
        a = m;
    else
        b = m;
    // point p
}
crossingPoint = (a + b) / 2;
```

About this code, we can say that:

1. Initially `a < b`.

2. If `b - a > 1e-10`, then the loop is entered for a first time; otherwise, a and b are already so close together that there is no need to enter the loop.

3. At point *p,* on the *k*th iteration through the loop, a < b and the crossing point lies between *a* and *b*.

4. This is true the first time through the loop, when *k* = 1.

5. This is true on each subsequent pass through the loop.

6. The looping stops because on each pass through the loop the distance between *a* and *b* is reduced by half. Thus, it is just a matter of time before the difference is less than 1*e*-10.

7. After the last iteration, a and b are very close together, so (a + b)/2 is a good approximation of the cube root of 107.

8. Therefore, it is fair to say that the code does exactly what was intended.

Summing a Series

The next example illustrates some useful computational techniques; however, it is significantly more complex than the preceding examples and may be skipped by the timid and math phobic.

The value of sin at *x* can be calculated as follows:

```
sin(x) = x - x³/3! + x⁵/5! - x⁷/7! + x⁹/9! - x¹¹/11! + ...
```

where x is expressed in radians. The more terms calculated, the greater the accuracy of the result. Before writing the code needed to perform the calculation, we make two useful observations about the series:

1. The terms of the series converge to zero because as *k* gets large the magnitude of *k*! rapidly overwhelms that of x^k.

2. The (*k* + 1)st term can be calculated from the *k*th term as follows:

$$\text{term}_{k+1} = - \text{term}_k * x * x / (2k * (2k + 1))$$

To gain some confidence in the correctness of this formula, we use it to generate several terms of the series (Table 8.3).

Table 8.3

Successive Terms in the Calculation of Sin		
k	**term**$_k$	**term**$_{k+1}$
1	+x¹/1!	-(+x¹/1!)*x*x / (2*3) = -x³/3!
2	-x³/3!	-(-x³/3!)*x*x / (4*5) = +x⁵/5!
3	+x⁵/5!	-(+x⁵/5!)*x*x / (6*7) = -x⁷/7!

The basic plan for the code is as follows:

1. Initialize sin to zero.

2. Enter a loop and on each pass through the loop increment sin by the next term in the series.

3. Stop when adding terms has no further effect.

In general, such a strategy for stopping a loop would be unwise, but it works in this situation because for any particular value of x:

1. The series converges, say, to y.

2. The terms of the series eventually become very small in comparison to y.

3. As demonstrated earlier in this chapter, floating-point arithmetic has limited precision and the sum of two numbers of vastly different magnitudes equals only the larger.

4. Therefore, adding additional terms eventually has no further effect.

Here is the code:

```
//Approximate sin(x)
int k;
double x;
double oldSin, sin;
double term;

x = ...;                 // Replace the dots with the desired value of x
oldSin = 999;
sin = 0;
k = 1;
term = x;
while (oldSin != sin){
   oldSin = sin;
   sin = sin + term;                        // point p
   term = -term*x*x / (2*k*(2*k+1)));
   k = k + 1;
}
```

About this code, we can say that:

1. Initially, `oldSin` and `sin` are unequal.

2. Consequently, the loop is entered for a first time.

3. At point p, on the kth iteration through the loop,

  a. `term` equals the kth term in the series

  b. `sin` equals the sum of the first k terms in the series

  c. `term` is then modified to become the $(k + 1)$st term of the series

4. This is true the first time through the loop, when $k = 1$, because

  a. `term = x`

  b. `sin = 0 + term`

  c. `term` is then modified to become $-$ `(x)x*x/(2*3)` $= -x^3/3$!

5. This is true on each subsequent pass through the loop because sum is increased by the now current term and `term` is then advanced correctly.

6. The looping stops because on each pass through the loop

   a. `term` is rapidly approaching 0 because $k!$ rapidly overwhelms x^k

   b. eventually, because of the limited precision of floating-point arithmetic, adding term to `sin` has no further effect on `sin`

   c. and on the next iteration, and not before, `sin` and `oldSin` are equal, after which the loop terminates

7. After the last iteration, `sin` provides a reasonable estimate of sin(x).

8. Therefore, it is fair to say that the code does exactly what was intended.

Once sin has been calculated, it is easy to calculate cos and tan using the trigonometric identities:

```
sin²(x) + cos²(x) = 1, which implies cos(x) = sqrt (1 - sin²(x))
tan(x) = sin(x) / cos(x)
```

Self-Test Questions

6. What is a loop invariant?

7. Use loop invariants and the method shown in this section to verify that the following loops are correct:

   a. Exponentiation, method 1:

```
int result = 1;
int base = 2;
int expo = 10;
while (expo > 0){
    result = result * base;
    expo = expo - 1;
}
```

   b. Exponentiation, method 2:

```
int result = 1;
int base = 2;
int expo = 10;
while (expo > 0){
    if (expo % 2 == 0){
        result = result * base * result * base;
        expo = expo / 2;
    }else{
        result = result * base;
        expo = expo - 1;
    }
}
```

8.4 String Utilities

In this section, we introduce two classes for working more efficiently and effectively with strings. The first of these, the `StringBuffer` class, allows us to improve computational efficiency at the cost of a small increase in programming complexity. The second, the `StringTokenizer` class, greatly reduces the programming effort needed to extract words, numbers, and other tokens from a string.

The `StringBuffer` Class

Strings contain a fixed number of characters when they are created; thus, they cannot grow to accommodate more characters. Nor can we modify a character at a given position in a string. The following code segment seems to tack new characters onto the end of a string, but the statement actually creates a new string and sets the variable to it:

```
String str = "Hi there";
str = str + ", Mary!";
```

The concatenation and assignment operators normally work well for this process, but if many such operations need to be performed, an object called a ***string buffer*** will work more efficiently. A string buffer is an instance of the Java class `StringBuffer`. String buffers behave like strings in many respects, but they can grow dynamically to accommodate more characters.

String buffers can be created in several ways, as the following code segment shows:

```
// Create a string buffer with capacity = 16, length = 0.
StringBuffer str1 = new StringBuffer();

// Create a string buffer with capacity = 80, length = 0.
StringBuffer str2 = new StringBuffer(80);

// Create a string buffer with capacity = 16, length = 9.
StringBuffer str3 = new StringBuffer("Hi there!");
```

A string buffer allows you to specify its initial capacity. Otherwise, Java uses a default initial capacity of 16 characters. The capacity is merely the maximum number of characters that the buffer can hold. The length, by contrast, is the number of characters the buffer is currently holding. If the capacity of the string buffer is exceeded, the capacity is automatically expanded to accommodate the additional characters. Note that the declaration of a string buffer differs slightly from what you have seen for strings. You must declare a variable of type `StringBuffer` and assign to it a `StringBuffer` object created with the `new` operator.

Once we have a string buffer object, it can be sent the `append` message. The `append` method appends its parameter to the string buffer starting at index *n*, where *n* is the length of the string buffer. For example, the code segment

```
StringBuffer str = new StringBuffer("There are ");
str.append(2);
str.append(" kinds of string types discussed thus far.");
```

creates a string buffer containing the characters "There are ", then appends the number 2 (after converting this to a string), and finally appends the string " kinds of string types discussed thus far." to the buffer. The parameter of `append` can be a string, data of any primitive type, an array of `char`, or an object of any type. When the parameter is an object, a string representation of the object is used. The `append` method returns the updated string buffer.

The method `toString` returns the string of characters contained in a string buffer. Thus, the code

```
str.toString()
```

added to the previous code segment would return the string "There are 2 kinds of string types discussed thus far."

In addition to the methods `length` and `charAt`, which you have seen used with strings, a string buffer implements several other methods, as shown in Table 8.4.

Table 8.4

Some Commonly Used `StringBuffer` Methods	
Method	**What It Does**
`StringBuffer append (aParm)`	Appends a string representation of `aParm`, where `aParm` can be a string, data of any primitive type, an array of `char`, or an object of any type.
`int capacity()`	Returns the capacity of the string buffer.
`char charAt(anInteger)`	Returns the character at the indicated position.
`StringBuffer insert (int index, aParm)`	Inserts the string representation of `aParm` beginning at the specified index, shifting any existing data to the right, where `aParm` can be a string, data of any primitive type, an array of `char`, or an object of any type.
`int length()`	Returns the number of characters currently in the string buffer.
`void setCharAt (int index, char newCh)`	Replaces the character at the given index with the new character.
`void setLength (int newCapacity)`	Sets the capacity of the string buffer. If the specified integer is less than the current number of characters in the buffer, Java truncates the buffer so that all characters beyond the new length are disregarded.
`String toString()`	Returns a string of the characters currently in the string buffer.

Java uses the `append` method in conjunction with the `toString` method to concatenate two `String` objects. For example, when the code

```
String str = "I hope" + " this works";
```

is executed, Java concatenates the two strings by performing

```
new StringBuffer().append("I hope").append(" this works).toString();
```

The `StringTokenizer` Class

Sentences are composed of individual words, or *tokens.* When you read, you automatically break a sentence into its individual tokens, usually using white space characters such as blanks, tabs, and newlines as delimiters. Java provides a `StringTokenizer` class (from the `java.util` package) that allows you to break a string into individual tokens using either the default delimiters (space, newline, tab, and carriage return) or a programmer-specified delimiter. The process of obtaining tokens from a string tokenizer is called *scanning.* Table 8.5 shows several `StringTokenizer` methods.

Table 8.5

Some Commonly Used `StringTokenizer` Methods	
Method	**What It Does**
`int countTokens()`	Returns the number of tokens in the string tokenizer.
`boolean hasMoreTokens()`	Returns `true` if there is still an unscanned token in the string tokenizer.
`String nextToken()`	Scans through the string tokenizer, returning the next available token.

For example, the following code displays each word of a sentence on a separate line in the terminal output stream:

```
String sentence = "Four score and seven years ago, our forefathers set " +
                "forth this great nation.";

StringTokenizer tokens = new StringTokenizer(sentence);

while (tokens.hasMoreTokens())
    writer.println (tokens.nextToken());
```

The preceding code produces a surprising result. The list of words displayed by `println` includes

```
ago,
nation.
```

rather than

```
ago
nation
```

The reason is simple. The delimiters are space, newline, tab, and carriage return. Punctuation marks are treated no differently than letters. To add punctuation marks to the list of delimiters, replace the second line of the preceding code with the following two lines:

```
String listOfDelimiters = ".,;?! \t\n\r";
StringTokenizer tokens = new StringTokenizer (sentence, listOfDelimiters);
```

Note: Remember to import `java.util.*`.

Self-Test Questions

8. Describe the differences between a string and a string buffer.
9. Assume that the `String` variable `str` refers to a string. Write the code to create a string tokenizer that recognizes decimal digits in `str` as delimiter characters.
10. Assume that the `String` variable `str` refers to a string. Write a code segment that uses a string tokenizer to remove the white space characters in `str`.
11. Generalize the method used in your answer to Question 10 to remove all the instances of any character from a string.

8.5 Formatted Output

Occasionally, a program must display tables of words and numbers. Unless these tables are formatted carefully, they can be unreadable (Figure 8.2). The `BreezySwing` package contains a `Format` class that enables us to create formatted output that is left justified, right justified, or centered within a field of some specified width. Table 8.6 shows a list of words and numbers justified in fields of width 10 using these three justification schemes.

To create such output, we first use the `justify` method to generate a string of length 10 with our number or word embedded appropriately. The unused portion of the string is filled with spaces. We then print the string. Here is a segment of code that embeds the word "cat" left justified in a string of length 8 together with several other examples:

```
import BreezySwing.*;
. . .
Format.justify ('l', "cat", 8);      // "cat" left justified in a string of
                                     // length 8 yields the string
                                     // "cat     "
```

Continues

Continued

```
Format.justify ('r', 45678, 7);        // 45678 right justified in a string of
                                       // length 7 yields the string
                                       // "  45678"


Format.justify ('c', "dog", 11);       // "dog" centered in a string of
                                       // length 11 yields the string
                                       // "    dog    "


Format.justify ('r', 2.534, 10, 2);    // 2.534 right justified in a string of
                                       // length 10 with a precision of 2 yields
                                       // "      2.53"
```

```
NAME SALES COMMISSION
Catherine 23415 2341.5
Ken 321.5 32.15
Martin 4384.75 438.48
Tess 3595.74 359.57
```

Version 1: Unreadable without formatting

```
NAME                    SALES      COMMISSION
Catherine            23415.00         2341.50
Ken                    321.50           32.15
Martin                4384.75          438.48
Tess                  3595.74          359.57
```

Version 2: Readable with formatting

Figure 8.2 A table of sales figures shown with and without formatting

Table 8.6

Words and Numbers Justified in Fields of Width 10		
Left	**Right**	**Centered**
0123456789	0123456789	0123456789
cat	cat	cat
dog	dog	dog
elephant	elephant	elephant
123	123	123
45678	45678	45678
3.14	3.14	3.14
155.76	155.76	155.76

In this code, the `justify` message is sent not to an object but to the class `Format`. This is not the first time we have seen messages sent to a class. When using the `justify` method, we need to be aware that it comes in four slightly different versions, as described in Table 8.7.

Table 8.7

The Four Versions of the `Format.justify` Method

Method	What It Does
`String justify (char alignment, String aString, int length)`	Returns a string of the indicated `length` with `aString` embedded and aligned to the left ('l'), center ('c'), or right ('r').
`String justify (char alignment, char aCharacter, int length)`	Returns a string of the indicated `length` with `aCharacter` embedded and aligned to the left ('l'), center ('c'), or right ('r').
`String justify (char alignment, long aLongInteger, int length)`	Returns a string of the indicated `length` with `aLongInteger`[a] embedded and aligned to the left ('l'), center ('c'), or right ('r').
`String justify (char alignment, double aDouble, int length, int precision)`	Returns a string of the indicated `length` with `aDouble` embedded and aligned to the left ('l'), center ('c'), or right ('r'). The `precision` specifies the number of digits displayed to the right of the decimal point.

[a] We have not discussed long integers yet, but for now suffice it to say that an integer can be used anytime a long integer is specified as a parameter.

To better illustrate the use of precision, Figure 8.3 shows the effect of printing the number 1.23456 in a field of width 10 with precisions that range from 0 to 9. Notice that the number is rounded up or extra zeros are added as appropriate. The field is filled with stars (*) if the width is insufficient to display the number with the requested precision. Here is the code that was used to create the demonstration:

```
i = 0;
while (i <= 9){
   str = "The number with precision " + i + ":"
      + Format.justify ('r', number, 10, i);
   writer.println (str);
   i = i + 1;
}
```

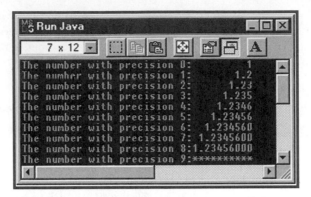

Figure 8.3 1.23456 displayed with precisions ranging from 0 to 9

Self-Test Questions

12. Write code segments to produce the following formatted strings:

   a. The value of `int` variable i, right-justified in a field of six columns.

   b. The value of `double` variable d, centered in a field of ten columns with a precision of 2.

8.6 Case Study: A Sales Table

We now write a program to capture sales data and display it in a formatted table.

Request. Write a program that allows the user to enter the names and annual sales figures for any number of salespeople. The program should display a formatted table of the names, sales, and commissions (at 10% of the sales amount) followed by the total of all sales and commissions.

Analysis. Figure 8.4 shows a proposed interface for this program. The user repeatedly:

- inputs a salesperson's name (no more than ten characters) in a text field
- inputs the salesperson's annual sales amount (a floating-point number) in a double field
- and then presses the **Enter** button

   Each time the user presses **Enter,** a new line of information is appended to a text area that contains the sales table. Finally, the user presses the **Display Totals** button, at which point the totals are displayed and both buttons are disabled, thereby preventing further user inputs or commands.

Figure 8.4 Proposed interface for the sales table program

Design. The data in the sales table are formatted as follows:

- names are left justified in a field of width 12
- sales, commissions, and totals are right justified in fields of width 15 with a precision of 2

Here is pseudocode for the `buttonClicked` method:

```
if (the Enter button is pressed) {
   read the salesperson's name and the sales amount
   calculate the commission
   format and display the name, sales amount, and commission
   increment the totals
}else{
   format and display the totals
   disable the command buttons
}
```

Implementation. Here is the complete code for the program. Notice the technique used for disabling a window object.

```
/* SalesTable.java
Display a table of names, sales, and commissions with totals.
```

Continued

```
1) The user enters each person's name and sales and presses the Enter
   button. The program then computes the commission as 10% of sales
   and appends this person's data to the table.
3) When the user presses the Display Totals button, the program displays
   the total sales and total commissions and blocks further user actions
   other than closing the window.
*/
import javax.swing.*;
import BreezySwing.*;
public class SalesTable extends GBFrame {

   // Define the table's header line
   String header = Format.justify('l', "NAME", 12) +
                   Format.justify('r', "SALES", 15) +
                   Format.justify('r', "COMMISSION", 15) + "\n";

   //Define the window objects
   JLabel       nameLabel    = addLabel        ("Name"            ,1,1,1,1);
   JLabel       salesLabel   = addLabel        ("Sales amount $"  ,2,1,1,1);
   JTextField   nameField    = addTextField    (""               ,1,2,1,1);
   DoubleField  salesField   = addDoubleField  (0                ,2,2,1,1);
   JButton      enterButton  = addButton       ("Enter"          ,3,1,1,1);
   JButton      totalsButton = addButton       ("Display Totals" , 3,2,1,1);
   JTextArea    output       = addTextArea     (header           ,4,1,3,4);

   //Define the instance variables
   double  totalSales = 0;            //The total of all sales
   double  totalCommissions = 0;      //The total of all sales commissions
   public void buttonClicked (JButton buttonObj){
   //Respond to a command button
   //  Preconditions  -- the user has pressed the desired button
   //  Postconditions -- the associated action has been completed

      if (buttonObj == enterButton)
        processInputs();
      else{
        enterButton.disable();        //Prevent further user action by
        totalsButton.disable();       //disabling the command buttons
        displayDashes();
        displayNumbers ("Totals", totalSales, totalCommissions);
      }
   }

   private void processInputs(){
   //Read the inputs, compute the commissions, format and display the
```

```
//name, sale, and commission.
//  Preconditions  -- the user has entered desired data in both input fields
//  Postconditions -- name, sale, and commission have been appended to the
//                     text area
//                  -- the totals have been incremented

   //Declare the local variables
   String name;                    //The salesperson's name
   double sales;                   //              sales
   double commission;              //              commission

   //Read the user input
   name = nameField.getText();
   sales = salesField.getNumber();

   //Calculate the commission.
   commission = sales * 0.10;

   //Display the name, sales, and commission
   displayNumbers (name, sales, commission);

   //Increment the totals
   totalSales += sales;
   totalCommissions += commission;
}

private void displayNumbers (String str, double num1, double num2){
//Format the input parameters and append to the text area.
//  Preconditions  -- none required
//  Postconditions -- the text area has been updated

   String numberLine = Format.justify ('l', str, 12) +
                       Format.justify ('r', num1, 15, 2) +
                       Format.justify ('r', num2, 15, 2);
   output.append (numberLine + "\n");
}

private void displayDashes(){
//Display dashes between the sales figures and the totals
//  Preconditions  -- none required
//  Postconditions -- the text area has been updated

   String dashLine = Format.justify ('l', " ", 12) +
                     Format.justify ('r', "----------", 15) +
                     Format.justify ('r', "----------", 15);
   output.append (dashLine + "\n");
```

Continues

Continued

```
   }

   public static void main (String[] args){
      SalesTable tpo = new SalesTable();
      tpo.setSize (350, 225);
      tpo.setVisible (true);
   }
}
```

8.7 Design, Testing, and Debugging Hints

- When designing and testing a complex Boolean expression, use a truth table to determine the possible values of the subexpressions. Be sure that the expression covers all of the possibilities.
- The use of loop invariants can help to verify that complex loops work correctly.

8.8 Summary

Several topics covered in this chapter involved techniques for reducing errors in programs. First, an awareness of the limits on the use of floating-point numbers can help to reduce errors associated with overflow and precision. Second, the ability to translate complex if statements to simpler ones can enhance confidence that we are using selection correctly. Third, we can use a method of induction with loop invariants to gain similar confidence with regard to the correctness of loops. Finally, we examined how two important string utilities—the string buffer and the string tokenizer—help to simplify the processing of text.

8.9 Key Terms

If you have difficulty finding the definitions of any key terms in the body of this chapter, turn to the Glossary at the end of the book.

arithmetic overflow	mathematical induction	string tokenizer
loop invariant	string buffer	

8.10 Answers to Self-Test Questions

1. Arithmetic overflow occurs when the magnitude of a number is too large to be represented by the number of bits available in computer memory.

2. The JVM responds to arithmetic overflow by converting the sign of the number. For example, adding 1 to the maximum allowable integer value results in converting the sign of this number.

3. In any comparison of two floating-point numbers, all of the available bits are compared. Thus, for example, the comparison $3.14 < 3.143$ might not produce the value true because the bits for the implicit digits to the right of 4 in the first number might be greater than those in the same positions for the second number.

4.
```
if (income >= 10000)
    rate = 0.20;
else if (income >= 5000)
    rate = 0.10;
else
    rate = 0.00;
```

5.
Value of Income	Value of Rate
10001	0.20
10000	0.20
9999	0.10
5001	0.10
5000	0.10
4099	0.00

6. A loop invariant is an assertion about a relationship between variables that remains true for all iterations of the loop. It is a statement that is true both before the loop is started, on each pass through the loop, and after the loop has ended.

7. For version a, let point p be `result = result * base`. Initially, `expo` is 10, so the loop is entered for the first time. At point p, on the kth iteration through the loop, `expo` equals $10 - k + 1$ and `result` equals 2^k. This is true for $k = 1$ through $k = 10$. The loop stops because `expo` is decremented by 1 on each pass and eventually equals 0. Therefore, the code does what is intended. This proof applies to the `else` part of version b, when `expo` is odd; for the `if` part, when `expo` is even, we can claim that `result` equals $(2^k)^2$ and `expo` is divided by 2 on each pass.

8. A string is immutable. None of its characters can be modified and it cannot be resized. A string buffer is mutable. Its characters can be modified and its size can be changed.

9.
```
StringTokenizer tokens = new StringTokenizer(str,
    "0123456789");
```

10.
```
StringTokenizer tokens = new StringTokenizer(str);
while (tokens.hasMoreTokens)
    str = str + tokens.nextToken();
```

11. ```
    String delimiters = "";
    delimiters = delimiters + <whatever character>;
    StringTokenizer tokens = new StringTokenizer(str, delimiters);
    while (tokens.hasMoreTokens)
        str = str + tokens.nextToken();
    ```

12. a. Format.justify('r', i, 6)

    b. Format.justify('c', d, 10, 2)

8.11 Programming Problems and Activities

1. Complete the two case studies in this chapter and test them.

2. Modify the program of Case Study 7.2 (rolling dice) so that it takes as an additional input the number of sides on a die (there need not be six sides). When the user clicks the **Roll** button, the program should use the number of sides to calculate the value of each die.

3. A simple text analyzer would display the following statistics:

   • the total number of words

   • the average length of a word

   • the longest word

   • the shortest word

   Write a program that allows the user to enter text in a text area. When the user clicks the **Analyze** button, the program displays, in a second text area, the statistics just listed. You should use a string tokenizer to process the data.

4. Most verbs form a participle by adding "ing" to the present singular. For example, the participle of "go" is "going" and of "eat" is "eating." In cases of verbs ending in "e," the "e" is dropped, as in "date"/"dating." Write a program that takes the present singular form of a verb as input and displays the participle form as output.

5. In ordinary conversation, one replies to a sentence by changing person. For example, I say, "I am going to town," and you might respond, "Did you say you are going to town?" Write a program that takes an input sentence and changes person. To keep it simple, the program should replace every instance of "I" with "you" and "am" with "are" in the input string and prepend a qualifier, such as "Did you say that", to this string before output.

6. Generalize the program of Problem 5 so it converts second-person words to first-person words. Where do you run into problems with this task?
    ```

9 Cooperating Classes

In this chapter, we return to a theme introduced in Chapter 6, namely, how to manage the complexities of writing large programs. The approach we chose in Chapter 6 was to apply the principle of divide and conquer, which led to the decomposition of large complex methods into hierarchies of smaller and simpler cooperating methods. We now take that principle one step further by decomposing our programs into systems of cooperating classes. We already know how to define a class, and we have already experienced the advantages of using classes created for us by others, so we are ready to take the obvious next step of dividing our programs into several classes. In this chapter, we start small and divide our programs into only two classes: one to manage the user interface and the other to encapsulate some other aspect of the overall task. In Chapters 10 and 11, we tackle more complex situations involving more than two classes. Most of this chapter focuses on basic syntactic and semantic issues involving classes and objects.

9.1 Classes and Objects

We introduced basic object-oriented terminology in Chapter 1 and have used it repeatedly since then. An object is a run-time entity that contains data and responds to messages. A class is a software package or template that describes the characteristics of similar objects. These characteristics are of two sorts: variable declarations that define an object's data requirements (instance variables) and methods that define its behavior in response to messages. The combining of data and behavior into a single software package is called encapsulation. An object is an instance of its class, and the process of creating a new object is called instantiation.

When a Java program is executing, the computer's memory must hold

- all class templates in their compiled form
- variables that refer to objects
- objects as needed

Each method's compiled byte code is stored in memory as part of its class's template. Memory for data, on the other hand, is allocated within objects. Although all class templates are in memory at all times, individual objects come and go. An object first appears and occupies memory when it is instantiated, and it disappears automatically when no longer needed. The JVM knows if an object is in use by keeping track of whether or not there are any variables referencing it. Because unreferenced objects cannot be used, Java assumes that it is okay to delete them from memory. Java does this during a process called *garbage collection.* In contrast, C++ programmers have the onerous responsibility of deleting objects explicitly. Forgetting to delete unneeded objects wastes scarce memory resources, and accidentally deleting an object too soon or more than once can cause programs to crash. In large programs, these mistakes are easy to make and difficult to find. Fortunately, Java programmers do not have to worry about the problem.

Three Characteristics of an Object

An object has three characteristics worth emphasizing. First, an object has *behavior* as defined by the methods of its class. Second, an object has *state,* which is another way of saying that at any particular moment its instance variables have particular values. Typically, the state changes over time in response to messages sent to the object. Third, an object has its own unique *identity,* which distinguishes it from all other objects in the computer's memory, even those that might momentarily have the same state. An object's identity is handled behind the scenes by the Java virtual machine and should not be confused with the variables that might refer to the object. Of these, there can be none, one, or several. When there are none, the garbage collector purges the object from memory. Shortly, we will see an example in which two variables refer to the same object.

Clients and Servers

When messages are sent, two objects are involved—the sender and the receiver, also called the *client* and *server.* A client's interactions with a server are limited to sending it messages; consequently, a client needs to know nothing about the internal workings of a server. The server's data requirements and the implementation of its methods are hidden from the client, an approach called information hiding in Chapter 1. Only a class's implementer needs to understand its internal workings. In fact, a class's implementation details can be changed radically without affecting any of its clients. Servers are also called *abstract data types* (ADTs). An ADT is abstract in that its clients need know only its interface—the messages it understands—and nothing about its implementation.

Self-Test Questions

1. What is the difference between a class and an object?
2. What happens to an object when it is no longer referenced by a variable?
3. List the three important characteristics of an object.
4. Describe the client–server relationship.
5. In what sense are abstract data types abstract?

9.2 A Student Class

The first class we develop in this chapter is called Student. We begin by considering the class from a client's perspective. Later we will show its implementation. From a client's perspective, it is enough to know that a student object stores a name and three test scores and responds to the messages shown in Table 9.1.

Table 9.1

Messages Understood by a Student Object	
Message	**Example**
setName(aString) returns void	Ex: stu.setName ("Bill"); Sets the name of stu to Bill.
getName() returns String	Ex: str = stu.getName(); Returns the name of stu.

setScore(whichTest,
       testScore)
   returns void
	Ex: stu.setScore (3, 95);
	Sets the score on test 3 to 95. If whichTest is not 1, 2, or 3, then 3 is substituted automatically.

getScore(whichTest) returns int	Ex: score = stu.getScore (3); Returns the score on test 3. If whichTest is not 1, 2, or 3, then 3 is substituted automatically.
getAverage() returns int	Ex: average = stu.getAverage(); Returns the average of the test scores.
getHighScore() returns int	Ex: highScore = stu.getHighScore(); Returns the highest test score.
toString() returns String	Ex: str = stu.toString(); Returns a string containing the student's name and test scores.

Using Student Objects

Some snippets of code illustrate how a client instantiates and manipulates student objects. First, we declare several variables, including two variables of type Student.

```
Student s1, s2;          // Declare the variables
String str;
int i;
```

As usual, we do not use variables until we have assigned them initial values. We assign a new student object to s1 using the operator new:

```
s1 = new Student();      // Instantiate a student and associate it with the
                         // variable s1
```

It is important to emphasize that the variable s1 is a reference to a student object and is *not* a student object itself.

A student object keeps track of the name and test scores of an actual student. Thus, for a brand new student object, what are the values of these data attributes? That depends on the class's internal implementation details, but we can easily find out by sending messages to the student object via its associated variable s1:

```
str = s1.getName();
writer.println (str);    // yields ""
i = s1.getHighScore();
writer.println (i);      // yields 0
```

Apparently, the name was initialized to an empty string and the test scores to zero. Now we set the object's data attributes by sending it some messages:

```
s1.setName ("Bill");     // Set the student's name to "Bill"
s1.setScore (1,84);      // Set the score on test 1 to 84
s1.setScore (2,86);      //                 on test 2 to 86
s1.setScore (3,88);      //                 on test 3 to 88
```

Messages that change an object's state are called **mutators.** To see if the mutators worked correctly, we use other messages to access the object's state (called **accessors**):

```
str = s1.getName();      // str equals "Bill"
i = s1.getScore (1);     // i equals 84
i = s1.getHighScore();   // i equals 88
i = s1.getAverage();     // i equals 86
```

The object's string representation is obtained by sending the toString message to the object:

```
str = s1.toString();
  // str  now equals
  // "Name:    Bill\nTest 1:  84\nTest2:  86\nTest3:  88\nAverage: 86"
```

When displayed in a text area (Figure 9.1), the string is broken into several lines as determined by the placement of the newline characters (`'\n'`). In addition to the explicit use of the `toString` method, there are other situations in which the method is called automatically. For instance, `toString` is called implicitly when a student object is concatenated with a string or is an argument in a `println` or `messageBox` message:

```
str = "The best student is: \n" + s1;
  // Equivalent to: str = "The best student is: \n" + s1.toString();
writer.println (s1);
  // Equivalent to: writer.println (s1.toString());
messageBox (s1);
  // Equivalent to: messageBox (s1.toString());
```

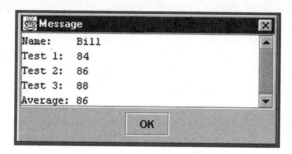

Figure 9.1 Implicit use of `toString` when a student object is sent to a message box

Because of these valuable implicit uses of the `toString` method, we frequently include this method in the classes we write. However, if we forget, Java provides a very simple version of the method through the mechanism of inheritance (discussed in Chapter 11). The simplified version does little more than return the name of the class to which the object belongs.

We close this demonstration by associating a student object with the variable `s2`. Rather than instantiating a new student, we assign `s1` to `s2`:

```
s2 = s1;                    // s1 and s2 now refer to the same student
```

The variables `s1` and `s2` now refer to the *same* student object. This might come as a surprise because we might reasonably expect the assignment statement to create a second student object equal to the first, but that is not how Java works. To demonstrate that `s1` and `s2` now refer to the same object, we change the student's name using `s2` and retrieve the same name using `s1`:

```
s2.setName ("Ann");     // Set the name
str = s1.getName();     // str equals "Ann". Therefore, s1 and s2 refer
                        // to the same object.
```

Table 9.2 shows code and diagrams that clarify the manner in which variables are affected by assignment statements. At any time, it is possible to break the connection between a variable and the object it references. Simply assign the value null to the variable:

```
Student s1;
s1 = new Student();       // s1 references the newly instantiated student
...                       // Do stuff with the student
s1 = null;                // s1 no longer references anything
```

Table 9.2

How Variables Are Affected by Assignment Statements

Code	Diagram	Comments
`int i, j;`	i ??? j ???	i and j are memory locations that have not yet been initialized, but which will hold integers.
`i = 3;` `j = i;`	i 3 j 3	i holds the integer 3. j holds the integer 3.
`Student s, t;`	s ??? t ???	s and t are memory locations that have not yet been initialized, but which will hold references to student objects.
`s = new Student();` `t = s;`	s t → student object	s holds a reference to a student object. t holds a reference to the same student object.

Structure of a Class Template

Having explored the Student class from a client's perspective, we now address the question of how to implement it. All classes have a similar structure consisting of four parts:

1. the class's name and some modifying phrases

2. a description of the instance variables

3. one or more methods that indicate how to initialize a new object (called *constructor* methods)

4. one or more methods that specify how an object responds to messages

The order of these parts can be varied arbitrarily provided part 1 comes first; however, for the sake of consistency, we will always adhere to the order listed, which yields the following class template:

```
public class <name of class> extends <some other class>{
    // Declaration of instance variables
    private <type> <name>;
    ...
    // Code for the constructor methods
    public <name of class>() {
        // Initialize the instance variables
        ...
    }
    ...
    // Code for the other methods
    public <return type> <name of method> (<parameter list>){
        ...
    }
    ...
}
```

Some of the phrases used in the template need to be explained:

public class: Class definitions usually begin with the keyword `public`, indicating that the class is accessible to all potential clients. There are some alternatives to `public` that we overlook for now.

<name of class>: Class names are user-defined symbols, and thus, they must adhere to the rules for naming variables and methods. It is common to start class names with a capital letter and variable and method names with a lowercase letter. There is one exception. Names of final variables (see Chapter 8) are usually completely capitalized.

extends <some other class>: Java organizes its classes in a hierarchy (see Chapter 1). At the root, or base, of this hierarchy is a class called `Object`. In the hierarchy, if class A is immediately above another class B, we say that A is the *superclass* or *parent* of B and B is a *subclass* or *child* of A (Figure 9.2). Each class, except `Object`, has exactly one parent and can have any number of children.

Whenever a new class is created, it must be incorporated into the hierarchy by extending an existing class. The new class's exact placement in the hierarchy is important because a new class inherits the characteristics of its superclass through a process called inheritance (Chapter 1). The new class

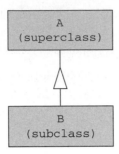

Figure 9.2 Relationship between superclass and subclass

then adds to and modifies these inherited characteristics, or in other words, the new class *extends* the superclass. If the clause `extends <some other class>` is omitted from the new class's definition, then by default, the new class is assumed to be a subclass of `Object`.

`private <type> <name>`: Instance variables are nearly always declared to be `private`. This prevents clients from referring to the instance variables directly. Making instance variables `private` is an important aspect of information hiding.

`public <return type> <name of method>`: Methods are usually declared to be `public`, which allows clients to refer to them.

`private` and `public` are called *visibility modifiers*. If both `private` and `public` are omitted, the consequences vary with the circumstances. Without explaining why, suffice it to say that in most situations omitting the visibility modifier is equivalent to using `public`. In earlier chapters, we did not bother to use a visibility modifier when declaring instance variables. From this point on, we will continue to omit visibility modifiers for window objects. We do this as a matter of convenience. The lines in which we define window objects are already so long that it is difficult to fit them on the pages of this book. However, we will use `private` for other instance variables unless there is some compelling reason to declare them `public`.

To illustrate the difference between `private` and `public`, suppose the class `Student` has a private instance variable `name` and a public method `setName`. Then

```
Student s;
s = new Student();
s.name = "Bill";       // Rejected by compiler because name is private
s.setName ("Bill")     // Accepted by compiler because setName is public
```

As a final note concerning our class template, notice that the constructor does not have a return type. All other methods do.

Implementation of the Student Class

Adhering to the format of our class template, we now implement the Student class. It is important to realize that other implementations are acceptable provided they adhere to the interface standards already established for the class:

```
/* Student.java
Manage a student's name and three test scores.
*/
public class Student {

    //Instance variables
    //Each student object will have a name and three test scores
    private String name;          //Student name
    private int test1;            //Score on test 1
    private int test2;            //Score on test 2
    private int test3;            //Score on test 3

    //Constructor method

    public Student(){
    //Initialize a new student's name to the empty string and the test
    //scores to zero.
        name = "";
        test1 = 0;
        test2 = 0;
        test3 = 0;
    }

    //Other methods

    public void setName (String nm){
    //Set a student's name
    // Preconditions  -- nm is not empty
    // Postconditions -- name has been set to nm
        name = nm;
    }

    public String getName (){
    //Get a student's name
    // Preconditions  -- none
    // Postconditions -- returns the name
        return name;
    }

    public void setScore (int i, int score){
    //Set the score on the indicated test
    // Preconditions  -- 1 <= i <= 3
```

Continued

```
//                    -- 0 <= score <= 100
//  Postconditions -- test i has been set to score
    if       (i == 1) test1 = score;
    else if (i == 2) test2 = score;
    else              test3 = score;
}

public int getScore (int i){
//Get the score on the indicated test
//  Preconditions  -- none
//  Postconditions -- returns the score on test i
    if       (i == 1) return test1;
    else if (i == 2) return test2;
    else              return test3;
}

public int getAverage(){
//Compute and return a student's average
//  Preconditions  -- none
//  Postconditions -- returns the average of the test scores
    int average;
    average = (int) Math.round((test1 + test2 + test3) / 3.0);
    return average;
}

public int getHighScore(){
//Compute and return a student's highest score
//  Preconditions  -- none
//  Postconditions -- returns the highest test score
    int highScore;
    highScore = test1;
    if (test2 > highScore) highScore = test2;
    if (test3 > highScore) highScore = test3;
    return highScore;
}

public String toString(){
//Return a string representation of a student's name, test scores
//and average.
//  Preconditions  -- none
//  Postconditions -- returns the string representation
    String str;
    str = "Name:    " + name  + "\n" +    // "\n" denotes a newline
          "Test 1:  " + test1 + "\n" +
          "Test 2:  " + test2 + "\n" +
          "Test 3:  " + test3 + "\n" +
          "Average: " + getAverage();
```

```
      return str;
   }
}
```

The meaning of the code is fairly obvious. All the methods, except the constructor method, have a return type, although the return type may be void, indicating that the method in fact returns nothing. Although each method's preconditions state what should be true when the method is called, no attempt is made to enforce the preconditions. Such code could be added, and an exception could be thrown anytime a precondition is violated (see Chapter 14 and Appendix F).

At the risk of being tedious, we repeat some observations made previously. When an object receives a message, the object activates the corresponding method. The method then manipulates the object's data by means of the instance variables. A method can also declare its own local variables. Whereas local variables retain their values only during the period in which the method is executing, an object's instance variables hold their values for the lifetime of the object.

Self-Test Questions

6. What are mutators and accessors? Give examples.
7. List two visibility modifiers and describe when they are used.
8. What is a constructor method?
9. Why do we include a toString method with a new user-defined class?
10. How can two variables refer to the same object?

9.3 Editing, Compiling, and Testing the Student Class

To use the Student class, we must save it in a file called **Student.java** and compile it by typing

```
javac Student.java
```

in a terminal window.[1] If there are no compile-time errors, the compiler creates the byte code file **Student.class.** Once the Student class has been compiled, applications can declare and manipulate student objects provided the code for the application and the Student class are in the same directory or the Student class is part of a package (see Appendix G). If we forget to compile **Student.java** or if we change it without remembering recompiling it, it will be compiled automatically in conjunction with the application that is using it.

---

[1] See the supplemental materials on the book's Web site for instructions specific to your development environment.

Here is a small program that uses and tests the Student class. Notice that for the first time we are using System.out.println rather than writer.println. We first mentioned the possibility of doing this in Chapter 2, and we give a complete explanation in Chapter 14. Figure 9.3 shows the results of running the program.

```java
public class TestStudent{

   public void run(){
      Student s1, s2;
      String str;
      int i;

      s1 = new Student();        // Instantiate a student object
      s1.setName ("Bill");       // Set the student's name to "Bill"
      s1.setScore (1,84);        // Set the score on test 1 to 84
      s1.setScore (2,86);        //                 on test 2 to 86
      s1.setScore (3,88);        //                 on test 3 to 88
      System.out.println("\nHere is student s1\n" + s1);

      s2 = s1;                   // s1 and s2 now refer to the same object
      s2.setName ("Ann");        // Set the name through s2
      System.out.println ("\nName of s1 is now: " + s1.getName());
   }

   public static void main (String[] args){
      TestStudent tpo = new TestStudent();
      tpo.run();
   }
}
```

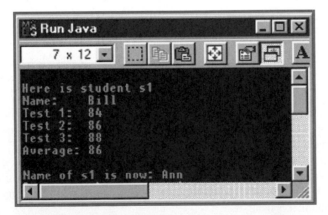

Figure 9.3 Output from the TestStudent program

Finding the Location of Run-Time Errors

Finding run-time errors in programs is no more difficult when there are several classes instead of just one. To illustrate, we introduce a run-time error into the Student class and then run the TestStudent program again. Here is a listing of the modified and erroneous lines of code. Figure 9.4 shows a snapshot of the error messages generated when the program runs.

```java
public int getAverage(){
//Compute and return a student's average
//   Preconditions  -- none
//   Postconditions -- returns the average of the test scores
    int average = 0;
    average = (int) Math.round((test1 + test2 + test3) / average);
    return average;
}
```

Figure 9.4 Divide by zero run-time error message

The messages indicate that

- an attempt was made to divide by zero in the Student class's getAverage method (line 64),
- which had been called from the Student class's toString method (line 89)
- which had been called by some methods we did not write
- which had been called from the TestStudent class's run method (line 13)
- which finally had been called from the TestStudent class's main method (line 22)

Here are the lines of code mentioned:

```
Student getAverage line 64 :
        average = (int) Math.round ((test1 + test2 + test3) / average);
Student toString line 89   :
        "Average: " + getAverage();
```

Continues

Continued

```
TestStudent run line 13          :
          System.out.println ("\nHere is student s1\n" + s1);
TestStudent main
          tpo.run();
```

Self-Test Questions

11. Write the form of the command that is used to compile a Java source program.

12. What type of file is generated when a Java source program compiles successfully?

9.4 `BreezySwing`: Titles and Menus

To this point, we have presented only the most rudimentary techniques for creating graphical user interfaces. Java's Swing toolkit includes many others, and BreezySwing supports the principal ones. Because making the transition from using these features in BreezySwing to using them in Swing is straightforward, we will occasionally present them in the hope that you will enjoy creating more professional looking GUIs. In this section, we show how to add titles and drop-down menus to a window. Titles do not change a program's functionality and can perhaps be considered a decorative feature. Drop-down menus provide an alternative to a confused jumble of command buttons.

Menus

Menus provide a convenient mechanism for entering commands into a program. A menu system consists of a menu bar, a number of menus, and for each menu, several selections. It is also possible to have submenus, but we ignore these for now. It is easy to add a menu system to an application. We simply declare a menu item object for each menu selection. For instance, the following code adds two menus to an application's interface:

```
JMenuItem highTest1MI    = addMenuItem ("HighStudent", "Test1");
JMenuItem highTest2MI    = addMenuItem ("HighStudent", "Test2");
JMenuItem highTest3MI    = addMenuItem ("HighStudent", "Test3");
JMenuItem highOverallMI  = addMenuItem ("HighStudent", "Overall");
JMenuItem highAverageMI  = addMenuItem ("HighStudent", "Average");

JMenuItem displayStudent1MI = addMenuItem ("Display", "Student1");
JMenuItem displayStudent2MI = addMenuItem ("Display", "Student2");
```

The first menu is called **HighStudent** and has five items, while the second, called **Display,** has two. When the user selects a menu item, the JVM sends a menuItemSelected message to the application, so we need to write the corresponding method. Here is an illustrative snippet of code from this method:

```
public void menuItemSelected (JMenuItem menuItemObj){
    if (menuItemObj == highTest1MI)
      ... do something appropriate ...
    else if (menuItemObj == highTest2MI){
      ... do something else ...

    etc.
}
```

The setTitle Method

Most applications include a title at the top of the window. To display a title in our applications, we need to add a constructor to the interface class and include the line:

```
setTitle (<"the title">);
```

We are now ready for the case study.

Self-Test Questions

13. Write the code that adds **File** and **Edit** menus to an interface with BreezySwing. Each menu should have at least three selections.

14. What happens when the user selects a menu item in a program written with BreezySwing?

9.5 Case Study: Student Test Scores

Request

Write a program that allows the user to compare test scores of two students. Each student has three scores.

Analysis

The proposed interface is shown in Figure 9.5. To use the interface:

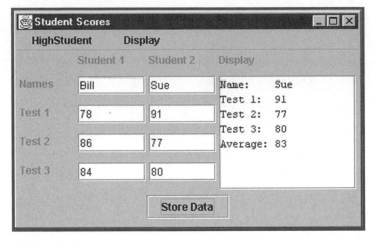

Figure 9.5 Proposed interface for the test scores program

1. Enter the names and test scores of two students and click the **Store Data** button. Anytime the data are updated, it is necessary to click the **Store Data** button again.

2. Select an option from either of the two menus described in Tables 9.3 and 9.4.

Table 9.3

Options in the HighStudent Menu

Menu Option	Explanation
Test1	Displays the name of the student who scored higher on test 1, unless the scores are equal. For instance:
Test2	Displays the name of the student who scored higher on test 2, unless the scores are equal.
Test3	Displays the name of the student who scored higher on test 3, unless the scores are equal.
Overall	Displays the name of the student who had the highest test score overall, unless they both have the same highest score.
Average	Displays the name of the student who had the higher average, unless they both have the same average. For instance:

Table 9.4

Options in the Display Menu	
Menu Option	**Explanation**
Student1	Displays the name, test scores, and average of student 1.
Student2	Displays the name, test scores, and average of student 2.

As a standard part of analysis, we determine which classes are needed to support the application, and we delineate each class's overall responsibilities. The nature of the current problem suggests the use of two classes:

1. `Student`: Not surprisingly, the `Student` class presented earlier exactly fits the needs of this program.

2. `StudentInterface`: This class supports the user interface and declares and manipulates two student objects.

Design

During analysis, we decided to base the implementation on two classes: `Student` and `StudentInterface`. Now, during design, we specify the characteristics of these classes in detail. This involves determining the data requirements of each class and the methods that will be needed by the clients of the classes. This process is usually straightforward. To illustrate, let us pretend for the moment that we have not already written the `Student` class.

Designing the `Student` Class

We know from the work completed during analysis that a student object must keep track of a name and three test scores. The high score and the average can be calculated when needed. Thus, the data requirements are clear. The `Student` class must declare four instance variables:

```
private String name;
private int test1;
private int test2;
private int test3;
```

To determine the `Student` class's methods, we look at the class from the perspective of the clients who will be sending messages to student objects. In this application, the interface is the only client. Here are the clues that help us pick the appropriate methods:

- The interface needs to instantiate two student objects. This indicates the need for a constructor method, which we always include anyway.

■ When the user clicks the **Store Data** button, the interface needs to tell each student object its name and three test scores. This can be handled by two mutator methods: `setName(theName)` and `setScore(whichTest, testScore)`.

■ When the user makes selections from the **HighStudent** menu, the interface needs to ask the student objects for the scores on specific tests, the highest score, or the average. This suggests three accessor methods: `getScore(whichTest)`, `getHighScore()`, and `getAverage()`.

■ When the user makes a selection from the **Display** menu, the interface needs a string representation of a student object, which can be provided by the method `toString()`.

We summarize our findings in a *class summary* box:

```
Class:
    Student extends Object
Private Instance Variables:
    String name
    int test1
    int test2
    int test3
Public Methods:
    constructors
    void setName (theName)
    String getName()
    void setScore (whichTest,
                    testScore)
    int getScore (whichTest)
    int getAverage()
    int getHighScore()
    String toString()
```

Normally, we would complete a class's design by writing pseudocode for methods whose implementation is not obvious, but we skip this step here.

Designing the `StudentInterface` Class

The design of an interface class is largely predetermined. There is little point in listing all the window objects required to support the interface. The person writing the code can easily determine these. However, it is necessary to note that two student objects will be needed. Let us call these `student1` and `student2`.

There must, of course, be a constructor and methods to handle button clicks and menu selections. These methods in turn can call helper methods. Here is pseudocode for the methods:

```
public StudentInterface(){
   // This is the constructor
   instantiate the student objects
   set the window's title to "Student Scores"
}
```

```
public void buttonClicked (buttonObj){
   get the data from the screen and use it to set data values for student1
   and student2
}
```

```
public void menuItemSelected (menuItemObj){
  if (menu item is "Test1")
    compareAndReport ("Test 1", score1 student1, score1 student2)
  else if (menu item is "Test2")
    compareAndReport ("Test 2", score2 student1, score2 student2)
  else if (menu item is "Test 3")
    compareAndReport ("Test 3", score3 student1, score3 student2)
  else if (menu item is "Overall")
    compareAndReport ("Overall", high score student1, high score student2)
  else if (menu item is "Average")
    compareAndReport ("Average", average student1, average student2)
  else if (menu item is "Display student 1")
    display string for student1 in text area
  else if (menu item is "Display student 2")
    display string for student2 in text area
}
```

```
private void compareAndReport (String description, int num1, int num2){
  if num1 == num2
    display description + "The students are equal"
  else if num1 > num2
    display description + name student1 + "scored higher"
  else
    display description + name student2 + "scored higher"
}
```

Here is the class summary box for the `StudentInterface` class:

Class:
    `StudentInterface extends GBFrame`
Private Instance Variables:
    `window objects as needed`
    `Student student1`
    `Student student2`
Public Methods:
    `constructor`
    `void buttonClicked (buttonObj)`
    `void menuItemSelected (menuItemObj)`
    `static void main (args)`
Private Methods:
    `void compareAndReport (description, num1, num2)`

Implementation

The code for the `Student` class has already been presented. Code for the `StudentInterface` class follows. Having by this point in the book established reasonable and useful standards for code documentation, we are now going to allow ourselves to be less thorough. Our code is always presented in the context of a great deal of additional explanation, so for the sake of brevity we now strip out the comments. Also, the declarations of the window objects are now so familiar that we omit those as well. Here then is the code:

```
import javax.swing.*;
import BreezySwing.*;

public class StudentInterface extends GBFrame{

   JLabel student1Label = addLabel ("Student 1",1,2,1,1);
   ... etc

   private Student student1;
   private Student student2;

   // Constructor
   public StudentInterface(){
      student1 = new Student();
      student2 = new Student();
      setTitle ("Student Scores");
   }

   // Other methods
   public void buttonClicked (JButton buttonObj){
      student1.setName (stud1NameField.getText());
      student1.setScore (1, stud1Test1Field.getNumber());
      student1.setScore (2, stud1Test2Field.getNumber());
      student1.setScore (3, stud1Test3Field.getNumber());

      student2.setName (stud2NameField.getText());
      student2.setScore (1, stud2Test1Field.getNumber());
      student2.setScore (2, stud2Test2Field.getNumber());
      student2.setScore (3, stud2Test3Field.getNumber());
   }

   public void menuItemSelected (JMenuItem menuItemObj){

      if      (menuItemObj == highTest1MI)
         compareAndReport ("Test 1", student1.getScore(1),
                                     student2.getScore(1));
      else if (menuItemObj == highTest2MI)
         compareAndReport ("Test 2", student1.getScore(2),
                                     student2.getScore(2));
      else if (menuItemObj == highTest3MI)
         compareAndReport ("Test 3", student1.getScore(3),
```

```
                                  student2.getScore(3));
      else if (menuItemObj == highOverallMI)
         compareAndReport ("Overall", student1.getHighScore(),
                                      student2.getHighScore());
      else if (menuItemObj == highAverageMI)
         compareAndReport ("Average", student1.getAverage(),
                                      student2.getAverage());
      else if (menuItemObj == displayStudent1MI)
         displayField.setText(student1.toString());
      else if (menuItemObj == displayStudent2MI)
         displayField.setText("" + student2);
   }

   private void compareAndReport (String description,
                                  int num1, int num2)
   {
      String str = description + ": ";
      if (num1 == num2)
         str = str + "the students are equal";
      else if (num1 > num2)
         str = str + student1.getName() + " scored higher.";
      else
         str = str + student2.getName() + " scored higher.";
      messageBox (str);
   }

   public static void main (String[] args){
      . . . the usual . . .
   }
}
```

Having introduced user-defined classes and worked our way through an example, we need to consider a few more details concerning their use.

9.6 The Static Modifier

The static modifier indicates that a variable or method applies to the class as a whole rather than to individual objects. Such variables and methods are called *class variables* and *class methods,* respectively. An example will help to clarify this somewhat vague description.

Counting the Number of Students Instantiated

Consider the Student class. Let us suppose we want to count all the student objects instantiated during the execution of an application. To do so, we introduce a variable, which we call studentCount. This variable will be incremented every time a student object is instantiated, and the natural place to do so is inside the class's constructor.

Clearly, this variable is independent of any particular student object and therefore cannot be an instance variable. Instead, it must be associated with the class as a whole and thus must be a class variable. In addition, we need two methods to manipulate the `studentCount` variable: one to initialize the variable to 0 at the beginning of the application and the other to return the variable's value on demand. These methods will be called `setStudentCount` and `getStudentCount`, respectively. Because these methods do not manipulate any particular student object, sending a message to a student object cannot activate them. Instead, they are activated when a message is sent to the class as a whole; hence, they are called class methods.

Modifying the `Student` Class

Here are the modifications needed to include the class variable and the two class methods in the `Student` class. Notice that the class variable and methods have been added at the end of the class's template. There is no rule that says they must be placed in that particular location, but it is as good as any other and is the one we usually use.

```
public class Student {

    private String name;
    ... rest of the instance variables go here ...

    public Student(){
        studentCount++;     // Increment the count when a student is
                            // instantiated
        name = "";
        test1 = 0;
        test2 = 0;
        test3 = 0;
    }

    public void setName (String nm){
        name = nm;
    }

    ... rest of the methods without change go here ...

    //--------------- class variables and methods ----------------
    static private int studentCount;

    static public void setStudentCount(int count){
        studentCount = count;
    }

    static public int getStudentCount(){
        return studentCount;
    }
}
```

Here is some code that illustrates the new capabilities of the `Student` class:

```
...
Student.setStudentCount (0);                // Initialize count to 0
s1 = new Student();                         // Instantiate a student object
...
s2 = new Student();                         // Instantiate a student object
...
s3 = new Student();                         // Instantiate a student object
messageBox (Student.getStudentCount());     // Displays 3
```

Notice that class messages are sent to a class and not to an object. Also, notice that we do not attempt to manipulate the studentCount variable directly because, in accordance with the good programming practice of information hiding, we declared the variable to be private.

Class Constants

By using the modifier final in conjunction with static, we can create a ***class constant.*** To illustrate the use of class constants, we modify the Student class again by adding two constants: MIN_SCORE and MAX_SCORE. Now, when a student's score is set, it will be held within the limits defined by these two constants. Such an approach is not ideal, but perhaps it is better than allowing a score to take a negative value or a ridiculously large value. Here then are the modifications needed for the Student class:

```
public class Student {

    private String name;
    ... rest of the instance variables go here ...

    ... no changes in the methods up to this point ...

    public void setScore (int i, int score){
        // Limit the score to the interval [MIN_SCORE, MAX_SCORE]
        score = Math.max (MIN_SCORE, score);
        score = Math.min (MAX_SCORE, score);

        if      (i == 1) test1 = score;
        else if (i == 2) test2 = score;
        else             test3 = score;
    }

    ... no changes in the methods here ...

//--------------- static variables and methods ----------------

    static final public int MIN_SCORE = 0;
    static final public int MAX_SCORE = 100;

    ... no changes in the rest of the static stuff ...
}
```

Note that we declare the two class constants as public because they cannot be changed by clients but might need to be accessed. Here is a snippet of code that illustrates the Student class's new features:

```
s = new Student();
s.setScore(1, -20);   // Too small, will be set to MIN_SCORE
s.setScore(2, 150);   // Too large, will be set to MAX_SCORE
s.setScore(3, 55);    // Value is acceptable
messageBox (s);       // Displays scores of 0, 100, and 55
System.out.println (Student.MIN_SCORE);     // Displays 0
System.out.println (Student.MAX_SCORE);     // Displays 100
```

Rules for Using the Static Modifier

There are two simple rules to remember when using the static modifier:

1. Class methods can reference static variables but never instance variables.
2. The other methods, called *instance methods,* can reference all variables.

The Math Class Revisited

By now, you may have guessed that all the methods and variables in the Math class are static. Math.PI refers to a static constant, while Math.max(MIN_SCORE, score) activates a static method.

The static Method main

All the many interface classes presented so far have included the static method main. Now we can understand more about how main works. Consider the following example:

```
import javax.swing.*;
import BreezySwing.*;

public class MyApp extends GBFrame{

    ... declare window objects ...
    ... declare instance variables ...

    public MyApp(){              // Constructor
        ...
    }

    public void buttonClicked (Button buttonObj){
        ...
    }

    public void menuItemSelected (MenuItem menuItemObj){
        ...
    }
```

```
    public static void main (String[] args){
        MyApp tpo = new MyApp();
        tpo.setSize (200,300);
        tpo.setVisible (true);
    }
}
```

When the user runs this program by typing

```
java MyApp
```

the following sequence of events occurs:

1. The Java interpreter sends the message main to the class MyApp.
2. The method main instantiates an object called tpo of type MyApp, at which point the MyApp constructor is activated.
3. The method main sends the object tpo two messages: setSize and setVisible.
4. The object tpo responds by setting its window size and displaying the interface.
5. Thereafter, the object tpo becomes inactive until the user clicks a button or selects a menu option, at which point the Java interpreter sends the tpo object either the message buttonClicked or menuItemSelected.

Notice that the methods main, buttonClicked, and menuItemSelected must be public, and the method main must also be static.

Writing Programs That Use Only Static Methods

It is possible, though generally not good programming practice, to write complete programs that use only static methods. The programs in the first few chapters could easily have been done this way. For instance, here is a rewrite of Chapter 2's temperature conversion program:

```
import TerminalIO.*;

public class Convert {
    public static void main (String [] args) {
        KeyboardReader reader = new KeyboardReader();
        ScreenWriter writer = new ScreenWriter();

        double fahrenheit;
        double celsius;

        writer.print ("Enter degrees Fahrenheit: ");
        fahrenheit = reader.readDouble();
        celsius = (fahrenheit - 32.0) * 5.0 / 9.0;
        writer.print ("The equivalent in Celsius is ");
        writer.println (celsius);
    }
}
```

We did not present the program in this form originally because from the outset we wished to establish a general structure that could be shared by terminal- and GUI-based programs; however, in the rest of the book, we will occasionally write short programs in this manner. We can also decompose a complex static method into a hierarchy of simpler static methods. As a trivial demonstration, we decompose main in the preceding program:

```
import TerminalIO.*;

public class Convert {

   private static KeyboardReader reader = new KeyboardReader();
   private static ScreenWriter   writer = new ScreenWriter();

   public static void main (String [] args) {
      printCelsius (convertToCelsius (readFahrenheit()));
   }

   private static double readFahrenheit(){
      writer.print ("Enter degrees Fahrenheit: ");
      return reader.readDouble();
   }

   private static double convertToCelsius (double fahrenheit){
      return (fahrenheit - 32.0) * 5.0 / 9.0;
   }

   private static void printCelsius (double celsius){
      writer.print ("The equivalent in Celsius is ");
      writer.println (celsius);
   }
}
```

Restriction on the Use of the messageBox Method

We have finally introduced enough terminology to state a restriction on the use of the messageBox method. The method can be used only in subclasses of GBFrame and then only in methods that are not static. We postpone the explanation of why until we have said more about inheritance in Chapter 11.

Self-Test Questions

15. What effect does the modifier static have on a variable?

16. What effect does the modifier static have on a method?

17. Write the form for declaring a static variable.

18. Why is it a good idea to declare a constant as static and public?

9.7 Constructors

In this chapter, we have seen the first use of constructors. The principal purpose of a constructor is to initialize the instance variables of a newly instantiated object. Constructors are activated when the keyword new is used and at no other time. A constructor is never used to reset instance variables of an existing object.

A class template can include more than one constructor, provided each has a unique parameter list; however, all the constructors must have the same name—that is, the name of the class. This is another example of overloaded methods, first encountered in Chapter 6. The constructors we have seen so far have had empty parameter lists and are called *default constructors*.

If a class template contains no constructors, the Java virtual machine provides a primitive default constructor behind the scenes. This constructor initializes numeric variables to zero and object variables to null, a special value that indicates the object variable currently references no object. However, if a class contains even one constructor, the Java virtual machine will no longer provide a default constructor automatically.

To illustrate these ideas, we add several constructors to the Student class. The code lists the original default constructor and two additional ones:

```
// Default constructor -- initialize name to the empty string and
// the test scores to zero.
public Student(){
    studentCount++;     // Increment the count when a student is
                        // instantiated
    name = "";
    test1 = 0;
    test2 = 0;
    test3 = 0;
}

// Additional constructor -- initialize the name and test scores
// to the values provided.
public Student(String nm, int t1, int t2, int t3){
    studentCount++;     // Increment the count when a student is
                        // instantiated
    name = nm;
    test1 = t1;
    test2 = t2;
    test3 = t3;
}

// Additional constructor -- initialize the name and test scores
// to match those in the parameter s.
```

Continues

Continued

```
    public Student(Student s){
        studentCount++;       // Increment the count when a student is
                              // instantiated
        name = s.name;
        test1 = s.test1;
        test2 = s.test2;
        test3 = s.test3;
    }
```

A class is easier to use when it has a variety of constructors. Here is some code that shows how to use the different Student constructors. In a program, we would use the constructor that best suited our immediate purpose:

```
Student s1, s2, s3;
s1 = new Student();                     // First student object has
                                        // name "" and scores 0,0,0

s2 = new Student ("Bill",70,80,90);     // Second student object has
                                        // name "Bill" and scores 70,80,90

s3 = new ·Student (s2);                 // Third student object also has
                                        // name "Bill" and scores 70,80,90

s3.setName ("Ann");                     // Third student object now has
s3.setScore (1,75);                     // name "Ann" and scores 75,80,90
```

There are now three completely separate student objects. For a moment, two of them had the same state—that is, the same values for their instance variables.

Self-Test Questions

19. How does a default constructor differ from other constructors?

20. What kinds of constructors are useful to include in a user-defined class?

9.8 Primitive Types, Reference Types, and the `null` Value

We mentioned earlier that two or more variables can refer to the same object. To better understand why this is possible, we need to consider how Java classifies types. In Java, all types fall into two fundamental categories:

1. *Primitive types*: int, double, boolean, char, and the shorter and longer versions of these

2. *Reference types*: all classes, for instance, String, Student, TextArea, GBFrame, and so on

As we first pointed out in Chapter 2, variables in these two categories are represented differently in memory. A variable of a primitive type is best viewed as a box that contains a value of that primitive type. In contrast, a variable of a reference type is thought of as a box that contains a pointer to an object. Thus, the state of memory after the following code

```
int number = 45;
String word = "Hi";
```

is executed could be depicted as in Figure 9.6.

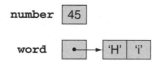

Figure 9.6 The difference between primitive and reference variables

What happens when no initial values are specified for these variables? An instance variable of a primitive type, such as `int`, is automatically assigned a standard default value, such as 0. An instance variable of a reference type, such as `String` or `Employee`, is assigned the special pointer value `null`. Thus, the code segment

```
int number;
String word;
```

could be depicted in memory as in Figure 9.7.

Figure 9.7 Default values for a primitive and a reference variable

Variables of all reference types can be assigned the `null` value. If a reference variable previously pointed to an object, and no other variable currently points to that object, the computer reclaims the object's memory during garbage collection. This situation is illustrated in the following code segment and in Figure 9.8:

```
Student student = new Student("Mary", 70, 80, 90);
student = null;
```

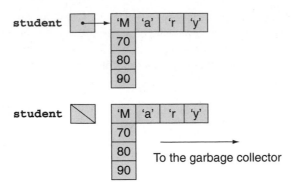

Figure 9.8 The student variable before and after it has been assigned the value null

A variable of any reference type can be compared to the null value, as follows:

```
if (student == null)
        // Don't try to run a method with that student!
else
        // Process the student
while (student != null)
        // Process the student
        // Obtain the next student from whatever source
```

When a program attempts to run a method with an object that is null, Java throws a ***null pointer exception,*** as in the following example:

```
String str = null;
System.out.println (str.length());   // OOPS! str is null, so Java throws a
                                     // null pointer exception.
```

Self-Test Questions

21. Explain the difference between a primitive type and a reference type and give an example of each.

22. What is the null value?

23. What is a null pointer exception?

9.9 Copying Objects

It is sometimes necessary to make copies of existing objects. We have already seen that assigning one object variable to another creates two references to a single object rather than two distinct but equal objects. Here is an illustration:

```
Student s1, s2;

s1 = new Student("Mary", 70, 80, 90);
s2 = s1;                                 // s1 and s2 refer to the same object
```

When the intent is to copy an object, we usually provide a method for doing so. Assuming that a `Student` method called `copy` exists, we can rewrite the foregoing code so as to create a copy of the student object s1:

```
Student s1, s2;

s1 = new Student("Mary", 70, 80, 90);
s2 = s1.copy();                          // s1 and s2 refer to distinct objects
```

The `copy` method does two things. First, it creates a new instance of `Student` with data values taken from the existing student. Second, it returns the new student object. Here is the code:

```
public Student copy(){
    Student s = new Student(name, test1, test2, test3);
    return s;
}
```

Java includes a `clone` method that is similar to the `copy` method presented here; however, its use involves concepts that are beyond this book's scope.

Self-Test Questions

24. Assume that *a* and *b* are two variables of type `String`. What happens as a result of the assignment expression `a = b`?

25. Why is it important to include a method for copying an instance in a user-defined class?

9.10 Comparing Objects for Equality

We are now in a position to understand why the operator `==` should never be used to compare strings for equality. Instead, we should use the `equals` method. We first mentioned this problem in Chapter 7. Consider the following code segment that compares three string variables:

```
String a = "cat", b = "ca", c = "dog";
b = b + "t";
System.out.println (a == b);         // Displays false     SURPRISE!!!
System.out.println (a.equals (b));   // Displays true      AS EXPECTED
System.out.println (a.equals (c));   // Displays false     AS EXPECTED
```

This code's rather unexpected behavior is explained as follows:

1. The variables a, b, and c reference three different objects even though two of these objects contain the same sequence of characters.

2. When applied to reference variables, the operator == compares the references, not the objects being referenced. Thus, if two references do not point to the same object in memory, == returns false. Because the two "cat" strings in our example are not the same object in memory, == returns false. For similar reasons, the != operator should not be used when comparing strings.

3. In contrast, the equals method compares objects and returns true if the objects contain the same sequence of characters. If the strings are of different lengths or if even one pair of characters fail to match, the equals method returns false.

As we have seen previously, the operator == can also be used with other types of objects, such as buttons and menu items. In these cases, the operator as usual tests for object identity—seeing if two variables reference the same object in memory. With window objects, the use of == is appropriate because we want to compare the references. For other types of objects, however, such as the student objects discussed in this chapter, the use of == should be avoided. To test two student objects for equality, it would be better to implement an equals method in the Student class. This method would compare the instance variables of two students for equality or would perhaps focus on a single privileged instance variable, such as the student's name. This privileged instance variable is sometimes called the object's **key field.**

Self-Test Questions

26. What is the difference between == and equals?

27. Write an equals method for the Student class.

9.11 The Methods `finalize` and `dispose`

For the sake of completeness, we now discuss the methods finalize and dispose, although you are unlikely to use them. Just as a class's constructors are called automatically when an object is instantiated, the method finalize, if defined, is called automatically when an object is swept away by the garbage collector. The method usually contains code to free certain types of computer resources that are not recovered by the garbage collector. File handles, about which you probably know nothing yet, are an example.

However, using finalize in this or any other way has a serious flaw. Programmers have no control over how long the garbage collector will wait before doing its job, and during the delay, an important resource may be unavailable. Consequently, programmers sometimes include a method called dispose. The dispose method is not called automatically, so it is the programmer's responsibility to call it when an object is no longer needed, which introduces the risk of calling it too soon. When included, both methods are declared public void and take no parameters.

CS Capsule: Reliability of Software Systems

As we pointed out in Chapter 8, the next time you step onto an airplane or lie down beneath an x-ray machine, you might ask yourself about the quality of the software that helps to run it. There are many measures of software quality, and we have already mentioned several in this book: readability, maintainability, correctness, and robustness. But perhaps the most important measure is *reliability.* Reliability should not be confused with correctness. Software is correct if its design and implementation are consistent with its specifications. For instance, it should produce the expected outputs when operating on inputs that fall within prespecified limits. However, software can be correct in this sense yet still be unreliable. Reliability is a measure of how often a system fails and the severity of these failures. An operating system is unreliable if it crashes after running for more than 10 days without being stopped and restarted. A word processor is unreliable if it destroys a document in response to an unexpected and thereby confusing sequence of inputs.

The military has been responsible for some of the most spectacular examples of unreliable software. The United States' early warning missile defense system is designed to detect a surprise nuclear missile attack; however, it once mistook the rising of the moon for such an attack, and on another occasion, it was mislead by a flock of geese. Although these failures have been infrequent, or so we are encouraged to believe, their consequences have come close to being catastrophic. Fortunately, for the safety of the world and all its inhabitants, this system is not connected to an automated missile launch controls system. There have also been spectacular failures of commercial software systems. For instance, the computer controlled Therac-25 x-ray machine gave several patients lethal doses of radiation before its problems were detected.

In general, standards for reliability should depend on a system's ability to do harm. While we accept unreliable PC software as a matter of course, we fervently hope that other more critical systems are written to a higher standard. A classic discussion of software reliability in military applications can be found in Alan Borning, "Computer System Reliability and Nuclear War," *Communications of the ACM,* Vol. 30, No. 2 (Feb. 1987), 112–131. Almost every textbook on computer ethics has case studies on computer reliability in commercial applications. A good place to start is Sara Baase, *A Gift of Fire* (Upper Saddle River, NJ: Prentice Hall, 1997), Chapter 4.

9.12 Design, Testing, and Debugging Hints

- When developing a user-defined class, write a short tester program that does the following:
  - creates objects of that class, using each of the different constructor methods
  - runs the accessor methods and displays the values of the objects' instance variables
  - runs the mutator methods and then displays the values of the variables once again
  - tests any class variables and class methods in a similar manner

- In general, it is useful for testing and debugging to write a `toString` method for each new user-defined class. The `toString` method returns a formatted string that contains the values of an object's instance variables.

- Be sure that each new object of a user-defined class has all of its instance variables initialized when the object is instantiated. Defining one or more constructor methods can do this.

- When clients will need to copy objects, provide a `copy` method. Beware that simple assignment of variables causes multiple references to the same object.

9.13 Summary

In this chapter, we have explored in detail how to define classes that cooperate in programs. In the analysis phase, the programmer decides what classes will be used and gives a broad outline of their roles and responsibilities in a program. In design, the methods and variables of a class are specified. Variables belong to two broad categories: instance variables and class variables. Likewise, methods can also be instance methods and class methods. Methods are further classified as accessors, which return the values of the variables, mutators, which modify the variables, and constructors, which initialize the variables during object instantiation. We also explored the implications of the fact that variables are references to objects. One consequence is that the `==` operator and the `equals` method behave differently. A second consequence is that the `=` operator and the `copy` method also produce different results.

9.14 Key Terms

If you have difficulty finding the definitions of any key terms in the body of this chapter, turn to the Glossary at the end of the book.

abstract data type	default constructor	null pointer exception
accessor	encapsulation	object
base	extend	parent
behavior	garbage collection	primitive type
black box	hierarchy	reference type
child	identity	reliability
class	information hiding	root
class constant	inheritance	server
class method	instance method	state
class summary	instance variable	subclass
class variable	instantiation	superclass
client	key field	visibility modifier
constructor	menu	
deep copying	mutator	

9.15 Answers to Self-Test Questions

1. A class is a template that describes the variables and the methods that define a set of objects. An object is an instance of a class.

2. An object's memory storage is returned to the computer by the garbage collector.

3. The three characteristics of an object are state, behavior, and identity.

4. Servers provide resources to clients. Clients obtain these services by instantiating a server and sending it messages.

5. Abstract data types are abstract in that the details of their methods and their data representation are hidden. This feature allows an ADT to be used with a minimum of learning and maintenance.

6. A mutator is a method that modifies a variable in a class or object. An accessor is a method that returns a value without modifying a variable in a class or object. An example of a mutator is a method `setScore(anInteger, anInteger)`, which sets the score at the position specified by the first parameter to the new score specified by the second parameter.

7. The visibility modifier `public` is used primarily for methods and makes these visible to all clients of a class. The visibility modifier `private` is use primarily for instance variables and makes these visible only within the implementation of a class.

8. A constructor method is run when an instance of a class is created. This method typically initializes an object's instance variables.

9. The `toString` method returns a string representation of an object, typically by concatenating the string representations of the values of its instance variables. This method is often used for debugging a class during development.

10. Two variables can refer to the same object after an assignment of that object to each variable. The object maintains its identity during assignment, which does not create a copy of the object.

11. `javac <program name>.java`

12. A byte code file with the name **<program name>.class**.

13.
```
JMenuItem newFileMI    = addMenuItem("File", "New");
JMenuItem openFileMI   = addMenuItem("File", "Open");
JMenuItem saveFileMI   = addMenuItem("File", "Save");
JMenuItem cutEditMI    = addMenuItem("Edit", "Cut");
JMenuItem copyEditMI   = addMenuItem("Edit", "Copy");
JMenuItem pasteEditMI  = addMenuItem("Edit", "Paste");
```

14. When the user selects a menu item, the message `menuItemSelected` is sent to the application. The application can implement this method to examine the parameter, which is the menu item selected, and take the appropriate action.

15. The modifier `static` specifies that a variable belongs to the entire class instead of an individual object. The variable can be accessed and modified by any instance.

16. The modifier `static` specifies that a method belongs to the entire class instead of an individual object. The method can be executed by any instance.

17. `static <type name> <variable name>;`

18. When a constant is `public`, it can be accessed by all clients, who cannot modify it anyway. When a constant is `static`, the storage necessary for it is not allocated anew every time an instance is created, but only once.

19. A default constructor expects no parameters. This constructor typically initializes instance variables to reasonable default values.

20. It is useful to have a default constructor, a copy constructor, and a constructor that expects values for instance variables as parameters.

21. A primitive type, such as int or double, is not a set of objects, but simply a set of values. A reference type, such as String, is a set of objects.

22. The null value is a special value that can be assigned to variables of any reference type. The null value indicates that a variable refers to no object.

23. A null pointer exception occurs when a client attempts to send a message to a variable that refers to no object and, hence, is null. This error commonly occurs when the programmer forgets to initialize a variable.

24. The assignment a = b results in the variables a and b referring to the exact same string object.

25. Objects are not copied with the assignment operator. Thus, if clients want to receive a copy of an object, the server must provide a distinct method that does this.

26. The operator == returns true when the two operands are the exact same (identical) object or false otherwise. That is, two objects may have the same state (all the values of their instance variables are the same) but == would still return false. The method equals, if it is included in a class, allows clients to determine whether two objects have the same state.

9.16 Programming Problems and Activities

1. Add the extra constructors and the copy method to the Student class of this chapter's Case Study, and test these methods thoroughly with a Tester program.

2. A student object should validate its own data. The client runs this method, called validateData(), with a student object, as follows:

```
String result = student.validateData();
if (result == null)
    <use the student>
else
    messageBox(result);
```

If the student's data are valid, the method returns the value null; otherwise, the method returns a string representing an error message that describes the error in the data. The client can then examine this result and take the appropriate action.

A student's name is invalid if it is an empty string. A student's test score is invalid if it lies outside the range from MIN_SCORE to MAX_SCORE, as discussed in this chapter. Thus, sample error messages might be

```
"SORRY: name required"
```

and

```
"SORRY: must have 50 <= test score <= 100".
```

Implement and test this method.

3. Redo the dice-playing program of Chapter 8 so that it uses dice objects. That is, design and implement a `Dice` class. Each instance of this class should have as attributes the die's current side, the total number of times it has been rolled, and the average all of the sides it has displayed. There should be accessor methods for all of these attributes, as well as a `toString` method. Two other methods, `roll` and `reset`, are the mutator methods. Be sure to test the `Dice` class in a simple tester program before incorporating it into the GUI-based application.

4. In the game of craps, a player provides an initial bankroll and bets from this amount on each roll of the dice. On each roll, the sum of the faces is taken. The outcomes are as follows:

   - If 7 or 11 is rolled, the player wins.
   - If 2, 3, or 12 is rolled, the player loses.
   - Otherwise, the number rolled becomes the player's point. The player rolls the dice repeatedly until the player wins by making point (getting the same number as on the first roll) or loses by crapping out (rolling a 7).

   Design and implement a craps machine that allows the user to play craps. This machine should be defined as a new class. The interface accepts an amount of money representing an initial bankroll. Before each roll of the dice, the user must make a bet. The interface should control the user's options by enabling and disabling the appropriate command buttons. At the end of the game, the program should display the amount of the user's current bankroll (after adding the gains and deducting the losses).

5. The game of blackjack is played with cards numbered 2 through 10, and the ace, king, queen, and jack. The last three cards each count 10, while the ace can count 1 or 11 depending on the total count in the player's hand. The object of the game for each player is to hit (be dealt cards that total) up to 21 without going over. A player who goes over 21 busts (loses). The player who has the count closest to 21 wins. Players may stay, or pass on further hits, when they get close to 21 and do not wish to risk a bust. When a player draws an ace, it counts as either 1 or 11 depending on which of these two values brings the count closest to 21 without going over. A hand containing an ace that currently counts as 11 is soft, because this ace's value may be changed to 1 after a subsequent hit. Thus, a hand may contain all four aces, but at most one of these can count as 11.

   The dealer has several restrictions. If the dealer's count is less than or equal to 16, the dealer must hit. If the dealer's count is greater than 16, the dealer must stay. Otherwise, the dealer plays the same as any other player.

   Design and implement three classes, `Card`, `Dealer`, and `Player`, that allow the user to play blackjack with the computer.

Each instance of the `Card` class should have one attribute, a point. A card's point is initialized with a random number between 1 and 11 when the card is instantiated. The `Card` class provides an accessor method for the point.

A `Player` object maintains a total count of the cards in a hand and a Boolean flag indicating whether or not the hand is soft (an ace counting as 11 rather than 1). These values are initially zero and false, respectively. The `Player` class provides an accessor method for the total count and a mutator method that adds a card's point to the total count.

A `Dealer` object maintains the same attributes as a player. However, the dealer is also responsible for generating cards and returning them to all players, including itself. An accessor method should be defined that does this.

Begin by defining each class and testing it with a short tester program. For example, you could create a dealer and ask it to hit until its count equals 16 or exceeds 16.

Then, provide an interface that allows the user to select two buttons, **Hit** or **Stay.** When the user selects **Hit,** a `Dealer` object generates a card and passes it to a `Player` object. A display area should show the player's card points and the total count after each hit.

Finally, make the dealer object a player also. If one of the two players busts, declare the other the winner. If one of the two players stays, let the other continue according to the rules until there is a winner.

6. The blackjack game program of Problem 5 has a shortcoming. There are 4 aces, 4 twos, 4 threes, and so on, but there are 16 worth ten (12 face cards plus 4 tens). The `Card` class uses a random number generator to instantiate a card whose point is between 1 and 10, making it equally likely that an ace will be dealt as a face card. Suggest a method for increasing the probability of dealing a face card and implement it in the program.

7. The blackjack game of Problem 5 has one other shortcoming. Using our current methods, there is a chance, though a remote one, that more than four of the cards dealt will be aces, or twos, or some other small nonface card. Suggest a method for solving this problem and implement it in the program. You will study an easy way to solve this problem with arrays in Chapter 10.

10 Arrays, Searching, and Sorting

There are situations in which programs need to manipulate many similar items, a task that would be extremely awkward using the language features encountered so far. The `Student` class in Chapter 9 gives a glimpse of the problem. Currently, a student has 3 test scores, but imagine how tedious and lengthy the code would become if a student had 20 scores. Fortunately, there is a way to handle this dilemma. Most programming languages, including Java, provide a data structure called an *array,* which consists of an ordered collection of similar items. An array, as a whole, has a single name, and the items in an array are referred to in terms of their position within the array. This chapter explains the mechanics of declaring arrays and presents many of the basic algorithms for manipulating them. Using an array, it is as easy to manipulate a million test scores as three.

10.1 Conceptual Overview

To demonstrate the need for arrays, let us consider how the `Student` class changes if there are no arrays and there are 20 rather than 3 test scores. The declarations for the instance variables now look like this:

```
private String name;
private int test1,  test2,  test3,  test4,  test5,
            test6,  test7,  test8,  test9,  test10,
            test11, test12, test13, test14, test15,
            test16, test17, test18, test19, test20;
```

and the computation of the average looks like this:

```
// Compute and return a student's average
public int getAverage(){
    int average;
    average = (test1 + test2  + test3  + test4  + test5 +
               test6  + test7  + test8  + test9  + test10 +
               test11 + test12 + test13 + test14 + test15 +
               test16 + test17 + test18 + test19 + test20) / 20;
    return average;
}
```

Other methods are affected in a similar manner; however, arrays restore sanity to the situation. The items in an array are called *elements,* and for any particular array, all the elements must be of the same type. The type can be any primitive or reference type. For instance, we can have an array of test scores, an array of names, or even an array of student objects. Figure 10.1 clarifies these ideas. In the figure, each array contains five elements, or has a *length* of five. The first element in the array test is referred to as test[0], the second as test[1], and so on. Here again we encounter Java's annoying convention of numbering from 0 rather than from 1, a convention that is guaranteed to cause us grief whenever we accidentally revert to our lifelong habit of counting from 1. Thus, the elements in an array of length 100 are numbered from 0 to 99. An item's position within an array is called its *index,* or *subscript.*

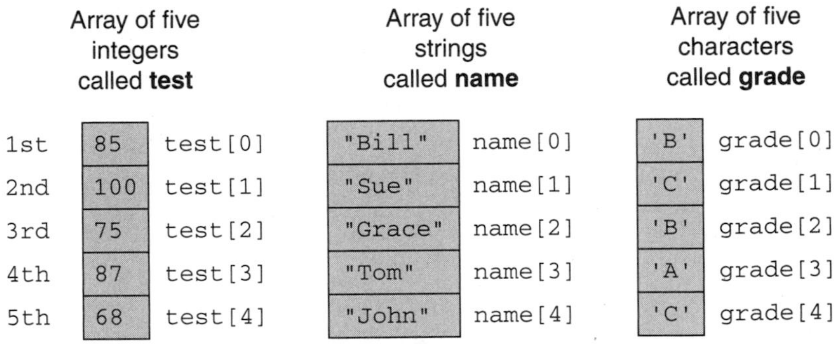

	Array of five integers called **test**		Array of five strings called **name**		Array of five characters called **grade**	
1st	85	test[0]	"Bill"	name[0]	'B'	grade[0]
2nd	100	test[1]	"Sue"	name[1]	'C'	grade[1]
3rd	75	test[2]	"Grace"	name[2]	'B'	grade[2]
4th	87	test[3]	"Tom"	name[3]	'A'	grade[3]
5th	68	test[4]	"John"	name[4]	'C'	grade[4]

Figure 10.1 Three arrays, each containing five elements

Self-Test Questions

1. How does an array solve the problem of having many variables to store and process data?

2. How does the programmer access an item in an array?

3. Mary is using an array of doubles to store an employee's wage amounts for each day of the week (Monday through Friday). Draw a picture of this array with sample items and references to each one.

10.2 Simple Array Manipulations

The mechanics of manipulating arrays are fairly straightforward as illustrated in the following snippets of code. First, we declare and instantiate an array of 500 integer values (Section 10.4 discusses array declarations in greater detail). By default, all of the values are initialized to 0:

```
int[] abc = new int[500];
```

Next, we declare some other variables:

```
int i = 3;
int temp;
double avFirstFive;
```

The basic syntax for referring to an array element has the form:

```
<array name>[<index>]
```

where `<index>` must be between 0 and the array's length less 1. The subscript operator (`[]`) has the same precedence as the method selector (`.`). To illustrate, we assign values to the first five elements:

```
abc[0] = 78;                    //1st element 78
abc[1] = 66;                    //2nd element 66
abc[2] = (abc[0] + abc[1]) / 2; //3rd element average of first two
abc[i] = 82;                    //4th element 82
abc[i + 1] = 94;                //5th element 94
```

When assigning a value to the 500th element, we must remember that its index is 499, not 500:

```
abc[499] = 76;                 //500th element 76
```

Fortunately, the JVM checks the values of subscripts before using them and throws an exception if they are out of bounds (less than 0 or greater than the array length less 1). This is similar to the JVM's behavior when a program attempts to divide by 0. In our present example, subscripts must be between 0 and 499. Later in the chapter, we will show how to work with arrays of any size and how to write loops that are not tied to a literal value (in this case, 500).

```
abc[-1] = 74;                 //NO! NO! NO! Out of bounds
abc[500] = 88;                //NO! NO! NO! Out of bounds
```

To compute the average of the first five elements, we could write:

```
avFirstFive = (abc[0] + abc[1] + abc[2] + abc[3] + abc[4])/5;
```

It often happens that we need to interchange elements in an array. To demonstrate, here is code that interchanges any two adjacent elements:

```
// Initializations
. . .
a[3] = 82;
a[4] = 95;
i = 3
. . .


// Interchange adjacent elements
temp = abc[i];                  // temp        now equals 82
abc[i] = abc[i + 1];            // abc[i]      now equals 95
abc[i + 1] = temp;              // abc[i + 1]  now equals 82
```

We frequently need to know an array's length, but we do not have to remember it. The array itself makes this information available by means of a public instance variable called `length`:

```
System.out.println ("The size of abc is: " + abc.length);
```

Self-Test Questions

4. Declare and instantiate array variables for the following data:

   a. An array of 15 doubles

   b. An array of 20 strings

5. Assume that the array a contains the five integers 34, 23, 67, 89, and 12. Write the values of the following expressions:

   a. `a[1]`

   b. `a[a.length - 1]`

   c. `a[2] + a[3]`

6. What happens when a program attempts to access an item at an index that is less than 0 or greater than or equal to the array's length?

10.3 Looping Through Arrays

There are many situations in which it is necessary to write a loop that iterates through an array one element at a time. Here are some examples based on the array abc of 500 integers. Later in the chapter, we will show how to work with arrays of any size and how to write loops that are not tied to a literal value (in this case, 500).

Sum the Elements

Here is code that sums the numbers in the array abc. Each time through the loop we add a different element to the sum. On the first iteration we add abc[0] and on the last abc[499].

```
int sum;
sum = 0;
for (i = 0; i < 500; i++)
    sum += abc[i];
```

Count the Occurrences

We can determine how many times a number x occurs in the array by comparing x to each element and incrementing count every time there is a match:

```
int x;
int count;
x = ...;                       //Assign some value to x
count = 0;
for (i = 0; i < 500; i++){
   if (abc[i] == x)
      count++;                 //Found another element equal to x
}
```

Determine Presence or Absence

To determine if a particular number is present in the array, we could count the occurrences, but alternatively, we could save time by breaking out of the loop as soon as the first match is found. Here is code based on this idea. The Boolean variable found indicates the outcome of the search:

```
int x;
boolean found;
x = ...;
found = false;             // Initially assume x is not present
for (i = 0; i < 500; i++){
   if (abc[i] == x){
      found = true;
      break;               // No point in continuing once x is found
```

Continues

Continued

```
    }                               // so break out of the loop
}
if (found)
    messageBox ("Found");
else
    messageBox ("Not Found");
```

Determine First Location

As a variation on the preceding example, we show how to find the first location of x in the array. The variable `loc` initially equals –1, meaning that we have not found x yet. We then iterate through the array, comparing each element to x. As soon as we find a match, we set `loc` to the location and break out of the loop. If x is not found, `loc` remains equal to –1.

```
int x;
int loc;
x = ...;
loc = -1;
for (i = 0; i < 500; i++){
    if (abc[i] == x){
        loc = i;
        break;
    }
}
if (loc == -1)
    messageBox ("Not Found");
else
    messageBox ("Found at index " + loc);
```

Locate Largest Number

To locate the largest number in an array, we begin by saying that the first element is the largest so far. On the first iteration through the loop, we compare the largest so far to the second element. If the second element is larger, we say it is the largest so far. On the second iteration, we compare the largest so far to third elements and so on. Sooner or later, we encounter the largest element and remember its location.

```
int loc = 0;                       // Largest so far is at index 0
for (i = 1; i < 500; i++){
    if (abc[i] > abc[loc])
        loc = i;                   // Largest so far is at index i
}
```

To illustrate this code, consider the array in Figure 10.2, whose largest element is 97. Initially, the largest so far is at location 0 (`loc` = 0). Thereafter:

During the 1st iteration compare   `abc[loc]` and `abc[1]`.

During the 2nd iteration compare   `abc[loc]` and `abc[2]`.

                                        And the largest so far is at location 2 (`loc` = 2).

During the 3rd iteration compare   `abc[loc]` and `abc[3]`.

. . .

During 120th iteration compare   `abc[loc]` and `abc[120]`.

                                        And the largest so far is at location 120 (`loc` = 120).

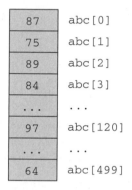

87	abc[0]
75	abc[1]
89	abc[2]
84	abc[3]
. . .	. . .
97	abc[120]
. . .	. . .
64	abc[499]

Figure 10.2 Finding the largest element in an array

Move Smallest Number to First Position

It is easy to move the smallest number in an array to the first position. Compare the first number to each of the remaining ones. Anytime a smaller number is found, interchange it with the first number and continue the comparisons. The smallest number will end up in the first position, and the rest of the numbers will be shuffled around a little:

```
int j;
int temp;
for (j = 1; j < 500; j++){
   if (abc[j] < abc[0]){
       temp = abc[j];
       abc[j] = abc[0];
       abc[0] = temp;
   }
}
```

Table 10.1 shows an illustration based on an array of five elements. The table shows the initial order of the numbers in the array and their order after each iteration through the loop. After the last iteration, the smallest number is at the top, and the remaining numbers are somewhat shuffled.

Table 10.1

Moving the Smallest Number to the Top of an Array					
	initial	j = 1	j = 2	j = 3	j = 4
abc[0]	24	15	15	10	10
abc[1]	15	24	24	24	24
abc[2]	20	20	20	20	20
abc[3]	10	10	10	15	15
abc[4]	16	16	16	16	16

Move Second Smallest Number to Second Position

Once we have moved the smallest number to the top, we can move the second smallest to the second position in a similar manner. This time we compare abc[1] to each of the numbers below it and interchange whenever we encounter a smaller number:

```
int j;
int temp;
for (j = 2; j < 500; j++){
    if (abc[j] < abc[1]){
        temp = abc[j];
        abc[j] = abc[1];
        abc[1] = temp;
    }
}
```

Sort in Ascending Order

The idea behind the two previous snippets of code can be extended to yield an algorithm for sorting the numbers in an array from smallest to largest. It is called a ***bubble sort***:

```
int i, j;
int temp;
for (i = 0; i < (500 - 1); i++){
    for (j = i + 1; j < 500; j++){
```

```
    if (abc[j] < abc[i]){
        temp = abc[j];
        abc[j] = abc[i];
        abc[i] = temp;
    }
  }
}
```

The outer loop is executed 499 times. This is only one of many different algorithms for sorting an array. In Chapter 12, we present one that is more difficult to understand but more efficient. Table 10.2 shows what happens on each pass through the outer loop and the corresponding range of activity for the inner loop:

Table 10.2

Sorting an Array of Numbers

Outer Loop Value of *i*	Inner Loop Range of Values for *j*	Inner Loop Elements Compared	Result Achieved by Inner Loop
0	1 . . . 499	abc[0] to abc[1 . . . 499]	abc[0] smallest
1	2 . . . 499	abc[1] to abc[2 . . . 499]	abc[1] next smallest
2	3 . . . 499	abc[3] to abc[3 . . . 499]	abc[2] next smallest
. . .	. . .	. . .	
498	499 . . . 499	abc[498] to abc[499]	abc[498] next smallest

Sort in Descending Order

A trivial modification of the preceding code yields an algorithm that sorts the numbers from largest to smallest. Simply replace

```
if. (abc[j] < abc[i]){
```

with

```
if (abc[j] > abc[i]){
```

Insert an Element

Sometimes only an array's initial slots are in use. For instance, an array might be capable of holding 500 integers, but only the first 154 positions might be occupied. Additional values can then be added to the array, either between values already present or after the last one. When inserting between existing values, care must be taken. All the values at and below the insertion point must first be moved down one position.

To illustrate, suppose that:

- The array `abc` can hold up to 500 numbers.
- The variable `indexLastElement` indicates the position of the last element currently in use.

Suppose further that:

- The array is not full (`indexLastElement < 499`).
- The variable `newValue` contains the value to insert.
- The variable `insertionPoint` indicates the insertion point, and `insertionPoint <= indexLastElement + 1`.

The code to perform the insertion is quite simple. Notice that the variable `i` decreases on successive iterations. The last element is the first one moved. The next to last element is then moved into the newly vacated slot and so forth. Finally, the new value is assigned to the array at the insertion point.

```
for (i = indexLastElement; i >= insertionPoint; i--)
    abc[i+1] = abc[i];
abc[insertionPoint] = newValue;
indexLastElement++;
```

Figure 10.3 illustrates the process and shows an array before and after the insertion of the number 6 at index position 3. The active or used portion of the array is shaded.

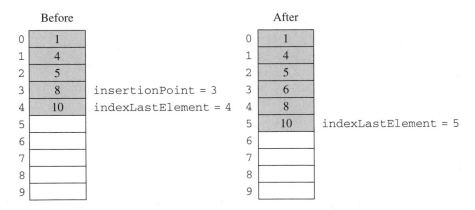

Figure 10.3 An array before and after the insertion of the value 6 at index position 3

Delete an Element

Deleting elements from partially full arrays is also a common task. Assume the situation is the same as in the previous example, but now we wish to delete the element at position `deletionPoint`. We assume that `0 <= deletionPoint <= indexLastElement`. Starting at the deletion point, the code overwrites each array element with the element below it.

```
for (i = deletionPoint; i < indexLastElement; i++)
    abc[i] = abc[i + 1];
indexLastElement--;
```

Figure 10.4 illustrates the process, showing an array before and after the deletion of the number 5. Notice that the array now contains two copies of the number 10; however, this does not cause a problem because the second instance is in the unused portion of the array.

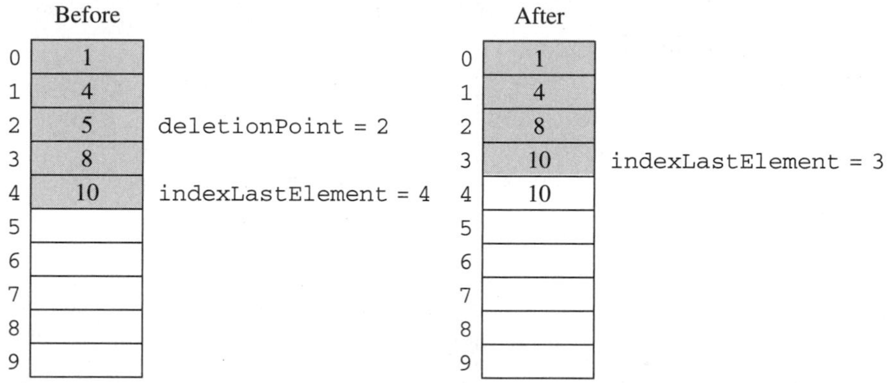

Figure 10.4 An array before and after the deletion of the element at index position 2

Self-Test Questions

7. Write a loop that prints all of the items in an array `a` to the terminal screen.

8. Write a loop that locates the first occurrence of a negative integer in an array `a`. When the loop is finished, the variable `pos` should contain the index of the negative number or the length of the array if there were no negative numbers in the array.

9. Discuss the problems posed by inserting and deleting items in an array.

10. When can one use the variable `length` in a loop with an array?

10.4 Declaring Arrays

Earlier, we declared an array of 500 integers as follows:

```
int[] abc = new int[500];
```

In doing so, we combined two separate statements:

```
int[] abc;              // Declare abc to be a variable that can
                        // reference an array of integers.
abc = new int[500];     // Instantiate an array of 500 integers for abc to
                        // reference.
```

Arrays are objects and must be instantiated before being used. Several array variables can be declared in a single statement like this:

```
int[] abc, xyz;
abc = new int[500];
xyz = new int[10];
```

or like this:

```
int[] abc = new int[500], xyz = new int[10];
```

Because arrays are objects, two variables can refer to the same array:

```
int[] abc, xyz;
abc = new int[10];             // Instantiate an array of 10 integers
xyz = abc;                     // xyz and abc refer to the same array
xyz[3] = 100;                  // Changing xyz changes abc as well.
System.out.println (abc[3]);   // 100 is displayed.
```

If we want abc and xyz to refer to two separate arrays that happen to contain the same values, we could copy all of the elements from one array to the other, as follows:

```
int[] abc, xyz;                // Declare two array variables
int i;
abc = new int[10];             // Instantiate an array of size 10
for (i = 0; i < 10; i++)       // Initialize the array
   abc[i] = i*i;               //    a[0]=0 and a[1]=1 and a[2]=4, etc.

xyz = new int[10];             // Instantiate another array of size 10
for (i = 0; i < 10; i++)       // Initialize the second array
   xyz[i] = abc[i];
```

Also, because arrays are objects, Java's garbage collector sweeps them away when they are no longer referenced:

```
int[] abc, xyz;
abc = new int[10];     // Instantiate an array of 10 integers.
xyz = new int[5];      // Instantiate an array of 5 integers.
xyz = null;            // The array of 5 integers is no longer referenced
                       // so the garbage collector will sweep it away.
```

Arrays can be declared, instantiated, and initialized in one step. The list of numbers between the braces is called an ***initializer list.***

```
int[] abc = {1,2,3,4,5} // abc now references an array of five integers.
```

As mentioned at the outset, arrays can be formed from any collection of similar items. Here then are arrays of doubles, characters, Booleans, strings, and students:

```
double[]   ddd = new double[10];
char[]     ccc = new char[10];
boolean[]  bbb = new boolean[10];
String[]   ggg = new String[10];
Student[]  sss = new Student[10];
String     str;

ddd[5] = 3.14;
ccc[5] = 'Z';
bbb[5] = true;
ggg[5] = "The cat sat on the mat.";
sss[5] = new Student();

sss[5].setName ("Bill");
str = sss[5].getName() + ggg[5].substring(7);
    // str now equals "Bill sat on the mat."
```

There is one more way to declare array variables, but its use can be confusing. Here it is:

```
int aaa[];               // aaa is an array variable.
```

That does not look confusing, but what about this?

```
int aaa[], bbb, ccc[];   // aaa and ccc are array variables.
                         // bbb is not. This fact might go unnoticed.
```

Instead, it might be better to write:

```
int[] aaa, ccc;          // aaa and ccc are array variables.
int bbb;                 // bbb is not. This fact is obvious.
```

Warning: Once an array is instantiated, its size cannot be changed, so make sure the array is large enough from the outset.

Self-Test Questions

11. What is an initializer list? Give an example of its use.

12. Why is it better to use the form `<type>[] <variable>` instead of `<type> <variable>[]` when declaring an array variable?

10.5 Parallel Arrays

There are situations in which it is convenient to declare what are called *parallel arrays*. Suppose we want to keep a list of people's names and ages. This can be achieved by using two arrays in which corresponding elements are related. For instance:

```
String[] name = {"Bill", "Sue", "Shawn", "Mary", "Ann"};
int[]    age  = {20    , 21    , 19     , 24     , 20};
```

Thus, Bill's age is 20 and Mary's is 24. There are many other uses for parallel arrays, but continuing on with our present example, here is a snippet of code that finds the age of a particular person:

```
String searchName;
int correspondingAge;
int i;

searchName = ...;                      // Set this to the desired name
for (i = 0; i < name.length; i++){     // name.length is the array's size
   if (searchName.equals (name[i]){
      correspondingAge = age[i];
      break;
   }
}
```

If for some reason the array of names must be sorted, the correspondence with the ages can be preserved. To achieve this, every time we switch two names, we switch the corresponding ages as well. Here is the relevant code. A snapshot of its output is in Figure 10.5.

```
String[] name = {"Bill", "Sue", "Shawn", "Mary", "Ann"};
int[]    age  = {20    , 21    , 19     , 24     , 20};

int i, j;
int tempAge;
String tempName;

for (i = 0; i < name.length - 1; i++){
   for (j = i + 1; j < name.length; j++){
      if (name[j].compareTo(name[i]) < 0){
         tempName = name[j];
         name[j] = name[i];
         name[i] = tempName;
         tempAge = age[j];
         age [j] = age [i];
         age [i] = tempAge;
      }
}
```

```
      }
  }
  for (i = 0; i < name.length; i++){
      System.out.println (name[i] + ":" + age[i]);
  }
```

Figure 10.5 A list of names with corresponding ages

Self-Test Questions

13. What are parallel arrays?

14. Describe an application in which parallel arrays might be used.

15. Declare and instantiate the variables for parallel arrays to track the names, ages, and Social Security numbers of 50 employees.

10.6 Two-Dimensional Arrays

Definition

The arrays we have been studying so far can represent only simple lists of items and are called *one-dimensional arrays.* For many applications, *multidimensional arrays* are more useful. A table of numbers, for instance, is best implemented as a *two-dimensional array.* Figure 10.6 shows a two-dimensional array with four rows and five columns.

An array of 20 numbers
arranged in 4 rows and 5 columns
called **table**

	col 0	col 1	col 2	col 3	col 4
row 0	00	01	02	03	04
row 1	10	11	12	13	14
row 2	20	21	22	23	24
row 3	30	31	32	33	34

Figure 10.6 A two-dimensional array with four rows and five columns

Suppose we call the array `table`; then to indicate an element in `table`, we specify its row and column position, remembering that indexes start at 0:

```
x = table[2][3]   // Set x to 23, the value in (row 2, column 3)
```

Sum the Elements

The techniques for manipulating one-dimensional arrays are easily extended to two-dimensional arrays. For instance, here is code that sums all the numbers in `table`. The outer loop iterates four times and moves down the rows. Each time through the outer loop, the inner loop iterates five times and moves across a different row.

```
int i, j;
int sum = 0;
for (i = 0; i < 4; i++){      // There are four rows: i = 0,1,2,3
   for (j = 0; j < 5; j++){ // There are five columns: j = 0,1,2,3,4
      sum += table[i][j];
   }
}
```

This segment of code can be rewritten without using the numbers 4 and 5. The value `table.length` equals the number of rows, and `table[i].length` is the number of columns in row `i`.

```
int i, j;
int sum = 0;
for (i = 0; i < table.length; i++){
   for (j = 0; j < table[i].length; j++){
      sum += table[i][j];
   }
}
```

Sum the Rows

Rather than accumulate all the numbers into a single sum, we now compute the sum of each row separately and place the results in a one-dimensional array called `rowSum`. This array has four elements, one for each row of the table. The elements in `rowSum` are initialized to 0.

```
int i, j;
int[] rowSum = {0,0,0,0};
for (i = 0; i < table.length; i++){
   for (j = 0; j < table[i].length; j++){
      rowSum[i] += table[i][j];
   }
}
```

Locate Largest Number

The next piece of code finds the location of the largest number in `table`. The technique is similar to the one used to find the largest number in a one-dimensional array. We begin by assuming that the largest number is at location (0,0). We then traverse `table`, comparing each value to the one at location (0,0). Whenever we encounter a larger value, we remember its location and use it in future comparisons.

```
int i, j;
int rowLoc = 0, colLoc = 0;
for (i = 0; i < table.length; i++){
    for (j = 0; j < table[i].length; j++){
        if (table[i][j] > table[rowLoc][colLoc]){
            rowLoc = i;
            colLoc = j;
        }
    }
}
```

Declare and Instantiate

Declaring and instantiating two-dimensional arrays are accomplished by extending the processes used for one-dimensional arrays:

```
int[][] table;          // The variable table can reference a
                        // two-dimensional array of integers
table = new int[4][5];  // Instantiate table as an array of size 4,
                        // each of whose elements will reference an array
                        // of 5 integers.
```

Figure 10.7 shows another diagram of `table` that illustrates the perspective revealed in the previous piece of code. The variable `table` references an array of four elements. Each of these elements in turn references an array of five integers. Although the diagram is complex, specifying an element in the resulting two-dimensional array is the same as before, for instance, `table[2][3]`.

Initializer lists can be used with two-dimensional arrays. This requires a list of lists. The number of inner lists determines the number of rows, and the size of each inner list determines the size of the corresponding row. The rows do not have to be the same size, but they are in this example:

```
int[][] table = {{ 0, 1, 2, 3, 4},    // row 0
                 {10,11,12,13,14},    // row 1
                 {20,21,22,23,24},    // row 2
                 {30,31,32,33,34}};   // row 3
```

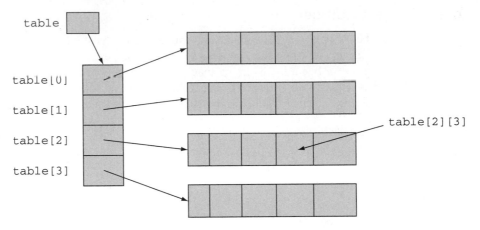

Figure 10.7 Another way of visualizing a two-dimensional array

Variable Length Rows

Occasionally, the rows of a two-dimensional array are not all the same length. Consider the following improbable declaration:

```
int[][] table;
table    = new int[4][];   // table has 4 rows
table[0] = new int[6];     // row 0 has 6   elements
table[1] = new int[10];    // row 1 has 10  elements
table[2] = new int[100];   // row 2 has 100 elements
table[3] = new int[1];     // row 3 has 1   element
```

Finally, remember that all the elements of a two-dimensional array must be of the same type, be they integers, doubles, strings, or whatever.

Self-Test Questions

16. What are two-dimensional arrays?

17. Describe an application in which a two-dimensional array might be used.

18. Write a code segment that searches a two-dimensional array for a given integer. The loop should terminate at the first instance of the integer in the array, and the variables row and col should be set to its position. Otherwise, the variables row and col should equal the number of rows and columns in the array (we assume that each row has the same number of columns).

10.7 Three-Dimensional Arrays and Higher

Java does not limit the number of dimensions for arrays. Here is the declaration and initialization of a three-dimensional array:

```
int[][][] threeD = {{{ 1, 2, 3}, { 4, 5, 6}},
                     {{ 7, 8, 9}, {10,11,12}},
                     {{13,14,15}, {16,17,18}}};
```

The array's elements fill a box whose dimensions are 3 by 2 by 3. To refer to an element, we indicate its position in the box, remembering as usual to start counting at 0. Thus, element 8 is at position (1,0,1) and is referred to as follows:

```
threeD[1][0][1]
```

Rather than attempting to visualize the array as a three-dimensional solid, we can instead represent it as shown in Figure 10.8. The first dimension has three subdivisions, each of which is further divided in two, and these sub-subdivisions finally contain three integers each.

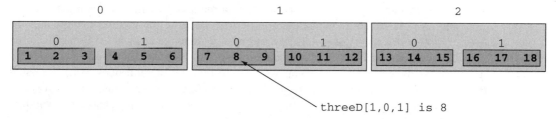

threeD[1,0,1] is 8

Figure 10.8 A three-dimensional array with dimensions 3, 2, 3

As a somewhat contrived example of a four-dimensional array, consider the task of tracking the sales of a worldwide sales force. We could record sales first by country, within country by region, within region by district, and within district by person. The declaration of the array might look like this:

```
double[][][][] sale;
```

When there is a new sale in country c, region r, district d, by person p, we record it as follows:

```
sale[c][r][d][p] += newSale;
```

At any moment, the total sales for the world can be computed as follows:

```
totalSales = 0;
for (c = 0; c < sale.length; c++){
   for (r = 0; r < sale[c].length; r++){
      for (d = 0; d < sale[c][r].length; d++){
         for (p = 0; p < sale[c][r][d].length; p++){
            totalSales += sale[c][r][d][p];
         }
      }
   }
}
```

Self-Test Question

19. Write a loop that prints the contents of a three-dimensional array to the terminal screen.

10.8 Arrays and Methods

An array can be passed as a parameter to a method. The method then manipulates the array in whatever manner is appropriate. Because the method manipulates the original array itself and not a copy, changes made to the array are still in effect after the method has completed its execution. Consequently, passing an array to a method can be dangerous, for how can we be sure that the method does exactly what is intended, and neither more nor less? A method can also instantiate a new array and return it using the `return` statement. Here are some illustrations based on examples presented earlier.

Sum the Elements

Here is a method that computes the sum of the numbers in an integer array. When the method is written, there is no need to know the array's size. The method works equally well with integer arrays of all sizes; however, the method cannot be used with arrays of other types, for instance, doubles. Notice that the method makes no changes to the array and therefore is "safe."

```
int sum (int[] a){
   int i, result = 0;
   for (i = 0; i < a.length; i++)
      result += a[i];
   return result;
}
```

Use of the method is straightforward:

```
int[] array1 = {10, 24, 16, 78, -55, 89, 65};
int[] array2 = {4334, 22928, 33291};
...
if (sum(array1) > sum(array2)) ...
```

Search for a Value

The code to search an array for a value is used so frequently in programs that it is worth placing in a method. Here is a method to search an array of integers. The method returns the location of the first array element equal to the search value and −1 if the value is absent:

```
int search (int[] a, int searchValue){
   int location;
   location = -1;
   for (i = 0; i < a.length; i++){
      if (a[i] == searchValue){
         location = i;
         break;
      }
   }
   return location;
}
```

Sort in Ascending Order

The code to sort an array can easily be packaged in a method:

```
void sort (int[] a){
   int i, j;
   int temp;
   for (i = 0; i < a.length - 1; i++){
      for (j = i + 1; j < a.length; j++){
         if (a[j] < a[i]){
            temp = a[j];
            a[j] = a[i];
            a[i] = temp;
         }
      }
   }
}
```

This method must be used with caution because it changes the array passed to it.

Sum the Rows

Here is a method that instantiates a new array and returns it. The method computes the sum of each row in a two-dimensional array and returns a one-dimensional array of row sums. The method works even if the rows are not all the same size. We also rely on the fact that Java provides a default value of 0 at each position in the new array.

```
int[] sumRows (int[][] a){
    int i, j;
    int[] rowSum = new int[a.length];
    for (i = 0; i < a.length; i++){
        for (j = 0; j < a[i].length; j++){
            rowSum[i] += a[i][j];
        }
    }
    return rowSum;
}
```

Here is code that uses the method. Notice that we do not have to instantiate the array oneD because that task is done in the method sumRows.

```
int[][] twoD = {{1,2,3,4}, {5,6}, {7,8,9}};
int[] oneD;

oneD = sumRows (twoD);      // oneD now equals {10, 11, 24}
```

Copy an Array

Earlier, we saw that copying an array must be done with care. Assigning one array variable to another does not do the job. It merely yields two variables referencing the same array. Here is a method that attempts to solve this problem. The first parameter represents the original array, and the second is the copy. The original is instantiated before the method is called, and the copy is instantiated in the method.

```
void copyOne (int[] original, int[] copy){
    int i;
    copy = new int[original.length];
    for (i = 0; i < original.length; i++){
        copy[i] = original[i];
    }
}
```

We now run this method in the following code segment:

```
int[] orig = {1,2,3,4,5};
int[] cp;
...
copyOne (orig, cp);
```

When `copyOne` terminates, we expect the variable `cp` to refer to an array of five integers. However, that does not happen. Even though the method created a copy of the original array and assigned it to the array parameter, the original variable `cp` was not changed. The only way to change the `cp` array is to change the contents of the cells within it, but the `cp` array had no cells of its own to begin with.

In a correct solution, the method returns the copy, as shown next:

```
int[] copyTwo (int[] original){
   int i;
   int[] copy = new int[original.length];
   for (i = 0; i < original.length; i++){
      copy[i] = original[i];
   }
   return copy;
}
```

Here is some code that illustrates the use of `copyTwo`:

```
int[] orig = {1,2,3,4,5};
int[] cp;
...
cp = copyTwo (orig);
```

Other Objects and Methods

Objects of all types, not just arrays, can be passed to and returned from methods. The lessons you have just learned when using arrays in this manner apply equally to all objects.

The Mysterious Parameter in Method `main`

We have finally reached a point at which we can explain the mysterious parameter in function `main`. Every program includes somewhere the code:

```
public static void main (String [] args)
```

We can now recognize this parameter as an array of strings. This array is built from the parameters specified in the command line when we run a Java program from inside a terminal window, as in:

```
c:\> java CommandLineDemo one 2.0 three
```

In this command line, there are three parameters and each is a string; however, a program processing these parameters will probably convert the second parameter to a floating-point value before using it. Here is a program that demonstrates the processing of the preceding command line parameters:

```
public class CommandLineDemo {
    public static void main (String [] args) {
        int i;
        for (i = 0; i < args.length; i++)
            System.out.println(args [i]);
    }
}
```

The output will be:

```
one
2.0
three
```

Self-Test Questions

20. What happens when one uses the assignment operator (=) with two array variables?

21. Discuss the issues involved with copying an array.

22. Write a method that performs the task of the code in Question 8, which is to search for a negative number.

23. Write a method rowSums that expects a two-dimensional array of integers as a parameter. The method should return a one-dimensional array whose items represent the sums of the items in the rows of the two-dimensional array.

24. Write a method that searches a two-dimensional array for a given integer. This method should return an object of class Point, which contains a row and a column. The constructor for Point is Point(anInteger, anInteger).

10.9 Case Study: Student Test Scores Again

In Chapter 9, we developed a program for keeping track of student test scores. We now build on that program in two ways:

1. We extend the program so that it allows the user to maintain an array of students.

2. We modify the Student class so that the three grades are stored in an array rather than in three separate instance variables.

Both changes illustrate the use of arrays to maintain lists of data.

Request. Modify the student test scores program of Chapter 9 so that it allows the user to maintain an array of students.

Analysis. As before, the interface displays the data for an individual student and allows the user to modify these data. However, the interface (see Figure 10.9) now provides a window on the current student in an array of students. The interface has buttons that support navigation through this array by moving to the first or last student in the array and by moving to the next or previous student in the array. The interface also has buttons that allow the user to add a student to the end of the array, insert a student before the current student, modify the current student, or delete the current student. The interface displays the index of the current student and the current length of the array. Finally, the interface provides menu options to sort the array of students by name or average test score. Table 10.3 explains each of these features in more detail.

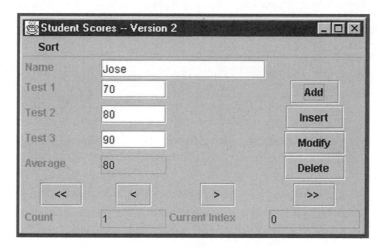

Figure 10.9 Interface for the new student test scores program

Table 10.3

Description of Buttons and Menu Options

Buttons and Menu Options	What It Does
Add	Creates a new student object with the data displayed and inserts it at the end of the array. The new student becomes the current student.
Insert	Creates a new student object with the data displayed and inserts it before the current student. The new student becomes the current student.
Modify	Replaces the current student's data with the data displayed.
Delete	Removes the current student from the array. If the array becomes empty or the deleted student was the last student, the data fields are cleared; otherwise, the next student becomes the current student.
<<	Moves to the first student in the array and displays its data.
<	Moves to the previous student in the array and displays its data.
>	Moves to the next student in the array and displays its data.
>>	Moves to the last student in the array and displays its data.
Sort/By Name	Sorts the array of students in ascending order by name and displays the first student.
Sort/By Average	Sorts the array of students in ascending order by average and displays the first student.

Design. We break the design into two parts, one for each class used in the program.

The **StudentTestScores** **Class:** This is the interface class, and it contains three private instance variables for the data:

- an array of Student objects
- the selected index (an int)
- the current number of students (an int)

The buttonClicked method calls one of several methods depending on which button was pressed. These methods either move through the list or update its contents in some way. We provide implementations of several of these methods and leave the others as exercises. There is also a method to validate the student's data before entering a new student in the array or modifying an existing student.

The **Student** **Class:** For this program, we make two major changes to the Student class described in Chapter 9:

1. The three test scores are stored in an array. This provides more flexibility than did the use of a separate instance variable for each test, and in the future, it will be easy to modify the class to deal with a larger number of tests.

2. The Student class provides a validateData method. Now any application that needs to validate student data can do so easily. If this code were placed in the interface class, it would need to be repeated in every interface that works with student objects, which would be wasteful, tedious, and difficult to maintain.

Implementation. Here is the code for the two classes. To save space, we have kept comments to a minimum; however, we have used descriptive names for variables and methods and hope you will find the code fairly self-documenting.

```
import javax.swing.*;
import BreezySwing.*;

public class StudentTestScores extends GBFrame{

    // Window objects ---------------------------------------

    JButton addButton      = addButton ("Add"    ,2,4,1,1);
    JButton insertButton   = addButton ("Insert",3,4,1,1);
    JButton modifyButton   = addButton ("Modify",4,4,1,1);
    JButton deleteButton   = addButton ("Delete",5,4,1,1);

    JLabel  blankLine1     = addLabel  (""   , 6,1,1,1);
    JButton firstButton    = addButton ("<<", 7,1,1,1);
    JButton previousButton = addButton ("<",  7,2,1,1);
    JButton nextButton     = addButton (">",  7,3,1,1);
    JButton lastButton     = addButton (">>", 7,4,1,1);

    JLabel nameLabel       = addLabel ("Name"     ,1,1,1,1);
```

```
JLabel test1Label    = addLabel ("Test 1"   ,2,1,1,1);
JLabel test2Label    = addLabel ("Test 2"   ,3,1,1,1);
JLabel test3Label    = addLabel ("Test 3"   ,4,1,1,1);
JLabel averageLabel  = addLabel ("Average"  ,5,1,1,1);

JTextField    nameField   = addTextField    ("",1,2,2,1);
IntegerField test1Field = addIntegerField  (0 ,2,2,1,1);
IntegerField test2Field = addIntegerField  (0 ,3,2,1,1);
IntegerField test3Field = addIntegerField  (0 ,4,2,1,1);
IntegerField averageField = addIntegerField (0 ,5,2,1,1);

JLabel       blankLine2
             = addLabel        (""              ,8,1,1,1);

JLabel       countLabel
             = addLabel        ("Count"         ,9,1,1,1);

IntegerField countField
             = addIntegerField (0               ,9,2,1,1);

JLabel       indexLabel
             = addLabel        ("Current Index" ,9,3,1,1);

IntegerField indexField
             = addIntegerField (-1              ,9,4,1,1);

JMenuItem sortByNameMI    = addMenuItem ("Sort","By Name");
JMenuItem sortByAverageMI = addMenuItem ("Sort","By Average");

// Other instance variables --------------------------------

private Student[] students = new Student[10];
private int indexSelectedStudent;
private int studentCount;

// Constructor----------------------------------------------

public StudentTestScores(){
   setTitle ("Student Scores -- Version 2");

   indexSelectedStudent = -1;
   studentCount = 0;

   averageField.setEditable (false);
   countField.setEditable (false);
   indexField.setEditable (false);

   displayCurrentStudent();
}

// buttonClicked method-------------------------------------
```

Continues

Continued

```
public void buttonClicked (JButton buttonObj){
   if      (buttonObj == addButton)       addStudent();

   // insert, modify, and delete are left as an exercise

   else if (buttonObj == firstButton)    displayFirstStudent();
   else if (buttonObj == previousButton) displayPreviousStudent();
   else if (buttonObj == nextButton)     displayNextStudent();
   else if (buttonObj == lastButton)     displayLastStudent();
}

// menuItemSelected method-----------------------------------

public void menuItemSelected (JMenuItem menuItemObj){

   if (menuItemObj == sortByNameMI){
      if (studentCount == 0) return;
      sortStudentsByName();
      indexSelectedStudent = 0;
      displayCurrentStudent();
   }

   // Sorting by average left as an exercise
}

// Private methods----------------------------------------------

private void addStudent(){
   if (studentCount == students.length){
      messageBox ("SORRY: student array is full");
      return;
   }

   Student stu = getDataOnScreen();
   String str = stu.validateData();
   if (str != null){
      messageBox (str);
      return;
   }

   students[studentCount] = stu;
   indexSelectedStudent = studentCount;
   studentCount++;

   displayCurrentStudent();
}

private Student getDataOnScreen(){
```

```java
      String nm = nameField.getText().trim();

   int[] tests = new int[Student.NUM_TESTS];
   tests[0] = test1Field.getNumber();
   tests[1] = test2Field.getNumber();
   tests[2] = test3Field.getNumber();

   Student stu = new Student (nm, tests);
   return stu;
}

private void displayFirstStudent(){
   if (studentCount == 0)
      indexSelectedStudent = -1;
   else
      indexSelectedStudent = 0;
   displayCurrentStudent();
}

private void displayPreviousStudent(){
   // Exercise
}

private void displayNextStudent(){
   if (studentCount == 0)
      indexSelectedStudent = -1;
   else
      indexSelectedStudent
          = Math.min (studentCount - 1, indexSelectedStudent + 1);
   displayCurrentStudent();
}

private void displayLastStudent(){
   // Exercise
}

private void displayCurrentStudent(){
   if (indexSelectedStudent == -1){
      nameField.setText ("");
      test1Field.setNumber (0);
      test2Field.setNumber (0);
      test3Field.setNumber (0);
      averageField.setNumber (0);
   }else{
      Student stu = students[indexSelectedStudent];
      nameField.setText (stu.getName());
      test1Field.setNumber (stu.getScore(1));
      test2Field.setNumber (stu.getScore(2));
      test3Field.setNumber (stu.getScore(3));
      averageField.setNumber (stu.getAverage());
```

Continued

```
        }
        countField.setNumber (studentCount);
        indexField.setNumber (indexSelectedStudent);
    }

    private void sortStudentsByName(){
        for (int i = 0; i < studentCount - 1; i++){
            String namei = students[i].getName();
            for (int j = i + 1; j < studentCount; j++){
                String namej = students[j].getName();
                if (namei.compareTo (namej) > 0){
                    Student temp = students[i];
                    students[i] = students[j];
                    students[j] = temp;
                }
            }
        }
    }

    public static void main (String[] args){
        StudentTestScores tpo = new StudentTestScores();
        tpo.setSize (400, 250);
        tpo.setVisible(true);
    }
}
```

```
public class Student {

    public final static int NUM_TESTS = 3;
    private final static int MIN_SCORE = 0;
    private final static int MAX_SCORE = 100;

    private String name;
    private int[] tests = new int[NUM_TESTS];

    public Student(){
        name = "";
        for (int i = 0; i < NUM_TESTS; i++)
            tests[i] = 0;
    }

    public Student(String nm, int[] t){
        name = nm;
        for (int i = 0; i < NUM_TESTS; i++)
            tests[i] = t[i];
    }

    public Student(Student s){
        name = s.name;
```

```
        for (int i = 0; i < NUM_TESTS; i++)
            tests[i] = s.tests[i];
    }

    public void setName (String nm){
        name = nm;
    }

    public String getName (){
        return name;
    }

    public void setScore (int i, int score){
    //Precondition -- 1 <= i <= NUM_TESTS
        tests[i - 1] = score;
    }

    public int getScore (int i){
    //Precondition -- 1 <= i <= NUM_TESTS
        return tests[i - 1];
    }

    public int getAverage(){
        int sum = 0;
        for (int i = 0; i < NUM_TESTS; i++)
            sum += tests[i];
        return sum / NUM_TESTS;
    }

    public int getHighScore(){
        int highScore;
        highScore = tests[0];
        for (int i = 1; i < NUM_TESTS; i++){
            highScore = Math.max (highScore, tests[i]);
        }
        return highScore;
    }

    public String toString(){
        String str;
        str = "Name:    " + name  + "\n";
        for (int i = 0; i < NUM_TESTS; i++){
            str += "tests " + i + ":  " + tests[i] + "\n";
        }
        str += "Average: " + getAverage();
        return str;
    }

    public String validateData(){
    //Returns null if there are no errors else returns
```

Continues

Continued

```
//an appropriate error message.
   if (name.equals ("")) return "SORRY: name required";
   for (int i = 0; i < NUM_TESTS; i++){
      if (tests[i] < MIN_SCORE || tests[i] > MAX_SCORE){
         String str = "SORRY: must have "+ MIN_SCORE
                     + " <= test score <= " + MAX_SCORE;
         return str;
      }
   }
   return null;
}
}
```

10.10 The Model/View Pattern

A large complex task is best accomplished by dividing it into simpler cooperating subtasks; however, we did not take full advantage of this precept in the preceding case study. We mixed code for controlling the interface with code for managing the application's underlying data. The StudentTestScores class manages a complex interface and at the same time performs basic manipulations on the array of students—adding, inserting, deleting, and sorting students in the array. Now we modify the case study by dividing the StudentTestScores class in two. The first class, StudentTestScoresView, will manage the interface, and the second class, StudentTestScoresModel, will support all manipulations of the student array.

The division of programs into a model and a view is used widely by computer professionals, and we strongly recommend it. It simplifies the task of writing complex applications and increases their maintainability. It is common for users to request changes to an application's interface, so it is advantageous to make these changes without becoming entangled in the intricacies of the model. Similarly, changes can be made to the model without worrying about the interface. The separation of model and view is also beneficial when an application requires several windows. A separate class supports each window, or view, and all views communicate with a common model.

In general, when we separate an application into a model and view, the responsibilities of the view are as follows:

1. Instantiate and arrange the window objects.

2. Instantiate and initialize the model.

3. Handle user-generated events such as button clicks and menu selections by sending messages to the model.

4. Accurately represent the model to the user.

The responsibilities of the model are as follows:

1. Define and manage the application's data (this usually requires coordinating the activities of several programmer-defined classes).

2. Respond to messages from the view.

The division of labor between the model and the view has proven itself useful in many different situations and is called a ***pattern.*** There are many other patterns in the realm of object-oriented programming. Each describes how a common programming situation can be handled by a collection of classes with predefined roles communicating in a predefined manner. In Chapter 18, we will see how the model/view pattern can be extended to the famous model/view/controller pattern, also called the MVC pattern.

Throughout the rest of the book, we invite you to modify the case studies so that they use the model/view pattern. On large projects, programmers can work independently on the view and the model, provided they specify ahead of time the public methods included in the model.

We now illustrate how a segment of code taken from the StudentTestScores class can be split between the classes StudentTestScoresView and StudentTestScoresModel. This will give you a feeling for how the separation is made between the model and view. The code deals with the task of adding a new student to the array of students. First, here is the code as it appears in the StudentTestScores class:

```
public void buttonClicked (JButton buttonObj){
   if (buttonObj == addButton) addStudent();
   ...
}


void addStudent(){
   // See if the array is full
   if (studentCount == students.length){
      messageBox ("SORRY: student array is full");
      return;
   }


   // Get the data from the screen and make sure they are valid
   Student stu = getDataOnScreen();
   String str = stu.validateData();
   if (str != null){
      messageBox (str);
      return;
   }


   // Place the new student in the array
   students[studentCount] = stu;
   indexSelectedStudent = studentCount;
```

Continues

Continued

```
    studentCount++;

    // Display the student just added
    displayCurrentStudent();
}
```

In this segment, the code is split fairly equally between managing the interface (getting data from the screen and displaying error messages) and manipulating the array (including worrying about whether or not the array is full and updating the student count and the index of the selected student).

The corresponding code in the StudentTestScoresView class follows. The code deals primarily with the interface and calls a method in the model to manipulate the data.

```
public void buttonClicked (JButton buttonObj){
    if (buttonObj == addButton){

        // Get the data from the screen
        Student stu = getDataOnScreen();

        // Ask the model to add the student to the array.
        // If model encounters any problems, it returns an error message
        // else it returns null.
        String str = model.addStudent (stu);
        if (str != null)
            messageBox (str);
        else
            displayCurrentStudent();
    }
    ...
}
```

Here is the code in the model. It is completely independent of the view. The code checks the length of the array and makes sure the data are valid before adding the student to the array. The model keeps track of the student count and the index of the selected student.

```
public String addStudent (Student stu){
    if (studentCount == students.length)
        return "SORRY: student array is full";

    String str = stu.validateData();
    if (str != null)
        return str;
```

```
        students[studentCount] = stu;
        indexSelectedStudent = studentCount;
        studentCount++;

        return null;
    }
```

Here are complete listings for the `StudentTestScoresView` and `StudentTestScoresModel` classes:

```
import javax.swing.*;
import BreezySwing.*;

public class StudentTestScoresView extends GBFrame{

    // Window objects -------------------------------------

    JButton addButton    = addButton ("Add"   ,2,4,1,1);
    JButton insertButton = addButton ("Insert",3,4,1,1);
    JButton modifyButton = addButton ("Modify",4,4,1,1);
    JButton deleteButton = addButton ("Delete",5,4,1,1);

    JLabel  blankLine1    = addLabel (""   , 6,1,1,1);
    JButton firstButton    = addButton ("<<", 7,1,1,1);
    JButton previousButton = addButton ("<",  7,2,1,1);
    JButton nextButton     = addButton (">",  7,3,1,1);
    JButton lastButton     = addButton (">>", 7,4,1,1);

    JLabel nameLabel    = addLabel ("Name"    ,1,1,1,1);
    JLabel test1Label   = addLabel ("Test 1"  ,2,1,1,1);
    JLabel test2Label   = addLabel ("Test 2"  ,3,1,1,1);
    JLabel test3Label   = addLabel ("Test 3"  ,4,1,1,1);
    JLabel averageLabel = addLabel ("Average" ,5,1,1,1);

    JTextField   nameField   = addTextField   ("",1,2,2,1);
    IntegerField test1Field = addIntegerField (0 ,2,2,1,1);
    IntegerField test2Field = addIntegerField (0 ,3,2,1,1);
    IntegerField test3Field = addIntegerField (0 ,4,2,1,1);
    IntegerField averageField = addIntegerField (0 ,5,2,1,1);

    JLabel       blankLine2
            = addLabel        (""            ,8,1,1,1);

    JLabel       countLabel
            = addLabel        ("Count"       ,9,1,1,1);
```

Continued

```
IntegerField countField
            = addIntegerField (0                    ,9,2,1,1);

JLabel        indexLabel
            = addLabel          ("Current Index" ,9,3,1,1);

IntegerField indexField
            = addIntegerField (-1                  ,9,4,1,1);

JMenuItem sortByNameMI    = addMenuItem ("Sort","By Name");
JMenuItem sortByAverageMI = addMenuItem ("Sort","By Average");

// Other instance variables --------------------------------

private StudentTestScoresModel model;

// Constructor----------------------------------------------

public StudentTestScoresView(){
   setTitle ("Student Scores -- Version 3");

   model = new StudentTestScoresModel();

   averageField.setEditable (false);
   countField.setEditable (false);
   indexField.setEditable (false);

   displayCurrentStudent();
}


// buttonClicked method-------------------------------------

public void buttonClicked (JButton buttonObj){
   if (buttonObj == addButton){
      Student stu = getDataOnScreen();
      String str = model.addStudent (stu);
      if (str != null)
         messageBox (str);
      else
         displayCurrentStudent();
   }

   // insert, modify, and delete are left as an exercise
```

```
      else if (buttonObj == firstButton){
         model.moveToFirstStudent();
         displayCurrentStudent();
      }
      else if (buttonObj == previousButton); // left as an exercise

      else if (buttonObj == nextButton){
         model.moveToNextStudent();
         displayCurrentStudent();
      }
      else if (buttonObj == lastButton);      // left as an exercise
   }

   // menuSelected method--------------------------------------

   public void menuItemSelected (JMenuItem menuItemObj){

      if (menuItemObj == sortByNameMI){
         model.sortStudentsByName();
         model.moveToFirstStudent();
         displayCurrentStudent();
      }

      // Sorting by average left as an exercise
   }

   // Private methods--------------------------------------------

   Student getDataOnScreen(){
      String nm = nameField.getText().trim();

      int[] tests = new int[Student.NUM_TESTS];
      tests[0] = test1Field.getNumber();
      tests[1] = test2Field.getNumber();
      tests[2] = test3Field.getNumber();

      Student stu = new Student (nm, tests);
      return stu;
   }

   void displayCurrentStudent(){
      Student stu = model.getCurrentStudent();
      if (stu == null){
         nameField.setText ("");
         test1Field.setNumber (0);
         test2Field.setNumber (0);
```

Continued

```
      test3Field.setNumber (0);
      averageField.setNumber (0);
   }else{
      nameField.setText (stu.getName());
      test1Field.setNumber (stu.getScore(1));
      test2Field.setNumber (stu.getScore(2));
      test3Field.setNumber (stu.getScore(3));
      averageField.setNumber (stu.getAverage());
   }
   countField.setNumber (model.getStudentCount());
   indexField.setNumber (model.getIndexSelectedStudent());
 }

 public static void main (String[] args){
    StudentTestScoresView tpo = new StudentTestScoresView();
    tpo.setSize (400, 250);
    tpo.setVisible(true);
 }
}
```

```
public class StudentTestScoresModel {

  // Instance variables --------------------------------

  private Student[] students = new Student[10];
  private int       indexSelectedStudent;
  private int       studentCount;

  // Constructor-----------------------------------------

  public StudentTestScoresModel(){
    indexSelectedStudent = -1;
    studentCount = 0;
  }

  public String addStudent (Student stu){
    if (studentCount == students.length)
      return "SORRY: student array is full";

    String str = stu.validateData();
    if (str != null)
      return str;

    students[studentCount] = stu;
    indexSelectedStudent = studentCount;
```

```
      studentCount++;

      return null;
   }

   public Student getCurrentStudent(){
      if (indexSelectedStudent == -1)
         return null;
      else
         return students[indexSelectedStudent];
   }

   public int getIndexSelectedStudent(){
      return indexSelectedStudent;
   }

   public int getStudentCount(){
      return studentCount;
   }

   void moveToFirstStudent(){
      if (studentCount == 0)
         indexSelectedStudent = -1;
      else
         indexSelectedStudent = 0;
   }

   void moveToPreviousStudent(){
      // Exercise
   }

   void moveToNextStudent(){
      if (studentCount == 0)
         indexSelectedStudent = -1;
      else
         indexSelectedStudent
            = Math.min (studentCount - 1, indexSelectedStudent + 1);
   }

   void moveToLastStudent(){
      // Exercise
   }

   void sortStudentsByName(){
      for (int i = 0; i < studentCount - 1; i++){
```

Continues

Continued

```
        String namei = students[i].getName();
        for (int j = i + 1; j < studentCount; j++){
          String namej = students[j].getName();
          if (namei.compareTo (namej) > 0){
            Student temp = students[i];
            students[i] = students[j];
            students[j] = temp;
          }
        }
      }
    }
}
```

Self-Test Question

25. Describe the roles and responsibilities of the model and the view in the model/view pattern.

10.11 Design, Testing, and Debugging Hints

- Three things should be done to set up an array:

  1. Declare an array variable.

  2. Instantiate an array object and assign it to the array variable.

  3. Initialize the cells in the array with data, as appropriate.

- When creating a new array object, try to come up with an accurate estimate of the number of cells for the data. If you underestimate, some data will be lost; if you overestimate, some memory will be wasted.

- To avoid range errors, remember that the index of an array cell ranges from 0 (the first position) to the length of the array minus 1.

- To access the last cell in an array, use the expression `<array>.length - 1`.

- As a rule of thumb, it is best to avoid aliasing—that is, having more than one array variable refer to the same array object. When you want to copy the contents of one array to another, do not use the assignment A = B; instead, write a copy method and use the assignment A = `arrayCopy(B)`.

- Aliasing is appropriate when an array is passed as a parameter to a method; in this case, the formal array parameter automatically serves as an alias for the actual array parameter.

10.12 Summary

This chapter has provided an introduction to the processing of arrays. An array is a collection of items that are accessed by index positions. We showed how to declare array variables and instantiate array objects, how to use loops to access all the items, and how to construct methods for array processing. We also covered arrays of more than one dimension—that is, arrays that use more than one index to access items.

10.13 Key Terms

If you have difficulty finding the definitions of any key terms in the body of this chapter, turn to the Glossary at the end of the book.

array	item	pattern
bubble sort	length (of an array)	position (within an array)
element	linear search	range bound error
index	multidimensional array	subscript
initializer list	parallel arrays	two-dimensional array

10.14 Answers to Self-Test Questions

1. An array can contain many items and still be treated as one thing. Thus, instead of having many variables for many items, an array requires just one variable and an operator to access each item within it.

2. To access an item in an array, the programmer uses the subscript operator `[]`.

3.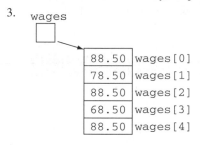

4. a. `double[] doubleArray = new double[15];`

   b. `String[] stringArray = new String[20];`

5. a. 23

   b. 12

   c. 156

6. Because each of these positions is outside of the range of allowable positions for this array, an error occurs, and Java throws an exception.

7.
```
for (int i = 0; i < a.length; i++)
    System.out.println(a[i]);
```

8.
```
int pos = 0;
for (pos = 0; pos < a.length; pos++)
    if (a[pos] < 0)
        break;
```

9. Insertion has a precondition that there is room on the array. Then one must open a hole for the new item by shifting all items to the right of the insertion point to the right by one. Deletion has a precondition that the array is not empty. Then one must shift all items to the right of the deletion point to the left by one.

10. One can use the variable `length` when one wants to visit all the items in an array.

11. An initializer list allows the program to specify the values that initially occupy positions in an array. An example of its use is `int[] a = {2, 4, 6};`

12. It is better to use the form `<type>[] <variable>` when declaring an array so as not to confuse it with the form `<type> variable` when declaring ordinary variables.

13. Parallel arrays are two or more arrays that have the same length and that use the same index values to establish logical connections among their items.

14. One might use parallel arrays to represent a phone book. The names occupy one array and the phone numbers occupy the other array.

15.
```
String[] names = new String[50];
int[] ages = new int[50];
String[] ssn = new String[50];
```

16. A two-dimensional array organizes items in rows and columns. Each item is accessed by specifying two index positions.

17. Representing a chessboard is one application of a two-dimensional array.

18.
```
int row = 0;
int col = 0;
bool found = false;
for (row = 0; row < a.length; row++){
    for (col = 0; col < a[row].length; col++)
        if (a[row][col] < 0){
            found = true;
            break;
        }
    if (found)
        break;
}
```

19.
```
for (int i = 0; i < a.length; i++)
    for (int j = 0; j < a[i].length; j++)
        for (int k = 0; k < a[i][j].length; k++)
            System.out.println(a[i][j][k]);
```

20. The assignment operator makes the two variables refer to the same array object.

21. As with other objects, arrays are not copied when the assignment operator is used. Thus, one must instantiate a new array of the same type and length as the original, transfer the items to the new array, and return the new array.

```
22. int findNeg(int[]a){
        int i = 0;
        for (i = 0; i < a.length; i++)
            if (a[i] < 0)
                break;
        return i;
    }
23. int[] rowSums(int[][] a){
        int[] result = new int[a.length];
        for (int row = 0; row < a.length; row++)
            for (int col = 0; col < a[row].length; col++)
                result[row] = result[row] + a[row][col];
        return result;
    }
24. Point search(int[][] a, int target){
        int row = 0;
        int col = 0;
        for (row= 0; row < a.length; row++)
            for (col = 0; col < a[row].length; col++)
                if (a[row][col] == target)
                    return new Point(row, col);
        return new Point(row, col);
    }
```

25. The responsibility of the model is to represent the data for an application. The responsibility of the view is to provide a view of the model to the user and to handle user requests for access to or modifications of the model.

10.15 Programming Problems and Activities

1. Write a program that takes ten integers as input. The program places the even integers into an array called evenList, the odd integers into an array called oddList, and the negative integers into an array called negativeList. The program displays the contents of the three arrays after all of the integers have been entered.

2. Write a program that takes ten floating-point numbers as inputs. The program displays the average of the numbers followed by all of the numbers that are greater than the average. As part of your design, write a method that takes an array of doubles as a parameter and returns the average of the data in the array.

3. Write a program that takes as input an unknown number of integer test scores. Assume that there are at most 50 scores and provide an **Enter** button to accept each score. When the user selects the **Results** button, the program displays the original list of scores, the scores sorted from low to high, the scores sorted from high to low, the highest score, the lowest score, and the average score. Write separate methods that take an array of integers as a parameter and compute each of these results.

4. The mode of a list of numbers is the number listed most often. Write a program that takes ten numbers as input and displays the mode of these numbers. Your program

should use parallel arrays and a method that takes an array of numbers as a parameter and returns the maximum value in the array.

5. The median of a list of numbers is the value in the middle of the list if the list is arranged in order. Add to the program of Problem 4 the capability of displaying the median of the list of numbers.

6. Modify the program of Problem 5 so that it displays not only the median and mode of the list of numbers but also a table of the numbers and their associated frequencies.

7. Write a text analyzer program that displays a table of the unique words typed in a text area and their associated frequencies. The words in the table should be in alphabetical order.

8. Design, implement, and test a class that represents a deck of cards. First, modify the Card class of Problem 5, Chapter 9, so that it maintains the suit of a card (spade, club, heart, or diamond). The constructor of this class should randomly generate not only the number but also the suit of a new card. Then, equip the Deck class with the following methods:

Method	What It Does
Deck()	Creates a new deck of 52 cards.
boolean empty()	Returns true if the deck has no cards left and false otherwise.
int size()	Returns the number of cards left in the deck.
Card [] deal(int number)	Precondition: The deck is not empty. Deals a hand (array) of cards from the top of the deck, reducing the size of the deck by the specified number.
Card deal()	Precondition: The deck is not empty. Deals the next card from the top of the deck, reducing the size of the deck by one.

Write a short tester program that creates two decks of cards. The program should deal one card at a time and display all 52 cards from the first deck; then it should deal four hands of 13 cards each and display them from the second deck.

9. Use the Deck class developed in Problem 8 to solve the problems mentioned in the blackjack program of Problems 6 and 7, Chapter 9.

10. Complete the student test scores application of Case Study 9.5 and test it thoroughly.

11. Develop a polynomial evaluator. The inputs should be the polynomial and a value for x. The output should be the value of the polynomial at x. You can use a terminal interface or a GUI with three fields and a button. The user will enter the polynomial as a string, subject to the following constraints:

- spaces separate terms and operators
- spaces separate items within terms, such as constants, variables, and exponents
- the operator is +
- the terms are in standard order, from the highest degree to the lowest degree

Thus, for example, the polynomial $3x^2 + 2x + 6$ is entered as the string $3 x ^ 2 + 2 x + 6$. Use a string tokenizer (see Chapter 8) to extract the terms from the string and an array to store the terms. An array of integers whose length is one greater than the degree of the polynomial will do. The index positions represent the exponents for each term, and the items at each position are the coefficients (use a coefficient of 0 for positions that are not in the input polynomial). To evaluate the polynomial, loop through this array.

12. Modify the program of Problem 11 to take two polynomials from the user. The program should have commands to evaluate each polynomial for a given value of x and to perform the arithmetic operations of addition, subtraction, multiplication, and division on them.

13. Write a program to keep statistics for a basketball team of 12 players. Statistics for each player should include shots attempted, shots made, and shooting percentage; free throws attempted, free throws made, and free throw percentage; offensive rebounds and defensive rebounds; assists; turnovers; and total points. Place these data in parallel arrays. Appropriate team totals should be listed as part of the output.

14. Modify the program of Problem 13 so that it uses a two-dimensional array instead of the parallel arrays for the statistics.

15. A magic square is a two-dimensional array of positive integers such that the sum of each row, column, and diagonal is the same constant. For example,

16	3	2	13
5	10	11	8
9	6	7	12
4	15	14	1

is a magic square whose constant is 34. Write a program that takes 16 integers as inputs. The program should determine whether or not the square is a magic square and display the result in a message box.

16. Pascal's triangle can be used to recognize coefficients of a quantity raised to a power. The rules for forming this triangle of integers are such that each row must start and end with a 1, and each entry in a row is the sum of the two values diagonally above the new entry. Thus, four rows of Pascal's triangle are

$$1$$
$$1 \quad 1$$
$$1 \quad 2 \quad 1$$
$$1 \quad 3 \quad 3 \quad 1$$

This triangle can be used as a convenient way to get the coefficients of a quantity of two terms raised to a power (binomial coefficients). For example,

$$(a + b)^3 = 1 \times a^3 + 3a^2b + 1 \times b^3$$

where the coefficients 1, 3, 3, and 1 come from the fourth row of Pascal's triangle.

Write a program that takes the number of rows as input and displays Pascal's triangle for those rows.

17. In the game of Penny Pitch, a two-dimensional board of numbers is laid out as follows:

```
1  1  1  1  1
1  2  2  2  1
1  2  3  2  1
1  2  2  2  1
1  1  1  1  1
```

A player tosses several pennies on the board, aiming for the number with the highest value. At the end of the game, the sum total of the tosses is returned. Develop a program that plays this game. The program should perform the following steps each time the user selects the **Toss** button:

- Generate two random numbers for the row and column of the toss.

- Add the number at this position to a running total.

- Display the board, replacing the numbers with Ps where the pennies land.

Hint: You should use a two-dimensional array of Square objects for this problem. Each square contains a number like those shown, and a Boolean flag that indicates whether or not a penny has landed on that square.

11 Inheritance, Abstract Classes, and Polymorphism

This chapter explores inheritance, abstract classes, and polymorphism. Two of these concepts were first encountered in Chapter 1.

Inheritance. Java organizes classes in a hierarchy. Classes inherit the instance variables and methods of the classes above them in the hierarchy. A class can extend its inherited characteristics by adding instance variables and methods and by overriding inherited methods. Thus, inheritance provides a mechanism for reusing code and can greatly reduce the effort required to implement a new class.

Abstract Classes. Some classes in a hierarchy must never be instantiated. They are called *abstract classes.* Their sole purpose is to define features and behavior common to their subclasses. The class Object, which is at the base or root of Java's class hierarchy, is an example of an abstract class.

Polymorphism. Methods in different classes, but with a similar function, are usually given the same name. This is called *polymorphism.* Polymorphism makes classes easier to use because programmers need to memorize fewer method names. In a well-designed class hierarchy, polymorphism is employed as much as possible. A good example of a polymorphic message is toString. Every object, no matter which class it belongs to, understands the toString message and responds by returning a string that describes the object.

We begin the chapter by examining these ideas in the context of a simple inheritance structure.

11.1 Implementing a Simple Shape Hierarchy

Suppose we need to perform some basic manipulations on circles and rectangles. These manipulations include positioning, moving, and stretching these basic geometric shapes. In addition, we want to determine a shape's area, and we want to be able to flip the dimensions of rectangles—that is, interchange a rectangle's width and height. For good measure, we require each shape to respond to the toString message by returning a description of the shape's attributes.

We proceed by defining classes for circles and rectangles. These classes will be called Circle and Rect, respectively. We do not use the more obvious name Rectangle because Java already includes a class with that name. To minimize the coding involved, we first implement a class Shape and from it derive subclasses Circle and Rect (Figure 11.1). Because we do not intend to instantiate a generic shape object, we designate the Shape class as abstract. Because we do intend to instantiate circles and rectangles, we call Circle and Rect *concrete classes.*

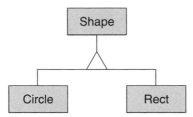

Figure 11.1 A hierarchy of shape classes

The implementation of these classes begins like this:

```
abstract public class Shape extends Object{
   ...
}

public class Circle extends Shape{
   ...
}

public class Rect extends Shape{
   ...
}
```

Notice the use of the word abstract at the beginning of the class definition for Shape.

Implementing the Shape Class

What characteristics are shared by the classes Circle and Rect? These can be extracted and defined in the Shape class:

- **Position**: All shapes have an *x, y* position in an underlying coordinate system. This position can be stored in instance variables xPos and yPos. The Shape class's constructors will initialize the variables, and accessor methods will make their values available to clients.

- **Movement**: All shapes are movable. Moving a shape is accomplished by changing its *x, y* coordinates. A method moveTo can perform the task.

- **Area Computation**: All shapes must be able to calculate their areas; however, this is done differently for circles and rectangles. Consequently, we cannot write code in the Shape class to perform the needed calculations, but we can designate in the Shape class that all subclasses must implement an area method. To do this, we declare area as an ***abstract method*** in the Shape class. Subsequently, the Java compiler will complain if a subclass of Shape forgets to implement an area method.

- **Stretching**: All shapes must be stretchable. This is achieved by changing a circle's radius or by changing a rectangle's width and/or height. The code cannot be written in the Shape class, so we declare an abstract method called stretchBy.

- **toString**: All shapes must respond to the toString message. The response should include a shape's position. Other details will differ for circles and rectangles. Therefore, the Shape class implements a toString method that indicates only the position. The subclasses will need to extend this method to include the other information.

That exhausts the list of attributes shared by circles and rectangles. Here is the complete listing for the Shape class:

```
abstract public class Shape{

    private double xPos;
    private double yPos;

    public Shape (){
        xPos = 0;
        yPos = 0;
    }

    public Shape (double x, double y){
        xPos = x;
        yPos = y;
    }

    abstract public double area();

    abstract public void stretchBy (double factor);

    public final double getXPos(){
        return xPos;
    }
}
```

Continued

```
    public final double getYPos(){
        return yPos;
    }

    public void moveTo (double xLoc, double yLoc){
        xPos = xLoc;
        yPos = yLoc;
    }

    public String toString(){
        String str = "(X,Y) Position: (" + xPos + "," + yPos + ")\n";
        return str;
    }
}
```

Notice these two new features in the listing:

1. *Abstract methods:* The methods area and stretchBy begin with the word abstract, end with a semicolon, and include no code. The purpose of an abstract method is to notify subclasses that they must implement the method or they will not compile successfully.

2. *Final methods:* In earlier chapters, you saw how programs define constants. A constant is specified as a final variable. This means that once it is defined, its value cannot be changed. A similar syntax is used to define methods that cannot be redefined in subclasses. For example, the accessor methods for the instance variables of the Shape class are defined as final:

```
    public final double getXPos(){
        return xPos;
    }

    public final double getYPos(){
        return yPos;
    }
```

The use of final in this code implies that subclasses of Shape cannot redefine these methods. Classes can also be declared as final. This implies that such classes cannot have subclasses.

Implementing the Circle Class

To implement the Circle class, we extend the Shape class. Only those features of a circle not shared with a rectangle need to be considered. Thus, the Circle class must do the following:

- Declare a variable to keep track of a circle's radius.
- Implement the abstract methods `area` and `stretchBy`.
- Extend `shape`'s constructors and `toString` method.

Here is the listing:

```java
public class Circle extends Shape{

    private double radius;

    public Circle(){
        super();
        radius = 0;
    }

    public Circle (double xLoc, double yLoc, double rds){
        super (xLoc, yLoc);
        radius = rds;
    }

    public double getRadius(){
        return radius;
    }

    public double area(){
        return Math.PI * radius * radius;
    }

    public void stretchBy (double factor){
        radius = radius * factor;
    }

    public String toString(){
        String str = "CIRCLE\n"
                    + super.toString()
                    + "Radius: " + radius + "\n"
                    + "Area: " + area();
        return str;
    }

}
```

The word `super` in the listing activates code in the superclass. The details of how this is done are different in constructors than in other methods.

Constructors and `super`

When an object is instantiated, a constructor is activated to initialize the object's variables. The constructor is, of course, located in the object's class. If variables are also declared in the superclass, these too need to be initialized. This initialization is achieved most easily by activating the constructor in the superclass. To activate the default constructor in the superclass, use the keyword `super`:

```
super();
```

To activate a different constructor in the superclass, use the keyword `super` together with the parameter list of the desired constructor. For instance,

```
super (xLoc, yLoc);
```

Other Methods and `super`

The `Circle` class also uses the keyword `super` but in a completely different manner. Any method can include code that looks like this:

```
super.<method name> (<parameter list>);
```

Such code activates the named method in the superclass. In comparison, the code

```
this.<method name> (<parameter list>);        // Long form
                                              //      or
<method name> (<parameter list>);             // Short form
```

activates the named method in the current class. We saw an example in the `Circle` class's `toString` method:

```
public String toString(){
    String str = "CIRCLE\n"
            + super.toString()              // <<<< super used here
            + "Radius: " + radius + "\n"
            + "Area: " + area();
    return str;
}
```

Implementing the `Rect` Class

The `Rect` class's implementation is similar to that of the `Circle` class, but there is one minor difference. The `Rect` class includes a method, `flipDimensions`, that is not part of either the `Shape` or `Circle` classes. Here is the code:

```
public class Rect extends Shape{

    private double width;
```

```
    private double height;

public Rect(){
    super();
    width = 0;
    height = 0;
}

public Rect (double xLoc, double yLoc, double wdth, double hght){
    super (xLoc, yLoc);
    width = wdth;
    height = hght;
}

public double area(){
    return width * height;
}

public void flipDimensions(){
    double temp = width;
    width = height;
    height = temp;
}

public void stretchBy (double factor){
    width = width * factor;
    height = height * factor;
}

public String toString(){
    String str = "RECTANGLE\n"
                + super.toString()
                + "Width & Height: " + width + " & " + height +"\n"
                + "Area: " + area();
    return str;
}

}
```

Protected Variables and Methods

In Chapter 9, we learned the difference between `public` and `private` visibility. A name declared `public` in a class is visible to the rest of an application, whereas a name declared `private` is visible only within that class's implementation. Subclasses cannot see `private` names declared in their parent classes. To make a method or variable visible to subclasses, but not to the rest of an application, we declare it as `protected`. To demonstrate, we could modify the `Shape` class as follows:

```
abstract public class Shape{

    protected double xPos;
    protected double yPos;
    ...
}
```

The variables `xPos` and `yPos` are now visible to all descendants of `Shape`, including `Circle`, so we can rewrite `Circle`'s constructors as follows:

```
public Circle (){
        xPos = 0;
        yPos = 0;
        radius = 0;
}

public Circle (double xLoc, double yLoc, double rds){
        xPos = xLoc;
        yPos = yLoc;
        radius = rds;
}
```

Obviously, this is not an improvement over our previous manner of coding `Circle`'s constructors. Generally, it is best to limit the visibility of instance variables as much as possible, so `private` instance variables are preferred to `protected` and `public` ones in most situations.

Implementation, Extension, Overriding, and Finality

From the foregoing discussion, we can see that there are four ways in which methods in a subclass can be related to methods in a superclass:

1. *Implementation* of an abstract method: As we have seen, each subclass is forced to implement the abstract methods specified in its superclass. Abstract methods are thus a means of requiring certain behavior in all subclasses.

2. *Extension*: There are two kinds of extension:

   a. The subclass method does not exist in the superclass.

   b. The subclass method invokes the same method in the superclass and then extends the superclass's behavior with its own operations.

3. *Overriding*: In this case, the subclass method does not invoke the superclass method. Instead, the subclass method is intended as a complete replacement of the superclass method.

4. *Finality*: The method in the superclass is complete and cannot be modified by the subclasses. We declare such a method to be `final`.

Self-Test Questions

1. What is a class hierarchy? Give an example.
2. What syntax is used to get one class to inherit data and behavior from another class?
3. What is an abstract class? Give an example.
4. How does the keyword `super` work with constructors?
5. How does the keyword `super` work with methods other than constructors?
6. What is the role of the visibility modifier `protected` in a class hierarchy?
7. Give an example of polymorphic methods.
8. What is a final method? Give an example.

11.2 Using the Shape Classes

Here is a short program that tests the shape classes:

```java
public class TestShapes {

    public static void main (String[] args){
        Circle circ;
        circ = new Circle (0, 0, 1);
        circ.moveTo (1, 2);
        circ.stretchBy (2);
        System.out.println ("\n" + circ.toString());

        Rect rect;
        rect = new Rect (0, 0, 1, 2);
        rect.moveTo (1, 2);
        rect.stretchBy (2);
        rect.flipDimensions();
        System.out.println ("\n" + rect.toString());
    }
}
```

The program produces the output shown in Figure 11.2.

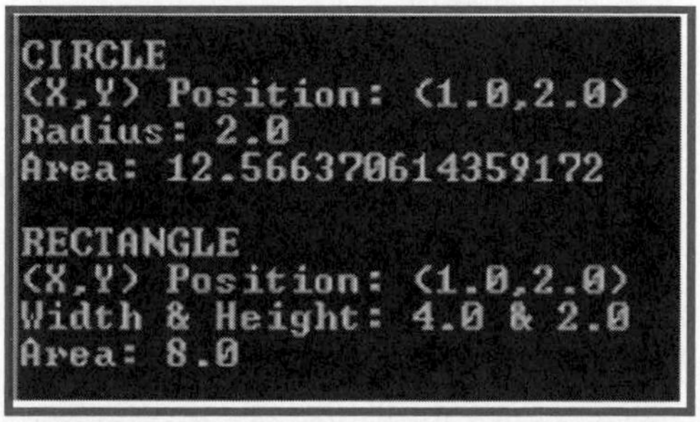

Figure 11.2 Output from the `TestShapes` program

Finding the Right Method

When a message is sent to an object, Java looks for a matching method. The search starts in the object's class and, if necessary, continues up the class hierarchy. Consequently, in the preceding program, when the `moveTo` message is sent to a circle or a rectangle, the `moveTo` method in the `Shape` class is activated. There is no `moveTo` method in either the `Circle` or `Rect` classes. On the other hand, when the `stretchBy` message is sent to a circle, Java uses the corresponding method in the `Circle` class.

Self-Test Question

9. Describe the process by which the JVM locates the right method to execute at run time.

11.3 Extending the Shape Hierarchy

We now introduce a new shape, cylinder, which looks like a soft drink can. We will implement the shape by means of a `Cylinder` class. A cylinder shares several characteristics with the other shapes. It has a position, but in a three-dimensional coordinate system. It has a surface area and can be moved and stretched. In addition, it has a new quality not seen before, volume. Because its dimensions are determined by the radius of its top and by its height, perhaps we can simplify the `Cylinder` class's implementation by extending the `Circle` class (Figure 11.3).

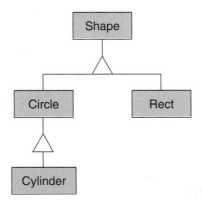

Figure 11.3 Extending the shapes hierarchy to include a cylinder

There is a possible objection to this approach. Although circles and rectangles are types of shapes, cylinders are not types of circles. In general, we must decide if we are basing a class hierarchy on coding convenience or on taxonomical accuracy. With this question in mind, an end of chapter exercise suggests two additional implementations and asks you to compare all three implementations. We are choosing the present implementation not for its merits but because it allows us to illustrate certain interesting aspects of class hierarchies.

Implementing the `Cylinder` Class

Here is the code for the `Cylinder` class:

```
public class Cylinder extends Circle{

   private double zPos;
   private double height;

   public Cylinder(){
      super();
      zPos = 0;
      height = 0;
   }

   public Cylinder (double xLoc, double yLoc, double zLoc,
                    double rds, double hght){
      super (xLoc, yLoc, rds);
      zPos = zLoc;
      height = hght;
   }

   public double area(){
      return 2 * super.area() + 2 * Math.PI * getRadius() * height;
   }

   public void moveTo (double xLoc, double yLoc, double zLoc){
      super.moveTo (xLoc, yLoc);
      zPos = zLoc;
   }

   public void stretchBy (double factor){
      super.stretchBy (factor);
      height = height * factor;
   }

   public double volume(){
      return super.area() * height;
   }

   public String toString(){
      String str = "CYLINDER\n"
               + "(X,Y,Z) Position: (" + getXPos() + ","
                                      + getYPos() + ","
                                      + zPos + ")\n"
               + "Radius & Height: "   + getRadius() + " & "
```

Continues

Continued

```
                                                 + height + "\n"
                     + "Area: " + area() + "\n"
                     + "Volume: " + volume();
        return str;
    }
}
```

More About the Use of `super`

Notice that in the `Cylinder` class, when we refer to a method in a superclass, sometimes we use the prefix `super` and sometimes we do not:

```java
public double volume(){
    return super.area() * height;                              // in Circle
}

public String toString(){
    String str = "CYLINDER\n"
                 + "(X,Y,Z) Position: (" + getXPos() + ","      // in Shape
                                + getYPos() + ","               // in Shape
                                + zPos + ")\n"
                 + "Radius & Height: "    + getRadius() + " & "  // in Circle
                                + height + "\n"
                 + "Area: " + area() + "\n"                      // in Cylinder
                 + "Volume: " + volume();
    return str;
}
```

Remember that Java normally starts its search for a method in the current class, which is `Cylinder` in the present example. The effect of the prefix `super` is to force the search to start in the current class's parent. For instance, because there is an `area` method in `Cylinder` and in `Circle`,

```
... area() ...          // Refers to the method in Cylinder
... super.area() ...    // Refers to the method in Circle
```

But because the `getRadius` method appears only in the `Circle` class, `super` is unnecessary:

```
... getRadius() ...          // Refers to the method in Circle
... super.getRadius()...     // Refers to the method in Circle
```

Testing the `Cylinder` Class

Here is a program that tests the `Cylinder` class; the program's output is in Figure 11.4.

```
public class TestShapes {
    public static void main (String[] args){
        Cylinder cyl;
        cyl = new Cylinder (0, 0, 0, 1, 2);
        cyl.moveTo (1, 2, 3);
        cyl.stretchBy (2);
        System.out.println ("\n" + cyl.toString());
    }
}
```

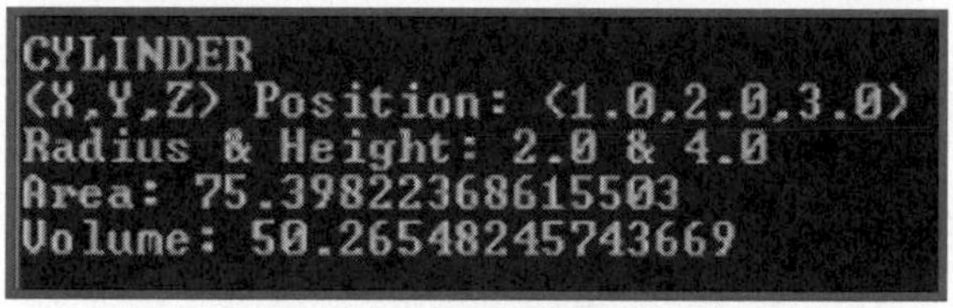

```
CYLINDER
<X,Y,Z> Position: <1.0,2.0,3.0>
Radius & Height: 2.0 & 4.0
Area: 75.39822368615503
Volume: 50.26548245743669
```

Figure 11.4 Output from the `Cylinder`'s `toString` method

Self-Test Question

10. When a programmer extends an existing class, which methods should the new class usually implement?

11.4 Arrays of Shapes

There are many situations in which we might want to work with arrays of shapes. In this section, we learn some simple rules that must be observed when doing so.

Declaring an Array of Shapes

Suppose we want to work with an array of circles. We might begin as follows:

```
Circle[] circles;                      // Declare an array variable.
circles = new Circle[10];              // Reserve space for 10 circles
circles[0] = new Circle (1,1,2);       // Assign a circle to the 1st element
circles[1] = new Circle (6,3,15);      // Assign a circle to the 2nd element
...
```

For greater flexibility we might instead prefer an array that can hold all the different types of shapes simultaneously—that is, circles, rectangles, and cylinders, as demonstrated next:

```
Shape[] shapes;                         // Declare an array variable
shapes = new Shape[10];                 // Reserve space for 10 shapes
shapes[0] = new Circle (1,1,1);         // Assign a circle to the 1st element
shapes[1] = new Rect (2,2,2,2);         // Assign a rectangle to the 2nd
shapes[2] = new Cylinder (3,3,3,3,3);   // Assign a cylinder to the 3rd
shapes[3] = new Rect (4,4,4,4);         // Assign a rectangle to the 4th
...
```

An important rule must be followed when objects of different classes are mixed in an array:

Rule for Mixing Objects of Different Classes in an Array. If we declare an array variable of type `ClassX`

```
ClassX[] theArray = new ClassX[10];
```

then we can store in the array objects of `ClassX` or objects of any class below `ClassX` in the class hierarchy.

```
theArray[0] = new ClassX();
theArray[1] = new ClassY(); // where ClassY is a subclass of ClassX
theArray[2] = new ClassZ(); // where ClassZ is a subclass of ClassY
... etc ...
```

A similar rule applies to nonarray variables:

Rule for Assigning Objects of Different Classes to a Variable. If we declare a variable of type `ClassX`

```
ClassX theVariable;
```

then we can assign to the variable objects of `ClassX` or objects of any class below `ClassX` in the class hierarchy.

```
theVariable = new ClassX();
theVariable = new ClassY(); // where ClassY is a subclass of ClassX
theVariable = new ClassZ(); // where ClassZ is a subclass of ClassY
... etc ...
```

Sending Messages to Objects in an Array of Shapes

Suppose we have an array of various shapes such as circles, rectangles, and cylinders. We can easily find the combined area of all the shapes by sending each an `area` message.

```
Shape[] shapes = new Shape[10];
shapes[0] = new Circle (...);
shapes[1] = new Cylinder (...);
...
totalArea = 0;
for (int i = 0; i < 10; i++)
   totalArea += shapes[i].area();
```

The `instanceof` Operator

In a similar manner, we might try to find the combined volume of all the shapes; however, we are now confronted with a problem. Some shapes do not have a volume and do not recognize the `volume` message. We can overcome this difficulty by sending the `volume` message to only those shapes that have a volume—that is, to the cylinder objects. Java provides an operator that allows us to determine an object's class. It is called `instanceof`. Here then is a first attempt at finding the total volume of all the shapes:

```
Shape[] shapes = new Shape[10];
shapes[0] = new Circle (...);
shapes[1] = new Cylinder (...);
...
totalVolume = 0;
for (int i = 0; i < 10; i++){
   if (shape[i] instanceof Cylinder)
      totalVolume += shapes[i].volume();    // <<<<<< Problem here
}
```

That looks good, but there is a problem in the indicated line. There is no `volume` method in the `Shape` class, so the Java compiler will complain. We did not have a similar problem when we were computing the `totalArea` because the `Shape` class does have an `area` method, even if it is an abstract method. Hence, the Java compiler accepts the line of code:

```
totalArea += shapes[i].area();
```

When the preceding line of code is executed, the `area` method used depends on the shape being processed at that moment—circle, rectangle, or cylinder.

Casting to the Rescue

We overcome our problem by using the cast operator. We replace the line of code

```
totalVolume += shapes[i].volume();                // <<<<<< Problem here
```

with the line

```
totalVolume += ((Cylinder)shapes[i]).volume();    // <<<<<< Problem gone
```

However, the cast operator must be used with caution, and two rules must be observed:

1. Before casting an object, we must be sure that the object is of the target type. Thus, before casting a generic shape to a cylinder, we must be certain that the shape is in fact a cylinder; otherwise, there will be a run-time error.

2. Never cast up; only cast down. Thus, it is okay to cast a `Shape` to a `Cylinder`, but not vice versa. Class `Cylinder` is below class `Shape` in the hierarchy.

A Short Example

A short example recaps the points we have been making:

```
public class TestShapes {
   public static void main (String[] args){
      Shape[] shapes = new Shape[3];
      shapes[0] = new Circle (0,0,1);        // Radius 1
      shapes[1] = new Rect (0,0,1,1);        // Width 1, height 1
      shapes[2] = new Cylinder (0,0,0,1,1);  // Radius 1, height 1

      double totalArea = 0;
      double totalVolume = 0;
      for (int i = 0; i < shapes.length; i++){
         totalArea += shapes[i].area();
         if (shapes[i] instanceof Cylinder)
            totalVolume += ((Cylinder)shapes[i]).volume();
      }
      System.out.println ("\nTotal area: " + totalArea);
      System.out.println ("Total volume: " + totalVolume);
   }
}
```

The output is shown in Figure 11.5.

```
Total area: 16.707963267948966
Total volume: 3.141592653589793
```

Figure 11.5 Total area and volume of an array of shapes

Self-Test Questions

11. State the rule for mixing objects of different classes in an array.

12. State the rule for assigning objects of one class to variables of another class.

13. What is a cast operator? Give an example.

14. What is the `instanceof` operator? When should it be used?

15. Suppose the array `a` contains objects of different classes. Write the code that assigns to the `String` variable `str` the object at position 3 in the array.

11.5 Shapes as Parameters and Return Values

Objects can be passed to and returned from methods. Actually, objects themselves are not passed, but references to objects are. We do not usually bother to make the distinction. Objects are passed to methods as parameters and passed back in `return` statements.

It is obvious that an object must exist before it is passed to a method. Less obvious is the fact that the changes the method makes to the object are permanent. The changes are still in effect after the method stops executing. In addition, an object returned by a method is usually created in the method, and the object continues to exist after the method stops executing.

If a parameter specifies that an incoming object belongs to `ClassX`, then an object of `ClassX` or of any subclass can be substituted. Similarly, if a method's return type is `ClassX`, then objects of `ClassX` or any subclass can be returned.

We now illustrate these ideas with some examples.

Rectangle In, Circle Out

For our first example, we write a method that takes a rectangle as an input parameter and returns a circle. The circle has the same area and position as the rectangle. The method makes no changes to the rectangle, and it has to instantiate the circle:

```
static private Circle makeCircleFromRectangle (Rect rectangle){
   double area = rectangle.area();
   double radius = Math.sqrt (area / Math.PI);
   Circle circle = new Circle (rectangle.getXPos(),
                               rectangle.getYPos(),
                               radius);
   return circle;
}
```

Here is a short program that shows the method in action:

```
public class TestShapes {

   public static void main (String[] args){
```

Continues

Continued

```
    Circle circ;
    Rect rect;

    rect = new Rect (1,1,4,6);
    circ = makeCircleFromRectangle (rect);

    System.out.println ("\nRectangle Area: " + rect.area() +
                        "\nCircle Area:    " + circ.area());
  }

  static private Circle makeCircleFromRectangle (Rect rectangle){
    ... code as shown above ...
  }
}
```

The output is shown in Figure 11.6.

```
Rectangle Area: 24.0
Circle Area:    24.0000000000000004
```

Figure 11.6 Areas of a rectangle and a circle made from the rectangle

Any Shape In, Circle Out

We now modify the previous method so that it accepts any shape as an input parameter—circles, rectangles, or cylinders. The fact that all shapes understand the area method makes the task easy:

```
static private Circle makeCircleFromAnyShape (Shape shape){
    double area = shape.area();
    double radius = Math.sqrt (area / Math.PI);
    Circle circle = new Circle (shape.getXPos(),
                                shape.getYPos(),
                                radius);
    return circle;
}
```

Any Shape In, Any Shape Out

It is also possible for a method to return an arbitrary rather than a specific shape. The next method has two input parameters. The first parameter is a shape, and the second indicates the type of shape to return:

```
static private Shape makeOneShapeFromAnother (Shape inShape, String type){
    Shape outShape;                              // declare outShape
    double area, radius, width, height;
    double x = inShape.getXPos();
    double y = inShape.getYPos();

    area = inShape.area();
    if (type.equals ("circle")){
        radius = Math.sqrt (area / Math.PI);
        outShape = new Circle (x, y, radius);    // assign a circle
    }
    else if (type.equals ("rectangle")){
        width = height = Math.sqrt (area);
        outShape = new Rect (x, y, width, height);   // assign a rectangle
    }
    else{
        radius = Math.sqrt (area / (Math.PI * 3));
        height = radius / 2;
        outShape = new Cylinder (x, y, 0,
                                 radius, height);    // assign a cylinder
    }
    return outShape;
}
```

In this code, notice that `outShape` is declared to be of type `Shape`, an abstract class; however, when it comes time to assign a value to `outShape`, one of the concrete shapes is used—`Circle`, `Rect`, or `Cylinder`. This is consistent with the rule stated earlier in the chapter:

> If we declare a variable of type `ClassX`, then we can assign to the variable objects of `ClassX` or objects of any class below `ClassX` in the class hierarchy.

Here is a test of the preceding method, with output shown in Figure 11.7.

```
public class TestShapes {

    public static void main (String[] args){
        Rect rect;
        Shape shape1, shape2, shape3;

        rect = new Rect (1,1,4,6);
        shape1 = makeOneShapeFromAnother (rect, "circle");
        shape2 = makeOneShapeFromAnother (rect, "rectangle");
        shape3 = makeOneShapeFromAnother (rect, "cylinder");

        System.out.println ("\nRectangle Area: " + rect.area() +
```

Continues

Continued

```
                              "\nCircle Area:     " + shape1.area() +
                              "\nRectangle Area: " + shape2.area() +
                              "\nCylinder Area:  " + shape3.area());
    }

    static private Shape makeOneShapeFromAnother (Shape inShape,
                                                  String     type){
    ... code as shown above ...
    }
}
```

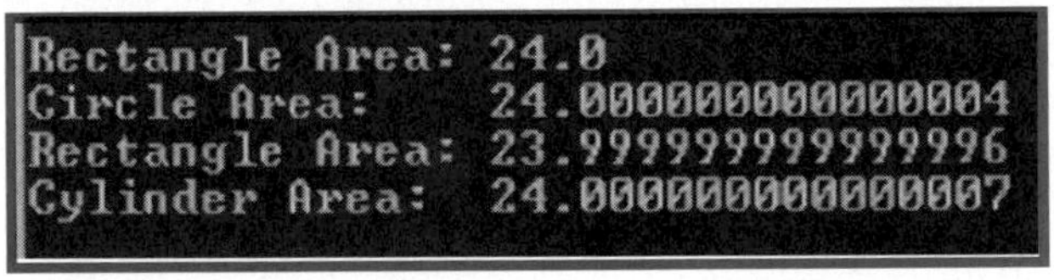

Figure 11.7 Areas of various shapes made from a rectangle

Self-Test Question

16. State the rule for passing a parameter of one class to a method that expects a parameter of another class.

11.6 An Employee Hierarchy

Well, enough about shapes already. Let us consider employees instead. Suppose a company has three types of employees: code testers, regular programmers, and lead programmers. Code testers are paid by the hour with overtime for hours over 40. Regular programmers are on salary. (Programmers work such long hours that the company would go broke if it had to pay them overtime.) Lead programmers are also on salary with a bonus for each programmer they supervise. The task is to design classes that can be used in a payroll system. The hierarchy of Figure 11.8 suggests itself.

In the hierarchy, the following are true:

- `Employee` is an abstract class that keeps track of name, number of dependents, deduction per dependent, and tax rate.

- `CodeTester` is a concrete class that keeps track of hourly rate and overtime rate.

- `Programmer` is a concrete class that keeps track of salary.

- `LeadProgrammer` is a concrete class that keeps track of the number of programmers supervised.

All the classes need to provide methods for manipulation of variables and a method to compute pay according to applicable rules.

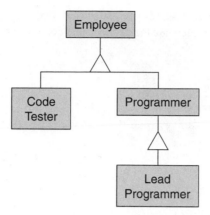

Figure 11.8 A hierarchy of employee classes

Here is a more complete specification of each class. The accessor and mutator methods needed for the class and instance variables are not shown.

```
abstract Employee extends Object
Class Variables
double DEDUCTION_PER_DEPENDENT
double TAX_RATE

Instance Variables
String name
int numDependents
double payRate
int unitsWorked

Instance Methods
protected double
  computeTax (double grossPay)
```

```
CodeTester extends Employee
Class Variables
double OVERTIME_FACTOR

Instance Variables
none, but here unitsWorked and
payRate represent hourly amounts

Instance Methods
public double
  computeNetPay (double
              hoursWorked)
```

```
Programmer extends Employee
Class Variables
none

Instance Variables
none, but here unitsWorked and
payRate represent weekly amounts

Instance Methods
public double computeNetPay ()
```

```
LeadProgrammer extends Programmer
Class Variables
double BONUS_PER_PROGRAMMER

Instance Variables
int numProgrammersSupervised

Instance Methods
public double computeNetPay ()
```

The implementation of these classes is straightforward. Only the rules for computing pay need further explanation. Here are the methods that compute an employee's pay:

In the `Employee` Class

```
protected double computeTax (double grossPay){
   double deductions = DEDUCTION_PER_DEPENDENT * numDependents;
   double tax = Math.max (0, (grossPay - deductions)) * TAX_RATE;
   return tax;
}
```

In the `CodeTester` Class

```
public double computeNetPay(double unitsWorked){
   double grossPay = 0;
   if (unitsWorked > 40){
      grossPay = (grossPay - 40) * payRate * (OVERTIME_FACTOR - 1);
      unitsWorked = 40;
   }
   grossPay += unitsWorked * payRate;
   double netPay = grossPay - computeTax (grossPay);
   return netPay;
}
```

In the `Programmer` Class

```
public double computeNetPay(){
   return payRate - computeTax (payRate * unitsWorked);
}
```

In the `LeadProgrammer` Class

```
public double computeNetPay(){
   double grossPay = payRate
                   + BONUS_PER_PROGRAMMER * numProgrammersSupervised;
   return grossPay - computeTax (grossPay);
}
```

11.7 `BreezySwing`: Check Boxes and Radio Buttons

To our growing list of window objects we now add check boxes and radio button groups. Before diving into the details, we present a simple demonstration interface.

A screenshot for a demo program is shown in Figure 11.9 and contains, among other window objects:

- Two *check boxes* labeled **Driver** and **Passenger** that are currently checked.
- A *radio button group* containing buttons labeled **Married**, **Single**, and **Divorced** with the option **Single** selected.

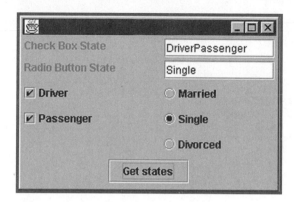

Figure 11.9 Some sample check boxes and radio buttons

Here is a listing of the demo program, which we discuss in the next two subsections:

```
import javax.swing.*;
import BreezySwing.*;

public class CheckBoxTester extends GBFrame{

    // Add fields to display states of boxes and buttons
    JLabel checkLabel = addLabel("Check Box State",    1,1,1,1);
    JLabel radioLabel = addLabel("Radio Button State", 2,1,1,1);
    JTextField checkField = addTextField("", 1,2,2,1);
    JTextField radioField = addTextField("", 2,2,2,1);


    // Add check boxes
    JCheckBox cbDriver    = addCheckBox("Driver",    3,1,1,1);
    JCheckBox cbPassenger = addCheckBox("Passenger", 4,1,1,1);

    // Add radio buttons
    JRadioButton rbMarried  = addRadioButton("Married",  3,3,1,1);
    JRadioButton rbSingle   = addRadioButton("Single",   4,3,1,1);
    JRadioButton rbDivorced = addRadioButton("Divorced", 5,3,1,1);

    JButton getStateBTN = addButton("Get states", 6,1,3,1);

    public CheckBoxTester(){
        // Mark the default check box and radio button
        cbDriver.setSelected (true);
        rbSingle.setSelected (true);
```

Continues

Continued

```
        // Add the radio buttons to a button group
        ButtonGroup bgMaritalStatus = new ButtonGroup();
        bgMaritalStatus.add(rbMarried);
        bgMaritalStatus.add(rbSingle);
        bgMaritalStatus.add(rbDivorced);
    }

    public void buttonClicked(JButton buttonObj){
        String cbStr = "", rbStr = "";
        if (cbDriver.isSelected())
           cbStr = "Driver";
        if (cbPassenger.isSelected())
           cbStr = cbStr + "Passenger";
        checkField.setText(cbStr);
        if (rbMarried.isSelected())
           rbStr = "Married";
        else if (rbDivorced.isSelected())
           rbStr = "Divorced";
        else if (rbSingle.isSelected())
           rbStr = "Single";
        radioField.setText(rbStr);
    }

    public static void main(String[] args){
        CheckBoxTester tpo = new CheckBoxTester();
        tpo.setSize (300, 200);
        tpo.setVisible (true);
    }
}
```

Check Boxes

Check boxes are declared in a now familiar manner. For instance,

```
JCheckBox cbDriver = addCheckBox ("Driver", 3,1,1,1);
```

Here are two frequently used `JCheckBox` and `JRadioButton` methods:

Name of Method	What It Does
setSelected (aBoolean)	If aBoolean is true, then mark the check box or radio button; else clear the check box or radio button.
isSelected() returns boolean	Return true if marked; else return false.

Unlike radio buttons, more than one check box can be selected simultaneously, so the `isSelected` method can return true for more than one check box at any given time. The code for `buttonClicked` in the demo program illustrates the different logic for testing the states of check boxes and radio buttons:

```
public void buttonClicked(JButton buttonObj){
    String cbStr = "", rStr = "";
    if (cbDriver.isSelected())
        cbStr = "Driver";
    if (cbPassenger.isSelected())
        cbStr = cbStr + "Passenger";
    checkField.setText(cbStr);
    if (rMarried.isSelected())
        rStr = "Married";
    else if (rDivorced.isSelected())
        rStr = "Divorced";
    else if (rSingle.isSelected())
        rStr = "Single";
    radioField.setText(rStr);
}
```

Radio Buttons

Radio buttons behave as a group, in so far as selecting one automatically deselects the others. To use radio buttons, one must declare a `ButtonGroup` and several radio buttons and then add each radio button to the group. In the demo program, radio buttons are declared as follows:

```
JRadioButton rbMarried  = addRadioButton("Married",  3,3,1,1);
JRadioButton rbSingle   = addRadioButton("Single",   4,3,1,1);
JRadioButton rbDivorced = addRadioButton("Divorced", 5,3,1,1);
```

The code to select a default radio button and to associate the radio buttons in a button group goes in the constructor method:

```
// Mark the default check box and radio button
cbDriver.setSelected (true);
rbSingle.setSelected (true);
// Add the radio buttons to a button group
ButtonGroup bgMaritalStatus = new ButtonGroup();
bgMaritalStatus.add(rbMarried);
bgMaritalStatus.add(rbSingle);
bgMaritalStatus.add(rbDivorced);
```

Later, when the program needs to know which radio button has been selected, it sends the `isSelected()` message to each radio button until one of them returns `true`.

11.8 Case Study: The Painter's Friend

We are now ready to present a case study that utilizes a hierarchy of classes.

Request. Write a program that allows a painter to estimate the number of gallons of paint needed to paint a house.

Analysis. We assume that a painter knows the following:

1. the number of square feet that a gallon of paint can cover
2. the number of coats of paint required
3. the dimensions of each wall, window, door, and gable

Thus, the interface should provide a way of entering these data and should display the total number of gallons of paint required. The proposed interface is in Figure 11.10. The program gives access to an array of different regions: walls, windows, gables, and doors. The user enters a new region by selecting the surface type, entering its width and height, and selecting either **Add** or **Insert.** The user can also modify, delete, or navigate to existing regions in the list by selecting the appropriate buttons. Finally, the user enters the square feet per gallon, the number of coats of paint required, and presses the **Compute Gallons Needed** button.

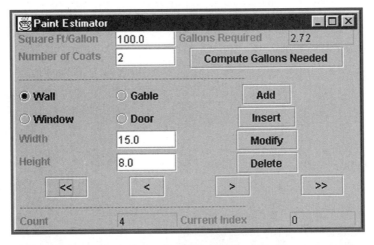

Figure 11.10 Interface for the paint estimator program

We will implement the program with the aid of seven classes:

- `PaintEstimatorView`: This class is responsible for setting up the view, handling user inputs, and updating the view with any changes.

- `PaintEstimatorModel`: This class is responsible for maintaining the data model of the program and computing the total gallons required. The data in the model are the array of regions, the number of square feet per gallon of paint, and the number of coats of paint.

- `Region`: This abstract class defines the common variables and methods of all regions.
- `Wall`, `Window`, `Door`, and `Gable`: These concrete classes define the variables and methods of the specific regions.

Design of `Region` and Its Subclasses. The data model for the application requires us to represent different kinds of regions. Each region has a height and width, which are set when the region is constructed. Each region also computes and returns its area. However, only walls and gables contribute to the surface area to be painted. The areas of windows and doors should be negative, so they can be deducted from the total surface area of a house. The fact that regions share some, but not all, properties suggests a hierarchy of classes in which `Region` is abstract and the other classes are concrete. Figure 11.11 shows the class hierarchy:

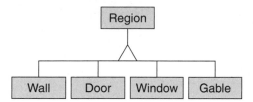

Figure 11.11 A hierarchy of regions

Here is a summary of the `Region` class:

Class:
  abstract Region
Protected Instance Variables:
  double width
  double height
Public Methods:
  constructors
  abstract double area()
  double getWidth()
  double getHeight()

Because the instance variables are `protected`, the subclasses `Wall`, `Window`, `Door`, and `Gable` have direct access to them, but classes outside the region hierarchy, such as the data model and interface, must call the `getWidth` and `getHeight` methods to access `height` and `width`.

The subclasses each implement the `area` method. Here is a summary of one of the subclasses:

Class:
  Wall extends Region
Public Methods:
  constructor
  double area()

Design of `PaintEstimatorModel`. The design of `PaintEstimatorModel` is similar to the design of the class `StudentTestScoresModel` discussed in Chapter 10. The `PaintEstimatorModel` supports the maintenance of an array of objects, with operations that allow insertions, deletions, and modifications to the array and changes to the array's current position indicator. Instance variables include the array of region, the index of the current object in the array, a count of the number of regions currently stored in the array, the square feet covered by a gallon of paint, and the number of coats of paint required. The model must provide mutator methods for these variables as well as a method that computes the total number of gallons required. Here is the class summary:

Class:
```
PaintEstimatorModel
```
Protected Instance Variables:
```
Region[] regions
int       indexSelectedRegion
int       regionCount
double    squareFeetPerGallon
int       numberOfCoats
```
Public Methods:
```
constructor
void    setNumberOfCoats (int noc)
double  getGallonsOfPaintNeeded()
Region  getCurrentRegion()
int     getRegionCount()
int     getIndexSelectedRegion()
void    moveToFirstRegion()
void    moveToPreviousRegion()
void    moveToNextRegion()
void    moveToLastRegion()
void    addRegion(Region rgn)
void    insertRegion(Region rgn)
void    modifyRegion(Region rgn)
void    deleteRegion(Region rgn)
```
Private Methods:
```
int area()
```

The array maintenance methods are essentially the same as the corresponding methods in the student test scores application in Chapter 10. The pseudocode for the methods `getGallonsOfPaintNeeded` and `area` follows:

```
getGallonsOfPaintNeeded
    a = area()
    if (a <= 0 || squareFeetPerGallon <= 0)
        return 0
```

```
    else
        return numberOfCoats * a / squareFeetPerGallon
```

area
```
    totalArea = 0
    for (i = 0; i < regionCount; i++)
        totalArea += regions[i].area()
    return totalArea
```

The design of the class `PaintEstimatorView` is similar to the design of the class `StudentTestScoresView` discussed in Chapter 10 and requires no further comment.

Implementation. Here is the code for the system. Comments have been omitted.

```
abstract public class Region {

    protected double width;
    protected double height;

    public Region(){
        width = 0;
        height = 0;
    }

    public Region (double w, double h){
        width = w;
        height = h;
    }

    abstract public double area();

    public double getWidth(){
        return width;
    }

    public double getHeight(){
        return height;
    }

}
```

```
public class Wall extends Region{

    public Wall (double width, double height){
        super (width, height);
    }

    public double area(){
```

Continued

```
         return width * height;
      }

   }
```

```
public class Gable extends Region{

   public Gable (double width, double height){
      super (width, height);
   }

   public double area(){
      return width * height / 2;
   }

}
```

```
public class Window extends Region{

   public Window (double width, double height){
      super (width, height);
   }

   public double area(){
      return - width * height;
   }
}
```

```
public class Door extends Region{

   public Door (double width, double height){
      super (width, height);
   }

   public double area(){
      return - width * height;
   }
}
```

```
import javax.swing.*;
import BreezySwing.*;

public class PaintEstimatorView extends GBFrame{

   // Window objects ------------------------------------

   JLabel sqrftLabel    = addLabel ("Square Ft/Gallon" ,1,1,1,1);
   JLabel numCoatsLabel = addLabel ("Number of Coats"  ,2,1,1,1);
   JLabel gllnReqLabel  = addLabel ("Gallons Required" ,1,3,1,1);
```

```
DoubleField sqrftField    = addDoubleField  (0,1,2,1,1);
IntegerField numCoatsField = addIntegerField (0,2,2,1,1);
DoubleField gllnReqField   = addDoubleField  (0,1,4,1,1);

JButton computeButton = addButton ("Compute Gallons Needed", 2,3,2,1);

JLabel separator1 = addLabel
("----------------------------------------------------------------"
, 3,1,4,1);

ButtonGroup rbgRegion = new ButtonGroup();
JRadioButton      rbWall   = addRadioButton ("Wall"  ,4,1,1,1);
JRadioButton      rbGable  = addRadioButton ("Gable" ,4,2,1,1);
JRadioButton      rbWindow = addRadioButton ("Window",5,1,1,1);
JRadioButton      rbDoor   = addRadioButton ("Door"  ,5,2,1,1);

JLabel widthLabel  = addLabel ("Width"  , 6,1,1,1);
JLabel heightLabel = addLabel ("Height", 7,1,1,1);

DoubleField widthField  = addDoubleField (0,6,2,1,1);
DoubleField heightField = addDoubleField (0,7,2,1,1);

JButton addButton    = addButton ("Add"   ,4,3,2,1);
JButton insertButton = addButton ("Insert",5,3,2,1);
JButton modifyButton = addButton ("Modify",6,3,2,1);
JButton deleteButton = addButton ("Delete",7,3,2,1);

JButton firstButton    = addButton ("<<", 8,1,1,1);
JButton previousButton = addButton ("<",  8,2,1,1);
JButton nextButton     = addButton (">",  8,3,1,1);
JButton lastButton     = addButton (">>", 8,4,1,1);

JLabel separator2 = addLabel
("----------------------------------------------------------------"
, 9,1,4,1);

JLabel        countLabel
          = addLabel        ("Count"        ,10,1,1,1);

IntegerField countField
          = addIntegerField (0              ,10,2,1,1);

JLabel        indexLabel
          = addLabel        ("Current Index" ,10,3,1,1);

IntegerField indexField
          = addIntegerField (-1             ,10,4,1,1);

// Other instance variables ----------------------------------
```

Continued

```
   private PaintEstimatorModel model;

   // Constructor---------------------------------------------------

   public PaintEstimatorView(){
      setTitle ("Paint Estimator");
      model = new PaintEstimatorModel();
      gllnReqField.setEditable (false);

      rbgRegion.add(rbWall);
      rbgRegion.add(rbGable);
      rbgRegion.add(rbWindow);
      rbgRegion.add(rbDoor);
      rbWall.setSelected (true);

      countField.setEditable (false);
      indexField.setEditable (false);
      displayCurrentRegion();
   }

   // buttonClicked method-----------------------------------------

   public void buttonClicked (JButton buttonObj){
      if (buttonObj == computeButton)
         computePaintNeeded();

      else if (buttonObj == addButton){
         Region rgn = getDataOnScreen();
         if (rgn != null){
            model.addRegion (rgn);
            displayCurrentRegion();
         }
      }

      // insert, modify, and delete are left as an exercise

      else if (buttonObj == firstButton){
         model.moveToFirstRegion();
         displayCurrentRegion();
      }
      else if (buttonObj == previousButton); // left as an exercise

      else if (buttonObj == nextButton){
         model.moveToNextRegion();
         displayCurrentRegion();
      }
      else if (buttonObj == lastButton);     // left as an exercise
   }

   // Private methods----------------------------------------------
```

```
private void computePaintNeeded(){
   double sqrftPerGal = sqrftField.getNumber();
   int numCoats = numCoatsField.getNumber();

   if (sqrftPerGal <= 0 || numCoats <= 0)
      messageBox ("SORRY: sqr ft/gl and num coats \n        must be > 0");
   else{
      model.setSquareFeetPerGallon (sqrftPerGal);
      model.setNumberOfCoats (numCoats);
      gllnReqField.setNumber (model.getGallonsOfPaintNeeded());
   }
}

private Region getDataOnScreen(){
   double width = widthField.getNumber();
   double height = heightField.getNumber();
   if (width <= 0 || height <= 0){
      messageBox ("SORRY: width and height \n        must be positive");
      return null;
   }

   Region reg;
   if (rbWall.isSelected())
      reg = new Wall (width, height);
   else if (rbGable.isSelected())
      reg = new Gable (width, height);
   else if (rbWindow.isSelected())
      reg = new Window (width, height);
   else
      reg = new Door (width, height);
   return reg;
}

void displayCurrentRegion(){
   Region rgn = model.getCurrentRegion();
   if (rgn == null){
      widthField.setNumber (0);
      heightField.setNumber (0);
   }else{
      if (rgn instanceof Wall)
         rbWall.setSelected (true);
      else if (rgn instanceof Gable)
         rbGable.setSelected (true);
      else if (rgn instanceof Window)
         rbWindow.setSelected (true);
      else
         rbDoor.setSelected (true);
      widthField.setNumber (rgn.getWidth());
      heightField.setNumber (rgn.getHeight());
   }
```

Continues

Continued

```java
      countField.setNumber (model.getRegionCount());
      indexField.setNumber (model.getIndexSelectedRegion());
   }

   public static void main (String[] args){
      PaintEstimatorView tpo = new PaintEstimatorView();
      tpo.setSize (400, 250);
      tpo.setVisible (true);
   }
}
```

```java
public class PaintEstimatorModel {

   private Region[] regions;
   private int indexSelectedRegion;
   private int regionCount;

   double squareFeetPerGallon;
   int numberOfCoats;


   public PaintEstimatorModel(){
      regions = new Region[5];
      regionCount = 0;
      indexSelectedRegion = -1;
   }

   public void setSquareFeetPerGallon (double sfpg){
      squareFeetPerGallon = sfpg;
   }

   public void setNumberOfCoats (int noc){
      numberOfCoats = noc;
   }

   public void addRegion (Region rgn){
      if (regionCount == regions.length){
         Region[] temp = new Region[regionCount + 5];
         for (int i = 0; i < regionCount; i++)
            temp[i] = regions[i];
         regions = temp;
      }
      regions[regionCount] = rgn;
      indexSelectedRegion = regionCount;
      regionCount++;
   }

   public double getGallonsOfPaintNeeded(){
      double a = area();
      if (a <= 0 || squareFeetPerGallon <= 0)
```

```java
         return 0;
      else
         return numberOfCoats * a / squareFeetPerGallon;
   }

   private double area(){
      double totalArea = 0;
      for (int i = 0; i < regionCount; i++)
         totalArea += regions[i].area();
      return totalArea;
   }

   public Region getCurrentRegion(){
      if (indexSelectedRegion == -1)
         return null;
      else
         return regions[indexSelectedRegion];
   }

   public int getRegionCount(){
      return regionCount;
   }

   public int getIndexSelectedRegion(){
      return indexSelectedRegion;
   }

   void moveToFirstRegion(){
      if (regionCount == 0)
         indexSelectedRegion = -1;
      else
         indexSelectedRegion = 0;
   }

   void moveToPreviousRegion(){
      // Exercise
   }

   void moveToNextRegion(){
      if (regionCount == 0)
         indexSelectedRegion = -1;
      else
         indexSelectedRegion
            = Math.min (regionCount - 1, indexSelectedRegion + 1);
   }

   void moveToLastRegion(){
      // Exercise
   }

}
```

11.9 Object-Oriented Analysis and Design Guidelines

Now that you are familiar with the major concepts of object-oriented programming, it is time to present some guidelines for object-oriented analysis and design.

Objects: A Universal Means of Representation

Objects can represent just about anything. We have seen examples of computational objects, such as buttons, text fields, menus, strings, and arrays. We have also seen examples of objects that represent "real" things, such as students and employees. Other examples include institutions, everyday objects (furniture, vehicles, animals, etc.), events, abstract concepts, and so on.

Analyzing Objects

Recall that analysis describes what a system will do, whereas design describes how the system will do it. Common sense dictates that analysis comes before design. During object-oriented analysis, we describe the objects or classes that will be used in a system, and we define the roles and responsibilities of each. We attempt to think in terms of objects or classes that are cohesive (i.e., have closely related responsibilities). During object-oriented design, we define the attributes (instance and class variables) and methods of each class. By the way, a class can have many methods and still be cohesive, provided those methods support a cohesive set of responsibilities.

As a rule of thumb, the nouns in the description of a system supply hints about the classes required. Each noun typically corresponds to a class. We must of course discount synonyms and nouns that are extraneous to the problem. If a system involves a natural or organizational hierarchy, the software includes a corresponding class hierarchy. Consider, for instance, a system involving managers, staff, and programmers. It might be realized as a hierarchy of classes rooted in an abstract employee class.

Designing Objects

During design, we start with the classes determined by analysis and add instance variables and methods to each class. Once again, there are some rules of thumb for determining class attributes and methods:

- Nouns in a problem description give a hint about attributes.
- Verbs in a problem description give a hint about methods.

Occasionally, a class is simply a convenient way of organizing a collection of related methods. Java's Math class is a good example, but more typically, a class is organized around related data and the methods needed for their management.

During design, we also determine the relationships among classes in the system. Objects (and their classes) are related in one of the following ways:

- Class A uses class B. This is true if a method of class A sends a message to an object of class B, or if a method of class A creates, receives, or returns an object of class B.

- Class A contains class B (sometimes called the "has-a" relation). This is true if class A defines an attribute (an instance variable) whose type is class B.

- Class A is a subclass of class B (sometimes called the "is-a" relation).

During design, we try to maximize the power of information hiding, inheritance, and polymorphism.

Maximizing Information Hiding

Here are some guidelines for taking advantage of information hiding:

- With the exception of some constants, all instance variables should be declared `private`.

- An object should always initialize its own instance variables when it is created.

- If an instance variable does not need an accessor or a mutator, the class should not provide it.

- If an instance variable should not be changed, it should be declared `final`.

Maximizing Inheritance

The most obvious way to make use of inheritance is to define new classes as subclasses of those already available in the standard Java packages. At other times, we attempt to organize related classes in a hierarchy, often based on an abstract superclass. An abstract class should define the data and methods that the subclasses have in common. Here are some guidelines for taking advantage of inheritance:

- Declare an instance variable or method `protected` when it should be visible to subclasses but not to the rest of the system.

- Declare a method `abstract` (in an abstract class) when that method must be implemented by all subclasses. Declare a method `final` when that method should be inherited but not overridden by any subclass.

- When overriding a superclass method, use `super` to invoke the superclass method when needed.

Maximizing Polymorphism

Use standard names (`draw` for drawing an image, `toString` for returning a string) for methods wherever possible. Provide abstract classes with abstract methods for situations in which you want to establish naming conventions for methods within a class hierarchy.

11.10 Summary

This chapter has explored in depth the ways in which inheritance and polymorphism can be exploited in Java programs. Java classes inherit data and behavior by extending other classes. An abstract class provides a repository of common behavior and data for several subclasses. The keyword `super` is used to run a constructor or other method in a superclass. We also examined the rules for storing different classes of objects in the same array, for assigning an object of one class to a variable of another class, and for passing parameters and returning objects in methods with mixed classes.

11.11 Key Terms

If you have difficulty finding the definitions of any key terms in the body of this chapter, turn to the Glossary at the end of the book.

abstract class   concrete class   overriding
abstract method   final method   polymorphism

11.12 Answers to Self-Test Questions

1. A class hierarchy is a set of classes in which one class is at the root and each class has zero or more subclasses. An example is a taxonomy of animals.

2. The inheriting class uses the syntax `class <name> extends <superclass name>`.

3. An abstract class serves as a repository of data and behavior common to a set of subclasses. Because this class is abstract, it cannot be instantiated. An example is the shape class, which is abstract and defines the behavior common to circles and rectangles.

4. To run a constructor of the same form in the superclass, one uses the form `super (<parameters>)` at the beginning of the corresponding constructor in the subclass.

5. With methods other than constructors, one uses the form `super.<method name> (<parameters>)`.

6. The visibility modifier `protected` allows subclasses in a hierarchy to access instance and class variables or methods of superclasses without allowing other clients in the system to access these items.

7. The method `toString` is polymorphic.

8. A final method cannot be overridden in a subclass. Examples are the accessors for variables that are defined in an abstract class. These methods should not be overridden by subclasses.

9. To locate the right method to execute, the JVM first looks in the class of the receiver object. If the method is not found there, the JVM looks at this class's superclass if there is one. This process is repeated until a method is found or an exception is thrown (if the method is not eventually found in the `Object` class).

10. When a programmer extends an existing class, the new class should at least have a constructor and a `toString` method.

11. Any object can go into an array of objects as long as the class of the new object is the same class or a subclass (descendant) of the array's element class.

12. An object can be assigned to a variable as long as the object's class is the same class as the variable's class or is a subclass (descendant) of the variable's class.

13. The cast operator allows the programmer to convert an object of one class to another class, essentially allowing it to masquerade as another type of object. The cast operator is most often used to convert a variable from a more inclusive class to a less inclusive class before assignment or sending a message. For example, if the `Shape` variable s contains an instance of `Circle`, one must use the cast `(Circle)` s before sending the message to get the radius.

14. The `instanceof` operator returns `true` if its right operand is an instance of its left operand or `false` otherwise. This operator should be used when the programmer must determine which class an object is.

15. `String str = (String) a[3];`

16. The rule for passing a parameter object is the same as the rule for assignment, namely, the class of the actual parameter must be the same as or less inclusive than the class of the formal parameter.

11.13 Programming Problems and Activities

1. Design a hierarchy of classes that models the taxonomy of your favorite region of the animal kingdom. Your hierarchy should be at most three classes deep and should employ abstract classes on the first two levels.

2. Design a hierarchy of classes that represents the taxonomy of artifacts, such as vehicles.

3. Implement the `Cylinder` class discussed in this chapter by moving it outside of the `Shape` hierarchy. An instance of `Circle` should be an instance variable in the `Cylinder` class.

4. Implement the `Cylinder` class discussed in this chapter as a subclass of `Shape`.

5. Discuss the advantages and disadvantages of the implementation strategies used in Programming Problems 3 and 4 of this chapter.

6. Complete the Case Study program of this chapter by finishing the methods marked as exercises.

7. Browse Java's class hierarchy on Sun's Web site (see Appendix A). Write an essay that describes the design ideas underlying a class hierarchy that you find interesting among Java's classes.

8. Redo the blackjack game of Chapter 9, Problem 7, so that the `Dealer` class is a subclass of the `Player` class.

12 Recursion, Complexity, and Searching and Sorting

In this chapter, we introduce three important computer science topics: recursion, complexity analysis, and searching and sorting. These topics are intertwined because searching and sorting involve recursion and complexity analysis. A recursive algorithm is one that is expressed in terms of itself in a manner that appears to be circular. Everyday algorithms, such as how to bake cake or change car oil, are rarely expressed recursively, but recursive algorithms are common in computer science. Complexity analysis is concerned with determining an algorithm's efficiency—that is, how its run time varies as a function of the quantity of data processed. Consider the searching and sorting algorithms presented in Chapter 10. When we test these algorithms on arrays of 10 to 20 elements, they are blindingly fast, but how fast can we expect them to be when the arrays are 100 times larger? Since painting two houses generally takes twice as long as painting one, we might guess that the same linear relationship between size and speed applies equally to sorting algorithms. However, we would be quite wrong, and in this chapter, we will learn techniques for analyzing algorithms more accurately. In later computer science courses, you will study this chapter's topics in greater depth.

12.1 Recursion

When asked to add the integers from 1 to N, we usually think of the process iteratively. We start with 0, add 1, then 2, then 3, and so forth until we reach N, or expressed differently

```
sum(N) = 1 + 2 + 3 + . . . + N, where N >= 1
```

Java's looping constructs make implementing the process easy. There is a completely different way to look at the problem, which at first seems very strange:

```
sum(1) = 1
sum(N) = N + sum(N - 1) if N > 1
```

At first glance, expressing `sum(N)` in terms of `sum(N - 1)` seems to yield a circular definition, but closer examination shows that it does not. Consider, for example, what happens when the definition is applied to the problem of calculating `sum(4)`:

```
sum(4) = 4 + sum(3)
       = 4 + 3 + sum(2)
       = 4 + 3 + 2 + sum(1)
       = 4 + 3 + 2 + 1
```

The fact that `sum(1)` is defined to be 1 without making reference to further invocations of `sum` saves the process from going on forever and the definition from being circular. Functions that are defined in terms of themselves in this way are called *recursive.* Here, for example, are two ways to express the definition of factorial, the first iterative and the second recursive:

1. `factorial(N) = 1 * 2 * 3 * . . . * N, where N >= 1`

2. `factorial(1) = 1`

`factorial(N) = N * factorial(N - 1) if N > 1`

No doubt the iterative definition is more familiar and thus easier to understand than the recursive one; however, such is not always the case. Consider the definition of Fibonacci numbers first encountered in Chapter 4. The first and second numbers in the Fibonacci sequence are 1. Thereafter, each number is the sum of its two immediate predecessors, as follows:

```
1   1   2   3   5   8   13   21   34   55   89   144   233 . . .
```

Or in other words:

```
fibonacci(1) = 1
fibonacci(2) = 1
fibonacci(N) = fibonacci(N - 1) + fibonacci(N - 2) if N > 2
```

This is a recursive definition, and it is hard to imagine how one could express it nonrecursively.

From these examples, we can see that recursion involves two factors. First, some function `f(N)` is expressed in terms of `f(N - 1)` and perhaps `f(N - 2)` and so on. Second, to prevent the definition from being circular, `f(1)` and perhaps `f(2)` and so on are defined explicitly.

Implementing Recursion

Given a recursive definition of some process, it is usually easy to write a ***recursive method*** that implements it. A method is said to be recursive if it calls itself. Let us start with a method that computes factorials.

```
int factorial (int N){
//Precondition N >= 1
    if (N == 1)
        return 1;
    else
        return N * factorial (N - 1);
}
```

For comparison, here is an iterative version of the method. As you can see, it is slightly longer and no easier to understand.

```
int factorial (int N){
    int i, product;
    product = 1;
    for (i = 2; i <= N; i++)
        product = product * i;
    }
    return product;
}
```

As a second example of recursion, here is a method that calculates Fibonacci numbers:

```
int fibonacci (int N){
    if (N <= 2)
        return 1;
    else
        return fibonacci (N - 1) + fibonacci (N - 2);
}
```

Turn back to Chapter 4 to see how difficult it is to write an iterative version of this method.

Tracing Recursive Calls

We can better understand recursion if we trace the sequence of recursive calls and returns that occur in a typical situation. Suppose we want to compute the factorial of 4. We call `factorial(4)`, which in turn calls `factorial(3)`, which in turn calls `factorial(2)`, which in turn calls `factorial(1)`, which returns 1 to factorial(2), which returns 2 to factorial(3), which returns 6 to factorial(4), which returns 24, or in other words:

```
factorial(4)
          calls factorial(3)
                            calls factorial(2)
                                              calls factorial(1)
                                              which returns 1
                            which returns 2*1 or 2
          which returns 3*2 or 6
which returns 4*6 or 24
```

At first, it seems strange to have all these invocations of the factorial method, each in a state of suspended animation, waiting for the completion of the ones further down the line. When the last invocation completes its work, it returns to its predecessor, which completes its work, and so forth up the line, until eventually the original invocation reactivates and finishes the job. Fortunately, we do not have to repeat this dizzying mental exercise every time we use recursion.

Guidelines for Writing Recursive Methods

Just as we must guard against writing infinite loops, so too we must avoid recursions that never come to an end. First, a recursive method must have a well-defined termination or ***stopping state.*** For the factorial method, this was expressed in the lines:

```
if (N == 1)
   return 1;
```

Second, the ***recursive step,*** in which the method calls itself, must eventually lead to the stopping state. For the factorial method, the recursive step was expressed in the lines:

```
else
   return N * factorial(N - 1);
```

Because each invocation of the factorial method is passed a smaller value, eventually the stopping state must be reached. Had we accidentally written

```
else
   return N * factorial(N + 1);
```

the recursion would have run out of control. Eventually, the user would notice and terminate the program, or else the Java interpreter would run out of memory, at which point the program would crash.

Here is a subtler example of a malformed recursive method:

```
int badMethod (int N){
   if (N == 1)
      return 1;
   else
      return N * badMethod(N - 2);
}
```

This method works fine if N is odd, but when N is even, the method passes through the stopping state and keeps on going. For instance,

```
badMethod(4)
  calls badMethod(2)
    calls badMethod(0)
      calls badMethod(-2)
        calls badMethod(-4)
          call badMethod(-6)
             . . .
```

When to Use Recursion

Recursion can always be used in place of iteration, and vice versa. Ignoring the fact that arbitrarily substituting one for the other is pointless and sometimes difficult, the question of which is better to use remains. Recursion involves a method repeatedly calling itself. Executing a method call and the corresponding return statement usually takes longer than incrementing and testing a loop control variable. In addition, a method call ties up some memory that is not freed until the method completes its task. Naïve programmers often state these facts as an argument against ever using recursion. However, there are many situations in which recursion provides the clearest, shortest, and most elegant solution to a programming task, as we shall soon see. As a beginning programmer, you should not be overly concerned about squeezing the last drop of efficiency out of a computer. Instead, you need to master useful programming techniques, and recursion ranks among the best.

We close this section by presenting two well-known and pleasing applications of recursion: the Towers of Hanoi and the Eight Queens problem.

Towers of Hanoi

Many centuries ago in the city of Hanoi, the monks in a certain monastery were continually engaged in what now seems a peculiar enterprise. Sixty-four rings of increasing size had been placed on a vertical wooden peg (Figure 12.1). Beside it were two other pegs, and the monks were attempting to move all the rings from the first to the third peg subject to two constraints:

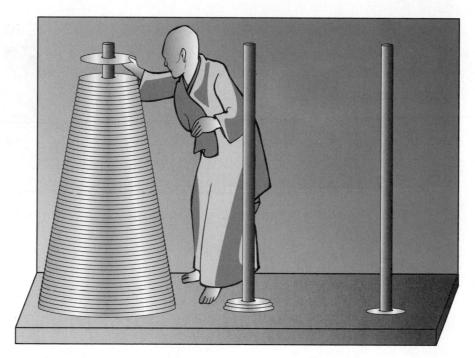

Figure 12.1 The Towers of Hanoi

- only one ring could be moved at a time
- a ring could be moved to any peg, provided it was not placed on top of a smaller ring

The monks believed that the world would end and humankind would be freed from suffering when the task was finally completed. The fact that the world is still here today and you are enduring the frustrations of writing computer programs seems to indicate the monks were interrupted in their work. They were, but even if they had stuck with it, they would not finish anytime soon. A little experimentation should convince you that for N rings, $2^N - 1$ separate moves are required. At the rate of one move per second, $2^{64} - 1$ moves take about 600 billion years.

It might be more practical to harness the incredible processing power of modern computers to move virtual rings between virtual pegs, thus bringing about the end of cyberspace. Just in case you are attracted to this ultimate act of cyber terrorism, we are willing to start you on your way by presenting a recursive algorithm for printing the required moves. In the spirit of moderation, we suggest that you begin by running the program for small values of N. Figure 12.2 shows the result of running the program with three rings. In the output, the rings are numbered from smallest (1) to largest (3). You might try running the program with different numbers of rings and satisfying yourself that the printed output is correct. The number of lines of output corresponds to the formula given earlier.

The program uses a recursive method called move. The first time this method is called, it is asked to move all N rings from peg 1 to peg 3. The method then proceeds

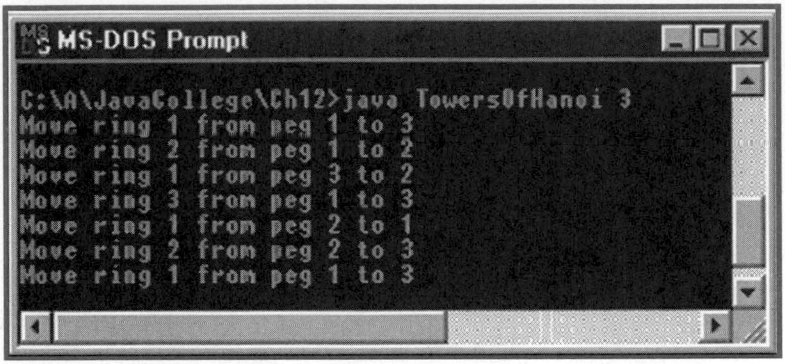

Figure 12.2 Running the `TowersOfHanoi` program with three rings

by calling itself to move the top $N - 1$ rings to peg 2, prints a message to move the largest ring from peg 1 to peg 3, and finally calls itself again to move the $N - 1$ rings from peg 2 to peg 3. Here is the listing:

```
/* TowersOfHanoi.java
Print the moves required to move the rings in the Towers of Hanoi problem.
1) Enter the number of rings as a command line parameter.
2) WARNING: Do not run this program with 64 rings.
*/

public class TowersOfHanoi {

   public static void main (String [] args) {
   //Obtain the number of rings from the first command line parameter.
   //Call the recursive move method to move the rings from peg 1 to peg 3
   //with peg 2 available for intermediate usage.
   //   Preconditions  -- number of rings != 64
   //   Postconditions -- the moves are printed in the terminal window

      int numberOfRings = Integer.valueOf (args[0]).intValue();
      move (numberOfRings, 1, 3, 2);
   }

   static void move (int n, int i, int j, int k){
   //Print the moves for n rings going from peg i to peg j
   //   Preconditions  -- none
   //   Postconditions -- the moves have been printed

      if (n > 0){                     //Stopping state is n == 0

         //Move the n - 1 smaller rings from peg i to peg k
         move (n - 1, i, k, j);
```

```
      //Move the largest ring from peg i to peg j
      System.out.println("Move ring " + n + " from peg " + i + " to " + j);

      //Move the n - 1 smaller rings from peg k to peg j
      move (n - 1, k, j, i);

      //n rings have now been moved from peg i to peg j.
    }
  }
}
```

Eight Queens Problem

The Eight Queens problem consists of placing eight queens on a chessboard in such a manner that the queens do not threaten each other. A queen can attack any other piece in the same row, column, or diagonal, so there can be at most one queen in each row, column, and diagonal of the board. It is not obvious that there is a solution, but the dimensions of a chessboard are 8×8 so there might be one. We now present a program that attempts to solve this problem and others of a similar nature. We call it the ManyQueens program, and it attempts to place N queens safely on an $N \times N$ board. The program either prints a solution or a message saying that there is none (Figure 12.3).

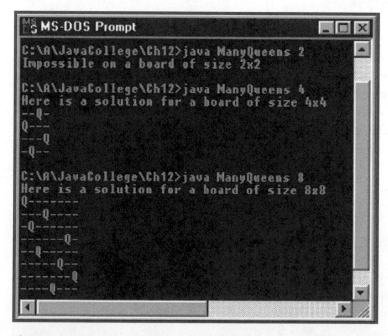

Figure 12.3 Output of the ManyQueens program for boards of size 2, 4, and 8

At the heart of the program is a recursive method called `canPlaceQueen`. Initially, the board is empty, and the first time the method is called, it places a queen at the top of column 1. It then calls itself to place a queen in the first safe square of column 2 and then again to place a queen in the first safe square of column 3 and so forth, until finally it calls itself to place a queen in the first safe square of the last column. If at some step (say, for column 5) the method fails, then it returns and processing resumes in the previous column by looking for the next safe square. If there is one, then onward to column 5 again or else back to column 3. And so it goes. Either a solution is found or all possibilities are exhausted. The program includes a second method called `attacked`. It determines if a queen placed in row r, column c is threatened by any queens already present in columns 1 to $c - 1$. Here is the code:

```
/* ManyQueens.java
Determine the solution to the many queens problem for a chessboard
of any size.
1) There is a single command line parameter indicating the size of the board.
2) If there is a solution display it else indicate that there is none.
*/

public class ManyQueens {

    public static void main (String [] args) {
    //Process the command line parameter. Call a recursive function
    //to determine if there is a solution. Print the results.
    //   Preconditions  -- the command line parameter is an integer greater
    //                      than or equal to 1
    //   Postconditions -- display a solution or a message stating that there
    //                      is none

        int i, j;           //Indices indicating board positions
        int boardSize;      //The size of the board, for instance, 8 would
                            //indicate an 8x8 board
        boolean[][] board;  //A two dimensional array representing the board.
                            //An entry of false indicates that a square is
                            //unoccupied.

        //Initialize the variables
        boardSize = Integer.valueOf (args[0]).intValue();
        board = new boolean[boardSize][boardSize];
        for (i = 0; i < boardSize; i++)
            for (j = 0; j < boardSize; j++)
                board[i][j] = false;

        //Determine if there is a solution
        if (! canPlaceQueen (0, board))

            //There is no solution
```

```
            System.out.println ("Impossible on a board of size " +
                               boardSize + "x" + boardSize);

      else{

         //There is a solution, so print it
         System.out.println ("Here is a solution for a board of size " +
                               boardSize + "x" + boardSize);
         for (i = 0; i < boardSize; i++){
            for (j = 0; j < boardSize; j++){
               if (board[i][j])
                  System.out.print ("Q");
               else
                  System.out.print ("-");
            }
            System.out.println();
         }

      }
}


static boolean canPlaceQueen (int col, boolean[][] board){
//Mark as true the first unattacked location in column col that
//permits a solution across the remaining columns.
//  Preconditions  -- 0 <= col < board.length
//  Postconditions -- if an entry in col gets marked true
//                     return true else return false

   int i;
   for (i = 0; i < board.length; i++){ //Iterate down the column
      if (! attacked (i, col, board)){ // if square is not under attack
         if (col == board.length -1){  //  if this is the last column
            board[i][col] = true;       //   end recursion! set square true
            return true;                //   recursive ascent true
         }else{                         //  else
            board[i][col] = true;       //   trial solution, set square true
                                        //   if recursive descent succeeds
            if (canPlaceQueen (col + 1, board))
               return true;             //    recursive ascent true
            else                        //   else
               board[i][col] = false;   //    trial solution didn't work
         }                              //   end if
      }                                 //  end if
   }
   return false;                        //  recursive ascent false
}


static boolean attacked (int row, int col, boolean[][] board){
```

Continues

Continued

```
//Determine if the square at location (row, col) is under attack.
//from any queen in columns 0 to col - 1
//   Preconditions  -- 0 <= row, col < board.length
//   Postconditions -- returns true if square under attack else false

   //Look for horizontal attack
   int i, j, k;
   for (j = 0; j < col; j++){
      if (board[row][j])
         return true;
   }


   //Look for attack from a descending diagonal
   i = row -- 1;
   j = col -- 1;
   for (k = 0; k <= Math.min(i, j); k++){
      if (board[i][j])
         return true;
      else{
         i--;
         j--;
      }
   }

   //Look for attack from an ascending diagonal
   i = row + 1;
   j = col - 1;
   for (k = 0; k <= Math.min(board.length - i - 1, j); k++){
      if (board[i][j])
         return true;
      else{
         i++;
         j--;
      }
   }

   return false;
   }
}
```

Self-Test Questions

1. What keeps a recursive definition from being circular?
2. What are the two parts of any recursive method?
3. Why is recursion more expensive than iteration?

4. What are the benefits of using recursion?

5. Consider the following definition of the method `raise`, which raises a given number to a given exponent:

```
int raise(int base, int expo){
   if (expo == 0)
      return 1;
   else
      return base * raise(base, expo - 1);
}
```

Draw a trace of the complete execution of `raise(2, 5)`.

6. Consider the following method:

```
int whatAMethod(int n){
   if (n == 0)
      return 1;
   else
      return whatAMethod(n);
}
```

What happens during the execution of `whatAMethod(3)`?

CS Capsule: Recursion Need Not Be Expensive

We have seen that the use of recursion has two costs: Extra time and extra memory are required to manage recursive function calls. These costs have led some to argue that recursion should never be used in programs. However, as Guy Steele has shown (in "Debunking the 'Expensive Procedure Call' Myth," *Proceedings of the National Conference of the ACM*, 1977), some systems can run recursive algorithms as if they were iterative ones, with no additional overhead. The key condition is to write a special kind of recursive algorithm called a ***tail-recursive*** algorithm. An algorithm is tail-recursive if no work is done in the algorithm after a recursive call. For example, according to this criterion, the factorial method that we presented earlier is not tail-recursive because a multiplication is performed after each recursive call. We can convert this version of the factorial method to a tail-recursive version by performing the multiplication before each recursive call. To do this, we will need an additional parameter that passes the accumulated value of the factorial down on each recursive call. In the last call of the method, this value is returned as the result:

```
int tailRecursiveFactorial (int N, int result){
   if (N == 1)
      return result;
   else
      return tailRecursiveFactorial (N - 1, N * result);
}
```

Note that the multiplication is performed before the recursive call of the method—that is, when the parameters are evaluated. On the initial call to the method, the value of `result` should be 1:

```
int factorial (int n){
   return tailRecursiveFactorial (n, 1);
}
```

Steele showed that a smart compiler can translate tail-recursive code in a high-level language to a loop in machine language. The machine code treats the method's parameters as variables associated with a loop and generates an *iterative process* rather than a recursive one. Thus, there is no linear growth of method calls, and extra stack memory is not required to run tail-recursive methods on these systems.

The catch is that a programmer must be able to convert a recursive method to a tail-recursive method and find a compiler that generates iterative machine code from tail-recursive methods. Unfortunately, some methods are difficult or impossible to convert to tail-recursive versions, and the needed optimizations are not part of most standard compilers. If you find that your Java compiler supports this optimization, you should try converting some methods to tail-recursive versions and see if they run faster than the original versions.

12.2 Complexity Analysis

There is an important question we should ask about every method we write. What is the effect on the method of increasing the quantity of data processed? Does doubling the data double the method's execution time, triple it, quadruple it, or have no effect? This type of examination is called *complexity analysis.* Let us consider some examples.

Sum Methods

First, consider the `sum` method presented in Chapter 10. This method processes an array whose size can be varied. To determine the method's execution time, beside each statement we place a symbol (`t1`, `t2`, etc.) that indicates the time needed to execute the statement. Because we have no way of knowing what these times really are, we can do no better.

```
int sum (int[] a){
   int i, result;
   result = 0;                          // Assignment: time = t1
   for (i = 0; i < a.length; i++){      // Overhead for going once around the
                                        // loop: time = t2
      result += a[i];                   // Assignment: time = t3
   }
   return result;                       // Return: time = t4
}
```

Adding these times together and remembering that the method goes around the loop *n* times, where *n* represents the array's size, yields:

```
executionTime
    = t1 + n*(t2 + t3) + t4
    = k1 + n*k2              where k1 and k2 are method-dependent
                            constants
    ≅ n*k2                   for large values of n
```

Thus, the execution time is linearly dependent on the array's length, and as the array's length increases, the contribution of `k1` becomes negligible. Consequently, we can say with reasonable accuracy that doubling the length of the array doubles the execution time of the method. Computer scientists express this linear relationship between the array's length and execution time using **big-O notation**:

```
executionTime = O(n).
```

Or phrased slightly differently, the execution time is of order *n*. Observe that from the perspective of big-O notation, we make no distinction between a method whose execution time is

```
1000000 + 1000000*n
```

and one whose execution time is

```
n/1000000
```

although from a practical perspective the difference is enormous.

Complexity analysis can also be applied to recursive methods. Here is a recursive version of the `sum` method. It too is O(*n*).

```
int sum (int[] a, int i){
    if (i >= a.length)          // Comparison: t1
        return 0;               // Return: t2
    else
        return a[i] + sum (a, i + 1);   // Call and return: t3
}
```

The method is called initially with `i` = 0. A single activation of the method takes time

```
t1 + t2      if  i >= a.length
```

and

```
t1 + t3      if  i < a.length.
```

The first case occurs once and the second case occurs the `a.length` times that the method calls itself recursively. Thus, if n equals `a.length`, then

```
executionTime
    = t1 + t2 + n*(t1 + t3)
    = k1 + n*k2              where k1 and k2 are method-dependent
                            constants
    = O(n)
```

Other O(*n*) Methods

Several of the other array processing methods presented in Chapter 10 are O(*n*). Here is the `search` method:

```
int search (int[] a, int searchValue){
    int location;
    location = -1;                      // Assignment: t1
    for (i = 0; i < a.length; i++){     // Loop overhead: t2
        if (a[i] == searchValue){       // Comparison: t3

            location = i;               // Assignment and break: t4
            break;                      //
        }
    }
    return location;                    // Return: t5
}
```

The analysis of the `search` method is slightly more complex than that of the `sum` method. Each time through the loop, a comparison is made. If and when a match is found, an assignment is made and the method breaks out of the loop. If we assume that the search is usually made for values present in the array, then on average we can expect that half the elements in the array are examined before a match is found. Putting all of this together yields:

```
executionTime
    = t1 + (n/2)*(t2 + t3) + t4 + t5
    = k1 + n*k2              where k1 and k2 are method-dependent
                            constants
    = O(n)
```

Now let us look at a method that processes a two-dimensional array:

```
int[] sumRows (int[][] a){
    int i, j;
    int[] rowSum = new int[a.length];       // Instantiation: t1
    for (i = 0; i < a.length; i++){         // Loop overhead: t2
        for (j = 0; j < a[i].length; j++){  // Loop overhead: t3
            rowSum[i] += a[i][j];           // Assignment: t4
        }
    }
    return rowSum;                          // Return: t5
}
```

Let n represent the total number of elements in the array and r the number of rows. For the sake of simplicity, we assume that each row has the same number of elements, say, c. The execution time can be written as:

```
executionTime
    = t1 + r*(t2 + c*(t3 + t4)) + t5
    = (k1 + n*k2) + (n/c)*t2 + n*(t3 + t4) + t5        where r = n/c
    = (k1 + n*k2) + n*(t2/c + t3 + t4) + t5
    = k2 + n*k3                        where k1, k2, k3, and k4 are constants
    = O(n)
```

Notice that we have replaced t1 by (k1 + n*k2). This is based on the perhaps unreasonable assumption that the JVM can allocate a block of memory for the array rowSum in constant time (k1) followed by the time needed to initialize all entries to zero (n*k2).

An $O(n^2)$ Method

Not all array processing methods are $O(n)$, as an examination of the sort method reveals.

```java
void sort (int[] a){
    int i, j;
    int temp;

    for (i = 0; i < a.length - 1; i++){   // Loop overhead: t1
        for (j = i+1; j < a.length; j++){ // Loop overhead: t2
            if (a[j] < a[i]){             // Comparison: t3

                temp = a[j];              // Assignments = t4
                a[j] = a[i];              //
                a[i] = temp;              //
            }
        }
    }
}
```

The outer loop of the sort method executes $n - 1$ times, where n is the length of the array. Each time the inner loop is activated, it iterates a different number of times. On the first activation, it iterates $n - 1$ times, on the second $n - 2$, and so on, until on the last activation it iterates once. Thus, the average number of iterations is $n / 2$. On some iterations, elements a[i] and a[j] are interchanged in time t4, and on other iterations, they are not. So on the average iteration, let's say time t5 is spent doing an interchange. The execution time of the method can now be expressed as:

```
executionTime
    = t1 + (n-1)*(t1 + (n/2)*(t2 + t3 + t5))
    = t1 + n*t1 - t1 + (n*n/2)(t2 + t3 + t5) - (n/2)*(t2 + t3 + t5)
    = k1 + n*k2 + n*n*k3
    ≅ n*n*k3                        for large values of n
    = O(n²)
```

Common Big-O Values

We have already seen several methods that are O(n) and one that is O(n^2). These are just two of the most frequently encountered big-O values. Table 12.1 lists common big-O values together with their names.

Table 12.1

Names of Some Common Big-O Values	
Big-O Value	**Name**
O(1)	Constant
O(log n)	Logarithmic
O(n)	Linear
O(n log n)	n log n
O(n^2)	Quadratic
O(n^3)	Cubic
O(2^n)	Exponential

As an example of O(1), consider a method that returns the sum of the first and last numbers in an array. This method's execution time is independent of the array's length. In other words, it takes constant time. Later in the chapter, we will see examples of methods that are logarithmic and n log n.

The values in Table 12.1 are listed from "best" to "worst." For example, given two methods that perform the same task, but in different ways, we tend to prefer the one that is O(n) over the one that is O(n^2). This statement requires some elaboration. For instance, suppose that the exact run time of two methods is

```
10,000 + 400n        // method 1
```

and

```
10,000 + n²          // method 2
```

For small values of n, method 2 is faster than method 1; however, and this is the important point, for all values of n larger than a certain threshold, method 1 is faster. The threshold in this example is 400. So if you know ahead of time that n will always be less than 400, you are advised to use method 2, but if n will have a large range of values, method 1 is superior.

To get a feeling for how the common big-O values vary with n, consider Table 12.2. We use base 10 logarithms. This table vividly demonstrates that a method might be useful for small values of n, but totally worthless for large values. Clearly, methods that take exponential time have limited value, even if it were possible to run them on the world's most powerful computer for billions of years. Unfortunately, there are many important problems for which even the best algorithms take exponential time.

You can achieve lasting fame by being the first person to replace one of these exponential time algorithms with one that takes less than exponential time.

Table 12.2

How Big-O Values Vary Depending on n							
n	1	log n	n	n log n	n^2	n^3	2^n
10	1	1	10	10	100	1,000	1,024
100	1	2	100	200	10,000	1,000,000	$\cong$ 1.3 e30
1,000	1	3	1,000	3,000	1,000,000	1,000,000,000	$\cong$ 1.1 e301

By the way, from the perspective of complexity analysis, we do not need to distinguish between base 2 and base 10 logarithms because they differ by only a constant factor:

```
log₂ n = log₁₀ n * log₂ 10
```

An O(r^n) Method

We have seen two algorithms for computing Fibonacci numbers, one iterative and the other recursive. The iterative algorithm presented in Chapter 4 is O(n). However, the much simpler recursive algorithm presented earlier in this chapter is O(r^n), where $r \cong$ 1.62. While O(r^n) is better than O(2^n), it is still exponential. It is beyond the book's scope to prove that the recursive algorithm is O(r^n). Nonetheless, it is easy to demonstrate that the number of recursive calls increases rapidly with n. For instance, Figure 12.4 shows the calls involved when we use the recursive method to compute the sixth Fibonacci number. To keep the diagram reasonably compact, we write (6) instead of fibonacci(6). Table 12.3 shows the number of calls as a function of n.

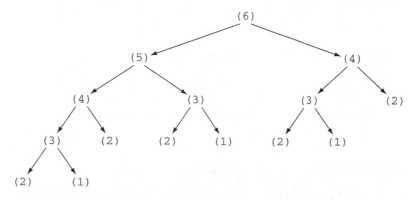

Figure 12.4 Calls needed to compute the sixth Fibonacci number recursively

Table 12.3

Calls Needed to Compute the *n*th Fibonacci Number Recursively	
n	Calls Needed to Compute *n*th Fibonacci Number
2	1
4	5
8	41
16	1973
32	4356617

The values in the table were obtained by running the following program:

```
public class Tester{
   static int count;

   public static void main (String[] args){
      int i, fibn, n;
      for (i = 1; i <= 5; i++){
         count = 0;
         n = (int)Math.pow(2,i);
         fibn = fibonacci(n);
         System.out.println ("" + n + ":" + count);
      }
   }

   static int fibonacci (int n){
      count++;
      if (n <= 2)
         return 1;
      else
         return fibonacci(n - 1) + fibonacci(n - 2);
   }
}
```

Programs such as this are frequently useful for gaining an empirical sense of an algorithm's efficiency.

Self-Test Questions

7. Using big-O notation, state the time complexity of the following recursive methods:

a. `factorial`

b. `raise` (see Question 5)

8. Recursive methods use stack space. Using big-O notation, state the space complexity of the following recursive methods:

a. `factorial`

b. `fibonacci`

9. State the time complexity of the following sort method:

```
void sort(int[] a){
    for (int j = 0; j < a.length() - 1; ++j)
    {
        int minIndex = j;
        for (int k = j + 1; k < a.length(); ++k)
            if (a[k] < a[minIndex])
                minIndex = k;
        if (minIndex != j){
            int temp = a[j];
            a[j] = a[minIndex];
            a[minIndex] = temp;
        }
    }
}
```

12.3 Binary Search

Searching is such a common activity that it is important to do it quickly. The search method presented earlier started at the beginning of an array and looked at consecutive elements until either the search value was located or the array's end was encountered. Imagine using this technique to find a number by hand in a list of 1 million entries. It would take forever.

Alternatively, if we know in advance that the list is in ascending order, we can quickly zero in on the search value or determine that it is absent using the **binary search algorithm.** We shall see that this algorithm is O(log *n*).

We start by looking at the middle of the list. We might be lucky and find the search value immediately. If not, we know whether to continue the search in the first or the second half of the list. Now we reapply the technique repeatedly. At each step, we reduce the search region by a factor of 2. Soon we must either find the search value or narrow the search down to a single element. A list of 1 million entries involves at most 20 steps.

Figures 12.5 illustrates the binary search algorithm. We are looking for the number 320. At each step we highlight the sublist that might still contain 320. Also at each step, all the numbers are invisible except the one in the middle of the sublist, which is the one that we are comparing to 320.

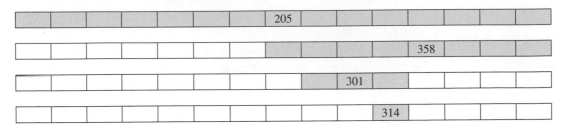

Figure 12.5 Binary search algorithm

After only four steps, we have determined that 320 is not in the list. Had the search value been 205, 358, 301, or 314 we would have located it in four or fewer steps. The binary search algorithm is guaranteed to search a list of 15 sorted elements in a maximum of four steps. Incidentally, the list with all the numbers visible looks like Figure 12.6.

15	36	87	95	100	110	194	205	297	301	314	358	451	467	486

Figure 12.6 Binary search algorithm list with all the numbers visible

Table 12.4 shows the relationship between a list's length and the maximum number of steps needed to search the list. To obtain the numbers in the second column, add 1 to the larger numbers in the first column and take the logarithm base 2. Hence, a method that implements a binary search is $O(\log n)$.

Table 12.4

Maximum Number of Steps Needed to Search Lists of Various Sizes

Binary Search Algorithm	
Length of List	**Maximum Number of Steps Needed**
1	1
2 to 3	2
4 to 7	3
8 to 15	4
16 to 31	5
32 to 63	6
64 to 127	7
128 to 255	8
256 to 511	9
512 to 1023	10
1024 to 2047	11
2^n to $2^{n+1} - 1$	$n + 1$

We now present two versions of the binary search algorithm, one iterative and one recursive, and both O(log *n*). We will forgo a formal analysis of the complexity. First, the iterative version:

```
// Iterative binary search of an ascending array
int search (int[] a, int searchValue){
    int left, middle, right;
    left = 0;
    right = a.length - 1;
    while (left <= right){
        middle = (left + right) / 2;
        if (a[middle] == searchValue)
            return middle;
        else if (a[middle] < searchValue)
            left = middle + 1;
        else
            right = middle - 1;
    }
    return -1;
}
```

Figure 12.7 illustrates an iterative search for 320 in the list of 15 elements. L, M, and R are abbreviations for `left`, `middle`, and `right`. At each step, the figure shows how these variables change. Because 320 is absent from the list, eventually (`left > right`) and the method returns –1.

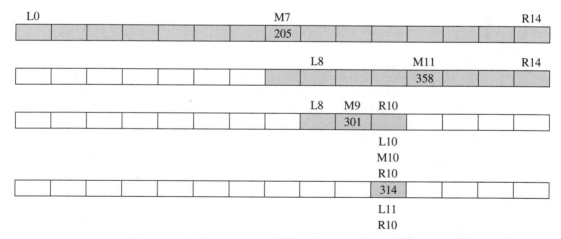

Figure 12.7 Steps in an iterative binary search for the number 320

Now for the recursive version of the algorithm:

```
// Recursive binary search of an ascending array
int search (int[] a, int searchValue, int left, int right){
```

Continues

Continued

```
   int middle;
   if (left > right)
      return -1;
   else{
      middle = (left + right) / 2;
      if (a[middle] == searchValue)
         return middle;
      else if (a[middle] < searchValue)
         return search (a, searchValue, middle+1, right);
      else
         return search (a, searchValue, left, middle-1);
   }
}
```

At heart, the two versions are similar, and they use the variables `left`, `middle`, and `right` in the same way. We conclude the discussion by showing how the two methods are called:

```
int[] a = {15,36,87,95,100,110,194,205,297,301,314,358,451,467,486};
int x = 320;
int location;

location = search (a, x);                  // Iterative version
location = search (a, x, 0, a.length-1); // Recursive version
```

Self-Test Questions

10. The efficiency of the method `raise` in Question 5 can be improved by the following changes. If the exponent is even, then raise the base to the exponent divided by 2 and return the square of this number. Otherwise, the exponent is odd, so raise the number as before. Rewrite the method `raise` using this strategy.

11. Draw a trace of the complete execution of `raise(2, 10)` as defined in Question 10.

12. What is the time complexity of `raise` in Question 10?

12.4 Quicksort

The bubble sort presented in Chapter 9 is $O(n^2)$. There are a number of variations on the algorithm, some of which are marginally faster, but they too are $O(n^2)$. In contrast, there are also several much better algorithms that are $O(n \log n)$. *Quicksort* is one of the simplest of these. The general idea behind quicksort is this: Break an array into two parts and then move elements around so that all the larger values are in one end and all the smaller values are in the other. Each of the two parts is then subdivided in the same manner and so on until the subparts contain only a single value, at which point the array is sorted. To illustrate the process, suppose an unsorted array, called a, looks like Figure 12.8.

Figure 12.8

| 5 | 12 | 3 | 11 | 2 | 7 | 20 | 10 | 8 | 4 | 9 |

Phase 1

1. If the length of the array is less than 2, then done.

2. Locate the value in the middle of the array and call it the **pivot.** The pivot is 7 in this example.

Figure 12.9

| 5 | 12 | 3 | 11 | 2 | **7** | 20 | 10 | 8 | 4 | 9 |

3. Tag the elements at the left and right ends of the array as i and j, respectively.

Figure 12.10

| 5 | 12 | 3 | 11 | 2 | 7 | 20 | 10 | 8 | 4 | 9 |
| i | | | | | | | | | | j |

4. While a[i] <= pivot value, increment i.
While a[j] >= pivot value, decrement j:

Figure 12.11

| 5 | 12 | 3 | 11 | 2 | 7 | 20 | 10 | 8 | 4 | 9 |
| | i | | | | | | | | j | |

5. If i > j, then
   end the phase
else
   interchange a[i] and a[j]:

Figure 12.12

| 5 | 4 | 3 | 11 | 2 | 7 | 20 | 10 | 8 | 12 | 9 |
| | i | | | | | | | | j | |

6. Increment i and decrement j.
If i > j, then end the phase:

Figure 12.13

| 5 | 4 | 3 | 11 | 2 | **7** | 20 | 10 | 8 | 12 | 9 |
| | | i | | | | | | j | | |

7. Repeat step 4; that is,
   While a[i] < pivot value, increment i.
   While a[j] > pivot value, decrement j:

Figure 12.14

| 5 | 4 | 3 | 11 | 2 | 7 | 20 | 10 | 8 | 12 | 9 |
| | | | i | | j | | | | | |

8. Repeat step 5; that is,
   If i > j, then
      end the phase
   else
      interchange a[i] and a[j]:

Figure 12.15

5	4	3	7	2	11	20	10	8	12	9
			i		j					

9. Repeat step 6; that is
   Increment i and decrement j.
   If i > j, then end the phase:

Figure 12.16

5	4	3	7	2	11	20	10	8	12	9
				ij						

10. Repeat step 4; that is,
   While a[i] < pivot value, increment i.
   While a[j] > pivot value, decrement j:

Figure 12.17

5	4	3	7	2	11	20	10	8	12	9
				j	i					

11. Repeat step 5; that is,
   If i > j, then
      end the phase
   else
      interchange a[i] and a[j].

12. This ends the phase. Split the array into the two subarrays a[0...j] and a[i...10]. For clarity, the left subarray is shaded. Notice that all the elements in the left subarray are less than or equal to the pivot, and those in the right are greater than or equal.

Figure 12.18

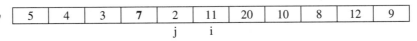

5	4	3	7	2	11	20	10	8	12	9

Phase 2 and Onward

Reapply the process to the left and right subarrays and then divide each subarray in two and so on until the subarrays have lengths of at most one.

Complexity Analysis

We now present an informal analysis of the quicksort's complexity. During phase 1, i and j moved toward each other. At each move, either an array element is compared to the pivot or an interchange takes place. As soon as i and j pass each other, the process stops. Thus, the amount of work during phase 1 is proportional to *n*, the array's length.

The amount of work in phase 2 is proportional to the left subarray's length plus the right subarray's length, which together yield *n*. And when these subarrays are divided, there are four pieces whose combined length is *n*, so the combined work is proportional to *n* yet again. At successive phases, the array is divided into more pieces, but the total work remains proportional to *n*.

To complete the analysis, we need to determine how many times the arrays are subdivided. We will make the optimistic assumption that each time the dividing line turns out to be as close to the center as possible. In practice, this is not usually the case. We already know from our discussion of the binary search algorithm that when we divide an array in half repeatedly, we arrive at a single element in about $\log_2 n$ steps. Thus, the algorithm is $O(n \log n)$ in the best case. In the worst case, the algorithm is $O(n^2)$.

Implementation

The quicksort algorithm can be coded using either an iterative or a recursive approach, but because we have described it recursively, we might as well implement it that way too.

```
void sort (int[] a, int left, int right){
   int i, j, pivotValue, temp;

   if (left >= right) return;

   i = left;
   j = right;
   pivotValue = a[(left + right)/2];
   while (i < j){
      while (a[i] < pivotValue) i++;
      while (pivotValue < a[j]) j--;
      if (i <= j){
         temp = a[i];
         a[i] = a[j];
         a[j] = temp;
         i++;
         j--;
      }
   }
   sort (a, left, j);
   sort (a, i, right);
}
```

Self-Test Questions

13. Describe the strategy of quicksort and explain why it can reduce the time complexity of sorting to $O(n \log n)$.

14. Why is quicksort not O(*n* log *n*) in all cases? Describe the worst-case situation for quicksort.

15. Describe three strategies for selecting a pivot value in quicksort.

12.5 Case Study: Comparing Sort Algorithms

For the benefit of those who are unconvinced by mathematical analysis, we now develop a program that compares the speed of our two sort algorithms.

Request. Write a program that allows the user to compare sort algorithms.

Analysis. The program compares bubble sort and quicksort. Because quicksort runs so much more quickly than bubble sort, we do not run both sorts on the same array. Instead, we run quicksort on an array that is 100 times longer than the array used with bubble sort. Also, because we have already compared these algorithms by counting their operations, we record run times and compare these instead. The proposed interface is shown in Figure 12.19. The user enters the size of the array of integers and clicks the **Sort** button. The program then performs these actions:

1. Loads two arrays with randomly generated integers ranging from 0 to 100,000. One array is of the size specified by the user, and the other array is 100 times that size.

2. Runs the bubble sort algorithm on the smaller array and the quicksort algorithm on the larger array, and records the run times of each sort in milliseconds.

3. Displays the array sizes and run times for each sort in labeled columns.

Design. The bubble sort and quicksort algorithms have already been presented in this text. There are two other primary tasks to consider:

1. Load an array with randomly generated numbers.

2. Obtain the run time of a sort.

We accomplish the first task by using the expression `(int)(Math.random() * (100000))` to generate the integer assigned to each cell in an array.

We accomplish the second task by using Java's `Date` class, as defined in the package `java.util`. When the program creates a new instance of `Date`, this object contains the current date down to the nearest millisecond, on the computer's clock. Thus, one can record the date at the beginning and end of any process by creating two `Date` objects, as follows:

```
Date d1 = new Date();   // Record the date at the start of a process.
<run any process>
Date d2 = new Date();   // Record the date at the end of a process.
```

To obtain the elapsed time between these two dates, one can use the `Date` instance method `getTime()`. This method returns the number of milliseconds from

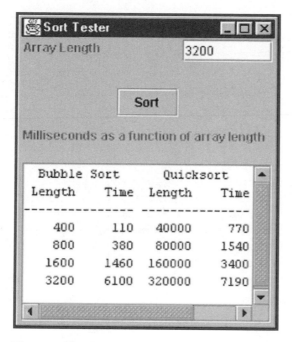

Figure 12.19 How run time varies with array length for bubble sort on the left and quicksort on the right

January 1, 1970, 00:00:00 GMT until the given date. Thus, the elapsed time in milliseconds for the example process can be computed as:

```
long elapsedTime = d2.getTime() - d1.getTime();
```

Implementation. To obtain the neatly formatted output shown in Figure 12.6, it is necessary to use the Format class as explained in Section 8.5. Here is the listing:

```
import javax.swing.*;
import java.util.*;
import BreezySwing.*;

public class ComparingSortAlgorithms extends GBFrame{

   JLabel arrayLengthLabel = addLabel ("Array Length",1,1,1,1);
   IntegerField arrayLengthField = addIntegerField (0,1,2,1,1);

   JButton sortButton = addButton("Sort",2,1,3,1);

   JLabel resultsLabel
```

Continues

Continued

```
          = addLabel ("Milliseconds as a function of array length",3,1,3,1);
   JTextArea resultsTextArea = addTextArea ("Area",4,1,3,4);

   public ComparingSortAlgorithms(){
      setTitle ("Sort Tester");

      //Set the text to column headers
      String str = Format.justify ('L', "  Bubble Sort", 15)
               + Format.justify ('L', "    Quicksort", 16) + "\n"
               + Format.justify ('R', "Length", 7)
               + Format.justify ('R', "Time", 8)
               + Format.justify ('R', "Length", 8)
               + Format.justify ('R', "Time", 8) + "\n"
               + Format.justify ('R', "---------------", 15)
               + Format.justify ('R', "---------------", 16) + "\n";
      resultsTextArea.setText (str);
   }


   public void buttonClicked (JButton buttonObj){

      //Get the array length and instantiate two arrays,
      //one of this length and the other a 100 times longer.
      int arrayLength = arrayLengthField.getNumber();
      int[] a1 = new int[arrayLength];
      int[] a2 = new int[arrayLength*100];

      //Initialize the first array
      for (int i = 0; i < a1.length; i++)
         a1[i] = (int)(Math.random() * (100000));
            // Random numbers between 0 and 100,000

      //Initialize the second array
      for (int i = 0; i < a2.length; i++){
         a2[i] = (int)(Math.random() * (100000));
      }

      //Declare timers
      Date d1, d2;
      long elapsedTime1, elapsedTime2;

      //Time bubble sort
      d1 = new Date();
      bubbleSort (a1);
      d2 = new Date();
```

```
      elapsedTime1 = d2.getTime() - d1.getTime();

      //Time quick sort
      d1 = new Date();
      quickSort (a2, 0, a2.length - 1);
      d2 = new Date();
      elapsedTime2 = (d2.getTime() - d1.getTime());

      //Display results in text area
      resultsTextArea.append
         ( Format.justify ('R', "" + arrayLength, 7)
         + Format.justify ('R', "" + elapsedTime1, 8)
         + Format.justify ('R', "" + arrayLength*100, 8)
         + Format.justify ('R', "" + elapsedTime2, 8) + "\n");
   }

   private void bubbleSort (int[] a){
   //Exchange sort
      for (int i = 0; i < a.length - 1; i++){
         for (int j = i + 1; j < a.length; j++){
            if (a[i] > a[j]){
               int temp = a[i];
               a[i] = a[j];
               a[j] = temp;
            }
         }
      }
   }

   private void quickSort (int[] a, int left, int right){
   //Quick sort
      int i, j, pivotValue, temp;

      if (left >= right) return;

      i = left;
      j = right;
      pivotValue = a[(left + right)/2];
      while (i < j){
         while (a[i] < pivotValue) i++;
         while (pivotValue < a[j]) j--;
         if (i <= j){
            temp = a[i];
            a[i] = a[j];
            a[j] = temp;
```

Continued

```
        i++;
        j--;
    }
  }
  quickSort (a, left, j);
  quickSort (a, i, right);
  return;
}

public static void main (String[] args){
    ComparingSortAlgorithms tpo = new ComparingSortAlgorithms();
    tpo.setSize (250, 300);
    tpo.setVisible(true);
  }
}
```

12.6 Design, Testing, and Debugging Hints

- When designing a recursive method, be sure that
    1. The method has a well-defined stopping state.
    2. The method has a recursive step that changes the size of the data so that the stopping state will eventually be reached.
- Recursive methods can be easier to write correctly than the equivalent iterative methods.
- More efficient code is usually more complex than less efficient code. Thus, it may be harder to write more efficient code correctly than less efficient code. Thus, before trying to make your code more efficient, you should demonstrate, through analysis, that the proposed improvement is really significant; for example, you will get $O(n \log n)$ behavior rather than $O(n^2)$ behavior.

12.7 Summary

This chapter has introduced several principal topics in computer science—recursion, complexity analysis, and sorting and searching. We examined the design and implementation of several classes of recursive algorithms, such as factorial and Fibonacci. We then explored two more complex and realistic uses of recursion in solving the Towers of Hanoi problem and the Eight Queens problem. This discussion led naturally into a discussion of analytical measurements of the run time of algorithms using big-O notation. Recursion and complexity analysis were further employed in an examination of improved sorting and searching algorithms.

12.8 Key Terms

If you have difficulty finding the definitions of any key terms in the body of this chapter, turn to the Glossary at the end of the book.

big-O notation	quicksort	recursive step
binary search algorithm	recursion	stopping state
complexity analysis	recursive definition	tail-recursive
iterative process	recursive method	

12.9 Answers to Self-Test Questions

1. The presence of a well-defined stopping state keeps a recursive definition from being circular. The stopping state is a test of a condition and an action that does not result in a recursive step.

2. A stopping state and a recursive step.

3. Recursion in most programming languages requires a run-time stack to track the data for each call of a recursive method. Each time a recursive method is called, the computer allocates memory for the method's information on the stack and copies the information into this memory. Thus, there is a cost of memory and time as well.

4. The primary benefit of using recursion is that the programmer can write solutions to some problems more easily and with less effort than solutions that use a loop. Some problems lend themselves quite naturally to recursive solutions and not at all naturally to iterative ones.

5. ```
raise(2, 5)
    raise(2, 4)
        raise(2, 3)
            raise(2, 2)
                raise(2, 1)
                    raise(2, 0)
                    returns 1
                returns 2
            returns 4
        returns 8
    returns 16
returns 32
```

6. The method `whatAMethod` is always called recursively with the same value, n. Thus, the stopping state, when n == 0, is never reached. The computer tolerates these recursive calls until there is no more stack space and then throws an exception.

7. a. The run time of `factorial` is O($n$).

   b. The run time of `raise` is O($n$).
```

8. a. The memory usage of `factorial` is O(n).

   b. The memory usage of `fibonacci` is O(n).

9. The run time of the sort method is O(n^2).

10.
```
int raise(int base, int expo){
    if (expo == 0)
        return 1;
    else if (expo % 2 == 0){
        int result = raise(base, expo / 2);
        return result * result;
    }else
        return base * expo(base, expo - 1);
}
```

11.
```
raise(2, 16)
    raise(2, 8)
        raise(2, 4)
            raise(2, 2)
                raise(2, 1)
                    raise(2, 0)
                    returns 1
                returns 2
            returns 4
        returns 16
    returns 256
returns 65536
```

12. For large n, `raise` tends to divide n by 2 on each recursive call, so the method is O($\log n$).

13. The strategy of quick sort is to select a pivot item and shift all of the smaller items to its left and all of the larger items to its right. This part of the process is linear. If the pivot item tends to be in the middle of the list, the number of times the shifting must occur is logarithmic, so that's why quicksort can be better than O(n^2).

14. Quicksort is not O($n \log n$) in all cases because the pivot item might be near the beginning or the end of the list, thus causing an uneven split of the list. If this situation occurs often enough, the run time of quicksort can degenerate to O(n^2) in the worst case.

15. Three methods to select a pivot value are to pick the item at the midpoint, to pick an item at a random position, and to pick the median of the first, last, and middle items.

12.10 Programming Problems and Activities

Note: Some of the problems ask you to implement a method and test it in a `Tester` program. Be sure that the method is defined as a `static` method; otherwise, you will get a syntax error.

1. Use a `Tester` program to implement and test a recursive method to compute the greatest common divisor (gcd) of two integers. The recursive definition of gcd is

```
gcd(a, b) = b, when a = 0
gcd(a, b) = gcd(b, a % b), when a > 0
```

2. Write a recursive method that displays a string backward in the terminal window and test the method with a `Tester` program. *Hint*: The string and the index position should be parameters. Recurse to the last index position in the string and display an individual character after each recursive call.

3. Design, implement, and test a recursive method that expects a positive integer parameter and returns a string representing that integer with commas in the appropriate places. The method might be called as follows:

```
String formattedInt = insertCommas(1000000);  // Returns "1,000,000"
```

Hint: Recurse by repeated division and build the string by concatenating after each recursive call.

4. The phrase "*N* choose *K*" is used to refer to the number of ways in which we can choose *K* objects from a set of *N* objects, where $N >= K >= 0$. For example, 52 choose 13 would express the number of possible hands that could be dealt in the game of bridge. Write a program that takes the values of *N* and *K* as inputs and displays as output the value *N* choose *K*. Your program should define a recursive method, `choose(n, k)`, that calculates and returns the result. *Hint*: We can partition the selections of *K* objects from *N* objects as the groups of *K* objects that come from $N - 1$ objects and the groups of *K* objects that include the *N*th object in addition to the groups of $K - 1$ objects chosen from among $N - 1$ objects.

5. Modify the Case Study of this chapter so that it counts comparison and exchange operations in both sort algorithms and displays these statistics as well. Run the program with two array sizes and make a prediction on the number of comparisons, exchanges, and run times for a third size.

6. Write a `tester` program to help assess the efficiency of the Towers of Hanoi program. This program should be similar to the one developed for the Fibonacci method.

7. Write a `tester` program to help assess the efficiency of the Eight Queens program. This program should be similar to the one developed for the Fibonacci method.

8. A permutation of a list of unique items is a way in which the items can be ordered in the list. Thus, the list that contains the items *a, b,* and *c* has the distinct permutations [*a,b,c*], [*b,c,a*], [*c,b,a*], [*b,a,c*], [*c,a,b*], and [*a,c,b*]. Write a program that determines the number of permutations of a given list of items. *Hint*: Use an array of unique integers to represent a list of items.

9. Modify the program of Problem 8 so that it returns a list of the permutations of a given list.

13 Simple Two-Dimensional Graphics

This chapter shows how to create simple two-dimensional graphics. The window objects used thus far are in fact nothing more than patterns of bits displayed on a two-dimensional bitmapped screen. Java provides classes and methods for manipulating bit patterns directly, and we will learn to use the most basic of these. Along the way, we will draw geometric shapes, graph data using line, bar, and pie charts, detect and respond to mouse events, manipulate fonts, and implement new graphics classes.

13.1 The Conceptual Framework for Computer Graphics

Underlying every graphics application is a *coordinate system.* Positions in this system are specified in terms of points. Points in a two-dimensional system have x and y coordinates. For example, the point (10, 30) has an x coordinate of 10 and a y coordinate of 30.

The x and y coordinates of a point express its position relative to the system's *origin* at (0, 0). Figure 13.1 presents some examples of points in the familiar *Cartesian coordinate system.* In this system, two perpendicular lines define an x-axis and a y-axis. The point of intersection is labeled (0, 0). Increasing values of x are to the right and increasing values of y are up.

In Java and most other programming languages, the coordinate system is oriented as in Figure 13.2. Note that the only quadrant shown is the one that defines the coordinates of the computer's screen. In the positive direction, it extends downward and to the right from the point (0, 0) in the upper left corner. The other three quadrants exist, but the points in them never appear on the screen.

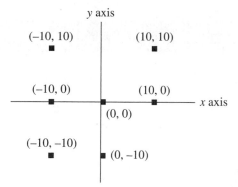

Figure 13.1 A Cartesian coordinate system

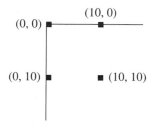

Figure 13.2 Orientation of Java's coordinate system

In a window-based application, each window has a coordinate system whose origin is located at the upper left outside corner of the window. Each integer point in this coordinate system, extending from the origin to the window's lower right corner, locates the position of a pixel, or picture element, in the window. By an integer point we mean a point both of whose coordinates are integers. One can also create rectangular regions within a window called ***panels.*** Each panel has its own coordinate system that is similar in form to the window's coordinate system. In fact, Java programmers usually draw images on panels and almost never on the window itself. Therefore, in the discussion that follows, we assume that we are drawing images on panels.

The `Graphics` Class

The package `java.awt` provides a `Graphics` class for drawing in a panel. A panel maintains an instance of this class, called a ***graphics context,*** so that the program can access and modify the panel's bitmap. The program sends messages to the graphics context to perform all graphics operations. Hereafter, we refer to the graphics context using the variable name `g`. Some commonly used `Graphics` drawing methods are listed in Table 13.1. The table also shows the results of running these methods in a window that has a single panel.

Table 13.1

Common Methods in the Graphics Class

Graphics Method	Example Call and Output	What It Does

drawLine(
  int x1,
  int y1,
  int x2,
  int y2)
	g.drawLine(10, 25, 40, 55)	Draws a line from point (x1, y1) to (x2, y2).

drawRect(
  int x,
  int y,
  int width,
  int height)
	g.drawRect(10, 25, 40, 30)	Draws a rectangle whose upper left corner is (x, y) and whose dimensions are the specified width and height.

drawOval(
  int x,
  int y,
  int width,
  int height)
	g.drawOval(10, 25, 50, 25)	Draws an oval that fits within a rectangle whose origin (upper left corner) is (x, y) and whose dimensions are the specified width and height. To draw a circle, make the width and height equal.

drawArc(
  int x,
  int y,
  int width,
  int height,
  int startAngle,
  int arcAngle)
	g.drawArc(10, 25, 50, 50, 0, 90)	Draws an arc that fits within a rectangle whose upper left corner is (x, y) and whose dimensions are the specified width and height. The arc is drawn from startAngle to startAngle + arcAngle. The angles are expressed in degrees. A start angle of 0 indicates the 3 o'clock position. A positive arc indicates a counterclockwise rotation, and a negative arc indicates a clockwise rotation from 3 o'clock.

drawPolygon(
  int x [],
  int y [],
  int n)
	int x [] = {10, 40, 60, 30, 40};
	int y [] = {25, 25, 50, 60, 40};
	g.drawPolygon(x, y, 5);
		Draws a polygon defined by n line segments, where the first n − 1 segments run from (x[i − 1], y[i − 1]) to (x[i], y[i]), for 1 <= i < n. The last segment starts at the final point and ends at the first point.

Table 13.1 *(continued)*

Graphics Method	Example Call and Output	What It Does

drawRoundRect(
  int x,
  int y,
  int width,
  int height,
  int arcWidth,
  int arcHeight)
	g.drawRoundRect(10, 25, 40, 30,
	                 20, 20)
		Draws a rounded rectangle.

drawString(
  String str,
  int x,
  int y)
	g.drawString("Java rules!",
	          10, 50)
	
	Java rules!
		Draws a string. The point (*x, y*) indicates the position of the base line of the first character.

In addition, there are the methods `fillArc`, `fillRect`, and `fillOval`, which draw filled shapes.

Adding a Panel to a Window

As mentioned earlier, panels are rectangular areas within a window. Each panel has its own coordinate system and graphics context for drawing images. `BreezySwing` provides the class `GBPanel` for defining panels. To write a graphics application, one should do two things:

1. Define a subclass of `GBPanel`. This class accesses the graphics context to create the drawing. The panel can draw images "on its own" or in response to messages sent to it from the main window.

2. Create an instance of the panel class and add this object to the application's window, in much the same manner as other window objects are added.

Let us assume that someone has defined a panel class named `ExamplePanel`. The following application adds an instance of this class to a window. Note that the panel is the only window object added, so it stretches across the entire width and height of the window below its title bar.

```
import BreezySwing.*;

public class GraphicsExamples extends GBFrame{
```

Continues

Continued

```
    GBPanel panel = addPanel(new ExamplePanel(), 1,1,1,1);

    public static void main (String[] args){
        GraphicsExamples tpo = new GraphicsExamples();
        tpo.setSize (200, 200);
        tpo.setVisible(true);
    }
}
```

The form of the method for adding a panel to a window is

```
GBPanel <variable name> = addPanel(<panel object>,
                              <row>, <col>, <width>, height>);
```

where <panel object> is an instance of a subclass of GBPanel or of GBPanel itself. The latter is rarely the case because new panels normally have behavior that is specific to an application. More often than not, we will use code such as

```
ExamplePanel panel = new ExamplePanel();

GBPanel p = addPanel(panel, 1,1,1,1);
```

This code provides a variable of the specific panel type so that messages can be sent to it without casting. The variable p, although it refers to the same object as panel, is then never used.

Implementing a Panel Class and the Method paintComponent

The responsibilities of a panel class are to draw images in response to messages from an application and also to redraw images whenever the window is refreshed. We discuss the refresh process here and examine how a panel receives messages from an application in a later section.

When a window opens, the JVM sends the message paintComponent to each window object. If the object has any images to draw, its paintComponent method accomplishes this. Thus, for example, when a window containing a button opens at program startup, the button's paintComponent method draws the image of the button on the screen. This process also occurs whenever the window is refreshed—for instance, after it is minimized and restored. The important point here is that the application never calls paintComponent directly; it is triggered automatically by the JVM in response to certain events. paintComponent receives the window object's graphics context as a parameter, so this object is accessible for drawing. The method is implemented in a superclass of the class GBPanel, so the programmer can override it to draw the appropriate images.

Here is the code for the implementation of the ExamplePanel class used earlier. Its paintComponent method draws a line segment when the window opens and whenever it is refreshed. The resulting window was shown in Figure 13.1.

```
import BreezySwing.*;                // Needed for GBPanel
import java.awt.*;                   // Needed for Graphics

public class ExamplePanel extends GBPanel{

    public void paintComponent (Graphics g){
        super.paintComponent(g);
        g.drawLine(10, 25, 40, 55);
    }
}
```

Note that the method first calls the same method in the superclass. The reason is that the method in the superclass paints the background of the component.

Finding the Height and Width of a Panel

Occasionally, it is useful to know the width and height of a panel. For instance, one might want to center an image in a panel and keep the image centered when the user resizes the window. The methods getWidth() and getHeight() return the current width and height of a panel, respectively. The following code would maintain a display of a panel's current width and height near the center of the panel:

```
public void paintComponent (Graphics g){
    super.paintComponent(g);
    g.drawString("(" + getWidth() + "," + getHeight() + ")",
                 getWidth() / 2, getHeight() / 2);
}
```

Self-Test Questions

1. Describe the difference between a screen coordinate system and the Cartesian coordinate system.

2. What is a graphics context?

3. Explain the meaning of the parameters for the method drawOval.

4. Write method calls with the Graphics object g to draw the following items:

   a. a rectangle at position (40, 30) with a width of 100 pixels and a height of 300 pixels

   b. a rectangle whose upper left corner is at (40, 30) and whose lower right corner is at (150, 160)

   c. a circle with a center point at (100, 100) and a radius of 25 pixels

   d. the statement "Graphics is easy in Java!" at position (200, 200)

5. Describe how the method paintComponent is used in a Java program.

13.2 The Method `repaint`

Before reapplying drawing commands, we normally want to erase the current drawing. The `repaint()` method provides the needed capability. This method, which is also implemented in one of `GBPanel`'s superclasses, first erases the current drawing in the panel and then calls `paintComponent`.

   `repaint` is also implemented in one of `GBFrame`'s superclasses. When sent to a window rather than a panel, this message does more. It tells all the window objects (text fields, labels, buttons, panels, etc.) to redisplay themselves. We illustrate the use of `repaint` in the next Case Study.

Self-Test Question

   6. Explain what happens when one calls the method `repaint`.

13.3 Case Study: Drawing Different Shapes

We are now ready to write a complete graphics program. We start with something very simple.

Request. Write a program that allows the user to draw different shapes.

Analysis. The application allows the user to enter the corner point, width, and height of the shape's bounding rectangle in integer fields. When the user selects a shape (**Oval** or **Rectangle**) from the **Shape** menu, the program draws the selected shape in the area to the right of the data fields after erasing the currently visible shape. The menu option **Shape/Clear** simply erases the current shape in the drawing area. The drawing area is clear at program startup. The proposed interface is shown in Figure 13.3.

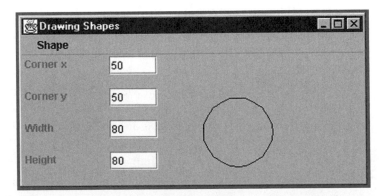

Figure 13.3 Interface for the shape drawing program

Classes. The program defines two classes: ShapeApp and ShapePanel. ShapeApp sets up the window objects and responds to the user's selection of menu options. ShapePanel draws the selected image or clears the panel.

Design. When the user selects a menu option, the menuItemSelected method in the ShapeApp class

- extracts the data from the input fields
- sends the message drawShape with these data and the menu option's name to the panel

The method drawShape in the ShapePanel class

- sets the panel's instance variables to the shape's type, corner point, width, and height (all parameters)
- calls repaint to refresh the panel

The method paintComponent in the ShapePanel class determines the type of shape to be drawn and calls the appropriate drawing method with the corner point, width, and height. If the type of shape is "clear," paintComponent does nothing, with the result that the panel is left empty.

Implementation. Here is the code for the two classes:

```
/* ShapeApp.java
Draw different shapes in a panel
*/
import javax.swing.*;
import BreezySwing.*;

public class ShapeApp extends GBFrame{

    // Set up the data fields for the size and position
    // of the shape
    JLabel xLabel           = addLabel("Corner x", 1,1,1,1);
    JLabel yLabel           = addLabel("Corner y", 2,1,1,1);
    JLabel widthLabel       = addLabel("Width",    3,1,1,1);
    JLabel heightLabel      = addLabel("Height",   4,1,1,1);
    IntegerField xField     = addIntegerField(0,   1,2,1,1);
    IntegerField yField     = addIntegerField(0,   2,2,1,1);
    IntegerField widthField = addIntegerField(0,   3,2,1,1);
    IntegerField heightField = addIntegerField(0,  4,2,1,1);

    // Must have a variable of type ShapePanel so one can
    // send the drawShape message
    ShapePanel shapePanel = new ShapePanel();
    GBPanel panel = addPanel(shapePanel, 1,3,1,4);

    // Set up the menu options
```

Continues

Continued

```
   JMenuItem ovalMI      = addMenuItem("Shape", "Oval");
   JMenuItem rectangleMI = addMenuItem("Shape", "Rectangle");
   JMenuItem clearMI     = addMenuItem("Shape", "Clear");

   public ShapeApp(){
      setTitle("Drawing Shapes");
   }

   public void menuItemSelected(JMenuItem mi){
      int x = xField.getNumber();
      int y = yField.getNumber();
      int width = widthField.getNumber();
      int height = heightField.getNumber();
      shapePanel.drawShape(mi.getText(), x, y, width, height);
   }

   public static void main (String[] args){
      ShapeApp tpo = new ShapeApp();
      tpo.setSize (400, 200);
      tpo.setVisible(true);
   }
}
```

```
import BreezySwing.*;
import java.awt.*;

public class ShapePanel extends GBPanel{

   private String shape = "clear";
   private int x, y, width, height;

   public void paintComponent (Graphics g){
      super.paintComponent(g);
      if (shape.equalsIgnoreCase("oval"))
         g.drawOval(x, y, width, height);
      else if (shape.equalsIgnoreCase("rectangle"))
         g.drawRect(x, y, width, height);
   }

   public void drawShape(String shape, int x, int y,
                         int width, int height){
      this.shape = shape;
      this.x = x;
      this.y = y;
      this.width = width;
```

```
      this.height = height;
      repaint();                  // Clear panel and call paintComponent
   }
}
```

13.4 The Method getGraphics

The program of Case Study 13.3 draws just one image at a time, and it erases that image before drawing the next one. Suppose, however, that onc wants to draw several images that remain in the panel. The program's policy of calling repaint to refresh the window with the new image will not work because the previous image is erased each time. Fortunately, Java provides another method, getGraphics(), which allows the programmer to access a panel's graphics object to draw without repainting. One uses this method as follows:

```
Graphics g = getGraphics();
<send messages to g to draw images>
```

The class ShapePanel can be modified to draw multiple shapes by

- omitting the method paintComponent
- placing the code to draw a shape in the method drawShape, which uses getGraphics to access the graphics object

To clear the panel, drawShape calls repaint, which clears the panel and calls the paintComponent method in a superclass that does nothing. Here is the code for the modified class:

```
import BreezySwing.*;
import java.awt.*;

public class ShapePanel extends GBPanel{

  // No instance variables are needed
  // No paintComponent method is needed
  // All drawing or clearing is done in drawShape

  public void drawShape(String shape, int x, int y,
                        int width, int height){
     Graphics g = getGraphics();
     if (shape.equalsIgnoreCase("oval"))
        g.drawOval(x, y, width, height);
     else if (shape.equalsIgnoreCase("rectangle"))
        g.drawRect(x, y, width, height);
```

Continues

Continued

```
    else
        repaint();                    // Clear panel and call paintComponent
  }
}
```

Graphics Methods and Constructors

We now need to mention a word of caution about using graphics methods. The graphics context of a window or window object is not available until after that component opens and is displayed. Therefore, the programmer should not attempt to use methods such as repaint and getGraphics, which rely on the graphics context, before this happens. In particular, one should not use these methods in constructor methods. Those who ignore this warning will be treated to a run-time exception.

The Transient Image Problem

The policy of using getGraphics instead of paintComponent works well for multiple images and is also more efficient because the entire panel is not repainted every time an image is drawn. However, suppose a user resizes or hides the window in some way. When that happens, the images in the panel disappear! The reason for this unpleasant event, called the **transient image problem,** is that no paintComponent method is available to redraw the images during a refresh. It seems that we now have a dilemma: either use paintComponent to draw one persistent image only or use getGraphics to draw multiple images that are transient. We will examine a way out of this dilemma that uses both methods in a later section of this chapter.

Self-Test Questions

7. Explain why one would use the method getGraphics for drawing images.
8. Describe the transient image problem and give an example of how it arises.

13.5 Color

A Java programmer can control the color of images by using the Color class, which is included in the package java.awt. The Color class provides the class constants shown in Table 13.3. For instance, the expression Color.red yields the Color constant for red. The Graphics class includes two methods for examining and modifying an image's color (Table 13.4). Images are drawn in the current color until the color is changed. Changing the color does not affect the color of previously drawn images. The next code segment draws a string in red and a line in blue in the graphics context g:

```
g.setColor (Color.red);
g.drawString ("Colors are great!", 50, 50);
g.setColor (Color.blue);
g.drawLine (50, 50, 150, 50);
```

Table 13.3

Constants in the Color Class	
Color Constant	**Color**
public static final Color red	red
public static final Color yellow	yellow
public static final Color blue	blue
public static final Color orange	orange
public static final Color pink	pink
public static final Color cyan	cyan
public static final Color magenta	magenta
public static final Color black	black
public static final Color white	white
public static final Color gray	gray
public static final Color lightGray	light gray
public static final Color darkGray	dark gray

Table 13.4

Two Methods in the Graphics Class for Manipulating an Image's Color	
Method	**What It Does**
Color getColor()	Returns the current color of the graphics context.
void setColor(Color c)	Sets the color of the graphics context to c.

Java allows the programmer finer control over colors by using RGB (red/green/blue) values. In this scheme, there are 256 shades of red, 256 shades of green, and 256 shades of blue. The programmer "mixes" a new color by selecting an integer from 0 to 255 for each color and passing these integers to a Color constructor as follows:

```
new Color (<int for red>, <int for green>, <int for blue>)
```

The next code segment shows how to create a random color with RGB values:

```
// Create a random color from randomly generated RGB values
int r = (int) (Math.random() * 256);
int g = (int) (Math.random() * 256);
int b = (int) (Math.random() * 256);
Color randomColor = new Color (r, g, b);
```

The value 0 indicates the absence of a color in the mixture, and the value 255 indicates the maximum saturation of that color. Thus, the color black has RGB (0, 0, 0), and the color white has RGB (255, 255, 255). There are $256 * 256 * 256 = 2^{24}$ possible colors in this scheme.

Setting a Panel's Background Color

In some applications, it is useful to see the area represented by a panel. For example, one could lay out a grid for several types of board games using panels, alternating white and black. A panel recognizes the message setBackGround(aColor), which changes its background color to the given color. The following short program displays a 2×2 grid of panels of four different colors, as shown in Figure 13.4.

```java
import javax.swing.*;
import BreezySwing.*;
import java.awt.*;

public class TestPanel extends GBFrame{

   GBPanel northWest = addPanel(new GBPanel(), 1,1,1,1);
   GBPanel southWest = addPanel(new GBPanel(), 1,2,1,1);
   GBPanel northEast = addPanel(new GBPanel(), 2,1,1,1);
   GBPanel southEast = addPanel(new GBPanel(), 2,2,1,1);

   public TestPanel(){
      northWest.setBackground(Color.red);
      southWest.setBackground(Color.blue);
      northEast.setBackground(Color.green);
      southEast.setBackground(Color.yellow);
   }

   public static void main (String[] args){
      TestPanel tpo = new TestPanel();
      tpo.setSize (200, 200);
      tpo.setVisible (true);
   }
}
```

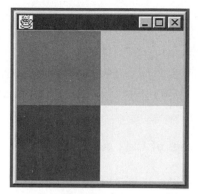

Figure 13.4 Setting the background color of panels

When the panel is a user-defined class, the background's color can be set in its constructor method. The next Case Study shows how to do this.

Self-Test Questions

9. Describe two ways to create a new color in Java.

10. How does the RGB system work?

11. Write a method `randomColor` that returns a randomly generated color using the RGB system.

13.6 Case Study: Fractals

Fractals are highly repetitive or recursive patterns. A fractal object appears geometric, yet it cannot be described with ordinary Euclidean geometry. Strangely, a fractal curve is not one-dimensional, and a fractal surface is not two-dimensional. Instead, every fractal shape has its own fractal dimension.

An ordinary curve has a precise finite length between any two points. By contrast, a fractal curve has an indefinite length between any two points. The apparent length depends on the level of detail considered. As we zoom in on a segment of a fractal curve, we can see more and more details, and its length appears greater and greater. Consider a coastline. Seen from a distance, it has many wiggles but a discernible length. Now put a piece of the coastline under magnification. It has many similar wiggles, and the discernible length increases. Self-similarity under magnification is the defining characteristic of fractals and is seen in the shapes of mountains, the branching patterns of tree limbs, and many other natural objects.

One example of a fractal curve is a *c-curve.* Figure 13.5 shows c-curves of the first 7 degrees. The level-0 c-curve is a simple line segment. The level-1 c-curve replaces the level-0 c-curve with two smaller level-0 c-curves meeting at right angles. The level-2 c-curve does the same thing for each the two line segments in the level-1 c-curve. This pattern of subdivision can continue indefinitely.

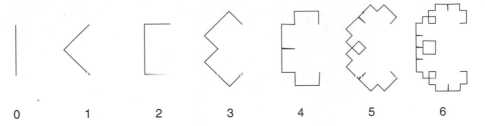

Figure 13.5 The first 7 degrees of the c-curve

Request. Write a program that allows the user to draw a particular c-curve in varying degrees.

Analysis. The proposed interface is shown in Figure 13.6. The user enters the level in a data field. The initial window displays a c-curve of level 0. The end points of this line segment are (150, 50) and (150, 150). This line segment is a good starting point for higher degree curves, all of which fit nicely within the initial window boundaries. The program has two menus:

1. The **Draw** menu has one selection, **Draw.** When the user selects **Draw,** the program clears the current image and draws a new one.

2. The **Color** menu has three selections, **Red, Black,** and **Blue,** which allow the user to change the color of the c-curve.

When the user resizes the window, the program refreshes the current image. Note that the drawing panel's background is white.

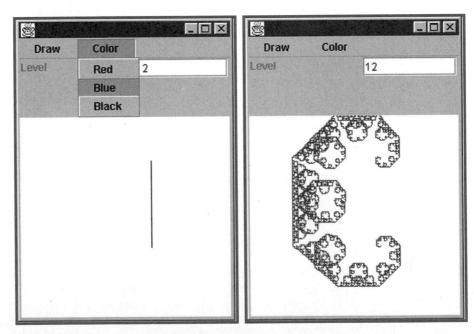

Figure 13.6 Interface for the c-curve program

Classes. As usual, we define a main window class to handle user input and menu selections and a panel class to do the drawing. We name these classes `FractalApp` and `FractalPanel`, respectively.

Design. We want the program to refresh the c-curve when the user resizes or hides the window. Consequently, the panel must use `paintComponent` and `repaint` to perform the drawing.

The `menuItemSelected` method performs these tasks:

- Sets the current level to the value in the input field.
- Sets the current color to the color indicated by a color selection.
- Sends the `drawCurve` message to the panel with this information.

The `drawCurve` method performs these tasks:

- Sets the color and level of the panel to the current values.
- Calls `repaint`.

The `paintComponent` method performs these tasks:

- Sets the color of the graphics context to the current color.
- Passes the level, the initial line segment (150, 100), (150, 200), and the graphics context to the `cCurve` method.

The `cCurve` method does the actual drawing and depends on the following recursive definition:

- A level-0 c-curve is a line segment $(x1, y1)$, $(x2, y2)$.
- Otherwise, a level-n c-curve consists of two level $n - 1$ c-curves constructed as follows:
  - Let xm be $(x1 + x2 + y1 - y2) / 2$.
  - Let ym be $(x2 + y1 + y2 - x1) / 2$.
  - The first level $n - 1$ c-curve uses the line segment $(x1, y1)$, (xm, ym), and level $n - 1$.
  - The second level $n - 1$ c-curve uses the line segment (xm, ym), $(x2, y2)$, and level $n - 1$.

In effect, as we showed in an earlier diagram, we replace each line segment by two shorter ones that meet at right angles.

Implementation. The following code shows the implementation of the class `FractalPanel`. The code for the class `FractalApp` is left as an exercise.

```
import BreezySwing.*;
import java.awt.*;


public class FractalPanel extends GBPanel{

   private Color color = Color.black;
```

Continues

Continued

```
    private int level = 0;

    public FractalPanel(){
        setBackground(Color.white);
    }

    public void paintComponent (Graphics g){
        super.paintComponent(g);
        g.setColor (color);
        cCurve (150, 100, 150, 200, level, g);
    }

    public void drawCurve(int level, Color color){
        this.color = color;
        this.level = level;
        repaint();
    }

    private void cCurve (int x1, int y1, int x2, int y2,
                         int level, Graphics g){
        if (level == 0)
            g.drawLine (x1, y1, x2, y2);
        else{
            int xm = (x1 + x2 + y1 - y2)/2;
            int ym = (x2 + y1 + y2 - x1)/2;
            cCurve (x1, y1, xm, ym, level - 1, g);
            cCurve (xm, ym, x2, y2, level - 1, g);
        }
    }
}
```

13.7 Graphing Data

A major application of graphics is the display of data in charts and graphs. Some common forms are line graphs, bar graphs, and pie charts.

Line Graphs

Line graphs are the easiest to conceptualize and implement. The data to be plotted might be listed in a table. For example, Table 13.5 lists the numbers of students receiving the letter grades A, B, C, D, and F in some class. A line graph of these data might look like the one in Figure 13.7.

Table 13.5

Distribution of Grades in a Class	
Letter Grade	**Number of Students**
A	5
B	7
C	10
D	6
F	2

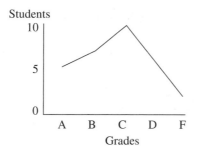

Figure 13.7 Line graph of student grades with a dot size of 1

To construct this line graph, we did the following:

- placed the letter grades along the *x* axis
- placed the numbers of these grades along the *y* axis
- drew a dot at the coordinates formed by each number/grade pair
- connected these dots

The major difficulty in drawing line graphs is figuring out the scale; that is:

- the number of pixels between each value on the *x* axis
- the number of pixels between each value on the *y* axis

The problem is solved by matching the range of values to the pixel dimensions of the graph. Suppose we plot grades on a 200 pixel-wide graph. Because there are five letter grades, there are 40 pixels between each value on the *x* axis. The general formula for calculating this increment is

```
x increment = width in pixels / number of values to plot
```

The increment for the *y* axis is calculated as follows:

```
if largest value to plot on the y axis equals 0
   y increment = 0
else
   y increment = total y pixels / largest value to plot on the y axis
```

A second problem is to determine the point in the panel corresponding to the origin of the graph. Because this point will lie at the lower left corner of the panel, the actual *x* coordinate will be zero, and the actual *y* coordinate will be the height of the panel minus one. For now, we simply assume that these values are given by the constants X_LEFT and Y_BOTTOM, respectively.

Now we can define two methods that convert data values in the table to pixel coordinates. The method getXCoordinate uses the position of the data value in the array (numbering from 1) and returns the *x* coordinate of the point to plot. In the code that follows

- xIncrement is the number of pixels between data points on the *x* axis
- i is a number from 1 to the number of values to plot, in this example, 5
- X_LEFT is the *x* coordinate of the graph's origin

```
private int getXCoordinate (int i, int xIncrement){
   return X_LEFT + xIncrement * i;
}
```

The method getYCoordinate returns the *y* coordinate of the point to plot. In the code that follows

- yIncrement is the number of pixels per data unit
- numStudents is the number of students being plotted at the current grade
- Y_BOTTOM is the *y* coordinate in the window of the bottommost point on the *y* axis

```
private int getYCoordinate (int numStudents, int yIncrement){
   return Y_BOTTOM - yIncrement * numStudents);
}
```

This method takes account of the fact that positive *y* coordinates extend downward rather than upward on a computer screen.

Let us assume that the array grades contains the data in Table 13.5's second column—that is, the column labeled **Number of Students.** The letter grades A, B, C, D, and F correspond to the index positions 0 through 4 of the array, as shown in Figure 13.8.

```
A  0  5
B  1  7
C  2  10
D  3  6
F  4  2
```

Figure 13.8

The following code segment plots these data in a dotted line graph:

```
int i, x, y, largestNumber, xIncrement, yIncrement;

// Compute the x and y increments.

largestNumber = findLargest(grades);
xIncrement = totalXPixels / grades.length;
if (largestNumber == 0)
    yIncrement = 0;
else
    yIncrement = totalYPixels / largestNumber;

// Compute and plot the data points.

for (i = 0; i < grades.length; i++){
    x = getXCoordinate (i + 1, xIncrement);
    y = getYCoordinate (grades[i], yIncrement);
    g.fillOval (x, y, 5, 5);
}
```

Note that we add 1 to the value of i before passing it to getXCoordinate because that method expects numbers from 1 to the size of the array.

To connect the dots, we draw line segments between them. We can also add a line segment between the graph's origin and the first dot. Because a line segment has two endpoints, the code requires an extra pair of int variables:

```
int i, x1, y1, x2, y2, largestNumber, xIncrement, yIncrement;

// Compute the x and y increments.

largestNumber = findLargest(grades);
xIncrement = totalXPixels / grades.length;
if (largestNumber == 0)
    yIncrement = 0;
else
```

Continues

Continued

```
    yIncrement = totalYPixels / largestNumber;

// Set the initial end point.

x1 = X_LEFT;
y1 = Y_BOTTOM;

// Compute and plot the data points.

for (i = 0; i < grades.length; i++){
   x2 = getXCoordinate (i + 1, xIncrement);
   y2 = getYCoordinate (grades[i], yIncrement);
   g.fillOval (x2, y2, 5, 5);                          //The dot size can be varied
   if (x1 != X_LEFT)
      g.drawLine (x1, y1, x2, y2);
   x1 = x2;
   y1 = y2;
}
```

In addition to the actual plot, we must take care of such details as drawing the axes, labeling them, and displaying any other information required by the users. These details are left as exercises.

Bar Graphs

A *vertical bar graph* shows the values as rectangular bars extending up from the *x* axis. A *horizontal bar graph* shows the bars as extending to the right from the *y* axis. In this section, we consider bars that are aligned vertically (Figure 13.9).

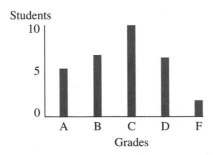

Figure 13.9 Vertical bar graph of student grades

We continue with the student grades example. To construct a bar graph, we must answer the following questions:

- How many bars are there? Our example needs five.
- How wide is a bar? The bar width in this example is ten pixels.

- How far apart are the bars? We use the same formula to calculate this increment as we did for the *x* increment of line graphs. We then center the bar on this value.
- How many pixels per unit of data are there? We use the same formula to calculate this increment as we did for the *y* increment of line graphs.

The following code segment brings these ideas together to display a bar graph of the student grades:

```
int i, x, y, height, largestNumber, xIncrement, yIncrement;

// Compute the x and y increments.

largestNumber = findLargest (grades);
xIncrement = totalXPixels / grades.length;
if (largestNumber == 0)
   yIncrement = 0;
else
   yIncrement = totalYPixels / largestNumber;

// Draw the bars.

for (i = 0; i < grades.length; i++){
   x = getXCoordinate (i + 1, xIncrement);
   y = getYCoordinate (grades[i], yIncrement);
   x = x - BAR_WIDTH / 2;
   height = BOTTOM_Y - y + 1;
   g.fillRect (x, y, BAR_WIDTH, height);
}
```

Pie Charts

A pie chart shows the relative sizes of the data as wedges of a pie (Figure 13.10). The size of a sector's central angle in a pie chart corresponds to a bar's height in a bar graph.

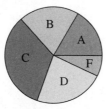

Figure 13.10 Pie chart of student grades

We continue with the student grades example. The angles for the data in our example are listed in Table 13.6. Because there are 30 students, 12 degrees (360 / 30) represents one student. Thus, the central angle for representing the 5 As is 5 *

12, or 60 degrees. In general, the expression for computing the degree increment for each unit of data is

```
if (totalUnits == 0)
   unitAngleSize = 0;
else
   unitAngleSize = 360.0 / totalUnits;
```

where `totalUnits` is the total number of units of data. We will assume that a method `sum(int[] a)` is available to compute this value.

Table 13.6

Angles Needed for Each Portion of the Student Grades Pie Chart		
Data Item	**Number of Items**	**Sector Size in Degrees**
A	5	60
B	7	84
C	10	120
D	6	72
F	2	24

The central angle corresponding to each kind of grade is then

```
centralAngle = (int) Math.round(unitAngleSize * grades[i]);
```

We must next determine how to start and end each sector. We set the starting angle for the first sector at 0 degrees, which is at 3 o'clock in the pie graph.

```
startAngle = 0;
```

After each sector is drawn, the starting angle of the next sector is computed by setting it to the current ending angle:

```
startAngle = startAngle + centralAngle;
```

We use the method `fillArc` to draw a filled arc in the current color of the graphics context. Before each call to `fillArc`, we set its color to a color generated by a programmer-defined method `intToColor`.

Finally, before we calculate the pie slices, we determine how large the pie will be and where it will be positioned in the panel. In this example, the radius of the pie will be slightly less than half of the panel's width. The pie will be positioned slightly above and to the left of the panel's center. To determine the center point of the window, we use the methods getWidth() and getHeight().

A complete code segment to draw the pie chart follows:

```
int totalUnits, centerX, centerY, radius, startAngle, i;
double unitAngleSize;

// Set up center point and radius of the pie, and the unit angle size.

totalUnits = sum(grades);
centerX = getWidth() / 2;
centerY = getHeight() / 2;
radius = centerX - centerX / 3;
centerX = radius;
centerY = centerY - centerY / 3;
if (totalUnits == 0)
   unitAngleSize = 0;
else
   unitAngleSize = 360.0 / totalUnits;
startAngle = 0;

// Draw the wedges in the pie.

for (i = 0; i < grades.length; i++){
   int centralAngle = (int) Math.round(unitAngleSize * grades[i]);
   g.setColor (intToColor(i));
   g.fillArc (centerX, centerY, radius, radius, startAngle, centralAngle);
   startAngle = startAngle + centralAngle;
}
```

13.8 Case Study: Multiple Views of Data

We now combine the previous techniques for graphing data into a Case Study.

Request. Write a program that allows the user to enter the numbers of students receiving the grades A, B, C, D, and F and to view these data in a line graph, a bar graph, or a pie chart.

Analysis. The proposed interface is shown in Figure 13.11. Above the graph display area are entry fields labeled with each letter grade. The default value for the number of students receiving each grade is 0. The user can display the graphs by selecting the **Graph** button. The data in the fields are transferred to an array of grades, and the three types of graphs are displayed in panels to the right of the data fields.

Note that we omit labels for the data in the graphs. That is left as an exercise.

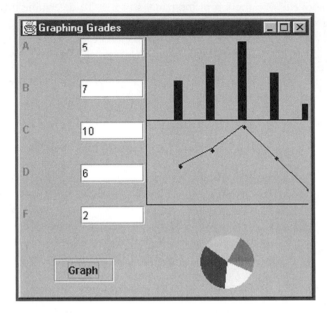

Figure 13.11 Three graphs of student grades

Classes. The program defines four classes. The class `GraphApp` is responsible for getting the inputs, responding to the button click, and sending messages to the graphing panels to draw the graphs. The classes `BarPanel`, `LinePanel`, and `PiePanel` are responsible for drawing bar, line, and pie graphs of the data, respectively.

Design. The method `buttonClicked` extracts the data from the fields and sends these in an array with the `drawGraph` message to the three graphing panels. Each graphing panel implements the `drawGraph` method, which transfers the array to an instance variable and calls `repaint`. The `paintComponent` method in turn uses the code developed earlier to draw the graph.

Implementation. We provide the code for the `GraphApp` class and leave the completion of the graphing panels as exercises. These are all straightforward adaptations of the code presented in the previous section.

```
/* GraphApp.java
Draw different graphs of data
*/
import javax.swing.*;
import BreezySwing.*;
import java.awt.*;

public class GraphApp extends GBFrame{
```

```java
   // Set up the data fields and command button
   JLabel aLabel         = addLabel ("A",        1,1,1,1);
   IntegerField aField = addIntegerField (0, 1,2,1,1);
   JLabel bLabel         = addLabel ("B",        2,1,1,1);
   IntegerField bField = addIntegerField (0, 2,2,1,1);
   JLabel cLabel         = addLabel ("C",        3,1,1,1);
   IntegerField cField = addIntegerField (0, 3,2,1,1);
   JLabel dLabel         = addLabel ("D",        4,1,1,1);
   IntegerField dField = addIntegerField (0, 4,2,1,1);
   JLabel fLabel         = addLabel ("F",        5,1,1,1);
   IntegerField fField = addIntegerField (0, 5,2,1,1);

   JButton graphBTN      = addButton("Graph",   6,1,2,1);

   // Set up the graphing panels
   BarPanel barPanel = new BarPanel();
   LinePanel linePanel = new LinePanel();
   PiePanel piePanel = new PiePanel();

   GBPanel p1  = addPanel(barPanel, 1,3,1,2);
   GBPanel p2 = addPanel(linePanel, 3,3,1,2);
   GBPanel p3  = addPanel(piePanel, 5,3,1,2);

   public static final int MAX_GRADES = 5;

   public GraphApp(){
      setTitle("Graphing Grades");
   }

   public void buttonClicked (JButton buttonObj){
      int[] grades = new int[MAX_GRADES];   // Transfer input data to
      grades[0] = aField.getNumber();       // graphing panels
      grades[1] = bField.getNumber();
      grades[2] = cField.getNumber();
      grades[3] = dField.getNumber();
      grades[4] = fField.getNumber();
      barPanel.drawGraph(grades);
      linePanel.drawGraph(grades);
      piePanel.drawGraph(grades);
   }

   public static void main (String[] args){
      GraphApp tpo = new GraphApp();
      tpo.setSize (500, 500);
      tpo.setVisible (true);
   }
}
```

13.9 Responding to Mouse Events

Until now, we have limited our use of the mouse to clicking on command buttons and selecting menu options. Everyone who has used a drawing program knows that much more can be done with the mouse, and in this section, we show how. Drawing applications usually detect and respond to the following mouse events: mouse clicks, mouse movement, and dragging the mouse (i.e., moving the mouse while a button is depressed). In addition, a program can respond to the mouse's entry into and exit from a given region. The GBPanel class includes methods for handling these events as described in Table 13.7. Notice that no distinction is made between the left and right mouse button. Each method has two parameters:

1. the *x* coordinate of the mouse when the event occurs

2. the *y* coordinate of the mouse when the event occurs

Table 13.7

Methods for Handling Mouse Events	
Method	**When It Is Called**
void mouseClicked (int x, int y)	when a mouse button is clicked
void mouseDragged (int x, int y)	when the mouse is moved while a button is depressed
void mouseEntered (int x, int y)	when the mouse enters a given region
void mouseExited (int x, int y)	when the mouse exits a given region
void mouseMoved (int x, int y)	when the mouse is moved
void mousePressed (int x, int y)	when a mouse button is pressed
void mouseReleased (int x, int y)	when a mouse button is released

To detect and handle mouse input, a subclass of GBPanel implements one or more of these methods. A mouse handling method typically transfers the values of the mouse coordinates to the panel's instance variables, performs some action, and updates the display with the results. For example, the following panel class tracks the position of a mouse press by displaying the mouse's coordinates. The mousePressed method stores the mouse coordinates in the instance variables mouseX and mouseY and then repaints the panel. paintComponent displays the values of mouseX and mouseY at that position.

```
import BreezySwing.*;
import java.awt.*;

public class MousePanel extends GBPanel{
```

```
    private int mouseX = 10, mouseY = 10;

    public void paintComponent (Graphics g){
        super.paintComponent(g);
        g.drawString("(" + mouseX + "," + mouseY + ")", mouseX, mouseY);
    }

    public void mousePressed(int x, int y){
        mouseX = x;
        mouseY = y;
        repaint();
    }
}
```

Self-Test Questions

12. List the different mouse events that GBPanel recognizes.

13. What does GBPanel do when a mouse event occurs?

14. One way to draw a rectangle with a mouse is to detect and respond to two clicks. One click designates the position of one corner and the other click designates the position of the opposite corner. Describe the problems with implementing this strategy using the mouseClicked method.

15. An alternative way to draw a rectangle is to press the mouse at one corner, drag it to the opposite corner, and then release the mouse. Describe how this process can be implemented with the GBPanel mouse-tracking methods.

13.10 Case Study: A Very Primitive Drawing Program

Drawing programs allow the mouse to be used as a pencil, paintbrush, or spray can. These programs range from the simple paint programs preinstalled on most computers to the sophisticated and expensive applications used by professional artists. All these programs have a common basis, the ability to draw a small dot at a location selected by the user. In the present Case Study, we show how this is done and in the process implement a very unspectacular drawing program.

Request. Write a program that allows the user to draw a figure by repeatedly clicking a mouse button.

Analysis. The panel class, called Sketchpad1, supports the simplest kind of drawing. When the user presses the mouse button in the panel, the program draws a pellet-sized dot on the screen at the current mouse position. The user constructs a figure by repeated applications of the process. The proposed interface, with drawing included, is in Figure 13.12.

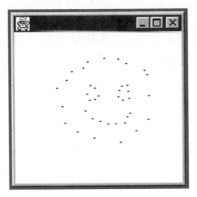

Figure 13.12 Interface for a very primitive pellet-based drawing program

Design. Because a single black pixel does not show up very well, we will represent each dot as a 2 × 2 block of pixels. The program's mousePressed method will draw such a block each time the user presses a mouse button.

Implementation. Here is the code:

```
import BreezySwing.*;
import java.awt.*;

public class Sketchpad1 extends GBPanel{

    public Sketchpad1(){
        setBackground(Color.white);
    }

    public void mousePressed (int x, int y){
        Graphics g = getGraphics();
        g.fillOval (x, y, 2, 2);
    }
}
```

Version 2. A slight modification to the program produces a big improvement in the results. The program now draws dots in response to mouse-dragged rather than mouse-pressed events. This means that the user does not have to press and release a mouse button for each dot. Instead, at the beginning of a drawing stroke, the user depresses a mouse button, a trail of dots is drawn as the user drags the mouse, and the stroke ends when the user releases the button. Figure 13.13 shows the results. Here is the code:

```
import BreezySwing.*;
import java.awt.*;

public class Sketchpad2 extends GBPanel{

    public Sketchpad2(){
        setBackground(Color.white);
    }

    public void mouseDragged(int x, int y){
        Graphics g = getGraphics();
        g.fillOval (x, y, 2, 2);
    }

}
```

Figure 13.13 An improved pellet-based drawing program

Version 3. The preceding pellet-drawing program leaves gaps in the strokes if the user drags the mouse too quickly. A simple line drawing program remedies the problem. As the user drags the mouse, line segments are drawn between successive mouse locations, thereby eliminating gaps in the stroke. Figure 13.14 illustrates the improvement (in everything except the author's artistry). A stroke begins with a mouse-pressed event, continues through a succession of mouse-dragged events, and ends when the user releases the button.

```
import BreezySwing.*;
import java.awt.*;

public class Sketchpad3 extends GBPanel{
```

Continues

Continued

```
   private int oldX, oldY;      //The beginning of a line segment

   public Sketchpad3(){
      setBackground(Color.white);
   }


   //Mark the beginning of a stroke's first line segment
   public void mousePressed (int x, int y){
     Graphics g = getGraphics();
     oldX = x;
     oldY = y;
   }

   //Draw line segments to connect successive locations within a stroke
   public void mouseDragged (int x, int y){
      Graphics g = getGraphics();
      g.drawLine (oldX, oldY, x, y);

      //Get ready for the next line segment
      oldX = x;
      oldY = y;
   }

   //Draw the last line segment in a stroke
   public void mouseReleased (int x, int y){
      Graphics g = getGraphics();
      g.drawLine (oldX, oldY, x, y);
   }
}
```

Figure 13.14 A simple line drawing program

13.11 Transient and Refreshable Images

Our sketchpad application suffers from the transient image problem. To draw a permanent or refreshable image—one that reappears when the window is resized—the application must maintain a record of the image and redraw it when necessary. As an illustration, we now modify Sketchpad2 as follows:

1. When the mousePressed method is invoked, the *x* and *y* coordinates are stored in two parallel arrays.

2. We implement a paintComponent method that loops through all the points stored in the arrays and draws the corresponding pellets.

The application handles the details of saving and displaying points in two new methods: savePoint(int x, int y) and displayPoints(Graphics g). Here is the listing of the modified program, called Sketchpad4:

```
import BreezySwing.*;
import java.awt.*;


public class Sketchpad4 extends GBPanel{

   private static int MAX_POINTS = 500;
   private int numPoints;
   private int[] xArray;
   private int[] yArray;

   public Sketchpad4(){
      setBackground(Color.white);
      numPoints = 0;
      xArray = new int[MAX_POINTS];
      yArray = new int[MAX_POINTS];
   }

   public void paintComponent (Graphics g){
      super.paintComponent(g);
      displayPoints (g);
   }

   public void mouseDragged (int x, int y){
      if (numPoints < xArray.length){
         Graphics g = getGraphics();
         g.fillOval (x, y, 2, 2);
         savePoint (x, y);
      }else
```

Continues

Continued

```
            new GBFrame().messageBox ("Sorry: cannot draw another pellet.");
     }

  private void displayPoints (Graphics g){
      int i;
      for (i = 0; i < numPoints; i++){
         g.fillOval (xArray[i], yArray[i], 2, 2);
      }
  }

  private void savePoint (int x, int y){
      xArray[numPoints] = x;
      yArray[numPoints] = y;
      numPoints++;
  }
}
```

Although this version of the program behaves correctly, there is still a problem. When the arrays of coordinates become full, the program can no longer accept mouse clicks, so the user sees a message box. There are several ways to deal with this problem. One way, which we leave as an exercise, is to resize the arrays when they become full, perhaps by adding 50 new cells each time this happens. Another way is to use lists to hold the coordinates. We examine lists in Chapter 15.

The technique just shown can also be applied with slight modification to Sketchpad3, the version that draws line segments. The trick is to insert in the arrays a special number that marks the boundary between strokes, for instance, –999.

Self-Test Question

16. How does one solve the transient image problem for a set of images?

13.12 Defining and Using a Geometric Class

Many applications implement classes to represent geometric objects such as points, lines, and circles. In this section, we develop a Circle class. A circle object has a center, a radius, and a color. Instances of class Circle recognize messages to access and modify these attributes and to draw themselves in a given graphics context. Table 13.8 lists the methods.

Table 13.8

Methods in Class `Circle`	
Method	**What It Does**
`Circle(int x, int y, int r, Color c)`	Constructor. Creates a circle with center point (x,y), radius r, and color c.
`int getX()`	Returns the x coordinate of the center.
`int getY()`	Returns the y coordinate of the center.
`int getRadius()`	Returns the radius.
`Color getColor()`	Returns the color.
`void setX(int x)`	Modifies the x coordinate of the center.
`void setY(int y)`	Modifies the y coordinate of the center.
`void setRadius(int r)`	Modifies the radius.
`Color setColor(Color c)`	Modifies the color.
`void draw(Graphics g)`	Draws the circle in the graphics context. The circle is filled with its color.
`void drawOutline(Graphics g)`	Draws an outline of the circle in the graphics context.
`boolean containsPoint(int x, int y)`	Returns true if the point (x,y) lies in the circle.
`void move(int xAmount, int yAmount)`	Moves the circle by xAmount horizontally and yAmount vertically. Negative amounts move to the left and up.

Here is an example of a `paintComponent` method that creates and draws a circle with center point (100, 100), radius 50, and color red:

```
public void paintComponent (Graphics g){
    super.paintComponent(g);
    Circle circle = new Circle (100, 100, 50, Color.red);
    circle.draw (g);
}
```

Implementation of the `Circle` Class

For the most part, the implementation of the `Circle` class is trivial and is left as an exercise. For now, we focus on just two methods: `draw` and `containsPoint`. The `draw` method uses `drawOval` to draw the circle. The `drawOval` method expects the position and extent of the circle's bounding rectangle, which can be derived from the circle's center and radius as shown next:

```
public void draw (Graphics g){
   // Save the current color of the graphics context
   // and set color to the circle's color.
   Color oldColor = g.getColor();
   g.setColor(color);

   // Translate the circle's position and radius
   // to the bounding rectangle's top left corner, width, and height.
   g.fillOval(centerX - radius, centerY - radius, radius * 2, radius * 2);

   // Restore the color of the graphics context.
   g.setColor(oldColor);
}
```

To determine if a point is in a circle, we consider the familiar equation for all points on the circumference of a circle

$$(x - xc)^2 + (y - yc)^2 = r^2 \qquad\qquad \text{(Eq. 1)}$$

or

$$(x - xc)^2 + (y - yc)^2 - r^2 = 0 \qquad\qquad \text{(Eq. 2)}$$

where (xc, yc) is the circle's center and r is its radius. A point (x, y) is then in the circle if the left side of Equation 2 is less than or equal to 0. For example, given a circle of radius 2 and center $(0, 0)$, the point $(1, 1)$ produces the result

$$1^2 + 1^2 - 2^2 = -2$$

implying that the point is in the circle.

Here is the method that results from this design:

```
public boolean containsPoint (int x, int y){
    int xSquared = (x - centerX) * (x - centerX);
    int ySquared = (y - centerY) * (y - centerY);
    int radiusSquared = radius * radius;
    return xSquared + ySquared - radiusSquared <= 0;
}
```

13.13 Case Study: Dragging Circles

We now present an application that uses our new `Circle` class in a program that responds to mouse events.

Request. Write a program that allows the user to drag circles in a window.

Analysis. The application draws some randomly generated circles at startup. When the user presses the mouse button in a circle, she can drag the circle to another position in the window. The proposed interface is shown in Figure 13.15. The application is based on three classes: the `Circle` class described in the previous section, a drawing panel class called `DragCirclesPanel`, and an application class called `DragCirclesApp`.

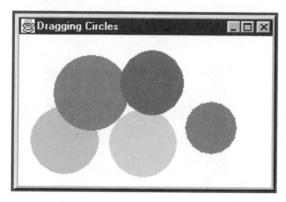

Figure 13.15 Interface for a circle dragging program

Design. The program maintains an array of the circle objects that appear in the drawing panel. When the user drags a circle, one of these objects is modified and redrawn. At all times, the program keeps track of the currently selected circle and the previous mouse position. During dragging, the program determines how far to move the selected circle by comparing the mouse's previous and current positions.

The design and implementation of the `Circle` class have already been discussed in the previous section. The two principal methods in the `DragCirclesPanel` class are `mousePressed` and `mouseDragged`. The `mousePressed` method begins by searching the array of circles to determine if the user has pressed the mouse button inside a circle. If she has, then

- a `Circle` variable, `selectedCircle`, is set to the circle that was selected
- the variables `previousX` and `previousY` are set to the mouse's current position

    The `mouseDragged` method

- determines the incremental amount by which the mouse has just moved by comparing the mouse's current position (`currentX`, `currentY`) to it previous position (`previousX`, `previousY`)
- calls the `move` method to move the circle by this amount
- invokes the `repaint` method, which clears the window and then calls `paintComponent` to redraw all the circles
- saves the new mouse position in the variables `previousX` and `previousY`

Implementation. Here is the code:

```
/* DragCirclesPanel.java
First draw five randomly generated circles. Thereafter, the user can use the
mouse to drag any circle around the window.
*/

import BreezySwing.*;
import java.awt.*;

public class DragCirclesPanel extends GBPanel{

   //Constants that control the characteristics of the randomly generated
   //circles.
   private final static int MAX_CIRCLES  = 5;   //Number of circles
   private final static int MIN_CENTER_X = 50;  //Range of x values for
   private final static int MAX_CENTER_X = 150; //circle centers
   private final static int MIN_CENTER_Y = 50;  //Range of y values for
   private final static int MAX_CENTER_Y = 150; //circle centers
   private final static int MIN_RADIUS   = 10;  //Range of values for the
   private final static int MAX_RADIUS   = 50;  //circle radii

   //Instance variables
   private int previousX, previousY  ; //Previous mouse position
   private    Circle selectedCircle;  //The selected circle or null if none.
   private    Circle[] circles = new Circle[MAX_CIRCLES];
                                      //The array of circles

   //Constructor -- initialize instance variables
   public DragCirclesPanel(){
      int i;
      setBackground(Color.white);
      selectedCircle = null;

      //Generate random circles
      for (i = 0; i < MAX_CIRCLES; i++){
         int centerX = randomInt(MIN_CENTER_X, MAX_CENTER_X);
         int centerY = randomInt(MIN_CENTER_Y, MAX_CENTER_Y);
         int radius = randomInt(MIN_RADIUS, MAX_RADIUS);
         Color color = randomColor();
         Circle circle = new Circle(centerX, centerY, radius, color);
         circles[i] = circle;
      }
   }

   //Redraw the circles. The last circle drawn appears topmost.
   public void paintComponent (Graphics g){
      super.paintComponent(g);
```

```
      int i;
      for (i = 0; i < MAX_CIRCLES; i++)
        circles[i].draw(g);
   }


   //Respond to the mouse pressed event by recording its position and by
   //determining if a circle has been selected.
   public void mousePressed (int x, int y){
      previousX = x;
      previousY = y;
      selectedCircle = findCircle(x, y);
   }


   //Respond to the mouse released event by indicating that no circle
   //is currently selected.
   public void mouseReleased (int x, int y){
      selectedCircle = null;
   }


   //Respond to the move dragged event by determining if a circle is
   //currently selected. If a circle is selected, then
   //  move it by an amount equal to the amount the mouse has moved,
   //  repaint the panel, and
   //  record the mouse's position in previousX and previousY.
   public void mouseDragged (int currentX, int currentY){
      if (selectedCircle != null){
         selectedCircle.move(currentX - previousX, currentY - previousY);
         repaint();
         previousX = currentX;
         previousY = currentY;
      }
   }


   //Return the topmost circle containing the point (x, y) or null if no
   //circle contains the point
   private Circle findCircle(int x, int y){
      int i;
      for (i = MAX_CIRCLES - 1; i >= 0; i--)
        if (circles[i].containsPoint(x, y)){
           return circles[i];
        }
      return null;
   }


   //Return a random integer between low and high inclusive.
   private int randomInt (int low, int high){
```

Continued

```
      return (int) (low + Math.random() * (high - low + 1));
   }


   //Return a random color.
   private Color randomColor(){
      Color color;
      int number = randomInt (1, 5);
      switch (number){
         case 1:
            color = Color.red;
            break;
         case 2:
            color = Color.blue;
            break;
         case 3:
            color = Color.green;
            break;
         case 4:
            color = Color.magenta;
            break;
         case 5:
            color = Color.cyan;
            break;
         default: color = Color.orange;
      }
      return color;
   }
}
```

Getting Rid of Flicker. This program has a problem. As we drag a circle around, the window seems to flicker. The cause lies in the mouseDragged method. Every time we move a circle, the repaint method is called. This method clears the window and then calls paintComponent to redraw the circles. Unless the computer is very fast, the human eye experiences the cycles of clear and redraw as flicker. Fortunately, there is a way to overcome the problem. Java allows drawing to be done in two different modes. In the default mode, which we have been using exclusively so far, images (lines, text, shapes) overwrite whatever happens to be underneath them. This mode is called *paint*. The second mode is called **XOR**. The result of drawing an image in XOR mode depends on two colors—the current color and the XOR color. Wherever the image overlays the XOR color, it is drawn in the current color, and vice versa. A consequence of this strange convention is that if an image is redrawn on top of itself, it disappears, and the window returns to its original appearance before the image was first drawn. Pixels of a different color (neither the current color nor the XOR color) underneath the image are changed in a manner too complex to explain here. However, redrawing over these pixels returns them to their original color too.

In the code that follows, we use the XOR mode to solve the flicker problem. When a circle is selected, we draw an outline of it in XOR mode. Then, as the user drags the mouse, we redraw the outline using XOR (restoring the pixels covered by the outline) and draw another outline in XOR mode at the mouse's new location. Drawing an outline involves so few pixels that the user sees no flicker and believes the outline is smoothly following the mouse around the window. When the user finally releases the mouse, we repaint the window. Here are the modifications to the program:

```
public void mousePressed (int x, int y){
   previousX = x;
   previousY = y;
   selectedCircle = findCircle(x, y);
   if (selectedCircle != null)
      selectedCircle.drawOutline(getGraphics());
}

public void mouseReleased (int x, int y){
   selectedCircle = null;
   repaint();
}

public void mouseDragged (int x, int y){
   if (selectedCircle != null){
      Graphics g = getGraphics();
      selectedCircle.drawOutline (g);                        // Old location
      selectedCircle.move (x - previousX, y - previousY);
      selectedCircle.drawOutline (g);                        // New location
      previousX = x;
      previousY = y;
   }
}
```

To complete the modifications, we must add a drawOutline method to the Circle class. Here is the code:

```
public void drawOutline (Graphics g){
   Color oldColor = g.getColor();
   g.setColor (Color.black);
   g.setXORMode (Color.white);
   g.drawOval (centerX - radius, centerY - radius, radius * 2, radius * 2);
   g.setColor (oldColor);
   g.setPaintMode();
}
```

13.14 Text Properties

From the perspective of a bitmapped display, text is drawn like any other image. A text image has several properties as shown in Table 13.9. These are set by adjusting the color and font properties of the graphics context in which the text is drawn. In this section, we first provide an overview of Java's Font class and then show some examples of its application.

Table 13.9

Text Properties	
Text Property	**Example**
Color	Red, green, blue, white, black, etc.
Font style	Plain, **bold,** *italic*
Font size	10 point, 12 point, etc.
Font name	Courier, Times New Roman, etc.

The Font Class

An object of class Font has three basic properties: a name, a style, and a size. The following code creates one Font object with the properties **Courier bold 12** and another with the properties ***Arial bold italic 10***:

```
Font courierBold12    = new Font("Courier", Font.BOLD, 12);
Font arialBoldItalic10 = new Font("Arial", Font.BOLD + Font.ITALIC, 10);
```

The Font constants PLAIN, BOLD, and ITALIC define the font styles. The font size is an integer representing the number of points, where one point equals 1/72 of an inch. The available font names depend on your particular computer platform. To see what they are, run the code segment

```
String fontNames[] = Toolkit.getDefaultToolkit().getFontList();
int i;
for (i = 0; i < fontNames.length; i++)
    System.out.println (fontNames[i]);
```

The code:
- declares the variable fontNames as an array of strings
- runs the Toolkit class method getDefaultToolkit, which returns the default toolkit for the particular computer platform

- runs the method `getFontList` on the toolkit. This method returns a list of the available font names
- sets the array `fontNames` to this list
- executes a loop that displays the contents of `fontNames` in the terminal window

Table 13.10 lists the principal `Font` methods.

Table 13.10

The Principal Font Methods	
Font Method	**What It Does**

`public Font`
   `(String name,`
    `int style,`
    `int size)`
	Creates a new `Font` object with the specified properties; `style` must be PLAIN, BOLD, ITALIC, or a combination of these using +.

`public String getName()`	Returns the current font name.
`public int getStyle()`	Returns the current font style.
`public int getSize()`	Returns the current font size.

Setting the Color and Font Properties of Text

The programmer sets the color and font properties of text by setting the color and font properties of the GUI object's graphics context. For example, assume that we want to display the text `"Hello world!"` in green with the font Courier bold 14. The following code would do this:

```
Font ourFont = new Font ("Courier", Font.BOLD, 14);
Color ourColor = Color.GREEN;
Graphics g = getGraphics();
g.setColor (ourColor);
g.setFont (ourFont);
g.drawString ("Hello world!", 100, 100);
```

Changing the font and color of a graphics context affects all subsequent graphics operations in that context but does not alter the font or color of existing images.

13.15 Design, Testing, and Debugging Hints

- Computer screen coordinates are not the same as conventional Cartesian coordinates. Computer screen coordinates place the origin (0, 0) in the upper left corner and get larger as they move to the right and to the bottom of the screen.

- The `repaint` method always clears the graphics context. Thus, any displayed images will be erased when `repaint` is invoked. This will occur automatically when the window is resized, unless you override the `paintComponent` method to redraw the images.

- Remember to call `super.paintComponent(g)` whenever you implement the method `paintComponent`. This guarantees that the window objects' background will be painted, thus clearing any images drawn in it.

- Never call a method that accesses a graphics context in a constructor method. This context is not yet available, and you will receive a run-time exception.

13.16 Summary

This chapter introduced the use of two-dimensional graphics in Java. We covered the basics of positioning images in a screen coordinate system and drawing them with methods from the `Graphics` class. We examined the transient image problem and showed how to solve it by using the methods `paintComponent`, `repaint`, and saving information about images. The tracking of mouse events allows users to interact with graphics-based programs, and the manipulation of color and text font properties expands the capabilities of these programs.

13.17 Key Terms

If you have difficulty finding the definitions of any key terms in the body of this chapter, turn to the Glossary at the end of the book.

Cartesian coordinate system	line graphs	transient image
c-curve	origin	vertical bar graph
fractal object	paint mode	XOR mode
graphics context	panel	
horizontal bar graph	refreshable image	

13.18 Answers to Self-Test Questions

1. In a Cartesian coordinate system, the origin is at the "center" of the system. The x and y coordinates increase as one moves to the east and to the north, respectively, and decrease as one moves to the west and to the south, respectively. In a screen coordinate system, the origin is at the upper left corner (northwest). The x and y coordinates increase as one moves to the east and to the south, respectively.

2. A graphics context is an object, associated with a window or a window object, to which messages are sent to draw images in the window or window object.

3. The first two parameters of the method `drawOval` represent the upper left corner of the rectangle that bounds the oval. The second pair of parameters represents the width and height of this bounding rectangle.

4. a. `g.drawRect(40, 30, 100, 300)`

   b. `g.drawRect(40, 30, 110, 130)`

   c. `g.drawOval(75, 75, 50, 50)`

   d. `g.drawstring("Graphics is easy in Java!", 200, 200)`

5. The method `paintComponent` is implemented for each window object. For most window objects, this method draws its image. For panels, this method paints the background. The JVM automatically calls `paintComponent` whenever a window object is refreshed. The programmer can override `paintComponent` in a user-defined class to draw application-specific images.

6. In the case of a window object, the method `repaint` first clears its image and then calls `paintComponent` to redraw it. In the case of a window, `repaint` first clears the window and then sends the message `repaint` to all of the window objects contained in it.

7. The method `getGraphics` is used to access a graphics context when the programmer does not wish to paint the entire window object with `repaint/paintComponent`. `getGraphics` thus allows the programmer to draw multiple images in a panel without clearing any of them.

8. The transient image problem appears when one resizes or covers a window containing an image. If no mechanism is provided for refreshing the image, the image disappears when the window is uncovered.

9. One way to create a color in Java is to use one of several `Color` class variables, such as `Color.red`. Another way is to instantiate a `Color` object using RGB values, such as new `Color(128, 128, 128)`.

10. The RGB system uses three integer values to specify each color. The integers represent the intensities of red, green, and blue that are mixed together, using the form (R,G,B). There are 256 integer values for each color component, for a total of 256^3 possible colors. The value (0,0,0) is black, or the absence of color. The value (255,255,255) is white, or total saturation. The value (255,0,0) is the most intense red, and so forth.

11. ```
Color randomColor(){
    int r = (int) (Math.random() * 256);
    int g = (int) (Math.random() * 256);
    int b = (int) (Math.random() * 256);
    return new Color (r, g, b);
}
```

12. The mouse events that `GBPanel` recognizes are mouse moved, mouse pressed, mouse released, mouse dragged, and mouse clicked.

13. When a mouse event occurs, `GBPanel` invokes a method that corresponds to the event, passing to the method as parameters the coordinates of the mouse when the event occurred. For example, if a mouse-moved event occurs, `BreezySwing` invokes the method `mouseMoved` with the current mouse coordinates as parameters.

14. One needs two sets of variables, say, `x` and `y` and `width` and `height`. The first pair of variables saves the coordinates of the first mouse click. When the second click occurs, the
```

program must use its coordinates and the coordinates of the first click to set the width and height and then draw the rectangle. The primary problem is how to distinguish the two clicks. One can used a `boolean` variable, say, `firstClick`, to record that the first click has occurred. This variable is set to `false` at program startup and after a second click. After a first click, the variable is set to `true`. The `mouseClicked` method must examine and modify `firstClick` to maintain the distinction between the two clicks.

15. The method `mousePressed` sets the variables representing the upper left corner of the rectangle. The method `mouseReleased` uses the current coordinates to compute the width and height and then draws the rectangle. There is no need to distinguish the events because a different method handles each one.

16. One solves the transient image problem for a set of images in two steps. First, one saves information about an image (coordinates, size, etc.) when the image is first drawn using `getGraphics`. Second, one implements a `paintComponent` method to access this information and refresh the window with the images.

13.19 Programming Problems and Activities

1. Write a program that allows the user to change the color of the application window and to view its size. The program should provide a menu of colors. When the user selects a color, the program sets the window's graphics context to that color. The program also displays the height and width of the window's graphics context at the center of the window. These values should be updated whenever the user resizes the window.

2. Modify the program of Problem 3, Chapter 9, so that it displays the faces of the dice on each roll. To do this, the `Dice` class should define a `draw` method. This method's parameters are a graphics context and a pair of coordinates representing the point at the center of the die's rectangular face. Thus, the application is responsible for computing the location of the dice, but the dice are responsible for drawing themselves. After each roll, the application should clear the window and redraw the dice.

3. Modify the program of Problem 9, Chapter 10, so that it displays the user's blackjack hand. To do this, the `Card` class should define a `draw` method. This method is similar to the `draw` method for dice in Problem 2 of this chapter. A card can be visualized as a rectangle that displays the card's number in the upper left corner and the lower right corner. In the case of the ace or a face card, use the letters A, K, Q, or J. In addition, you should display the name of the suit (spade, club, heart, or diamond) in the middle of the rectangle. When the suit of the card is a spade or club, the information displayed within the rectangle should be black; otherwise, this information should be red.

4. The 20th-century Dutch painter Piet Mondrian developed a style of abstract painting that exhibited simple recursive patterns. For example, an "idealized" pattern from one of his paintings might look like that shown in Figure 13.16:

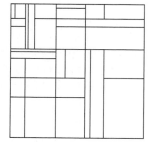

Figure 13.16

To generate such a pattern with a computer, an algorithm would begin by drawing a rectangle and then repeatedly draw two unequal subdivisions, as shown in Figure 13.17. As you can see, the algorithm continues this process of subdivision for a number of levels, until an "aesthetically right moment" is reached. In this version, the algorithm appears to divide the current rectangle into portions representing one-third and two-thirds of its area, and it appears to alternate the subdivisions randomly along the horizontal and vertical axes. Design, implement, and test a program that uses a recursive method to draw such patterns. The user should be able to draw several pictures with different levels.

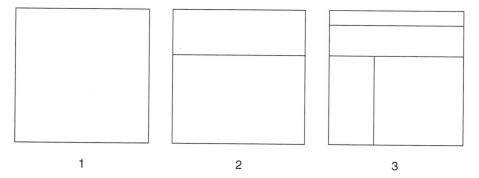

Figure 13.17

5. Modify the program in Problem 4 so that it fills the rectangular areas in the picture with randomly generated colors.

6. The programs in Problems 4 and 5 use constant factors of one-third and two-thirds to subdivide the rectangle on the recursive steps. Modify the program in Problem 5 so that the factors randomly alternate among one-fifth and four-fifths, one-quarter and three-quarters, and one-third and two-thirds.

7. Modify the salary schedule program of Problem 9, Chapter 4, so that it displays a bar graph of the salary schedule.

8. In the `Sketchpad4` program Case Study, saving the points in arrays causes a problem: The size of the arrays is fixed when they are created, so the number of pellets the user can draw is limited. Modify the program so that the arrays can accommodate any number of points. When the arrays become full, invoke a method that creates two new arrays that are 50 cells larger than the old arrays, copy the data from the old arrays to the new arrays, and reset the instance variables to the new arrays. Test the program thoroughly.

9. Modify the `Sketchpad4` program Case Study so that it supports freehand drawing, as suggested in the text. Also, add a menu that allows the user to select the width of a pellet (1, 3, or 5 pixels).

10. The freehand drawing program of Problem 9 works well as long as the user drags the mouse slowly. However, when dragging speeds up, large gaps appear between the pellets. To solve this problem, modify the program so that it draws lines between the points during dragging. Simply pressing the mouse should still draw a pellet. The two arrays should contain the coordinates of these pellets, as well as the coordinates of the endpoints of each line segment. To distinguish a pellet from a line segment, use the value –1 as a separator in each array. For example, if the user draws a pellet at (100, 100) and then two line segments at (100, 100), (150, 160) and (150, 160), (200, 45), the two arrays should contain the values

   100 –1 100 150 –1 150 200

   100 –1 100 160 –1 160 45

   You should continue to use the method `fillOval` to draw pellets, but use `drawLine` to draw line segments.

11. Sketching programs typically allow users to draw lines, rectangles, and ovals by selecting an item from a menu and clicking the mouse in the desired area of the sketchpad. Write a program that supports this kind of drawing. The program should have a **Shape** menu and a **Color** menu. When the user selects **Shape/Line**, for example, two mouse clicks in the drawing area will establish the endpoints of a line. Other lines can then be drawn until the user selects a different shape. This program does not have to refresh the images when the window size is modified.

12. Modify the program of Problem 11 so that it can refresh the images. To do this, define the classes `Line`, `Circle`, and `Rect` and maintain arrays of each kind of shape. Each of these classes should have a `draw` method.

13. A *scattershot diagram* allows a user to visualize data as points in a two-dimensional graph. In a simple case, we might plot integer values from an array along the *y* axis and their index positions along the *x* axis. This image allows us to visualize the movement of data in an array as it is being sorted. Modify the sorting program Case Study of Chapter 12 so that it displays the data in this manner as they are being sorted. When the user enters a new number of data values, the program refreshes the window by displaying a scattershot of these data. When a sort algorithm exchanges two values in the array, the program redraws these values in the scattershot. The program should not have to repaint the entire scattershot when only two values are exchanged.

14. Complete the implementation of the `Circle` class of Section 13.12 and test it with a tester program.

15. As you probably know, the game of tic-tac-toe is played with a 3×3 grid of squares and each player takes turns marking an X or an O until three letters line up in a row, column, or diagonal. Write a program that plays this game with a user. The program makes the first move, at random, with an X. The user places an O by selecting a square with the mouse. The program should prevent entries in squares already occupied and should make its own entries at random. The program displays a message box announcing the winner when a game is over and allows the user to reset the board by selecting a menu item. *Hint*: Use an array of panels to represent the board.

14 Files

Data stored in variables are temporary, existing for at most the lifetime of an application. Data that must last longer are saved in files on secondary storage devices, such as magnetic disks, optical disks (CDs), and magnetic tapes. When needed again later, the data are read from the files back into variables. Dealing directly with directory structures and file layouts on disk is a complex process, so operating systems provide a layer of software to hide the messy details. In addition, Java has built a hierarchy of classes on top of this layer to give it an object-oriented interface. When working with files, a program deals with these Java classes, which in turn manage the actual transfer of data between memory and secondary storage. In Figure 14.1, the boxes labeled "Input file" and "Output file" represent instances of these Java classes.

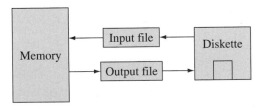

Figure 14.1 File objects manage the movement of data between memory and secondary storage devices

Java supports two types of file access: sequential and random. If we imagine a file as a long sequence of contiguous bytes, then random access allows a program to retrieve a byte or group of bytes from anywhere in a file. Sequential access forces a program to retrieve bytes sequentially starting from the beginning of a file. Thus, to retrieve the 100th byte, a program must first retrieve the preceding 99. Despite this restriction, sequential file access is extremely useful and is the topic of this chapter.

14.1 File Classes

At the lowest level, Java views the data in files as a stream of bytes. A stream of bytes from which data are read is called an ***input stream,*** and a stream of bytes to which data are written is called an ***output stream.*** Java provides classes for connecting to and manipulating data in a stream. The classes are defined in the package `java.io` and are organized in a large complex hierarchy, a small portion of which is shown in Figures 14.2 and 14.3. The concrete classes are shown in light blue and the abstract classes in dark blue. Although the number of these classes looks intimidating, we will use them in a few simple combinations as summarized in Table 14.1. The rest of the chapter is devoted to explaining how to use these combinations.

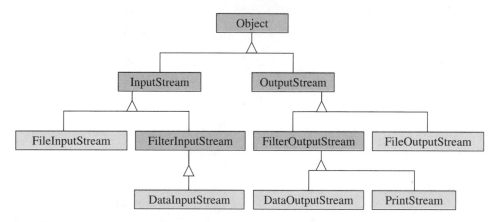

Figure 14.2 A portion of the hierarchy for stream classes

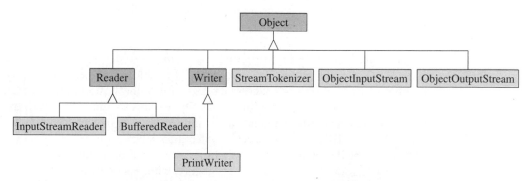

Figure 14.3 A few other I/O oriented classes

Table 14.1

Combinations of Classes Used in Several Common I/O Situations	
Task	**Combination of Classes Used**
Read one character at a time from a text file	`InputStreamReader` on `FileInputStream`
Read one line at a time from a text file	`BufferedReader` on `InputStreamReader` on `FileInputStream`
Read one word at a time from a text file	`StreamTokenizer` on `BufferedReader` on `InputStreamReader` on `FileInputStream`
Write `int`, `double`, `char`, `String`, etc. to a text file	`PrintWriter` on `FileOutputStream`
Write `int`, `double`, `char`, `String`, etc. to a nontext file	`DataOutputStream` on `FileOutputStream`
Read `int`, `double`, `char`, `String`, etc. from a nontext file	`DataInputStream` on `FileInputStream`
Write a complete object to a file	`ObjectOutputStream` on `FileOutputStream`
Read a complete object from a file	`ObjectInputStream` on `FileInputStream`
Read keyboard input	`System.in` which is a `BufferedReader` on `InputStreamReader` on `InputStream`
Write console output	`System.out` and `System.err` which are `PrintStream` objects

The table's second column requires some explanation. For instance, the entry

`InputStreamReader` on `FileInputStream`

means that an `InputStreamReader` object is wrapped around a `FileInputStream` object. As indicated in the table, nearly all input operations involve a `FileInputStream`; however, an object of this type has the rather limited capability of reading raw bytes from a file. To treat this stream of raw bytes as characters or lines or words, we must pass it through objects that translate it appropriately. Thus, an `InputStreamReader` object translates raw bytes into characters in some designated encoding scheme. In a similar manner, nearly all output operations involve a `FileOutputStream` in combination with other classes that translate data in various forms to the raw bytes processed by a `FileOutputStream`.

To help you better understand this approach, here are short summaries of some of the classes taken verbatim from Sun's Java documentation. The documentation is downloadable from Sun's Web site (see Appendix A).

> **InputStream** — this abstract class is the superclass of all classes representing an input stream of bytes.

FileInputStream — obtains input bytes from a file in a file system.

Reader — abstract class for reading character streams.

InputStreamReader — a bridge from byte streams to character streams: It reads bytes and translates them into characters according to a specified character encoding. The encoding that it uses may be specified by name, or the platform's default encoding may be accepted.

BufferedReader — read text from a character-input stream, buffering characters so as to provide for the efficient reading of characters, arrays, and lines.

StreamTokenizer — takes an input stream and parses it into "tokens", allowing the tokens to be read one at a time.

OutputStream — this abstract class is the superclass of all classes representing an output stream of bytes. An output stream accepts output bytes and sends them to some sink.

FileOutputStream — an output stream for writing data to a `File`.

Writer — abstract class for writing to character streams.

PrintWriter — prints formatted representations of objects to a text-output stream.

We now turn to the details.

Self-Test Questions

1. Why are file classes needed?
2. How does Java represent data to be transferred to and from a file?
3. Why are so many file classes needed?

14.2 File Input

We begin our discussion of file input by writing a program that reads a text file, converts all alphabetical characters to uppercase, and displays the result in a text area (Figure 14.4). To use the program, type a file name in the text field and select the **Display the Contents** button. We will present four versions of this program. In the first, a stub replaces the method for reading and processing the file. In the other three versions, we show how to read the file one character, one line, and one word at a time.

A typical file input process is described in the following pseudocode algorithm:

```
Open an input connection to a file
Read the data from the file and process them
Close the input connection to the file
```

Figure 14.4 Interface for the text conversion program

Here is the program with a stub taking the place of the method `readAndProcessData`:

```
import javax.swing.*;
import java.io.*;
import BreezySwing.*;

public class ConvertText extends GBFrame{

    //Window objects
    JLabel nameLabel        = addLabel       ("File Name:"              ,1,1,1,1);
    JTextField nameField = addTextField (""                            ,1,2,1,1);
    JButton displayButton = addButton     ("Display the Contents",2,1,2,1);
    JTextArea output       = addTextArea     (""                        ,3,1,2,6);


    //Constructor
    public ConvertText(){
        nameField.requestFocus();                //Move cursor to nameField
        output.setEditable(false);      //Prevent user from modifying output
        setTitle("Convert Text to Uppercase");     //Give the window a title
    }

    //Respond to the command button
    public void buttonClicked(JButton buttonObj){
```

```
        //Get the name of the text file
        String fileName = nameField.getText();

        try{

            //Open an input connection on the file, read and process the file,
            //close the file.
            FileInputStream stream = new FileInputStream(fileName);
            readAndProcessData(stream);
            stream.close();

        }catch(IOException e){

            //If cannot open the file, then inform the user.
            messageBox("Error in opening input file:\n" + e.toString());

        }

        //Get ready for the user's next input
        nameField.requestFocus();       //Move cursor to nameField
        nameField.selectAll();          //and select all text in the field
    }


    //Read and process the data (this is a stub)
    private void readAndProcessData(FileInputStream stream){
        messageBox("Running readAndProcessData\n" +
                "File opened successfully");
    }

    public static void main (String[] args){
        ConvertText tpo = new ConvertText();
        tpo.setSize(300, 300);
        tpo.setVisible(true);
    }
}
```

We now explain the details.

Exception Handling

Java responds to run-time errors by throwing exceptions. In earlier chapters, we saw examples of divide by 0 exceptions and array subscript exceptions. When these exceptions occurred, the JVM displayed system-defined error messages in a terminal window and stopped. The try-catch statement provides a mechanism for handling exceptions under program control without forcing the program to stop. In the discussion that follows, we are concerned only with exceptions related to files. Similar techniques for handling other kinds of exceptions are presented in Appendix F.

Opening and Closing a `FileInputStream`

The `buttonClicked` method in our previous example program

- opens a file input stream on the user's file name
- passes the stream to a method for reading and processing the data
- closes the stream

The code is embedded in a `try-catch` statement and consists of two parts:

1. A `try` clause: A block of code is included here. If a run-time error occurs in this block, Java throws an exception and control passes immediately to a `catch` clause.

2. One or more `catch` clauses: Each `catch` clause is qualified by a particular kind of exception that might be thrown in the `try` statement. In this case, an `IOException`, such as a failure to find the file, can occur. Our example has just one `catch` clause, which expects an instance of `IOException`, here named e, as a parameter. When the `catch` clause is invoked, the code in our example sends the `toString` message to the object e, thus obtaining information about the error. Our example then displays this information in a message box.

The code for opening and closing a file stream is always embedded in a `try-catch` statement; otherwise, there is a compile-time error.

Reading Data from a Text File

After a file input stream has been successfully opened, we can read data from it. We now examine the input of data from ***text files***. A text file is one that contains nothing but characters. Java provides several ways to read characters from a file:

1. one character at a time, using the class `InputStreamReader`
2. one line at a time, using the class `BufferedReader`
3. one word at a time, using the class `StreamTokenizer`

To utilize the desired type of input, the Java programmer uses the appropriate class and methods. We now show how this is done in the context of our example program.

Reading Data One Character at a Time

The next code segment shows how the method `readAndProcessData` is coded to read text from a file one character at a time:

```
private void readAndProcessData (FileInputStream stream){
   InputStreamReader reader = new InputStreamReader (stream);
   int asciiValue;
   char ch;
   try{
```

```
      output.setText("");
      asciiValue = reader.read();                         //read returns an int
      while (asciiValue != -1){                  //-1 indicates end of stream
         ch = Character.toUpperCase ((char)asciiValue);     //cast and convert
         output.append (String.valueOf(ch));        //convert a char to a String
         asciiValue = reader.read();
      }
   }catch(IOException e){
      messageBox ("Error in file input:\n" + e.toString());
   }
}
```

First, the method instantiates an `InputStreamReader` on a `FileInputStream` object. The result is shown in Figure 14.5.

Figure 14.5 Combination of objects needed to read text one character at a time

The method uses a `try-catch` statement to read data from the stream. The form of the input loop is fairly general:

```
get the first datum from the stream
while (the datum does not indicate that the end of stream has been reached)
   process the datum
   get the next datum from the stream
}
```

Note three other points:

1. The `read` method returns –1 on reaching the end of the stream.
2. The `read` method returns a value of type `int`, which corresponds to the ASCII value of the character in the file. This value is cast to `char` before further processing.
3. The `catch` clause handles any `IOException` that might occur as the stream is read.

Reading Data One Line at a Time

The next version of the `readAndProcessData` method reads text from a file one line at a time:

```
private void readAndProcessData (FileInputStream stream){
   InputStreamReader iStrReader = new InputStreamReader (stream);
   BufferedReader reader = new BufferedReader (iStrReader);
```

Continues

Continued

```
    String line;
    try{
       output.setText("");
       line = reader.readLine();
       while (line != null){                    //null indicates end of stream
          line = line.toUpperCase();
          output.append (line + "\n");
          line = reader.readLine();
       }
    }catch(IOException e){
       messageBox ("Error in file input:\n" + e.toString());
    }
}
```

To set up the reader, we proceed as before by first connecting an input stream reader to the file input stream. To the input stream reader we then connect an instance of `BufferedReader`. The result is shown in Figure 14.6.

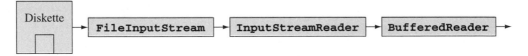

Figure 14.6 Combination of objects needed to read text one line at a time

Once again, the method uses a `try-catch` statement. The structure of the input process is the same as before. However, note the following differences:

1. We now call the method `readLine` to obtain a string representing the next line of text in the stream.

2. When this string has the value `null`, we have reached the end of the stream.

3. We use the `String` instance method `toUpperCase` to convert the entire string to uppercase.

4. The newline character is not part of the string obtained from `readLine`, so we append a newline to the string before outputting it.

The use of a `BufferedReader` not only allows us to work with whole lines of text, but also can improve the speed at which the data are input. When the programmer uses a `BufferedReader` for input, Java uses an area of memory called a **buffer** to read large chunks of text from the file rather than single characters.

Reading Data One Word at a Time

Sequences of characters separated by whitespace characters (blanks, tabs, newlines) can be processed as words or **tokens.** For example, suppose a file contains the sequence "16 cats sat on 4 mats." It contains the separate tokens

16

cats

sat

on

4

mats

Java provides a `StreamTokenizer` class for reading tokens from a file. The behavior of a stream tokenizer is similar to the behavior of the string tokenizer discussed in Chapter 8. The next code segment revisits our example program to show how tokens are read from a file stream:

```
private void readAndProcessData (FileInputStream stream){
   InputStreamReader iStrReader = new InputStreamReader (stream);
   BufferedReader bufReader = new BufferedReader (iStrReader);
   StreamTokenizer reader = new StreamTokenizer (bufReader);

   //Add periods, commas, semicolons, and exclamation marks to the
   //standard set of whitespace characters.
   reader.whitespaceChars  ('.', '.');
   reader.whitespaceChars  (',', ',');
   reader.whitespaceChars  ('!', '!');
   reader.whitespaceChars  (';', ';');

   String token = "";
   try{
      output.setText("");
      reader.nextToken();
      while (reader.ttype != StreamTokenizer.TT_EOF){
         if (reader.ttype == StreamTokenizer.TT_WORD){
            token = reader.sval;
            token = token.toUpperCase();
         }else if (reader.ttype == StreamTokenizer.TT_NUMBER)
            token = reader.nval + "";
         output.append (token + "\n");
         reader.nextToken();
      }
   } catch (IOException e){
      messageBox ("Error in file input:\n" + e.toString());
   }
}
```

The setup of the stream extends our previous setup by connecting an instance of `StreamTokenizer` to a buffered reader. The combination is illustrated in Figure 14.7. The code uses three instance variables in the class `StreamTokenizer`. These are:

ttype   An int variable containing the type of the current token. Tokens can be of four types: end of file, end of line, word, and number, represented by the constants TT_EOF, TT_EOL, TT_WORD, and TT_NUMBER, respectively.

sval   A String containing the current token if it is a word.

nval   A double containing the current token if it is a number.

The method nextToken() reads the next token from the input stream and updates the tokenizer's instance variables with information about the type and value of the token. The nextToken method skips whitespace between words and numbers. Notice that it is possible to treat additional characters as whitespace.

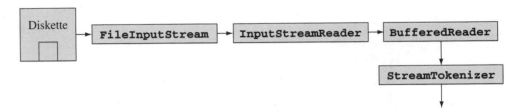

Figure 14.7 Combination of objects needed to read text one token at a time

Self-Test Questions

4. List the specific stream classes from which one can read the following items:

   a. individual characters

   b. individual lines of text

   c. individual words of text

5. Write the code that is necessary to open a file for the input of individual characters, using the file name "myfile."

6. Assume that an appropriate stream has been set up for input. Write the pseudocode form of the loop for reading the following items from the input stream:

   a. individual characters

   b. individual lines of text

7. How does a try-catch statement work with file streams?

8. Explain how the instance variables ttype, sval, and nval are used with a StreamTokenizer.

14.3 Case Study: A Text Analyzer

To illustrate the use of input streams, we write a simple text analyzer.

Request. Examine a text file and determine the word count, the longest word, and the length of the longest word.

Analysis. The program uses essentially the same interface as our previous program (Figure 14.8). When the user selects the **Analyze** button, the program opens the indicated text file, counts the number of words, and determines which word is the longest. The program then displays the word count, the longest word, and the length of the longest word in the text area.

Figure 14.8 Interface for a text analyzer program

For example, assume that the file **words.dat** contains the following text:

This is a short file. There
are only a few words in it. The
longest word has 7 letters.

Then an analysis produces the results shown in Figure 14.9. Special considerations include these:

- If the file name provided by the user is not on disk, the program displays a message box with an error message.
- A default file name, **words.dat,** appears in the text field initially.
- Numbers in the file will be ignored.

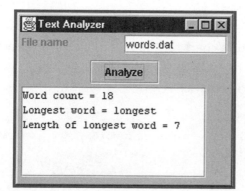

Figure 14.9 Analysis of a sample text

Design. The following pseudocode describes the operations performed in the `buttonClicked` method:

```
Open a file input stream with the file name provided by the user
Initialize the counter to 0 and the longest word to the empty string
Call the method analyzeFile to read and process the words in the file
Close the file input stream
Call the method printStatistics to display the statistics
```

The `analyzeFile` method reads words and computes statistics as follows:

```
Open an input stream reader on the file input stream
Open a stream tokenizer on the input stream reader
Read the first token
While (there are more tokens){
   If (the token is a word){
      Increment the word count
      If (the length of the word is greater than the longest word)
         Set the longest word to the word just input
   }
   Read the next token
}
```

A structure chart illustrates the program's design, as shown in Figure 14.10.

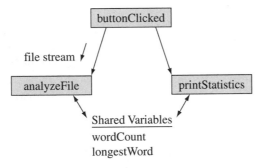

Figure 14.10 Structure chart for the text analyzer program

Implementation. Here is the code:

```
/* TextAnalyzer.java
Analyze a text file and determine the number of words, the longest word,
and the length of the longest word. Ignore numbers.
*/


import javax.swing.*;
```

```java
import BreezySwing.*;
import java.io.*;

public class TextAnalyzer extends GBFrame{


   //Window objects
   JLabel fileLabel      = addLabel      ("File name",1,1,1,1);
   JTextField fileField = addTextField ("words.dat",1,2,1,1);
   JButton doReport      = addButton     ("Analyze"  ,2,1,2,1);
   JTextArea outputArea = addTextArea  (""           ,3,1,2,3);

   //Instance variables
   private int wordCount;            //The number of words in the text
   private String longestWord;       //The longest word in the text


   //Constructor
   public TextAnalyzer() {
      setTitle("Text Analyzer");
   }


   //Analyze the text
   public void buttonClicked (JButton buttonObj){

      //Get the file name and initialize the instance variables
      String fileName = fileField.getText();
      wordCount = 0;
      longestWord = "";

      try{

         //Instantiate a file stream on the text file, analyze, and
         //print the results
         FileInputStream fileStream = new FileInputStream(fileName);
         analyzeFile(fileStream);
         fileStream.close();
         printStatistics();

      }catch (IOException e){

         //Report error conditions
         messageBox("File not opened\n" + e.toString());

      }
```

Continued

```
    }


    //Instantiate a stream tokenizer on the file stream, process the stream
    //one token at a time, count the tokens, and identify the longest token.
    private void analyzeFile(FileInputStream fileStream){

        //Declare and initialize local variables
        int tokenType = 0;
        String word = "";

        //Instantiate the stream tokenizer
        InputStreamReader reader = new InputStreamReader(fileStream);
        StreamTokenizer tokens = new StreamTokenizer(reader);

        //Treat periods as whitespace
        tokens.whitespaceChars  ('.', '.');

        try{

            //Read and process the tokens
            tokens.nextToken();
            while (tokens.ttype != StreamTokenizer.TT_EOF){

                if (tokens.ttype == StreamTokenizer.TT_WORD){
                    word = tokens.sval;
                    wordCount++;
                    if (word.length() > longestWord.length())
                        longestWord = word;
                }
                tokens.nextToken();


            }

        }catch (IOException e){
            messageBox("Data not read properly " + e.toString());
        }
    }

    //Print the results of the analysis
    private void printStatistics(){
        outputArea.setText("");
        outputArea.append ("Word count = " + wordCount + "\n");
        outputArea.append("Longest word = " + longestWord + "\n");
        outputArea.append("Length of longest word = "
```

```
                                + longestWord.length() + "\n");
   }

   public static void main (String[] args){
      TextAnalyzer tpo = new TextAnalyzer();
      tpo.setSize (250, 200);
      tpo.setVisible(true);
   }
}
```

14.4 File Output

We now turn our attention to file output. The file output process conforms to the following pattern:

```
Open an output connection to a file
Write data to the file
Close the output connection to the file
```

Here are the details.

Opening and Closing a `FileOutputStream`

The following code segment

- opens a file output stream on a file named **test.out**
- passes the stream to a method for writing the data
- closes the stream

```
try{
   FileOutputStream stream = new FileOutputStream ("test.out");
   writeData (stream);
   stream.close();
}catch(IOException e){
   messageBox ("Error opening output file " + e.toString());
}
```

Writing Data to a `PrintWriter`

The class `PrintWriter` writes data to a file output stream as encoded characters. The resulting file can be read with a text editor or an input stream reader. The `PrintWriter` methods `print` and `println` each take a single parameter, which can be an int, a double, a String, or any other type. If the parameter is an object, then the string representation of the object is printed as determined by the object's toString method. The println method appends a newline character ('\n') to the print stream. Figure 14.11 shows the flow of data from memory to a print writer to a file output stream to disk.

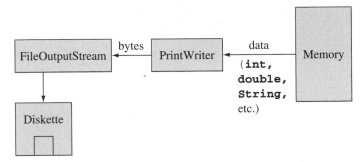

Figure 14.11 Combination of objects needed to write data as text

The following code implements the writeData method invoked in the previous code segment. This method

- opens a print writer on the file output stream
- writes a header message followed by a newline to the print writer
- writes 10 random integers between 1 and 10, separated by spaces, to the print writer

```
void writeData(FileOutputStream fileOutputStream){
    int i;
    PrintWriter printWriter = new PrintWriter (fileOutputStream, true);
    printWriter.println ("Here are 10 random integers: ");

    for (i = 1; i <= 10; i++)
        printWriter.print ((int) (1 + Math.random() * 10) + " ");
}
```

The preferred constructor for a print writer takes a Boolean parameter that indicates whether or not the application desires the output stream to be flushed. Flushing sends any data left in the output buffer to the disk. A print writer throws no exceptions, so a try-catch statement is not necessary.

Self-Test Questions

9. List the steps required for writing string data to an output stream.
10. What type of data can be output with the method println?
11. What does it mean to flush an output stream?

14.5 Case Study: Employees and Payroll

There are many situations in which it is necessary to read several files in synchronization and simultaneously write results to an output file. We illustrate a problem of this type in this Case Study.

Request. Write a program that reads two text files and writes a third. The first file contains employee names and pay rates, the second contains hours worked by each employee during the last payroll period, and the third has each employee's wage for the period. There is a one-to-one correspondence between lines in the employee and hours files. Thus, the hours worked by the *i*th employee in the employee file are recorded in the *i*th line of the hours file.

Analysis. Programs of this type are often accompanied by a ***data flow diagram*** that shows the flow of information into and out of the program. The inputs can come from the console, files, and other programs. Likewise outputs can go to the console, files, and other programs. In a complex application involving many programs, these diagrams are quite involved; however, that is not the case in the current situation (Figure 14.12). In accordance with the standard conventions for data flow diagrams, file names are sandwiched between parallel lines, and program names are placed in ellipses. Keyboard inputs and screen outputs are not enclosed in any manner. Arrows indicate the direction in which information flows—for instance, from a file into a program, or vice versa. Thus, Figure 14.12 indicates that there are two input files, employee data and hours worked, and an output file for the payroll report. The program, called `EmployeePayroll`, obtains the actual file names from the console at run time.

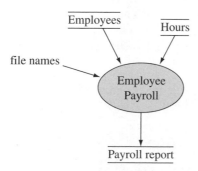

Figure 14.12 Data flow diagram for the payroll program

Before writing the program, we must agree on file formats. The text in each file is broken into lines, and the lines are formatted as follows:

Employee file   <last name> <first name> <number of dependents> <hourly rate>

Hours file   <last name> <first name> <regular hours> <overtime hours>

Payroll report   <employee name> <regular pay> <overtime pay> <gross pay> <tax> <net pay>

When the payroll report is printed, it needs to be highly readable. For this reason, we organize the names and numbers in formatted columns. Here are sample data that conform to the described file formats:

Employee file

```
Lambert Ken 7 5.50
Osborne Martin 3 6.75
```

Hours file

```
Lambert Ken 40 4
Osborne Martin 40 6
```

Report file

Employee Name	Dependents	Reg. Pay	O.T. Pay	Gross Pay	Tax	Net Pay
------------	----------	--------	--------	---------	---	-------
Lambert, Ken	7	220.00	33.00	253.00	2.53	250.47
Osborne, Martin	3	270.00	60.75	330.75	29.77	300.98

Notice that report file begins with explanatory column headers. Chapter 8 describes techniques for achieving the report's neat appearance.

There are a few remaining details to establish. Figure 14.13 shows the proposed interface for the program. An `Employee` class represents employees, and an `Employee` object is responsible for reading an employee's name and hours worked, computing his pay, and writing the results to the report file. Overtime hours are paid at 1.5 times the regular hourly rate. The base tax rate is 15% of the gross pay with a 2% deduction in the tax rate for each dependent. Net pay equals gross pay less tax.

Figure 14.13 Interface for the payroll program

Design. We use stream tokenizers for input and a print writer for output. The interface class, EmployeePayroll, follows the usual format. Here is pseudocode for the two principal methods:

```
buttonClicked
    Open a file input stream on the employee file
    Open a file input stream on the hours worked file
    Open a file output stream on the report file
    Call the method processFiles with the streams as parameters
    Close the files
```

```
processFiles
    Open a stream tokenizer on the employee file stream
    Open a stream tokenizer on the hours worked file stream
    Open a print writer on the report file stream
    Write the header to the report file
    While (a next line is read successfully from the employee file){
        If (a matching line is NOT read from the hours file){
            display an error message
            and break out of the loop
        }
        compute and print an employee's pay
    }
```

In the preceding method, the reading, calculating, and writing is done by methods in the Employee class. Here is a summary of the class:

Class:
```
    Employee extends Object
```
Private Class Constant:
```
    static final double TAX_RATE = 0.15
    static final double DEDUCTION = 0.02
```
Private Instance Variables:
```
    String firstName
    String lastName
    int dependents
    double hourlyRate
    int regularHours
    int overtimeHours
```
Public Methods:
```
    String toString()
    boolean readEmployee(StreamTokenizer stream)
    boolean readHoursWorked(StreamTokenizer stream)
    void computeAndPrintPay(PrintWriter stream)
    void printHeader(PrintWriter stream)
```

The method `readEmployee` attempts to read a line of data from the employee file and returns a Boolean indicating whether it succeeded. Similarly, the method `readHoursWorked` attempts to read a line of data from the hours file. In addition, this method checks to see if the name read from the hours file matches the employee's name.

Implementation. Here is the code for the two classes:

```
/* EmployeePayroll.java
Create a payroll report file by reading an employee file and a
corresponding hours file.
*/

import javax.swing.*;
import BreezySwing.*;
import java.io.*;

public class EmployeePayroll extends GBFrame{

   //Window objects
   JLabel employeeLabel     = addLabel      ("Employee file",1,1,1,1);
   JTextField employeeField = addTextField ("employee.dat" ,1,2,1,1);
   JLabel hoursLabel        = addLabel      ("Hours file"   ,2,1,1,1);
   JTextField hoursField    = addTextField ("hours.dat"    ,2,2,1,1);
   JLabel reportLabel       = addLabel      ("Report file"  ,3,1,1,1);
   JTextField reportField   = addTextField ("report.dat"   ,3,2,1,1);
   JButton doReport         = addButton     ("Compute Pay"  ,4,1,2,1);

   //Constructor
   public EmployeePayroll(){
      setTitle("Employee Payroll");
   }


   //Compute the payroll.
   public void buttonClicked (JButton buttonObj){

      //Read the names of the files
      String employeeFileName = employeeField.getText();
      String hoursFileName    = hoursField.getText();
      String reportFileName   = reportField.getText();

      //Open streams on the files, process the data, close the files.
      try{
         FileInputStream employeeFile = new FileInputStream(employeeFileName);
         FileInputStream hoursFile    = new FileInputStream(hoursFileName);
```

```
        FileOutputStream reportFile  = new FileOutputStream(reportFileName);
        processFiles(employeeFile, hoursFile, reportFile);
        employeeFile.close();
        hoursFile.close();
        reportFile.close();
    }catch (IOException e){
        messageBox("File not opened\n" + e.toString());
    }
}


//Process the files.
private void processFiles(FileInputStream  employeeFile,
                          FileInputStream  hoursFile,
                          FileOutputStream reportFile){

    //Attach tokenizers to the input streams and a print writer to the
    //output stream.
    InputStreamReader employeeReader = new InputStreamReader(employeeFile);
    StreamTokenizer   employeeStream = new StreamTokenizer(employeeReader);
    InputStreamReader hoursReader    = new InputStreamReader(hoursFile);
    StreamTokenizer   hoursStream    = new StreamTokenizer(hoursReader);
    PrintWriter       reportStream   = new PrintWriter(reportFile, true);

    //Write the column headers to the report file
    Employee employee = new Employee();
    employee.printHeader(reportStream);

    //Process each line of the employee file
    while (employee.readEmployee(employeeStream)){

        //Read a corresponding line from the hours file
        if (!employee.readHoursWorked(hoursStream)){
            messageBox ("Matching data missing from the\n" +
                        "hours file for " + employee.getName());
            break;
        }

        //Compute and print an employee's pay
        employee.computeAndPrintPay(reportStream);
    }

    messageBox ("Processing completed");
}

public static void main (String[] args){
    EmployeePayroll tpo = new EmployeePayroll();
```

Continues

Continued

```
      tpo.setSize (300, 200);
      tpo.setVisible(true);
   }
}
```

```
/* Employee.java
 An employee knows how to
 1) read his name and basic payroll information from an employee file,
 2) read his hours worked from an hours file,
 3) write column headers to a report file, and
 3) compute and write the wages to the same report file.
*/

import java.io.*;
import BreezySwing.Format;         //Import just the Format class from BreezySwing

public class Employee extends Object{

   private static final double TAX_RATE  = 0.15; //Base tax rate
   private static final double DEDUCTION = 0.02; //Deduction per dependent
   private String firstName = "";              //First name
   private String lastName = "";               //Last name
   private int    dependents;                  //Number of dependents
   private int    regularHours;                //Regular hours worked
   private int    overtimeHours;               //Overtime hours worked
   private double hourlyRate;                   //Hourly pay rate


   //Get the employee's name
   public String getName(){
      return firstName + " " + lastName;
   }

   //Return a string representation of an employee.
   public String toString(){
      return lastName     + " "
          + firstName    + " "
          + hourlyRate   + " "
          + dependents   + " "
          + regularHours + " "
          + overtimeHours;
   }

   //Read an employee's name, dependents, and pay rate.
   //Return true if the data are read successfully else return false.
```

```
public boolean readEmployee(StreamTokenizer stream){
   try{
      stream.nextToken();   lastName   = stream.sval;
      stream.nextToken();   firstName  = stream.sval;
      stream.nextToken();   dependents = (int) stream.nval;
      stream.nextToken();   hourlyRate = stream.nval;
      return (stream.ttype != StreamTokenizer.TT_EOF);
   }catch (Exception e){
      return false;
   }
}


//Read an employee's name and hours.
//Return true if data are read successfully else return false.
//The name read from the file must match the employee's name.
public boolean readHoursWorked(StreamTokenizer stream){
   String tempFirstName = "", tempLastName = "";
   try{
      stream.nextToken();   tempLastName  = stream.sval;
      stream.nextToken();   tempFirstName = stream.sval;
      stream.nextToken();   regularHours  = (int) stream.nval;
      stream.nextToken();   overtimeHours = (int) stream.nval;
      if (stream.ttype == StreamTokenizer.TT_EOF)
         return false;
      return (tempLastName.equals(lastName) &&
              tempFirstName.equals(firstName));
   }catch(Exception e){
      return false;
   }
}


//Compute and print the employee's pay.
//Net pay = gross pay - taxes.
//Gross pay = hourly rate times regular hours + one and half the hourly
//            rate for overtime hours.
//The tax rate equals TAX_RATE less DEDUCTION per dependent.
public void computeAndPrintPay(PrintWriter stream){
   double regPay = hourlyRate * regularHours;
   double overPay = hourlyRate * 1.5 * overtimeHours;
   double grossPay = regPay + overPay;
   double tax =
         Math.max (0, grossPay * (TAX_RATE - dependents * DEDUCTION));
   double netPay = grossPay - tax;
   stream.println(
      Format.justify('l', lastName + ", " + firstName, 15)
    + Format.justify('r', dependents                 , 12)
```

Continues

Continued

```
         + Format.justify('r', regPay          , 10, 2)
         + Format.justify('r', overPay         , 10, 2)
         + Format.justify('r', grossPay        , 11, 2)
         + Format.justify('r', tax             ,  7, 2)
         + Format.justify('r', netPay          ,  9, 2));
   }


   //Write column headers to the report file.
   public void printHeader(PrintWriter stream){
      stream.println(
           Format.justify('l', "Employee Name", 15)
         + Format.justify('r', "Dependents"    , 12)
         + Format.justify('r', "Reg. Pay"      , 10)
         + Format.justify('r', "O.T. Pay"      , 10)
         + Format.justify('r', "Gross Pay"     , 11)
         + Format.justify('r', "Tax"           ,  7)
         + Format.justify('r', "Net Pay"       ,  9));
      stream.println(
           Format.justify('l', "-------------", 15)
         + Format.justify('r', "----------"    , 12)
         + Format.justify('r', "--------"      , 10)
         + Format.justify('r', "--------"      , 10)
         + Format.justify('r', "---------"     , 11)
         + Format.justify('r', "---"           ,  7)
         + Format.justify('r', "-------"       ,  9));
   }
}
```

Note that the `Employee` methods `readEmployee` and `readHoursWorked` catch an exception of type `Exception` instead of `IOException`. Specifying the most general type of exception allows the methods to catch errors that might be caused by incorrect formats in the files.

14.6 Other Input/Output Situations

We have now covered the basics of file I/O, but there are several other common situations to discuss.

Data Input and Output Streams

When `print` and `println` methods write a number to a `PrintWriter`, they transform the number to its humanly readable character string representations. If the number needs to be read later by another program, the string representing the number is first read and then converted back to the appropriate numeric data type. Data input and output streams avoid the need for conversion. A primitive type or string written to a `DataOutputStream` is represented in binary format that is not humanly readable, but which can be read back into a program using a `DataInputStream` without conversion. Table 14.2 lists several useful methods in these two classes.

Table 14.2

Methods in the Classes `DataInputStream` and `DataOutputStream`	
Method	**What It Does**
`char readChar()`	Reads a `char` from a `DataInputStream`.
`double readDouble()`	Reads a `double` from a `DataInputStream`.
`int readInt()`	Reads an `int` from a `DataInputStream`.
`String readUTF()`	Reads a `String` from a `DataInputStream`.
`void writeChar (char ch)`	Writes a `char` to a `DataOutputStream`.
`void writeDouble (double d)`	Writes a `double` to a `DataOutputStream`.
`void writeInt (int i)`	Writes an `int` to a `DataOutputStream`.
`void writeUTF (String s)`	Writes a `String` to a `DataOutputStream`.

A program reading from a data input stream must know the order and types of data expected at each moment. To illustrate, we present a sample program that

- generates a user-specified number of random integers (the number is entered as a parameter in the command line)
- writes these integers to a data output stream
- reads them back in from a data input stream
- outputs the integers to the terminal window

```
/* TestDataStreams.java
1) Write randomly generated integers to a data output stream. A command line
   parameter specifies the number of integers to generate.
2) Read them back in using a data input stream and display them in
   the terminal window.
*/

import java.io.*;

public class TestDataStreams{

   public static void main (String[] args){
```

Continues

Continued

```
    //Obtain the number of ints from the command line parameters.
    int number = Integer.valueOf(args[0]).intValue();

    //Generate random ints and write them to a data output stream.
    try{
        FileOutputStream foStream = new FileOutputStream("ints.dat");
        DataOutputStream doStream = new DataOutputStream(foStream);
        int i;
        for (i = 0; i < number; i++)
            doStream.writeInt((int) (Math.random() * number + 1));
        doStream.close();
    }catch(IOException e){
        System.err.println("Error during output: " + e.toString());
    }

    //Read the ints from a data input stream and display them in
    //a terminal window.
    try{
        FileInputStream fiStream = new FileInputStream("ints.dat");
        DataInputStream diStream = new DataInputStream(fiStream);
        while (true){
            int i = diStream.readInt();
            System.out.println(i);
        }
    }catch(EOFException e){
        System.out.println("\nAll done.");
    }catch(IOException e){
        System.err.println("Error in input" + e.toString());
    }
  }
}
```

A data input stream is processed within an ***exception-driven loop.*** Using the expression `while (true)`, the loop continues until an `EOFException` occurs. This exception is not viewed as an error but rather as a good reason to exit the loop. The `catch` statement in this example prints a reassuring message.

Now that we have seen two different ways to handle file input and output, it is natural to ask when to use each one. Here are two rules of thumb:

1. It is appropriate to use a print writer for output and a stream tokenizer for input when the file must be viewed or created with a text editor or when the order and types of data are unknown.

2. It is appropriate to use a data input stream for input and a data output stream for output when the file need not be viewed or created with a text editor and when the order and types of data are known.

Serialization and Object Streams

Until now, we have focused on reading and writing primitive data types and strings. Java also provides methods for reading and writing complete objects. This makes it easy to save a program's state before closing it and to restore the state when the program is run again. Objects that are saved between executions of a program are said to be **persistent,** and the process of writing them to and reading them from a file is called **serialization.** To use serialization, a programmer must do two things:

1. Make classes serializable. We explain how momentarily.

2. Write objects using an `ObjectOutputStream` and read them later using an `ObjectInputStream`.

For example, consider the student test scores program of Chapter 10. This program was written using a model/view pattern in which the model encapsulates the program's data requirements and the view manages the user interface. The data model in turn consists of the two classes `Student` and `StudentTestScoresModel`. To serialize these classes, we import the package `java.io` and add the qualifier "`implements Serializable`" to each class's definition. The changes are in bold type:

```
import java.io.*;

public class StudentTestScoresModel implements Serializable{

   // Instance variables
   Student[] students = new Student[10];
   int       indexSelectedStudent;
   int       studentCount;

   . . .

}
```

```
import java.io.*;

public class Student implements Serializable{

   // Instance variables
   private String name;
   private int[] tests = new int[NUM_TESTS];

   . . .

}
```

The interface for the program declares an object called `model` that is of type `StudentTestScoresModel`. Saving and restoring the program's data involve nothing more than serializing this single object, which we do in the methods `saveModel` and `loadModel`. These methods are activated when the user selects the menu options **File/Save** and **File/Open,** respectively. The additions to the view are in bold type:

```
import java.io.*;
import javax.swing.*;
import BreezySwing.*;

public class StudentTestScores extends GBFrame{
   . . .
   JMenuItem saveModelMI = addMenuItem ("File","Save");
   JMenuItem loadModelMI = addMenuItem ("File","Open");
   . . .
   private StudentTestScoresModel model;
   . . .


   public void menuItemSelected (JMenuItem menuItemObj){
      . . .
      else if (menuItemObj == saveModelMI)
         saveModel();
      else if (menuItemObj == loadModelMI)
         loadModel();
      . . .
   }


   . . .


   private void saveModel(){
      String outputFileName;
      . . . use a file dialog to ask the user for the name
            of the output file as explained soon . . .
      try{
         FileOutputStream foStream = new FileOutputStream (outputFileName);
         ObjectOutputStream ooStream = new ObjectOutputStream (foStream);
         ooStream.writeObject (model);
         foStream.flush();
         foStream.close();
      }catch (IOException e){
         messageBox ("Error during output: " + e.toString());
      }
   }


   private void loadModel(){
```

```
    String inputFileName;
    . . . use a file dialog to ask the user for the name
        of the input file as explained soon . . .
    try{
        FileInputStream fiStream = new FileInputStream (inputFileName);
        ObjectInputStream oiStream = new ObjectInputStream (fiStream);
        model = (StudentTestScoresModel) oiStream.readObject();
        fiStream.close();
    }catch (Exception e){
        messageBox ("Error during input: " + e.toString());
    }
}

    . . .
}
```

In this code, the method `writeObject` outputs the `model` object to the object output stream, which in turns triggers automatic serialization of the array of students and each individual student in the array. Likewise, the method `readObject` inputs the `model` object and all its constituent parts from the object input stream. Note that:

- the method `readObject` returns an `Object`, which is cast to a `StudentTestScoresModel` before it is stored in the variable.

- the methods `readObject` and `writeObject` can throw several different types of exceptions. To catch all of these in a single `catch` clause, we use the generic `Exception` object as a parameter.

The methods `readObject` and `writeObject` can be used with objects of any type such as strings, arrays, or user-defined objects. When reading an object, the programmer must be aware of its type and its position in the input stream and must cast and store it in the appropriate type of variable. As you can see, object streams and serialization are powerful and convenient tools for managing persistence.

Terminal Input and Output

We are finally in a position to explain previously hidden details involved in terminal I/O. The stream object `System.out` is an instance of the class `PrintStream`. Another instance of this class, `System.err`, is used to display error messages in a terminal window (which, by default, is the same as the terminal window used by `System.out`). The stream object `System.in` is an instance of the class `InputStream` and is used to read input from the keyboard. The two output streams understand the easy-to-use `print` and `println` methods; however, using the terminal input stream is quite complicated and usually involves the following steps:

1. Open an `InputStreamReader` on the object `System.in`.
2. Open a `BufferedReader` on the resulting input stream reader.

3. Use the method `readLine()` to read a line of text (a `String`) from the buffered reader.

4. Convert this string to a primitive data type as appropriate.

The next program uses the three terminal streams in a brief interaction with the user:

```
/* TestTerminal.java
A simple demonstration of terminal I/O.
*/

import java.io.*;

public class TestTerminal{

    public static void main (String[] args){
        String name;
        int age;
        double weight;

        while (true){
            try{
                //Instantiate a buffered reader on System.in
                InputStreamReader reader = new InputStreamReader(System.in);
                BufferedReader buffer = new BufferedReader(reader);

                //Prompt the user for a name.
                //Read the name and save it in a string variable.
                System.out.print("\nEnter your name or \"quit\": ");
                name = buffer.readLine();

                //Break if name equals "quit"
                if (name.equals ("quit")) break;

                //Prompt the user for an age.
                //Read the age as a string, convert it to an integer, and
                //store it in an int variable.
                System.out.print("Enter your age: ");
                age = (Integer.valueOf(buffer.readLine())).intValue();

                //Prompt the user for a weight.
                //Read the weight as a string, convert it to a double,
                //and store it in a double variable.
                System.out.print("Enter your weight: ");
                weight = (Double.valueOf(buffer.readLine())).doubleValue();
```

```
        //Output the results
        if (age <= 15)
            System.err.println
            ("Sorry: use of this program is restricted to those over 15!");
        else
            System.out.println
            (name + ", age " + age + ", weight " + weight);

    }catch(Exception e){

        //Flag input errors
        System.err.println("Input error -- " + e.toString());

    }
    }


    System.out.println("Done");
    }
}
```

A sample session with this program is shown in Figure 14.14. From this example, we get a fair indication of the coding needed to support the `ScreenWriter` and `KeyboardReader` classes.

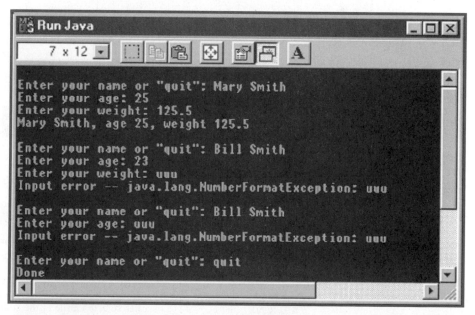

Figure 14.14 A sample session with the `TestTerminal` program

File Dialogs

Until now in this chapter, file names have been hard coded into the programs or have been entered into a text field. Problems can arise if the specified file does not exist or if the user cannot remember a file's name. These problems are avoided if a file dialog is used. The user can then browse through the computer's directory structure to find a desired file name or can back out by canceling the dialog. Figure 14.15 shows a typical file dialog as supported by Swing's JFileChooser class. Table 14.3 lists important JFileChooser methods.

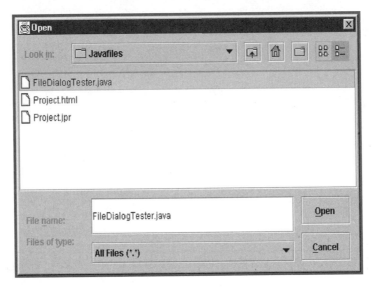

Figure 14.15 A typical file dialog

Table 14.3

Important JFileChooser Methods	
Constant or Method	**What It Does**
JFileChooser ()	Constructor that creates a file dialog that is attached to the user's home directory.
JFileChooser (String directoryPathName)	Constructor that creates a file dialog that is attached to the specified directory.
int showOpenDialog (JFrame parent)	Opens a file dialog for an input file. Returns the JFileChooser constant APPROVE_OPTION if the user has selected a file or the constant. CANCEL_OPTION if the user has canceled.
int showSaveDialog (JFrame parent)	Opens a file dialog for an output file. Returns the JFileChooser constant APPROVE_OPTION if the user has selected a file or the constant. CANCEL_OPTION if the user has canceled.
File getSelectedFile()	Returns the selected file.

The following code segment displays a file dialog for an input file. After the dialog closes, the code displays the file name if the user did not cancel the dialog; otherwise, the code displays a message saying the dialog was canceled. At instantiation, the dialog is attached to the directory **c:\Javafiles** (on a PC). The parent frame passed to the method `showOpenDialog` is the variable `this`, which refers to the application's view class.

```
JFileChooser chooser = new JFileChooser();
int result = chooser.showOpenDialog(this);
if (result = JFileChooser.CANCEL_OPTION)
   messageBox ("The dialog was cancelled.");
else
   try{
       File file = chooser.getSelectedFile();
       messageBox ("File name: " + file.getName());
   }catch(Exception e){
       messageBox("Error opening input file " + e.toString());
   }
```

As usual, we must use a `try-catch` statement when opening a file. Here is a segment that combines opening the file and processing its data:

```
JFileChooser chooser = new JFileChooser();
int result = chooser.showOpenDialog(this);
if (result == JFileChooser.APPROVE_OPTION)
   try{
      File file = chooser.getSelectedFile();
      FileInputStream stream = new FileInputStream (file);
      processData (stream);
      stream.close();
   }catch (IOException e){
      messageBox ("Error opening input file " + e.toString());
   }
```

Self-Test Questions

12. When would one use data output and input streams instead of text-based streams?

13. What is serialization? Describe situations that call for serialization.

14. Under what circumstances would serialization be a poor choice?

15. Describe the steps required to create a stream for terminal input.

CS Capsule: Programming Language Translation

Each time you compile and run a program, a large number of software tools come into play. Two programs in particular, a compiler and a run-time interpreter, play the most significant roles.

The compiler's primary task is to translate the expressions in a source program to a form that can be evaluated by the run-time interpreter. A compiler for a full-blown programming language must analyze many different kinds of expressions (loops, conditionals, assignments, function calls, declarations, etc.) and report specific syntax errors to the programmer.

In addition to a large variety of expressions, a compiler must deal with a complex vocabulary and be capable of generating target expressions that will execute efficiently at run time. A compiler delegates the task of recognizing words in the source program to a module called the scanner, and it delegates the task of generating efficient object code to a module called the code generator. The work of syntax analysis and error checking falls to a module called the parser. Most parsers make use of a table of syntax rules and a pushdown stack to handle backtracking during the processing of expressions.

Most of the real work in compiler design now focuses on the so-called "back end" or code generator. Aside from the task of producing the most efficient code (code that is not only fast but also small), designers face the challenge of generating code for multiple hardware platforms. As you know, a Java compiler generates platform-independent code called byte code. Each major hardware platform is then responsible for providing an interpreter that understands byte code.

When the executable program is in the machine language of the computer, the computer executes the program's instructions directly; when the executable program is in an intermediate language, such as byte code, the interpreter must decode the program's instructions and invoke the appropriate machine operations. Most interpreters access a program's data in an area of memory called a run-time stack. This stack is also used to store intermediate values of expressions and data belonging to function calls that are currently being evaluated.

Two other software tools that enable compiled programs to be executed are a linker and a loader. The linker combines the code from different modules, such as libraries, into a single executable program. This work usually includes verifying that the functions called in one module have unique definitions in the system. After successful linkage, the loader prepares the run-time system for execution by formatting memory into segments for the program's instructions and for the run-time stack.

Recent advances in programming language translation have led to advances in hardware design. For example, the design of a reduced instruction set (RISC) chip for microprocessors was made possible by new methods of compiler optimization. Thus, programming language translation is an important area of computer science and will become a focus of study as you proceed through upper-level computer science courses.

14.7 Design, Testing, and Debugging Hints

- Attempts to open file streams must be embedded within `try-catch` statements. These statements will catch and respond to errors in I/O operations.

- When reading data from an input stream, the first datum must be read before testing for the end of the stream. Thus, the form of such a process is

```
Get the next datum from the stream
While not at the end of the stream
    Process the datum
    Get the next datum from the stream
```

14.8 Summary

This chapter has described many ways in which data can be saved to and loaded from files. All of the files considered were sequential access. Input operations exist to read individual characters, lines, or words from text files. Output operations exist to write data of any primitive type or strings to text files. Data streams are used for the input and output of specific types of data, and serialization allows the programmer to transfer object models to or from disk without worrying about conversions to text format. File dialogs provide a means of browsing directories for files, and terminal I/O uses many of the same classes and methods as file I/O.

14.9 Key Terms

If you have difficulty finding the definitions of any key terms in the body of this chapter, turn to the Glossary at the end of the book.

buffer	file	serialization
data input stream	file input stream	text files
data output stream	file output stream	token
exception-driven loop	print stream	

14.10 Answers to Self-Test Questions

1. File classes are needed to translate data from machine-dependent devices to a standard form that can be used in a program.

2. Java represents data that are transferred to and from a file as a stream of bytes.

3. Many different classes are needed to translate data from a stream of bytes to more specific forms, such as characters, integers, strings, or objects.

4. a. `InputStreamReader`

   b. `BufferedReader`

   c. `StreamTokenizer`

5. `InputStreamReader = new InputStreamReader(new FileInputStream("myfile"));`

6. a.
```
read an int from the stream
while the int != -1{
    cast the int to a char and process it
    read an int from the stream
}
```
   b.
```
read a string from the stream
while the string != null{
    process the string
    read a string from the stream
}
```

7. The `try-catch` statement is used when a stream is opened and when a datum is read from an input stream. The `try` clause attempts to perform an operation. If Java throws an exception during this operation, control is given to the `catch` clause. Otherwise, the `catch` clause is skipped.

8. The instance variable `ttype` contains a constant that indicates either that the end of stream has been reached or the type of datum that has just been input. The instance variable `sval` contains a string that has just been input. The instance variable `nval` contains the value of a number, as a `double`, that has just been input.

9. Step 1. Open a `FileOutputStream` with a string representing the file name.

   Step 2. Create a `PrintWriter` with the `FileOutputStream` as a parameter.

   Step 3. Send the message `print` or `println` with data to the `PrintWriter`.

10. Any of the primitive types or `String`.

11. During output, some data might be left in an output buffer, so a flush guarantees that these data will also be written to the disk.

12. Data input and output streams are useful when one is dealing with a specific type of data, such as integers or doubles. One does not have to worry about the format of a file because the operators take care of recognizing the delimiters between data items. However, because the files are not text files, one cannot create them or view them with a word processor.

13. Serialization is a means of making a data model persistent. Objects in a data model can be saved to and loaded from a file as objects. Serialization relieves the programmer of the need to translate the contents of objects to a format for text streams or data streams.

14. There are two primary problems with serialization. First, one cannot read a serialized file with a word processor. Second, when changes are made to the object model, all of the data bases must be re-created and saved from scratch.

15. Step 1. Create a new `InputStreamReader` with the object `System.in` as a parameter.

    Step 2. Create a new `BufferedReader` with the `InputStreamReader` as a parameter.

    Step 3. Send the message `readLine()` to the `BufferedReader`.

    Step 4. If necessary, convert the resulting string to the appropriate data type.

14.11 Programming Problems and Activities

1. Write a program that reads names from a text file. The names are separated by new-line characters, are in sorted order, and some are duplicated names. The program should write the names to a different text file without the duplicated names. Allow the user to specify the file names in text fields.

2. A text file contains a list of salespersons and their total annual sales amounts. Each line of the file contains the person's last name, followed by a blank space, followed by a floating-point number. Write a program that reads the data from such a file, sorts them according to name (ascending order) and then according to sales amount (descending order), and outputs the results of the sorts to two different text files. Allows the user to specify the file names in text fields.

3. Merging the contents of two files is a common operation. Write a program that reads words from two text files. You may assume that the words in each input file are sorted in ascending order. Write all of these words to a third file so that the contents of this file are also sorted in ascending order.

4. Add a command to the program of Problem 4 that concatenates two files. This operation should place the results in a third file.

5. Add a checkbox labeled **Save to Disk** to the TidBit Computer Store program of Problem 11, Chapter 4. When the user checks this box, the program saves the loan schedule to a text file named **loan.dat.**

6. Add a **File** menu to the circle drawing program of Chapter 13. The menu should have the options **New, Open,** and **Save.** When the user selects **New,** the drawing area is cleared, and a new group of randomly generated circles is drawn. When the user selects **Open,** the program clears the drawing area, reads circles from a file, and displays these. When the user selects **Save,** the program writes the currently displayed circles to a file. Use the classes `DataInputStream` and `DataOutputStream` in this program.

7. Modify the program of Problem 6 so that it uses serialization.

15 Collections

A *collection* is a container for other objects. To be useful, a collection must provide methods for accessing the objects it contains, including adding and removing objects. Collections vary in terms of the types of items they contain and in the manner in which they organize their contents. In earlier chapters, we discussed strings and arrays. Both are examples of *linear collections.* The items in a linear collection are ordered by position. Each item except the first has a unique predecessor, and each item except the last has a unique successor. Everyday examples of linear collections are grocery lists, stacks of dinner plates, and customers waiting in line at a bank. We begin this chapter by presenting a linear collection called a *list.*

The chapter also presents an *unordered collection* called a *map.* As the name implies, items in an unordered collection are in no particular order, and we cannot meaningfully speak of an item's predecessor or successor. A bag of marbles is an example of an unordered collection. Although we can put marbles into and take marbles out of a bag, once in the bag the marbles are in no particular order.

A map is characterized by the fact that each item is associated with a unique identifying key at the time it is added to the collection. Later, an item is retrieved from a map by specifying its key. For instance, if the items are employees, the keys could be their Social Security numbers. Most implementations of maps have the rather astounding capability of being able to search for and retrieve items in constant time independent of the number of items currently stored in the map. This contrasts sharply with arrays in which the time required to search for an item depends on the array's size.

Lists and maps are part of `java.util`, one of Java's standard packages. The chapter's last section presents some additional aspects of `java.util` and serves as an introduction to data structures as studied in CS 2 courses.

15.1 Lists

As we have seen in previous chapters, arrays provide a convenient mechanism for working with ordered collections. However, arrays do have drawbacks:

- The length of an array is declared when the array is instantiated, and the length cannot be changed thereafter.
- If an array is not full, the programmer must keep track of the last position currently in use.
- Inserting a new item into an array necessitates pushing down the elements at and below the insertion point.
- Similarly, deleting an item from an array necessitates pulling elements up to fill the gap.

For the convenience of arrays without their drawbacks, Java provides *lists*.[1] More precisely, Java provides an ***interface*** named `List`. An interface consists of a set of public method headers without any implementing code. A class is said to ***implement*** an interface if it implements all of the methods specified in the interface. More than one class can implement the same interface, and `java.util` provides several different implementations of the `List` interface. Each implementation has particular performance characteristics that make it more or less suitable for use in a given situation.

In `java.util`, the two principal implementations of `List` are called `ArrayList` and `LinkedList`. We are not going to concern ourselves with the performance differences between the two implementations at present but will instead use `ArrayList` throughout the chapter. We will look at coding details that distinguish the two implementations and discuss their significance in Chapter 16. In this chapter, it will be convenient to think of a list as an array that grows and shrinks dynamically depending on how many elements it contains.

Comparison of Arrays and Lists

We have already hinted that insertions and deletions are done more easily in lists than in arrays. Here are some snippets of code that compare the two.

Declare and Instantiate. Declare and instantiate a collection of students:

```
int indexEnd = -1;
Student a[] = new Student[100];   // Create an array that can hold up to
                                  // 100 student objects.

List list = new ArrayList();      // Create a list of indeterminate size.
                                  // The interface is List and the
                                  // implementation is ArrayList
```

---

[1] Lists were added to Java in version 1.2. Before that, Java provided a similar mechanism called vectors.

Add. Add a student to the end of the collection:

```
if (indexEnd + 1 < a.length){      // Add to the array if space is available
   indexEnd++;
   a[indexEnd] = stu;
}


list.add (stu);                    // Lists use the add method, and
                                   // space is always available.
```

Store. Store a student `stu` at position `pos`:

```
a[pos] = stu;                      // Arrays use the bracket notation.

list.set (pos, stu);               // Lists use the set method.
```

Access. Access the student at position `pos`:

```
s = a[pos];                        // Arrays use the bracket notation.

s = list.get (pos);                // Lists use the get method.
```

Insert. Insert a student at position `insertPos`:

```
if (indexEnd + 1 < a.length){                // Make sure the array has room.
   for (i = indexEnd; i >= insertPos; i--)// Move elements down to open up
      a[i + 1] = a[i];                       // a gap in the array.
   a[insertPos] = s;                         // Put the new item in the gap
   indexEnd++;                               // Increment the index
}


list.add (insertPos, s);                     // Lists use the add method
```

Notice the following points:

- The list variable is declared to be of type `List`, the name of the interface, but it is instantiated as an object of type `ArrayList`.
- An initial size for the list need not be specified when the list is instantiated, although it can be. Regardless of its initial size, a list grows as needed.
- An element's type is not specified when a list is instantiated. In fact, a list can hold elements of many types simultaneously, provided only that they are all objects. Thus, a list is considered to be a collection of generic objects.
- Elements in a list are stored and accessed by sending messages to the list.
- The shifting of elements necessitated by insertions and deletions is handled automatically in `ArrayList`.

Cast When Accessing. Because the items in a list are viewed as generic objects, they must be cast to their actual types before being sent messages, as illustrated in the next code segment:

```
// Add a string and a student to a list.

List list = new ArrayList();
list.add ("Hi there!");          // Add a string.
list.add (new Student());        // Add a student.

// Retrieve the string and the student from the list and process them.

String str;
Student stu;

str = (String) list.get (0);
. . . can now send String messages to str . . .

stu = (Student) list.get (1);
. . . can now send Student messages to stu . . .
```

As this code illustrates, we must remember an item's type when adding it to a list so that we can cast it correctly when retrieving it later. If we forget to cast an object when we retrieve it from a list and if we subsequently send it a message, the Java compiler flags an error. If we cast incorrectly, the Java virtual machine throws an exception at run time.

List Methods

Java provides many methods for manipulating lists. These are defined in the package `java.util`, and applications must import this package if they use lists. Table 15.1 shows some commonly used `List` methods.

Note the following points:

- Some methods are index-based insofar as they manipulate an item at a given position in the list. Each list method that expects an index parameter throws a range bound exception if the index is out of range (counting from 0 to the size of the list minus 1).

- Some methods are object-based insofar as they manipulate a given item in the list without regard to its actual position. Object-based methods are founded on the premise that two objects are equal if the expression `object1.equals(object2)` returns `true`, where `equals` is a method in the class of `object1`. Because `equals` is a method in the class `Object`, all classes inherit this method; however, the version in class `Object` only considers two objects equal if they are identical. It is often useful to use a more relaxed standard for equality, such as considering two objects equal if they are equal on some identifiable attribute.

Table 15.1

Commonly Used List Methods	
List Method	**What It Does**
boolean add(Object obj)	Adds the object to the end of the list, increasing the list's size by one, and returns true.
void add(int index, Object obj)	Inserts the object at the specified index position.
void clear()	Removes all objects from the list.
boolean contains(Object obj)	Returns true if the object is among the values stored in the list or false otherwise.
Object get(int index)	Returns the object at the specified index position.
int indexOf(Object obj)	Returns the index position of the first instance of the object in the list or −1 if the object is not in the list.
int indexOf(Object obj, int index)	Same as above, but starts the search from the specified index.
boolean isEmpty()	Returns true if the list contains no objects or false otherwise.
Iterator iterator()	Returns an iterator on the list (more about iterators in Section 15.7).
boolean remove(Object obj)	Removes the first occurrence of the specified object.
Object remove(int index)	Removes the object at the specified index position.
void set(int index, Object obj)	Replaces the object already stored at the specified index position with the specified object.
int size()	Returns the number of objects currently stored in the list.
Object[] toArray()	Returns an array of the objects in the current list order.

Self-Test Questions

1. Describe three shortcomings of arrays that do not occur with lists.
2. What is an interface? How is it used in conjunction with classes?
3. Give two examples of index-based list methods.
4. Give two examples of object-based list methods.
5. Write a code segment to display all of the items in a list called list on the terminal screen.
6. What issues must be kept in mind when inserting items into a list and accessing items in a list?

15.2 `BreezySwing`: **Scrolling Lists and Dialogs**

In preparation for the next Case Study, we add scrolling lists and dialogs to our growing repertoire of GUI features. A scrolling list is basically a mechanism that allows users to view and interact with an underlying list of strings. We have already encountered two examples of dialogs, namely, message boxes and file dialogs. In this section, we will show how to construct customized dialogs.

Scrolling Lists

Figure 15.1 illustrates the use of a ***scrolling list.*** Scrolling lists are instances of the class `JList` as defined in the package `javax.swing`. When the user clicks on an entry in a scrolling list, the entry is automatically highlighted, thus giving the user visual feedback. At the same time, the program is notified of a single click event. When the user double clicks on an entry, again it is highlighted, but the program is notified of two events—a single click event followed by a double click event.

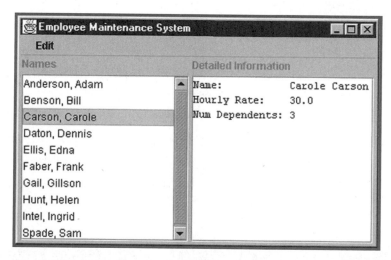

Figure 15.1 An interface containing a scrolling list of names

Java sets up a scrolling list according to the model/view pattern introduced in Chapter 10. Associated with a scrolling list window object is a ***list model,*** which contains the data displayed in the scrolling list. When the programmer adds a scrolling list to an interface with the method `addList`, `BreezySwing` automatically creates an instance of the class `DefaultListModel` and associates it with the scrolling list. The programmer can then send messages to either the scrolling list or its model to accomplish such tasks as asking which item, if any, has been selected or selecting or highlighting an entry. In addition, a program can add entries to and remove entries from a scrolling list. Table 15.2 describes many of the most useful methods for manipulating a scrolling list, and Table 15.3 describes the methods for responding to single and double click events.

Table 15.2

The Most Useful Methods for Scrolling Lists and Their Models	
JList Method	**What It Does**
ListModel getModel()	Returns the model for the list. You should cast the result to a DefaultListModel.
int getSelectedIndex()	Returns the position of the selected item.
Object getSelectedValue()	Returns the selected item.
void setSelectedIndex(int index)	Selects the item at the given index.
void setSelectedValue(Object obj, boolean shouldScroll)	Selects the given item.
DefaultListModel Method	**What It Does**
add(int index, Object obj)	Inserts an item at the given position.
addElement(Object obj)	Adds an item to the end of the list.
void clear()	Makes the list empty.
Object get(int index)	Returns the item at the given position.
Object remove(int index)	Removes the item at the given position.
boolean removeElement(Object obj)	Removes the first instance of the given item.
Object set(index i, Object obj)	Replaces the item at the given position with the given item.
int size()	Returns the number of items in the list.
Object[] toArray()	Returns an array of the items.

Table 15.3

Two BreezySwing Methods for Responding to List Events	
Name of the Method	**What It Does**
listItemSelected (JList listObj) returns void	The framework invokes this method when the user selects a list item with a single click or a double click. Applications are not required to include this method, but if they do not, the single click event is ignored. The parameter is the list containing the selected entry.
listDoubleClicked (JList listObj, String itemClicked) returns void	The framework invokes this method when a list item is double clicked. Applications are required to include this method but may leave it blank if no programmatic response is required. The parameters are the list and the list item where the event occurred. *Note*: This method is invoked *after* the method listItemSelected.

Dialogs

Usually, a dialog is *modal,* meaning that the rest of the application is inaccessible as long as the dialog is active. Users quit most dialogs by clicking an **OK** or a **Cancel** button. The **OK** button closes a dialog and transmits data entered by the user back to the rest of the application, whereas the **Cancel** button closes a dialog and discards the data.

Dialogs are implemented in much the same way as application windows, but by extending the class GBDialog rather than GBFrame.[2] We now illustrate the implementation and use of dialogs by borrowing some code from the next Case Study. Figure 15.2 shows the application's main window and accompanying dialog. The dialog is activated when the user selects menu option **Edit/Add** or **Edit/Modify,** at which point the dialog is activated and passed an employee object. The dialog then retains control of the application until the user clicks the dialog's **OK** or **Cancel** button. If the user clicks **OK,** the employee object is updated with the data on the screen, but if the user clicks **Cancel,** no changes are made to the employee object. In either event, the dialog then closes and control returns to the main window.

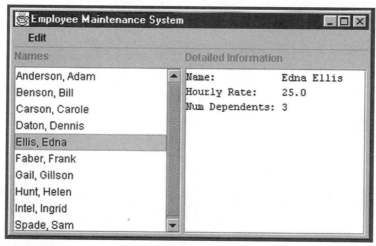

Main Window

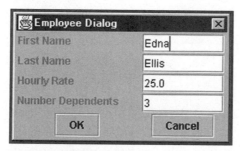

Employee Dialog

Figure 15.2 A program with a modal dialog

---

[2] In Chapter 18, we show how to create dialogs using the standard Java classes.

First, we show the code for instantiating and opening the dialog. This code is located in the class for the main window. The comments explain the details:

```
. . .
public class EmployeeSystem extends GBFrame{
. . .
   //Instantiate the dialog passing it
   //  this    -- a reference to the application object itself
   //  employee -- a reference to an employee object
   EmployeeDialog employeeDialog
                 = new EmployeeDialog (this, tempEmp);

   //Tell the dialog to show itself, thereby giving it control until
   //the user clicks either the OK or Cancel button.
   employeeDialog.show();

   //As soon as the dialog closes, control returns to this point.
   //We now ask the dialog whether the user clicked the OK or the
   //Cancel button.
   if (employeeDialog.getDlgCloseIndicator().equals ("OK")){
      . . . the user clicked the OK button . . .
   }else{
      . . . the user clicked the Cancel button . . .
   }
. . .
```

Here is the code for the dialog. Again, comments explain the details:

```
/*  EmployeeDialog.java

1) This is the dialog for the employee system.
2) It displays the employee passed to it.
3) The user can then change the data in the dialog's window.
4) If the user clicks the OK button, the employee is updated with
   the data in the window provided the data are valid.
5) If the user clicks the Cancel button, the dialog closes and returns
   without modifying the employee.
*/

import javax.swing.*;
import BreezySwing.*;

public class EmployeeDialog extends GBDialog{

   //Window objects
   JLabel lbFirstName    = addLabel ("First Name"      ,1,1,1,1);
```

```
JLabel lbLastName       = addLabel ("Last Name"        ,2,1,1,1);
JLabel lbHourlyRate     = addLabel ("Hourly Rate"      ,3,1,1,1);
JLabel lbNumDependents = addLabel ("Number Dependents",4,1,1,1);

JTextField tfFirstName      = addTextField    ("",1,2,1,1);
JTextField tfLastName       = addTextField    ("",2,2,1,1);
DoubleField dfHourlyRate    = addDoubleField  (0 ,3,2,1,1);
IntegerField ifNumDependents = addIntegerField (0, 4,2,1,1);

JButton btnOK     = addButton ("OK"    ,5,1,1,1);
JButton btnCancel = addButton ("Cancel",5,2,1,1);

//Instance variables
private Employee        employee;        //The employee being modified

public EmployeeDialog (JFrame f, Employee emp){
//Constructor
//  Preconditions  -- the input parameters are not null
//  Postconditions -- the dialog's window is initialized
//                 -- the employee variable is set
//                 -- the employee's data are displayed in the
//                    dialog's window

   //Housekeeping required in every dialog
   super (f);

   //Set the dialog's size and title
   setSize (250,150);
   setTitle ("Employee Dialog");

   //Set the dialog's default value for the close indicator to Cancel.
   //If the user closes the dialog without clicking either the OK or
   //Cancel button, the default takes effect.
   setDlgCloseIndicator ("Cancel");


   //Save the employee reference and display the employee data in the
   //dialog's window.
   employee = emp;
   tfFirstName.setText      (employee.getFirstName());
   tfLastName.setText       (employee.getLastName());
   dfHourlyRate.setNumber   (employee.getHourlyRate());
   ifNumDependents.setNumber (employee.getNumDependents());
}

public void buttonClicked (JButton buttonObj){
```

Continues

Continued

```
//Responds to the OK and Cancel buttons.
//  Preconditions  -- one of the two buttons has been clicked
//  Postconditions -- if the Cancel button then
//                        the employee is not modified
//                        the close indicator equals Cancel
//                        the dialog is closed
//                        control returns to the caller
//               -- if the OK button but the user input is invalid then
//                        an error message is displayed
//                        the dialog remains active
//               -- if the OK button and the user input is valid then
//                        the employee is modified
//                        the close indicator equals OK
//                        the dialog is closed
//                        control returns to the caller


   //Get the data from the screen
   String    firstName    = tfFirstName.getText().trim();
   String    lastName     = tfLastName.getText().trim();
   double    hourlyRate    = dfHourlyRate.getNumber();
   int       numDependents = ifNumDependents.getNumber();
   String    validationErrors;


   if (buttonObj == btnCancel)              //Cancel button

      //Close the dialog and return to the caller
      dispose();


   else{                                    //OK button

      //Validate the data by calling a static method in the Employee
      //class
      validationErrors = Employee.validate
         (firstName, lastName, hourlyRate, numDependents);

      if (validationErrors != "")           //Screen data invalid

         //Display an error message
         messageBox (validationErrors);

      else{                                 //Screen data valid

         //Update the employee with the screen data
         employee.setAllVariables
```

```
                (firstName, lastName, hourlyRate, numDependents);

            //Set the close indicator to OK, close the dialog, and
            //return to the caller.
            setDlgCloseIndicator ("OK");
            dispose();
        }
    }
  }
}
```

Self-Test Questions

7. Describe how the model/view pattern applies to scrolling lists.
8. Describe how an application transfers information to and from a dialog.

15.3 Case Study: The Employee Maintenance System

We have already had a preview of this Case Study. It brings together lists and dialogs in an application we call the employee maintenance system. The application uses two lists. The first is a list of employee objects and acts as our internal data store. The second is a scrolling list of employee names and is part of the user interface. Each name in the scrolling list of employee names corresponds to an object in the employee list, first to first, second to second, and so forth. One of the application's main challenges consists of keeping these two lists in synchronization.

Request. Write a program that allows the user to maintain a list of employees.

Analysis. The employee objects are similar to those described in the Case Study of Chapter 14. Each employee has a first and last name, an hourly rate, and some number of dependents. We already presented the interface in Figure 15.2. The main window displays employee names in a scrolling list, and when the user selects a name by clicking on it, the corresponding employee object is displayed in the text area. In addition, the main window provides an **Edit** menu with the following options:

- **Add** a new employee. This menu option pops up a dialog that allows the user to enter the information for a new employee. When the user clicks **OK,** the dialog closes, the new employee object is added to the end of the employee list, and his or her name is added to the end of the name list and highlighted. If the user clicks **Cancel,** the employee is not added.

- **Modify** the selected employee. This menu option pops up the dialog again and allows the user to change the selected employee's information. The **OK** button modifies the selected employee, and the **Cancel** button discards the changes if any.

■ **Delete** the selected employee. This menu option removes the selected employee from the lists. No name is now selected in the name list.

Finally, double clicking on a name in the list has the same effect as selecting the menu option **Edit/Modify.**

The application is based on three classes:

■ `Employee`, which is similar to the `Employee` class presented in Chapter 14

■ `EmployeeSystem`, which supports the main window and the lists of employee objects and names

■ `EmployeeDialog`, which allows the user to insert information for a new employee or modify information for an existing employee

We now present the design and implementation of the first two classes. The `EmployeeDialog` class was presented in the previous section.

Design of the `EmployeeSystem` Class. In addition to variables for the window objects, the `EmployeeSystem` class has two instance variables:

■ `employeeList`, which is a list of the employee objects

■ `selectedEmployee`, which is an employee object corresponding to the currently selected name

Here is a class summary box for the `EmployeeSystem` class:

Class:
```
EmployeeSystem extends GBFrame
```
Private Instance Variables:
```
window objects as needed
List employeeList
Employee selectedEmployee
```
Public Methods:
```
constructor
void listItemSelected(listObj)
void listDoubleClicked(listObj, listItem)
void menuItemSelected(menuItemObj)
static void main(args)
```
Private Methods:
```
void addNewEmployee()
void modifySelectedEmployee()
void deleteSelectedEmployee()
void displaySelectedEmployee()
```

Before looking at the listing, we present pseudocode for the two most difficult methods:

```
void addNewEmployee(){
    create a new Employee object
```

```
    create an employee dialog and pass it
       "this" and the new employee object
    send the employee dialog the show message
    if the user closes the dialog with the OK button then{
       add the new employee's name to the end of the
          scrolling list of names and select the name
       add the new employee to the list of employees
       make the new employee the selectedEmployee
       display the employee's information in the text area
    }
}


void modifySelectedEmployee(){
    if no employee name is selected then
       display a message "SORRY: must select before modify"
    else{
       create an employee dialog and pass it
          this and the selected employee
       send the employee dialog the show message
    }
    if the user closes the dialog with the OK button then{
       update the scrolling list with the new name and
          select the name
       redisplay the employee's information in the text area
    }
}
```

Implementation of the EmployeeSystem Class. Here is the code for the EmployeeSystem class:

```
/* EmployeeSystem.java

1) This program maintains a list of employees and displays their names
   in a scrolling list control.
2) Single clicking on a name displays the employee's information.
3) Double clicking on a name allows the employee's information to be
   changed.
4) Other operations are supported by means of an Edit menu with the options:
   Add    -- adds a new employee to the end of the list and selects the
             name in the scrolling list
   Modify -- modifies the selected employee
   Delete -- deletes the selected employee
5) The selected employee is the one corresponding to the highlighted
   name in the scrolling list control.
*/
```

Continued

```java
import javax.swing.*;
import java.util.*;
import BreezySwing.*;

public class EmployeeSystem extends GBFrame{

   //Window objects
   JLabel namesLB              = addLabel ("Names"               ,1,1,1,1);
   JLabel detailedInfoLB       = addLabel ("Detailed Information",1,2,2,1);

   java.awt.List nameList      = addList    (              2,1,1,5);
   JTextArea detailedInfoField = addTextArea (""            ,2,2,2,4);


   JMenuItem addMenuItem    = addMenuItem ("Edit", "Add");
   JMenuItem modifyMenuItem = addMenuItem ("Edit", "Modify");
   JMenuItem deleteMenuItem = addMenuItem ("Edit", "Delete");

   //Instance variables
   private JList employeeList;           //List of employee objects
   private Employee selectedEmployee;    //Selected employee if there is one

   public EmployeeSystem(){
   //Constructor
   //  Preconditions  -- none
   //  Postconditions -- title of window set
   //                 -- instance variables initialized

      setTitle ("Employee Maintenance System");
      employeeList = new ArrayList();                //Instantiate a new list
      selectedEmployee = null;                       //No employee is selected
   }

   public void listItemSelected (JList listObj){
   //Displays the information for the employee whose name is selected.
   //  Preconditions  -- a name in the name list is single clicked
   //  Postconditions -- the employee corresponding to the name
   //                    is selected and her info is displayed

      int index = nameList.getSelectedIndex();
      selectedEmployee = (Employee)employeeList.get(index);
      displaySelectedEmployee();
   }
```

```java
public void listDoubleClicked (JList listObj, String itemClicked){
//Opens a modify dialog on the employee whose name is selected.
//Note: double clicking on a name automatically triggers the single click
//       event first.
//  Preconditions  -- a name in the list is double clicked
//  Postconditions -- see the modifySelectedEmployee method

   modifySelectedEmployee();
}


public void menuItemSelected (JMenuItem mi){
//Responds to a menu selection
//  Preconditions  -- none
//  Postconditions -- see the methods corresponding to the menu items

   if      (mi == addMenuItem)    addNewEmployee();
   else if (mi == modifyMenuItem) modifySelectedEmployee();
   else if (mi == deleteMenuItem) deleteSelectedEmployee();
}


private void addNewEmployee(){
//Adds a new employee.
//  Preconditions  -- none
//  Postconditions -- if the user cancels the dialog, then no change
//                 -- else the new employee is selected
//                       she is added to the end of the employee list
//                       her name is added to the end of the name list
//                       her info is displayed
//                       she becomes the selected item in both lists
   int index;

  Employee tempEmp = new Employee();
  EmployeeDialog employeeDialog
               = new EmployeeDialog (this, tempEmp);
  employeeDialog.show();
  if (employeeDialog.getDlgCloseIndicator().equals ("OK")){
     selectedEmployee = tempEmp;
     employeeList.add (selectedEmployee);
     DefaultListModel model = (DefaultListModel) nameList.getModel();
     model.addElement (selectedEmployee.getName());
     index = employeeList.size() - 1;
     nameList.setSelectedIndex (index);
     displaySelectedEmployee();
  }
}
```

Continued

```
private void modifySelectedEmployee(){
//Allows modifications to the selected employee.
//   Preconditions  -- none
//   Postconditions -- if there is no selected employee, then
//                      display an error message
//                   -- if the user cancels the dialog, then no change
//                   -- else the employee data are changed
//                         her name, which may be modified, overwrites her
//                         previous name in the name list and the name
//                         is selected
//                         her info is redisplayed

    int index;
    String name;

    if (selectedEmployee == null){
       messageBox ("SORRY: must select before modify");
       return;
    }
    EmployeeDialog employeeDialog
                = new EmployeeDialog (this, selectedEmployee);
    employeeDialog.show();
    if (employeeDialog.getDlgCloseIndicator().equals ("OK")){
       index = nameList.getSelectedIndex();
       name = selectedEmployee.getName();
       DefaultListModel model = (DefaultListModel) nameList.getModel();
       model.set (index, name);
       nameList.setSelectedIndex (index);
       displaySelectedEmployee();
    }
}

private void deleteSelectedEmployee(){
//Deletes the selected employee.
//   Preconditions  -- none
//   Postconditions -- if there is no selected employee, then
//                      display an error message
//                   -- else the employee is removed from the employee list
//                         her name is removed from the name list
//                         no name is highlighted in the name list
//                         no employee is selected in the employee list
//                         the info area is cleared

    if (selectedEmployee == null){
       messageBox ("SORRY: must select before delete");
```

```
            return;
        }
        employeeList.remove (selectedEmployee);
        int index = nameList.getSelectedIndex();
        DefaultListModel model = (DefaultListModel) nameList.getModel();
        model.remove (index);
        selectedEmployee = null;
        displaySelectedEmployee();
    }

    private void displaySelectedEmployee(){
    //Displays the selected employee's info in the info area
    //   Preconditions  -- none
    //   Postconditions -- if there is no selected employee, then no change
    //                  -- else the selected employee's info is displayed

        String str = "";
        if (selectedEmployee != null)
            str = selectedEmployee.toString();
        detailedInfoField.setText (str);
    }

    public static void main (String[] args){
    //Instantiates, sizes, and displays the application's main window

        EmployeeSystem tpo = new EmployeeSystem();
        tpo.setSize (350, 200);
        tpo.setVisible (true);
    }
}
```

Implementation of the `Employee` Class. This class is straightforward. A static method is included for validating data values that might be assigned to an employee object. Here is the code:

```
/*  Employee.java

An employee class with basic accessor and mutator methods
plus a static data validation method.
*/

public class Employee {

    //Instance variables
    String    firstName;                      //First name
```

Continues

Continued

```
String    lastName;                          //Last name
double    hourlyRate;                        //Hourly pay rate
int       numDependents;                     //Number of dependents


public static String validate (String fName, String lName,
                               double hRate, int nDependents)
{
//Determines if the parameters have valid values for an employee.
//  Preconditions  -- none
//  Postconditions -- if the parameters are valid then
//                    returns the empty string
//                 -- else returns a string that indicates the problems

   String errors = "";
   if (fName.trim().equals(""))
      errors = "First name must not be blank\n";
   if (lName.trim().equals(""))
      errors +="Last name must not be blank\n";
   if (hRate <= 0)
      errors += "Hourly rate must be > 0\n";
   if (nDependents < 0)
      errors += "Number of dependents must be >= 0\n";

   return errors;
}

public Employee (){
//Default constructor
//  Preconditions  -- none
//  Postconditions -- a new employee is instantiated with all
//                    instance variables equal to either zero or
//                    the empty string

   firstName = "";
   lastName = "";
   hourlyRate = 0;
   numDependents = 0;
}

public Employee(String frstNm, String lstNm, double rate, int numDep){
//Constructor
//  Preconditions  -- none
//  Postconditions -- a new employee is instantiated with the
//                    instance variables equal to the parameter values
```

```
        firstName = frstNm;
        lastName = lstNm;
        hourlyRate = rate;
        numDependents = numDep;
    }


    public void setAllVariables(String frstNm, String lstNm,
                              double rate, int numDep){
    //Sets all instance variables.
    //   Preconditions  -- none
    //   Postconditions -- the instance variables are set to the
    //                      parameter values

        firstName = frstNm;
        lastName = lstNm;
        hourlyRate = rate;
        numDependents = numDep;
    }


    public String getLastName() {
    //Gets the employee's last name.
    //   Preconditions  -- none
    //   Postconditions -- returns the last name

        return lastName;
    }


    public String getFirstName() {
    //Gets the employee's first name.
    //   Preconditions  -- none
    //   Postconditions -- returns the first name

        return firstName;
    }


    public String getName(){
    //Gets the employee's last and first names.
    //   Preconditions  -- none
    //   Postconditions -- returns the concatenation of last and first name

        return (lastName + ", " + firstName);
    }


    public double getHourlyRate() {
    //Gets the employee's hourly pay rate.
```

Continued

```
//  Preconditions  -- none
//  Postconditions -- returns the hourly pay rate

    return hourlyRate;
}

public int getNumDependents(){
//Gets the number of the employee's dependents.
//  Preconditions  -- none
//  Postconditions -- returns the number of dependents

    return numDependents;
}

public String toString(){
//Gets a string representation of the employee's data.
//  Preconditions  -- none
//  Postconditions -- returns a string representation of the
//                    employee's data

    return
        "Name:            " + firstName + " " + lastName + "\n" +
        "Hourly Rate:     " + hourlyRate + "\n" +
        "Num Dependents: " + numDependents;
}
}
```

15.4 Maps

When objects are stored in a collection, it is often convenient to associate with each object a unique value called a *key.* These keys are then used later to retrieve their associated objects from the collection. For instance, a collection of employee objects could use employee ID numbers as keys. A collection that associates keys with objects in this way is called a *map,* a *table,* or a *dictionary.*

Parallel arrays provide one mechanism for implementing a map. In this implementation, the first array holds the keys and the second the corresponding objects. For instance, Figure 15.3 shows a map that associates the keys s1, s2, s3, and s4 with student objects. The keys are held in the first array and the student objects in the second. To use this map, we would:

- search for a key in the first array and then
- use the index position of the key to retrieve the corresponding student in the second array

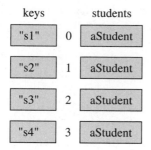

Figure 15.3 A map implemented as two parallel arrays

Working with parallel arrays is effective but tedious, so Java provides a `Map` interface and several implementing classes in the package `java.util`. A Java `Map` associates keys with objects using a mechanism that is hidden from programmers (Figure 15.4). The keys in a `Map` can be objects of any type, provided only that their values are unique. The objects associated with the keys, on the other hand, can be duplicates.

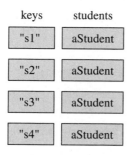

Figure 15.4 Java's `Map` interface associates keys with values using a hidden mechanism

Java provides two implementations of the `Map` interface, and in the code that follows, we will use the `HashMap` implementation. Here we initialize a map with the data in Figure 15.4:

```
Map studentMap = new HashMap();      //Declare and instantiate a map
int i;
Student stu;

for (i = 1; i <= 4; i++){
   stu = new Student();              //Instantiate a new student
   stu.setId ("s" + i);             //Set the student's attributes
   stu.setName . . .                //. . .
   stu.setScore . . .               //. . .
   studentMap.put ("s" + i, stu);   //Add the student to the map using
                                    //the student's id as the key
}
```

Notice that a student's ID, being a string, is in fact an object. Notice also that a student ID is both one of its attributes and its key. It is common practice to choose an object's key from among its attributes.

An object is retrieved from a map using the get method, as illustrated in this statement which retrieves and displays the student whose key is s1:

```
System.out.println (studentMap.get ("s1"));
```

Table 15.4 lists and describes the most frequently used Map methods. In this table, the object associated with a key is called its *value.*

Table 15.4

The Most Frequently Used Map Methods	
Method	**What It Does**
void clear()	Removes all keys and values from a map.
boolean containsKey(Object key)	Returns true if the map contains the indicated key or false otherwise.
boolean containsValue (Object value)	Returns true if the map contains at least one instance of the indicated value or false otherwise.
Object get(Object key)	Returns the value associated with the indicated key if the key is in the map or null otherwise.
boolean isEmpty()	Returns true if the map is empty or false otherwise.
Object put(Object key, Object value)	If the key is already in the map, replaces the previous value with the new value and returns the previous value; otherwise, adds the key and the associated value to the map and returns null.
Object remove(Object key)	If the key is in the map, removes the key value pair from the map and returns the value; otherwise, returns null.
int size()	Returns the number of key value pairs currently in the map.

Self-Test Questions

9. How does a map differ from a list?

10. List two applications that call for the use of maps.

15.5 Case Study: The Therapist

To illustrate the use of maps, we offer an amusing program that will allow you to earn a fortune as a nondirective psychotherapist.

Request. Write a program that emulates a nondirective psychotherapist. The practitioner of this kind of therapy is essentially a good listener who responds to a patient's statements by rephrasing them or indirectly asking for more information.

Analysis. Figure 15.5 shows the system's interface as it changes throughout a sequence of exchanges with the user. When the user enters a statement, the program responds in one of two ways:

1. With a randomly chosen hedge, such as "Please tell me more."
2. By changing some key words in the user's input string and appending this string to a randomly chosen qualifier. Thus, to "My professor always plays favorites," the program might reply with "Why do you say that your professor always plays favorites?"

The program consists of two classes: TherapistInterface and Therapist. A TherapistInterface object controls the GUI, passes user inputs to a Therapist object, and displays that object's reply. A Therapist object does the actual work of constructing a reply from the user's statement.

Design of the TherapistInterface Class. The TherapistInterface class creates a new Therapist object at program startup, displays a prompt, and waits for user input. Here is pseudocode for the buttonClicked method:

```
void buttonClicked(JButton buttonObj){
    get the string from the patient field
    ask the therapist object for its reply to this string
    clear the patient field
    display the therapist's reply in the therapist field
}
```

Design of the Therapist Class. The Therapist class stores hedges and qualifiers in two lists and stores keywords and their replacements in a map. These collections are initialized when a therapist object is instantiated. The principal method in the Therapist class is called reply. The structure chart in Figure 15.6 shows the relationship between the reply method and its subordinate methods.

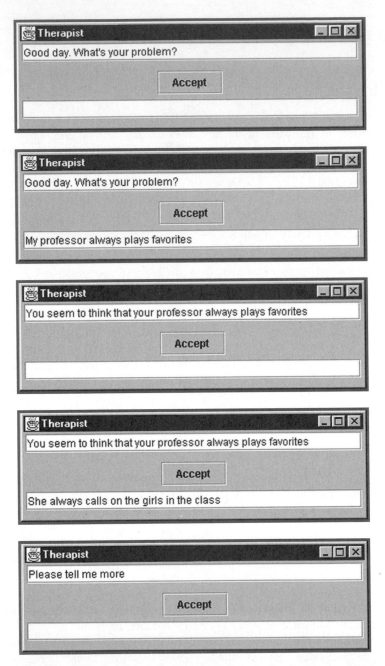

Figure 15.5 A sequence of interactions between a user and the therapist program

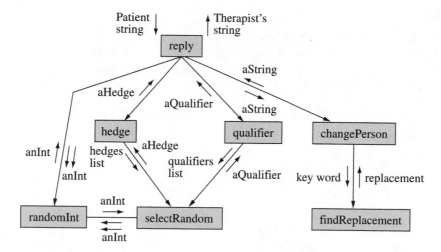

Figure 15.6 Structure chart for the `reply` method

Here is pseudocode for the methods in the structure chart:

```
String reply(String patientString){
   pick a random number between 1 and 3
   if the number is 1
      call the hedge method to return a randomly chosen hedge
   else{
      call the qualifier method to randomly choose a qualifying phrase
      call the changePerson method to change persons in the patient's string
      return the concatenation of these two strings
   }
}

String hedge(){
   randomly select a number between 0 and the size of the hedges list - 1
   return the string at that index position in the hedges list
}

String qualifier(){
   randomly select a number between 0 and the size of the qualifiers list - 1
   return the string at that index position in the qualifiers list
}

String changePerson(String patientString){
   open a string tokenizer on the patientString (see Chapter 8)
   create a string buffer
   while the tokenizer has more tokens
      get the next token
```

Continued

```
      find the replacement word for that token
      append the replacement word to the string buffer
   }
   return the contents of the string buffer
}


String findReplacement(String word){
   if the word is a key in the replacements map
      return the value stored at that key
   else
      return the word
}


String selectRandom(List list){
   generate a random number between 0 and one less than the list's size
   use this number as an index into the list
   return the indexed item
}


int randomInt(int low, int high){
   use Math.random to generate a random double 0 <= x < 1
   map x to an integer low <= i <= high
   return i
}
```

We are now ready to present the Java code for the classes.

Implementation of the `TherapistInterface` Class

```
/* TherapistInterface.java
1) This class provides the interface to the therapist system.
2) The user makes a statement and presses the Accept button.
3) The system displays the therapist's response.
*/


import javax.swing.*;
import BreezySwing.*;

public class TherapistInterface extends GBFrame{

   //Window objects
   JTextField therapistField =
         addTextField("Good day. What's your problem?", 1, 1, 1, 1);
   JButton acceptButton       = addButton("Accept"        , 2, 1, 1, 1);
   JTextField patientField   = addTextField(""            , 3, 1, 1, 1);
```

```java
    //Instance variable
    private Therapist therapist;        //The therapist object

    public TherapistInterface(){
    //Constructor
    //  Preconditions  -- none
    //  Postconditions -- the window's title is set
    //                 -- a therapist object is instantiated

       setTitle("Therapist");
       therapist = new Therapist();
    }

    public void buttonClicked (JButton buttonObj){
    //Responds to the Accept button
    //  Preconditions  -- the Accept button is clicked
    //  Postconditions -- the therapist's response is displayed
    //                 -- the patientField is cleared
    //                 -- focus is set to the patientField

       String patientString = patientField.getText();
       String therapistString = therapist.reply(patientString);
       therapistField.setText(therapistString);
       patientField.setText("");
       patientField.requestFocus();
    }

    public static void main (String[] args){
    //Instantiates, sizes, and displays the application's main window

       TherapistInterface tpo = new TherapistInterface();
       tpo.setSize (400, 125);
       tpo.setVisible(true);
       ((TherapistInterface)tpo).patientField.requestFocus();
    }
}
```

Implementation of the `Therapist` Class

```java
/* Therapist.java
1) This class emulates a nondirective psychotherapist.
2) The major method, reply, accepts user statements and generates
   a nondirective reply.
*/
```

Continued

```java
import java.util.*;

public class Therapist extends Object{


    private List hedgeList;            //The list of hedges
    private List qualifierList;        //The list of qualifiers
    private Map  replacementMap;       //The map of replacement words

    public Therapist(){
    //Constructor
    //  Preconditions  -- none
    //  Postconditions -- the two lists and the map are instantiated
    //                    and initialized

       hedgeList = new ArrayList();
       hedgeList.add("Please tell me more");
       hedgeList.add("Many of my patients tell me the same thing");
       hedgeList.add("It's getting late, maybe we had better quit");

       qualifierList = new ArrayList();
       qualifierList.add("Why do you say that ");
       qualifierList.add("You seem to think that ");
       qualifierList.add("So, you're concerned that ");

       replacementMap = new HashMap();
       replacementMap.put("i", "you");
       replacementMap.put("me", "you");
       replacementMap.put("my", "your");
       replacementMap.put("am", "are");
    }

    public String reply(String patientString){
    //Replies to the patient's statement with either a hedge or
    //a string consisting of a qualifier concatenated to
    //a transformed version of the patient's statement.
    //  Preconditions  -- none
    //  Postconditions -- returns a reply

       String reply = "";               //The therapist's reply
       int choice = randomInt(1, 3); //Generate a random number between 1 and 3

       //If the patient says nothing, then encourage him.
       if (patientString.trim().equals(""))
```

```
        return "Take your time. Some things are difficult to talk about.";

    //Else reply with a hedge or a qualified response
    switch (choice){
       case 1:
          reply = hedge(hedgeList);              //Hedge 1/3 of the time
          break;
       case 2:
       case 3:
          reply = qualifier(qualifierList) +   //Build a qualified response
                  changePerson(patientString); //2/3 of the time
          break;
    }
    return reply;
}

private String hedge(List hedgeList){
//Selects a hedge at random
//  Preconditions  -- the hedge list has been initialized
//  Postconditions -- returns a randomly selected hedge

   return (String) selectRandom(hedgeList);
}

private String qualifier(List qualifierList){
//Selects a qualifier at random
//  Preconditions  -- the qualifier list has been initialized
//  Postconditions -- returns a randomly selected qualifier

   return (String) selectRandom(qualifierList);
}

private String changePerson(String str){
//Returns a string created by swapping i, me, etc. for you, your, etc.
//in the string str
//  Preconditions  -- none
//  Postconditions -- returns the created string

   StringTokenizer tokens = new StringTokenizer(str);        //Tokenize str
   StringBuffer buffer = new StringBuffer();    //Create a response buffer

   //Build the response from replacements of the tokens
   while (tokens.hasMoreTokens()){
      String keyWord = tokens.nextToken();
      String replacement = findReplacement(keyWord);
      buffer.append(replacement + " ");
```

Continued

```
    }
    return buffer.toString();
}

private String findReplacement(String keyWord){
//Returns the value associated with the keyword or the keyword itself
//if the keyword is not in the map.
//   Preconditions  -- the replacement map has been initialized
//   Postconditions -- returns the replacement

  keyWord = keyWord.toLowerCase();
  if (replacementMap.containsKey(keyWord))
     return (String) replacementMap.get(keyWord);
  else
     return keyWord;
}

private Object selectRandom(List list){
//Selects an entry at random from the list
//   Preconditions  -- the list is not empty
//   Postconditions -- returns the random entry

  int index = randomInt(0, list.size() - 1);
  return list.get(index);
}

private int randomInt(int low, int high){
//Generate a random number between low and high
//   Preconditions  -- low <= high
//   Postconditions -- returns the random number

  return (int) (low + Math.random() * (high - low  + 1));
}
}
```

15.6 **Primitive Types and Wrapper Classes**

Java distinguishes between primitive data types (numbers, characters, Booleans) and objects (instances of String, Employee, Student, etc.). Variables and arrays can refer either to primitive data types or to objects, as in:

```
int x;                  // An integer variable
int nums[];             // An array of integers
Student student;        // A Student variable
Student students[];     // An array of Students
```

However, the items in a list must all be objects, as must the keys and values in a map. Thus:

```
List list = new ArrayList();
list.add (3.14);          // Invalid (compile-time error), 3.14 is not
                          // an object
list.add (new Student()); // Valid
```

However, there are occasions when we desire to store primitive data types in lists and maps, which we can do if we first convert them to objects. Java provides *wrapper classes* for this purpose. Here is an example that illustrates how to convert an integer to and from its wrapper class Integer:

```
Integer intObject;        // Variable for wrapper object
int i, j;
i = 3;
intObject = new Integer (i); // Wrap 3 in an Integer wrapper object
j = intObject.intValue();    // Unwrap 3 from the Integer wrapper object
```

As you can see from this code, the wrapper object intObject serves as a container in which the integer value 3 is stored or wrapped. The intValue method retrieves or unwraps the value in intObject. The wrapper classes for all the primitive data types are listed in Table 15.5.

Table 15.5

Primitive Data Types and Their Corresponding Wrapper Classes

Primitive Data Type	Wrapper Class	Method for Unwrapping
boolean	Boolean	boolean booleanValue()
char	Character	char charValue()
byte	Byte	byte byteValue()
short	Short	short shortValue()
int	Integer	int intValue()
long	Long	long longValue()
float	Float	float floatValue()
double	Double	double doubleValue()

Manipulating Primitive Types in a List

We now present several code segments in which we manipulate a list containing wrapper objects. In the first example, we retrieve a value of a primitive type from a list. The steps involved are:

1. Access the object at the desired position in the list.

2. Cast the object to the appropriate wrapper object.

3. Apply the appropriate accessor method to unwrap the object.

Here is the equivalent code:

```
int x;
Integer intObj;
List list = new ArrayList();
. . .
intObj = (Integer)list.get(3);     // Access and cast the object.
i = intObj.intValue();             // Unwrap the object.
```

As a second example, we add together the first two doubles in a list and store the result back into the list's first location:

```
int x, y;
x = ((Double) list.get(0)).doubleValue();    //Get, cast, and unwrap
y = ((Double) list.get (1)).doubleValue();   //Get, cast, and unwrap
list.set (0, new Double(x + y));             //Add, wrap, and store
```

Finally, here is a method that returns the sum of the integers in a list:

```
int sum (List list){
   int s, i;
   s = 0;
   for (i = 0; i < list.size(); i++)
      s = s + ((Integer) list.get(i)).intValue();
   return s;
}
```

Self-Test Questions

11. Why is there a need for wrapper classes?

12. Write a code segment that inserts the numbers 1 through 10 into the list `list`.

13. Write a code segment that prints the numbers contained in the list of Question 12.

15.7 A Further Look at Java Collections (Optional)

Lists and maps are not the only useful classes in the package `java.util`. In this section, we give a brief overview of sets and iterators and show how to use the `Collection` interface. These topics are covered thoroughly in courses on data structures,[3] so here we present only a quick overview.

Sets

In mathematics, sets are collections that contain no duplicate items. In Java, two objects are duplicates if the expression `object1.equals(object2)` returns `true`. From a programmer's perspective, the items in a set are in no particular order. The major operations on a set are adding elements, removing elements, asking whether an element is contained in the set, examining the set's size, and determining whether the set is empty. There is also an `iterator` method that permits a traversal of all items in a set. We will discuss the use of the `iterator` method shortly. The various set operations are specified in Java's `Set` interface, whose major methods are listed in Table 15.6.

Table 15.6

Some Commonly Used Methods in the `Set` Interface	
Method	**What It Does**
`boolean add(Object obj)`	If the object is not already in the set, then adds the object to the set, increasing the sets size by one, and returns `true`; otherwise, returns `false`.
`void clear()`	Removes all elements from the set.
`boolean contains(Object obj)`	Returns `true` if the object is in the set; else `false`.
`boolean isEmpty()`	Returns `true` if the set contains no objects; else `false`.
`Iterator iterator()`	Returns an iterator on the set.
`boolean remove(Object obj)`	If the object is in the set, removes it and returns `true`; otherwise, returns `false`.
`int size()`	Returns the number of objects currently in the set.

---

[3] See Kenneth A. Lambert and Martin Osborne, *Java: A Framework for Program Design and Data Structures* (Pacific Grove, CA: Brooks/Cole, 2000).

The Set interface is implemented by the class HashSet. Here is a trivial illustration:

```
Set s = new HashSet();

s.add("Bill");
s.add("Mary");
s.add("Jose");
s.add("Bill");                          // Duplicate element

System.out.println(s.size());           // Prints 3
System.out.println(s.contains("Jose")); // Prints true
s.clear();
System.out.println(s.size());           // Prints 0
```

Iterators

All Java collections support an object called an ***iterator***. An iterator supports retrieval of items from a collection one at a time so that they can be processed in some manner. This type of processing usually takes the form:

```
open an iterator object on some collection
while the iterator has more items{
    get the next item from the iterator
    cast and process the item
}
```

We now present three examples based on this approach.

Printing the Items in a Set

Suppose we have a set of names. By creating an iterator on the set, we can retrieve the names one by one and print them:

```
Set s = new HashSet();
String name;

s.add("Bill");
s.add("Mary");
s.add("Jose");

Iterator iter = s.iterator();

while (iter.hasNext()){
    name = (String)iter.next();
    System.out.println (name);
}
```

An iterator resembles an internal stream of objects. The two principal methods in the preceding code are described in Table 15.7.

Table 15.7

The `Iterator` **Methods** `hasNext` **and** `next`	
Name of Method	**What It Does**
`boolean hasNext()`	Returns `true` if there are more elements and `false` otherwise.
`Object next()`	Returns the current element in the iterator and advances to the next element.

Forming the Intersection of Two Sets

As a second example, here is a method that uses an iterator to create the intersection of two sets. The intersection of two sets is a new set containing only the items the two sets have in common. Here is the code:

```
Set intersection(Set a, Set b){

    Set result = new HashSet();
    Iterator iter = a.iterator();

    while (iter.hasNext()){
        Object obj = iter.next();
        if (b.contains(obj))
            result.add(obj);
    }

    return result;
}
```

Printing the Items in a Map

As a third example, we use an iterator to print the contents of a map. The steps in this process are:

- Send the `keySet()` message to the map, obtaining a set of keys.
- Send the `iterator()` message to the set of keys, obtaining an iterator object.
- Loop through this iterator using each key to access the associated value in the map.
- Print the key and the value.

Here is the equivalent code:

```
Set s = map.keySet();
Object key, value;
Iterator iter = s.iterator();
while (iter.hasNext()){
    key = iter.next();
    value = map.get (key);
    System.out.println ("Key = "      + key.toString() +
                             "\nValue = " + value.toString());

}
```

Sorted Sets and Sorted Maps

Sets and maps are unordered collections; however, there is sufficient need for sorted versions of these that Java includes the interfaces `SortedSet` and `SortedMap` and the implementations `TreeSet` and `TreeMap`, respectively. Iterators on these collections access the items in a sorted order, but there is a catch. All the items must be ***mutually comparable,*** which is to say, for any two items in the collection, `e1.compareTo(e2)` returns a negative integer, zero, or a positive integer depending on whether `e1` is less than, equal to, or greater than `e2`. Strings satisfy this requirement, as does any class that implements the `Comparable` interface.

Consider, for example, the problem of sorting a list of unique items. We could use one of the sort methods from Chapters 10 or 12, rewritten, of course, to manipulate a list. But another way to proceed is to transfer the items from the list to a sorted set and then transfer the items back to the list. A precondition is that the list contains unique, comparable items. Here is the code:

```
// Sort a list of unique items

List list = new ArrayList();

. . . add unique items to the list . . .

SortedSet set = new TreeSet();

for (int i = 0; i < list.size(); i++)     // Copy the items to the sorted set
    set.add(list.get(i));

Iterator iter = set.iterator();            // Copy the items back to the list
list.clear();
while (iter.hasNext())
    list.add(iter.next());
```

The `Collection` Interface

Java organizes the interfaces for lists and sets into a hierarchy (Figure 15.7). An interface hierarchy behaves in the same manner as a class hierarchy in that interfaces lower in the hierarchy extend those above them by adding extra methods. At the top of the collection hierarchy is the most general interface, called `Collection`. This interface specifies methods, such as `clear`, `add`, and `size`, that sets and lists have in common. The `Collection` interface also specifies several methods that are useful for manipulating entire collections, as shown in Table 15.8.

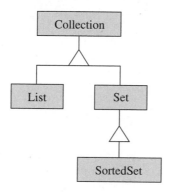

Figure 15.7 The `Collection` and `Map` hierarchies

Table 15.8

Some Frequently Used `Collection` Methods	
Method	**What It Does**
`boolean addAll(Collection c)`	Adds all of the elements in the specified collection to this collection. Returns `true` if the collection changed as a result of this call or `false` otherwise.
`boolean containsAll(Collection c)`	Returns `true` if the collection contains all of the elements in the specified collection or `false` otherwise.
`boolean removeAll(Collection c)`	Removes all this collection's elements that are also contained in the specified collection. Returns `true` if the collection changed as a result of this call or `false` otherwise.
`boolean retainAll(Collection c)`	Retains only the elements in this collection that are contained in the specified collection. Returns `true` if the collection changed as a result of this call or `false` otherwise.

The receivers and parameters for the methods in Table 15.8 can be any mixture of lists, sets, and sorted sets. For example, we can remove all the items from a list that are in a set, or conversely. Here we illustrate the use of these methods by writing code segments that generate the union and intersection of two collections:

```
// Let c be the union of a and b

Set c = new HashSet();

c.addAll(a);
c.addAll(b);
```

```
// Let c be the intersection of a and b

Set c = new HashSet();

c.addAll(a);
c.retainAll(b);
```

The classes that implement the various `Collection` interfaces include constructors that take a `Collection` of any type as a parameter. This facilitates some powerful shortcuts when working with collections. Consider the situation we presented earlier of sorting the items in a list. Here is a much shorter version:

```
list = new ArrayList(new TreeSet(list));   // Sort a list of unique items
```

In this example,

- The list to be sorted is passed to the constructor for `TreeSet`, which transfers the list's items to a sorted set object.
- The sorted set is passed to the constructor for `ArrayList`, which transfers the items (now in sorted order) to a new array list object.
- The list variable is set to the new array list object.

Self-Test Questions

14. How do sets differ from lists and maps?
15. What is the purpose of an iterator?
16. Write a code segment that prints the items in a set.
17. Describe how to sort the items in a list of unique items without using a sort method.

15.8 Design, Testing, and Debugging Hints

- Lists throw range bound exceptions just like arrays; be sure that a list index is within the range of indexes for that list.
- Any object can be inserted directly into a list or a map. However, an object extracted from a list or a map must be cast to an appropriate class before further processing.

- Values of simple types (`int`, `double`, `char`) must first be inserted into the corresponding wrapper objects (`Integer`, `Double`, `Character`) before being inserted into a list or a map.

15.9 Summary

In this chapter, we provided an introduction to several collection classes that provide capabilities that arrays do not possess. Unlike arrays, all of these collections can grow or shrink in size. One type of collection, the list, orders the items by position. Two other types of collections, maps and sets, are unordered. A map associates a set of unique keys with values. A set contains unique items. Each collection class also has a set of high-level methods for insertions, removals, searches, and other operations. The collection classes can contain any objects, but clients must place values of primitive types such as `int` in wrapper objects before storing them in collections. Finally, the collection classes support iterators that allow clients to perform traversals of the items in the collections.

15.10 Key Terms

If you have difficulty finding the definitions of any key terms in the body of this chapter, turn to the Glossary at the end of the book.

collection	keyed list	sorted map
dialog	list	sorted set
dictionary	map	table
iterator	modal	wrapper class
key	set	

15.11 Answers to Self-Test Questions

1. Three shortcomings of arrays that one does not find in lists are that lists can be resized, items can be inserted or removed with a single method call, and users need not keep track of unused positions.

2. An interface is a set of methods that clients of a class can use. Classes that implement an interface must implement all of the methods in that interface. An interface is a means of expressing an abstract view of operations, whereas the different implementing classes provide different performance characteristics in realizing the same set of operations.

3. The methods `add(index, obj)` and `set(index, obj)` are two examples of index-based list methods.

4. The methods `contains(obj)` and `remove(obj)` are two examples of object-based list methods.

5. ```
   for (int i = 0; i < list.size(); i++)
       System.out.println(list.get(i));
   ```

6. Any objects can be inserted into a list. After accessing an object in a list, that object must be cast to the appropriate class before sending it a message.

7. The model/view pattern is realized in the use of a list model with a scrolling list. The model keeps track of the items, whereas the scrolling list displays them.

8. An application sends information to a dialog by passing an object as a parameter to a dialog constructor. The dialog class saves a reference to this object in an instance variable. While the dialog is active, mutations can occur to this object. The application thus receives these changes. An application also can send the message getDialogCloseIndicator to a dialog to access information, typically about how the dialog was closed.

9. Unlike a list, a map is an unordered collection of items. One can think of a map's items as a set of keys. Each key is associated with a value.

10. A map could represent a phone book or a dictionary.

11. Wrapper classes are needed when storing values of primitive types in data structures that contain objects. One wraps a primitive value in the appropriate object and inserts it into the data structure. For access, one retrieves the object and unwraps the primitive value contained in it.

12. ```
    for (int i = 1; i <= 10; ++i)
        list.add(new Integer(i));
    ```

13. ```
    for (int i = 0; i < list.size(); ++i)
        System.out.println(((Integer)list.get(i))intValue());
    ```

14. Sets are unordered collections of unique items, whereas lists are ordered collections of items and maps are unordered collections of key/value pairs.

15. An iterator is an object that allows a client to visit each item in a collection.

16. ```
    Iterator iter = set.iterator();
    while (iter.hasNext())
        System.out.println(iter.next());
    ```

17. The easiest way to sort a list of unique items is to transfer them to a sorted set, open an iterator on the set, clear the list, and transfer the items from the iterator back to the list.

15.12 Programming Problems and Activities

1. Modify the shape drawing program of Problem 12, Chapter 13, so that it stores shapes in a list rather than an array.

2. Modify the employee maintenance system (the first Case Study in this chapter) so that the user can transfer the list of employees to and from a file using serialization. A **File** menu with options **New, Open,** and **Save** would be appropriate.

3. Modify the employee maintenance system (the first Case Study in this chapter) by adding an **Insert** option to the **Edit** menu. This option allows the user to insert a new employee before the selected employee in the list.

4. The employee maintenance system currently allows the user to enter duplicate names in the list. Fix the program so that the dialog does not allow this to happen.

Hint: Define a public method in the `EmployeeSystem` class that searches for a given name in the list.

5. Add a **Sort** menu to the employee maintenance system. This menu should have the options **By Name** and **By Wage.**

6. Modify the employee maintenance system so that it uses a map instead of a list to store the employee objects.

7. There are several ways to make the therapist's responses more realistic in the program of this chapter's second Case Study:

    a. Add five more hedges and five more qualifying phrases to the lists of hedges and qualifiers.

    b. When the user makes a statement by addressing the therapist in the second person ("you said that . . ."), arrange for the therapist to reply by changing person, as usual.

    c. The focus often shifts to a much earlier topic in a conversation. Create a history list of the user's sentences and occasionally have the therapist select a topic from these to generate a reply.

    d. Add a mechanism that allows the therapist to spot certain keywords in the user's sentences and make the appropriate responses when these keywords are found. For example, when the user's sentence contains the keyword "mother," the therapist would pick from among several replies that are associated with that term, such as, "You seem to think a lot about your parents" or "Tell me more about your parents."

    Make several of these modifications to the therapist program.

8. Write a program that maintains a dictionary. The interface should have the following components:

    a. a **Word** menu containing the options **Add** and **Delete**

    b. a list containing an alphabetical list of the words

    c. a text area containing the definition of the currently selected word in the list

    d. a text field to allow user input of new words

    When the user selects a word in the list, the program updates the text area with the word's definition. When the user selects **Word/Delete,** the program removes the selected word from the list, selects the first word in the list, and updates the text area. When the user selects **Word/Add,** the program adds the word in the text field and the definition in the text area to the dictionary, displays the updated list of words, and selects the word just added.

    You should store the words and their definitions in a hash table.

9. Add a **File** menu to the program of Problem 8. This menu should have the standard options **New, Open,** and **Save,** and use dialogs to obtain file names from the user. These operations are similar to those you have seen in previous problems.

10. A confirmation dialog asks a question of the user, who responds by choosing between buttons labeled **Yes** and **No.** The application that uses this dialog should implement a `confirmationResponse` method that takes a Boolean parameter. This parameter will be true if the user selects **Yes** and false if the user selects **No.** Design, implement, and test a class named `ConfirmationDialog`.

16 Array and Linked Implementations of Lists

This chapter presents several different implementations of lists and compares their performance characteristics. These implementations fall into two categories: array-based lists and link-based lists. The linked-based implementations are in turn of two types: singly linked lists and doubly linked lists. A variety of other linked structures are used in the implementation of collection classes, and the study of singly and doubly linked lists provides a good foundation for their study. In the chapter, we also introduce stacks and queues, which are closely related to lists.

16.1 Interfaces, Abstract Data Types, and Prototypes

A class has two aspects: its interface as seen by clients and its internal implementation. The interface is defined by the class's public methods. The internal implementation depends on the class's choice of instance variables and the coding details of its methods. From a client's perspective, it is important that a class's interface provide useful services in a clear, concise, and stable manner. The third characteristic, stability, is critical because changing a class's interface necessitates recoding its clients. On the other hand, changing a class's internal implementation does not disturb the class's clients and may in fact be highly beneficial if it results in greater computing efficiency.

Before the first object-oriented language appeared, computer scientists realized the advantages of separating a resource's interface from its underlying implementation. They called this concept an *abstract data type* (*ADT*). Early programming languages lacked mechanisms to support the easy development of ADTs, so they were used only with difficulty and less frequently than warranted. Now, however, with the widespread acceptance of object-oriented languages, the use of ADTs has become pervasive and automatic.

The `List` interface of Chapter 15 is a good example of an ADT. Although we did not examine list implementations in Chapter 15, we did mention that Java provides two, namely, `ArrayList` and `LinkedList`. In this chapter, we develop some simplified versions of these two implementations and in the process clarify the distinction between interfaces and implementations.

As we saw in Chapter 15, a list ADT is a linear collection of objects ordered by position. At any given moment, each object in a list, except the first, has a unique predecessor and each object, except the last, has a unique successor. Java's list classes provide three types of access to the items they contain:

1. **Indexed-based access.** Methods such as `get`, `set`, `add`, and `remove` expect an integer index as a parameter. This value specifies the position, counting from 0, at which the access, replacement, insertion, or removal occurs.

2. **Object-based access.** Methods such as `contains`, `indexOf`, and `remove` expect an object as a parameter and search the list for the given object. Actually, there are two versions of `remove`, one index-based and the other object-based.

3. **Position-based access.** Position-based methods support moving to the first, last, next, or previous item in a list. Each of these methods establishes a current position in the list, and we can then access, replace, insert, or remove the item at this current position. We did not illustrate any of these methods in Chapter 15, but will do so in this chapter.

Java's `List` interface includes the index-based and object-based operations, and Java's `ListIterator` interface supports the position-based operations.

Before writing large complex systems, computer scientists sometimes implement a ***prototype.*** A prototype is a simplified version of a system that includes only the most essential features of the real thing. By experimenting with a prototype, computer scientists are able to explore a system's core issues in a simplified context, free from distracting details. With that idea in mind, in the rest of the chapter, we are going to define and implement prototypes for lists, list iterators, stacks, and queues. The prototypes will be sufficiently complex to allow us to explore the trade-offs between different implementations yet simple enough to keep the classes small.[1] We will define all our prototypes in terms of interfaces, and we will then implement these interfaces in several different ways. Table 16.1 gives an overview.

---

[1] Those who are interested in the full implementations can read Sun's downloadable Java source code.

Table 16.1

An Overview of This Chapter's Interfaces and Implementations		
Interface	**Implementation**	
IndexedList	FSAIndexedList	— fixed size array indexed list
	SLIndexedList	— singly linked indexed list
PositionalList	FSAPositionalList	— fixed size array positional list
	DLPositionalList	— doubly linked positional list
Stack	LBStack	— list-based stack
Queue	LBQueue	— list-based queue

Self-Test Questions

1. What is an abstract data type? Give two examples.
2. Describe the difference between index-based access and position-based access to items in a list.
3. What is a prototype?

16.2 `IndexedList` Interface

Our first prototype consists of a subset of the index-based methods in Java's `List` interface plus a few others as described in Table 16.2. If a method's preconditions are not satisfied, it throws an exception. We show how to throw exceptions in Section 16.3.

An interface contains method headers, and each implementation is obliged to define all the corresponding methods. An interface can also include comments that state the preconditions and postconditions for each method. Here is a listing of the `IndexedList` interface:

```
// File: IndexedList.java
// Interface for the indexed list prototype

public interface IndexedList {

    public void add(int index, Object obj);
    // Preconditions:  The list is not full and
    //                 0 <= index <= size
    // Postconditions: Inserts obj at position index and
    //                 increases the size by one.


    public Object get(int index);
```

```
    // Preconditions:  0 <= index < size
    // Postconditions: Returns the object at position index.

    public boolean isEmpty();
    // Postconditions: Returns true if the list is empty or false otherwise.

    public boolean isFull();
    // Postconditions: Returns true if the list is full or false otherwise.

    public Object remove(int index);
    // Preconditions:  0 <= index < size
    // Postconditions: Removes and returns the object at position index.

    public void set(int index, Object obj);
    // Preconditions:  0 <= index < size
    // Postconditions: Replaces the object at position index with obj.

    public int size();
    // Postconditions: Returns the number of objects in the list

    public String toString();
    // Postconditions: Returns the concatenation of the string
    //                 representations of the items in the list.
}
```

Table 16.2

Public Methods in the IndexedList Interface

Method	Preconditions	Postconditions
void add(int index, Object obj)	The list is not full and 0 <= index <= size	Inserts obj at position index and increases the size by one.
Object get(int index)	0 <= index < size	Returns the object at position index.
boolean isEmpty()	None	Returns true if the list is empty and false otherwise.
boolean isFull()	None	Returns true if the list is full and false otherwise.
Object remove(int index)	0 <= index < size	Removes and returns that object at position index.
void set(int index, Object obj)	0 <= index < size	Replaces the object at position index with obj.
int size()	None	Returns the number of objects in the list.
String toString()	None	Returns the concatenation of the string representations of the items in the list.

Self-Test Questions

4. What is the purpose of an interface?

5. Why do we include preconditions and postconditions in an interface?

16.3 Fixed Size Array Implementation of `IndexedList`

It is easy to implement an indexed list using an array. Figure 16.1 shows an array implementation of the list (D1, D2, D3). The array contains three data items and has two cells unoccupied. In an array implementation of a list, it is crucial to keep track of both the list's size (three in this case) and the array's length (five in this case). We track the list's size in an integer variable that is initially set to 0. Once the list's size equals the array's length, the list is full and no more items can be added. Consequently, clients should always check to see if a list is full before adding items to a fixed size array-based implementation. Alternatively, it is possible to move a list into a larger array once the existing array becomes full, but we leave this modification as an exercise. When a list is instantiated, it must in turn instantiate its underlying array using some predefined length, such as 10.

Figure 16.1 An array implementation of a list

The next listing shows part of our `FSAIndexedList` class. We have completed only the constructor. Completion of the other methods is left as an exercise. All the needed techniques were presented in Chapter 10.

```java
// File: FSAIndexedList.java

import java.io.*;                       // Needed for serialization

public class FSAIndexedList implements IndexedList, Serializable{

    private static int DEFAULT_CAPACITY = 10;   // Array's length

    private Object[] items;                       // The array of objects
    private int listSize;                         // The list size
```

```
public FSAIndexedList(){
    items = new Object[DEFAULT_CAPACITY];
    listSize = 0;
}

public void add(int index, Object obj){
    if (isFull())
        throw new RuntimeException("The list is full");
    if (index < 0 || index > listSize)
        throw new RuntimeException
        ("Index = " + index + " is out of list bounds");
    . . .
}

public boolean isEmpty(){. . .}

public boolean isFull(){. . .}

public Object get(int index){. . .}

public Object remove(int index){. . .}

public void set(int index, Object obj){. . .}

public int size(){. . .}

public String toString(){. . .}
}
```

Note that the class FSAIndexedList implements two interfaces: IndexedList and Serializable. The latter interface is required so that lists can be stored easily on disk (see Chapter 14). Note also that the add method contains code to test for its preconditions. When a precondition is violated, the implementation throws an exception. Instead, we could rely on the fact that the underlying array throws an exception if an index violates the array bounds; however, we obtain greater control over the error messages if we detect error conditions explicitly and then throw an appropriate exception. In general, such code has the following form:

```
if (<precondition violated>)
    throw new <exception type>(<optional message string>);
```

In this chapter, we restrict ourselves to the RuntimeException, but there are other alternatives, which you can explore by reading the Java documentation.

Self-Test Questions

6. The size of a list might not be the same as the length of the array that implements it. Describe the problems that this fact poses for the users and implementers of a list.

7. Why does a list class implement the `Serializable` interface?

8. Describe the use of exceptions in a list implementation.

9. Complete the code for the `FSAIndexedList` method `get`.

16.4 Singly Linked Implementation of `IndexedList`

Linked structures provide a frequently used mechanism for implementing lists. As the name implies, a linked structure consists of objects linked to other objects. The fundamental building block of such a structure is called a *node.* A node has two parts: an object and references, or *pointers,* to other nodes. Of the many different linking schemes, the *singly linked list* is the simplest. In a singly linked list, each node contains an object and a pointer to a successor node. The structure as a whole is accessed via a variable called the *head* that points to the first node. Figure 16.2 shows a singly linked list containing the objects D1, D2, and D3. The last node in a singly linked list has no successor, which is indicated by a backslash or *null pointer.*

Figure 16.2 A singly linked list

Coding with Nodes

In Java, the nodes in a singly linked list are instances of a `Node` class, which we define as follows:

```java
public class Node {

  public Object value;     //Object stored in this node
  public Node   next;      //Reference to the next node

  public Node(){
     value = null;
     next = null;
  }

  public Node(Object value, Node next){
     this.value = value;
```

```
        this.next = next;
    }
}
```

To keep the discussion that follows as simple as possible, we declare the attributes as public. Later, we will change them to private. We now present some code segments that illustrate how to use the Node class in a singly linked list.

Building a Linked List. First, we build a singly linked list containing the three strings:

```
Throw
the
ball
```

```
// Build a singly linked representation of the list
// ("Throw", "the", "ball")

// Declare some Node variables
Node head, node0, node1, node2;      //We count from 0 as usual

// Instantiate the nodes
node0 = new Node();
node1 = new Node();
node2 = new Node();

// Put an object in each node and link the nodes together
head = node0;

node0.value = "Throw";
node0.next  = node1;

node1.value = "the";
node1.next  = node2;

node2.value = "ball";
```

Figure 16.3 shows the result of this effort.

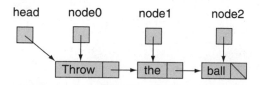

Figure 16.3 Singly linked representation of the list ("Throw", "the", "ball")

Building the Linked List Again. We can achieve the same result more concisely as illustrated next:

```
// More concise code for building the list
// ("Throw", "the", "ball")

// Declare some Node variables
Node head, node0, node1, node2;

// Initialize and link the nodes
node2 = new Node ("ball" , null);      //Warning: a node must be created
node1 = new Node ("the"  , node2);     //before it is used in a link.
node0 = new Node ("Throw", node1);
head  = node0;
```

Building the Linked List for the Last Time. We can even build the list without declaring the variables node0, node1, and node2:

```
// Most concise code for building the list
// ("Throw", "the", "ball")

// Declare the head variable
Node head;

// Initialize and link the nodes
head = new Node ("ball" , null);
head = new Node ("the"  , head);
head = new Node ("Throw", head);
```

Traversing a Linked List. Now suppose that we know only the head of the list and are asked to print the third word. To do this, we have to traverse the list and follow the pointers as we go.

```
// Print the string in node 2

Node pointer;

pointer = head;               //Now pointing at node 0
pointer = pointer.next;       //Now pointing at node 1
pointer = pointer.next;       //Now pointing at node 2

System.out.println (pointer.value);   //Print the string in node 2
```

To generalize the preceding code, we print the string in node *i*:

```
// Print the string node i, i = 0, 1, 2, . . .

int  index, i = 2;

pointer = head;                          //Start at the beginning of the list
for (index = 0; index < i; index++)   //Traverse the list
      pointer = pointer.next;

System.out.println (pointer.value);   //Print the string in node i
```

Searching a Linked List. We illustrate the basic technique for searching a linked list by looking for the word "cat" and printing "found" or "not found" depending on the outcome:

```
// Search a list for the word "cat" and print "found" or "not found"
// depending on the outcome.

Node pointer;
String str;

for (pointer = head; pointer != null; pointer = pointer.next){
   str = (String)(pointer.value);
   if (str.equals("cat")
      break;
}
if (pointer == null)
   System.out.println ("not found");
else
   System.out.println ("found");
```

Null Pointer Exceptions. A common error occurs when writing code to manipulate linked structures. It is called a ***null pointer exception,*** and it happens when the code treats null as if it were an object. For instance, consider the following code fragment:

```
Node node0;
. . .
node0.value = "Throw";   //This will generate a null pointer exception if
                          //node0 does not refer to an object.
```

If node0 is used with the dot operator before it has been associated with an object, then a null pointer exception is thrown. There are three ways to deal with this situation. First, we can use the try-catch mechanism to handle the exception immediately or at a higher level:

```
//Handling the exception immediately.
Node node0;
. . .
try{
   node0.value = "Throw";
}catch (NullPointerException e){
    . . . some corrective action goes here . . .
}
//Handling the exception at a higher level
. . .
try{
    . . . call a method that works with nodes and that might throw
        a null pointer exception . . .
}catch (NullPointerException e){
    . . . some corrective action goes here . . .
}
```

Second, we can detect the problem before it occurs:

```
Node node0;
. . .
if (node0 != null){
   node0.value = "Throw";
}else{
    . . . some corrective action goes here . . .
}
```

Third, we can ignore the exception, in which case the JVM prints an error message in the terminal window.

The `SLIndexedList` Class

We now have sufficient background to understand the singly linked implementation of the `IndexedList` prototype. Here is an outline of the class. For now most of the methods are empty, but in the subsections that follow, we will fill them in. Notice that the `Node` class is defined inside the `SLIndexedList` class. Thus, it is called a *private inner class.* There are several advantages to using a private inner class. First, it is accessible only to code within the enclosing class. Second, even though its attributes and methods are private, they are visible to the enclosing class. Third, if two classes give their inner class the same name, there is no naming conflict.

```
// File: SLIndexedList.java

import java.io.*;                    // Needed for serialization

public class SLIndexedList implements IndexedList, Serializable{
```

```
   private Node head;              // Pointer to first node
   private int listSize;           // The list size
   private Node nodeAtIndex;       // The node at index position or null if
                                   // past the end of the list.
   private Node nodeBefore;        // The node before index position or null
                                   // if before the beginning of the list

   public SLIndexedList(){
      head = null;
      listSize = 0;
   }

   public void add(int index, Object obj){}

   public boolean isEmpty(){
      return listSize == 0;
   }

   public boolean isFull(){
      return true;
   }

   public Object get(int index){. . .}

   public Object remove(int index){. . .}

   public void set(int index, Object obj){. . .}

   public int size(){
      return listSize;
   }

   public String toString(){
      String str = "";
      for (Node node = head; node != null; node = node.next)
          str += node.value + " ";
      return str;
   }

   private void locateNode(int index){. . .}

   // ----------------- Private inner class for Node -----------------

   private class Node {
```

Continues

Continued

```
    private Object value;      //Object stored in this node
    private Node    next;      //Reference to the next node

    private Node(){
       value = null;
       next = null;
    }

    private Node(Object value, Node next){
       this.value = value;
       this.next = next;
    }
  }
}
```

The `locateNode` Method

To locate node i ($i = 0, 1, 2, \ldots$) in a linked list, we must start at the head node and visit each successive node until we reach node i. This traversal process is used in the methods `get`, `set`, `add`, and `remove`, so to save time, we write a private helper method, `locateNode`, to implement the process. This helper method takes an index i as a parameter and sets the variable `nodeAtIndex` to node i. In addition, it sets the variable `nodeBefore` to node $i - 1$. The latter variable is used by the methods `add` and `remove`. Figure 16.4 shows the outcome of calling `locateNode(2)`. If the index equals the list size, the method sets `nodeBefore` to the last node and `nodeAtIndex` to `null`.

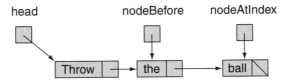

Figure 16.4 The outcome of calling `locateNode(2)`

Here is the code for `locateNode`:

```
private void locateNode(int index){
//Obtain pointers to the node at index and its predecessor
//Preconditions    0 <= index <= listSize
//Postconditions   nodeAtIndex points to the node at position index
//                  or null if there is none
//                  nodeBefore points at the predecessor or null
//                  if there is none
```

```
    nodeBefore = null;
    nodeAtIndex = head;
    for (int i = 1; i < listSize && i <= index; i++){
        nodeBefore = nodeAtIndex;
        nodeAtIndex = nodeAtIndex.next;
    }
    if (index == listSize){
        nodeBefore = nodeAtIndex;
        nodeAtIndex = null;
    }
}
```

The `get` and `set` Methods

The methods `get` and `set` use `locateNode` to access the node at a given index position. The `get` method then retrieves the value in the node, whereas the `set` method changes the value. Here is the code for `get`. The `set` method is left as an exercise.

```
public Object get(int index){
    if (index < 0 || index >= listSize)
        throw new RuntimeException
        ("Index = " + index + " is out of list bounds");

    locateNode(index);
    return nodeAtIndex.value;
}
```

The `remove` Method

The `remove` method locates an indicated node, deletes it from the linked list, and returns the value stored in the node. A node is deleted by adjusting pointers. There are two cases to consider.

1. To delete the first node, set the `head` pointer to the first node's `next` pointer (Figure 16.5).

2. To delete any other node, locate it. Then set the predecessor's `next` pointer to the deleted node's `next` pointer (Figure 16.6).

Step 1. Locate the node (the first one).

Step 2. Set the head pointer to the first node's next pointer.

Step 3. The garbage collector removes the deleted node from memory.

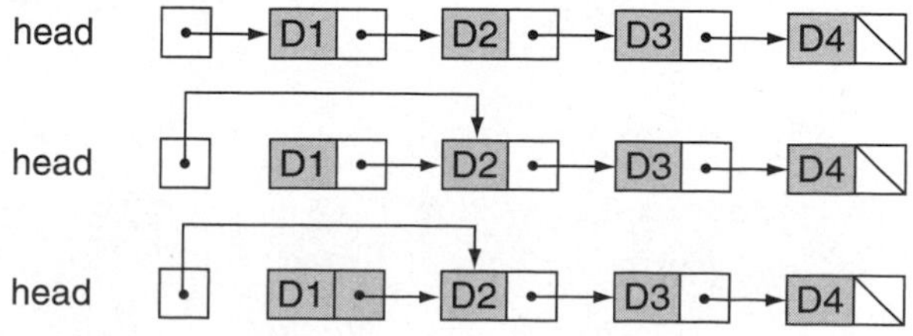

Figure 16.5 Removing the first node from a linked list

Step 1. Locate the node (say, node 2).

Step 2. Set the predecessor's next pointer to the deleted node's next pointer.

Step 3. The garbage collector removes the deleted node from memory.

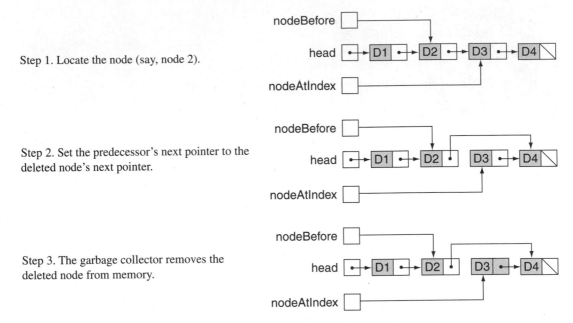

Figure 16.6 Removing any node other than the first from a linked list

In the second case, if the deleted node is the last one, then the predecessor's `next` pointer is set to `null`. Here is the code for the `remove` method:

```
public Object remove(int index){
    if (index < 0 || index >= listSize)        // Check precondition
        throw new RuntimeException
        ("Index = " + index + " is out of list bounds");

    Object removedObj = null;

    if (index == 0){                           // Case 1: item is first one
        removedObj = head.value;
        head = head.next;
    }else{
        locateNode(index);
        nodeBefore.next = nodeAtIndex.next;
        removedObj = nodeAtIndex.value;
    }

    listSize--;
    return removedObj;
}
```

The `add` Method

The `add` method must deal with the following situations:

Case 1: If the index is 0, the new node becomes the first node in the list. To accomplish this, the new node's `next` pointer is set to the old `head` pointer, and the `head` pointer is then set to the new node. Figure 16.7 shows a node with the object D2 being inserted at the beginning of a list.

Case 2: If the index is greater than 0, the new node is inserted between the node at position index −1 and the node at position index or after the last node if the index equals the list size. To accomplish this, we locate the node at position index. We then aim the new node's `next` pointer at the node at position index and the predecessor's `next` pointer at the new node. Figure 16.8 shows a node containing the object D3 being inserted at position 1 in a list.

Before the node D2 is inserted at the beginning of the list.

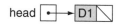

After the node is inserted.

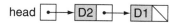

Figure 16.7 Adding a new node at the beginning of a linked list

Step 1. Locate the node before and the node at the index.

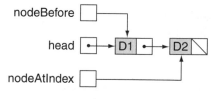

Step 2. Aim the new node's next pointer at the node at the index.

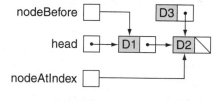

Step 3. Aim the predecessor's next pointer at the new node.

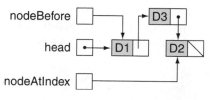

Figure 16.8 Adding a new node to a linked list at position 1

Here is the code for the `add` method:

```
public void add(int index, Object obj){
    if (index < 0 || index > listSize)        // Check precondition
        throw new RuntimeException
        ("Index = " + index + " is out of list bounds");

    if (index == 0)                            // Case 1: Head of list
        head = new Node(obj, head);
    else{                                      // Case 2: Other positions
        locateNode(index);
        nodeBefore.next = new Node(obj, nodeAtIndex);
    }
    listSize++;
}
```

Self-Test Questions

10. What is a node?

11. What is the null pointer exception?

12. Draw a diagram of the linked structure that is formed by running the following code, which uses the Node class defined in this section:

    ```
    Node node = null;
    for (int i = 1; i <= 5; i++)
        node = new Node("" + i, node);
    ```

16.5 Testing the `IndexedList` Implementations

Having developed two implementations of an IndexedList, we address the problem of testing them. We want to make sure that the implementations are free of bugs before we use them in an application. A good test program will exercise all the features of an IndexedList in a clear-cut manner and produce output that is easy to interpret. Anytime we make changes to the implementations, we should run the test program again, and if new features are added, we should extend the test program to include them. Proper testing is extremely important, so we include a complete listing of the test program. Some significant modifications are recommended in the exercises.

```
/* File: IndexedListTester.java

Test the fixed size array and the singly linked implementations of an
indexed list.

*/
```

```java
import java.io.*;

public class IndexedListTester{

   public static void main(String[] args){

      IndexedList list;                      // Declare list variable

      //Test the fixed size array implementation
      list = new FSAIndexedList();
      System.out.println ("Test of FSAIndexedList");
      System.out.println ("----------------------");
      testImplementation (list);

      //Test the singly linked implementation
      list = new SLIndexedList();
      System.out.println ("Test of SLIndexedList");
      System.out.println ("---------------------");
      testImplementation (list);
   }

   private static void testImplementation (IndexedList list){
      int i, n;                              // Loop control variables
      Integer wrap;                          // Wrapper for integers
      int sum;                               // Sum of the values in the list

      //Print the list. It should be empty
      System.out.println ("\nTest 1: Expect an empty list");
      System.out.println ("Size: " + list.size() + " List: " + list);
      pause();

      //Add 0,1,2,3,4 to the list and print.
      for (i = 0; i < 5; i++){
         wrap = new Integer(i);
         list.add(i, wrap);
      }
      System.out.println ("\nTest  2: Expect the list 0 1 2 3 4");
      System.out.println ("Size: " + list.size() + " List: " + list);
      pause();

      //Sum the values in the list and print.
      sum = 0;
      for (i = 0; i < list.size(); i++)
         sum += ((Integer)list.get(i)).intValue();
      System.out.println ("\nTest 3: Expect 10");
      System.out.println ("sum = " + sum);
```

Continues

Continued

```
      pause();

      //Change all the list entries and print.
      //The list will contain 1,2,3,4,5
      n = list.size();
      for (i = 0; i < n; i++){
         wrap = new Integer(i+1);
         list.set(i, wrap);
      }
      System.out.println ("\nTest 4: Expect the list 1 2 3 4 5");
      System.out.println ("Size: " + list.size() + " List: " + list);
      pause();

      //Add at the beginning and interior of the list. Then print.
      //The list will contain 91,1,92,2,3,4,5
      list.add(0, new Integer(91));
      list.add(2, new Integer(92));
      System.out.println ("\nTest 5: Expect the list 91 1 92 2 3 4 5");
      System.out.println ("Size: " + list.size() + " List: " + list);
      pause();

      //Remove from the beginning, interior, and end of list. Then print.
      //The list will contain 1,2,3,4
      list.remove(0);
      list.remove(1);
      list.remove(list.size() - 1);
      System.out.println ("\nTest 6: Expect the list 1 2 3 4");
      System.out.println ("Size: " + list.size() + " List: " + list);
      pause();

      //Remove remaining items from the list, sum, and print.
      sum = 0;
      while (! list.isEmpty())
         sum += ((Integer)list.remove(0)).intValue();
      System.out.println ("\nTest 7: Expect an empty list and then 10");
      System.out.println ("Size: " + list.size() + " List: " + list);
      System.out.println ("sum = " + sum);
      pause();

      //At this point we should include tests that make sure all exceptions
      //are thrown as intended; however, for the sake of brevity we include
      //just two and leave the rest as an exercise.

      //Add to the list using an invalid index
```

```java
        list.add (0, new Integer(0));          //List should now contain 0
        System.out.println
           ("\nTest 8: Expect 'Index out of list bounds' error");
        try{
           list.add(2, new Integer(3));       //0 or 1 would be valid
        }catch (RuntimeException e){
           System.out.println (e.toString());
        }
        pause();

        //Add enough objects to the list to cause an 'Array is full' error
        //when using the fixed size array implementation
        System.out.println ("\nTest 9: Expect 'The list is full' error if FSA");
        try{
           for (i = 1; i < 20; i++){
              wrap = new Integer(i);
              list.add(i, wrap);
           }
        }catch (RuntimeException e){
           System.out.println (e.toString());
        }
        pause();

        //See if the list is full
        System.out.println ("\nTest 10: Expect true if FSA imp else false");
        System.out.println ("Full = " + list.isFull());
        pause();

        //Print the list
        System.out.println ("\nExpect 0-9 if FSA else 0-19");
        System.out.println ("Size: " + list.size() + " List: " + list);
        pause();
    }

    private static void pause() {
        BufferedReader reader =                 // Keyboard input
           new BufferedReader (new InputStreamReader (System.in));
        try{
           System.out.println ("Press Enter to continue . . .");
           reader.readLine();
        }catch (IOException e){
           System.out.println (e.toString());
        }
    }
}
```

16.6 Complexity Analysis of Indexed Lists

Users of indexed lists face a dilemma. Which of the two implementations should they use? An understanding of the memory usage and run-time efficiency of the implementations provides an answer. We begin with an analysis of the memory usage.

Memory Usage

Java maintains a region of memory, called **dynamic memory,** from which it allocates space for objects. Memory for an object is not allocated until the object is instantiated, and when the object is no longer referenced, the memory is reclaimed in a process called **garbage collection.**

When a FSAIndexedList is instantiated, a single contiguous block of memory is allocated for the list's underlying array. If the array is too small, then it fills up, and if it is too large, there is much unused space. In the first instance, an application may fail because at some point it can no longer add items to a list, and in the second instance, it may hog so much memory that the computer's overall performance is degraded. The space occupied by the array depends on two factors: the array's length and the size of each entry. As the array contains references to objects and not the actual objects themselves, each entry is exactly the same size, or 4 bytes on most computers. The total space occupied by a list equals the space needed by the objects plus $4n$ bytes, where n represents the array's length.

With a SLIndexedList, memory is allocated one node at a time and is recovered each time a node is removed. Each node contains two references: one to an object in the list and the other to the next node in the linked structure. Consequently, the total space occupied by a list equals the space needed by the objects plus $8m$ bytes, where m represents the list's length.

We can now compare the memory usage of the two implementations. When the underlying array is less than half full, the array implementation occupies more memory than the corresponding linked implementation. Beyond the halfway point, the array implementation holds the advantage. Consequently, if we can accurately predict the maximum size of our list and if we do not expect the list's size to vary greatly, then an array implementation makes better use of memory. At other times, the linked implementation has the advantage.

Run-Time Efficiency

There are several factors that affect the run-time efficiency of the two implementations. First, consider the problem of accessing an item at a particular position within a list. The entries in an array are contiguous, which makes it possible to access an entry in constant time. Figure 16.9 shows an array in which each entry is 4 bytes long. The array's **base address** (i.e., the address of the array's first byte) is at location 100, and each successive entry starts 4 bytes past the beginning of the previous one. When we write code that refers to array element a[i], the following computation is performed:

```
Address of array entry i = base address + 4 * i
```

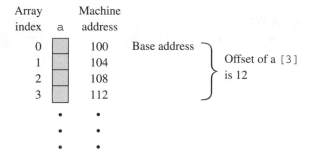

Figure 16.9 Memory map for an array with base address 100 and entry size of 4 bytes

The quantity 4 * i is called the ***offset*** and equals the difference between the base address and the location of the desired entry. Once the computation has been completed, the array element is immediately accessible. Because the address computation is performed in constant time, accessing array elements is an O(1) operation.

In contrast, the nodes in a linked structure are not necessarily in physically adjacent memory locations. This implies that a node cannot be accessed by adding an offset to a base address but, instead, is located by following a trail of pointers, beginning at the first node. Thus, the time taken to access a node is linearly dependent on its position within the linked structure or O(n). From this discussion we conclude that the get and set methods are O(1) for an array implementation and O(n) for a linked implementation.

Next consider the problem of adding an item to a list. In an array implementation, insertion is preceded by shifting all the array entries at and below the insertion point down one slot. This is an O(n) operation and is followed by the O(1) operation of storing a new reference in the array at the insertion point. Thus, the operation is O(n) overall. For a linked list, locating the insertion point requires a traversal and is an O(n) operation. This is followed by instantiating a new node and tying it into the linked structure, which is an O(1) operation. Thus, the operation is O(n) overall.

A similar analysis shows that removing an item from a list is O(n) for both implementations. The toString method involves traversing the list from beginning to end and is an O(n) operation for both implementations, while the remaining operations (isEmpty, isFull, and size) are obviously O(1). Table 16.3 summarizes these findings.

In conclusion, we see that the fixed size array implementation provides better run-time performance than the singly linked implementation; however, in situations where we cannot predict a list's maximum size, the array implementation incurs the risk of either running out of space or wasting it. This drawback is overcome by using dynamic rather than fixed size arrays. When a dynamic array fills, it is replaced by a larger array, and when it shrinks beyond a certain point, it is replaced by a smaller array. Each time this happens, the entries are copied from the old to the new array. While this approach solves the memory problem, it reintroduces a performance problem. Copying entries between arrays is an O(n) operation, but it is experienced only occasionally. In fact, we can show that on average add and remove remain O(1), provided dynamic arrays grow and shrink by a factor of 2.

Table 16.3

The Running Times of the Indexed List Implementations		
	Complexity	
Method	**Fixed Size Array** (`FSAIndexedList`)	**Singly Linked List** (`SLIndexedList`)
`boolean isEmpty()`	O(1)	O(1)
`boolean isFull()`	O(1)	O(1)
`int size()`	O(1)	O(1)
`void add(int i, Object o)`	O(n)	O(n)
`Object get(int i)`	O(1)	O(n)
`Object remove(int i)`	O(n)	O(n)
`Object set(int i, Object o)`	O(1)	O(n)
`String toString()`	O(n)	O(n)

Self-Test Questions

13. How are arrays represented in memory, and what effect does this representation have on the performance of array processing?

14. How are linked structures represented in memory, and what effect does this representation have on the performance of linked structure processing?

16.7 `PositionalList` Interface

A positional list has a more complex interface than an indexed list, and in contrast to an indexed list, it does not provide direct access to an item based on an index. Instead, a client moves a pointer called the ***current position indicator*** forward or backward through the list until a desired position is reached. Other operations can then replace, insert, or remove an item relative to the current position. Table 16.4 gives an overview of the methods organized by category. In the rest of this section, we explain these methods and their use more fully.

We call our interface `PositionalList`, and it is similar to Java's standard `ListIterator` interface. Iterators (see Section 15.7) are closely tied to a class over which they iterate; however, the implementation of iterators involves technical details that are beyond this book's scope. Consequently, we implement `PositionalList` not as an iterator but as a stand-alone class.

Table 16.4

Overview of the `PositionalList` Interface	
Method Categories	**Method Names**
Move	`moveToHead, moveToTail, next, previous`
Check position	`hasNext, hasPrevious`
Modify content	`add, remove, set`
Other	`isEmpty, isFull, size, toString`

Navigating

The current position indicator is part of the state of a positional list, and provided the list is not empty, it always has a value. To navigate in a positional list, a client

- moves to the head or the tail of the list using the methods `moveToHead` and `moveToTail`
- determines if either end of the list has been reached using the methods `hasNext` and `hasPrevious`
- moves to the next or previous item in the list using the methods `next` and `previous`

To illustrate, consider Table 16.5, which shows the effect of navigating in a list of three items. In the table, an arrow represents the current position indicator.

Table 16.5

Navigation in a List of Three Items					
Action	hasNext	hasPrevious	Effect		
`moveToHead`	`true`	`false`	D1 ↑	D2	D3
`next`	`true`	`true`	D1	D2 ↑	D3
`next`	`true`	`true`	D1	D2	D3 ↑
`next`	`false`	`true`	D1	D2	D3 ↑

Here is a code segment that traverses a positional list from beginning to end:

```
list.moveToHead();
while (list.hasNext()){
    Object item = list.next();
    <do something with the item>
}
```

Alternatively, we can traverse a list in the opposite direction:

```
list.moveToTail();
while (list.hasPrevious()){
    Object item = list.previous();
    <do something with the item>
}
```

An exception is thrown if `next` or `previous` is called when `hasNext` or `hasPrevious` is false, respectively.

Adding an Object

The `add` method expects an object as a parameter, and provided the list is not full, it does one of the following:

- if the list is empty, adds the object to the list and places the current position indicator immediately after the object
- otherwise, inserts the object immediately before the current position indicator

The following code segment adds the numbers from 1 to 5 to a positional list:

```
for (int i = 1; i < 5; i++)
    list.add(new Integer(i));              // list contains 1 2 3 4 5
```

Removing an Object

The `remove` method deletes the current object if there is one. The ***current object*** is the object returned by the most recent `next` or `previous` operation, provided there have been no intervening `add`, `remove`, `moveToHead`, `moveToTail`, or `toString` operations. The following code segment removes the second object from a list of at least two objects:

```
list.moveToHead();
list.next();
list.next();
list.remove();
```

The `remove` method locates the current position indicator in the space vacated by the removed object.

Setting an Object

The set method replaces the current object with the object specified in the method's parameter. The replacement then becomes the current object, and the current position indicator does not change. Here is an example that sets the second object in a list:

```
list.moveToHead();
list.next();
list.next();
list.set (anObject);
```

An Extended Example

Table 16.6 presents an extended example of using a positional list. Letters of the alphabet indicates the objects in the list, and a comma represents the current position indicator. During the course of the example we illustrate the use of the methods in a variety of circumstances.

Table 16.6

An Extended Example of Positional List Manipulations

Operation	Current Position After the Operation	State of the List After the Operation "," indicates the current position and bold indicates the current object	Value Returned	Comment
instantiate a new positional list that contains the objects a b c	0	,a b c	a positional list object	Initially, the list contains **a**, **b**, and **c**, and the current position equals 0.
hasNext()	0	,a b c	true	There are items following the current position.
next()	1	**a**,b c	a	Return **a** and advance the current position.
next()	2	a **b**,c	b	Return **b** and advance the current position.
remove()	1	a,c	void	Remove **b**, the last item returned by previous or next. Note the location of the current position.
add(b)	2	a b,c	void	Insert **b** immediately to the left of the current position indicator.

Continues

Table 16.6 *(continued)*

Operation	Current Position After the Operation	State of the List After the Operation "," indicates the current position and bold indicates the current object	Value Returned	Comment
next()	3	a b **c**,	c	Return **c** and advance the current position.
next()	3	a b c,	exception	The current position is at the end of the list; therefore, it is impossible to retrieve a next item.
hasNext()	3	a b c,	false	The current position is at the end of the list; therefore, there is no next item.
hasPrevious()	3	a b c,	true	There are items preceding the current position.
previous()	2	a b,**c**	c	Return **c** and move the current position backward.
remove()	2	a b,	void	Remove **c**, the last item returned by previous or next. Note the location of the current position.
previous()	1	a,**b**	b	Return **b** and move the current position backward.
set(e)	1	a,**e**	void	Replace **b**, the last item returned by previous or next. The item **e** is now current.
add(b)	2	a b,e	void	Insert **b** immediately to the left of the current position indicator.
add(c)	3	a b c,e	void	Insert **c** immediately to the left of the current position indicator.
remove()	3	a b c,e	exception	There is no current object because add has occurred since the last next or previous.
previous()	2	a b,**c** e	c	Return **c** and move the current position backward.
previous()	1	a,**b** c e	b	Return **b** and move the current position backward.

The Interface

Having established a clear picture of how positional lists work, we now present the interface. Table 16.7 describes the methods. If a method's preconditions are not satisfied, it throws an exception.

Table 16.7

The Methods in the `PositionalList` Interface

Method	Preconditions	Postconditions
A default constructor	None	An empty positional list is instantiated. The current position is not defined.
A constructor that takes an `IndexedList` as a parameter	The size of the indexed list is not greater than the maximum capacity of a positional list.	A positional list is instantiated and contains the same objects as are in the `IndexedList`. The current position immediately precedes the first object.
`void add(Object obj)`	The list is not full.	Inserts `obj` at the current position in a nonempty list or simply adds it to an empty list. The current position indicator is located after the object just inserted.
`boolean hasNext()`	None	Returns `true` if the current position indicator is followed by an object and `false` otherwise.
`boolean hasPrevious()`	None	Returns `true` if the current position indicator is preceded by an object and `false` otherwise.
`boolean isEmpty()`	None	Returns `true` if the list is empty and `false` otherwise.
`boolean isFull()`	None	Returns `true` if the list is full and `false` otherwise.
`void moveToHead()`	None	Moves the current position indicator immediately before the first object if there is one.
`void moveToTail()`	None	Moves the current position indicator immediately after the last object if there is one.
`Object next()`	`hasNext` returns `true`.	Returns the object after the current position indicator and then moves the indicator after the object.
`Object previous()`	`hasPrevious` returns `true`.	Returns the object before the current position indicator and then moves the indicator before the object.
`Object remove()`	There is a current object.	Removes the current object.
`void set(Object obj)`	There is a current object.	Replaces the current object with `obj`.
`int size()`	None	Returns the number of objects in the list.
`String toString()`	None	Returns a string that is the concatenation of the string representations of the objects in the list.

Here is the Java code for the interface:

```java
// File: PositionalList.java
// Interface for the positional list prototype

/* At all times a current position indicator (cpi) is associated with
   the list.
   In a nonempty list the indicator is either:
     Before the first item
     Between two items
     After the last item
   In an empty list the indicator exists without any items.
*/

public interface PositionalList {

   public void add(Object obj);
   // Preconditions:  The list is not full.
   // Postconditions: obj is inserted immediately before the cpi

   public boolean hasNext();
   // Postconditions: Returns true if there is an object after the
   //                 cpi and false otherwise

   public boolean hasPrevious();
   // Postconditions: Returns true if there is an object before the
   //                 cpi and false otherwise

   public boolean isEmpty();
   // Postconditions: Returns true if the list contains no items
   //                 and false otherwise

   public boolean isFull();
   // Postconditions: Returns true if the list cannot take another item
   //                 and false otherwise

   public void moveToHead();
   // Postconditions: Moves the cpi before the first object if
   //                 the list is not empty

   public void  moveToTail();
   // Postconditions: Moves the cpi after the last object if
   //                 the list is not empty

   public Object next();
   // Preconditions:  hasNext returns true
```

```
    // Postconditions: Returns the object following the cpi
    //                   and moves the cpi after that object.

    public Object previous();
    // Preconditions:   hasPrevious returns true
    // Postconditions: Returns the object preceding the cpi
    //                   and moves the cpi before that object

    public Object remove();
    // Preconditions:   None of add, remove, moveToHead, moveToTail, toString
    //                   have been called since the last successful call
    //                   to next or previous
    // Postconditions: Removes the object encountered by the most
    //                   recent next or previous.
    //                   The cpi retains its position relative to the items
    //                   that are left in the list.

    public void set(Object obj);
    // Preconditions:   None of add, remove, moveToHead, moveToTail, toString
    //                   have been called since the last successful call to
    //                   next or previous
    // Postconditions: Replaces the object returned by the most
    //                   recent next or previous

    public int size();
    // Postconditions: Returns the number of items in the list

    public String toString();
    // Postconditions: Returns a string representation of the list by
    //                   concatenating the string representations of the
    //                   individual items in the list.
}
```

Self-Test Questions

15. How does one navigate through a positional list?

16. Assume that the positional list `list` has been instantiated and that the objects a, b, and c have been added to it. Write code segments that accomplish the following tasks:

    a. remove item b

    b. add item d after the last item in the list

    c. replace item a with item e

16.8 Fixed Size Array Implementation of `PositionalList`

There are two primary problems to solve when implementing a positional list:

1. keeping track of the interacting preconditions and postconditions of all the operations
2. keeping track of the current position and current object

In the fixed size array implementation, we solve these problems by means of the instance variables `curPos` and `lastItemPos`. As the name suggests, `curPos` is the current position indicator. It equals i if the current position is immediately before the item at index position i in the list ($i = 0, 1, 2, \ldots$), and it equals the list size if the current position is after the last item. The variable `lastItemPos` equals the index of the last item returned by `next` or `previous` or –1 if there has been an intervening `add`, `remove`, `moveToHead`, `moveToTail`, or `toString` operation. It also equals –1 initially. Thus, when `lastItemPos` equals –1, the methods `remove` and `set` are blocked because we know their preconditions are not satisfied. Here is a partial listing of the fixed size array implementation of a positional list:

```
import java.io.*;                    // Needed for serialization

public class FSAPositionalList implements PositionalList, Serializable{

   private static int DEFAULT_CAPACITY = 10;    // Maximum list size

   private Object[] items;                       // The array of objects
   private int listSize;                         // The list size

   private int curPos;
       //Current position indicator
       //Equals i if immediately before the item at index i
       //Equals listSize if after the last item

   private int lastItemPos;
       //Equals index of last item returned by next or previous
       //Equals -1 initially and after add, remove, moveToHead,
       //and moveToTail


   //Constructors

   public FSAPositionalList(){
      items = new Object[DEFAULT_CAPACITY];
      listSize = 0;
      curPos = 0;
      lastItemPos = -1;      //Block remove and set until after a successful
```

```
                                                      //next or previous
    }

    public FSAPositionalList(IndexedList list){
        // Exercise
    }



    // Methods that indicate the state of the list

    public boolean isEmpty(){
        return listSize == 0;
    }

    public boolean isFull(){
        return listSize == items.length;
    }

    public boolean hasNext(){
        return curPos < listSize;
    }

    public boolean hasPrevious(){
        return curPos > 0;
    }

    public int size(){
        return listSize;
    }

    // Methods that move the current position indicator

    public void moveToHead(){
        curPos = 0;
        lastItemPos = -1;      //Block remove and set until after a successful
                                                      //next or previous
    }

    public void  moveToTail(){
        curPos = listSize;
        lastItemPos = -1;      //Block remove and set until after a successful
                                                      //next or previous
    }

    // Methods that retrieve items

    public Object next(){
        if (!hasNext())
```

Continued

```java
        throw new RuntimeException
        ("There are no more elements in the list");

    lastItemPos = curPos;    //Remember the index of the last item returned
    curPos++;                                //Advance the current position
    return items[lastItemPos];
}

public Object previous(){
    if (!hasPrevious())
        throw new RuntimeException
        ("There are no more elements in the list");

    lastItemPos = curPos - 1;            //Remember the index of the last item
                                                        //returned
    curPos--;                            //Move the current position backward
    return items[lastItemPos];
}

// Methods that modify the list's contents

public void add(Object obj){
    // Exercise
}

public Object remove(){
    // Exercise
}

public void set(Object obj){
    if (lastItemPos == -1)
        throw new RuntimeException (
                "There is no established item to set.");

    items[lastItemPos] = obj;
}

//Method that returns a string representation of the list.

public String toString(){
    String str = "";
    for (int i = 0; i < listSize; i++)
        str += items[i] + " ";
    return str;
}
}
```

Self-Test Question

17. Write the code for the FSAPositionalList constructor method that expects an IndexedList as a parameter.

16.9 Doubly Linked Implementation of PositionalList

We never use a singly linked structure to implement a positional list because it provides no convenient mechanism for moving one node to the left—that is, to a node's predecessor. In a singly linked list, moving left requires repositioning to the head of the list and then traversing right. The cost of doing this is O(n). In a doubly linked list, it is equally easy to move left and right. Both are O(1) operations. Figure 16.10 shows a doubly linked structure with three nodes.

head

Figure 16.10 A doubly linked structure with three nodes

It turns out that the code needed to manipulate a doubly linked list is simplified if one extra node is added at the head of the list. This node is called a ***sentinel node,*** and it points forward to what was the first node and backward to what was the last node. The head pointer now points to the sentinel node. The resulting structure is called a ***circular linked list.*** The sentinel node does not contain a list item, and when the list is empty, the sentinel remains. Figure 16.11 shows an empty circular linked list and a circular linked list containing three items.

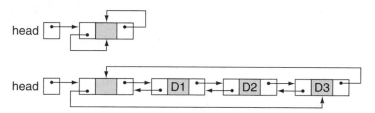

head

head

Figure 16.11 Two circular doubly linked lists with sentinel nodes

The basic building block of a doubly linked list is a node with two pointers: next which points right and previous which points left. We define the node in a private inner class called Node. As in the array implementation, we rely heavily on the variables curPos and lastItemPos; however, they now represent two-way nodes rather than integers. Here is a partial listing of the class DLPositionalList. The missing parts are left as exercises.

```java
import java.io.*;                    // Needed for serialization

public class DLPositionalList implements PositionalList, Serializable{

    private Node head;
        //Sentinel head node

    private Node curPos;
        //Current position indicator
        //Points at the node which would be returned by next
        //The current position is considered to be immediately
        //before this node
        //If curPos == head then at end of list
        //If curPos.previous == head then at beginning of list

    private Node lastItemPos;
        //Points at the last item returned by next or previous
        //Equals null initially and after add, remove, moveToHead,
        //moveToTail, and toString

    private int listSize;
        //The number of items in the list

    //Constructor

    public DLPositionalList(){
        head = new Node(null, null, null);
        head.next = head;
        head.previous = head;
        curPos = head.next;
        lastItemPos = null;
        listSize = 0;
    }

    public DLPositionalList (IndexedList list){
        // Exercise
    }

    // Methods that indicate the state of the list

    public boolean isEmpty(){
        return listSize == 0;
    }

    public boolean isFull(){
        return false;
```

```
}


   public boolean hasNext(){
      return curPos != head;
   }


   public boolean hasPrevious(){
      return curPos.previous != head;
   }


   public int size(){
      return listSize;
   }



   // Methods that move the current position indicator

   public void moveToHead(){
      curPos = head.next;
      lastItemPos = null;        //Block remove and set until after a
                                 //successful next or previous
   }

   public void  moveToTail(){
      curPos = head;
      lastItemPos = null;        //Block remove and set until after a
                                 //successful next or previous
   }



   // Methods that retrieve items

   public Object next(){                              //Returns the next item
      if (!hasNext())
         throw new RuntimeException
         ("There are no more elements in the list");

      lastItemPos = curPos;    //Remember the index of the last item returned
      curPos = curPos.next;                    //Advance the current position
      return lastItemPos.value;
   }

   public Object previous(){                      //Returns the previous item
      if (!hasPrevious())
         throw new RuntimeException
         ("There are no more elements in the list");
```

Continues

Continued

```java
    lastItemPos = curPos.previous;    //Remember the index of the last item
                                                          //returned
    curPos = curPos.previous;              //Move the current position backward
    return lastItemPos.value;
}


// Methods that modify the list's contents

public void add(Object obj){
    // To be discussed
}

public Object remove(){
    // Exercise
}

public void set(Object obj){
    if (lastItemPos == null)
        throw new RuntimeException (
                    "There is no established item to set.");

    lastItemPos.value = obj;
}


//Method that returns a string representation of the list.

public String toString(){
    String str = "";
    for (Node node = head.next; node != head; node = node.next)
        str += node.value + " ";
    return str;
}

// ----------------- Private inner class for Node -----------------

private class Node implements Serializable {
    private Object value;        //Value stored in this node
    private Node   next;         //Reference to next node
    private Node   previous;     //Reference to previous node

    private Node(){
```

```
            value = null;
            previous = null;
            next = null;
        }

    private Node(Object value){
            this.value = value;
            previous = null;
            next = null;
        }

    private Node(Object value, Node previous, Node next){
            this.value = value;
            this.previous = previous;
            this.next = next;
        }
    }
}
```

The add Method

Figure 16.12 shows the steps required to insert a node into a doubly linked list. The new node is inserted immediately before the one pointed to by curPos.

The same steps are required even when there are no data nodes already in the list. In that case, the header node is both the successor and the predecessor of the new node. Here is the code for the add method:

```
public void add(Object obj){
    //Create new node for object obj (steps 2 and 3 in Figure 16.12)
    Node newNode = new Node(obj, curPos.previous, curPos);

    //Link the new node into the list (steps 4 and 5 in Figure 16.12)
    curPos.previous.next = newNode;
    curPos.previous = newNode;

    //curPos does not change

    listSize++;
    lastItemPos = null;    //Block remove and set until after a successful
                                             //next or previous
}
```

The add method is remarkably simple; however, without a sentinel node, the code becomes considerably more complex.

Step 1. The list before insertion

Step 2. Set the previous pointer of the new node to `curPos.previous`

Step 3. Set the next pointer of the new node to `curPos`

Step 4. Set the next pointer of the predecessor node to the new node

Step 5. Set the previous pointer of the successor node to the new node

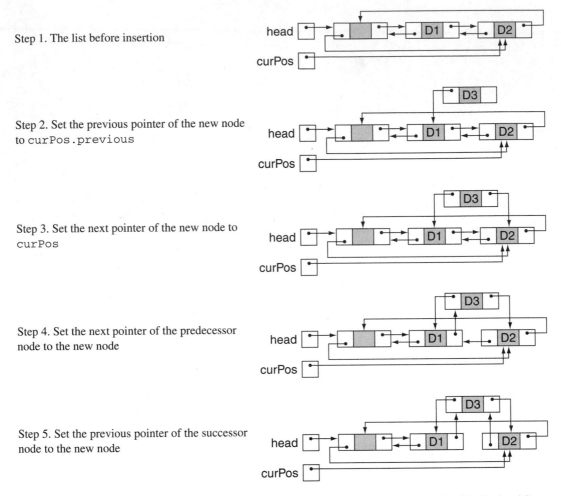

Figure 16.12 Steps required to insert a node into a doubly linked list

Self-Test Questions

18. What advantages does a doubly linked list have over a singly linked list?
19. What advantages does a circular linked list with a sentinel node have over a plain linked list?

16.10 Complexity Analysis of Positional Lists

The memory requirements of positional and indexed lists are similar. The only difference is that the nodes in doubly linked lists utilize two pointers rather than one. Table 16.8 summarizes the run times of the positional list implementations. The unfilled slots are left as exercises. Because an item is added, removed, or replaced at the current position indicator, no search is required to locate the position. The self-test question at the end of the section asks you to complete Table 16.8 and to compare the two types of lists and their various implementations.

Table 16.8

The Run Times of the Positional List Implementations		
	Complexity	
Method	**Fixed Size Array (FSAPositionalList)**	**Doubly Linked List (DLPositionalList)**
`boolean isEmpty()`	O(1)	O(1)
`boolean isFull()`	O(1)	O(1)
`int size()`	O(1)	O(1)
`boolean hasNext()`	O(1)	O(1)
`boolean hasPrevious()`	O(1)	O(1)
`void moveToHead()`	O(1)	O(1)
`void moveToTail()`	O(1)	*Exercise*
`Object next()`	O(1)	O(1)
`Object previous()`	O(1)	O(1)
`void add(Object o)`	*Exercise*	*Exercise*
`void remove(Object o)`	*Exercise*	*Exercise*
`void set(Object o)`	*Exercise*	*Exercise*

Self-Test Question

20. Complete the analysis in Table 16.8.

16.11 Stacks and Queues

Computer scientists have developed abstract data types for almost every purpose. Two of these that are in widespread use and that you will see in further computer science courses are stacks and queues. We now give a brief overview of each.

Stacks

A *stack* is a restricted list in which objects are added and removed at just one end, called the *top.* This restriction imposes a last-in, first-out (LIFO) ordering on additions and removals. The addition and removal operations are called *push* and *pop,* respectively. The trays at a lunch counter provide an everyday example of a stack. Customers remove trays from the top of this stack, and likewise the dishwasher returns clean trays back to the top. It is even possible that trays near the bottom of the stack are never used.

Stacks are used widely in computer science. A method's local variables are stored in a stack of activation records. There is one activation record for each method call, and it contains space for all the method's local variables. Each time one method calls another, the stack grows; and each time a method returns to its caller, the stack shrinks. When a recursive method calls itself, there are multiple activation records for the method. The activation record for the currently executing method is always at the top of the stack. Recursive algorithms can always be replaced by nonrecursive ones that use stacks, and backtracking algorithms rely on stacks. You will learn more about backtracking algorithms in subsequent computer science courses. There are many other examples.

The `Stack` interface is given in Table 16.9. If a method's preconditions are not satisfied, the method throws an exception.

Table 16.9

The `Stack` Interface		
Method	**Preconditions**	**Postconditions**
`boolean isEmpty()`	None	Returns `true` if the stack is empty and `false` otherwise.
`boolen isFull()`	None	Returns `true` if the stack is full and `false` otherwise.
`void push(Object obj)`	The stack is not full.	Adds the object to the top of the stack.
`Object pop()`	The stack is not empty.	Removes the object at the top of the stack and returns a reference to this object.

Here is a listing of the interface:

```
// File: Stack.java
// Interface for the stack prototype

public interface Stack {

    public boolean isEmpty();
    // Postconditions: Returns true if the stack is empty, false otherwise.

    public boolean isFull();
    // Postconditions: Returns true if the stack is full, false otherwise.
```

```
    public void push (Object obj);
    // Preconditions:  The stack is not full.
    // Postconditions: obj has been added to the top of the stack.

    public Object pop();
    // Preconditions:  The stack is not empty.
    // Postconditions: The top object is removed from the stack and returned.
}
```

List-Based Implementation of Stacks

Arrays and singly linked structures provide obvious implementations of stacks; however, it is also possible to implement a stack by using a list. That is the approach we take here. The other approaches are left as an exercise.

```java
import java.io.*;

public class LBStack implements Stack, Serializable{

    private IndexedList list;

    public LBStack(){
        list = new SLIndexedList();
    }

    public boolean isEmpty(){
        return list.isEmpty();
    }

    public boolean isFull(){
        return list.isFull();
    }

    public void push (Object obj){
        if (isFull())
            throw new RuntimeException("Stack is full");
            //This won't happen when SLIndexedList is used.
        list.add(0, obj);
    }

    public Object pop(){
        if (isEmpty())
            throw new RuntimeException("Stack is empty");
        return list.remove(0);
    }
}
```

Java defines its own Stack class in the package java.util. However, it is implemented as a subclass of Vector, which is an earlier version of List. This means that clients of Stack can use all of the Vector methods to access and modify the contents of a stack, including adding and removing in the middle of a stack. The implementation in java.util violates the definition of a stack by allowing manipulations that are inappropriate for a stack. In short, Stack should not be treated as a subclass of List.

Queues

A *queue* is a restricted list in which items are removed from one end, called the *front,* and added to the other end, called the *rear.* Thus, a queue imposes a first-in, first-out (FIFO) ordering on additions and removals. The operation of adding is called *enqueue* and of removing is called *dequeue.* The line at a ticket counter is a queue. The first person in line is the first one served. Imagine the frustration of waiting in line for hours to buy a ticket to a big concert only to discover that the line is a stack rather than a queue.

Queues are used widely in computer science. Two common applications are in scheduling algorithms and simulations. Table 16.10 describes the interface.

Table 16.10

The Queue Interface		
Method	**Preconditions**	**Postconditions**
boolean isEmpty()	None	Returns true if the queue is empty and false otherwise.
boolean isFull()	None	Returns true if the queue is full and false otherwise.
void enqueue(Object obj)	The queue is not full.	Adds the object to the rear of the queue.
Object dequeue()	The queue is not empty.	Removes the object at the front of the queue and returns a reference to this object.

Here is a listing of the interface:

```java
// File: Queue.java
// Interface for the queue prototype

public interface Queue {

   public boolean isEmpty();
   // Postconditions: Returns true if the queue is empty, false otherwise.

   public boolean isFull();
```

```
// Postconditions: Returns true if the queue is full, false otherwise.

public void enqueue (Object obj);
// Preconditions:  The stack is not full.
// Postconditions: obj has been added to the rear of the queue.

public Object dequeue();
// Preconditions:  The queue is not empty.
// Postconditions: The front object is removed from the queue and returned.
}
```

List-Based Implementation of Queues

We confront the same choices when implementing queues as stacks. We can either start from scratch or utilize a list. Again, we choose a list and leave the other alternative as an exercise. For our list, we use a doubly linked implementation of a positional list and in the exercises ask you to consider the pros and cons of using any of the alternative lists.

```java
import java.io.*;

public class LBQueue implements Queue, Serializable{

    private PositionalList list;

    public LBQueue(){
        list = new DLPositionalList();
    }

    public boolean isEmpty(){
        return list.isEmpty();
    }

    public boolean isFull(){
        return list.isFull();
    }

    public void enqueue (Object obj){
        if (isFull())
            throw new RuntimeException("Queue is full");
            //This won't happen when DLPositionalList is used
        list.moveToTail();
        list.add(obj);
    }
```

Continues

Continued

```
public Object dequeue(){
    if (isEmpty())
        throw new RuntimeException("Queue is empty");
    list.moveToHead();
    list.next();
    return list.remove();
}
}
```

Self-Test Questions

21. What is a stack?

22. Write a code segment that transfers the items from an indexed list to a stack.

23. What is a queue?

24. Write a code segment that transfers items from a queue to an indexed list.

16.12 Summary

In this chapter, we examined the trade-offs when implementing lists with arrays and linked structures. We found that arrays nicely support the implementation of index-based lists, whereas linked structures do better with positional lists. These trade-offs in turn depend on the way in which arrays and linked structures are represented in memory.

16.13 Key Terms

If you have difficulty finding the definitions of any key terms in the body of this chapter, turn to the Glossary at the end of the book.

abstract data type (ADT)	linked structure	random access data structures
base address	node	rear
contiguous memory	offset	sequential access
current position indicator	pointer	sequential access structures
doubly linked structure	positional list	singly linked structure
dynamic memory	private inner class	stack
front	queue	top
indexed list	random access	

16.14 Answers to Self-Test Questions

1. An abstract data type is a set of objects that are defined by means of the operations on them. Two examples are lists and strings.

2. Index-based access allows a programmer to locate an item by giving its position in a list. Position-based access requires a programmer to navigate to an item from a given position.

3. A prototype is a simplified version of a software component that includes only the most essential features of the real thing. A prototype allows a programmer to explore behavior and performance free from the distractions of implementation details.

4. An interface allows users and implementers of a class or ADT to share information about the class or ADT.

5. We include preconditions and postconditions in an interface so that users and implementers are clearly aware of the conditions for and results of the correct use and implementation of methods.

6. If a list is correctly designed as an ADT, the only problem that arises for a user is that the static array implementation of a list might become full. The problems for an implementer are that the list might become full and that there might be a large amount of wasted space.

7. A list class implements the `Serializable` interface so that clients can save lists in files.

8. It is helpful to throw exceptions when the preconditions of a method are violated. For example, the method `get` in an indexed list throws an exception when it receives a parameter that is not in the range of positions in the list.

9.
```
public Object get(int index){
    if (index < 0 || index >= listSize)
        throw new RuntimeException
        ("Index = " + index + " is out of list bounds");
    return items[index];
}
```

10. A node is an object that contains at least two parts: a data item and a reference to another node.

11. A null pointer exception is thrown when a program attempts to send a message to a variable that contains the `null` pointer, instead of a reference to an object.

12. node

13. Array cells are represented as a block of adjacent memory cells. This representation allows the computer to locate a position in the array in constant time.

14. Nodes in linked structures are represented as distinct chunks of memory in the system heap. Because their locations in memory are independent of their positions in a linked structure, the computer cannot locate a position in a linked structure in constant time.

15. To navigate through a positional list, one can move to its head and then run the next operation until one reaches the desired object of position. Alternatively, one can move to its tail and run the previous operation.

16. a.
```
list.moveToHead();
list.next();
list.next();
list.remove();
```

b. `list.moveToTail();`
   `list.add(d);`

c. `list.moveToHead();`
   `list.next();`
   `list.set(e);`

17.
```
public FSAPositionalList(IndexedList list){
    for (int i = 0; i < list.size(); i++)
        add(list.get(i));
}
```

18. A doubly linked list allows the programmer to move to the previous node in constant time.

19. A circular linked list with a header node allows the programmer to treat insertions and removals at the head and tail in the same way as other insertions.

20.

`void moveToTail()`	O(1)	**O(1)**
`void add(Object o)`	**O(n)**	**O(1)**
`void remove(Object o)`	**O(n)**	**O(1)**
`void set(Object o)`	**O(1)**	**O(1)**

21. A stack is an ADT in which items are accessed at one end, called the top. Items are accessed in last in, first-out order.

22.
```
for (int i = 0; i < list.size(); i++)
    stack.push(list.get(i));
```

23. A queue is an ADT in which items are added at one end, called the rear, and removed from the other end, called the front. Items are accessed in first-in, first-out order.

24.
```
while (! queue.isEmpty())
    list.add(queue.dequeue());
```

16.15 Programming Problems and Activities

1. Modify the `IndexedList` test program so that:
   - it tests all exceptions
   - it only produces printed output for a test if the results of the test are incorrect

2. A set is a collection of unique objects in no particular order. The basic operations on sets are `member`, `add`, `remove`, `size`, `isEmpty`, and the combiners `union`, `intersection`, and `difference`. Design a `Set` class, implement it with a one-way list, and discuss any performance issues that arise.

3. Modify the shape drawing program of Chapter 13 so that it represents the list of shapes as a list. Discuss any performance issues that arise.

4. Write a program that reads the words from one text file and writes them, in reverse order, to another text file. The program should use a list to accomplish the transfer.

5. Identify earlier Case Studies and problems that might be better implemented using a positional list and then modify one of them to use a positional list.

6. Complete the fixed size array implementation of an indexed list. Test it with the program in Section 16.5.

7. Modify the fixed size array implementation of an indexed list so that the array grows and shrinks in response to the list size.

8. Complete the implementations of a positional list and write a tester program that verifies there are no bugs.

9. Implement the doubly linked positional list without using a sentinel node.

10. Write a dynamic array implementation for the positional list.

11. Characterize situations in which indexed lists are a better choice than positional lists, and vice versa. Are there situations in which each implementation is preferred? Explain.

12. Perform a complexity analysis on our implementations of Stack and Queue.

13. Discuss the pros and cons of using different types of lists in our implementations of Stack and Queue.

14. Implement Stack and Queue from scratch using arrays and linked structures. Test the implementations and provide a complexity analysis.

15. What performance penalty, if any, do we pay when we implement Stack and Queue using lists rather than implementing them from scratch?

17 Introduction to HTML and Applets

17.1 Hypertext, Hypermedia, and the World Wide Web

In 1945, Vannevar Bush, a scientist at MIT, published a prophetic essay, "As We May Think," in the *Atlantic Monthly*. According to Bush, though computers were already wonderful for number crunching, they would soon be used for data storage, data manipulation, and logical reasoning. These predictions came to pass in the 1950s and 1960s, with the advent of such branches of computer science as database management and artificial intelligence.

Bush also raised and attempted to answer the following question: How could we improve the way in which we consult our information sources during research? The traditional researcher used indexing schemes, such as card catalogs, but this method restricts the user to a linear or binary search. By contrast, the human mind uses association to search its own memory bank. For example, when I hear the word "wife," I instantly think of a particular person, namely, my own wife. My mind does not go through a complex search process to retrieve the associated information. Somehow, it just gets it.

Bush proposed to use computer technology to link chunks of information associatively. The keyed list or map structure that we discussed in Chapter 15 uses associative indexing. Now imagine that the entries in such a table also contain embedded links to other entries in other tables. Bush called his imaginary machine a *memex.* Each individual would have a desktop memex, as a virtual extension of his or her memory. The memex would receive chunks of information from a photocopy machine, a keyboard, or a stylus. The information would be stored on microfilm. The user would establish links between chunks of information by means of a few simple keystrokes.

The computer would maintain these ***associative links*** and also traces of the user's explorations of them. The user could come back to that trail or give it to another user to link into a more general trail. Research would involve following the trails blazed by the masters, not just the examination of their end products.

Hypertext and Hypermedia

By the late 1960s, the technology for realizing Bush's dream became available. In 1967, Theodor Holm Nelson coined the term ***hypertext*** to refer to Bush's machine. A hypertext is a structure consisting of nodes and the links between them. Each node is a document or chunk of text. Normally, links to other nodes are displayed to the user as embedded, highlighted terms within a given chunk of text. The user moves to a node by using an arrow key or mouse to select an associated term.

Early hypertext systems were

- Douglas Englebart's NLS/Augment (1968)
- Cognetics Corporation's Hyperties (mid-1980s)

In 1987, Apple Computer released Hypercard, one of the first hypermedia platforms. Hypermedia is like hypertext, but adds

- GUIs
- images
- sound
- animation
- applications.

For example, a link might appear as an icon or image rather than as highlighted text. The targeted chunk of information might be a full-screen image, a movie, a musical recording, or a computer application, such as a database program.

Networks and the World Wide Web

All of the early hypertext systems ran on separate stand-alone machines, which maintained data storage for the individual user. With the development of the Internet, people began to think of sharing hypertext across a network of communicating machines. Chunks of information, or pages as they are now called, could be stored on many different physical machines around the world. Each page would be linked in a gigantic hypermedia system, the World Wide Web. The Web is now a reality, taken for granted by millions of users.

The Web consists of two kinds of machines:

- servers, on which pages of information reside
- clients, which run browsers to access information on the servers

In some cases the client and server reside on the same machine.

When one opens a browser, one is presented with an initial page of information. Embedded in this page are links to other nodes. When one selects a link, the following occurs:

- The browser sends a message to the node's machine, requesting a transfer of its information.

- If the request is successful, the information at the node is downloaded to the user's browser.

Because there are different types of computers, a networked hypermedia system requires a uniform means of

- representing information using a machine-independent hypertext markup language

- designating node addresses using machine-independent *uniform resource locators* (URLs)

- transmitting information from site to site using machine-independent network transmission protocols

- displaying information with browsers from different vendors, subject to the restriction that all the browsers behave in a similar manner

Self-Test Questions

1. Describe the basic ideas underlying hypertext.
2. What is the difference between hypertext and hypermedia?
3. What is a URL?

17.2 Overview of the Hypertext Markup Language

The *hypertext markup language* (HTML) was developed as a machine-independent way of representing information in a networked-based hypermedia system. Early word processing systems, such as WordStar, bracketed text with codes that specified print formats. For example, the code ^I (control I) indicated italics and ^B bold. To illustrate, the text

```
Bush, Vannevar, ^BAs We May Think^B, ^IAtlantic Monthly^I, July, 1945.
```

would have been printed as

```
Bush, Vannevar, As We May Think, Atlantic Monthly, July, 1945.
```

HTML uses a similar scheme. Codes, called *markup tags,* can indicate the format of textual elements or links to other nodes. Browsers interpret these codes as commands and display the text in the desired format. Figure 17.1 shows the relationship between authors and users of HTML documents.

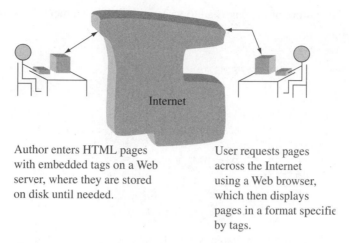

Author enters HTML pages with embedded tags on a Web server, where they are stored on disk until needed.

User requests pages across the Internet using a Web browser, which then displays pages in a format specified by tags.

Figure 17.1 The Internet

A Short Example

As a first example of using HTML, we will show you how to create the Web page shown in Figure 17.2. The page includes markup tags for

- a title
- a heading
- two paragraphs of text

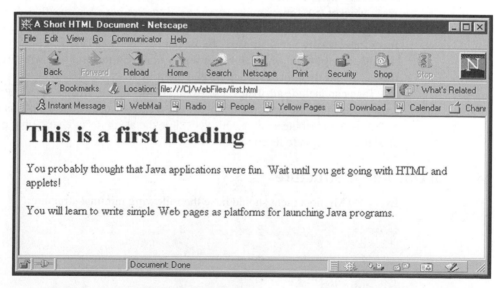

Figure 17.2 A simple Web page

The author of the page had to write an HTML document that looks like this:

```
<html>
<head>
<TITLE>A Short HTML Document</TITLE>
</head>
<body>
<H1>This is a first heading</H1>
<P>You probably thought that Java applications were fun. Wait until
you get going with HTML and applets!</P>
<P>You will learn to write simple Web pages as platforms
for launching Java programs.</P>
</body>
</html>
```

When a browser displays the document, the title appears at the top of the browser's window. There is a blank line between the heading and the first paragraph and between the two paragraphs. The browser uses word wrap to fit the text within the window's boundaries. A typical HTML document consists of multiple HTML pages.

The document must be stored in a file having the extension .html on a UNIX system and .htm on a Windows system. Pages can be any size, from a few to many hundreds of lines. We now turn to a discussion of the tags that define the HTML protocol.

Markup Tags

A markup tag in HTML begins with a left angle bracket (<) and ends with a right angle bracket (>), for example, <title>. Tags are not case sensitive. For instance, the tags <title>, <TITLE>, and <TiTlE> are equivalent, though not equally readable. Tags usually occur in pairs, for example, <title> and </title>. The start tag tells the browser where to begin the format, and the end tag, which includes a slash (/), tells the browser where to end the format.

Tags can include attributes. For example, the tag <P ALIGN=CENTER> tells the browser to align the next paragraph in the center of the window. In this example, ALIGN is the attribute's name and CENTER is the attribute's value. Some commonly used markup tags are listed in Table 17.1.

Minimal Document Structure

Every HTML document should have the following minimal structure:

```
<html>
<head>
<TITLE> the title goes here </TITLE>
</head>
<body>
the text for the document goes here
</body>
</html>
```

Table 17.1

Basic HTML Markup Tags	
Markup Tag	**What It Does**
HTML	Designates an HTML document.
HEAD	Designates the head of the document.
BODY	Designates the contents of the document.
TITLE	Designates the title that appears in the browser's window.
P	Designates a paragraph of text.
H1, H2, etc.	Designates a heading. There are six levels of headings.
PRE	Designates text to be formatted literally.
BR	Indicates a line break.
UL	Designates a bulleted list.
OL	Designates a numbered list.
LI	Indicates an item within a list.

Note the following points:

1. The HTML tag informs the browser that it is dealing with an HTML document.

2. The HEAD tag identifies the first part of the document.

3. The TITLE tag identifies the document's title. The title is displayed at the top of the browser's window and is used during searches for the document. The title is also displayed in bookmark lists (a list of the user's favorite links). We recommend short descriptive titles.

4. The BODY tags enclose the information provided by the HTML document.

5. Browser ignores extra whitespace, such as blank lines and tab characters.

Commenting an HTML Document

Authors often add comments to an HTML document. The browser does not interpret comments or show them to the reader. The form of a comment is

```
<!-- text of comment -->
```

In the following example, we have modified the first example by inserting blank lines and comments to make it more readable. However, a browser will display this page exactly as before.

```
<html>
<!-- Authors: Kenneth A. Lambert and Martin Osborne
     Last update: November 30, 2000                -->

<hcad>
<TITLE>A Short HTML Document</TITLE>
</head>

<body>
<H1>This is a first heading</H1>

<P>You probably thought that Java applications were fun. Wait until
you get going with HTML and applets!</P>

<P>You will learn to write simple Web pages as platforms
for launching Java programs.</P>

</body>
</html>
```

Self-Test Questions

4. What does HTML stand for?
5. What is the purpose of HTML tags?
6. Write an HTML code segment that shows the minimal HTML document structure for a Web page.
7. What is an HTML comment? Give an example.

17.3 Simple Text Elements

Headings

HTML provides six levels of document headings, numbered H1 through H6. The form of a heading is

```
<Hnumber>Text of heading</Hnumber>
```

Headings are displayed in a different font size and style from normal text. The browser inserts a blank line after each heading.

Paragraphs

The end tag </P> may be omitted. The browser then ends the paragraph at the beginning of the next paragraph or heading tag. The browser uses word wrap to fit a paragraph within the borders of the browser's window. Most browsers insert a blank line after the end of each paragraph; however, they ignore blank lines within a paragraph.

The browser recognizes the following alignment attributes:

- LEFT (the default)
- RIGHT
- CENTER

The next example uses headings of several sizes and paragraphs with different alignments:

```
<H1>The first level heading</H1>
<P ALIGN=RIGHT>The first paragraph.</P>
<H2>The second level heading</H2>
<P ALIGN=CENTER>The second paragraph.</P>
<H3>The third level heading</H3>
<P>The third paragraph.</P>
```

The results of this example are shown in Figure 17.3.

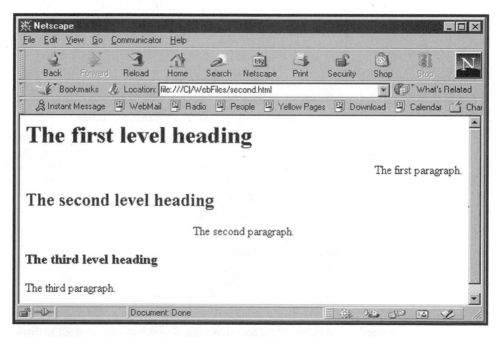

Figure 17.3 Headings and paragraphs

Forced Line Breaks

Occasionally, an author would like to display several lines of text without word wrap. The line break tag, <BR>, is used for this purpose. For example, the following HTML segment would display the author's address:

```
Department of Computer Science<BR>
Washington and Lee University<BR>
Lexington, VA 24450<BR>
```

Because a line break tag tells the browser where to break a line, no end tag is required.

Preformatted Text

Suppose you want the browser to display text "as is," with line breaks, extra spaces, and tabs. The <PRE> tag accomplishes this. For example, the following HTML segment displays some Java program code with the indicated indentation and line breaks:

```
<PRE>
    public static void main (String[] args){
        Frame frm = new FahrenheitToCentigrade();
        frm.setSize (200, 150);
        frm.setVisible (true);
    }
</PRE>
```

In general, you should not use other markup tags within a chunk of preformatted text.

Self-Test Questions

8. Why does the HTML programmer need to use forced line breaks?
9. When do we use preformatted text in an HTML document?
10. Write an HTML code segment that shows a level 1 heading and a level 2 heading.

17.4 Character-Level Formatting

HTML provides some control over the format of characters. Table 17.2 lists some of the commonly used tags and their effects.

Escape Sequences

HTML treats <, >, and & as special characters. For example, the characters < and > are treated as the delimiters of an HTML tag. If you want the browser to display these characters rather than interpret them, you must use the escape sequences listed in Table 17.3.

Self-Test Questions

11. What happens if you forget to close the markup tag for italic on a piece of text?
12. What is the purpose of the escape sequences in HTML? Give an example.

Table 17.2

Some Character Format Tags

Markup Tag	What It Does	Example HTML	Displayed Text
EM	Emphasis, usually italics.	`<EM>Italics</EM>`, for emphasis.	*Italics,* for emphasis.
STRONG	Strong emphasis, usually bold.	`<STRONG>Bold</STRONG>`, for more emphasis.	**Bold,** for more emphasis.
CITE	Used for titles of books etc., usually italics.	Plato's `<CITE>Republic</CITE>`	Plato's *Republic*
B	Bold text.	`<B>Bold</B>` text.	**Bold** text.
I	Italic text.	`<I>Italic</I>` text.	*Italic* text.
TT	Typewriter text, a fixed-width font.	`<TT>Typewriter</TT>` text.	`Typewriter` text.

Table 17.3

Some Escape Sequences

Character	Escape Sequence	Example HTML	Displayed Text
<	`&lt;`	The character `&lt;` begins an HTML markup tag.	The character < begins an HTML markup tag.
>	`&gt;`	The character `&gt;` ends an HTML markup tag.	The character > ends an HTML markup tag.
&	`&amp;`	`&amp;` is an ampersand.	& is an ampersand.

17.5 Lists

HTML supports the display of three kinds of lists:

- unnumbered (bulleted) lists—tag UL
- numbered (ordered) lists—tag OL
- definition (association) lists—tag DL

For bulleted and numbered lists, you perform the following steps:

1. Start with the desired list tag (UL or OL).
2. For each item, enter the LI (list item) tag followed by the text of the item. No closing tags are needed for the items.
3. End with the desired list tag.

An Unnumbered List Example

The next HTML segment displays a bulleted list of courses that one of the authors taught last year (Figure 17.4).

```
<UL>
<LI>Fundamentals of Data Structures
<LI>Programming Language Design
<LI>Operating Systems
<LI>Artificial Intelligence
</UL>
```

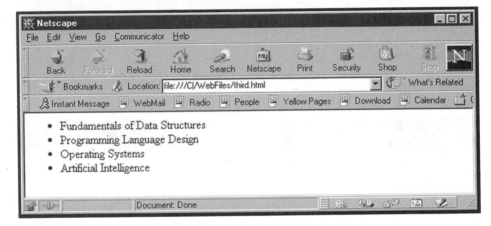

Figure 17.4 An unnumbered list

A Definition List Example

A *definition list* displays terms and their associated definitions. Several tags are used with these lists:

- The tag <DL> begins the definition list and ends it.
- The tag <DT> precedes each term in a definition list.
- The tag <DD> precedes each definition in a definition list.

The following example uses a definition list to add course numbers to the course list (Figure 17.5):

```
<DL>

<DT>CSCI111
<DD>Fundamentals of Data Structures

<DT>CSCI312
```

```
<DD>Programming Language Design

<DT>CSCI330
<DD>Operating Systems

<DT>CSCI315
<DD>Artificial Intelligence

</DL>
```

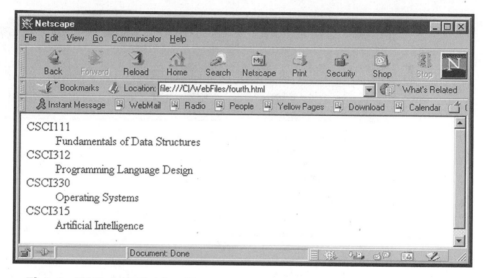

Figure 17.5 A definition list

A Nested List Example

Lists can be nested within other lists to any depth, but more than three levels deep can be difficult to read. The following HTML segment nests a numbered list in an unnumbered one (Figure 17.6):

```
<UL>
<LI>Fundamentals of Data Structures

<!--The nested, numbered list begins here. -->
<OL>
<LI>Analysis of algorithms
<LI>Collections
<LI>Linked lists
<LI>Stacks
<LI>Queues
```

Continues

Continued

```
<LI>Recursion
<LI>Binary search trees
</OL>
<!--The nested list ends here. -->

<LI>Programming Language Design
<LI>Operating Systems
<LI>Artificial Intelligence
</UL>
```

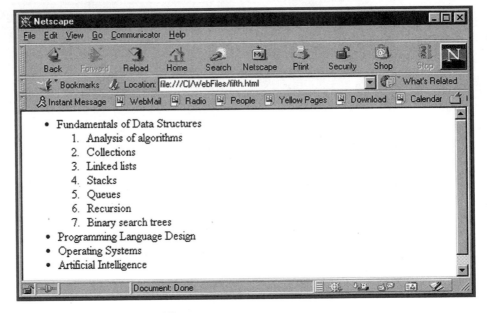

Figure 17.6 A nested list

Self-Test Questions

13. List three types of HTML lists and describe their characteristics.
14. Write an HTML code segment that uses a list to display the names of your grandparents and your parents. The list should be organized to show the relationships clearly.

17.6 Linking to Other Documents

Links, also called *hyperlinks* or hypertext references, allow readers to move to other pages in the Web. The markup tag for a link is <A>, which stands for anchor. Placing a link in an HTML document involves the following steps:

1. Identify the target document that will be at the other end of the link. This identifier should be a path name or a URL (see the discussion in the next subsection).
2. Determine the text that labels the link in the browser.
3. Place this information within an anchor, using the following format:

```
<A HREF=target document identifier>text of link</A>
```

For example, the next HTML anchor sets up a link to the file `courses.html` and labels the link "`courses last year`":

```
<A HREF="courses.html">courses last year</A>
```

Links or anchors can appear within any HTML element. They are often embedded as items in a list or as terms in a paragraph. For example, the following segment displays a link to the file `courses.html` in a sentence that mentions the author's courses:

```
<P>
My <A HREF="courses.html">courses last year</A> were Fundamentals of Data
Structures, Programming Language Design, Operating Systems, and
Artificial Intelligence.
</P>
```

When the user browses this page, the link is highlighted in blue and underlined, as in Figure 17.7. When the user clicks on the link, the browser retrieves and displays the target document, provided that the document has been placed at the appropriate location.

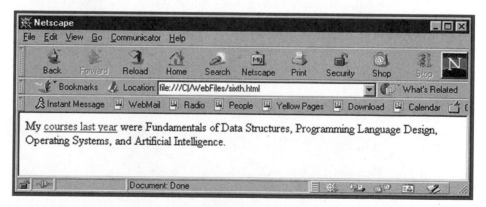

Figure 17.7 A link to another page

Path Names

Note the path name in the `Location` field in the header portion of the Figure 17.7 screenshot. The path name specifies the path to the file `sixth.html` on the author's computer. This file contains the page currently being displayed. The path name is said to be *absolute* because it specifies the exact or absolute position of the file in the computer's directory structure.

In HTML anchors, we can use absolute or *relative* path names to specify the location of a target document. A relative path name specifies a document's position relative to that of the currently displayed document. Here are some examples that show the relative path name to `MyPage.html`:

Position of `MyPage.html` Relative to Current Page	Relative Path Name
In the same directory	`MyPage.html`
Below, in a subdirectory called **Sub1**	`/Sub1/MyPage.html`
In the directory immediately above	`../MyPage.html`
In the directory two levels above	`../../MyPage.html`
In a directory **Twin1,** which up one and then down one from the current directory	`../Twin1/MyPage.html`

In general, relative path names are easier to use than absolute path names, because

- they are shorter and require less figuring out and typing
- they need not be changed when a group of documents is moved, even to another computer, provided the documents retain their relative positions

URLs

When a target document resides on another server in the network, a path name no longer suffices to locate the document. Instead, we use a *uniform resource locator* (URL) to locate the document on another machine. A URL to another Web site (called a host) has the following format:

```
http://server name/document path name
```

For instance, the URL for Ken Lambert's home page is:

```
<A HREF="http://www.wlu.edu/~lambertk">Ken Lambert</A>
```

Please feel free to visit.

Self-Test Questions

15. Write the form of the markup tag for links.
16. What is an absolute path name? Give an example.
17. What is a relative path name? Give an example.
18. Write the format of a URL to another Web site.

17.7 Multimedia

HTML supports the presentation of a range of nontextual information such as images, sound, and movies.

Inline Images

Inline images are graphical images that are displayed when the user opens a page. The form of the markup tag for an inline image is

```
<IMG SRC=ImageLocation>
```

where *ImageLocation* is a URL or path name. Images can be encoded in the GIF or JPEG format and are stored in files whose extensions are .gif, .jpg, or .jpeg.

Several parameters can be used with the markup tag of an inline image:

- Size attributes: These specify the height and width of the image in pixels. For example:

```
<IMG SRC="mypicture.gif" HEIGHT=100 WIDTH=100>
```

- Alignment attribute: This specifies the position of text relative to the image. By default, text that follows an image starts at the image's lower right corner. The text moves to the top right or to the center right of the image when TOP or CENTER are specified. For example:

```
<IMG SRC="mypicture.gif" ALIGN=CENTER>
```

To detach an image from surrounding text, place the image in a separate paragraph. For instance:

```
<p ALIGN=CENTER>
<IMG SRC="mypicture.gif">
</p>
```

External Images

Inline images increase a document's size and slow its transfer across the Net. For that reason, documents sometimes provide links to *external images,* which are not displayed until the user clicks on a link. The following HTML segment shows two ways of linking to an external image. The first link is a string of text. The second link is a smaller version of the image (sometimes called a thumbnail):

```
<A HREF="mypicture.gif">Sample picture</A>

<A HREF="mypicture.gif"><IMG SRC="mythumbnail.gif"</A>
```

This kind of strategy is also used with other media, such as sound recordings and movies.

Colors and Backgrounds

Browsers normally display black text on a gray background with links highlighted in blue. However, an HTML author can easily change the colors of these elements. Background, text, and link colors are controlled by the BGCOLOR, TEXT, and LINK attributes of the BODY tag. For example, the following tag sets the background to black, text to white, and links to red:

```
<BODY BGCOLOR="#000000" TEXT="#FFFFFF" LINK="#FF0000">
```

A string of three two-digit hexadecimal numbers specifies a color by indicating the RGB (red, green, blue) components of the color. The first two digits represent the red component, the second the green, and the third the blue. Thus, a total of 2^{24} colors is possible. The string "#000000" indicates black, a total absence of any color, while "#FFFFFF" represents white, a total saturation of all colors. Bright red is "#FF0000" and bright green "#00FF00".

Another way to customize a background is to display an image on it. The following tag shows how to use an image as a background:

```
<BODY BACKGROUND="mybackground.jpg">
```

If the image is small, the browser fills the window with the image by a process called tiling, which repeatedly displays the image across and down the screen, thus creating a wallpaperlike effect.

Other Media

Table 17.4 shows file name extensions for some typical media used in HTML documents.

Table 17.4

Some Hypermedia File Name Extensions	
File Name Extension	**Type of Medium**
.au	AU sound file
.wav	WAV sound file
.mov	QuickTime movie
.mpeg or .mpg	MPEG movie

Self-Test Questions

19. What is the difference between an inline image and an external image?
20. Write the simplest version of the format of the markup tag for an inline image.
21. Write a markup tag that loads an inline image in the file **image.gif** that centers the image and scales its size to 200 pixels x 200 pixels.
22. What are two ways of tagging an external image? Give an example of each.

17.8 Tables

HTML allows authors to organize information in tables (Figure 17.8).

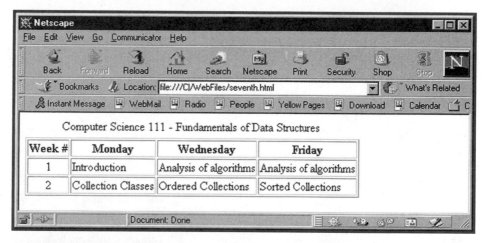

Figure 17.8 A table

As you have seen in earlier chapters, tables provide a highly structured way of accessing information. This is true of tables in user interfaces as well.

Tables usually contain the following elements:

- A caption or title, normally at the top of the table.
- A first row containing column headers. Each header describes the kind of data contained in the column beneath it.
- Several rows of data. The cells in a row can contain any HTML elements (text, images, links, etc.).

Table 17.5 provides a list of the HTML markup tags used with tables.

The tags accept the attributes shown in Table 17.6. Cell attributes override row attributes, and row attributes override table attributes.

Table 17.5

Table Format Tags	
Table Markup Tag	**What It Does**
<TABLE>	Defines a table.
<CAPTION>	Defines the title of the table. The default position of the title is at the top of the table, but ALIGN=BOTTOM can also be used.
<TR>	Defines a row within a table.
<TH>	Defines a table header cell.
<TD>	Defines a table data cell.

Table 17.6

Table Attributes		
Attribute	**Tag**	**What It Does**
BORDER	<TABLE>	Display a border.
ALIGN (LEFT, CENTER, RIGHT)	All except <CAPTION>	Horizontal alignment of elements in cells.
VALIGN (TOP, MIDDLE, BOTTOM)	All except <CAPTION>	Vertical alignment of cells.
ROWSPAN=n	<TD>	The number of rows that a cell spans.
COLSPAN=n	<TD>	The number of columns that a cell spans.
NOWRAP	All except <CAPTION>	Turn off word wrap within a cell.

Typical Table Format

The format of a typical table follows. The blank lines between rows increase readability but do not affect the manner in which the table is displayed:

```
<TABLE>
<CAPTION> title of the table </CAPTION>


<TR>
<TH> header of first column </TH>
.

.
<TH> header of last column </TH>
</TR>
```

```
<TR>
<TD> contents of first data cell </TD>
 .
 .
<TD> contents of last data cell </TD>
</TR>
 .
 .
<TR>
<TR>
<TD> contents of first data cell </TD>
 .
 .
<TD> contents of last data cell </TD>
</TR>
</TABLE>
```

A Simple Example

The table shown in Figure 17.8 at the beginning of this section was created using the following HTML code:

```
<TABLE BORDER>

<CAPTION ALIGN=CENTER>
Computer Science 111 - Fundamentals of Data Structures
</CAPTION>

<TR>
<TH>Week #</TH>
<TH>Monday</TH>
<TH>Wednesday</TH>
<TH>Friday</TH>
</TR>

<TR>
<TD ALIGN=CENTER>1</TD> <TD>Introduction</TD>
<TD>Analysis of algorithms</TD> <TD>Analysis of algorithms</TD>
</TR>

<TR>
<TD ALIGN=CENTER>2</TD> <TD>Collection Classes</TD>
<TD>Ordered Collections</TD> <TD>Sorted Collections</TD>
</TR>

</TABLE>
```

Self-Test Questions

23. Describe how one creates a table using the HTML table tags.

24. Write an HTML code segment that displays a 3 × 3 table whose rows are numbered

    1 2 3
    4 5 6
    7 8 9

17.9 Applets

As mentioned in Chapter 5, an applet is a Java application that runs in a Web page. Two components are needed to run an applet:

1. an HTML document that contains an applet markup tag

2. a byte code file for the applet—that is, a compiled Java applet in a `.class` file

An applet markup tag has the following form:

```
<APPLET CODE=byte code file name WIDTH=width HEIGHT=height></APPLET>
```

The width and height are the width and height, respectively, of the applet's screen area in pixels.

Example

Let us assume that the Fahrenheit/Celsius converter of Chapter 5 has already been rewritten as a Java applet. It might appear in a Web page as shown in Figure 17.9.

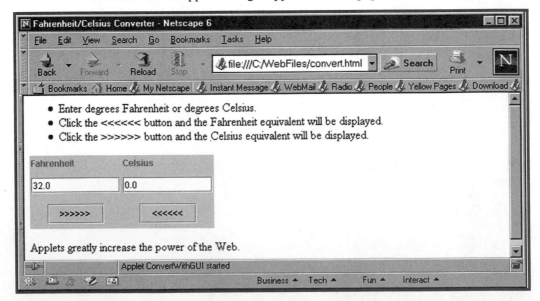

Figure 17.9 An applet within a Web page

Here is the HTML code for the example:

```
<html>
<head>
<TITLE>Fahrenheit/Celsius Converter</TITLE>
</head>

<body>

<UL>
<LI>Enter degrees Fahrenheit or degrees Celsius.
<LI>Click the <STRONG><<<<<<</STRONG> button and the
Fahrenheit equivalent will be displayed.
<LI>Click the <STRONG>>>>>>></STRONG> button and the
Celsius equivalent will be displayed.
</UL>

<APPLET CODE="ConvertWithGUI.class" WIDTH=250 HEIGHT=100>
</APPLET>

<P>
Applets greatly increase the power of the Web.

<body>
</html>
```

Converting an Application to an Applet

Throughout this text, we have used the class `GBFrame` to provide the framework for GUI-based applications. We now show how to use a similar class, `GBApplet`, to write GUI-based applets. To convert Java applications to applets, we must do four things:

1. Replace the name `GBFrame` with the name `GBApplet` at the beginning of the class definition.

2. Delete the method `main`.

3. Eliminate any use of the `setTitle` method.

4. Replace the constructor, if any, by the method `init`:

```
public void init(){
    ...
}
```

The following listing shows these changes:

```
/* ConvertWithGUI.java
This GUI-based temperature conversion program can convert from
Fahrenheit to Celsius and vice versa.
*/

import javax.swing.*;
import BreezySwing.*;

public class ConvertWithGUI extends GBApplet{   // Change superclass


    //Declare and instantiate the window objects
    JLabel       fahrenheitLabel  = addLabel       ("Fahrenheit" ,1,1,1,1);
    JLabel       celsiusLabel     = addLabel       ("Celsius"    ,1,2,1,1);
    DoubleField fahrenheitField   = addDoubleField (32.0         ,2,1,1,1);
    DoubleField celsiusField      = addDoubleField (0.0          ,2,2,1,1);
    JButton      fahrenheitButton = addButton      (">>>>>>"     ,3,1,1,1);
    JButton      celsiusButton    = addButton      ("<<<<<<"     ,3,2,1,1);

    //Declare other instance variables
    double fahrenheit;          //Number of degrees Fahrenheit
    double celsius;             //Number of degrees Celsius

    //This method responds to button clicks
    public void buttonClicked (JButton buttonObj){

        //When more than one button, determine which one was clicked
        if (buttonObj == fahrenheitButton){

            //Convert from Fahrenheit to Celsius
            fahrenheit = fahrenheitField.getNumber();
            celsius = (fahrenheit  - 32.0) * 5.0 / 9.0;
            celsiusField.setNumber (celsius);

        }else{

            //Convert Celsius to Fahrenheit
            celsius = celsiusField.getNumber();
            fahrenheit = celsius * 9.0 / 5.0 + 32.0;
            fahrenheitField.setNumber (fahrenheit);
        }
    }


    // Delete method main
}
```

Using the Applet Viewer

Sun's JDK comes with a tool called an applet viewer. This tool allows the programmer to run an applet and view just its GUI, without the surrounding Web page. To use the applet viewer, you must

1. compile the Java source program as usual

2. create an HTML file with at least the minimal applet tag for the applet

3. at the command line prompt, run the command

```
appletviewer <html file name>
```

Figure 17.10 shows the converter applet running within the applet viewer.

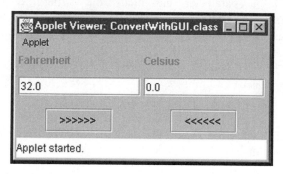

Figure 17.10 An applet within the applet viewer

Constraints on Applets

There are several major differences between applets and applications:

1. Applets do not have menu bars and, consequently, no pull-down menus; however, buttons often provide an acceptable substitute.

2. To ensure security on the user's machine, applets cannot access files. Imagine how dangerous it would be to download applets across the Web if the applets could trash the files on your computer.

3. Applets and the HTML documents that use them should be placed in the same directory. This rule can be violated, but doing so is beyond the scope of this book. Java programs, whether they are standalone applications or applets, frequently utilize classes in addition to those in the standard Java libraries. These classes, which might include the BreezySwing package, should be in the same directory as the applet.

4. The programs in this book use Java 2, so only Web browsers that support Java 2 can run the applets in this chapter. One such browser is available from www.sun.com.

5. The technique for defining dialogs to use in applications, as described in Chapter 15, applies to applets, with three qualifications:

a. The parameter of the dialog's constructor should not be the applet, but instead an anonymous frame. Thus, the value passed to the constructor could simply be `new Frame()`.

b. You will see a warning message at the bottom of the dialog.

c. The dialog does not prevent you from returning to the Web page. Once there, you cannot interact with the applet, but you can browse to other pages, quit the browser, and perhaps hang the computer.

Passing Parameters to Applets

It is possible to send information from an HTML page to an applet. The information is passed in HTML parameter tags and is retrieved in the applet's code. In the following example, a parameter tag binds the string `"5"` to the name "numberOfCourses." The parameter tag must appear between the opening and closing applet tag:

```
<APPLET CODE="Courses.class" WIDTH=150 HEIGHT=100>
<PARAM NAME=numberOfCourses VALUE="5">
</APPLET>
```

At any point within the applet, the method `getParameter` can retrieve the parameter's value, but always as a string:

```
String str = getParameter ("numberOfCourses");
int num = (new Integer(str)).intValue();
```

A common location for such code is in the `init` method.

If there are several parameters, each requires its own tag.

Self-Test Questions

25. Describe the simplest format of an HTML applet tag. Give an example.

26. How is an application converted to an applet using `BreezySwing`?

27. What can an application do that an applet cannot do?

17.10 Design, Testing, and Debugging Hints

- The paragraph (P) tag ignores blanks lines but inserts one.
- Be sure to test your document whenever you add a new link.

17.11 Summary

In this chapter, we introduced the basics of Web page construction with HTML. Web pages allow the user to view text in various formats, such as paragraphs, lists, and tables, as well as images, sound, and video. These items are organized as chunks of information that can be accessed via embedded links. Web pages can also contain applets, or Java applications that are downloaded from a Web server and run in the user's Web browser. We examined some simple steps to convert a Java application to an applet and include information in a Web page to run the applet. Applets have most of the functionality of applications, including the GUI, but they lack drop-down menus and file access to the user's disks.

17.12 Key Terms

If you have difficulty finding the definitions of any key terms in the body of this chapter, turn to the Glossary at the end of the book.

absolute pathname
associative link
definition list
external image
hyperlinks

hypermedia
hypertext
hypertext markup language
    (HTML)
inline image

markup tag
memex
uniform resource locator
    (URL)

17.13 Answers to Self-Test Questions

1. Hypertext consists of chunks of text linked together so that readers can move from chunk to chunk by following the links. This process emulates associative memory, whereby one recalls a content that is associated with a term. That content can contain other terms that lead to further contents and so on.

2. Hypertext consists of chunks of text only, whereas hypermedia consists of any information that can be digitized, including text, images, sound, video, and computer programs.

3. A URL stands for uniform resource locator, which is the label that identifies a page of information on the World Wide Web.

4. HTML stands for hypertext markup language, in which Web pages are written.

5. An HTML tag is used to express a command to a Web browser, such as formatting text or loading an image.

6.
```
<html>
<head>
<TITLE> the title goes here </TITLE>
</head>
<body>
```

```
the text for the document goes here
</body>
</html>
```

7. An HTML comment is not treated as text or a command by browsers. Instead, a comment provides a way to document a Web page's source code for the benefit of programmers. Here is an example:

```
<!-- Authors: Kenneth A. Lambert and Martin Osborne
     Last update: November 30, 2000                 -->
```

8. Forced line breaks are needed when lines must be skipped on a page between paragraphs or within paragraphs. Line breaks that simply appear within a paragraph in source code are not treated as such by browsers.

9. Preformatted text is used when we want source text to appear literally in the format that it's in.

10.
```
<H1>The first level heading</H1>
<H2>The second level heading</H2>
```

11. If one forgets to close the markup tag for italic, the italic style will affect all of the text following the opening until the end of the page.

12. An escape sequence asks the browser to treat a character used to delimit a tag as a literal character to be displayed instead. For example, the escape sequence $gt; asks the browser to display the character >.

13. An unnumbered list formats the items in the list by prefixing them with bullets. A numbered list formats the items in the list by numbering them. A definition list formats the items by associating a term with a definition.

14.
```
<UL>
<LI>Mother: Jeanne Redel
<UL>
<LI>Mother: Luretta Brong
<LI>Father: Walter Redel
</UL>
<LI>Father: Kenneth Lambert
<UL>
<LI>Mother: Lola Peters
<LI>Father: Kenneth Lambert
</UL>
</UL>
```

15. The markup tag for links has the form <A HREF=*target document identifier*>*text of link*</A>.

16. An absolute path name specifies the exact or absolute position of a file in the computer's directory structure. An example on a PC is C:\books\CS1Java\Chapter1.html.

17. A relative path name specifies the position of a file relative to the current directory in the computer's directory structure. An example on a PC is ..\CS1Java\Chapter1.html. The current directory is on the same level as CS1Java.

18. A URL to another Web site has the form *server name/document path name*.

19. An inline image displays when a Web page that contains its tag opens. An external image does not display until the user selects a link.

20. The simplest form of a tag for an inline image is `<IMG SRC=`*`image file name`*`>`.

21. `<IMG SRC="image.gif" HEIGHT=200 WIDTH=200 ALIGN = CENTER>`

22. One way to tag an external image is to provide a textual link:

    `<A HREF="mypicture.gif">Sample picture</A>`

    Another way is to provide a thumbnail:

    `<A HREF="mypicture.gif"><IMG SRC="mythumbnail.gif"</A>`

23. Tables are usually constructed from three parts: a caption or title, a first row containing column headers, and several rows of data, using the tags `<TABLE>`, `<CAPTION>`, `<TR>`, `<TH>`, and `<TD>`.

24.
```
<TABLE BORDER>
<TR>
<TD>1</TD>
<TD>2</TD>
<TD>3</TD>
</TR>

<TR>
<TD>4</TD>
<TD>5</TD>
<TD>6</TD>
</TR>

<TR>
<TD>7</TD>
<TD>8</TD>
<TD>9</TD>
</TR>

</TABLE>
```

25. The simplest form of an applet tag is

    `<APPLET CODE=`*`byte code file name`*` WIDTH=`*`an integer`*` HEIGHT=`*`an integer`*`>`
    `</APPLET>`

    An example tag is

    `<APPLET CODE="FahrenheitToCentigrade.class" WIDTH=200 HEIGHT=150>`
    `</APPLET>`

26. To convert an application to an applet, replace `GBFrame` with `GBApplet`, delete method `main`, change all drop-down menus to buttons, and remove all references to files.

27. Unlike an applet, an application can have drop-down menus and can manage files.

17.14 Programming Problems and Activities

For a fairly complete reference on HTML and Web page design, enter the following URL in your Web browser:

```
www.ncsa.uiuc.edu/General/Internet/WWW/HTMLPrimer.html
```

1. If you have not done so already, create a home page on your local Web server. Include a title, a brief paragraph that states who you are, and a picture of your favorite pastime.

2. Add to your home page a list of courses in which you are enrolled this term.

3. Make each item in the list of Problem 2 a link to a page that describes that item. Create these pages and test your hypertext thoroughly.

4. Add links to the pages created in Problem 3 that return the user to your home page.

5. Add a link to a page that runs the therapist program of Chapter 15. You must convert this program to an applet to run it from HTML.

6. Write an applet that plays the game of tic-tac-toe with the user. The interface should display a 3 × 3 grid of empty buttons at the beginning of a new game. The applet also selects the two letters used by the players at random. When the user selects an empty button, the applet displays the user's letter on that button and displays its own letter on a randomly selected empty button. After each button is selected, the applet determines if there is a winner. If so, the applet displays a message box and then clears the buttons for a new game. You should use the methods `getText` and `setText(String)` to examine and change the label of a button.

7. Select an application that uses a menu, such as one of the sketching applications of Chapter 13, and discuss how to convert it to an applet. This will require that you think of a way to display commands other than by means of a menu. Test the resulting program on a Web page.

18 Swing and AWT

pplications with a graphical user interface are based ultimately on Java's *Abstract Windowing Toolkit* (*AWT*) and *Swing toolkit.* However, for the sake of simplicity, we have until now avoided using them. Instead, we have made all of our stand-alone programs subclasses of GBFrame and our applets subclasses of GBApplet. These are two of the major classes in the BreezySwing package. Although BreezySwing makes it easy to create GUI-based programs, it blocks access to the full power of Java's GUIs. Fortunately, we have not noticed the deprivation, but with an eye to your future as Java programmers, we now present Swing and AWT in some detail.

18.1 The Swing and AWT Philosophy

Traditional programming languages such as Pascal and C++ provide no standard features for programming graphical user interfaces, so GUI code must often be rewritten when GUI applications are ported to different machines. Moreover, the GUI features themselves may vary from platform to platform. Java's originators developed Swing and the Abstract Windowing Toolkit to solve these problems.

The toolkits are abstract in two senses:

1. They provide classes and methods that are platform independent. Write once, run anywhere.

2. They create user interfaces whose look and feel are platform independent. Run anywhere, look similar.

Applications that use Swing and AWT involve the use of four categories of classes. Table 18.1 briefly describes each category. Later we will explore the categories in detail and show how they work together to support a graphical user interface. Most of the layout managers are in AWT. Event classes and listener classes are in both Swing and AWT. AWT and Swing have similar component classes, and we explore the Swing versions in this chapter.

Table 18.1

Classes Used in GUI-Based Applications	
Categories	**What They Do**
GUI component classes	GUI components include such basic window objects as buttons, text fields, and menu items. Also included in this category are frames, applets, and dialogs, which act as containers for the basic window objects.
Layout manager classes	When objects, such as buttons, are added to a window, their placement is determined by a layout manager. For instance, GBFrame and GBApplet use a grid bag layout. The other layout managers are flow, border, grid, and card.
Event classes	Event classes define the events that are triggered when users do such things as click buttons, select menu items, and move the mouse.
Listener classes	*Listener* classes contain methods that are activated when events occur.

We use these classes to define a graphical user interface as follows:

1. Add window objects to the interface under the control of a layout manager.
2. Decide which events each object should handle by adding listeners for the event to the object.

We can get a feel for all of this by revisiting the Fahrenheit to Celsius conversion program of Chapter 5 and comparing how it is implemented with GBFrame versus directly with Swing and AWT.

Self-Test Questions

1. In what two senses are Swing and AWT abstract?
2. What are the four types of classes used in building GUIs, and what are their roles and responsibilities?

18.2 Conversion Program Implemented with GBFrame

Figure 18.1 shows a version of the following program implemented with GBFrame:

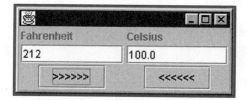

Figure 18.1 The conversion program with GBFrame

```
/* ConvertWithGUI.java
This GUI-based temperature conversion program can convert from
Fahrenheit to Celsius and vice versa.
*/


import javax.swing.*;
import BreezySwing.*;

class ConvertWithGUI extends GBFrame{


   //Declare and instantiate the window objects
   JLabel        fahrenheitLabel  = addLabel       ("Fahrenheit" ,1,1,1,1);
   JLabel        celsiusLabel     = addLabel       ("Celsius"    ,1,2,1,1);
   DoubleField   fahrenheitField  = addDoubleField (32.0         ,2,1,1,1);
   DoubleField   celsiusField     = addDoubleField (0.0          ,2,2,1,1);
   JButton       fahrenheitButton = addButton      (">>>>>>"     ,3,1,1,1);
   JButton       celsiusButton    = addButton      ("<<<<<<"     ,3,2,1,1);

   //Declare other instance variables
   double fahrenheit;              //Number of degrees Fahrenheit
   double celsius;                 //Number of degrees Celsius

   //This method responds to button clicks
   public void buttonClicked (JButton buttonObj){

      //When more than one button, determine which one was clicked
      if (buttonObj == fahrenheitButton){

         //Convert from Fahrenheit to Celsius
         fahrenheit = fahrenheitField.getNumber();
         celsius = (fahrenheit  - 32.0) * 5.0 / 9.0;
         celsiusField.setNumber (celsius);

      }else{
```

Continues

Continued

```
        //Convert Celsius to Fahrenheit
        celsius = celsiusField.getNumber();
        fahrenheit = celsius * 9.0 / 5.0 + 32.0;
        fahrenheitField.setNumber (fahrenheit);
    }
  }

  public static void main (String[] args){
     ConvertWithGUI tpo = new ConvertWithGUI();
     tpo.setSize (250, 100);      //Set the window's size in pixels
     tpo.setVisible (true);       //Make the window visible
  }
}
```

From the perspective of this chapter, there are several points to notice about the code:

1. The program extends `GBFrame`.

2. The window objects, or GUI components, are instantiated and laid out in the window.

3. The program responds to events that are triggered by the user. In this example, the events of interest are

- clicking on the >>>>>> button
- clicking on the <<<<<< button
- closing the window by clicking on the **X** in the window's top right corner

4. There is code to respond to the events. The underlying Java framework activates this listener code when an event occurs. The listener code for the click button event is in the method `buttonClicked`, while that for handling the window close event is handled out of sight inside `GBFrame`.

18.3 Conversion Program Implemented with Swing and AWT

Now, in contrast, let's look at the program implemented using Swing and AWT without `GBFrame`. The program is spread out over four files:

`ConversionWithSwing.java`   This file contains the program's main class. It defines the GUI and contains code that does the conversion between Fahrenheit and Celsius.

`CelsiusButtonListener.java`   This file defines the listener for the <<<<<< button.

`FahrenheitButtonListener.java`   This file defines the listener for the >>>>>> button.

`GenericWindowListener.java`   This file defines the listener for closing the window when the **X** button is clicked.

The Interface

The interface (Figure 18.2) appears essentially the same as it did earlier when we used GBFrame. The cause of the minor differences will become clear when we discuss layout managers.

Figure 18.2 The conversion program with Swing

The File ConversionWithSwing.java

The listing is broken by extensive comments that must be read carefully for a proper understanding of how the Swing/AWT classes work together to support a GUI.

We begin as usual by importing the swing package:

```
import javax.swing.*;
```

Because we are now dealing directly with layouts and listeners, we also import the awt package:

```
import java.awt.*;
```

We then extend JFrame rather than GBFrame:

```
public class ConversionWithAWT extends JFrame {
```

The variables that reference the window objects are declared next:

```
    private JLabel      fahrenheitLabel;
    private JTextField  fahrenheitField;
```

Swing/AWT has no integer fields, so in the preceding line, we use a text field instead.

```
    private JLabel      celsiusLabel;
    private JTextField  celsiusField;
    private JButton     fahrenheitButton;
    private JButton     celsiusButton;
```

There are a number of tasks that must be performed in the constructor:

```
public ConversionWithAWT(){
```

First, instantiate the window objects:

```
fahrenheitLabel  = new JLabel ("Fahrenheit");
fahrenheitField  = new JTextField ("212", 6);    // 6 columns wide
celsiusLabel     = new JLabel ("Celsius");
celsiusField     = new JTextField ("100", 6);    // 6 columns wide
fahrenheitButton = new JButton (">>>>>>");
celsiusButton    = new JButton ("<<<<<<");
```

Second, before adding and positioning window objects, we must instantiate the layout:

```
FlowLayout layout = new FlowLayout();
```

Third, we must get the frame's content pane and set its layout:

```
Container mainWindow = getContentPane();
mainWindow.setLayout (layout);
```

Fourth, we add the window objects under the influence of the layout, which controls their actual placement. There are several different types of layouts, flow layout being the simplest. A flow layout displays components in the order in which they are added. As many components as possible are displayed on each line. Those that do not fit on a given line wrap around onto the next line.

```
mainWindow.add (fahrenheitLabel);
mainWindow.add (celsiusLabel);
mainWindow.add (fahrenheitField);
mainWindow.add (celsiusField);
mainWindow.add (fahrenheitButton);
mainWindow.add (celsiusButton);
```

Fifth, it is necessary to tell the buttons where their listener code is located. This is done by instantiating listener objects and associating them with the buttons. The Java framework sends messages to the listener objects when the buttons are clicked. The listener object for the first button is an instance of the class FahrenheitButtonListener, and for the second button it is an instance of the class CelsiusButtonListener. The need for the parameter this will be explained soon.

```
fahrenheitButton.addActionListener
                        (new FahrenheitButtonListener (this));
celsiusButton.addActionListener
                        (new CelsiusButtonListener (this));
```

Sixth, a listener is needed to close the window. The listener is activated when the user clicks the **X** in the window's top right corner. We call the listener class `GenericWindowListener`. Here we instantiate the listener object and associate it with the window.

```
        addWindowListener (new GenericWindowListener());
    }
```

The conversion from Celsius to Fahrenheit is done in the method that follows. The `FahrenheitButtonListener` object calls this method. We will see the details soon. Note that the method's code is straightforward:

- The code retrieves a string from the Celsius field and converts it to a number.
- The code then converts the number to its Fahrenheit equivalent, converts that back to a string, and displays the string in the Fahrenheit field.

The conversions between strings and numbers are necessary because Swing/AWT does not include the numeric fields that are part of `GBFrame` and `GBApplet`. Instead, we must use Swing's `JTextField`.

```
public void computeFahrenheit(){
    String str = celsiusField.getText().trim();
    int celsius = (new Integer (str)).intValue();
    int fahrenheit = celsius * 9 / 5 + 32;
    fahrenheitField.setText ("" + fahrenheit);
}
```

The conversion from Fahrenheit to Celsius is handled by the next method. It is similar to the preceding one.

```
public void computeCelsius(){
    String str = fahrenheitField.getText().trim();
    int fahrenheit = (new Integer (str)).intValue();
    int celsius = (fahrenheit - 32) * 5 / 9;
    celsiusField.setText ("" + celsius);
}
```

The method `main` is similar, but the window is made a bit narrower:

```
public static void main (String[] args){
    JFrame frm = new ConversionWithSwing();
    frm.setSize (150, 150);
    frm.setVisible (true);
}
}
```

That ends the code for `ConversionWithSwing.java`. We now examine the code for the listener classes.

The File `FahrenheitButtonListener.java`

When a user clicks on the button to compute Celsius, the Java framework sends the `actionPerformed` message to the `FahrenheitButtonListener` object that we saw instantiated in the earlier code. Here is an annotated listing of the class.

We begin by importing the package `java.awt.event`:

```
import java.awt.event.*;
```

The class `FahrenheitButtonListener` implements the `ActionListener` interface. The `ActionListener` interface declares just one method, namely, `actionPerformed`, and the `FahrenheitButtonListener` class must provide code to define this method. A button would be nonfunctional if the main GUI class failed to associate it with an `ActionListener` object.

```
public class FahrenheitButtonListener implements ActionListener{
```

Listeners often need to send messages back to the main GUI class. This listener is designed to send a message back to the view, an instance of the class `ConversionWithSwing`. To do so, it must declare a variable of type `ConversionWithSwing`.

```
    private ConversionWithSwing theGUI;
```

In the constructor that follows we assign a value to the variable `theGUI`. The value being assigned corresponds to the word "`this`" in the main GUI class. Here is the line of code, copied from the previous main GUI class, that activates the constructor:

```
fahrenheitButton.addActionListener
    (new FahrenheitButtonListener (this));
```

And now here is the constructor itself:

```
    public FahrenheitButtonListener (ConversionWithSwing gui){
        theGUI = gui;
    }
```

As already mentioned, the Java framework sends the `actionPerformed` message to the `FahrenheitButtonListener` object when the button to compute Celsius is clicked. An event object is passed to the method as a parameter. The event object contains information about the event, such as the identity of the button that triggered the event, which in this case we already know is the button to compute Celsius.

```
    public void actionPerformed (ActionEvent e){
```

Listener code is often very simple. In this example, all it does is send a message back to the main GUI class, requesting the main GUI class to compute and display the degrees Celsius.

```
        theGUI.computeCelsius();
    }
}
```

The File `CelsiusButtonListener.java`

This file is so similar to the listener just discussed that we present the listing without further discussion.

```java
import java.awt.event.*;

public class CelsiusButtonListener implements ActionListener{

    private ConversionWithSwing theGUI;

    public CelsiusButtonListener (ConversionWithSwing gui){
        theGUI = gui;
    }

    public void actionPerformed (ActionEvent e){
        theGUI.computeFahrenheit();
    }
}
```

The File `GenericWindowListener.java`

A window listener's principal task is to close the window when the user clicks the window's **X** button, which in turn triggers the window's closing event. However, there are several other window events that can be handled in a window listener class. These include iconifying and deiconifying the window and activating and deactivating the window. The listener has a separate method for handling each type of window event. When one of these events occurs, the Java framework sends the appropriate message to the window listener object. As in many applications, this window's closing event is the only one of concern. However, all the methods must be included in the listing, even if some have no code. Here is the listing:

```java
import java.awt.event.*;

public class GenericWindowListener implements WindowListener{

    public void windowClosing (WindowEvent e){
```

Continues

Continued

```
        System.exit(0);
    }

    public void windowActivated (WindowEvent e){}
    public void windowClosed (WindowEvent e){}
    public void windowDeactivated (WindowEvent e){}
    public void windowDeiconified (WindowEvent e){}
    public void windowIconified (WindowEvent e){}
    public void windowOpened (WindowEvent e){}
}
```

As you can readily see, the difference between writing GUI application with and without GBFrame is dramatic.

Self-Test Questions

3. Describe the roles and responsibilities of the different classes written in the ConversionWithSwing program.

4. Which parts of the ConversionWithSwing program are hidden in the version that uses BreezySwing?

18.4 Variations on Implementing with Swing and AWT

The preceding example illustrates one of several different ways to implement the conversion program using Swing and AWT. In this section, we explore several variations. Each variation has pros and cons, and the variation you think best for the conversion program might not be best in another situation. Just remember that, when you write programs, you want to strive for simplicity, clarity, and maintainability.

Simplifying the GenericWindowListener Class

The GenericWindowListener class listed earlier included a number of empty methods. The need to include the empty methods can be avoided if the GenericWindowListener extends the WindowAdapter class instead of implementing the WindowListener interface. The WindowAdapter class is part of the package java.awt.event. Its code is shown below. As you can see, its code implements the WindowListener interface and consists of nothing but empty methods:

```
public abstract class WindowAdapter implements WindowListener {
    public void windowOpened(WindowEvent e) {}
    public void windowClosing(WindowEvent e) {}
```

```
    public void windowClosed(WindowEvent e) {}
    public void windowIconified(WindowEvent e) {}
    public void windowDeiconified(WindowEvent e) {}
    public void windowActivated(WindowEvent e) {}
    public void windowDeactivated(WindowEvent e) {}
}
```

Here is the GenericWindowListener written as an extension of the WindowAdapter class. Only one method now needs to be implemented.

```
import java.awt.event.*;

public class GenericWindowListener extends WindowAdapter{

    public void windowClosing (WindowEvent e){
        System.exit(0);
    }
}
```

Altogether there are 11 listener interfaces in AWT. We have seen two, ActionListener and WindowListener, and will examine some of the remaining ones soon. Listeners with more than one method have a corresponding adapter, thus providing programmers with the convenience of extending the adapter rather than implementing the interface.

Incorporating the Listeners into the Main GUI Class

Listeners do not have to be in separate classes but can be incorporated into the main GUI class. This is achieved by having the main GUI class implement the desired listeners in addition to extending the JFrame class. We illustrate the process by incorporating the button and window listeners. We will, of course, need to implement all the methods in the ActionListener and the WindowListener interfaces. By the way, a class can extend only one other class but can implement any number of interfaces. Here is the code with some comments included:

```
import javax.swing.*;
import java.awt.*;
import java.awt.event.*;

public class ConversionWithSwing extends JFrame
                                 implements ActionListener,
                                            WindowListener{

    private JLabel     fahrenheitLabel;
    private JTextField fahrenheitField;
```

Continues

Continued

```
private JLabel      celsiusLabel;
private JTextField celsiusField;
private JButton     fahrenheitButton;
private JButton     celsiusButton;


public ConversionWithSwing(){
    fahrenheitLabel  = new JLabel ("Fahrenheit");
    fahrenheitField  = new JTextField ("212", 6);     // 6 columns wide
    celsiusLabel     = new JLabel ("Celsius");
    celsiusField     = new JTextField ("100", 6);     // 6 columns wide
    fahrenheitButton = new JButton (">>>>>>");
    celsiusButton    = new JButton ("<<<<<<");

    FlowLayout layout = new FlowLayout();
    Container mainWindow = getContentPane();
    mainWindow.setLayout (layout);
    mainWindow.add (fahrenheitLabel);
    mainWindow.add (celsiusLabel);
    mainWindow.add (fahrenheitField);
    mainWindow.add (celsiusField);
    mainWindow.add (fahrenheitButton);
    mainWindow.add (celsiusButton);
```

We still need to associate the buttons and the window with listener objects. But now the only listener object is the application itself, namely, this.

```
        fahrenheitButton.addActionListener (this);
        celsiusButton.addActionListener (this);
        addWindowListener (this);
    }
```

A class that implements the ActionListener must include the method actionPerformed.

```
    public void actionPerformed (ActionEvent e){
        String str;
        int fahrenheit, celsius;
        JButton btn = (JButton)e.getSource();

        if (btn == celsiusButton){
            str = celsiusField.getText().trim();
            celsius = (new Integer (str)).intValue();
            fahrenheit = celsius * 9 / 5 + 32;
            fahrenheitField.setText ("" + fahrenheit);
```

```
        }
        else{
            str = fahrenheitField.getText().trim();
            fahrenheit = (new Integer (str)).intValue();
            celsius = (fahrenheit - 32) * 5 / 9;
            celsiusField.setText ("" + celsius);
        }
    }
```

A class that implements the `WindowListener` must include the seven methods that follow, even if most of them are empty.

```
public void windowClosing (WindowEvent e){
    System.exit(0);
}
public void windowActivated (WindowEvent e){}
public void windowClosed (WindowEvent e){}
public void windowDeactivated (WindowEvent e){}
public void windowDeiconified (WindowEvent e){}
public void windowIconified (WindowEvent e){}
public void windowOpened (WindowEvent e){}
```

Fortunately, some things never change. Here is the familiar method `main`.

```
public static void main (String[] args){
    JFrame frm = new ConversionWithSwing();
    frm.setSize (150, 150);
    frm.setVisible (true);
}
}
```

This completes our overview of the workings of Swing and AWT. We now turn to some of the details, beginning with a discussion of GUI components and layouts.

Self-Test Questions

5. What is an adapter class? Give an example.
6. Describe the structure of an application that incorporates listeners into the main class.

18.5 GUI Components

The first category of classes used in developing windows-based applications is the GUI components. The visible objects that constitute a window fall into this category.

These objects include buttons, text fields, text areas, lists, menu items, and so forth. You can find complete documentation for all of the GUI component classes at the Java Web site, as described in Appendix A.

The `Component` Class Hierarchy

All of the GUI component classes, whether in Swing or AWT, are subclasses of an abstract class in AWT called `Component`. This class specifies the most basic attributes and behavior of all GUI objects. For example, every ***component*** has attributes that define its size (width and height in pixels), background color, foreground color, text font, and visibility. Commonly used methods for modifying these attributes are shown in Table 18.2. The `Component` class also includes methods for adding listener objects to a component, as illustrated earlier in the conversion program.

Table 18.2

Some Commonly Used `Component` Methods	
Component Method	**What It Does**
`void setBackground(Color c)`	Sets the background color of the component.
`void setEnabled(boolean b)`	Enables or disables the component.
`void setFont(Font f)`	Sets the font of the component.
`void setForeground(Color c)`	Sets the foreground color of the component.
`void setSize(int w, int h)`	Sets the width and height of the component.
`void setVisible(boolean b)`	Displays or hides the component.

Figure 18.3 shows a portion of the Swing branch of the `Component` class hierarchy. Note the following points about the figure:

- The two classes at the top of the hierarchy are in `java.awt`, whereas the rest of the classes are in `javax.swing`.
- The concrete classes are shaded, whereas the abstract classes are not.

The classes `DoubleField` and `IntegerField`, which we have defined in the `BreezySwing` package, are subclasses of the `JTextField` class, and thus understand all `JTextField` messages. You are already familiar with the capabilities and behavior of many of the component classes, but several deserve further explanation.

Panels

`JPanel` is the parent class of the `BreezySwing` class `GBPanel`. As we saw in Chapter 13, a panel represents a rectangular area within a window. This area can be painted and repainted independently of the rest of the window.

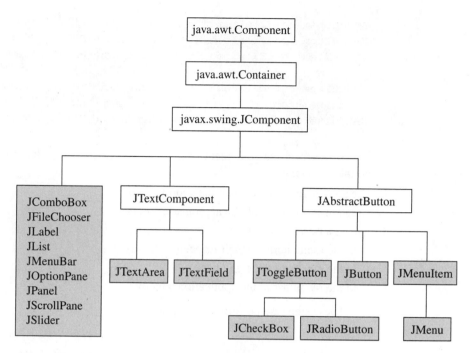

Figure 18.3 A portion of the swing classes in the component hierarchy

Scroll Bars

You have seen **scroll bars** along the sides of list box and text area components. However, scroll bars are not automatically provided for these components. To add scroll bars to a list box or text area, you must wrap an instance of JScrollPane around it, as shown in the following code segment:

```
Container c = getContentPane();
TextArea ta = new JTextArea();    // Create a text area
c.add(new JScrollPane(ta));       // Wrap it in scroll bars and add to GUI
```

Sliders

A **slider** is used to enter an input value, usually a number, by dragging the mouse along a ticked ruler. Sliders are instances of the class JSlider. A Case Study later in the chapter uses sliders and a panel to create a color meter for your computer.

Menu Components

In earlier chapters, BreezySwing hid the details of menu setup. For example, the following code segment uses BreezySwing to set up a **File** menu and an **Edit** menu with appropriate options:

```
JMenuItem newFileItem   = addMenuItem("File", "New");
JMenuItem openFileItem   = addMenuItem("File", "Open");
JMenuItem saveFileItem   = addMenuItem("File", "Save");


JMenuItem cutEditItem    = addMenuItem("Edit", "Cut");
JMenuItem copyEditItem   = addMenuItem("Edit", "Copy");
JMenuItem pasteEditItem = addMenuItem("Edit", "Paste");
```

To perform the equivalent task without BreezySwing, the programmer must do the following:

1. Create new menu items with the appropriate labels.
2. Create new menus with the appropriate labels.
3. Create a new menu bar.
4. Add the menu items to their respective menus.
5. Add the menus to the menu bar.
6. Add the menu bar to the application window.

These steps are performed in the next code segment:

```
// Create the menu items.
JMenuItem newFileItem   = new JMenuItem ("New");
JMenuItem openFileItem   = new JMenuItem ("Open");
JMenuItem saveFileItem   = new JMenuItem ("Save");
JMenuItem cutEditItem    = new JMenuItem ("Cut");
JMenuItem copyEditItem   = new JMenuItem ("Copy");
JMenuItem pasteEditItem = new JMenuItem ("Paste");

// Create the menus and the menu bar.
JMenu fileMenu = new JMenu ("File");
JMenu editMenu = new JMenu ("Edit");
JMenuBar menuBar = new JMenuBar();

// Add the menu items to the menus.
fileMenu.add (newFileItem);
fileMenu.add (openFileItem);
fileMenu.add (saveFileItem);
editMenu.add (cutEditItem);
editMenu.add (copyEditItem);
editMenu.add (pasteEditItem);

// Add the menus to the menu bar.
menuBar.add (fileMenu);
menuBar.add (editMenu);

// Add the menu bar to the application window.
setJMenuBar (menuBar);
```

The menu classes also support the creation of submenus. To create a submenu, you simply add one menu as an item to another.

The programmer sets up listeners for menu events in the same way as shown earlier for button events, by implementing the interface `ActionListener`. In this case, an action listener is added to each menu item.

Option Panes

Option panes provide a set of commonly used dialogs, such as prompters, message boxes, and confirmation dialogs. They are created by sending messages to the class `JOptionPane`. Table 18.3 lists some typical messages.

Table 18.3

Some `JOptionPane` Methods	
`JOptionPane` Method	**What It Does**
`int showConfirmDialog(Component parent, String message)`	Pops up a confirmation dialog with the options **Yes, No,** and **Cancel** and the title "Select an Option." Returns the `JOptionPane` constants `YES_OPTION`, `NO_OPTION`, and `CANCEL_OPTION`.
`String showInputDialog(Component parent, String message)`	Pops up a prompter dialog with the message. Returns `null` if canceled; otherwise, returns the string entered.
`void showMessageDialog(Component parent, String message)`	Pops up a message dialog with the message and the title "Confirm."

There are several variations of each method that allow the client to specify the title, the type of message (error, warning, etc.), and so forth. The following code segment shows the use of a confirmation dialog:

```
int choice = JOptionPane.showConfirmDialog(this, "Want to quit?");
if (choice == JOptionPane.YES_OPTION)
   System.out.println("Yes");
else if (choice == JOptionPane.NO_OPTION)
   System.out.println("No");
else if (choice == JOptionPane.CANCEL_OPTION)
   System.out.println("Cancel");
```

Container Classes

Container objects are so called because they contain other window objects, including other containers. Figure 18.4 shows Swing's primary container classes, and Table 18.4 describes their uses.

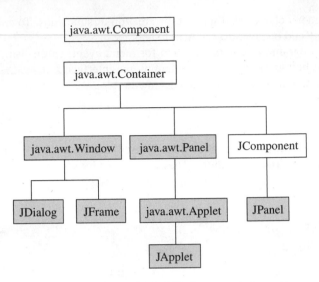

Figure 18.4 The primary Swing container classes

Table 18.4

The Uses of Swing's Container Classes

Container Class	What It Does
JFrame	Displays components in an application window. All stand-alone GUI applications must extend JFrame (or GBFrame when using BreezySwing).
JApplet	Displays components in a Web browser. Applets have neither a menu bar nor a border. All Web-based applications must extend JApplet (or GBApplet when using BreezySwing).
JDialog	Displays components in a dialog window. Dialogs are used as auxiliary windows in stand-alone applications and applets. They can be either modal or nonmodal. Until it is dismissed, a modal dialog blocks user interaction with the rest of an application. Dialogs extend JDialog (or GBDialog when using BreezySwing).
JPanel	Organizes a set of components as a group. Panels can factor complex interfaces into modular chunks. An applet, frame, or dialog can contain several panels, which in turn can contain buttons, text fields, lists, etc., and even other panels. Panels extend JPanel (or GBPanel in BreezySwing).

A container must use a layout manager that determines the arrangement of the components within it. The different types of layouts are discussed next.

Self-Test Questions

7. Write a code segment that uses a JOptionPane method to prompt the user for her name.

8. What are container classes? Give three examples.

18.6 Layouts

In many programming environments, one must specify the location and size of window objects in terms of pixel positions and pixel dimensions. Although this approach provides precise control over a window's appearance, it has a drawback. When a window is resized, its components remain fixed in position and size. Consequently, if the window is too small, some of the components cannot be seen, and if it is too large, the components seem to huddle in the window's top left corner. In contrast, components in a Java window distribute themselves to fill the available space. The exact manner of this distribution depends on what is called the window's layout, as defined by one of Java's layout manager classes. Although you have had no way of knowing it, GBFrame and GBApplet use the layout manager GridBagLayout. Figure 18.5 lists the layout manager classes with an illustration and overview of each.

Layout Manager	Illustration	Overview
BorderLayout		A border layout divides a window into five regions, positioned as shown. Each region can contain one component. This is the default layout for frames and dialogs.
CardLayout		A card layout consists of a stack of components. Only one component can be seen at a time, but it is possible to switch between components.
FlowLayout		A flow layout displays components in the order in which they are added. As many components as possible are displayed on each line. Those that do not fit on a given line wrap around onto the next line. This is the default layout for panels and applets.
GridLayout		A grid layout organizes components in a grid of equal sized cells.

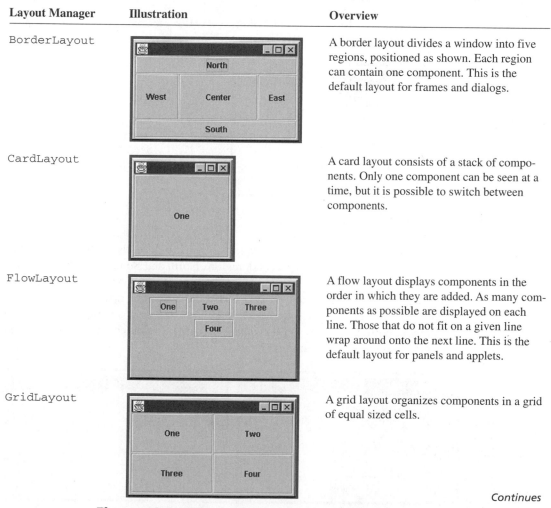

Continues

Figure 18.5 The layout manager classes in AWT

Layout Manager	Illustration	Overview
GridBagLayout	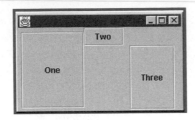	A grid bag layout also organizes components in a grid, but the grid can be adjusted in many ways. Components occupy rectangular blocks of cells, cells can be empty, and the size of cells can vary. All of this gives the programmer a great deal of control over a layout's appearance

Figure 18.5 The layout manager classes in AWT *(continued)*

A more detailed description of each layout manager follows.

Border Layouts

The default layout for frames and dialogs is BorderLayout. The layout of Figure 18.6 divides a container into five regions.

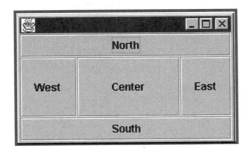

Figure 18.6 A border layout

A region's size is based on several factors. First it depends on the preferred size of the component placed in it. Second, regions North and South are expanded horizontally to fill the container's width, and regions East and West are expanded vertically. Third, the Center region expands to fill the remaining space. Not all regions need to be present. If the Center region is omitted, it leaves an empty space in the container; however, if any of the other regions are omitted, the central region expands to fill the vacated space (Figure 18.7).

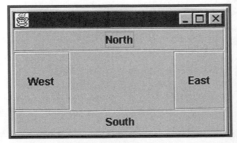 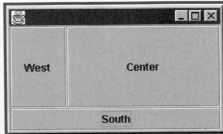

Figure 18.7 Border layouts that are not filled

A component is added to a region using the `add` method:

```
add (<component>, <region>)
```

where `<region>` is one of the strings "North", "South", "East", "West", and "Center".

For example, the following code segment creates the border layout shown in Figure 18.6, which includes all five regions. The usual place for this sort of code is in a constructor.

```
// Create and set the layout
BorderLayout layout = new BorderLayout();
Container mainWindow = getContentPane();
mainWindow.setLayout (layout);

// Add components under control of the layout
mainWindow.add (new JButton("North"), "North");
mainWindow.add (new JButton("East"), "East");
mainWindow.add (new JButton("South"), "South");
mainWindow.add (new JButton("West"), "West");
mainWindow.add (new JButton("Center"), "Center");
```

In the code, the first and third lines can be omitted when using a frame or a dialog.

Flow Layouts

The default window layout for panels and applets is `FlowLayout`. A flow layout displays components in horizontal lines in the order in which they are added. Components that do not fit on a line wrap around onto the next (Figure 18.8).

Figure 18.8 A flow layout

When a user resizes a window, the wrapping points shift, and the appearance of the window changes dramatically. For instance, the two windows in Figure 18.9 were created by the same program.

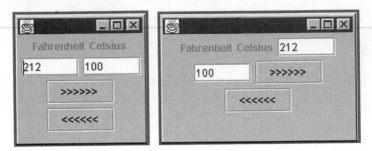

Figure 18.9 Two views of the same program with a flow layout

By default, a flow layout centers the components in each row and separates them horizontally and vertically by five pixels. The flow layout shown in Figure 18.8 can be created as follows:

```
FlowLayout layout = new FlowLayout();
Container mainWindow = getContentPane();
mainWindow.setLayout (layout);

mainWindow.add (new JButton("One"));
mainWindow.add (new JButton("Two"));
mainWindow.add (new JButton("Three"));
mainWindow.add (new JButton("Four"));
```

The first two lines are optional in panels and applets. The programmer has some minor control over a flow layout. One can align the components to the left, center, or right using the constants

```
FlowLayout.LEFT
FlowLayout.CENTER
FlowLayout.RIGHT
```

For instance, to align the components at the left (Figure 18.10), the programmer writes

```
FlowLayout layout = new FlowLayout (FlowLayout.LEFT);
Container mainWindow = getContentPane();
mainWindow.setLayout (layout);

// Now add the components
```

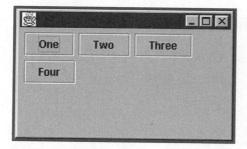

Figure 18.10 A flow layout with components aligned to the left

The programmer can control the horizontal and vertical spacing between components. The following example centers window objects with horizontal gaps of 10 and vertical gaps of 15 pixels (Figure 18.11):

```
FlowLayout layout = new FlowLayout (FlowLayout.CENTER, 10, 15);
Container mainWindow = getContentPane();
mainWindow.setLayout (layout);

// Now add the components
```

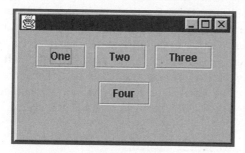

Figure 18.11 A flow layout with fixed spacing and components aligned to the center

Grid Layouts

A regular pattern of objects, such as a table of buttons, is easily displayed with a grid layout. To use a grid layout:

1. Create a new instance of class `GridLayout` with the desired number of rows and columns.

2. Set the container's layout to this instance.

3. Add the components to the container.

The components are positioned in the grid from left to right and top to bottom, in the order added, and each cell in the grid is the same size. The following code segment creates the grid layout displayed in Figure 18.12:

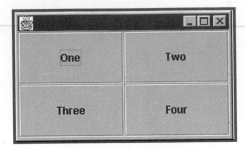

Figure 18.12 A grid layout

```
mainWindow.setLayout (new GridLayout(2, 2));
mainWindow.add (new JButton("One"));
mainWindow.add (new JButton("Two"));
mainWindow.add (new JButton("Three"));
mainWindow.add (new JButton("Four"));
```

Grid Bag Layouts

The *grid bag layout* is the most versatile and most complex layout manager. It treats the display area as a grid of cells. The grid begins with no cells and adds cells as needed to accommodate the components. Components occupy rectangular blocks of cells called display areas. Cells can be empty, and their size can vary. In Figure 18.13, a grid has been superimposed on the window. The button **One** occupies two cells. Each of the other buttons occupies a single cell. The remaining cells are empty. Notice that the cells differ markedly in size, and the components fill their display areas in varying degrees. The classes GBFrame, GBApplet, and GBDialog use a grid bag layout.

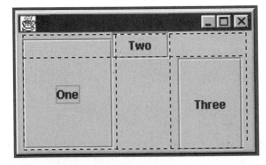

Figure 18.13 The grid within a grid bag layout

Class GridBagLayout must always be used in conjunction with another class: GridBagConstraints. A constraints object specifies the manner in which a component occupies the grid. This is done by assigning values to the constraints object's public instance variables. Here is an illustrative code segment:

```
GridBagLayout layout = new GridBagLayout();
Container mainWindow = getContentPane();
mainWindow.setLayout (layout);

constraints = new GridBagConstraints();
constraints.gridy = 0;          // row 0
constraints.gridx = 0;          // column 0
constraints.gridheight = 2;
constraints.fill = GridBagConstraints.BOTH;
constraints.insets = new Insets (6,4,3,0);
constraints.weightx = 100;

JButton button1 = new JButton ("One");
layout.setConstraints (button1, constraints);
mainWindow.add (button1);
```

The public instance variables are described in Table 18.5.

Table 18.5

The Grid Bag Constraints

Public Instance Variable	Description
anchor	When a component is smaller than its display area, an anchor specifies how to position the component in the area. The valid values are CENTER (the default), NORTH, NORTHEAST, EAST, SOUTHEAST, SOUTH, SOUTHWEST, WEST, and NORTHWEST. These values must be preceded by the name of the class—for instance, GridBagConstraints.NORTH.
fill	When a component's requested size is smaller than its display area, the fill attribute can be used to stretch the component. The valid values are:

NONE	Do not stretch the component. This is the default.
HORIZONTAL	Stretch the component as much as possible horizontally.
VERTICAL	Stretch the component as much as possible vertically.
BOTH	Stretch the component as much as possible horizontally and vertically.

These values must be preceded by the name of the class—for instance, GridBagConstraints.VERTICAL.

gridx, gridy	Use gridx and gridy to specify the top left cell in a component's display area. Numbering begins at 0. The value GridBagContraints.RELATIVE (the default value) can be used instead of a number. This value indicates that a component is to be positioned relative to the last component added, to the right for gridx and below for gridy.
gridwidth, gridheight	These variables specify the width and height of a component's display area, as measured in cells. The default value is 1. The values REMAINDER and RELATIVE can be used to specify that the component is the last or next to last, respectively, in a row or column.

Continues

Table 18.5 *(continued)*

Public Instance Variable	Description
ipadx, ipady	These variables are used to increase a component's minimum size by the specified number of pixels on the left and right (ipadx) and on the top and bottom (ipady). The default values are 0.
insets	Insets specify how much empty space, as measured in pixels, should be placed between a component and the edges of its display area. The default is 0. Here is an example:
	`constraints.insets = new Insets (top,left,bottom,right);`
	where top, left, bottom, and right are nonnegative integers.
weightx, weighty	In a grid bag layout, not all cells need to be the same size. Their sizes can vary depending on values assigned to weightx and weighty. These values do not specify absolute dimensions for a cell, merely a relative size. Thus, all things being equal, a cell with weightx = 100 is twice as wide as one with weightx = 50, while a cell with weightx = 0 is just wide enough to display its component. Of course, all things are seldom equal. The algorithm used for determining a cell's dimensions is not described in Java's online documentation, so one must acquire an intuitive sense for what happens through experimentation. By the way, if all the weights are 0 (the default), the components huddle together in the center of the container.

Here is code to create the grid bag layout shown in Figure 18.13.

```
// Create and set the layout
   GridBagLayout layout = new GridBagLayout();
   Container mainWindow = getContentPane();
   mainWindow.setLayout (layout);

// Create a constraints object
   GridBagConstraints constraints;

// Create three button objects.
   JButton button1 = new JButton ("One");
   JButton button2 = new JButton ("Two");
   JButton button3 = new JButton ("Three");

// Set the constraints object for button1, indicating that
// button1:
//    starts in row 0, column 0
//    has a height of 2 cells
//    fills its display area in both directions
//    is inset within its display area by 6, 4, 3, and 0
//    has a horizontal weighting factor of 100
```

```
// with the remaining constraints taking their default values
   constraints = new GridBagConstraints();
   constraints.gridy = 0;          // row 0
   constraints.gridx = 0;          // column 0
   constraints.gridheight = 2;
   constraints.fill = GridBagConstraints.BOTH;
   constraints.insets = new Insets (6,4,3,0);
   constraints.weightx = 100;
   layout.setConstraints (button1, constraints);
   mainWindow.add (button1);

// Set the constraints object for button2, indicating that
// button2:
//    starts in row 0, column 1
// with the remaining constraints taking their default values
   constraints = new GridBagConstraints();
   constraints.gridy = 0;          // row 0
   constraints.gridx = 1;          // column 1
   layout.setConstraints (button2, constraints);
   mainWindow.add (button2);

// Set the constraints object for button3, indicating that
// button3:
//    starts in row 1, column 2
//    fills its display area in the vertical directions
//    has a horizontal weighting factor of 50
//    has a vertical weighting factor of 100
// with the remaining constraints taking their default values
   constraints = new GridBagConstraints();
   constraints.gridy = 1;          // row 1
   constraints.gridx = 2;          // column 2
   constraints.weightx = 50;
   constraints.weighty = 100;
   constraints.fill = GridBagConstraints.VERTICAL;
   layout.setConstraints (button3, constraints);
   mainWindow.add (button3);
```

Card Layouts

A card layout consists of a stack of components. Only one component can be seen at a time, but it is possible to switch between components. When a card layout is created, the top component is visible. Figure 18.14 illustrates a card layout, and here is the code that created it:

Figure 18.14 A card layout

```
CardLayout layout = new CardLayout();
Container mainWindow = getContentPane();

setLayout (layout);
mainWindow.add ("One", new JButton("One"));
mainWindow.add ("Two", new JButton("Two"));
mainWindow.add ("Three", new JButton("Three"));
mainWindow.add ("Four", new JButton("Four"));
```

Several methods are used to move between components. These are first, last, next, previous, and show. Here is some code that demonstrates these methods in action. The word this refers to the container in which the code is running, a frame in this example. At other times, this might be replaced by a variable name that refers to the container associated with the layout.

```
layout.first (this);
layout.next (this);
layout.previous (this);
layout.last (this);
layout.show (this, "Three");
```

Panels

For the sake of simplicity, all of the components in the preceding discussion were buttons. We could equally well have used lists, text areas, and even panels. A panel is a container that can contain other components, including other panels. Fancy graphical user interfaces can be built by combining panels and other components in an imaginative manner. Figure 18.15, for instance, shows an example that is plenty fancy and more than a bit silly.

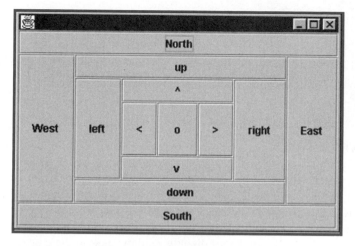

Figure 18.15 The use of panels

Here is the code that laid out the GUI in the figure:

```
BorderLayout layout = new BorderLayout();
Container mainWindow = getContentPane();
mainWindow.setLayout (layout);

mainWindow.add (new JButton ("North"), "North");
mainWindow.add (new JButton ("East"), "East");
mainWindow.add (new JButton ("South"), "South");
mainWindow.add (new JButton ("West"), "West");

JPanel panel = new JPanel();
mainWindow.add (panel, "Center");

BorderLayout layout2 = new BorderLayout();
panel.setLayout (layout2);
panel.add (new JButton ("up"), "North");
panel.add (new JButton ("down"), "South");
panel.add (new JButton ("left"), "West");
panel.add (new JButton ("right"), "East");

JPanel panel2 = new JPanel();
panel.add (panel2, "Center");

BorderLayout layout3 = new BorderLayout();
panel2.setLayout (layout3);
panel2.add (new JButton ("^"), "North");
panel2.add (new JButton ("v"), "South");
panel2.add (new JButton ("<"), "West");
panel2.add (new JButton (">"), "East");
panel2.add (new JButton ("o"), "Center");
```

Self-Test Questions

9. What is a panel? Give an example of its use.

10. List the major layout manager classes and their primary features.

11. What are the default layouts of frames, applets, and dialogs?

18.7 Events

When developing a graphical user interface, the programmer is concerned not only with the layout of the window objects but also with handling the events they trigger. If we use `BreezySwing`, then we handle events very easily in methods such as `buttonClicked` and `menuItemSelected`. But life becomes complicated when we use Java's GUI packages directly, as illustrated in the conversion program earlier in the chapter. In this section, we give a brief overview of the relationships between events, listeners, and components. For an exhaustive survey of all of the events, listeners, and components supported by Swing and AWT, see Sun's documentation.

Events and Components

From our work with the conversion program, we know that certain events can be associated with certain components. For instance, the action event can be associated with buttons, and keyboard events can be associated with text fields. Table 18.6 lists

■ three different classes of events

■ their associated components

■ the conditions that trigger the events

For example, the table indicates that the `ActionEvent`

■ is limited to buttons, lists, menu items, and text fields

■ can be triggered by clicking a button, double clicking an item in a list, selecting a menu item, or pressing the **Enter** key in a text field

Events and Listeners

An event is ignored unless the originating component has added a listener to handle the event. In the conversion program we used the `addActionListener` method to add listeners to buttons. Table 18.7 lists some events in AWT, their associated listeners, and how to add/remove these listeners. We did not have any reason to remove a component's listener in the conversion program, but the table shows that we could have done so. Table 18.7 also lists the methods included in each listener interface.

Table 18.6

Some Events and Their Associated Components

Event Class	Associated Components	Triggered When

`ActionEvent`	`JButton`
	`JList`
	`JMenuItem`
	`JTextField`
		The button is clicked.
		An item in the list is double clicked.
		The menu item is selected.
		The user presses the **Enter** key in the field.

`MouseEvent`
`extends`
`InputEvent`
	`Component`	■ A mouse button is pressed in the component.
		■ A mouse button is released in the component (provided it was pressed in the same component).
		■ A mouse button is clicked in the component (i.e., pressed and then released).
		■ The mouse enters the component.
		■ The mouse exits the component.
		■ The mouse is dragged in the component (i.e., moved while a button is depressed).
		■ The mouse is moved in the component.

`WindowEvent`	`Window`	■ The window is activated. ■ The window is closed. ■ The window is closing. ■ The window is deactivated. ■ The window is deiconified. ■ The window is iconified. ■ The window is opened.

Table 18.7

Some Events and Their Associated Listeners

Event Class	Associated Listener Interface	Is There an Adapter Class?	Methods to Add / Remove Listener	Listener Interface Methods
Action Event	Action Listener	No	addActionListener () removeActionListener ()	actionPerformed (ActionEvent)
Mouse Event extends InputEvent	Mouse Listener	Yes	addMouseListener () removeMouseListener ()	mousePressed (MouseEvent) mouseReleased (MouseEvent) mouseClicked (MouseEvent) mouseEntered (MouseEvent) mouseExited (MouseEvent)
	Mouse Motion Listener	Yes	addMouse MotionListener () removeMouse MotionListener ()	mouseDragged (MouseEvent) mouseMoved (MouseEvent)

Continues

Table 18.7 *(continued)*

Event Class	Associated Listener Interface	Is There an Adapter Class?	Methods to Add / Remove Listener	Listener Interface Methods
Window Event	Window Listener	Yes	addWindowListener () removeWindow Listener ()	windowActivated (WindowEvent) windowClosed (WindowEvent) windowClosing (WindowEvent) windowDeactivated (WindowEvent) windowDeiconified (WindowEvent) windowIconified (WindowEvent) windowOpened (WindowEvent)

Events and Their Methods

When an event occurs, the event object, e, is passed as a parameter to the appropriate listener method, and the listener method can then send messages to the event object. For instance, consider the following code segment:

```
JButton btn = (JButton) e.getSource();
```

The getSource message is understood by all events and returns the object in which the event originated—a button in the preceding example. Table 18.8 lists several different classes of events and the most useful methods in each class.

Table 18.8

Some Events and Their Associated Methods

Event Class	Event Methods	Description
All events	Object getSource() String toString()	Gets the object in which the event originated. Returns a string representation of the event.
MouseEvent extends InputEvent	int getClickCount()	Returns the number of mouse clicks associated with the event. Could be 0, 1, or 2.
	Point getPoint()	Returns the *x, y* position of the mouse where the event occurs relative to the top left corner of the component in which the event occurs.
	int getX()	Returns the *x* position of the mouse where the event occurs relative to the top left corner of the component in which the event occurs.
	int getY()	Returns the *y* position of the mouse where the event occurs relative to the top left corner of the component in which the event occurs.
	boolean isPopup Trigger()	Returns true if this mouse event triggers the pop-up menu else false.
WindowEvent	getWindow()	Returns the window in which the event occurred.

Self-Test Question

12. Describe how components, listeners, and events cooperate in an application.

18.8 Dialogs

In Chapter 15, we examined how to construct dialogs with the BreezySwing class GBDialog. In a real Java application or applet, you would use the Swing class JDialog. Like the JFrame class, which is used to implement application windows, JDialog is a subclass of the Window class. Thus, dialogs are like frames in many ways, but with two important exceptions:

1. A dialog can be *modal*; that is, it can prevent the user from accessing the rest of the application before quitting the dialog.

2. A dialog must have a *parent*—that is, a frame to which it can refer after it is created.

A dialog can also have a title. There are several constructors that allow the programmer to specify these attributes:

```
public JDialog (JFrame parent, String title, boolean modal)
public JDialog (JFrame parent, String title)
public JDialog (JFrame parent, boolean modal)
public JDialog (JFrame parent)
```

Dialogs are modal by default. The reference to the parent frame allows a dialog to send messages to the application.

The programmer must use Swing and AWT to lay out a dialog's window objects and set up their listeners, just as with frames. To show how this is done, we redo the dialog example presented in Chapter 15. The interface of the revised dialog is shown in Figure 18.16.

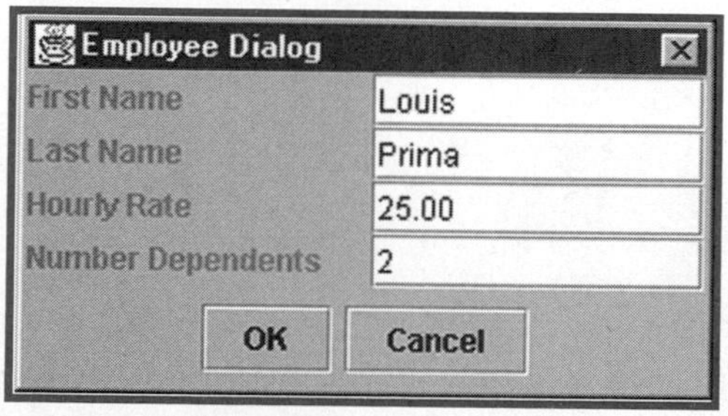

Figure 18.16 A sample dialog

Here is the portion of the application's main interface class that involves the use of the dialog. For convenience, we use GBFrame.

```
private void modifySelectedEmployee(){
//Allows modifications to the selected employee.
//  Preconditions  -- none
//  Postconditions -- if there is no selected employee, then
//                          display an error message
//                 -- if the user cancels the dialog, then no change
//                 -- else the employee data are changed
//                       her name, which may be modified, overwrites her
//                       previous name in the name list and the name
//                       is selected
//                       her info is redisplayed


    int index;
    String name;

    if (selectedEmployee == null){
       messageBox ("SORRY: must select before modify");
       return;
    }
    EmployeeDialog employeeDialog
                 = new EmployeeDialog (this, selectedEmployee);
    employeeDialog.show();
    if (employeeDialog.getDlgCloseIndicator().equals ("OK")){
       index = nameList.getSelectedIndex();
       name = selectedEmployee.getName();
       DefaultListModel model = (DefaultListModel) nameList.getModel();
       model.set (index, name);
       nameList.setSelectedIndex (index);
       displaySelectedEmployee();
    }
  }
```

Here is a listing of the revised dialog class. We use Swing and AWT directly.

```
/*  EmployeeDialog.java

1) This is the dialog for the employee system.
2) It displays the employee passed to it.
3) The user can then change the data in the dialog's window.
4) If the user clicks the OK button, the employee is updated with
   the data in the window provided the data are valid.
5) If the user clicks the Cancel button, the dialog closes and returns
   without modifying the employee.
*/


import javax.swing.*;
```

```java
import java.awt.*;
import java.awt.event.*;

public class EmployeeDialog extends JDialog
                            implements ActionListener{

    //Window objects
    JLabel lbFirstName      = new JLabel("First Name");
    JLabel lbLastName       = new JLabel("Last Name");
    JLabel lbHourlyRate     = new JLabel("Hourly Rate");
    JLabel lbNumDependents  = new JLabel("Number Dependents");

    JTextField tfFirstName      = new JTextField(12);
    JTextField tfLastName       = new JTextField(12);
    JTextField tfHourlyRate     = new JTextField(12);
    JTextField tfNumDependents  = new JTextField(12);

    JButton btnOK     = new JButton("OK");
    JButton btnCancel = new JButton("Cancel");

    //Instance variables
    private Employee    employee;       //The employee being modified
    private String      closeIndicator; //The dialog close indicator

    public EmployeeDialog (JFrame f, Employee emp){
    //Constructor
    //  Preconditions  -- the input parameters are not null
    //  Postconditions -- the dialog's window is initialized
    //                  -- the employee variable is set
    //                  -- the employee's data are displayed in the
    //                     dialog's window

        //Housekeeping required in every dialog
        super (f);

        //Set the dialog's size and title
        setSize (275,150);
        setTitle ("Employee Dialog");

        // Add the window objects to the appropriate layout

        JPanel labelPanel = new JPanel(new GridLayout(4, 1));
        JPanel fieldPanel = new JPanel(new GridLayout(4, 1));
        JPanel buttonPanel = new JPanel();
        Container mainWindow = getContentPane();
        mainWindow.add("West", labelPanel);
```

Continues

Continued

```
    mainWindow.add("East", fieldPanel);
    mainWindow.add("South", buttonPanel);
    labelPanel.add(lbFirstName);
    labelPanel.add(lbLastName);
    labelPanel.add(lbHourlyRate);
    labelPanel.add(lbNumDependents);
    fieldPanel.add(tfFirstName);
    fieldPanel.add(tfLastName);
    fieldPanel.add(tfHourlyRate);
    fieldPanel.add(tfNumDependents);
    buttonPanel.add(btnOK);
    buttonPanel.add(btnCancel);

    // Add the action listeners to the buttons

    btnOK.addActionListener(this);
    btnCancel.addActionListener(this);

    //Set the dialog's default value for the close indicator to Cancel.
    //If the user closes the dialog without clicking either the OK or
    //Cancel button, the default takes effect.
    setDlgCloseIndicator ("Cancel");

    //Save the employee reference and display the employee data in the
    //dialog's window.
    employee = emp;
    tfFirstName.setText      (employee.getFirstName());
    tfLastName.setText       (employee.getLastName());
    tfHourlyRate.setText     ("" + employee.getHourlyRate());
    tfNumDependents.setText ("" + employee.getNumDependents());
}

public void setDlgCloseIndicator(String s){
    closeIndicator = s;
}

public String getDlgCloseIndicator(){
    return closeIndicator;
}

public void actionPerformed (ActionEvent e){
//Responds to the OK and Cancel buttons.
//  Preconditions  -- one of the two buttons has been clicked
//  Postconditions -- if the Cancel button then
//                      the employee is not modified
```

```
//                     the close indicator equals Cancel
//                     the dialog is closed
//                     control returns to the caller
//           -- if the OK button but the user input is invalid
//                     then an error message is displayed
//                     the dialog remains active
//           -- if the OK button and the user input is valid then
//                     the employee is modified
//                     the close indicator equals OK
//                     the dialog is closed
//                     control returns to the caller


  //Get the data from the screen
  String    firstName    = tfFirstName.getText().trim();
  String    lastName     = tfLastName.getText().trim();
  double    hourlyRate   =
     Double.valueOf(tfHourlyRate.getText().trim()).doubleValue();
  int       numDependents =
     Integer.valueOf(tfNumDependents.getText().trim()).intValue();
  String    validationErrors;
  JButton buttonObj = (JButton) e.getSource();


  if (buttonObj == btnCancel)                //Cancel button

     //Close the dialog and return to the caller
     dispose();

  else{                                      //OK button

     //Validate the data by calling a static method in the Employee
     //class
     validationErrors = Employee.validate
        (firstName, lastName, hourlyRate, numDependents);

     if (validationErrors != "")             //Screen data invalid

        //Display an error message
        JOptionPane.showMessageDialog (this, validationErrors);

     else{                                   //Screen data valid

        //Update the employee with the screen data
        employee.setAllVariables
           (firstName, lastName, hourlyRate, numDependents);

        //Set the close indicator to OK, close the dialog, and
```

Continues

Continued

```
        //return to the caller.
        setDlgCloseIndicator ("OK");
        dispose();
    }
  }
 }
}
```

The critical code to notice in the main interface class is

```
EmployeeDialog employeeDialog
            = new EmployeeDialog (this, selectedEmployee);
employeeDialog.show();
if (employeeDialog.getDlgCloseIndicator().equals ("OK")){
   <update the model and interface>
}
```

The dialog is activated in line 2, at which point the main interface is blocked until the user closes the dialog. After the dialog is closed, execution resumes at line 4. Here the application determines the manner in which the user closed the dialog and then in line 5 takes the appropriate action.

You have seen similar code for the action listener earlier in this chapter. Note the following points, however:

1. The constructor method calls the `JDialog` constructor (`super`) with the parent and the title parameters.

2. A dialog's default layout is `BorderLayout`.

3. This particular dialog sets its own size.

18.9 The Model/View/Controller Pattern

In Chapter 10, we introduced the idea of separating an application into a model and a view. Now we take the idea one step further and show how to divide an application into a model, a view, and a controller, where the controller represents all the application's listener classes. This division of responsibilities is well suited to handling the complexities of large applications, although it will appear a little awkward in the small Case Study that we present next.

In the *model/view/controller pattern,* also called the MVC pattern, it is the view's responsibility to:

1. instantiate the window objects, position them in the interface, and attach listeners to them as needed

2. instantiate and initialize the model

3. accurately represent the model to the user

The responsibilities of the model are to:

1. define and manage the application's data (this usually requires coordinating the activities of several programmer-defined classes)

2. respond to messages from the listeners

3. inform the view of changes to the model's internal state

The responsibilities of controller are to:

1. implement the necessary listeners

2. send messages to the model in response to user-generated events

Here then is an illustration of the model/view/controller pattern.

18.10 Case Study: A Color Meter Application

Request. Create an application that allows the user to view a color by mixing red, green, and blue (RGB) values.

Analysis. The proposed interface is shown in Figure 18.17. A color has three components (red, blue, green). The user manipulates each component separately by means of one of the sliders. Each slider takes on values in the range 0 . . . 255. The rectangular patch below the sliders changes color in response to changes in the sliders. In addition, the RGB values are displayed to the right of the sliders.

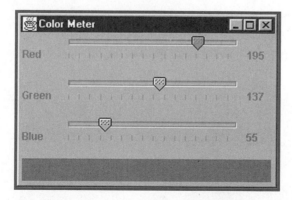

Figure 18.17 The interface for the color meter application

The application uses the seven classes listed in the following table:

Class	Role in the Program
ColorMeterView	The view class defines the window's layout, associates listeners with the sliders, instantiates the model, and redisplays the color when requested by the model.
ColorMeterModel	The model knows the current color, changes the color in response to messages from the listeners, and informs the view when the color display needs to be changed.
GenericWindow Listener	The controller contains one instance of the GenericWindowListener encountered earlier in the chapter. This listener closes the application's window when the user clicks the **X** button.
SliderListener	The controller contains three slider listeners, one attached to each slider. The listeners detect changes in the sliders and inform the model. The listener classes are organized in a hierarchy whose abstract class is SliderListener and whose concrete classes follow.
RedSliderListener	The listener for red sliders.
BlueSliderListener	The listener for blue sliders.
GreenSliderListener	The listener for green sliders.

Design and Implementation of `ColorMeterView`. The constructor has these tasks to perform:

- instantiates the model, passes it a pointer back to the view, and initializes the color to pure red
- instantiates the window objects and adds them to a grid bag layout
- initializes the appearance of the view to match the model
- attaches listeners to the sliders and to the window

The method `public void update (Color color)`

- is called by the model whenever the color changes
- redisplays the color patch and the numbers beside the sliders to reflect the latest color

```java
import javax.swing.*;
import java.awt.*;

public class ColorMeterView extends JFrame{

    // Declare variables for the window objects
    private JLabel      redLabel;
    private JLabel      greenLabel;
    private JLabel      blueLabel;
    private JSlider     redSlider;
    private JSlider     greenSlider;
```

```java
private JSlider        blueSlider;
private JLabel         redValue;
private JLabel         greenValue;
private JLabel         blueValue;
private JPanel         colorPanel;

// Declare a variable for the model
private ColorMeterModel model;

// Constructor
public ColorMeterView(){

  // Set the title
  setTitle ("Color Meter");

  // Instantiate the model
  model = new ColorMeterModel (this, new Color (255,0,0));

  // Instantiate the window objects
  redLabel    = new JLabel("Red");
  greenLabel  = new JLabel("Green");
  blueLabel   = new JLabel("Blue");
  redSlider   = createSlider();
  greenSlider = createSlider();
  blueSlider  = createSlider();
  redValue    = new JLabel("   ");
  greenValue  = new JLabel("   ");
  blueValue   = new JLabel("   ");
  colorPanel  = new JPanel();

  // Instantiate and set a grid bag layout
  GridBagLayout layout = new GridBagLayout();
  getContentPane().setLayout(layout);

  // Add the window objects to the layout.
  //                       row,col,width,height
  addComponent(layout, redLabel    , 0, 0, 1, 1);
  addComponent(layout, greenLabel  , 1, 0, 1, 1);
  addComponent(layout, blueLabel   , 2, 0, 1, 1);
  addComponent(layout, redSlider   , 0, 1, 1, 1);
  addComponent(layout, greenSlider , 1, 1, 1, 1);
  addComponent(layout, blueSlider  , 2, 1, 1, 1);
  addComponent(layout, redValue    , 0, 2, 1, 1);
  addComponent(layout, greenValue  , 1, 2, 1, 1);
```

Continues

Continued

```
   addComponent(layout, blueValue   , 2, 2, 1, 1);
   addComponent(layout, colorPanel  , 3, 0, 3, 10);

   // Initialize the appearance of the view to match the model
   redSlider.setValue (255);
   greenSlider.setValue (0);
   blueSlider.setValue (0);
   update (new Color (255,0,0));

   // Add listeners to three scrollsliders
   redSlider.addChangeListener
         (new RedSliderListener(model));
   greenSlider.addChangeListener
         (new GreenSliderListener(model));
   blueSlider.addChangeListener
         (new BlueSliderListener(model));

   // Add a listener to the window
   addWindowListener(new GenericWindowListener());
}

private JSlider createSlider(){
   JSlider slider = new JSlider(SwingConstants.HORIZONTAL, 0, 255, 16);
   slider.setBackground(getBackground());
   slider.setPaintTicks(true);
   slider.setPaintTrack(true);
   slider.setMajorTickSpacing(16);
   return slider;
}

// Add a component to the layout in the indicated row and column
// with the indicated height and width.
private void addComponent(GridBagLayout layout,
                          Component component,
                          int row, int col,
                          int width, int height){

   GridBagConstraints constraints = new GridBagConstraints();

   constraints.fill = GridBagConstraints.BOTH;
   constraints.insets.bottom = 2;
   constraints.insets.top    = 2;
   constraints.insets.left   = 2;
   constraints.insets.right  = 2;
```

```
        constraints.weightx = 100;
        constraints.weighty = 100;

        constraints.gridx = col;
        constraints.gridy = row;
        constraints.gridwidth = width;
        constraints.gridheight = height;
        layout.setConstraints(component, constraints);
        getContentPane().add (component);
    }


    // The model calls this method whenever the model wants
    // to update the view. It updates the number to the right of
    // each slider and repaints the panel in the current color.
    public void update(Color color){
        redValue.setText("" + color.getRed());
        greenValue.setText("" + color.getGreen());
        blueValue.setText("" + color.getBlue());
        colorPanel.setBackground(color);
    }

    public static void main (String[] args){
        JFrame frm = new ColorMeterView();
        frm.setSize (300, 200);
        frm.setVisible (true);
    }
}
```

Design and Implementation of `ColorMeterModel`. Two instance variables are needed:

1. `color`, which indicates the current color

2. `view`, which points back to the view class, thus allowing the model to send messages to the view

The constructor

- initializes the variable that points back to the view
- initializes the variable that holds the color

The method `public void setRedValue(int value)`

- is called by the red slider listener
- has a parameter that indicates the red component's new value
- sets the specified component to the value indicated and tells the view to update itself

The methods `setGreenValue(anInt)` and `setBlueValue(anInt)` are similar.

```java
import java.awt.*;

public class ColorMeterModel{

    private Color color;
    private ColorMeterView view;

    public ColorMeterModel(ColorMeterView vw, Color initialColor){
        view = vw;
        color = initialColor;
    }

    // Change the red component of the color.
    // value -- indicates the new red component.
    public void setRedValue(int value){

        // Get the current component colors;
        int greenValue = color.getGreen();
        int blueValue = color.getBlue();

        // Reset the meter's color
        color = new Color(value, greenValue, blueValue);

        // Update the view to reflect the change in color
        view.update (color);
    }

    // Change the green component of the color.
    // value -- indicates the new green component.
    public void setGreenValue(int value){

        // Get the current component colors;
        int redValue = color.getRed();
        int blueValue = color.getBlue();

        // Reset the meter's color
        color = new Color(redValue, value, blueValue);

        // Update the view to reflect the change in color
        view.update (color);
    }

    // Change the blue component of the color.
    // value -- indicates the new blue component.
    public void setBlueValue(int value){
```

```
        // Get the current component colors;
        int redValue = color.getRed();
        int greenValue = color.getGreen();

        // Reset the meter's color
        color = new Color(redValue, greenValue, value);

        // Update the view to reflect the change in color
        view.update (color);
    }
}
```

Design and Implementation of the Listener Classes. The abstract `SliderListener` class implements the `ChangeListener` interface. A slider listener object declares the protected instance variable `model` which refers to the model. Here is the code:

```
// SliderListener

import javax.swing.event.*;

abstract public class SliderListener implements ChangeListener{

    protected ColorMeterModel model;

}
```

When the user interacts with a slider, a `ChangeEvent` occurs. This event is passed to the `stateChanged` method, which is implemented in the subclasses `RedSliderListener`, `GreenSliderListener`, and `BlueSliderListener`. The `stateChanged` method

- extracts the integer value from the slider's event
- runs the model's method for changing the appropriate color with this integer as a parameter

Here is the code for the class `RedSliderListener`:

```
// RedSliderListener

import javax.swing.*;
import javax.swing.event.*;

public class RedSliderListener extends SliderListener{

    public RedSliderListener(ColorMeterModel cmmdl){
```

Continues

Continued

```
        model = cmmdl;
    }

    public void stateChanged(ChangeEvent e) {
        JSlider slider = (JSlider)e.getSource();
        int value = Math.min (255, slider.getValue());
        model.setRedValue(value);
    }
}
```

18.11 Applets, Swing, and AWT

We have already seen how to convert stand-alone programs into applets when GBFrame and GBApplet are used. The conversion process follows the same pattern when Swing/AWT is used. Here are a few points to remember:

1. Window objects are created and added to the interface in an init() method rather than in a constructor.

2. There is no method main.

3. Because applets are embedded in Web pages, the Web browser handles the applet's closing. Thus, there is no need for a WindowListener.

4. Like stand-alone applications, applets need listeners to detect and handle events in components.

5. Applets can be split between a view and a model in the same manner as before.

To illustrate the conversion process, here is the ConversionWithSwing program from the beginning of the chapter rewritten as an applet:

```
import javax.swing.*;
import java.awt.*;
import java.awt.event.*;

public class ConversionWithSwing extends JApplet
                                 implements ActionListener{

    private JLabel     fahrenheitLabel;
    private JTextField fahrenheitField;
    private JLabel     celsiusLabel;
    private JTextField celsiusField;
    private JButton    fahrenheitButton;
    private JButton    celsiusButton;

    public void init(){
```

```
    fahrenheitLabel  = new JLabel ("Fahrenheit");
    fahrenheitField  = new JTextField ("212", 6);      // 6 columns wide
    celsiusLabel     = new JLabel ("Celsius");
    celsiusField     = new JTextField ("100", 6);      // 6 columns wide
    fahrenheitButton = new JButton (">>>>>>");
    celsiusButton    = new JButton ("<<<<<<");

    Container mainWindow = getContentPane();
    mainWindow.setLayout(new FlowLayout());
    mainWindow.add (fahrenheitLabel);
    mainWindow.add (celsiusLabel);
    mainWindow.add (fahrenheitField);
    mainWindow.add (celsiusField);
    mainWindow.add (fahrenheitButton);
    mainWindow.add (celsiusButton);

    fahrenheitButton.addActionListener (this);
    celsiusButton.addActionListener (this);
  }

  public void actionPerformed (ActionEvent e){
    String str;
    int fahrenheit, celsius;
    JButton btn = (JButton)e.getSource();

    if (btn == celsiusButton){
      str = celsiusField.getText().trim();
      celsius = (new Integer (str)).intValue();
      fahrenheit = celsius * 9 / 5 + 32;
      fahrenheitField.setText ("" + fahrenheit);
    }
    else{
      str = fahrenheitField.getText().trim();
      fahrenheit = (new Integer (str)).intValue();
      celsius = (fahrenheit - 32) * 5 / 9;
      celsiusField.setText ("" + celsius);
    }
  }
}
```

18.12 Setting the Look and Feel

As mentioned in Chapter 5, the programmer can set the look and feel of a GUI-based program written with Swing. BreezySwing users accomplish this by calling the method setLookAndFeel within a subclass of GBFrame, GBDialog, or GBApplet. Here is the code for the method, which you can place in any subclass of JFrame, JDialog, or JApplet as well:

```
public void setLookAndFeel(String type){
    int value = 0;
    UIManager.LookAndFeelInfo[] looks;
    looks = UIManager.getInstalledLookAndFeels();
    if (type.equalsIgnoreCase("METAL"))
        value = 0;
    else if (type.equalsIgnoreCase("MOTIF"))
        value = 1;
    else
        value = 2;
    try{
        UIManager.setLookAndFeel(looks[value].getClassName());
        SwingUtilities.updateComponentTreeUI(this);
    }catch(Exception e){
        messageBox("Error: \n" + e.toString());
    }
}
```

18.13 Summary

This chapter has given an overview of the use of Swing and AWT to create GUI applications. We covered several examples of each of the categories of classes used in these applications: components, layout managers, events, and listeners.

18.14 Key Terms

Abstract Windowing Toolkit (AWT)
component
container
grid bag layout

interface
listener
modal
model/view/controller pattern
parent

scroll bar
slider
Swing

18.15 Answers to Self-Test Questions

1. Swing and AWT are abstract in the sense that they allow the programmer to write the program once and run it on any platform and in the sense that the same program has a similar look and feel on any platform.

2. The four types of classes in a GUI application are components, layout managers, events, and listeners. Components represent windows and window objects. Layout managers define the

styles of organizing components in a window. Events represent things that occur in components during the execution of a program, such as mouse clicks. Listeners detect events and respond to them.

3. The responsibility of `ConversionWithSwing` is to create the window objects, lay them out in the interface, add listeners to them, and implement methods to respond to requests from the listeners. The responsibility of the two button listeners is to detect button clicks and respond by calling the appropriate methods in the view. The responsibility of the window listener is to detect a window closing event and exit the application.

4. The listeners, the layout manager, and the code for creating the window objects are hidden in the `BreezySwing` version of the program.

5. An adapter class implements an interface with stub methods. Thus, a class that extends an adapter class does not have to implement all of the methods in the interface if they are not needed. `WindowAdapter` is an example of an adapter class.

6. The main class must implement all of the interfaces of the listeners that are incorporated. This means that the main class must also implement all of the listener methods.

7. `String name = JOptionPane.showInputDialog(this, "Enter your name");`

8. A container class is a type of component that can hold other window objects. Examples of container classes are frames, dialogs, and applets.

9. A panel is a rectangular area that can contain other window objects. For example, one might divide a window into three panels: one for labels, one for fields, and one for buttons.

10. The major layout manager classes are flow layout, border layout, grid layout, card layout, and grid bag layout. A border layout has five areas designated by direction (north, south, east, west, and center). A flow layout uses a wrap around. A grid layout uses a two-dimensional grid of fixed-sized cells. A grid bag layout uses a two-dimensional grid of variable-sized cells. A card layout presents window objects on a stack with the top item visible.

11. The default layout of frames and dialogs is border layout. The default layout of applets is flow layout.

12. An event occurs in a component. If a listener for that event is attached to the component, the appropriate method in the listener is called and passed the event as a parameter. This method then handles the event according to the needs of the application.

18.16 Programming Problems and Activities

1. Redo the Fahrenheit to Celsius application with Swing/AWT so that your program adheres to the model/view/controller pattern.

2. Redo the shapes drawing program of Chapter 13 using Swing/AWT.

3. Modify the shapes drawing program of Problem 2 so that the user can select the color from a dialog that displays a color meter.

4. A robust integer field would allow the user to type only digits and provide methods to get and set the integer value. Explore Sun's documentation for `JTextField` and develop a subclass that satisfies the requirements of an integer field.

5. Develop a double field class.

Java Resources

Sun Microsystems maintains an excellent Web site where programmers can find complete documentation for the Java API (Application Programming Interface) and download a free JDK (Java Development Kit). Here are some of the items that you can access on the Web:

- **Sun's top-level Java page** (http://www.javasoft.com). This page contains news about events in the Java world and links to documentation, Java-related products, program examples, and free downloads of the JDK.

- **Products and APIs** (http://www.javasoft.com/products/). This page allows you to select the version of JDK that matches your computer and to begin the download process. You can also download the documentation if you do not want to access it on the Web.

- **Documentation and Training** (http://developer.java.sun.com/developer/infodocs/). This page introduces you to the documentation for the Java API and describes the most effective ways to browse this documentation.

- **Package index** (http://java.sun.com/j2se/1.3/docs/api/). This page has links to all of the packages in JDK 1.3.

We suggest that you bookmark all of these links and use the last one on a daily basis. You might even bookmark the links to the most commonly used packages, such as `java.lang`, `java.awt`, and `javax.swing`. When you visit a package, you can browse all of the classes in that package. When you visit a class, you can browse all of the variables and methods defined in that class. There are numerous cross-references to superclasses and related classes in a given package.

If you decide to download the JDK, be sure to select JDK 1.3 (`BreezySwing` cannot be used with versions earlier than JDK 1.2). Note that at the time of this writing, the most current version of JDK was JDK 1.3. After downloading, you install the JDK on your computer by running the installation program. You should print the **Readme** file for further reference. The installation will leave the directory

JDK1.3 on your disk. To use `BreezySwing` and `TerminalIO`, you should copy files **BreezySwing.jar** and **TerminalIO.jar** from this text's CD to the **jre\lib\ext** directory within JDK1.3.

Place the following command in the **autoexec.bat** file and restart your machine.

```
path=%path%;c:\;c:\jdk1.3\bin
SET CLASSPATH=c:\jdk1.3\classes;.
```

Be sure to terminate CLASSPATH with ";.".

Before you use JDK, make sure that all of your Java source program (**.java**) files are in the current directory (this can be any directory on your computer). You can define more than one class in a source file, but the usual procedure is to have one source file for each class. Each source file should begin with the same name as the class that it contains and should end with **.java**. Remember that Java class names and file names are case sensitive. If you want to run an applet, the appropriate **html** file should also be in this directory.

You can then do the following at the system command prompt:

- **Compile a program.** The basic syntax is `javac <filename>`, where `<filename>` is a Java source file name (ending in **.java**). Java locates and compiles all of the files required by your program. Any syntax error messages are displayed in the command window, and a byte code (**.class**) file is generated for each class defined in your program.

- **Run an application.** The basic syntax is `java <filename>`, where `<filename>` is the name of the class that defines the `main` method of your program. Note that the **.class** extension must be omitted. Run-time error messages are displayed in the command window.

- **Run an applet.** The basic syntax is `appletviewer <filename>`, where `<filename>` is the name of an **html** file that links to your applet.

Using Borland JBuilder Foundation

Borland JBuilder Foundation is an integrated application that enables you to create Java programs and applets, compile them, debug them, and run them in one environment. The following sections give you the basic information you need to run the programs in this book in the JBuilder Foundation environment. As of this writing, the most recent version of JBuilder Foundation is JBuilder4 Foundation (hereafter called JBuilder4), which is included on the CD that comes with this text.

Installation

To install JBuilder4 on your PC, follow these steps:

1. Insert the CD from this book and follow the instructions to install JBuilder4 Foundation.

2. Open the Windows Explorer and you should see the JBuilder4 directory under the C drive. Drag the files **BreezyGUI.jar** and **TerminalIO.jar** from the CD into this directory. These files contain the I/O packages used in the text.

3. Visit Borland's Website (www.JBuilder.4.Trial.Registration@borland.com) to obtain a key and serial number for your copy of JBuilder4. Launch JBuilder4 and enter the serial number and key. The development environment window will pop up with a default project. You should close this project by selecting menu option **File/Close Projects** (Figure A.1).

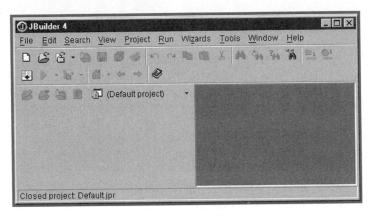

Figure A.1   The JBuilder4 development environment window

4. Add the two I/O libraries **BreezySwing.jar** and **TerminalIO.jar** by selecting menu option **Tools/Configure Libraries** and following the steps shown in Figures A.2, A.3, and A.4. In the dialog, select the **Required Libraries** tab, select the **Add** button, select the two libraries, and select **OK**. Now you can create a project and JBuilder4 will know where to find these libraries.

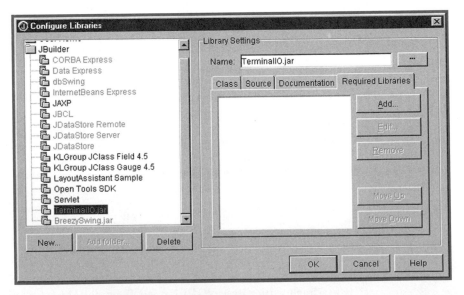

Figure A.2   The configure libraries dialog

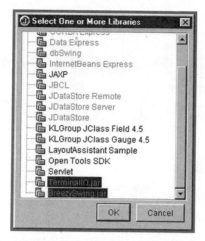

Figure A.3 Selecting the two I/O libraries

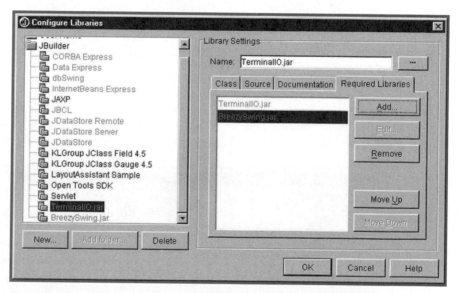

Figure A.4 The two libraries have been added

Setting Up a New Project

JBuilder4 requires you to create a new project to hold the files for a program. To start a new project, follow these steps:

Step 1: Launch JBuilder4 and then select the menu option **File/New Project**. The Project Wizard dialog will pop up (Figure A.5). JBuilder4 specifies a path to the project file **untitled1.jpr** within the directory **C:/WINDOWS/jbproject**. You can change these names or just click **Next** to move to the next step. Note that JBuilder4 sets up directories for source files, byte code files, and backup files under your project directory.

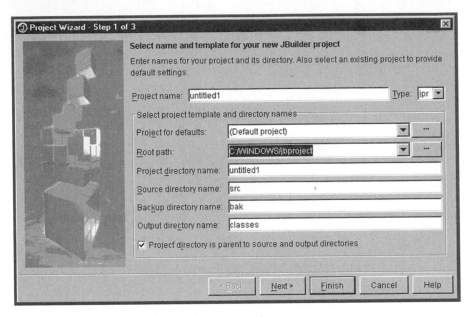

Figure A.5   The JBuilder project wizard

Step 2: After you have selected **Next** in the Project Wizard, you should see a list of the required libraries. This list should contain the I/O libraries that you entered when you installed JBuilder4 (Figure A.6). Select **Next** and move to the next step.

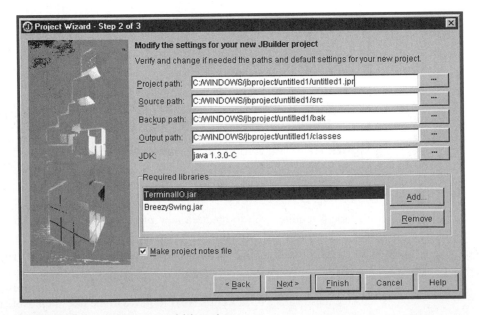

Figure A.6   The required libraries

Step 3: This step allows you to enter documentation about the project, such as its title, your name, and a brief description (Figure A.7). Select **Finish** and move to the next step.

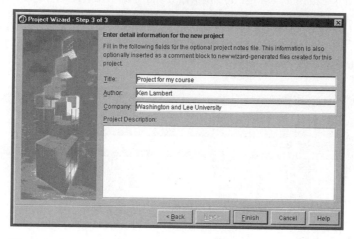

Figure A.7 Project documentation

Step 4: After you have selected **Finish** in the Project Wizard, the Project window opens. A list of the project files appears in the left pane. Note that the file icon **untitled1.html** appears beneath the file icon **untitled.jpr.** The **.html** file contains the documentation that was entered during the Project Wizard dialog. You use the **.jpr** file to reopen the project from the Explorer or from the JBuilder4 **File** menu. To view the documentation about the new project in the Project Notes pane at the right side of the window, double click on the **.html** file in the list to the left (Figure A.8).

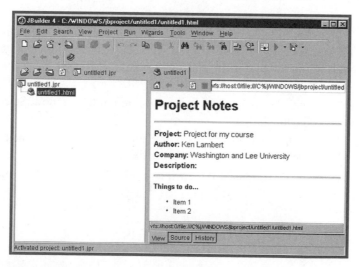

Figure A.8 The Project window

Adding Source Files to the Project

In this example, we use the program file **ConvertWithGUI.java** from Chapter 5. You should copy the directory **Code5** from the CD to the C drive. Then click the little folder labeled **+** above the left pane of the Project window. A file dialog will open and you can navigate to the **Code5** directory (Figure A.9). In this example, you select the **ConvertWithGUI.java** file and press Enter.

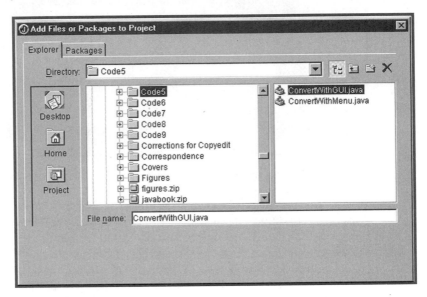

Figure A.9   The dialog for adding files to a project

Figure A.10 shows the updated Project window. Note that a little folder labeled **–** has appeared above the left pane. Clicking this icon removes the selected file from the project (but does not delete it from the directory). Note also the three main display areas:

1. A list box with the project files in the upper left of the window. Select a file to display its contents.

2. A list box with the names of classes, variables, and methods in the lower left of the window. Select a name to locate it in the file.

3. A text area in the right half of the window. This area displays the selected file.

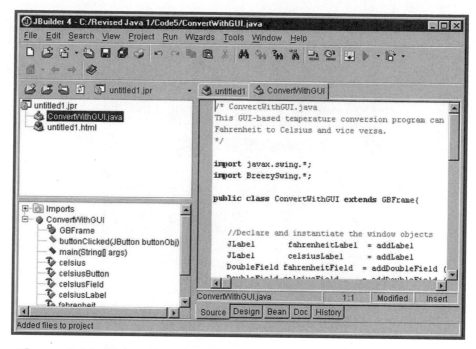

Figure A.10   The Project window after Java source file has been added to the project

Compiling and Starting an Application

After you have added the files necessary for the project, you are ready to run it. Simply select the menu option **Run/Run Project** or click the green arrow icon in the menu bar. If there are syntax errors, the error messages will appear in a pane at the bottom of the project window, and the line of code with the first error is highlighted in the editor pane. If there are no syntax errors, the Runtime Properties dialog will pop up asking you for the name of the main Java class (Figure A.11). Select the **. . .** button to the right of **Main class,** enter the name **ConvertWithGUI** in the field, and select **OK** (Figure A.12). Then the program's GUI should pop up, as shown in the text.

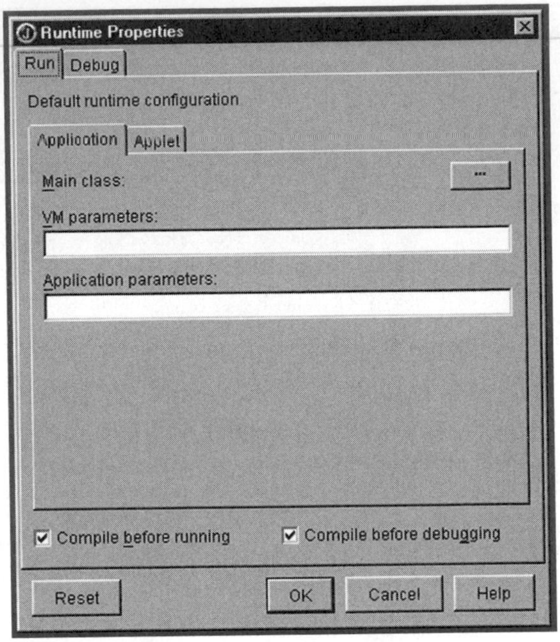

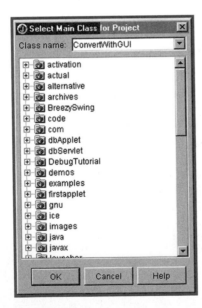

Figure A.11 The runtime properties dialog

Figure A.12 Setting the main class

When you run the compiler the first time, JBuilder4 creates the directory **classes** under your project directory. The byte code files for your Java programs are written to and executed from this directory.

When you are finished with a program, remove all source files from the project and add new ones or start a new project and repeat the earlier steps to create new programs.

Running Applets with JBuilder

To run an applet with JBuilder4, follow these steps:

1. Copy the **BreezySwing** directory from the CD to the **classes** directory under your project directory.
2. Copy the **.html** file for the applet to the **classes** directory under your project directory. We use the file **convert.html** in the directory **Code17** in this example.
3. Add the Java source file (**ConvertWithGUI.java** in **Code17**) and the **.html** file for the applet to the project.
4. Select the menu item **Project/Properties.**
5. Select the **Run** tab.
6. Select the **Applet** tab.
7. Select the **HTML file:** radio button.
8. Select the **. . .** button to the right and browse to your applet's HTML file, which should be in the **classes** directory.
9. Double click this file. The dialog should now look like the one in Figure A.13.

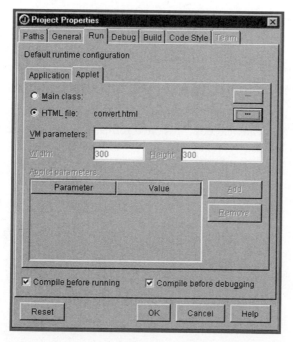

Figure A.13 Configuring JBuilder4 to run an applet

10. Select the menu item **Project/Rebuild Project** to compile the program.

11. To run the applet in the applet viewer, select the menu item **Project Run Project.**

12. Alternatively, to run the applet from its HTML file, double click on this file in the Project list pane. You should see the Web page in the text area to the right (Figure A.14).

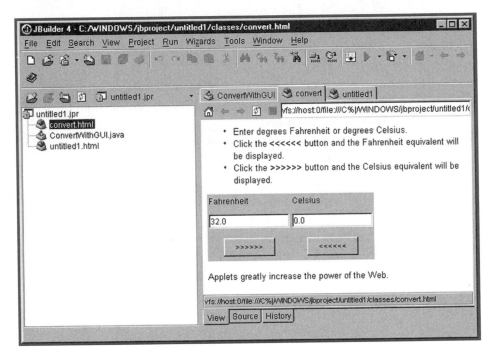

Figure A.14 Viewing a Web page with an applet in JBuilder4

Note that you can also edit, save, and refresh your Web pages simply by toggling between **View** and **Source** with an HTML file selected.

B Reserved Words

The words in **bold** are not discussed in this book. For a discussion of them, see the references on Sun's Web site.

abstract	double	import	private	**throws**
boolean	else	**inner**	protected	**transient**
break	extends	instanceof	public	try
byte	final	int	**rest**	**var**
case	**finally**	interface	return	void
catch	float	long	short	**volatile**
char	for	**native**	static	while
class	**future**	new	super	
const	**generic**	null	switch	
continue	**goto**	operator	**synchronized**	
default	if	**outer**	this	
do	implements	**package**	**throw**	

C Operator Precedence

The operators in **bold** are not discussed in this book. For a discussion of them, see the references on Sun's Web site.

Operator	Function	Association
( )	Parentheses	Left to right
[ ]	Array subscript	
.	Object member selection	
++	Increment	Right to left
--	Decrement	
+	Unary plus	
-	Unary minus	
!	Boolean negation	
~	**Bitwise negation**	
(*type*)	Type cast	
*	Multiplication	Left to right
/	Division	
%	Modulus	
+	Addition or concatenation	Left to right
-	Subtraction	
<<	**Bitwise shift left**	**Left to right**
>>	**Bitwise shift right**	
>>>	**Bitwise shift right, sign extension**	

Operator	Function	Association
 <= > >= instanceOf	Less than Less than or equal to Greater than Greater than or equal to Class membership	Left to right
== !=	Equal to Not equal to	Left to right
&	**Boolean AND (complete)** **Bitwise AND**	**Left to right**
^	**Boolean exclusive OR** **Bitwise exclusive OR**	**Left to right**
|	**Boolean OR (complete)** **Bitwise OR**	**Left to right**
&&	Boolean AND (partial)	Left to right
||	Boolean OR (partial)	Left to right
?:	**Ternary conditional**	**Right to left**
= += -= *= /= %= **<<=** **>>=** **>>>=** **&=** **|=** **^=**	Assign Add and assign Subtract and assign Multiply and assign Divide and assign Modulo and assign **Shift left and assign** **Shift right, sign extension, and assign** **Shift right, no sign extension, and assign** **Boolean or bitwise AND and assign** **Boolean or bitwise OR and assign** **Boolean or bitwise exclusive OR and assign**	Right to left

D ASCII Character Set

The following table shows the ordering of the ASCII character set. The printable characters range from ASCII 33 to ASCII 126. The values from ASCII 0 to ASCII 32 and ASCII 127 are associated with whitespace characters, such as the horizontal tab (HT), or nonprinting control characters, such as the escape key (ESC). The digits in the left column represent the leftmost digits of the ASCII code, and the digits in the top row are the rightmost digits. Thus, the ASCII code of the character R at row 8, column 2, is 82.

	0	1	2	3	4	5	6	7	8	9
0	NUL	SOH	STX	ETX	EOT	ENQ	ACK	BEL	BS	HT
1	LF	VT	FF	CR	SO	SI	DLE	DC1	DC2	DC3
2	DC4	NAK	SYN	ETB	CAN	EM	SUB	ESC	FS	GS
3	RS	US	SP	!	"	#	$	%	&	`
4	(	)	*	+	,	-	.	/	0	1
5	2	3	4	5	6	7	8	9	:	;
6	<	=	>	?	@	A	B	C	D	E
7	F	G	H	I	J	K	L	M	N	O
8	P	Q	R	S	T	U	V	W	X	Y
9	Z	[	\	]	^	_	'	a	b	c
10	d	e	f	g	h	i	j	k	l	m
11	n	o	p	q	r	s	t	u	v	w
12	x	y	z	{	|	}	~	DEL		

E Number Systems

When we make change at the store, we use the decimal (base 10) number system. The digits in this system are the characters 0 through 9. Computers represent all information in the binary (base 2) system. The digits in this system are just the characters 0 and 1. Because binary numbers can be very long strings of 1s and 0s, programmers also use the octal (base 8) and hexadecimal (base 16) number systems, usually for low-level programming in assembly language. The octal digits range from 0 to 7, and the hexadecimal digits include the decimal digits and the letters A through F. These letters represent the numbers 10 through 15, respectively.

To identify the system being used, one can attach the base as a subscript to the number. For example, the following numbers represent the quantity 414 in the binary, octal, decimal, and hexadecimal systems:

```
414 in binary notation              110011110₂
414 in octal notation               636₈
414 in decimal notation             414₁₀
414 in hexadecimal notation         19E₁₆
```

414 in binary notation — 110011110_2
414 in octal notation — 636_8
414 in decimal notation — 414_{10}
414 in hexadecimal notation — $19E_{16}$

Note that as the size of the base grows, either the number of digits or the digit in the largest position might become smaller.

Each number system uses positional notation to represent a number. The digit at each position in a number has a positional value. The positional value of a digit is determined by raising the base of the system to the power specified by the position. For an n-digit number, the positions (and exponents) are numbered 0 through $n - 1$, starting with the rightmost digit and moving to the left. For example, as the next figure illustrates, the positional values of a three-digit decimal number are 100 (10^2), 10 (10^1), and 1 (10^0), moving from left to right in the number. The positional values of a three-digit binary number are 4 (2^2), 2 (2^1), and 1 (2^0).

base 10

positional values | 100 | 10 | 1 |

positions   2   1   0

base 2

positional values | 4 | 2 | 1 |

positions   2   1   0

The quantity represented by a number in any system is determined by multiplying each digit (as a decimal number) by its positional value and adding the results. The following examples show how this is done for numbers in several systems:

```
414 base 10 =
4 * 10² + 1 * 10¹ + 4 * 10⁰ =
4 * 100 + 1 * 10 + 4 * 1 =
400      + 10      + 4 = 414
```

```
110011110 base 2 =
1 * 2⁸ + 1 * 2⁷ + 0 * 2⁶ + 0 * 2⁵ + 1 * 2⁴ + 1 * 2³ + 1 * 2² + 1 * 2¹ + 0 * 2⁰ =
1 * 256 + 1 * 128 + 0 * 64 + 0 * 32 + 1 * 16 + 1 * 8 + 1 * 4 + 1 * 2 + 0 * 1 =
256      + 128      + 0       + 0       + 16      + 8      + 4      + 2      + 0 = 414
```

```
636 base 8 =
6 * 8² + 3 * 8¹ + 6 * 8⁰ =
6 * 64 + 3 * 8 + 6 * 1 =
384      + 24      + 6 = 414
```

```
19E base 16 =
1 * 16² + 9 * 16¹ + E * 16⁰ =
1 * 256 + 9 * 16 + 14 * 1
256       + 144      + 14 = 414
```

Each of these examples appears to convert from the number in the given base to the corresponding decimal number. To convert a decimal number to a number in a given base, we use division and remainder rather than multiplication and addition. The process works as follows:

1. Find the largest power of the given base that divides into the decimal number.
2. The quotient becomes the digit at that power's position in the new number.
3. Repeat steps 1 and 2 with the remainder until the remainder is less than the number.
4. If the last remainder is greater than 0, the remainder becomes the last digit in the new number.
5. If you must skip a power of the base when performing step 3, then put a 0 in that power's position in the new number.

To illustrate, let us convert the decimal number 327 to the equivalent binary number.

The highest power of 2 by which 327 is divisible is 256 or 2^8. Thus, we'll have a nine-digit binary number, with 1 in position 8:

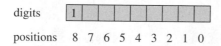

digits

positions   8 7 6 5 4 3 2 1 0

The remainder of the first division is 71. The highest power of 2 by which 71 is divisible is 64 (2^6). Thus, we have skipped 128 (2^7), so we write 0 in position 7 and 1 in position 6:

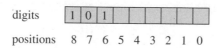

digits

positions   8 7 6 5 4 3 2 1 0

The remainder of the second division is 7. Thus, as you can see, we skip 3 more powers of 2—32, 16, and 8—on the next division in order to use 4. So, we place 0s at positions 5, 4, and 3, and 1 at position 2 in the new number:

digits

positions   8 7 6 5 4 3 2 1 0

The remainder of the third division is 3. This is divisible by the next power of 2, which is 2, so we put 1 at position 1 in the new number. The remainder of the last division, 1, goes in position 0:

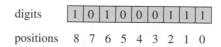

digits

positions   8 7 6 5 4 3 2 1 0

One reason that programmers prefer to use octal or hexadecimal notation instead of binary notation is that octal and hexadecimal are more expressive (one can say more with less). Another reason is that it is very easy to convert an octal number or a hexadecimal number to the corresponding binary number. To convert octal to binary, one assumes that each digit in the octal number represents three digits in the corresponding binary number. One then starts with the rightmost octal digit and writes down the corresponding binary digits, padding these to the left with 0s to the count of 3, if necessary. One proceeds in this manner until all of the octal digits have been converted. The following examples show such conversions:

Octal   547   372

Binary   101 100 111   11 111 010

The conversion of hexadecimal numbers to binary numbers works in a similar way, except that each hexadecimal digit translates to four binary digits.

Java Exception Handling

Java divides run-time errors into two broad categories: errors and exceptions. Errors are serious run-time problems that usually should not be handled by the programmer. For example, if a method gets stuck in an infinite recursion, as described in Chapter 12, Java will throw a `StackOverflowError`. Java defines a separate class for each type of error. You can browse through these in Sun's Web site, as described in Appendix A, starting with the class `Error` in the package `java.lang`.

Exceptions come in two varieties: those that Java requires the programmer to handle, such as `IOException`, and those that the programmer may or may not handle, such as `ArithmeticException` and `ArrayIndexOutOfBoundsException`. To explore Java's `Exception` class hierarchy on Sun's Web site, select the desired package in the package index and scroll to the bottom of the page. Most of the exception classes are defined in `java.lang`, but several important ones are also defined in `java.io` and `java.util`.

Chapter 14 showed how to use the `try-catch` statement to handle exceptions associated with file streams. The next code segments show how one might handle exceptions in the cases of division and array subscripting:

```
// Catch an attempt to divide by zero

try{
    quotient = dividend / divisor;
    System.out.println("Successful division");
}
catch (ArithmeticException e){
    System.out.println("Error1: " + e.toString());
}
```

```
// Catch an attempt to use an array index that is out of range

try{
   a[x] = 0;
   System.out.println("Successful subscripting");
}
catch (ArrayIndexOutOfBoundsException e){
   System.out.println("Error2: " + e.toString());
}
```

When Java detects an error and throws an exception, control is immediately transferred from the offending instruction in the `try` statement to the `catch` statement. Thus, the output of the first message would be skipped if an exception occurs in either of the preceding code segments. If the `try` statement completes successfully, the `catch` statement is not executed.

A `try` statement can be followed by more than one `catch` statement. For example, the next code segment combines the exception handling of the previous two segments:

```
// Catch an attempt to divide by zero and to use an array index
// that is out of bounds

try{
   quotient = dividend / divisor;
   System.out.println("Successful division");
   a[x] = quotient;
   System.out.println("Successful subscripting");
 }
catch (ArithmeticException e){
   System.out.println("Error1: " + e.toString());
}
catch (ArrayIndexOutOfBoundsException e){
   System.out.println("Error2: " + e.toString());
}
```

The same two exceptions are possible in this example, but Java will get to throw only one of them. When this occurs, control shifts to the first `catch` statement following the `try` statement. If the class of the exception thrown is the same as or is a subclass of the class of that `catch` statement's parameter, then the code for the `catch` statement executes. Otherwise, Java compares the exception thrown to the parameter of the next `catch` statement and so on.

It is possible (and often desirable) to define new kinds of exceptions that can be thrown by methods in user-defined classes. We showed some examples of throwing exceptions in Chapter 15. The complete rules for doing this are beyond the scope of this book but can be found on Sun's Web site.

G Java Packages

A Java package is a name that stands for a set of related classes. For example, the package `java.io` stands for all of the Java file stream classes. Exceptions (discussed in Chapter 14) and interfaces (discussed in Chapters 15, 16, and 18) can also be parts of a package. You can browse Java's packages by following the procedure described in Appendix A.

The package `java.lang` contains many commonly used classes, such as `Math` and `String`. This package is implicitly imported into every Java program file, so no `import` statement is required. To use any other package, such as `java.io`, in a program file, the programmer must explicitly import the package with an `import` statement.

The program examples in this book import all of the classes in a given package using the form

```
import <package name>.*;
```

It is also possible to import selected classes from a given package and omit others. For example, the following line would import only the `StringTokenizer` class from the `java.util` package and omit the others:

```
import java.util.StringTokenizer;
```

This statement has the effect of making the `StringTokenizer` class visible to the program file, but it leaves the rest of the classes in the `java.util` package invisible.

It is possible (and desirable) to create packages of related classes that you have designed and implemented. For example, one might put the list classes discussed in Chapter 16 into a single package called `ListPrototype`. The rules for doing this are beyond the scope of this book, but they can be found on Sun's Web site.

BreezySwing and TerminalIO

This appendix provides a quick reference to classes and methods that support terminal- and GUI-based I/O. Methods that are part of AWT and Swing are so noted. For more details, byte code, source code, a tutorial, and a related package (BreezyGUI) that uses only AWT components, see the book's Web site at www.wlu.edu/~lambertk/java/.

H.1 BreezySwing

Programs that use BreezySwing should import the package as follows:

```
import BreezySwing.*;
```

To use BreezySwing in a Java application, define the application class as an extension of the class GBFrame.

BreezySwing provides the following features:

1. A grid bag layout and methods for creating and positioning window objects.
2. Abstract methods for handling typical events, such as button selections, menu item selections, list item selections, and mouse events. The programmer overrides these methods for use in particular applications.
3. Specialized data entry field classes for integers and floating-point numbers.
4. Methods for displaying message boxes.
5. A class for formatting strings and numbers with centered, left justified, or right justified.

To use `BreezySwing` in a Java applet, define the applet class as an extension of `GBApplet`. Applets do not have a method `main`, and they use an `init` method instead of a constructor method. `GBApplet` provides the same functionality as above, but without menus. To use `BreezySwing` in a dialog, define the dialog class as an extension of `GBDialog`.

Methods to Initialize a Window

There are three methods to set up almost every application window. They are part of AWT.

`void setSize(int width, int height)`

Action: Adjusts the size of the window to the specified width and height in pixels.

Example: `frm.setSize(200, 200);`

`void setTitle(String title)`

Action: Adds the specified title to the title bar of the window.

Example: `frm.setTitle("Shape Drawing program");`

`void setVisible(int width, int height)`

Action: Makes the window visible or invisible.

Example: `frm.setVisible(true);`

H.2 Method Specifications for Classes `GBFrame`, `GBApplet`, and `GBDialog`

The following methods are used in classes that extend `GBFrame`, `GBApplet`, and `GBDialog`. When adding window objects to a window, the `row` and `col` parameters specify a row and a column in the window's underlying grid bag layout (counting from 1). The `width` and `height` parameters specify the number of columns and rows through which a window object extends. Window objects include labels, buttons, lists, menu items, and data entry fields. A window automatically adjusts the size and spacing between objects when it is resized.

Methods That Add Window Objects to a Window

`JLabel addLabel(String text, int row, int col, int width, int height)`

Action: Creates a new label with the given text, places the label in the framework at the given location, and returns the label.

Example: `JLabel radiusLabel = addLabel("Radius", 1, 1, 1, 1);`

JButton addButton(String label, int row, int col,
                    int width, int height)

Action: Creates a new button with the given label, places the button in the framework at the given location, and returns the button.

Example: JButton calculateButton = addButton("Calculate", 1, 1, 1, 1);

IntegerField addIntegerField(int number, int row, int col,
                                int width, int height)

Action: Creates a new integer field with the given number, places the integer field in the framework at the given location, and returns the integer field.

Example: IntegerField radiusField = addIntegerField(0, 1, 1, 2, 1);

DoubleField addDoubleField (double number, int row,
                              int col, int width,
                              int height)

Action: Creates a new double field with the given number, places the ouble field in the framework at the given location, and returns the double field.

Example: DoubleField areaField = addDoubleField(0.0, 1, 1, 2, 1);

JTextField addTextField(String text, int row, int col,
                          int width, int height)

Action: Creates a new text field with the given text, places the text field in the framework at the given location, and returns the text field.

Example: JTextField nameField = addTextField("Sandy", 1, 1, 3, 1);

JTextArea addTextArea(String text, int row, int col,
                        int width, int height)

Action: Creates a new text area with the given text, places the text area in the framework at the given location, and returns the text area.

Example: JTextArea resultArea = addTextArea("", 1, 1, 5, 2);

JList addList(int row, int col, int width, int height)

Action: Creates a new list, places the list in the framework at the given location, and returns the list.

Example: JList nameList = addList(1, 1, 5, 1);

JCheckBox addCheckBox (String text, int row, int col,
                      int width, int height)

Action: Creates a new check box with the given text, places the check box
          in the framework at the given location, and returns the check box.

Example: JCheckBox marriedBox = addCheckBox ("Married", 1,
          1, 1, 1);

JMenuItem addMenuItem(String menuLabel, String itemLabel)

Action: Creates a menu with the specified label if one does not exist, then
          creates a menu item with the specified label, adds the menu item to
          the menu, and returns the menu item. *Note*: Not available for
          GBApplet and GBDialog.

Example: JMenuItem saveFileItem = addMenuItem("File", "Save");

JRadioButton addRadioButton (String text, int row,
                            int col, int width,
                            int height)

Action: Creates a new radio button with the given text, places the radio button
          in the framework at the given location, and returns the radio button.

Example: JRadioButton marriedBTN = addRadioButton
          ("Married", 1, 1, 1, 1);

GBPanel addPanel (GBPanel, int row, int col, int width,
                  int height)

Action: Creates a new panel with the given panel, places the panel in the
          framework at the given location, and returns the panel.

Example: GBPanel testPanel = addPanel (new GBPanel(), 1, 1,
          1, 1);

Methods That Display Message Boxes

Message boxes are used to pop up messages. They are typically used to display
short text outputs such as error messages.

void messageBox(String message)

Action: Displays a message box with the specified string.

Example: messageBox("Computation completed.");

void messageBox(Double number)

Action: Displays a message box with the specified number.

Example: messageBox(3.14);

void messageBox(Object obj)

Action: Displays a message box with the string representation of the object.

Example: messageBox(new Student());

void messageBox(String message, int width, int height)

Action: Displays a message box with the specified string in a window with the specified dimensions.

Example: `messageBox("Computation completed.", 200, 50);`

void messageBox(Double number, int width, int height)

Action: Displays a message box with the specified number in a window with the specified dimensions.

Example: `messageBox(3.14, 50, 50);`

void messageBox(Object obj, int width, int height)

Action: Displays a message box with the string representation of the object in a window with the specified dimensions.

Example: `messageBox(new Student(), 300, 300);`

Methods for Handling Events in Window Objects

When an event (e.g., a button click, menu selection, list selection, mouse move, etc.) occurs, the JVM calls one of the following methods.

void buttonClicked(JButton buttonObj)

Action: The framework invokes this method when a button is selected. The application should override this method to take the appropriate action. The parameter is the button where the event occurred.

void listDoubleClicked(JList listObj, String itemClicked)

Action: The framework invokes this method when a list item is double clicked. The application should override this method to take the appropriate action. The parameters are the list and the list item where the event occurred. *Note*: This method is invoked *after* the method `listItemSelected` (see below).

void listItemSelected(JList listObj)

Action: The framework invokes this method when a list item is selected with a single click or a double click. The application may or may not override this method to take the appropriate action. The parameter is the list in which the item was selected. The programmer can use the `JList` methods `getSelectedValue()` and `getSelectedIndex()` to determine the selected item and its position.

void menuItemSelected(JMenuItem mI)

Action: The framework invokes this method when a menu item is selected. The application should override this method to take the appropriate

action. The parameter is the menu item where the event occurred.
Note: Not available for GBApplet and GBDialog.

H.3 Method Specifications for Class GBDialog

The following messages are unique to class dialog and are not shared by classes GBFrame or GBApplet.

GBDialog(JFrame f)

Action: This is the constructor. Its use is required in the constructor of a GBDialog subclass, and it is invoked by calling super. The constructor's parameter is the parent frame of the dialog. When the dialog is used by an application, the parent frame is a reference to the application. When the dialog is used by an applet or by another dialog, the parent frame is an anonymous frame.

String getDlgCloseIndicator()

Action: Returns the dialog's closing indicator. The value of this indicator is "Cancel" by default.

Example: String indicator =
        theDialog.getDlgCloseIndicator();

void setDlgCloseIndicator(String s)

Action: Sets the dialog's closing indicator to the given string.

Example: theDialog.setDlgCloseIndicator("OK");

H.4 Method Specifications for Class GBPanel

GBPanel is a BreezySwing extension of JPanel. GBPanel provides several default methods for handling mouse events.

void mouseClicked(int x, int y)

Action: The framework invokes this method when a mouse button is clicked. The panel should override this method to take the appropriate action. The parameters represent the panel coordinates of the mouse when the event occurred.

void mousePressed(int x, int y)

Action: The framework invokes this method when a mouse button is pressed. The panel should override this method to take the appropriate action. The parameters represent the panel coordinates of the mouse when the event occurred.

void mouseReleased(int x, int y)

Action: The framework invokes this method when a mouse button is
released. The panel should override this method to take the appropriate action. The parameters represent the panel coordinates of the
mouse when the event occurred.

void mouseMoved(int x, int y)

Action: The framework invokes this method when the mouse is moved. The
panel should override this method to take the appropriate action.
The parameters represent the panel coordinates of the mouse when
the event occurred.

void mouseDragged(int x, int y)

Action: The framework invokes this method when the mouse is dragged
(i.e., moved while a button is pressed). The panel should override
this method to take the appropriate action. The parameters represent
the panel coordinates of the mouse when the event occurred.

void mouseEntered(int x, int y)

Action: The framework invokes this method when the mouse enters the
panel. The panel should override this method to take the appropriate
action. The parameters represent the panel coordinates of the mouse
when the event occurred.

void mouseExited(int x, int y)

Action: The framework invokes this method when the mouse exits the
panel. The panel should override this method to take the appropriate
action. The parameters represent the panel coordinates of the mouse
when the event occurred.

H.5 Method Specifications for Class Format

The class Format allows a programmer to center, left justify, or right justify data
within a number of columns.

```
static String justify(char justification, String text,
                      int width)
static String justify(char justification, char ch,
                      int width)
static String justify(char justification, long number,
                      int width)
static String justify(char justification, double number,
                      int width, int precision)
```

Action: Formats and returns the string representation of the given data, where justification is `'l'`, `'r'`, or `'c'`. The data are centered, left justified, or right justified within the given width.

Examples: `String strOutput   = Format.justify('r', "Hi`
`there!", 34);`

`String charOutput = Format.justify('c', 'A', 10);`

`String intOutput   = Format.justify('l', 21, 80);`

`String dollars    = Format.justify('r', 3.1416,`
`10, 2);`

H.6 Method Specifications for Window Objects

All the classes described in this section are defined in `java.io` except for `IntegerField` and `DoubleField`, which are `BreezySwing` extensions of Java's `TextField` class. Additional information can be found in Sun's standard Java documentation.

Methods Common to All Window Objects

The method `setVisible(aBoolean)` (described in section H.1) also works with any window object to make it appear or disappear. The method `setEnabled(aBoolean)` works with such window objects as buttons, menu items, and fields. This method enables or disables the actions of a button or the input or output of fields. The method `requestFocus()` sends the cursor to a field or makes a button ready to be pressed.

Method Specifications for Classes `JLabel` and `JButton`

The method `setText(aString)` modifies the text associated with a label or a button. The method `getText()` returns this text.

Method Specifications for Class `JtextField`

`String getText()`
Action: Returns the text field's contents.
Example: `String data = theField.getText();`

`void setText(String str)`
Action: Replaces the contents of the text field with the given string.
Example: `theField.setText("Jane Roe");`

void setEditable(boolean)

Action: Enables or disables editing of the field.

Example: `theField.setEditable(false);`

Method Specifications for Class `JtextArea`

void append(String str)

Action: Appends the given string to the text already displayed in the text area.

Example: `theArea.append("A string with a newline\n");`

String getText()

Action: Returns the text area's contents.

Example: `String data = theArea.getText();`

void setText(String str)

Action: Replaces the contents of the text area with the given string.

Example: `theArea.setText("Jane Roe");`

void setEditable(boolean)

Action: Enables or disables editing of the text area.

Example: `theArea.setEditable(false);`

Method Specifications for Class `IntegerField`

`IntegerField` is a `BreezySwing` extension of `TextField`.

int getNumber()

Action: Returns the integer currently stored in the integer field or 0 if the integer is malformed.

Example: `int radius = radiusField.getNumber();`

void setNumber(int number)

Action: Displays the specified number in the integer field.

Example: `radiusField.setNumber(2316);`

boolean isValid()

Action: Returns true if the integer in the field is well formed and false otherwise.

Example: `if (radiusField.isValid())`

Method Specifications for Class `DoubleField`

`DoubleField` is a `BreezySwing` extension of `TextField`.

`double getNumber()`

Action: Returns the floating-point number currently stored in the double field or 0 if the number is malformed.

Example: `double velocity = velocityField.getNumber();`

`void setNumber(double number)`

Action: Displays the specified number in the double field.

Example: `areaField.setNumber(527.32);`

`boolean isValid()`

Action: Returns true if the floating-point number in the field is well formed and false otherwise.

Example: `if (velocityField.isValid())`

`void setPrecision(double number)`

Action: Sets the number of digits to be displayed after the decimal point in the double field.

Example: `salaryField.setPrecision(2);`

`int getPrecision()`

Action: Returns the number of digits to be displayed after the decimal point in the double field.

Example: `System.out.println("Precision = " +`
            `salaryField.getPrecision());`

Method Specifications for Check Boxes, Radio Buttons, and Button Groups

Check boxes and radio buttons support the methods `setText(aString)` and `getText()`, for changing and examining their labels, and the methods `setSelected(aBoolean)` and `isSelected()`, for selecting, deselecting, and examining their selection status. To group radio buttons in a manner that allows only one at a time to be selected, one adds them to an instance of `JButtonGroup` with the method `add(aRadioButton)`.

Method Specifications for the Classes `JList` and `DefaultListModel`

To manipulate the contents of scrolling lists, one must use methods from the `JList` and `DefaultListModel` classes. Here are the `JList` methods:

`JList` Method	What It Does
`ListModel getModel()`	Returns the model for the list. You should cast the result to a `DefaultListModel`.
`int getSelectedIndex()`	Returns the position of the selected item.
`Object getSelectedValue()`	Returns the selected item.
`void setSelectedIndex(int index)`	Selects the item at the given index.
`void setSelectedValue(Object obj, boolean shouldScroll)`	Selects the given item.

Here are the `DefaultListModel` methods:

`DefaultListModel` Method	What It Does
`add(int index, Object obj)`	Inserts an item at the given position.
`addElement(Object obj)`	Adds an item to the end of the list.
`void clear()`	Makes the list empty.
`Object get(int index)`	Returns the item at the given position.
`Object remove(int index)`	Removes the item at the given position.
`boolean removeElement(Object obj)`	Removes the first instance of the given item.
`Object set(index i, Object obj)`	Replaces the item at the given position with the given item.
`int size()`	Returns the number of items in the list.
`Object[] toArray()`	Returns an array of the items.

H.7 `TerminalIO`

Programs that use `TerminalIO` should import the package as follows:

```
import TerminalIO.*;
```

The package provides objects and methods for reading from the keyboard and writing to the terminal window.

Method Specifications for the Class `KeyboardReader`

This class provides methods for reading user input entered at the keyboard. Such input is automatically echoed in the terminal window. In what follows, assume that `reader` is an instance of the class `KeyboardReader`.

`void pause()`

Action: Prompts the user to press the **Enter** key and waits for the user to do so. This method can be used to pause output in the terminal window and to keep the terminal window from closing in non-GUI programs.

Example: `reader.pause();`

`char readChar(String userPrompt)`

Action: Displays `userPrompt` in the terminal window and waits for the user's input. Returns a character that represents the user's input from the terminal window.

Example: `char letter = reader.readChar("Please enter a letter: ");`

`char readChar()`

Action: Same as the preceding except there is no prompt.

`double readDouble(String userPrompt)`

Action: Displays `userPrompt` in the terminal window and waits for the user's input. Returns a `double` that represents the user's input as echoed in the terminal window. Throws a `NumberFormatException` if the user's input does not represent a `double`.

Example: `double d = reader.readDouble("Please enter a real number: ");`

`double readDouble()`

Action: Same as the preceding except there is no prompt.

`double readInt(String userPrompt)`

Action: Displays `userPrompt` in the terminal window and waits for the user's input. Returns an `int` that represents the user's input as echoed in the terminal window. Throws a `NumberFormatException` if the user's input cannot represent an `int`.

Example: `int i = reader.readInt("Please enter an integer: ");`

`double readInt()`

Action: Same as the preceding except there is no prompt.

String readLine(String userPrompt)

Action: Displays userPrompt in the terminal window and waits for the user's input. Returns a string that represents the user's input as echoed in the terminal window.

Example: String name = reader.readLine
                          ("Please enter your name: ");

String readLine()

Action: Same as the preceding except there is no prompt.

Method Specifications for the Class ScreenWriter

This class provides methods for writing program output to the terminal window. The class and its methods can be avoided by sending print and println messages to System.out. The class's only purpose is to increase the parallelism between keyboard input and terminal output in the book's early chapters. Here is a list of the methods. We omit explanations.

void print(boolean x)

void print(char x)

void print(char[] x)

void print(double x)

void print(float x)

void print(int x)

void print(long x)

void print(Object x)

void print(String x)

void println()

void println(boolean x)

void println(char x)

void println(char[] x)

void println(double x)

void println(float x)

void println(int x)

void println(long x)

void println(Object x)

void println(String x)

Glossary

abstract Simplified or partial, hiding detail.

abstract class A class that defines attributes and methods for subclasses but is never instantiated.

abstract data type (ADT) A class of objects, a defined set of properties of those objects, and a set of operations for processing the objects.

abstract method A method that is specified but not implemented in an abstract class. The subclasses must implement this method.

Abstract Windowing Toolkit (AWT) A Java package that contains the definitions of all of the classes used to set up graphical user interfaces.

accessor A method used to examine an attribute of an object without changing it.

accumulator A variable used for the purpose of summing successive values of some other variable.

activation record An area of computer memory that keeps track of a method call's parameters, local values, return value, and the caller's return address. *See also* **run-time stack.**

actual parameter A variable or expression contained in a method call and passed to that method. *See also* **formal parameter.**

adapter class A Java class that allows another class to implement an interface class without implementing all of its methods. *See also* **interface.**

address An integer value that the computer can use to reference a location. Often called address of a memory location. *See also* **value.**

algorithm A finite sequence of effective statements that, when applied to a problem, will solve it.

alias A situation in which two or more names in a program can refer to the same memory location. An alias can cause subtle side effects.

analysis The phase of the software life cycle in which the programmer describes what the program will do.

applet A Java program that can be downloaded and run on a Web browser.

application software Programs designed for a specific use.

argument A value or expression passed in a method call.

arithmetic/logic unit (ALU) The part of the central processing unit that performs arithmetic operations and evaluates expressions.

arithmetic overflow A situation that arises when the computer's memory cannot represent the number resulting from an arithmetic operation.

array A data structure whose elements are accessed by means of index positions.

array index The relative position of the components of an array.

ASCII character set The American Standard Code for Information Interchange ordering for a character set (see Appendix D).

assembly language A computer language that allows the programmer to express operations and memory addresses with mnemonic symbols.

assertion Special comments used with `if` statements and loops that state what you expect to happen and when certain conditions will hold.

assignment statement A method of putting values into memory locations.

association list A collection of items that can be accessed by specifying key values. *See also* **keyed list.**

associative link A means of recognizing and accessing items in a network structure, such as the World Wide Web.

attribute A property that a computational object models, such as the balance in a bank account.

behavior The set of actions that a class of objects supports.

big-O notation A formal notation used to express the amount of work done by an algorithm or the amount of memory used by an algorithm.

binary digit A digit, either 0 or 1, in the binary number system. Program instructions are stored in memory using a sequence of binary digits. *See also* **bit.**

binary search The process of examining a middle value of a sorted array to see which half contains the value in question and halving until the value is located.

bit A binary digit.

bitmap A data structure used to represent the values and positions of points on a computer screen or image.

block An area of program text, enclosed in Java by the symbols {}, that contains statements and data declarations.

Boolean expression An expression whose value is either true or false. *See also* **compound Boolean expression** and **simple Boolean expression.**

border layout A Java layout class that allows the programmer to place window objects in five areas (north, south, west, east, and center) of a window. Border layout is the default layout for Java applications.

bottom-up implementation A method of coding a program that starts with lower-level modules and a test driver module.

buffer A block of memory into which data are placed for transmission to a program, usually with file or string processing.

buffered file input The input of large blocks of data from a file.

bus A group of wires imprinted on a circuit board to facilitate communication between components of a computer.

button A window object that allows the user to select an action by clicking a mouse.

byte A sequence of bits used to encode a character in memory. *See also* **word.**

byte code The kind of object code generated by a Java compiler and interpreted by a Java virtual machine. Byte code is platform independent.

call Any reference to a method by an executable statement. Also referred to as **invoke.**

call stack The trace of method calls that appears when Java throws an exception during program execution.

cancellation error A condition in which data are lost because of differences in the precision of the operands.

card layout A Java layout class that allows the programmer to manipulate the window as a stack of cards.

cast An operator that is used to convert a value of one type to a value of a different type (e.g., `double` to `int`).

c-curve A fractal shape that resembles the letter C.

central processing unit (CPU) A major hardware component that consists of the arithmetic/logic unit and the control unit.

character set The list of characters available for data and program statements.

check box A window object that allows the user to check a labeled box.

class A description of the attributes and behavior of a set of computational objects.

class constant A constant that is visible to all instances of a class and, if public, is accessed by specifying the class name. For example, `Math.PI` is a class constant.

class constructor A method used to create and initialize an instance of a class.

class method A method that is invoked when a message is sent to a class. For example, `Math.sqrt` is a class method. *See also* **message.**

class variable A variable that is visible to all instances of a class and, if public, is accessed by specifying the class name.

client A computational object that receives a service from another computational object.

client/server relationship A means of describing the organization of computing resources in which one resource provides a service to another resource.

coding The process of writing executable statements that are part of a program to solve a problem. *See also* **implementation.**

cohesive method A method designed to accomplish a single task.

combo box A window object that allows the user to select from a pull-down list of options.

comment A nonexecutable statement used to make a program more readable.

compatible type Expressions that have the same base type. A formal parameter and an actual parameter must be of compatible type, and the operands of an assignment statement must be of compatible type.

compilation error An error detected when the program is being compiled. *See also* **design error, run-time error,** and **syntax error.**

compiler A computer program that automatically converts instructions in a high-level language to machine language.

complexity For algorithms, the formula that expresses the rate of growth of work or memory as a function of the size of the data or problem that it solves. *See also* **big-O notation.**

compound assignment An assignment operation that performs a designated operation, such as addition, before storing the result in a variable.

compound Boolean expression Refers to the complete expression when logical connectives and negation are used to generate Boolean values. *See also* **Boolean expression** and **simple Boolean expression.**

compound statement Uses the symbols { and } to group several statements and data declarations as a unit. *See also* **block.**

concatenation An operation in which the contents of one data structure are placed after the contents of another data structure.

concrete class A class that can be instantiated. *See also* **abstract class.**

conditional statement *See* **selection statement.**

conjunction The connection of two Boolean expressions using the logical operator **&&** (AND), returning false if at least one of the expressions is false or true if they are both true.

constant A symbol whose value cannot be changed.

contained class A class that is used to define a data object within another class.

container A Java class that allows the programmer to group window objects for placement in a window.

contiguous memory Computer memory which is organized so that the data are accessible in adjacent cells.

control structure A structure that controls the flow of execution of program statements.

control unit The part of the central processing unit that controls the operation of the rest of the computer.

coordinate system A grid that allows a programmer to specify positions of points in a plane or of pixels on a computer screen.

counter A variable used to count the number of times some process is completed.

data The particular characters that are used to represent information in a form suitable for storage, processing, and communication.

data abstraction The separation between the conceptual definition of a data structure and its eventual implementation.

data input stream A Java class that supports the input of data from a binary file.

data output stream A Java class that supports the output of data to a binary file.

data type A formal description of the set of values that a variable can have.

data validation The process of examining data prior to its use in a program.

debugging The process of eliminating errors, or "bugs," from a program.

decrement To decrease the value of a variable.

default constructor A method that Java provides for creating objects of a class. The programmer can override this method to do extra things.

definition list An HTML structure that allows an author to display a keyed list on a Web page.

design The phase of the software life cycle in which the programmer describes how the program will accomplish its tasks.

design error An error such that a program runs, but unexpected results are produced. Also referred to as a logic error. *See also* **compilation error**, **run-time error**, and **syntax error.**

dialog A type of window that pops up to display information or receive it from the user.

dictionary A data structure that allows the programmer to access items by specifying key values. *See also* **association list.**

disjunction The connection of two Boolean expressions using the logical operator | | (OR), returning TRUE if at least one of the expressions is TRUE or FALSE if they are both FALSE.

divide-and-conquer algorithms A class of algorithms that solves problems by repeatedly dividing them into simpler problems. *See also* **recursion.**

double A Java data type used to represent numbers with a decimal point.

doubly linked list A linked list in which each node has a pointer to the previous node and a pointer to the next node.

do-while loop A posttest loop examining a Boolean expression after causing a statement to be executed. *See also* **for loop**, **loops**, and **while loop.**

driver A method used to test other methods.

dynamic memory Memory allocated under program control from the heap and accessed by means of pointers. *See also* **heap** and **pointer.**

dynamic structure A data structure that may expand or contract during execution of a program. *See also* **dynamic memory.**

echo checking A debugging technique in which values of variables and input data are displayed during program execution.

empty link *See* **null value.**

empty statement A semicolon used to indicate that no action is to be taken. Also referred to as a **null statement.**

encapsulation The process of hiding and restricting access to the implementation details of a data structure.

end-of-file marker A special marker inserted by the machine to indicate the end of the data file.

end-of-line character A special character (`'\n'`) used to indicate the end of a line of characters in a string or a file stream.

entrance-controlled loop *See* **pretest loop.**

enumeration A Java class that allows the programmer to process a sequence of objects.

error *See* **compilation error, design error**, **logic error, run-time error,** and **syntax error.**

event An occurrence, such as a button click or a mouse motion, that can be detected and processed by a program.

event-driven loop A process, usually hidden in the operating system, that waits for an event, notifies a program that an event has occurred, and returns to wait for more events.

exception An abnormal state or error that occurs during run time and is signaled by the operating system.

exception-driven loop The use of exceptions to implement a normal loop, usually for file input.

execute To carry out the instructions of a program.

exit-controlled loop *See* **posttest loop.**

expanding capabilities implementation A coding strategy that begins with a running but incomplete program and gradually adds features until the program is complete.

explicit type conversion The use of an operation by a programmer to convert the type of a data object.

exponential form *See* **floating-point.**

extended if statement Nested selection where additional **if-else** statements are used in the **else** option. *See also* **nested if statement.**

external image An image displayed when the user selects a link on a Web page.

external pointer A special pointer that allows users to access the nodes in a linked list.

Fibonacci numbers A series of numbers generated by taking the sum of the previous two numbers in the series. The series begins with the numbers 1 and 2.

field width The number of columns used for the output of text. *See also* **formatting.**

file A data structure that resides on a secondary storage medium.

file input stream A Java class used to connect a program to a file for input.

file output stream A Java class used to connect a program to a file for output.

final method A method that cannot be implemented by a subclass.

fixed-point A method of writing decimal numbers where the decimal is placed where it belongs in the number. *See also* **floating-point.**

floating-point A method for writing numbers in scientific notation to accommodate numbers that may have very large or very small values. *See also* **fixed-point.**

flow layout A Java layout class that allows the user to place window objects in wrap-around rows in a window. Flow layout is the default layout for applets.

flowchart A diagram that displays the flow of control of a program. *See also* **control structure.**

font The kind of typeface used for text, such as Courier and Times Roman.

for loop A structured loop consisting of an initializer expression, a termination expression, an update expression, and a statement.

formal parameter A name, introduced in a method definition, that is replaced by an actual parameter when the method is called.

formal specification The set of preconditions and postconditions of a method.

formatting Designating the desired field width when displaying text. *See also* **field width.**

fractal geometry A theory of shapes that are reflected in various phenomena, such as coastlines, water flow, and price fluctuations.

frame A Java class that defines the window for an application. *See also* **application software.**

garbage collection The automatic process of reclaiming memory when the data of a program no longer need it.

global identifier A name that can be used by all of the methods of a class.

global variable *See* **global identifier.**

graphical user interface (GUI) A means of communication between human beings and computers that uses a pointing device for input and a bitmapped screen for output. The bitmap displays images of windows and window objects such as buttons, text fields, and pull-down menus. The user interacts with the interface by using the mouse to directly manipulate the window objects. *See also* **window object.**

grid bag layout A Java layout class that allows the user to place window objects in a two-dimensional grid in the window and to have control over how the window objects occupy the cells in that grid.

grid layout A Java layout class that allows the user to place window objects in a two-dimensional grid in the window.

hardware The computing machine and its support devices.

hash table A data structure that allows the programmer to access items by specifying key values and that supports very fast lookups.

heap An area of computer memory where storage for dynamic data is available.

heap underflow A condition in which memory leakage causes dynamic memory to become unavailable.

high-level language Any programming language that uses words and symbols to make it relatively easy to read and write a program. *See also* **assembly language** and **machine language.**

hypermedia A data structure that allows the user to access different kinds of information (text, images, sound, video, applications) by traversing links.

hypertext A data structure that allows the user to access different chunks of text by traversing links.

hypertext markup language (HTML) A programming language that allows the user to create pages for the World Wide Web.

Hypertext Transport Protocol (HTTP) The scheme used to provide addresses for pages on the World Wide Web.

identifiers Words that must be created according to a well-defined set of rules but can have any meaning subject to these rules.

identity The property of an object that it is the same thing at different points in time, even though the values of its attributes might change.

if-else statement A selection statement that allows a program to perform alternative actions based on a condition.

implementation The phase of the software life cycle in which the program is coded in a programming language.

increment The process of increasing a number by 1.

index *See* **array index.**

infinite loop A loop in which the controlling condition is not changed in such a manner to allow the loop to terminate.

information hiding A condition in which the user of a module does not know the details of how it is implemented, and the implementer of a module does not know the details of how it is used.

inheritance The process by which a subclass can reuse attributes and behavior defined in a superclass. *See also* **subclass** and **superclass.**

initializer list A means of expressing a set of data that can be assigned to the cells of an array in one statement.

inline image An image that is loaded when the user accesses a Web page.

input Data obtained by a program during its execution.

input assertion A precondition for a loop.

input device A device that provides information to the computer. Typical input devices are a mouse, keyboard, disk drive, microphone, and network port. *See also* **I/O device** and **output device.**

instance A computational object bearing the attributes and behavior specified by a class.

instance method A method that is called when a message is sent to an instance of a class. *See also* **message.**

instance variable Storage for data in an instance of a class.

instantiation The process of creating a new object or instance of a class.

integer arithmetic operations Operations allowed on data of type `int`. These include the operations of addition, subtraction, multiplication, division, and modulus to produce integer answers.

integer overflow A condition in which an integer value is too large to be stored in the computer's memory.

interface A formal statement of how communication occurs between the user of a module (class or method) and its implementer.

interface A Java file that simply specifies the methods to be implemented by another class. A class that implements several interfaces can thus adopt the behavior of several classes.

invariant expression An assertion that is true before the loop and after each iteration of the loop.

invoke *See* **call.**

I/O device Any device that allows information to be transmitted to or from a computer. *See also* **input device** and **output device.**

iteration *See* **loops.**

justification The process of aligning text to the left, the center, or the right within a given number of columns.

key The value used to access data in a keyed list.

keyed list A data structure that allows the programmer to access items by using key values. *See also* **association list.**

keywords See **reserved words.**

library A collection of methods and data organized to perform a set of related tasks. *See also* **class** and **package.**

lifetime The time during which a data object or method call exists.

linear An increase of work or memory in direct proportion to the size of a problem.

linear search *See* **sequential search.**

linked list A list of data items in which each item is linked to the next one by means of a pointer.

listener A Java class that detects and responds to events.

literal An element of a language that expresses itself, such as 34 or "hi there."

loader A system software tool that places program instructions and data into the appropriate memory locations before program startup.

local identifier A name whose value is visible only within a method or a nested block.

local variable *See* **local identifier.**

logarithmic An increase of work in proportion to the number of times that the problem size can be divided by 2.

logic error *See* **design error.**

logical operator Either logical connective (`&&`, `||`) or negation (`!`).

logical size The number of data items actually available in a data structure at a given time. *See also* **physical size.**

logical structure The organization of the components in a data structure, independent of their organization in computer memory.

long A Java data type used to represent large integers.

loop invariant An assertion that expresses a relationship between variables that remains constant throughout all iterations of the loop.

loop variant An assertion whose truth changes between the first and final execution of the loop.

loop verification The process of guaranteeing that a loop performs its intended task.

loops Program statements that cause a process to be repeated. *See also* **do-while loop**, **for loop**, and **while loop.**

low-level language *See* **assembly language.**

machine language The language used directly by the computer in all its calculations and processing.

main (primary) memory Memory contained in the computer. *See also* **memory** and **secondary memory.**

main unit A computer's main unit contains the central processing unit (CPU) and the main (primary) memory; it is hooked to an input device and an output device.

mainframe Large computers typically used by major companies and universities. *See also* **microcomputer** and **minicomputer.**

manifest interface The property of a method such that, when the method is called, the reader of the code can tell clearly what information is being transmitted to it and what information is being returned from it.

mantissa/exponent notation A notation used to express floating-point numbers.

markup tag A syntactic form in the hypertext markup language used to create different elements displayed on a Web page.

mathematical induction A method of proving that parts of programs are correct by reasoning from a base case and an induction hypothesis to a general conclusion.

matrix A two-dimensional array that provides range checking and can be resized.

megabyte Shorthand for approximately 1 million bytes.

memory The ordered sequence of storage cells that can be accessed by address. Instructions and variables of an executing program are temporarily held here. *See also* **main memory** and **secondary memory.**

memory location A storage cell that can be accessed by address. *See also* **memory.**

menu item A window object that displays as an option in a pull-down menu or pop-up menu.

merge The process of combining lists. Typically refers to files or arrays.

message A symbol used by a client to ask an object to perform a service. *See also* **method.**

method A chunk of code that can be treated as a unit and invoked by name. A method is called when a message is sent to an object. *See also* **class method** and **instance method.**

method heading The portion of a method implementation containing the function's name, parameter declarations, and return type.

microcomputer A computer capable of fitting on a laptop or desktop, generally used by one person at a time. *See also* **mainframe** and **minicomputer.**

minicomputer A small version of a mainframe computer. It is usually used by several people at once. *See also* **mainframe** and **microcomputer.**

mixed-mode Expressions containing data of different types; the values of these expressions will be of either type, depending on the rules for evaluating them.

modal A state in which the computer user cannot exit without explicitly signaling the computer, usually with an "Accept" or "Cancel" option.

model/view/controller pattern A design plan in which the roles and responsibilities of the system are cleanly divided among data management (model), user interface display (view), and user event handling (controller) tasks.

modem A device that connects a computer to a telephone system to transmit data.

module An independent unit that is part of a larger development. Can be a method or a class (set of methods and related data).

module specifications In the case of a method, a description of data received, information returned, and task performed by a module. In the case of a class, a description of the attributes and behavior.

mutator A method used to change the value of an attribute of an object.

negation The use of the logical operator ! (not) with a Boolean expression, returning TRUE if the expression is FALSE, and FALSE if the expression is TRUE.

nested if statement A selection statement used within another selection statement. *See also* **extended if statement.**

nested loop A loop as one of the statements in the body of another loop.

nested selection Any combination of selection statements within selection statements. *See also* **selection statement.**

network A collection of resources that are linked together for communication.

node A component of a linked list, consisting of a data item and a pointer to the next node.

null statement *See* **empty statement.**

null value A special value which indicates that no object can be accessed.

object A collection of data and operations, in which the data can be accessed and modified only by means of the operations.

object code *See* **object program.**

object-oriented programming The construction of software systems that use objects.

object program The machine code version of the source program.

off-by-one error Usually seen with loops, this error shows up as a result that is one less or one greater than the expected value.

one-dimensional array An array in which each data item is accessed by specifying a single index.

one-way list A list that supports navigation in one direction only.

operating system A large program that allows the user to communicate with the hardware and performs various management tasks.

ordinal data type A data type ordered in some association with the integers; each integer is the ordinal of an associated value of the data type.

output Information that is produced by a program.

output assertion A postcondition for a loop.

output device A device that allows you to see the results of a program. Typically, it is a monitor, printer, speaker, or network port. *See also* **input device** and **I/O device.**

overflow In arithmetic operations, a value may be too large for the computer's memory location. A meaningless value may be assigned or an error message may result. *See also* **underflow.**

overloading The process of using the same operator symbol or identifier to refer to many different functions. *See also* **polymorphism.**

overriding The process of reimplementing a method already implemented in a superclass.

package A group of related classes in a named directory.

panel A window object whose purpose is to contain other window objects.

parallel arrays Arrays of the same length but with different component data types.

parameter *See* **argument.**

parameter list A list of parameters. An actual parameter list is contained in a method call. A formal parameter list is contained in a method heading.

parent The immediate superclass of a class.

peripheral memory *See* **memory** and **secondary memory.**

persistence The property of a data model that allows it to survive different runs of an application. *See also* **serialization.**

physical size The number of memory units available for storing data items in a data structure. *See also* **logical size.**

pivot A data item around which an array is subdivided during quicksort.

pixel A picture element or dot of color used to display images on a computer screen.

pointer A reference to an object that allows one to access it.

polymorphism The property of one operator symbol or method identifier having many meanings. *See also* **overloading.**

pop-up menu A window object that allows the user to pop up and select from a list of menu items. *See also* **menu item.**

portable Able to be transferred to different applications or computers without changes.

postcondition A statement of what is true after a certain action is taken.

posttest loop A loop where the control condition is tested after the loop is executed. A `do-while loop` is a posttest loop. Also referred to as an **exit-controlled loop.**

precondition A statement of what is true before a certain action is taken.

pretest condition A condition that controls whether the body of the loop is executed before going through the loop.

pretest loop A loop where the control condition is tested before the loop is executed. A `while loop` is a pretest loop. Also referred to as an **entrance-controlled loop.**

primary memory *See* **main memory** and **memory.**

priming input statement An input statement that must be executed before a loop control condition is tested.

primitive data type A data type such as `char`, `int`, `double`, or `boolean` whose values are stored directly in variables of that type. Primitive data types are always passed by value when they are parameters in Java and copied during assignment statements.

print stream A Java class that sends text output to the terminal window.

private method A method that is accessible only within the scope of a class definition.

private variable A variable that is accessible only within the scope of a class definition.

procedural programming A style of programming that decomposes a program into a set of methods or procedures.

program A set of instructions that tells the machine (the hardware) what to do.

program proof An analysis of a program that attempts to verify the correctness of program results.

program walk-through The process of carefully following, using pencil and paper, steps the computer uses to solve the problem given in a program. Also referred to as a **trace.**

programming language Formal language that computer scientists use to give instructions to the computer.

protected variable A variable that is accessible only within the scope of a class definition, within the class definition of a subclass, or within the class's package.

pseudocode A stylized half-English, half-code language written in English but suggesting Java code.

public method A method that is accessible to any program component that uses the class.

public variable A variable that is accessible to any program component that uses the class.

pull-down menu A window object that allows the user to pull down and select from a list of menu items. *See also* **menu item.**

quadratic An increase of work or memory in proportion to the square of the size of the problem.

queue A data structure that allows the programmer to insert items only at one end and remove them from the other.

quicksort A relatively fast sorting technique that uses recursion. *See also* **exchange sort.**

radio button A type of check box that permits the user to select only one check box in the group. *See also* **check box.**

random access data structure A data structure in which the time to access a data item does not depend on its position in the structure.

range-bound error The situation that occurs when at attempt is made to use an array index value that is less than 0 or greater than or equal to the size of the array.

recursion The process of a subprogram calling itself. A clearly defined stopping state must exist. Any recursive subprogram can be rewritten using iteration.

recursive data structure A data structure that has either a simple form or a form that is composed of other instances of the same data structure. *See also* **linked list.**

recursive step A step in the recursive process that solves a similar problem of smaller size and eventually leads to a termination of the process.

recursive subprogram *See* **recursion.**

reference type A data type such as array, String, or any other Java class, whose instances are not stored directly in variables of that type. References or pointers to these objects are stored instead. References to objects are passed when they are parameters in Java, and only the references, not the objects, are copied during assignment statements.

refreshable image An image that is redisplayed when the user resizes or minimizes a window.

relational operator An operator used for comparison of data items of the same type.

repetition *See* **loops.**

representational error A condition in which the precision of data is reduced because of the order in which operations are performed.

reserved words Words that have predefined meanings that cannot be changed. A list of reserved words for Java is in Appendix B.

return type The type of value returned by a method.

robust The state in which a program is protected against most possible crashes from bad data and unexpected values.

round-off error A condition in which a portion of a real number is lost because of the way it is stored in the computer's memory.

run-time error An error detected when, after compilation is completed, an error message results instead of the correct output. *See also* **compilation error, design error, exception,** and **syntax error.**

run-time stack An area of computer memory reserved for local variables and parameters of method calls.

scanning The process of picking words or tokens out of a stream of characters.

scope of identifier The largest block in which the identifier is available.

scroll bar A window object that allows the user to select a value from a continuous range.

scrolling list A window object that displays a selectable list of strings.

secondary memory An auxiliary device for memory, usually a disk or magnetic tape. *See also* **main memory** and **memory.**

selection The process by which a method or a variable of an instance or a class is accessed.

selection sort A sorting algorithm that sorts the components of an array in either ascending or descending order. This process puts the smallest or largest element in the top position and repeats the process on the remaining array components. *See also* **quicksort.**

selection statement A control statement that selects some particular logical path based on the value of an expression. Also referred to as a **conditional statement.**

self-documenting code Code that is written using descriptive identifiers.

semantics The rules for interpreting the meaning of a program in a language.

sentinel value A special value that indicates the end of a set of data or of a process.

sequential access data structure A data structure in which the time to access a data item depends on its position in the structure.

sequential search The process of searching a list by examining the first component and then examining successive components in the order in which they occur. Also referred to as a **linear search.**

sequential traversal The process of visiting each data item in an array or a linked list from beginning to end.

serialization A mechanism that maintains the persistence of objects in a data model. *See also* **persistence.**

server A computational object that provides a service to another computational object.

short A Java data type used to represent small integers.

short-circuit evaluation The process whereby a compound Boolean expression halts evaluation and returns the value of the first subexpression that evaluates to true, in the case of | |, or false, in the case of &&.

side effect A change in a variable that is the result of some action taken in a program, usually from within a method.

simple Boolean expression An expression in which two numbers or variable values are compared using a single relational operator. *See also* **Boolean expression** and **compound Boolean expression.**

software Programs that make the machine (the hardware) do something, such as word processing, database management, or games.

software engineering The process of developing and maintaining large software systems.

software life cycle The process of development, maintenance, and demise of a software system. Phases include analysis, design, coding, testing/verification, maintenance, and obsolescence.

software reuse The process of building and maintaining software systems out of existing software components.

source program A program written by a programmer.

stack A dynamic data structure in which access can be made from only one end. Referred to as a LIFO (last-in, first-out) structure.

stand-alone program A Java program that runs directly on a computer without the aid of a Web browser. *See also* **application.**

state The set of all the values of the variables of a program at any point during its execution.

statement block (synonym compound statement) A form by which a sequence of statements and data declarations can be treated as a unit.

stepwise refinement The process of repeatedly subdividing tasks into subtasks until each subtask is easily accomplished. *See also* **structured programming** and **top-down implementation.**

stopping state The well-defined termination of a recursive process.

stream A channel in which data are passed from sender to receiver.

stream tokenizer A Java class that allows the programmer to input text from a file one word at a time.

string An abbreviated name for a string literal.

string buffer A Java class that allows the programmer to modify the contents of a string and efficiently increase its size.

string literal One or more characters, enclosed in double quotes, used as a constant in a program.

string tokenizer A Java class that allows the programmer to access text in a string one word at a time.

structure chart A graphical method of indicating the relationship between modules when designing the solution to a problem.

structured programming Programming that parallels a solution to a problem achieved by top-down implementation. *See also* **stepwise refinement** and **top-down implementation.**

stub programming The process of using incomplete functions to test data transmission among them.

subclass A class that inherits attributes and behavior from another class.

subscript *See* **array index.**

substring A string that represents a segment of another string.

superclass The class from which a subclass inherits attributes and behavior. *See also* **inheritance** and **subclass.**

syntax The rules for constructing well-formed programs in a language.

syntax error An error in spelling, punctuation, or placement of certain key symbols in a program. *See also* **compilation error, design error,** and **run-time error.**

system software The programs that allow users to write and execute other programs, including operating systems such as Windows and MacOS.

tail-recursive The property that a recursive algorithm has of performing no work after each recursive step. *See also* **recursion.**

text area A window object that provides a scrollable region within which the user can view or enter several lines of text.

text field A window object in which the user can view or enter a single line of text.

token An individual word or symbol.

top-down implementation A method for coding whereby you start with a top-level task and implement subtasks. Each subtask is then subdivided into smaller subtasks. This process is repeated until each remaining subtask is easily coded. *See also* **stepwise refinement** and **structured programming.**

trace *See* **program walk-through.**

transient image An image that is lost when the user resizes or minimizes a window.

truth table A means of listing all of the possible values of a Boolean expression.

two-dimensional array An array in which each data item is accessed by specifying a pair of indexes.

two-way list A list that supports navigation in both directions.

type *See* **data type.**

type promotion The process of converting a less inclusive data type, such as int, to a more inclusive data type, such as double.

underflow A value that is too small to be represented by a computer; it is automatically replaced by its negation. *See also* **overflow.**

Unicode A character set that uses 16 bits to represent over 65,000 possible characters. These include the ASCII character set as well as symbols and ideograms in many international languages. *See also* **ASCII character set.**

uniform resource locator (URL) The address of a page on the World Wide Web.

user-defined class A new data type introduced and defined by the programmer.

user-defined method A new function introduced and defined by the programmer.

user-friendly Describes an interactive program with clear, easy-to-follow messages for the user.

value The contents of a memory location. *See also* **address.**

variable A memory location, referenced by an identifier, whose value can be changed during a program.

vector A one-dimensional array that supports resizing, insertions, and removals.

virtual machine A software tool that behaves like a high-level computer.

visibility modifier A symbol (**public, protected,** or **private**) that specifies the kind of access that clients have to a server's data and methods.

void method A method that returns no value.

waterfall model A series of steps in which a software system trickles down from analysis to design to implementation. *See also* **software life cycle.**

while loop A pretest loop that examines a Boolean expression before causing a statement to be executed.

window A rectangular area of a computer screen that can contain window objects. Windows typically can be resized, minimized, zoomed, or closed. *See also* **frame.**

window object A computational object that displays an image, such as a button or a text field, in a window and supports interaction with the user.

word A unit of memory consisting of 1 or more bytes. Words can be addressed.

wrapper class A class designed to contain a primitive data type so that the primitive type can behave like a reference type. *See also* **primitive data type** and **reference type.**

writing to a file The process of entering data to a file.

Case Studies Index

Java Classes Index

Note that the classes DoubleField, Format, GBApplet, GBDialog, GBFrame, GBPanel, and IntegerField belong to the BreezySwing package and the classes ScreenWriter and KeyboardReader belong to the package TerminalIO rather than to standard Java, but are included for your reference.

Subject Index

abstract class, 307–308
abstract data type (ADT), 224, 508
abstract method, 309–310
Abstract Windowing Toolkit (AWT), 585
accessor method, 226
actual parameter, 134
adapter class, 595
address, 12
algorithm, 54
analysis, 15, 53, 239
applet, 25, 576–580, 630–631
application software, 7
arithmetic
    expression, 48–50
    overflow, 196
array, 261
artificial intelligence, 95
ASCII, 9–10, 648
assembler, 14
assembly language, 14
assignment statement, 39
associative link, 557
bar graph, 400
base address, 528
behavior, 224
big-O notation, 359
binary
    digit, 3
    numbers, 7–8
    search, 365–368
bit, 3
boolean type, 163
border layout, 604
bottom-up implementation, 156

boundary conditions, 85
break statement, 181
BreezySwing, 45, 236, 328, 471, 577
bubble sort, 268
buffer, 436
button, 118
byte, 3
byte code, 25
byte type, 167
call stack, 153
card layout, 611
cast, 169, 321
central processing unit (CPU), 3
char type, 164
check box, 330
child, 229
class, 19, 223
    constant, 245
    constructor, 249
    method, 243, 246–248
    hierarchy, 229, 308
    summary box, 240
    variable, 243
client, 224
coding, 15
cohesion, 141
collection, 466
    linear, 466
    unordered, 466
color, 390–392
combinatorial explosion, 94
comments, 64
compiler, 15
complete code coverage, 84
complexity analysis, 358

component, 598
concatenation, 110
concrete class, 308
constant, 168, 245
container, 601
contiguous memory, 529
continue statement, 182
coordinate system, 380
copying objects, 252–253
coupling, 141
cryptanalysis, 190
cryptography, 190
data
    input stream, 452
    output stream, 452
    type, 44
debugging, 62, 91
decimal numbers, 8, 649
declaration statement, 44
decrement, 171
default constructor, 249
definition list, 566
design, 15, 239
dialog, 473, 617
dictionary, 486
double type, 46
doubly linked list, 541
do-while statement, 177
driver, 156
dynamic memory, 528
editing a program, 32
element, 262
encapsulation, 19, 223
equality, 253
equivalence classes, 84
errors, 56

681

Borland®

JBuilder™ 4 Foundation
Upgrade Information

This book includes a full version of JBuilder 4 Foundation, the leading cross-platform environment for learning Java™ programming and personal application development. JBuilder includes an integrated editor, debugger, compiler, visual designers, wizards, and tutorials.

Borland also offers JBuilder Professional and JBuilder Enterprise for advanced Java development.

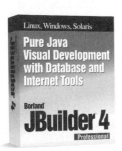

Upgrade to JBuilder Professional for:

- Database application development
- Web application development using JSP™ and servlets
- Advanced debugging
- JDK™ switching
- 250+ JavaBeans® components with source code
- Additional wizards and samples
- Source revision management

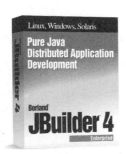

Upgrade to JBuilder Enterprise for everything in JBuilder Professional plus:

- Enterprise JavaBeans™ development
- Application deployment to J2EE™ application servers including Borland® AppServer™ and BEA® WebLogic® Server
- Free Borland AppServer developer license
- Team development support
- Remote debugging

Upgrade Now! Shop online at shop.borland.com or call 1-800-252-5547. For educational pricing, see www.borland.com/education.

For more information on the features of JBuilder Professional and Enterprise, visit the Borland JBuilder Web site at www.borland.com/jbuilder.

Promotion code: J5001